LYSIAS
Selected Speeches

Oklahoma Series in Classical Culture

Oklahoma Series in Classical Culture

Series Editor

Susan Ford Wiltshire, *Vanderbilt University*

Advisory Board

LYSIAS

Selected Speeches

XII, XVI, XIX, XXII, XXIV, XXV,
XXXII, XXXIV

Edited
With Introduction, Notes, and Appendices
By Charles Darwin Adams

Foreword by A. J. Heisserer

UNIVERSITY OF OKLAHOMA PRESS : NORMAN AND LONDON

INTERNATIONAL STANDARD BOOK NUMBER: 0–8061–1396–0

LIBRARY OF CONGRESS CATALOG CARD NUMBER: 79–123339

Lysias: Selected Speeches is Volume 3 of the Oklahoma Series in Classical Culture.

Reprinted 1970 by the University of Oklahoma Press, Publishing Division of the University, Norman, from the edition originally published 1905 by American Book Company, New York. First paperback printing, 1976.

4   5   6   7   8   9   10   11   12   13

TO MY FATHER
Daniel Emerson Adams

Contents

I

Foreword

IT is a pleasure for the University of Oklahoma Press to be able to reissue once again the fine classroom book on *Lysias: Selected Speeches,* by Charles Darwin Adams. Lysias has always been a favorite among classicists who are looking for a suitable Attic speech writer for undergraduate students. His diction and direct style will always find a welcome audience among serious students of Attic oratory. His speeches provide the modern reader with an invaluable glimpse into the world of Athenian politics and society at the end of the fifth and the beginning of the fourth century B.C. Indeed, they reveal much about Greek life everywhere during this period, especially various legal aspects. For the student of rhetoric, the ancient historian, and the legal scholar, Lysias will remain always an indispensable source.

The present edition by Adams has long been a favorite of teachers of Greek oratory. Adams went to great lengths to offer the most helpful notations for students; invariably he was able to anticipate precisely those places where the syntax would occasion difficulty and to obviate the difficulty by a clear explanation of the grammar involved. These notations are at the bottom of each page. Adams also provided several appendices intended to facilitate understanding of esoteric elements referred to in these speeches, e.g., cf. the Appendices on "Athenian Legal Procedure" and "Money and Prices at Athens" (for the latter the reader must take into account the inflation that has occurred since the original edition). Altogether, then, this is a splendid contribution to classical studies, one that we feel instructors will be happy to have in their hands.

A. J. HEISSERER
Oklahoma Series in Classical Culture

Preface

THIS volume has been prepared primarily for the use of college freshmen. On the side of grammar I have tried to provide in the notes for the understanding of unusual constructions, and for a somewhat systematic study of certain matters which, while entirely regular, require more observation and reflection than can be counted upon before the first year in college. I have laid especial emphasis upon the force of the tenses. The feeling for the finer distinctions of the Greek tenses is more difficult of attainment than the understanding of the moods, and these distinctions often baffle translation. The force of the particles is another difficulty that can be met only by constant observation and comparison in reading. In many instances I have given in a single note a systematic review of the uses of a given particle, and have then attempted by repeated references to this note to provide for frequent review and discrimination. I have treated many of the uses of prepositions in the same way.

Rhetorical matters have received especial attention. In Lysias we have the first really successful application of rhetorical theory to practical speech. The more vehement and showy style of Demosthenes, imitated by Cicero, and through him passed on to the modern world, long dominated English oratory. But in our own time, with the marked tendency toward simplicity and directness in public speech, we are ready for a new appreciation of Lysias, and for the study of his style as a most valuable training in the art of combining simplicity with distinction in prose composition. I have added to the Introduction to each speech a chapter on its Argument and Style, designed to be studied section by section as the reading advances.

5

I have attempted to bring all of the matter in the notes within the ready understanding of the young students for whom the volume is designed. Nothing can be more valuable to advanced students than constant reference to other Greek authors and to the standard modern authorities, but to fill notes for young students with such matters is only to discourage them in the attempt to use the notes at all.

The notes have been prepared upon the assumption that either the twelfth or the sixteenth speech will be the first to be read.

In the preparation of this volume I have made constant use of the stores of material in the great edition of Frohberger-Gebauer and the hardly less valuable edition of Rauchenstein-Fuhr. Thalheim's critical edition of 1901 has made the task of establishing and commenting on the text much simpler than that of my predecessors. For the treatment of Lysias's Ethopoiia I have depended especially on the studies of the late Ivo Bruns, whose brilliant work, *Das Literarische Porträt der Griechen*, has made all students of Greek literature his debtors. And in all departments of my work I have turned constantly to the *Attische Beredsamkeit* of Friedrich Blass, the man who more than all others in our time has broadened the foundations for the study of Greek oratory.

I am indebted to Professor Herbert Weir Smyth for valuable suggestions and criticisms, and to my colleague, Professor Richard Wellington Husband, who has read nearly all of the volume in proof, and whose criticism has been of constant service.

CHARLES DARWIN ADAMS

LYSIAS
Selected Speeches

Introduction

THE LIFE OF LYSIAS

[Dionysius begins his essay on Lysias with a brief biography. We have a critical edition of this essay in Usener-Radermacher, *Dionysii Halicarnasei Opuscula*, Lips. 1899. We have also a biography in the *Lives of the Ten Orators*, handed down to us under the false ascription to Plutarch; the unknown author is cited as Pseudo-Plutarch. A critical edition of this text, together with that of Dionysius's essay, is contained in Thalheim's text edition of Lysias.

A brief life of Lysias is appended to the discussion of his works in Photius, *Bibl.* 262, but it offers nothing that is not found in Pseudo-Plutarch.

Suidas, *s.v.* Λυσίας, gives a very condensed life, but adds nothing to the statements of Dionysius.

Harpocration refers to a speech of Lysias Περὶ τῶν ἰδίων εὐεργεσιῶν (*s.vv.* Κεῖοι, μεταπύργιον, Φηγαιεῦσι). From this speech *On his Services*, lost to us, the biographers probably obtained some of their facts about his life.]

LYSIAS was the son of Cephalus, a Syracusan who had settled at the Piraeus by invitation of Pericles.[1] The family was prosperous and honored, but by the Athenian consti- **The family** tution neither Cephalus nor his sons could become **of Cephalus** Athenian citizens except by special act of the Ecclesia. They probably did receive the rank of privileged metics (ἰσοτελεῖς) by which they were freed from the small, but humiliating, tax on foreigners, and from the requirement that they be enrolled as under the formal protection of an Athenian patron (προστάτης). They came under the same military and financial obligations to the state as though they had been citizens, and we have Lysias's testimony to the fact that these duties were fully performed (**12.**

[1] Lys. 12. 4; Plato, *Republic*, 328 b.

9

20). They also received the privilege — not always granted even to ἰσοτελεῖς — of holding real estate.[1]

That Cephalus's home was one of refinement and a gathering place of the most cultured men of the time is evident from the fact that Plato chooses it as the scene of his great dialogue, the *Republic*.[2] Plato draws a charming picture of the aged man, sitting in the center of an eager circle, talking with Socrates about the infirmities and the compensating pleasures of old age. He says that he has the comfort of knowing that the ample fortune which had come down from his grandfather, Cephalus, and his father, Lysanias, will pass on undiminished to his sons. He admits that wealth is a comfort to old age, but insists that without a calm and happy spirit wealth would be worthless to an old man. Of the advantages that wealth gives he holds the greatest to be that it enables a man to fulfill all his obligations to gods and men, and so to face the unknown world beyond death with the good hope of which Pindar sings.[3]

The boy Lysias, brought up in such a home, had every advantage of contact with the leaders in the literary life of the city, and **Lysias's** of education with the sons of the best families.[4] But **Education** at the age of fifteen he set forth with his older brother, Polemarchus,[5] for the new colonial city Thurii, in southern Italy.

[1] We have explicit testimony to the fact that Lysias was ἰσοτελής (Ps.-Plut. 836 A), and the fact that the family owned real estate in Attica (12. 18) implies the same status for the others. (Inscriptions seldom show ἔγκτησις γῆς καὶ οἰκίας except as added to a grant of ἰσοτέλεια or προξενία.)

[2] Plato does not take pains to secure exact chronological accuracy in the setting of the dialogue. If he thought of it as held before the departure of Polemarchus for Thurii, Lysias and Euthydemus would hardly have been of an age to warrant their mention with the company gathered ; but if we place the dialogue after Polemarchus's return from Thurii, as is now commonly done, we must probably assume that Plato forgets or ignores the fact that at this time Cephalus had been dead several years.

[3] Plato, *Republic*, 328–332.

[4] Dionys. *Lysias*, § 1 ; Ps.-Plut. 835 C.

[5] Pseudo-Plutarch (835 D) says that Lysias had three brothers, Pole-

Here, near the site of old Sybaris, a new city was rising, to which men prominent in every profession were flocking from **Removal to** all Greece. Athens took the lead in founding the col- **Thurii** ony, but she treated it as a pan-Hellenic enterprise, and settlers were welcomed from every city. Hippodamus of Miletus, the greatest architect of the day, laid out the plan of the orderly streets; Protagoras of Abdera, the greatest of the sophists, the poet-philosopher Empedocles of Agrigentum, Tisias of Syracuse, chief expounder of the new Sicilian art of Rhetoric, Herodotus the historian, Cleandridas the Spartan statesman, were among the famous men who joined in founding the new city.

It is possible that Lysias and his brother were among the first colonists, in 443 B.C.,[1] but it is more likely that they went much later, about the beginning of the Peloponnesian War.[2]

marchus, Euthydemus, and Brachyllus. Dionys. (§ 1) says that two brothers went with him to Thurii, but according to Ps.-Plut. he went σὺν τῷ πρεσβυτάτῳ ἀδελφῶν Πολεμάρχῳ (835 D). In the opening of the *Republic* (328 B) Plato says, ᾖμεν οὖν οἴκαδε εἰς τοῦ Πολεμάρχου, καὶ Λυσίαν τε αὐτόθι κατε-λάβομεν καὶ Εὐθύδημον, τοὺς τοῦ Πολεμάρχου ἀδελφούς. Brachyllus was probably the husband of Lysias's sister (Blass, *Attische Beredsamkeit,* I.[2] 346).

[1] On the date of the colonization of Thurii see Busolt, *Griechische Geschichte,* III. 1. 523.

[2] The question of the date of the removal to Thurii is bound up with the unsettled question of the year of Lysias's birth. The data for **Birth** the year of birth are the following statements:

RELIABLE STATEMENTS

a. Cephalus settled in Athens by persuasion of Pericles; Lys. 12. 4.

b. Cephalus lived at Athens thirty years ; Lys. 12. 4.

STATEMENTS THAT ARE PROBABLY RELIABLE

c. Lysias was born at Athens; Dionys. § 1 ; Ps.-Plut. 835 C ; Cicero, *Brutus,* 16. 63.

d. Lysias was considerably older than Isocrates, who was born 436 B.C. ; Plato, *Phaedrus,* 228 A, 279 A.

e. Lysias removed to Thurii at the age of fifteen ; Dionys. § 1 ; Ps.-Plut. 835 D.

Here Polemarchus received the citizenship that had been beyond his reach at Athens, and Lysias too became a citizen in

f. Lysias and his brother returned to Athens during the rule of the Four Hundred, 411 B.C.; Ps.-Plut. 835 E; Dionys. § 1.

STATEMENTS OF DOUBTFUL VALUE

g. Lysias was born in the archonship of Philocles (459/8); Ps.-Plut. 835 C. But this date would easily be the result of a computation of one who did not know the birth year, but assumed the removal to Thurii to have been in 444/3 (444/3 + 15 = 459/8).

h. Lysias went to Thurii when the colony was founded; Dionys. § 1; Ps.-Plut. 835 D. But any one who did not know the date of the removal would naturally assume this.

i. Lysias was forty-seven years old when he returned to Athens; Dionys. § 1. But this may be only a reckoning of the number of years between the computed date 459/8 and 412/11. That it was so obtained is probable from Dionysius's qualifying words, ὡς ἄν τις εἰκάσειεν.

j. Cephalus died before Lysias went to Thurii; Ps.-Plut. 835 D. But by Pseudo-Plutarch's own statement that the removal was in 444/3 the coming of Cephalus to Athens is thus carried back before 474/3, a date too early for the influence of Pericles. The death of Cephalus before Lysias's removal would be a natural assumption to account for the migration of so young a boy.

The traditional date, 459/8, based on *g*, is consistent with the data as given above, but it forces us to the conclusion that Lysias's extraordinary professional activity fell between the years of fifty-five and seventy-eight. The improbability of so productive an old age, occupied with a profession taken up so late in life, has led many scholars to reject the date 459/8 and to seek other points of reckoning.

If we try to bring the birth year down to a later date, we must stop well before 436/5, the birth year of Isocrates (*d*). If we assume 446 as the approximate date, we have the coming of Cephalus (*a, c*) at a time when Pericles's influence was fully established, the removal to Thurii at about the beginning of the Peloponnesian War (= 446 − 15), and the death of Cephalus before 416 (= 446 − 30). This would bring the beginning of Lysias's professional work into the prime of his life.

By bringing the birth year down to 444, as is oftener done, we bring the possible date of Cephalus's death down to about 414, a time that allows the possibility of his having been seen by the boy Plato (b. 427). But the boy's knowledge of the old gentleman could hardly account for the beautiful

due time. The brothers prospered and acquired property.[1] We may safely conjecture that they were engaged in manufacture, as they were later at the Piraeus.

But the intellectual advantages open to the brothers in the new colony were no less attractive than their opportunities in politics and business. Polemarchus was committed to the study of Philosophy,[2] but Lysias turned to the new art of Rhetoric.

Rhetorical studies

In his school years at Athens his training had been in poetry only, the great epics and lyrics. He had doubtless heard, too, some of the works of the great dramatists ; but prose literature was still in its infancy. He might have read some of the work of the Ionian chroniclers, the undeveloped beginnings of historical writing, and he may well have heard, shortly before his departure for Thurii, some of the earliest work of Herodotus from his own lips. He had heard powerful speeches, — probably he had heard Pericles himself, — but at this time public men had no thought of publishing their speeches ; speech writing was only just coming to be regarded as a literary art, and the new art had not yet passed from the first theorists to the speakers in courts and ecclesia.

But at Thurii Lysias found himself in the midst of a new and vigorous literary movement, centering in the teaching of Tisias, the Syracusan rhetorician.

Corax of Syracuse had been the first to treat speech writing as an object of systematic study. We have only vague accounts of his work, but we know that, out of the mass of litigation that had come from revolutions and counterrevolutions in the Sicilian cities, the practice of the law courts had developed more rapidly than in the rest of Hellas, and that Corax

The Sicilian rhetoric

description in the *Republic*. It is more likely that Plato wrote of what he had learned from others.

For the detailed discussion of the whole question and the views of modern scholars, see Blass, *Attische Beredsamkeit*, I.[2] 339 ff.

[1] Dionys. § 1 ; Ps.-Plut. 835 D.

[2] Plato, *Phaedrus* 257 B.

had formulated certain principles of pleading. His greatest service was his study of the art of argument from " probabilities," an art which would enable one to plead upon scanty evidence, or even against overwhelming evidence of his opponent. He had made some progress, too, toward a theory of the effective disposition of matter in a speech — at least he had developed a theory of the structure of the proem. Tisias, his pupil, succeeded to the master's place, and reduced his teachings to a system, embodying them in a formal treatise ($T\acute{\epsilon}\chi\nu\eta$).

Tisias

Tisias, then, the young Lysias found at Thurii, and under his instruction he entered upon the study of the art of argumentation and speech writing (Ps.-Plut. 835 D).

But these studies were doubtless furthered by the influence of another great teacher, the greatest of the sophists, Protagoras. He had come to Thurii with the first colonists, and had helped draft their constitution. From him, or at least from pupils of his, Lysias would receive training no less valuable than that of Tisias. Protagoras did not aim so much at the production of a formal speech, but he professed to enable his pupils to conquer their opponents in any disputation, and this by his famous art of making the weaker the stronger argument, $\tau\grave{o}\nu$ $\mathring{\eta}\tau\tau\omega$ $\lambda\acute{o}\gamma o\nu$ $\kappa\rho\epsilon\acute{\iota}\tau\tau\omega$ $\pi o\iota\epsilon\hat{\iota}\nu$. The whole art of dialectic and eristic was his, and he professed to be able to corner the professor of any science on his own ground, without himself knowing the facts of the science on which he was disputing. This brilliant training in argumentation fitted exactly into Tisias's more limited teaching. It was, moreover, accompanied by other teaching which was lacking in Tisias's course, the systematic study of language. Grammar and vocabulary received careful treatment at the hands of Protagoras, so that his pupils were trained not only in the invention of argument, but in its correct expression.

Protagoras

Lysias came under these influences just as he was passing from boyhood to manhood, the age when he was best fitted to profit by the instruction which his abundant means and leisure opened to him. He devoted himself to the study of prose composition in the form of speech writing, not at all as a means of livelihood, but purely as a literary accomplishment.

The prosperous life of the brothers at Thurii continued about twenty years ;[1] but in 413 came the terrible disaster to the Athenian army before Syracuse, and the complete triumph **Expulsion** of the anti-Athenian party in Sicily. One result was **from Thurii** the expulsion from Thurii of some three hundred Athenian sympathizers, Polemarchus and Lysias being among the number.[2] The brothers naturally returned to their former home at Athens, where their mother was still living,[3] and where their father had left a large property.[4] Here, at the Piraeus, the **Return to** brothers conducted a shield manufactory operated by **Athens** more than a hundred slaves (12. 19). Lysias, and perhaps Polemarchus, lived at the Piraeus.[5]

On his return to the Piraeus Lysias had found the Four Hundred in power. They were supported at the first by the more intelligent and wealthy citizens, the class with whom **Political** Lysias's social and intellectual connections would be **conditions** most intimate. But as metics Lysias and Polemarchus could have no direct share in the stirring political movements of the summer of 411, which ended with the triumph of the conservative aristocracy. The next year saw the restoration of the radical democracy, and then followed the tremendous exertions of the exhausted state in its determined effort to ward off the inevitable result of the long-protracted war. In the great financial sacrifices demanded in these last years of the war, Lysias and his brother bore their full share. But they had inherited sufficient property, their busi-

---

[1] Upon the supposition that Lysias was born *c.* 446. The earlier birth year gives a residence of about thirty years. See p. 11.

[2] Dionys. *Lysias*, § 1; Ps.-Plut. 835 E.

[3] [Dem.] 59. 22.

[4] For the father's death, see p. 12.

[5] For the question of Polemarchus's residence, see on 12. 16. The brothers together owned three houses (12. 18).

ness was prosperous, and they came to the close of the war with better fortunes than did many of their associates.

The life of Lysias during these seven years was by no means that of a manufacturer hard pressed by the daily cares of his **Lysias's** business. The men of his class knew little of the **rhetorical** slavery that comes with the pressure of modern busi- **pursuits** ness methods. While he operated a successful manu- factory, the larger interests of his life were intellectual. His own study of rhetoric in the years at Thurii enabled him now, in the prime of life, to take his place at once among the most prominent writers at Athens. And in no department of lit- erature would excellence find quicker recognition at just this time than in rhetoric. For during the years of Lysias's ab- sence in Italy the same development of prose writing that had been going on at Thurii had advanced even more rapidly at Athens.

Even before the Peloponnesian War Protagoras had given his pupils at Athens the same training in language and in the art of **Rhetoric at** disputation which he gave at Thurii, and the lesser **Athens** sophists had worked effectively along the same lines, to train skilled debaters and to teach the art of polished expres- sion. But in the distinctive art of rhetoric two men, greater than any of Lysias's teachers, had been doing brilliant work at Athens, Thrasymachus of Chalcedon and Gorgias of Leontini.[1] Into the circle of their pupils Lysias now came.

Thrasymachus was one of the sophists and rhetoricians who went from city to city offering instruction in the new learning. He **Thrasyma-** was already well known at Athens about the beginning **chus of** of the Peloponnesian War[2] and became one of the **Chalcedon** great rhetorical teachers there, the most influential in the ultimate development of prose writing.[3] We have only a sin-

---

[1] It is entirely possible that Lysias had heard both Thrasymachus and Gorgias at Thurii; but the biographers name neither as his teacher.

[2] Aristophanes has his fling at him in 427 B.C., Frag. 198. 7.

[3] For a detailed study of Thrasymachus and his permanent influence on

gle fragment of his writing,[1] but from statements of ancient critics
we learn that he developed a clear and pure style of speech,
avoiding, on the one hand, the artificial stiffness of other rhetoricians, and, on the other, the undignified speech of the untrained
man ; that he was probably the first to perfect the rounded, periodic sentence, gathering the separate thoughts into one compact
whole ; and that he added to this periodic structure the beauty of
a fitting prose rhythm. Thrasymachus also taught his pupils the
effectiveness of the appeal to the feelings, in distinction from the
appeal to the reason only. The art of disputation as taught by
the other rhetoricians awakened the admiration of the hearers,
but it did not move them ; Thrasymachus taught how to reach the
will through the feelings. All of this work was sound, and it laid
a permanent foundation for that dignified, forcible, noble Attic
style which his pupil Isocrates later brought to perfection.

But during the same period, from 427 on, another, more popular, teacher of Rhetoric was coming from time to time to Athens,
Gorgias of Leontini, an exponent of the Sicilian rheto- **Gorgias of**
ric, with its elaborate arguments from probability, but **Leontini**
still more prominently the exponent of a new method of expression. Gorgias's invention was that of a new form of composition,
intermediate between poetry and prose. Poetry had the beauty
of the grouping of words in symmetrical verses determined by
meter ; Gorgias developed a form of prose in which short clauses
of almost or quite equal length were ranged in pairs, each pair
marked by an antithesis of thought, and often by rhyme of the
final syllables. Poetry had also the beauty of a vocabulary of its
own, raised above the common speech, and enriched by the free
word formations of the poet ; Gorgias transferred this rich vocabulary to his prose. To compensate for the loss of the rhythm of
poetry, he pleased the ear with constant assonance of syllables,
and with every sort of play on the sounds of words.

Attic prose, see Drerup, *Untersuchungen zur älteren griechischen Prosalittera-
tur*, p. 225 ff.

[1] A proem of thirty-seven lines preserved by Dionys. *Demosthenes*, § 3.

The young Athenians were carried away by this novel style of composition. They flocked to his lectures and vied with one another in imitating his prettily balanced antitheses and his cunning play of sounds. No writer of the time entirely escaped his influence. It formed an irresistible current setting toward all that was artificial in speech.

Yet a third man had been molding Attic prose style in these same years, Antiphon, an Athenian by birth. Under the influence **Antiphon** of the earlier Sicilian teachers, Antiphon took up the study and teaching of rhetoric, and that in the most practical form. His work, like that of Thrasymachus and Gorgias, commenced about the beginning of the Peloponnesian War. He published a systematic treatise on rhetoric ($T\acute{\epsilon}\chi\nu\eta$), and a series of model speeches to illustrate methods of handling both sides of typical cases at law. But Antiphon was more than a theorist ; he was an active politician, — the real intellectual force back of the oligarchy of the Four Hundred, — and he wrote speeches for litigants to deliver in actual cases in the courts. He further treated these speeches not simply as pleas to accomplish their immediate purpose in the court room, but as literary masterpieces, to be published and circulated afterward.[1]

In style Antiphon was neither poetic like Gorgias, nor clear and noble like Thrasymachus, but he had a dignity of expression which, with his strength in argument, gave him a commanding position. His mature work represents the earlier, strong type of Athenian speech of the Periclean time, modified, but not controlled, by the refinements of Thrasymachus and Gorgias.[2]

Now when Lysias returned to Athens in 411 he found the **The amateur study of rhetoric** influence of these three men at its height. All had published treatises on the theory of rhetoric, and speeches by all were in circulation among students of oratory. The most mature work of each of the three falls near

---

[1] The sophists and rhetoricians were freely publishing their model speeches and rhetorical exercises, but Antiphon was the first to publish speeches that had been actually used in court.   [2] Drerup, pp. 293, 296, 350.

this date. Lysias found also a body of men of his own age and younger, trained under these teachers, enthusiasts in the art of speech writing. Many men had taken up the work as a money-earning profession, and were prospering as speech writers (λογο-γράφοι) for the political assemblies and the courts. But they were looked upon only as tradesmen, and hardly had access to the inner circle of the gentlemen who were cultivating the new art for art's sake. Into this inner circle Lysias came, and was soon recognized as its ablest representative.

Of his work in this period we obtain invaluable knowledge through the *Phaedrus* of Plato, his younger contemporary. Plato represents Socrates as meeting his young friend Phae- **The Phaedrus** drus all aglow from the hearing of a wonderful dis- **of Plato** course of Lysias at the house of a friend. Upon Socrates's request that Phaedrus recite the speech to him, Phaedrus replies, " Do you suppose that I, a layman in the art, could give the speech from memory in a way that would be worthy of Lysias, the ablest writer of the day, a composition on which he has worked long and at his leisure ? I would give much if I could ! " After some byplay of insistence and refusal Socrates discovers that Phaedrus has Lysias's manuscript hidden under his cloak. So, seated under a plane-tree, Phaedrus proceeds to read aloud Lysias's discourse on Love. At the close of the reading Socrates finds his young friend in a fine frenzy, carried away by the charm of the language. After a bit of mock sympathy with his ravings, Socrates turns to a sharp criticism of the speech, both as to form and content.[1]

We may think of Lysias, then, in these last years of the Peloponnesian War, as occupying his abundant leisure with the composition of speeches and essays designed to be read to a circle of his private friends, and perhaps to be published. It is not likely,

[1] Whether the discourse of Lysias in the *Phaedrus* was a part of a published speech which Plato incorporated in his dialogue as a subject for criticism, or only a discourse written by Plato in the manner of Lysias, has been much disputed. The prevailing opinion now is that it is the work of Lysias himself. So Jebb, *Attic Orators*, I. 305 ff.; Blass, *o.c.* p. 424 ff.

though it is possible, that he was already beginning to give courses
of lectures on rhetoric. His written discourses were ranked with
the best work of Thrasymachus and Gorgias.

But the prosperity of these years after the return from Thurii
was suddenly interrupted. The disastrous close of the war was
followed by the political revolution which put the
The Thirty Thirty into complete control of the city, while this
body itself soon fell under the domination of a reckless and desperate faction headed by the returned exile Critias. The Thirty
found themselves with an empty treasury, with no subject states to
furnish tribute as of old, with their own citizens terribly impoverished by the twenty-seven years' war; and they had to meet, not
only the ordinary expenses of the state, but the expense of the
employment of a standing Spartan garrison. They could not
safely put heavy financial burdens upon those of their own citizens
who had still some property remaining, for it was upon the good-
will of these richer citizens that the administration had to depend
for moral support. The obvious resort was the seizure of the
property of the wealthy metics, who formed a large class of the
men engaged in business and manufacture.

False charges against a group of these metics were formulated
and their condemnation pushed through the Senate, without warning or opportunity of defense for the accused. Among
The seizure the victims of this lawless attack were the brothers
of Polemar- Polemarchus and Lysias. In his twelfth speech Lysias
chus and
Lysias gives the detailed account of their arrest, the seizure
of their property, the execution of his brother, and his own narrow
escape and flight to Megara.

When the democratic exiles who had been banished by the
Thirty gathered on the frontier and moved down upon Piraeus,
"The Re- establishing themselves in camp at Munychia, Lysias
turn" joined them and became an active helper in the
Return.[1] After the restoration of the democracy Thrasybulus, the

---

[1] 12. 53 implies that Lysias was with the exiles at Piraeus. Ps.-Plutarch
(835 F) says that he furnished 2000 drachmas and 200 shields; that he hired

great leader of the Return, carried a motion in the Ecclesia[1] that citizenship be granted to all who had joined in the return of the democrats.[2] This would have given to Lysias the full rights of a citizen, but the decree was attacked as illegal by Archinus, another of the democratic leaders, and was defeated in the courts (see XXXIV, Introd.).[3]

Failure to receive citizenship

Immediately after the restoration of the democracy Lysias came before the courts in the prosecution of Eratosthenes, the member of the Thirty who had arrested his brother, Polemarchus. To this prosecution Lysias brought the perfected skill in argument and arrangement of matter and the facility in expression which he had been acquiring in his years of rhetorical training. This prosecution, while probably not successful in securing the condemnation of Eratosthenes, brought Lysias prominently before the public, and opened the way for him to enter at once upon a career as a λογογράφος, or professional writer of

Prosecution of Eratosthenes

Beginning of career as a professional speech writer

---

300 mercenaries (presumably Ps.-Plutarch means at his own expense), and secured a gift of two talents for the cause from Thrasydaeus, an Elean friend. If these statements are true, Lysias must have saved something from the wreck of his property. The statements may have come from Lysias's speech "On his Services."

[1] On the date, see Chron. 401 B.C.

[2] μετεδίδου τῆς πολιτείας πᾶσι τοῖς ἐκ Πειραιέως συγκατελθοῦσι, ὧν ἔνιοι φανερῶς ἦσαν δοῦλοι, Arist. *Resp. Ath.* 40. 2.

[3] The account of the biographers rests upon a misunderstanding of this motion of Thrasybulus. Pseudo-Plutarch says (835 F) that Thrasybulus moved that citizenship be given to Lysias, that it was so voted by the people, but that their action was annulled by the courts as illegal, not being based on a recommendation of the Senate (cp. Phot. 4. 172 C; Schol. Aesch. 3. 195; Schol. Hermog., Walz V. 343). The tradition has evidently represented as a special proposition in the case of Lysias what was really a proposition for all who had shared in the Return. The effect of a γραφὴ παρανόμων was to suspend any decree against which it was brought, pending the decision of the courts (Meier u. Schömann, *Der attische Process*, p. 435). Archinus probably brought his action immediately upon the passage of the decree, so that we can hardly suppose that Lysias enjoyed even a few weeks of citizenship.

speeches for others to deliver in the courts or political assemblies. What had before been the occupation of scholarly leisure now became the means of restoring his fortunes.

With remarkable literary insight Lysias was able to turn from the artificial style which he, like all rhetoricians of the time, had cultivated for purposes of display, and to perfect a type of plain, practical speech, which soon placed him at the head of his profession.

It was probably at this time that he also began the work of **Lysias as a** formal teaching. We have Aristotle's testimony [1] that **teacher of** Lysias at first taught rhetoric, but that finding in **rhetoric** Theodorus of Byzantium a rival who was his superior in rhetorical theory, he turned to the work of a λογογράφος.[2]

Another rival also soon appeared in the person of his younger contemporary, Isocrates, who returned about 400 B.C. from a **His work as** course of rhetorical training under Gorgias in Thessaly. **a speech** Isocrates, with his artificial style and his refined ele- **writer** gance of expression, proved no match for Lysias in speech writing for court or ecclesia, and soon abandoned this field, turning to the teaching of rhetoric, and the publication of political pamphlets, cast for the most part in the form of speeches.

Lysias was thus left as the recognized master of practical speech writing. As a metic he was excluded from personal activity in politics, and thus he turned the more toward the one pursuit of writing for others. The fact of the superiority of his rivals in the department of teaching rhetoric tended to the same result. The twenty years after the restoration of the democracy show remarkable activity of Lysias in this professional work. In the first cen-

[1] Cited by Cicero, *Brutus*, § 48.

[2] It is quite possible (Blass, p. 347, holds it as certain) that his work as a teacher falls in the period before the Thirty, but it seems more probable that this money-earning work began with his work as a paid speech writer after the loss of his property. The title, ὁ σοφιστής, applied to him in [Dem.] 59. 21, probably comes from this work as a teacher.

tury A.D. more than two hundred of his published speeches were in circulation.[1]

Only once do we find Lysias coming forward personally in public affairs. In 388 the Corinthian War was still dragging along, indecisive and burdensome to both sides ; but rumors were abroad that a coalition was forming on the side of Sparta, between Persia and Dionysius, tyrant of Syracuse. At the Olympic Games of that year a splendidly equipped delegation from Dionysius appeared, and a band of rhapsodists chanted the poems of the tyrant.

Against this glorification of the tyrant of his father's native city Lysias delivered before the assembled Greeks his Olympic oration. The Greeks were urged to give up their ruinous strife with one another, and to join against their common enemies, the tyrants. So effective is the speech said to have been that the crowds rushed upon the gold-bedecked tent of the Syracusans and plundered it.[2]

Of Lysias's private life after the Return, we know only that his wife was a daughter of his sister, and that he was a lover of the *hetaera* Metanira, for whom he secured initiation into the Eleusinian Mysteries.[3]

Private life

As we can trace his professional work down to about 380 B.C., we conclude that he died not long after that date.[4]

Death

[1] Pseudo-Plutarch (836 A) says that 425 speeches were current under the name of Lysias, of which Dionysius and Caecilius held 233 to be genuine. It was only natural that many speeches of unknown authorship came in time to be ascribed to so fertile and popular an author.

[2] Diodor. 14. 109 ; Dionysius, *Lysias*, § 29 ; Ps.-Plut. 836 D. For the story of a mission of Lysias to the court of Dionysius, based upon a probably corrupt Ms. reading, see crit. note on 19. 19.

[3] [Dem.] 59. 21, 22.

[4] We have the statement of Pseudo-Plutarch (836 A) that Lysias died at Athens ὀγδοήκοντα τρία ἔτη βιούς, ἢ ὥς τινες ἐξ καὶ ἑβδομήκοντα, ἢ ὥς τινες ὑπὲρ ὀγδοήκοντα, a statement which shows only that the biographers had no reliable knowledge of the date.

THE WORKS OF LYSIAS

Our manuscripts of Lysias [1] have preserved thirty-one speeches,
of which twenty-three are now commonly held to be genuine.

Collections Parts of three other speeches are preserved in our
of Lysias's manuscripts of Dionysius of Halicarnassus,[2] being
speeches inserted by him as specimens of Lysias's style. To
these is to be added the fragment in Plato's *Phaedrus*.[3]

The ancient critics made the following classification of speeches :

Λόγοι
- δικανικοί, *court speeches* { δημόσιοι *in public cases.* / ἰδιωτικοί *in private cases.*
- συμβουλευτικοί, *deliberative speeches in political assemblies.*
- ἐπιδεικτικοί, *exhibition speeches,* including rhetorical exercises, eulogies, speeches for public festivals, *etc.*

Twenty-four of the twenty-six extant speeches fall under the
first class, the department in which Lysias especially excelled.
Of greatest historical interest is the group of speeches for public
cases arising out of the question of reconstruction after the rule
of the Thirty — cases which involved the vital question how far the
supporters of the oligarchy were to be restored to political influence under the restored democracy.[4] The political questions
involved naturally give to these speeches much of the tone and
manner of deliberative oratory, and in the most important, the
Speech against Eratosthenes (XII), Lysias speaks in his own
person.

We have only four speeches written for litigants in private
cases : X is for the prosecution in a libel suit ; XVII is for a
claimant of disputed property ; XXIII, a preliminary suit to determine the legal status of an alleged citizen, to clear the way for
the prosecution of a private claim ; XXXII, a suit of an heir
against his guardian, to force the relinquishment of an estate.

Of speeches of the second main division, the deliberative, we

[1] See App. V.   [2] See XXXII, first crit. note.
[3] Blass (p. 375) classes this with ἐπιστολαί, after Hermias.
[4] For the fuller discussion of these cases, see p. 39 ff.

have only one, and that probably incomplete (XXXIV). It is a speech written for a citizen who, immediately after the overthrow of the Thirty, opposed a proposition before the Ecclesia to restrict the franchise to owners of real estate.[1]

The third main division is represented in our extant speeches only by the proem of the *Olympic Speech*.[2]

THE STYLE OF LYSIAS

Lysias stands in the judgment of the Greek and Roman critics as the greatest representative of the Plain Style[3] in prose composition.[4] The Grand Style of Thucydides and the florid, poetic mannerisms of Gorgias stand at one extreme; the simple, straightforward style of Lysias, at the other. Lysias took the plain, direct speech of daily life, purified it of its colloquialisms and vulgarities, and shaped it into a perfect medium for the expression of his thought. His language is the current speech of his own day, neither elevated by occasional words from the vocabulary of the older generation, nor enriched by the diction of the poets, nor made striking by newly formed compounds. Even metaphorical language he seldom used.[5]

Lysias a representative of the Plain Style

Vocabulary

---

[1] See XXXIV, Introd.   [2] See p. 23.

[3] For discussion of the three " Styles," see App. § 37 ff.

[4] Modern criticism of the style of Lysias naturally follows the generally sound observations of Dionysius of Halicarnassus. In his treatise on Lysias he extols his Purity of Language (§ 2), Simplicity of Language (§ 3), Clearness (§ 4), Brevity (§ 5), Compact and Rounded Composition (§ 6), Vividness (§ 7), Ethopoiia (§ 8), Adaptedness (§ 9), Persuasiveness (§ 10), and Charm (§ 10 ff.). It must be remembered that Dionysius had a large body of Lysias's works where we have but a few, and that he had a broader basis for comparison in the possession of many more of the works of his contemporaries than have come down to us.

[5] In 24. 14 we have a brief simile, heightened by personification. In 24. 3 ἰᾶσθαι is a simple metaphor. But this speech is throughout in mock-rhetorical style. Other metaphorical expressions are the simple and common ones of

To this simplicity of vocabulary was added a skill in phrase and sentence structure that produced remarkable clearness. In
Sentence structure. Clearness reading Thucydides or Antiphon we are often puzzled to catch the meaning of a sentence, though every individual word may be simple. Lysias seldom perplexes us ; he expresses the relations of words as well as the words themselves ; phrases follow in the natural order of thought ; and the sentences are seldom too long to be carried in the mind as a whole.

And yet this clearness is consistent with brevity both in thought and language. From the union of this simplicity and
Brevity brevity, together with a fine appreciation of the striking details in a story, comes the vividness of Lysias's narrative style — a department in which he was never surpassed.

But the simplicity of Lysias's composition, even in much of his narrative, is not the monotonous simplicity of the pure " running
Periodic structure style."[1] The art of periodic composition had already become the subject of careful study at Athens before Lysias returned from Thurii.[2] While we have no knowledge of Lysias's own theories of the rhetorical " period," we certainly find him to be master of a style that made full use of the compact and rounded form that we properly call periodic,[3] without sacrifice of grace and simplicity.

This effect is due to the brevity and simplicity of his periods, and to the fact that he seldom casts the whole sentence in periodic form. Within the limits of one sentence we often find one, or two, or even more, short periods, but united with other clauses that remain outside the periodic structure. Comparatively few

22. 8 μαχομένων ; 22. 15 πολιορκούμεθα ; 25. 25 καρπωσαμένους ; 32. 22 πολεμῶσι.

We find personification in 12. 14 πρόθυμον δύναμιν ; 12. 23 παρανομίᾳ ; 12. 36 ἀρετῇ ; 12. 78 πονηρίας ; 32. 23 πονηρίαν.

[1] For the full discussion of the running and the periodic styles, see App. § 37 ff

[2] Cp. p. 17.

[3] On the ancient and modern use of the term "period" see App. § 52 ff.

sentences are entirely without periodic form, yet in comparatively few does the periodic structure embrace the whole thought. In many sentences again the periodic structure is that of form only, the formal subordination of clauses that are logically coördinate.[1]

The periodic structure in a speech of Lysias is thus seldom obtrusive. We do not often, as in Isocrates regularly, find sentence after sentence shaped in a stiff periodic mold, nor do we often come upon periods so strong and compact that they challenge attention, as they so often do in the speeches of Demosthenes. In Lysias the periodic structure runs through all, giving tone to all, yet usually subordinate to the natural logical flow of the thought.[2]

The periodic language is most marked, as is fitting, in proems and the more earnest appeals, while in narrative it is either of a simplified type or is abandoned altogether.

Yet there is a difference in the periodic composition of the several speeches. Lysias was too good an artist to put into the mouth of the ordinary client a speech that would, by its very phraseology, remind the hearer that the speaker was only declaiming a purchased plea. For the plain man he wrote in a plain style that so concealed its art as to seem the natural expression of the man himself. But for the more mature or experienced client, from whose lips the more rhetorical style would not seem unfitting, and especially in cases that dealt with public questions, he sometimes wrote in a manner distinctly more formal, with no little use of the mannerisms of the current rhetoric in the structure of sentence and period.[3]

[1] See App. § 50.

[2] In this fact we find the explanation of the apparently contradictory statements of Dionysius that Lysias's composition is smooth and simple (συντίθησί γε αὐτὴν ἀφελῶς πάνυ καὶ ἁπλῶς, ὁρῶν ὅτι οὐκ ἐν τῇ περιόδῳ καὶ τοῖς ῥυθμοῖς, ἀλλ' ἐν τῇ διαλελυμένῃ λέξει γίνεται τὸ ἦθος, Lysias § 8), and yet that he is a master of "compact and rounded expression" (ἡ συστρέφουσα τὰ νοήματα καὶ στρογγύλως ἐκφέρουσα λέξις, § 6).

[3] The twenty-fifth speech is a notable example of this. Its style is far removed from that of the sixteenth.

When writing for his own delivery, as in the *Speech against Eratosthenes*, Lysias was free to follow his own ideal of oratory, and

The "Gorgian figures" it is in precisely this speech that we find him making largest use of the rhetorical devices of the day.[1] Here we find, especially in proem and epilogue, the frequent use of antithetic and parallel structure of periods, set off by some of the so-called "Gorgian figures" of speech.[2] When, therefore, we speak of Lysias as the representative of the Plain Style of composition it must be with the qualification that this statement applies strictly to his sentence structure in those speeches only where he is writing for the plain man or for the commonplace issue. In other cases, while always far from the grand style, he does show distinctly and repeatedly the artificial traits of the rhetorical style.

Another chief characteristic of Lysias's work is implied in what has just been said. This is his Ethopoiia, such adaptation of sen-

Ethopoiia timent, argument, and language to the personality ($\mathring{\eta}\theta o\varsigma$) of the client, that it seems to the hearers the natural expression of the speaker's own thought. In this Lysias has no rival. And this effect was produced by no mechanical imitation of speech or character.[3] Lysias did not put into the mouth of an uncultured man the ungrammatical or coarse language that he might easily have imitated, nor did he restrict himself to the narrow range of thought which such a client might have had. Both speech and thought are often above the level of the speaker's own powers. And yet they are so nicely fitted to his case, they express so clearly his own feelings, and they so easily carry the hearer along by their apparent candor and sim-

---

[1] The twenty-fourth speech is so manifestly mock-rhetorical in form that it should not be considered as in the same class with the others.

[2] For detailed statements as to these "figures" and Lysias's use of them see App. § 56 ff.

[3] See Bruns's enlightening discussion of the meaning and method of Ethopoiia, *Literarisches Porträt*, p. 440 ff. The best treatment of the subject in English is the dissertation by Devries, *Ethopoiia*, Baltimore, 1892.

plicity, that we forget the professional writer and think only of the speaker.

This perfection of art could have come only from a rare ability to enter into the feelings of the client, to grasp the essential points of his case, and to see in talking with him what sentiments would seem natural and unaffected as coming from his lips ; and then artfully to embody all of this in language in which all art should be concealed.[1]   Not every speech offers opportunity for Ethopoiia. The prosecutor does not make his own personality prominent, and defendants have more occasion to emphasize their own personality in some cases than in others.   It is in cases of defense on δοκι-μασία, like those of the sixteenth and twenty-fifth speeches, that Lysias finds his perfect opportunity to embody his client's personality in his speech.[2]

Closely allied to Ethopoiia is the portraiture of other persons involved in a case.   Here Lysias is no less successful.   With a few strokes he gives a picture that stands as a perma-nent character in literature.   Such are the portraits of **Portraiture** Theramenes in the twelfth speech, of Aristophanes in the nine-teenth, of the speaker and his father in the same speech, of the politician in the twenty-fifth, of Diogiton and his daughter in the thirty-second.

To the qualities already discussed Dionysius adds *adaptedness*, τὸ πρέπον.   This is in some measure included in Ethopoiia, but it means more than that, for it includes adaptedness of   **" Adapted-** the speech to all the conditions under which it is   **ness "** spoken.   We have a good example in the twelfth speech, where there is no occasion for Ethopoiia, but where the plea is adapted with great skill to appeal to the two very different factions in the jury.

---

[1] For the discussion of Ethopoiia as shown in individual speeches, see *Notes on Argument and Style*.   For the possible imitation of personal peculi-arities of language, see on 19. 15.

[2] See Bruns's discriminating treatment of Lysias's pleas in prosecution and defense, p. 438 ff.

Last of all, as the crowning quality of Lysias's style, and a quality so pervasive that it alone would serve to distinguish
Charm genuine from spurious speeches of Lysias, Dionysius names a certain indefinable *charm*, χάρις. This is only to give a name to the final impression produced by all of the qualities that have been mentioned. It is the result of the combined purity and simplicity and vividness of diction, with the fine adaptation of all to speaker and occasion.

Dionysius admits what all readers must feel, that Lysias is not strong in the appeal to the feelings. He presents his case in a
Weakness in way that secures conviction, but he seldom arouses
appeal to the anger or fear. The pathos of simplicity he does have,
feelings through his marvelous power in narrative. But when we think how, in a case like that of the twelfth speech, Demosthenes would have poured out his wrath upon Eratosthenes, and how he would have swept all before his flood of indignation, we feel that even here, where Lysias is most stirred, his language is too cold and calm.

Nor has Lysias the power of Isocrates or Demosthenes to lift the hearer up to high planes of moral or political thought. He makes no attempt to raise a case from the range of small and temporary considerations to that of great principles.

But within these limits Lysias has unexcelled skill in the discovery and invention of arguments.[1] He has the Greek shrewd-
Invention of ness in turning a point for or against a man at will.
argument When a rich man has performed large financial services for the state, if he is Lysias's client, the services are a proof of his noble loyalty ;[2] but if he is Lysias's opponent, they are a proof of the rapidity with which the fellow has enriched himself from the public funds, and of his shameless effrontery.[3] If influential friends plead for the acquittal of the accused, Lysias urges the

---

[1] The early Greek Rhetoric was divided into three departments: εὕρεσις, *invention ;* λέξις, *expression ;* and τάξις, *arrangement.* See *Volkmann, Rhetorik der Griechen und Römer,* p. 28.

[2] 21. 1 ff.   [3] 27. 10.

jury to be as zealous in punishing the public enemy as these men are in trying to save their personal friend.[1] When Lysias's client finds that he is the only man to appear as prosecutor on a charge of embezzlement, this becomes a proof of the extent of the defendant's stealings — that he has been able to buy off all prosecutors save one.[2] If the opponent of Lysias's client is a rich man, the jury must condemn him to show that no man is rich enough to buy their votes ;[3] if the opponent is eloquent, he must be condemned as a warning to the whole class of demagogues, who try to deceive the people by their powers of speech.[4]

Lysias is always resourceful, shrewd in covering his own weak point, and as shrewd in finding or inventing the weakness of his opponent. He has the respectable moderation of his **Moderation in attack** time in refraining from the vulgar invective and outright lying that marred the legal practice of Demosthenes and his contemporaries a generation later,[5] but he does not hesitate to put false construction upon the actions of his opponent, and to play upon unworthy prejudices of the jury. He is, so far as invention of argument is concerned, a typical product of that rhetorical school which prided itself upon " making the weaker, the stronger case."

In the arrangement of matter and the structure of the framework of his speeches, Lysias is less successful. There is little variation in his plan — a proem to catch the attention **Arrangement of matter** and favor of the jury, a brief statement of the case (unless it is already before the jury), often a simple narrative of facts, then detailed arguments followed by a brief and seldom effective epilogue. He has little skill in so arranging his several arguments as to make them converge to one point, or lead up to a climax of conviction or feeling. In the shorter speeches we do not feel this weakness, but in a long plea like the nineteenth it is noticeable ; our conviction is stronger at the middle than at the close.

---

[1] 30. 33. [2] 29. 1. [3] 28. 9.
[4] 27. 5. [5] Cp. Bruns, pp. 470, 552–6.

The Revolutions of 411 and 404 B.C.

THE public activity of Lysias began immediately after the overthrow of the Thirty Tyrants. Several of his earliest and most
Relation of Lysias to the political revolutions
important speeches were written for the prosecution or defense of men who had been engaged in the revolutions of 411 and 404 B.C. The understanding of many of his speeches requires a knowledge of both attempts of the richer and more intelligent classes to set aside the democracy of Pericles, as it had been modified in effect, if not in principle, by his successors, and to establish a conservative form of government, with limited franchise, which should deprive the masses of their political power.

Both of our traditional terms, "The Oligarchy of the Four Hundred" and "The Thirty Tyrants," are misleading. It is true
The origin of the two "Revolutions"
that the administration of the Four Hundred did become a mere oligarchy, and that of the Thirty, outright tyranny; but it was because in each case a small clique of unprincipled men gained control of a movement which originated in an attempt at genuine political reform, and which was at the outset supported by the best intelligence and character of the city.[1]

While the immediate occasion of the revolution of 411 was the offer of Alcibiades to rescue the city from its imminent danger, by securing Persian help, upon condition of the disfranchisement of the Demos, yet the real force back of the whole movement was the profound conviction among intelligent and loyal citizens that the existing democracy was a failure.

[1] For outline of events, see Chron. Appendix.

Athens had been plunged into a terrible war to gratify the personal ambition, as many believed, of the great democratic leader. Since the death of Pericles (in 429) the leadership had been neither energetic nor intelligent, except during brief intervals. When, by the trapping of a Spartan force on the island of Sphacteria (in 425), Sparta was brought to propose peace on terms which would have left Athens in full possession of her own power, and would surely have broken up the Peloponnesian confederacy, Cleon carried the crowd in the assembly against the peace proposals. When, after Cleon's death, the Peace of Nicias had been negotiated by the conservative leader on terms which preserved to Athens a fair equivalent of her former power (in 421), and when Sparta had gone so far as to seek a defensive alliance with her, — a turn of events full of unexpected promise, — peace was again snatched from the state by the masses, carried away by the influence of their latest and most dangerous leader, Alcibiades, with the help of Hyperbolus, Cleon's worthy successor. Then came the great democratic enterprise, the Sicilian expedition, with its dazzling promises and terrible failure, draining the city of men and ships and money. At last, in 412, crippled in resources, depleted in troops, weary of years of fighting, the state was facing dire peril. Against her stood the united Peloponnesians, supported now by Syracuse, and with the promise of Persian gold and ships ; her control of the sea was no longer secure ; a permanent Lacedaemonian army of occupation at Decelea controlled the outlying Attic districts, and forced the city to maintain a vigilant defense of her own walls ; and now the allies, long restive under the arbitrary and shortsighted domination of Athens, were making haste to revolt and to put themselves under the protection of Sparta.

The attitude of the masses toward the Peloponnesian War

There was never a more imperative call for wise and efficient statesmanship ; for an administration which could carry on large military enterprises, handle the finances of a hard-pressed state, conduct the most delicate foreign negotiations, and call out the hearty support and confidence of all the citizens. The democratic administration was notoriously lacking in all of **The failures** these qualities. Both Senate and Ecclesia expressed **of the demo-** for the most part the changing will of the masses. **cratic ad-** Only in special emergencies, and not always then, **ministration** could the better element be rallied with strength enough to overcome the popular vote. The demagogues had been steadily increasing in power since the beginning of the war, and the "sycophants"—politicians turned blackmailers—were on every side threatening the men of property. This new generation of democratic leaders, trained in the popular arts of rhetoric, was the more dangerous by reason of the perfection of its tools. The courts were in the hands of demagogues and sycophants, and their verdict no longer carried moral weight. And all the **Financial** time the war, long maintained against the protests of **burdens** the middle and upper classes, was bearing down upon them. Agriculture was destroyed, manufactures crippled by the loss of thousands of slave artisans and by the call for free men of the laboring class for service in the fleet ; foreign trade was gone with the closing of the ports of the Athenian league, and the transference of the seat of war to the Aegean. And now heavy direct war taxes began to press upon all who had any considerable property left. The cutting off of the tribute by the revolt of the cities of the league threw the whole cost of the war upon the citizens themselves. To the whole body of the richer citizens financial ruin seemed inevitable.

Another influential class too was ripe for action against the radical democracy. The intellectual leaders, full of the new **Aristocratic** learning of the sophists, were in the full tide of revolt **sentiments** against the authority of tradition in politics, as in reli- **of the edu-** gion ; every institution had to meet their challenge **cated men** and justify itself to their reason. Among these men the incompetence of the Demos was taken for granted, and they were eagerly discussing theories of government and ideal constitutions. Some saw in the Spartan oligarchy the ideal form of government. Yet few had lost faith in the entire democratic idea ; most believed that citizenship must be limited, and their watchword had already become " Return to the constitution of the fathers." To some this meant the constitution of Solon ; to others, the moderate democracy of Clisthenes ; to all it meant the cutting loose from the domination of the masses.

In this repudiation of the extreme democracy the men of the new culture found themselves in perfect agreement with the very men to whom in religious and literary questions they were most opposed, the representatives of the conservative aristocracy. Thus the anti-democratic idea was fostered by men like Antiphon, now a man of nearly seventy years, the ablest representative of the new profession of the law, and a leading theorist in the new political science ; Thucydides, the scholarly representative of the property holding aristocracy ; Socrates, the philosopher, and many of his circle ; Euripides, the poet of the new culture, and his bitterest critic, Aristophanes, the champion of the "good old " beliefs and customs. The reaction against the existing democracy is prominent in all that is best in the thought of the time.

It was under these conditions, with dissatisfaction with the actual working of democracy pervading all the more intelligent circles, and under the impending ruin of the propertied classes **The Revolution of 411 B.C.** by the continuance of the war, that the proposition came from Alcibiades for a change in the government. The result was the Revolution of 411, which put the Four Hundred into power. The movement was supported by the best and wisest men in the state.

But even in its preliminary stages the revolution betrayed signs of fatal weakness. The honorable and patriotic men among the leaders allowed the hot-headed younger men to take the lead in putting down opposition. More than one democratic opponent was assassinated, and a policy of general terrorism was followed, as the easiest means of clearing the way for the new movement.

The revolutionary government once set up, it was inevitable

that the control should fall still more into the hands of the " practical politicians." The existence of a well-organized system of party clubs enabled their leaders to set aside the representative government that they had promised.

The failure to win the fleet to the support of the new movement threw the aristocratic leaders into grave danger, for there **Dangers of** was every reason to fear a successful democratic reac-**the new** tion. The leaders, instead of meeting this danger by **government** carrying out their earlier. promises, and so drawing together the whole body of conservative citizens, made the fatal mistake of withdrawing more closely into their own small group, **Treason of** and seeking their personal safety and the support of **the leaders** their government by plans for a treacherous surrender of the city to Sparta.

Their attempt was thwarted only just in time by the prompt **Theramenes** action of one of their own party, Theramenes, who organized a revolt against the leaders of the Four Hundred within their own number, and succeeded in bringing **The modified** into power the real conservative aristocracy, under a **aristocracy** limited franchise along the lines at first proposed by the reformers.

But now the fleet under its democratic leaders won a series **The demo-** of brilliant victories on the Hellespont, which so **cratic fleet** turned the tide of feeling at home that it soon swept away the moderate administration of Theramenes and restored the old democratic constitution. The attempt at a **Restoration** reform of the democracy was at an end, and the **of democ-** Demos, led by Cleophon, a typical demagogue, was **racy** again in complete control.

For six years (410–404) the democracy went on as of old, led now by Cleophon, now by Alcibiades, — welcomed back to the **Last years** city as the idol of the people, only to be repudiated **of the war** on his first reverse at sea, — then led again by Cleophon and his radicals. All of the abuses of the democracy were once more in full swing. The demagogues attacked the moderate and conservative supporters of the Four Hundred, and inflicted upon them banishment or confiscation of property or disfranchisement; advantageous peace proposals from Sparta were rejected; victorious and patriotic generals were put to death under the hot anger of the populace at the loss of their friends in the storm off the Arginusae (406); and at last the fleet in which had been staked, by one supreme effort, the last resources of the impoverished city was lost at Aegospotami — betrayed by the treachery or the incompetence of its generals. And still the radical democratic leaders refused to talk of peace. It was only when the Peloponnesian fleet under Lysander had closed their harbor, and the land force had moved in upon the suburbs of the city, and when hunger was beginning to press hard upon them, that the conservative element succeeded in making itself heard, and its leader, Theramenes, was entrusted with negotiations for peace.

With the surrender of the city to Sparta the political situation was entirely changed. Whether or not the terms of surrender included the express provision that the democracy be **Effect of** set aside, it was certainly no part of the Spartan pro- **the sur-** gramme to leave the Athenian Demos, with its unyield- **render** ing hatred of Sparta, anything of its old power. It was fully understood between the aristocratic leaders and the Spartans that a new government was to be set up, which should exclude the masses from political power.

When the Spartan Lysander entered the city upon its surrender, he brought with him a body of exiled Athenians, men who had been banished for their support of the government of **Restoration** the Four Hundred, and who now stood under the **of exiled** definite protection of Sparta. They at once united **oligarchs** with the aristocratic element in the city in perfecting arrangements for a new aristocratic revolution. The old political clubs were reorganized under even more efficient central control; the extreme oligarchs, under the lead of Critias, made common cause with the moderate faction of Theramenes; and finally, supported by

Lysander in person, they carried through, without violence, a com-
Establish-   plete revolution.   Nominally the board of Thirty Com-
ment of the   missioners who were appointed were to draw up a new
Thirty   constitution and to administer the government only
until that should be adopted, but in fact they became an irrespon-
sible governing board, with a Senate entirely subservient to them.
The popular courts and the Ecclesia, the real strongholds of democratic power, were abolished outright.

   This new oligarchy of 404 B.C. was thus in part thrust upon the
city by Spartan dictation, and was in part due to the attempt of
the returned oligarchical exiles to secure their own safety.   But
beyond these causes was a real revival of the old movement of the
intelligent and substantial citizens to rid the city of the abuses of
the radical democracy.   Doubtless some of the supporters of the
former oligarchy had lost hope of reform, had become convinced
that a limited democracy was impracticable, and had decided that
the evils of the old democracy were less than those of any government which could be secured in its place.   But a large body of
honest citizens supported the new movement, expecting it to result, not in an oligarchy at all, but in a democracy with franchise
limited to the three upper property classes.[1]

   But almost from the start the new administration fell under the
control of its own worst elements, the returned exiles of the
Critias   extreme oligarchical faction, led by Critias.   Return-
against   ing with the most violent hatred of the democracy
Theramenes   which had banished him, Critias conducted the administration in disregard of all rights of person and property.   A
minority, led by Theramenes, attempted to stand against this crim-
Exile and   inal exercise of power, as Theramenes had success-
return of   fully stood against the abuses of the Four Hundred ;
the patriots but the attempt failed, and Theramenes lost his

   [1] This was what the Thirty professed to have as their aim, and the fact
that they had the support of so intelligent and patriotic a body as the Knights
shows that many citizens had confidence in their purpose and ability to carry
out their promise.

life.   The faction of Critias pushed on, throwing off all pretense of reform, and took forcible possession of the city, killing or expelling all who opposed them.   The result was the rally of the democratic exiles under Thrasybulus, and the restoration of democratic government.

The struggle of the exiled democrats to win their return had brought to the front a democratic leader of the best type, Thrasybulus.   It was fortunate for the restored democracy **Thrasybulus** that it was to begin its new career, not under men of the Cleon-Cleophon type, but led by a man of real power, of broad views, and of unquestioned patriotism.   Thrasybulus saw that the first problem of the new government was to help conservative and democrat to forget the bloody attacks and reprisals of the past eight years, and to persuade the long-separated factions to unite, loyally and generously, as one people.   The am- **The am-** nesty had provided for the exclusion of the extreme **nesty** oligarchs from the city, for the peaceable withdrawal to Eleusis of all who preferred to cast in their lot with them, and for the ample protection of those of their former supporters who were ready to resume their allegiance to the democracy.   Thrasybulus's problem now was to persuade the excitable, passionate people to abide faithfully by these terms of amnesty, to live up to its spirit as well as its letter.   And this was no easy task : exiles of the democrats came back to live side by side with men who had actively supported an administration which had murdered their brothers, confiscated their property, and driven them and their families homeless into foreign cities.   It was hard to see these men of the city party living unpunished, prosperous, possessed of all the rights of citizenship, and gradually resuming their places in the administrative offices or the Senate.   Even the great influence of Thrasybulus was not sufficient to prevent attacks in the courts upon former members of the city party.

One of the first of these attacks came from Lysias himself. Eratosthenes, the member of the board of Thirty who was commonly believed to be least compromised by their crimes, ventured to take advantage of a special provision of the amnesty by **Lysias's attack on Eratosthenes** which any member of that board might remain in the city if he would submit to the regular accounting for his conduct in office. Lysias, whose brother had been arrested by Eratosthenes in person, when he might, perhaps, have prevented his death, attacked him in the court of accounting (Speech XII, *Against Eratosthenes*, 403 B.C.), and made every effort to arouse the hostility of the jury against the conservative members of the late government. We do not know the outcome of the trial, but it is probable that the conservative influence in the jury was strong enough to restrain them from taking the vengeance for which Lysias pleaded.

Some three years later Lysias was employed to write a speech for a substantial citizen who had been a supporter of the Thirty, **Lysias's speeches in other cases growing out of the revolution** and who was now a candidate for office. He was attacked at his δοκιμασία on the ground that the supporters of the oligarchy ought to be considered ineligible for office under the restored democracy. Lysias (Speech XXV, *Apologia, c.* 400 B.C.) warns the democracy that such a policy will only perpetuate division and weaken their own administration, and he vigorously attacks the petty politicians who are trying to stir up party strife as a means of maintaining their own unworthy leadership.

Shortly after this Lysias was retained to prepare a speech for the prosecution of Nicomachus, on the ground of unjustifiable delay in completing a revision of the laws, for which he was a special commissioner. Lysias in this speech (XXX, *Against Nicomachus*, 399/8 B.C.) makes an incidental, but serious, charge that the defendant had helped pave the way for the establishment of the Thirty. He thus tries to revive the old bitterness, for the advantage of his client, in a case which has no connection with the events of 404.

About the same time he was employed to write the main speech for the prosecution of Agoratus, a man of servile origin, who had received citizenship for supposed services to the democracy at the time of the first oligarchy (Speech XIII, *Against Agoratus, c.*

398 B.C.). Before the establishment of the Thirty, Agoratus had sworn away the lives of certain prominent democratic opponents of the movement. He is now prosecuted by the family of one of these victims, and Lysias makes every effort to excite the anger of the jury against the Thirty and all of their tools. The defendant was probably guilty enough, and a political adventurer who deserved little mercy, but he was fairly under the protection of the amnesty, and the attack upon him was a menace to the harmony of the reunited factions. Lysias, as a paid advocate, was arousing passions which had been allayed only by patient effort, and was showing himself a better pleader than statesman.

About this time he wrote another speech (Speech XXXI, *Against Philon, c.* 398 B.C.) for a client who was to attack a man who had been exiled by the Thirty, but who did not take up arms with the other exiles to secure the return. This man Philon was now a candidate for the Senate. Most of Lysias's attack is based upon Philon's failure to help overthrow the Thirty. The appeal is to the old enmities, though pressed less forcibly than in some of the other speeches.

Some years after these attacks we find Lysias on the other side, writing a speech in defense of Mantitheus, a young knight who was accused of having served in the cavalry of the Thirty (Speech XVI, *For Mantitheus,* 394–389 B.C.). His enemies now seek to exclude him from office on this ground. In his skillful defense Lysias almost entirely ignores the political principle involved, merely appealing briefly to the fact that many of the cavalry of the Thirty had already held office since the restoration. We are disappointed to find no frank discussion of the political question, and no appeal on the ground of living up to the spirit of the amnesty.

Twenty-one years after the fall of the Thirty, Lysias was again employed to prepare a speech attacking an active supporter of that administration (Speech XXVI, *Against Evander,* 382 B.C.). Evander, an office-holder under the Thirty, was now a candidate for the archonship. In a vigorous attack upon him Lysias maintains that such a man should be excluded from office, and that he should be grateful that he is permitted to vote and sit on juries. He lays down the principle that those who held office in the oligarchy should be absolutely excluded from office in the democracy, a principle opposed to the whole spirit of the amnesty, and to the earnest conviction of the ablest democratic leaders.

The extant speeches of Lysias are only a fragment of his works, and probably give only a partial idea of his activity in connection with the questions growing out of the restoration of the democracy. As a foreigner Lysias had no direct share in politics, but as an advocate, writing speeches for others, he had a strong influence. From the extant speeches it would appear that his influence was, on the whole, against the harmony of the old factions; that, while his pen was occasionally at the service of men of the city party unjustly attacked, yet his most hearty service was rendered in seeking revenge on the aristocrats. There is in these speeches no sign of large, broad political views, of a grasp of the real issues involved, or of a great desire to see a united Athens.

The Speech Against Eratosthenes

INTRODUCTION

THIS speech was delivered soon after the overthrow of the Thirty, probably in the autumn of 403 B.C. It is an attack upon Eratosthenes, one of the Thirty, and involves the discussion of the whole administration of that body, and to some extent of that of the Four Hundred, the oligarchy of 411 B.C.[1]

Eratosthenes had been a supporter of the first oligarchy and a member of the second.[2] Early in the administration of the Thirty he had set forth with others of their number to arrest certain rich metics. It fell to him to seize Polemarchus, Lysias's brother, who was immediately put to death (§§ 5–25). When, after the battle at Munychia (Spring, 403), most of the Thirty retired to Eleusis, Eratosthenes, with one other of their number, remained in Athens, though not as a member of the new governing board of Ten. In the final amnesty between the two parties it was provided that any one of the Thirty who was willing to risk a judicial examination of his conduct as a member of the late administration might remain in the city. Otherwise all were obliged to settle at Eleusis or remain permanently in exile.[3] Eratosthenes, believing himself to be less compromised than the others of the Thirty, ventured to remain and submit to his " accounting." [4]

---

[1] For an account of the two oligarchies, see Introd. p. 32 ff., and Chron. Appendix.

[2] For the doubtful claim that he was a member of the Central Committee that planned the second movement, see on § 43.

[3] Arist. *Resp. Ath.* 39. 6.

[4] The office that the Thirty had held was nominally that of Συγγραφεῖς, commissioners for revision of the constitution.

The constitution provided an elaborate system of accounting by all public officers at the close of their year of office. This involved the examination of their record by a board of state auditors ($\Lambda o\gamma\iota\sigma\tau\alpha\iota$), a review of their findings by a jury of five hundred, and the fullest opportunity for prosecution of complaints against them by any private citizen. The accounting included not only their handling of public funds, but every act of their administration.[1]   But it is possible that for the accounting of members of the late oligarchical administration a special tribunal was established.   We know that in one respect the jury was peculiar, for Aristotle tells us (*Resp. Ath.* 39. 6) that it was provided in the amnesty that their accounting should be before a jury taken from the three upper property classes — a wise provision for securing a fair hearing.[2]

The regular time for accounting was at the close of the civil year, July–August, but as the democracy came back to power early in October, it is in every way probable that the court, whether by ordinary or extraordinary process, was immediately summoned, and that they heard not only the accounting of Eratosthenes, but that of subordinate members of the late administration.[3]   Before this court Lysias appeared, charging Eratosthenes with the murder of Polemarchus, and demanding the penalty of death.[4]   He could count on the support of the radical democrats, who found it by no means easy to accept the terms of amnesty dictated by Sparta.   But this element was in the minority in a jury made up as this was.   The more moderate democrats, notably Thrasybulus, the hero of the Return, were totally opposed to any attempt

[1] On the details of the system of accounting, see Gilbert, *Greek Constitutional Antiquities*, 224 ff. ; Gardner and Jevons, *Manual of Greek Antiquities*, 466–468.

[2] See Wilamowitz, *Aristoteles und Athen*, II. 217 ff.

[3] That other cases were before the court appears from §§ 2, 33, 35, 36, 37, 79, 91, 100.

[4] As an $\iota\sigma o\tau\epsilon\lambda\eta s$ Lysias had full privileges before the Athenian courts. Other metics were under the formal restriction that they could introduce suits only through their $\pi\rho o\sigma\tau\alpha\tau\eta s$ (see p. 9).

to strike back at the city party.   With these there were also on
the jury some of the former supporters of the Thirty.[1]

The task then which Lysias undertook was difficult.   He had
to convince the jury that the one man of the Thirty who was commonly believed least responsible for their crimes was so guilty
that he was not to be forgiven, at a time when the watchword
of the leaders of both parties was " Forgive and forget."   He
had to reopen questions which had been settled, arouse resent-
ments which had been allayed with great sacrifice of personal
feeling, and urge the jury to act upon a principle which, if
further extended in the treatment of members of the city party,
would be fraught with the gravest danger.   For at this crisis
everything depended upon holding together the long-contending
aristocratic and democratic parties.   The real question of the day
was as to the power of the democracy to regain the confidence
and support of the great conservative middle class, men who
had formerly been represented by Theramenes, and later by
Eratosthenes.   If these men could be convinced that the restored
democracy would use its power moderately, foregoing revenge for
the past, turning its back upon the demagogue and the political
blackmailer ($\sigma\nu\kappa o\phi\acute{a}\nu\tau\eta s$), there was hope for the future.

But if the jury should support the attack on Eratosthenes, it
would seem like a declaration of the opposite policy.   No one
could blame the Sicilian Lysias for seeking his personal revenge, —
he could hardly be expected to put the good of the Athenian state
before the satisfaction of his personal feelings, — but the question
for the Athenian jurymen was whether to begin a policy of revenge
at the moment when the policy of forgiveness had brought rest
after a long and bitter struggle.   It is this larger political aspect of the case which gives to the speech against Eratosthenes
its historical interest.   It was one of the first tests — perhaps the
first — of the genuineness of the reconciliation.   Nothing could
be more just than to declare that the man who had stood with the
Thirty in their guilty prosperity, however reluctantly, must fall

[1] See §§ 92–95.

with them under their penalty; but nothing could be more
unwise. To distinguish between those of the Thirty who had
sought to establish personal tyranny, and those who had honestly
striven for a reformed, conservative democracy, was of first importance. The question of the hour was how to bring together the
triumphant popular party and the large body of honest, patriotic
citizens who had failed in their two attempts to establish a government better than the democracy, and had been betrayed into the
attitude of supporting an outrageous tyranny.

Men there were of the late administration who were to be punished, — the men who had used the movement for their personal
power and enrichment and to gratify personal hatred. But the
great body of their supporters, and perhaps some of the leaders
themselves, were to be so treated as to make it clear that the restored democracy was to be a government for the whole people,
not another tyranny of class over class.

OUTLINE

I. Προοίμιον, *Exordium*, §§ 1–3.
The novel difficulties of this prosecution.

II. Διήγησις, *Narratio*, §§ 4–19.
The honorable record of Lysias's family, § 4. The story of the
crime of the Thirty against the family, §§ 5–19.

III. Παρέκβασις, *Egressio*, §§ 20–23.
Denunciation of the defendants by means of a summary contrast between the patriotic services of Lysias's family and the
crimes of the Thirty.

IV. Πρόθεσις, *Propositio*, in the form of ἐρώτησις, §§ 24–25.

V. Πίστεις, *Argumentatio*, §§ 26–80.

A. Arguments based on the immediate charge, §§ 26–37.

1. The claim that Eratosthenes opposed the arrest is contra-
dicted by his conduct. (Addressed to Eratosthenes.) § 26.

2. The answer that he was forced to make the arrest is insufficient, §§ 27–34.

3. The verdict will have far-reaching influence (*a*) on citizens, (*b*) on foreigners, § 35.

4. It would be inconsistent to have executed the generals of Arginusae and now to spare these men, § 36.

5. Enough is already proven. No punishment could be adequate to their crimes, § 37.

B. Argument based on the general career of Eratosthenes, §§ 38–61.

Introductory : Eratosthenes cannot plead, as so many do, that past services should outweigh present guilt, §§ 38–40.

1. Attack upon Eratosthenes's conduct in the time of the Four Hundred, §§ 41–42.

2. Attack upon his conduct in the establishment of the Thirty, §§ 43–47.

3. Attack upon his conduct as one of the Thirty, §§ 48–52.

4. Attack upon his conduct in the time of the Ten, §§ 53–61.

C. Argument to counteract the defense that Eratosthenes was a friend and supporter of Theramenes. Attack on the career of Theramenes, §§ 62–78.

Introductory, §§ 62–64.

1. Attack upon Theramenes's conduct in connection with the Four Hundred, §§ 65–66.

2. Attack upon his conduct after the rule of the Four Hundred, § 67.

3. Attack upon his conduct in the making of the peace, §§ 68–70.

4. Attack upon his conduct in the establishment of the Thirty, §§ 71–77.

5. Conclusion : This is the man whose past friendship the defendants cite as a proof of their loyalty, § 78.

D. General conclusion of Πίστεις.

The time has come to bring Eratosthenes and his fellow-rulers to justice, §§ 79–80.

VI. Ἐπίλογος, *Peroratio*, §§ 81–100.

A. The utmost penalty that you could inflict would be inadequate to balance your charges against these men, §§ 81–84.

B. Attack upon the men who will plead for the defendants or give testimony for them, §§ 84–89.

C. To acquit the defendants will be to proclaim that you approve their conduct, §§ 90–91.

D. Appeal to the representatives of the two parties on the jury, §§ 92–98.

1. To the men ἐξ ἄστεως, §§ 92–94.

2. To the men ἐκ Πειραιῶς, §§ 95–98.

E. Conclusion : Summary of the crimes of the accused, and appeal to the jurors to avenge the dead, §§ 99–100.

COMMENTS ON ARGUMENT AND STYLE

I. Προοίμιον, *Exordium*, §§ 1–3.

In the opening words of a speech an expression of perplexity as to how to begin, in view of the difficulty of the task, was a commonplace of the rhetoricians. Lysias gives a bright turn and challenges attention by reversing the thought, and saying — with exaggeration — that his only difficulty will be to find an end. Cicero uses the same device, Manilian Law, § 3, Huius autem orationis difficilius est exitum quam principium invenire. Ita mihi non tam copia quam modus in dicendo quaerendus est.

In § 2 attention is quickened by another reversal of an ordinary thought. " Sycophancy " had become so much of a trade that it was quite a matter of course for the prosecutor to explain at the outset that he had good reason for appearing in the case, some personal or family injury to avenge, or some obligation of friendship to the persons aggrieved. Lysias recalls this custom, but uses it in a novel way to arouse at the outset the resentment of the jury against the defendant and his friends. But before he leaves the point he really follows the custom, alludes to his motives, and adds that in this he is in reality the representative of the interests of the jury themselves.

§ 3 concludes the proem with another commonplace expression of perplexity, based on his inexperience in pleading.

The proem is thus made up largely of commonplace, formal pleas of the ˙rhetorical schools, but is made effective by novel turns of the thought.

The sentence structure is at the beginning artificial ; parallelism of cola,[1] with antithesis, pervades the first two sections :

> οὐκ ἄρξασθαί μοι δοκεῖ ἄπορον εἶναι ὦ ἄνδρες
>   [δικασταὶ τῆς κατηγορίας
> ἀλλὰ παύσασθαι λέγοντι
>
> τοιαῦτα αὐτοῖς τὸ μέγεθος
> καὶ τοσαῦτα τὸ πλῆθος εἴργασται
>
>   ὥστε μήτ᾽ ἂν ψευδόμενον
> δεινότερα τῶν ὑπαρχόντων κατηγορῆσαι
>   μήτε τἀληθῆ βουλόμενον εἰπεῖν
> ἅπαντα δύνασθαι
>
> ἀλλ᾽ ἀνάγκη
>   ἢ τὸν κατήγορον ἀπειπεῖν
>   ἢ τὸν χρόνον ἐπιλιπεῖν.

Here the balance of cola is repeatedly strengthened by similarity of sound in words holding like position in the two cola (cp. App. § 57. 3) :

— ἄρξασθαι	τοιαῦτα τὸ μέγεθος	— ἀπειπεῖν
— παύσασθαι	τοσαῦτα τὸ πλῆθος	— ἐπιλιπεῖν

While these formal devices give a distinctly rhetorical tone to the opening, they are less formal and less obtrusive than the devices in the openings of Gorgias or Antiphon. The members of a pair of cola are in only one case (the last pair) precisely symmetrical, and the length of the cola — in strong contrast with those of

---

[1] For the terms " colon " and " period," see App. § 44.

Gorgias — is sufficient to give dignity and to prevent the impression of petty play on sound.

II. Διήγησις, *Narratio*, §§ 4–19.

Lysias does not need to state the case, for the clerk of the court has read to the jury the formal complaint. The speaker can pass at once to the narrative of the conduct upon which he bases his attack. And here he is at his best. In the simplest language he describes the life of his own family and their suffering at the hands of the Thirty. As the narrative proceeds, the sentences become very short, significant details of the story follow rapidly, and the hearer is made to see the events as if passing before his eyes.[1] The devices of the rhetorician do now and then appear in artificial pairs of cola :

§ 6. $\begin{cases} \underline{τιμωρεῖσθαι} \ μὲν \ \underline{δοκεῖν} \\ \underline{τῷ \ δ' \ ἔργῳ \ χρηματίζεσθαι} \end{cases}$

(Note the chiastic order.)

§ 6. $\begin{cases} τὴν \ μὲν \ πόλιν \ πένεσθαι \\ τὴν \ δ' \ ἀρχὴν \ δεῖσθαι \ χρημάτων \end{cases}$

§ 7. $\begin{cases} ἀποκτιννύναι \ μὲν \ . \ . \ . \ περὶ \ οὐδενὸς \ \underline{ἡγοῦντο} \\ λαμβάνειν \ δὲ \ . \ . \ . \ περὶ \ πολλοῦ \ \underline{ἐποιοῦντο} \end{cases}$

The rhymed ending adds to the artificial structure of this pair, as of the next (see App. § 57. 3 f.) ;

§ 7. $\begin{cases} \underline{ὡς \ οὐ \ χρημάτων \ ἕνεκα \ ταῦτα \ πέπρακται} \\ \underline{ἀλλὰ \ συμφέροντα \ τῇ \ πολιτείᾳ \ γεγένηται.} \end{cases}$

But as he reaches the climax of his own ill treatment in §§ 10 and 11, and that of his brother's family in §§ 18 and 19, he passes over into strong periodic structure.

III. Παρέκβασις, *Egressio*, §§ 20–23.

The term " digression " applies to this section only as an interruption of the strictly logical order, which would require the presentation of the arguments (Πίστεις) before the attempt to move the feelings of the jury by denunciation. But it is a wise

---

[1] For a full discussion of the narrative style, see App. § 42.

order that Lysias chooses. With the narrative fresh in the minds of the jury he hastens to play upon the feeling of indignation that the narrative has aroused, and so to bring the jury to the hearing of his formal arguments with minds strongly prejudiced against the defendant. He does this by emphatic and indignant — sometimes pathetic — comments on the conduct that he has just described. (For similar use of the Παρέκβασις, see on 24. 7–9.)

The structure is for the most part periodic, with much of antithesis and amplification.

The summary statement of the crimes of the Thirty (§ 21) illustrates the periodic effect which may be given purely by similarity of form to a group of coördinate cola. (See App. § 46.)

IV. Πρόθεσις, *Propositio*, §§ 24–25.

After the proem and immediately before or after the " narrative " (with its possible " digression ") the rhetoricians prescribed the Πρόθεσις, the statement of what the speaker proposes to prove. But here the narrative has already brought out the charge, showing it to rest upon an act which cannot be denied. Lysias's argument must therefore be directed to answering the excuses that Eratosthenes will urge. This Lysias brings before the jury in the Ἐρώτησις.

V. Πίστεις, *Argumentatio*, §§ 26–80.

A. Arguments based on the immediate charge, §§ 26–37.

In the form of a direct personal attack Lysias confronts Eratosthenes with the inconsistency between his claim that he tried in council to save Polemarchus and his conduct in seizing him. In this attack (§ 26) everything is marshaled in balanced antitheses ; only in the middle period do the cola extend beyond the briefest, most emphatic forms :

> εἶτ᾽ ὦ σχετλιώτατε πάντων
> ἀντέλεγες μὲν ἵνα σώσειας
> συνελάμβανες δὲ ἵνα ἀποκτείνειας ;

> καὶ ὅτε μὲν τὸ πλῆθος ἦν ὑμῶν κύριον . . . τῆς ἡμετέρας
> ἀντιλέγειν φῂς τοῖς βουλομένοις ἡμᾶς ἀπολέσαι

ἐπειδὴ δὲ ἐπὶ σοὶ μόνῳ ἐγένετο καὶ σῶσαι . . . καὶ μή
εἰς τὸ δεσμωτήριον ἀπήγαγες;

εἶθ' ὅτι μέν, ὡς φής, ἀντειπὼν οὐδὲν ὠφέλησας
ἀξιοῖς χρηστὸς νομίζεσθαι

ὅτι δὲ συλλαβὼν ἀπέκτεινας
οὐκ οἴει δεῖν ἐμοὶ καὶ τουτοισὶ δοῦναι δίκην;

After this vigorous outburst Lysias settles down to the detailed argument addressed to the jury in answer to the defendant s claim that he acted against his will.

The language of §§ 27–36 is of a third Lysian type, differing from the set antitheses of the proem, and equally from the running style of the narrative. It is the natural form of argument, the sentence structure clear and simple, without padding to secure symmetry of form. The frequent use of questions of appeal enlivens the argument.

In the culminating passage in §§ 32–34, turning again to Eratosthenes, Lysias comes back to the more antithetic form of the previous attack (§ 26), but the antitheses are more those of short phrases than of whole cola :

§ 32. $\begin{cases} οὐχ\ ὡς\ ἀνιωμένου \\ ἀλλ'\ ὡς\ ἡδομένου \end{cases}$

§ 33. $\begin{cases} ἃ\ ἴσασι\ γεγενημένα \\ τῶν\ τότε\ λεγομένων \end{cases}$

§ 33. $\begin{cases} πάντα\ τὰ\ κακὰ\ εἰργασμένοις\ τὴν\ πόλιν \\ πάντα\ τἀγαθὰ\ περὶ\ αὑτῶν\ λέγειν \end{cases}$

B. §§ 38–61. Lysias now passes from the crimes against his own family to the attack upon Eratosthenes's career as one of the oligarchs. He knows that there is a general belief that Eratosthenes was opposed to the worst crimes of the Thirty. He therefore tries to throw upon him the reproach of constant support of their action.

One period in the opening (§§ 39–40) is noteworthy for its even balance of cola :

> ἐπεὶ κελεύετε αὐτὸν ἀποδεῖξαι
> ὅπου τοσούτους τῶν πολεμίων ἀπέκτειναν
> ὅσους τῶν πολιτῶν
>
> ἢ ναῦς ὅπου τοσαύτας ἔλαβον
> ὅσας αὐτοὶ παρέδοσαν
>
> ἢ πόλιν ἥντινα τοιαύτην προσεκτήσαντο
> οἵαν τὴν ὑμετέραν κατεδουλώσαντο.[1]
>
> ἀλλὰ γὰρ ὅπλα τῶν πολεμίων τοσαῦτα ἐσκύλευσαν
> ὅσα περ ὑμῶν ἀφείλοντο
>
> ἀλλὰ τείχη τοιαῦτα εἷλον
> οἷα τῆς ἑαυτῶν πατρίδος κατέσκαψαν.

All of the specific attacks of this section (§§ 42–61) have a plausible sound, but no one of them is well sustained. Even if Eratosthenes did labor for the establishment of the Four Hundred, that was only what most of the best men in the city were doing ; in their evil government he had no part. The charge that Eratosthenes was one of the prime movers in the second oligarchy (§§ 43–47) is vaguely supported and is not in itself probable. Apparently the charge is made in the attempt to put Eratosthenes into close connection with the detested Critias.

In the review of Eratosthenes's conduct as one of the Thirty (§§ 48–52), Lysias can bring no specific charge beyond that of the arrest of Polemarchus. He tries to forestall the plea of Eratosthenes that he actively opposed certain of the crimes of the Thirty by the shrewd claim that this would only prove that he could safely have opposed them all. He finally (§§ 53–61) tries to give the impression that Eratosthenes was connected with the bad administration of the Board of Ten, a charge that seems to be entirely without foundation.

---

[1] On the ὁμοιοτέλευτον, see App. § 57. 4.

To a jury already prejudiced by the affecting narrative of the arrest, and hurried on from one point to another, this whole attack was convincing ; but the modern reader finds little of real proof, and an abundance of sophistry.

The language is clear and natural, in Lysias's characteristic argumentative style.

C. §§ 62–78.

Lysias comes now to the refutation of the main argument of the defense, that Eratosthenes was a member of that honorable minority among the Thirty who opposed the crimes of Critias's faction, and whose leader, Theramenes, lost his life in the attempt to bring the administration back to an honest course.

Whatever we may think of the real motives of Theramenes, there can be no question that at the time of this trial the people were already coming to think of him as a martyr for popular rights.   All knew that Eratosthenes was his friend and supporter. Lysias saw therefore that he must blacken the character of Theramenes.   He accordingly turns to a rapid review of his career. In a few clear-cut sentences he pictures Theramenes at each crisis, always the same shrewd, self-seeking, unscrupulous man, always pretending to serve the state, always ready to shift to the popular side, always serving his own interests.

The attack is a masterpiece.   There is no intemperate language, no hurling of epithets.   " He accuses by narrating.   The dramatically troubled time from 411 to 403 rises before us in impressive pictures.   At every turn Theramenes appears as the evil genius of the Athenians.   His wicked egoism stands out in every fact." [1]

Regarded as a product of rhetorical art, the attack on Theramenes merits only admiration ; but is this picture of Theramenes true to the facts?   In his narrative Lysias selects those acts only upon which he can put a bad construction.   He fails to tell us what appears so clearly in the narrative of Thucydides,[2] and in the defense put into the mouth of Theramenes by Xenophon in

---

[1] Bruns, *Das literarische Porträt der Griechen*, p. 493.

[2] Thuc. 8. 89 ff.

his answer to Critias before the Senate,[1] that his opposition to the extreme faction of the Four Hundred was, whatever may have been his motive, an efficient cause of their overthrow, at a time when there was reason to fear that they were on the point of betraying the city to the Peloponnesians.   Lysias has nothing to say of the period which immediately followed, during which Theramenes was at the head of a successful administration by a limited democracy,[2] except to accuse him of treachery to his friends for securing the punishment of some of his former colleagues, a punishment which may have been fully deserved.   He misrepresents Theramenes's responsibility for the hard terms of the peace, and he ignores the fact that the final opposition to Critias which cost him his life was in every particular what would have been demanded of the most patriotic citizen.   It is, indeed, possible to see in every act of Theramenes a cool, deliberate egoism, but it is also true that he sought his own advancement in every case save one by a policy which was in the interest of the conservative middle class.[3]

Thucydides has a high opinion of his ability,[4] but while he gives no explicit estimate of his moral character, he seems to look upon his opposition to the other faction of the Four Hundred as the result of personal ambition.[5]   His praise of the administration after the Four Hundred is rather praise of the form of government than of its leader.[6]

Xenophon nowhere gives his own estimate of Theramenes, but he puts into his mouth[7] an answer to Critias which is so complete, and which so well represents the true policy for the conservative middle class, that it seems impossible that Xenophon looked upon

---

[1] Xen. *Hell.* 2. 3. 46.   [2] Thuc. 8. 97. 1 f.

[3] In the one case, the prosecution of the generals for the failure to rescue the drowning men after the battle of Arginusae, he certainly sought to throw off the unjust censure that was falling upon himself by a deliberate and unjust attack upon other men.

[4] Thuc. 8. 68. 4.   [5] Thuc. 8. 89. 3.

[6] Thuc. 8. 97. 2.   [7] Xen. *Hell.* 2. 3. 35-49.

him as an unworthy leader of the party to which Xenophon himself belonged.

The tragic death of Theramenes soon led to the feeling that he had died a martyr to the rights of the people against the tyrants. Lysias evidently feels the danger of such a conviction even among the democrats of the jury. In the next generation opinions were sharply divided as to the character of Theramenes. Aristotle, to whom he stood as the representative of the ideal government by the upper classes, places him among the great men of Athens.[1]

This section (§§ 62–78) presents a style of narrative very different from that of §§ 4–19, the story of the arrest. There we have the simplest statement of facts; the power of the narrative lies in the vividness with which we see the events, and the certainty of our feelings being stirred at the sight. Here Lysias is dealing with more complicated acts, and those which do not make their own appeal. He therefore at every step throws in with the narrative of the events his own interpretation of motive and result. By a phrase here, a single invidious word there, he shrewdly colors the medium through which we see the events. Every statement is so turned as to become an argument. It is a type of narrative which the effective speaker must master, an instrument the more effective because so subtle in its working.

---

[1] *Resp. Ath.* 28. 5, *The best of the statesmen at Athens, after those of early times, seem to have been Nicias, Thucydides, and Theramenes. As to Nicias and Thucydides, nearly every one agrees that they were not merely men of birth and character, but also statesmen, and that they acted in all their public life in a manner worthy of their ancestry. On the merits of Theramenes opinion is divided, because it so happened that in his time public affairs were in a very stormy state. But those who give their opinion deliberately find him, not, as his critics falsely assert, overthrowing every kind of constitution, but supporting every kind so long as it did not transgress the laws; thus showing that he was able, as every good citizen should be, to live under any form of constitution, while he refused to countenance illegality and was its constant enemy* (Kenyon's trans.). For a summary of the modern discussions as to the character of Theramenes, see Busolt, *Griechische Geschichte,* III. ii. 1463.

The language of the section is simple, free from rhetorical forms ; even antitheses are only sparingly used.

It is only in the concluding paragraph that the speaker passes over to the artificial, rhetorical form, in balanced periods. The *amplification* at the opening of § 78, with the striking repetition of καί in the long series (see App. § 58. 4), marks the change of style :

καὶ τοσούτων καὶ ἑτέρων κακῶν καὶ αἰσχρῶν
καὶ πάλαι καὶ νεωστὶ
καὶ μικρῶν καὶ μεγάλων
αἰτίου γεγενημένου
τολμήσουσιν αὐτοὺς φίλους ὄντας ἀποφαίνειν
οὐχ ὑπὲρ ὑμῶν ἀποθανόντος Θηραμένους
ἀλλ᾽ ὑπὲρ τῆς αὐτοῦ πονηρίας

καὶ δικαίως μὲν ἐν ὀλιγαρχίᾳ δίκην δόντος
ἤδη γὰρ αὐτὴν κατέλυσε
δικαίως δ᾽ ἂν ἐν δημοκρατίᾳ
δὶς γὰρ ὑμᾶς κατεδουλώσατο

τῶν μὲν παρόντων καταφρονῶν
τῶν δὲ ἀπόντων ἐπιθυμῶν

καὶ τῷ καλλίστῳ ὀνόματι χρώμενος
δεινοτάτων ἔργων διδάσκαλος καταστάς.

Here, as the period advances, every part falls into the artificial, balanced form, culminating in the four formal cola which sum up Theramenes's character with the brevity and sharpness of an epigram.[1]

VI. Ἐπίλογος, *Peroratio*, §§ 81–100.

The peroration opens with a vigorous appeal to the resentment of the people against the Thirty. By ignoring the specific charge against Eratosthenes, Lysias is able to throw upon him the hatred of the jury for the crimes of the whole administration.

[1] See Rn.-F. on § 78.

He then arouses suspicion against any who may appear as witnesses or supporters of Eratosthenes in his defense, by trying to make the jury believe that the city is still in danger from oligarchical plots. To the plea that Eratosthenes was the best man among the Thirty, he makes the keen reply of the rhetorician, "That only proves him to be worse than any other citizen."

After shrewdly warning the jury that to acquit Eratosthenes will be to convict themselves of approving the conduct of the Thirty, Lysias makes a direct appeal to the representatives of each of the two parties. It is a most effective plea, and as a summing up against the Thirty worthy only of admiration. But as a summing up against Eratosthenes it has the fault of the whole speech, the unfair heaping upon him of crimes which he did not instigate, and in the commission of which he probably took even a passive part only by compulsion.

The final section (§§ 99–100), addressed to men already deeply moved by the recital of their wrongs, brings them in the most solemn way face to face with their duty to avenge the dead, and, by an appeal that works upon the most profound feelings, warns them of the presence and earnest watchfulness of the spirits who look to them for the punishment of their murderers. It is a fine artistic sense which leads the speaker, after raising the feelings of the jury to such a pitch, to close with words of absolute simplicity, — Παύσομαι κατηγορῶν. ἀκηκόατε, ἑωράκατε, πεπόνθατε, — ἔχετε · δικάζετε.

The language suited to a peroration is different from that of narrative or argument. It is addressed more to the feelings ; and as holding the formal place of dignity at the close, it admits of more formal structure. Both considerations tend to throw the thought into periodic form. The thought of §§ 81–84 is of itself an antithesis, and the antithetic structure inevitably pervades the passage. It is dignified, with less apparent striving for formal balance of phrase and colon than we sometimes find in Lysias's antitheses. The questions of appeal are especially fitting to a peroration (§§ 82 close –84).

In the section §§ 84–89 there is a steady advance in balance of form until from § 87 on almost every sentence has its pair of antithetic cola.

The final section (§§ 99–100) falls almost entirely within periodic forms, but without any petty play on sound or artificial balance to mar the earnestness of the appeal.

The study of the style of this speech is especially interesting because it is the only extant speech which Lysias wrote for his own delivery,[1] and one of the first in his career as a practical speech writer. In preparing each of his other speeches he had to adapt the speech to the man who was to deliver it ; in this he was free to follow his judgment of what a speech should be. He was already well known as a student of rhetoric ; he now undertook to apply his rhetorical theory to a practical case which was of the utmost importance to himself, and which involved great public questions.

[1] The *Olympic Speech* (XXXIII) was probably spoken by Lysias, but we have a mere fragment of it.

ABBREVIATIONS

B.   = Babbitt's *Grammar of Attic and Ionic Greek*, 1902.
G.   = Goodwin's *Greek Grammar* (revised edition), 1892.
GMT. = Goodwin's *Syntax of the Moods and Tenses of the Greek Verb* (enlarged edition), 1890.
Gl.   = Goodell's *School Grammar of Attic Greek*, 1902.
GS.   = Gildersleeve's *Syntax of Classical Greek* (first part), 1900.
HA.   = Hadley's *Greek Grammar* (revised by Allen), 1884.

XII

ΚΑΤΑ ΕΡΑΤΟΣΘΕΝΟΥΣ
ΤΟΥ ΓΕΝΟΜΕΝΟΥ ΤΩΝ ΤΡΙΑΚΟΝΤΑ, ΟΝ
ΑΥΤΟΣ ΕΙΠΕ ΛΥΣΙΑΣ

1 Οὐκ ἄρξασθαί μοι δοκεῖ ἄπορον εἶναι, ὦ ἄνδρες
δικασταί, τῆς κατηγορίας, ἀλλὰ παύσασθαι λέγοντι·
τοιαῦτα αὐτοῖς τὸ μέγεθος καὶ τοσαῦτα τὸ πλῆθος εἴρ-
γασται· ὥστε μήτ᾽ ἂν ψευδόμενον δεινότερα τῶν ὑπαρ-

1. **λέγοντι**: as the inf. παύσασθαι takes its subject from μοι,
the partic. λέγοντι is assimilated
in case to μοι. HA. 941 ; G. 928.
1 ; B. 631 ; Gl. 543 a (1). Cp.
ἔλεγεν ὡς . . . συμβουλεύσειεν
αὐτοῖς παύσασθαι φιλονικοῦσιν *he
said that he advised them to stop
contending*, 22. 8. — **αὐτοῖς**: plural,
because the denunciation of Eratosthenes will involve an attack
on all of the Thirty and their tools ;
αὐτοῖς rather than τούτοις because
most of those included in the word
are absent. — **τοιαῦτα . . . εἴργασται** : this clause stands in an
unusual balance between the preceding and the following ; it serves
as an emphatic statement of the
ground of the preceding assertion,
and at the same time it gives the
ground of the statement expressed

by the ὥστε clause. See Crit. Note.
— **ἄν** : the force of ἄν extends to
both κατηγορῆσαι and δύνασθαι :

$$\text{ὥστε ἄν} \begin{cases} \text{μήτε ψευδόμενον . . . κατ-} \\ \text{ηγορῆσαι} \\ \text{μήτε βουλόμενον . . . δύ-} \\ \text{νασθαι.} \end{cases}$$

The verbs are thrown into the
infin. by ὥστε ; otherwise they
would be optative, apodoses of ψευ-
δόμενος and βουλόμενος. GMT.
592 ; HA. 964 a ; G. 1308 ; B.
595 ; Gl. 579. The two clauses may
be so combined as to make both
κατηγορῆσαι and εἰπεῖν depend on
δύνασθαι, but this breaks the parallelism of the cola, which is
heightened by the play on sound
(see App. § 57. 3). — **τῶν ὑπαρχόντων**: *the facts*. 'No charges that
one could invent could be worse
than the crimes *that are*.' On the

5 χάντων κατηγορῆσαι, μήτε τἀληθῆ βουλόμενον εἰπεῖν
ἅπαντα δύνασθαι, ἀλλ' ἀνάγκη ἢ τὸν κατήγορον ἀπει-
2 πεῖν ἢ τὸν χρόνον ἐπιλιπεῖν. τοὐναντίον δέ μοι δοκοῦμεν πείσεσθαι ἢ ἐν τῷ πρὸ τοῦ χρόνῳ. πρότερον μὲν
γὰρ ἔδει τὴν ἔχθραν τοὺς κατηγοροῦντας ἐπιδεῖξαι, ἥτις
10 εἴη πρὸς τοὺς φεύγοντας· νυνὶ δὲ παρὰ τῶν φευγόντων
χρὴ πυνθάνεσθαι, ἥτις ἦν αὐτοῖς πρὸς τὴν πόλιν ἔχθρα,
ἀνθ' ὅτου τοιαῦτα ἐτόλμησαν εἰς αὐτὴν ἐξαμαρτάνειν.
οὐ μέντοι ὡς οὐκ ἔχων οἰκείας ἔχθρας καὶ συμφορὰς

various meanings of ὑπάρχειν see on § 23.

2. πείσεσθαι : πάσχω has here its simplest meaning, *experience*. πάσχω = *I am acted upon* in distinction from ποιῶ *I act*. The idea of "suffering" would come only from the context or the addition of a specific word (*e.g.* κακῶς). — ἐν τῷ πρὸ τοῦ χρόνῳ : other expressions for the same idea are ἐν τῷ πρόσθεν χρόνῳ 21. 25 ; ἐν τῷ ἔμπροσθεν χρόνῳ 19. 45, 19. 53 ; ἐν τῷ τέως χρόνῳ 7. 12, 21. 19, 27. 16, 28. 3. The form πρὸ τοῦ is a relic of the Homeric demonstrative τοῦ. HA. 655 d ; G. 984 ; B. 443. 4 ; Gl. 549 c. — γάρ : explicative γάρ, see on 19. 12. — τὴν ἔχθραν : a modern prosecutor would certainly not tell the jury that he is a personal enemy of the man whom he is prosecuting. But in Athens "sycophancy" had become such a trade that when one man accused another in court, the pre-

sumption often was that it was a case of blackmail (cp. on 22. 1). Hence as a precaution against that supposition an honest prosecutor regularly tries to show to the jury at the outset that he or his family or his close friends have personal reasons for wishing to see the defendant punished. — τοὺς κατηγοροῦντας : the prosecutor is usually called ὁ διώκων (cp. 10. 11), or ὁ κατηγορῶν, or ὁ κατήγορος (cp. § 1). The defendant is ὁ φεύγων (cp. ἐφύγομεν § 4). — πυνθάνεσθαι : *inquire*, the conative present of πυθέσθαι *to learn*. HA. 825 ; G. 1255 ; B. 523 ; Gl. 454 c ; GMT. 25 ; GS. 192. — ὅτου : the antecedent is really the preceding clause, but ἀνθ' ὅτου has come to be felt almost as a conjunction, *wherefore*. HA. 999 ; Gl. 619. — εἰς : for this use of εἰς in hostile sense see 32. 19 Crit. Note. — ἐξαμαρτάνειν : the present tense, a course of action. — ὡς : for sub-

14 τοὺς λόγους ποιοῦμαι, ἀλλ' ὡς ἅπασι πολλῆς ἀφθο-
3 νίας οὔσης ὑπὲρ τῶν δημοσίων ὀργίζεσθαι. ἐγὼ μὲν
οὖν, ὦ ἄνδρες δικασταί, οὔτ' ἐμαυτοῦ πώποτε οὔτε
ἀλλότρια πράγματα πράξας νῦν ἠνάγκασμαι ὑπὸ τῶν
γεγενημένων τούτου κατηγορεῖν, ὥστε πολλάκις εἰς

jective ὡς see on 16. 8. — τοὺς
λόγους ποιοῦμαι : a slightly more
formal expression than λέγω ; cp.
English, " I make the statement "
and " I speak." The thought underlying the sentence is, 'Do not
imagine that I am emphasizing
their hostility to the whole city
from any lack of personal complaints of my own. I, the metic,
wish to call your attention to the
complaints which you all have, before I proceed to present my personal and family wrongs.' — ἀλλ' ὡς
ἅπασι κτλ. : but assuming that all
have great abundance (of matter)
for anger because of their public
acts. — ἀφθονίας ὀργίζεσθαι : abundance for anger ; in this expression the English demands the more
precise statement, abundance of
matter for, abundance of cause
for, but we too use the vague
expression in " abundance for his
support," "abundance for eating
and drinking." — ὑπέρ : force, see
on ὀργίζεσθε § 80.

3. ἐγὼ μὲν οὖν : now I. μὲν
οὖν originally connected its clause
with the preceding through οὖν,
and set it in contrast with some-

thing following through μέν (the
weaker form of μήν), as in § 12.
But it has come to have often a
mere transitional force, often without connection with the preceding,
and often with no correlative to
μέν. A. Marking transition to a
new topic, 12. 3, 19. 2, 19. 11,
24. 5. and often. B. Marking
transition to a new fact in a narrative, 12. 9, 12. 12, 32. 18.
C. Marking the close of a topic
in the discussion, 12. 47, 19. 24,
19. 53, 19. 55, 19. 56, 19. 60, 22. 4,
24. 4. For τοίνυν = μὲν οὖν see
on 16. 7 (D). For οὖν = μέν οὖν see
on 19. 7 (B). — πράγματα : here in
the technical sense, law-business,
L. & S. s.v. III, 4. On the fact cp.
Introd. p. 19. — ὑπὸ τῶν γεγενημένων : the use of ὑπό, the preposition proper to the voluntary
agent, gives to the non-personal
word a touch of personification.
GS. 166. Cp. 24. 17. 32. 10, 32.
18. — τούτου : as Lysias passes
now to his personal complaint,
he turns from speaking of the
Thirty in general to the one man
against whom he brings his formal
charge. Before the speech began

πολλὴν ἀθυμίαν κατέστην, μὴ διὰ τὴν ἀπειρίαν ἀναξίως
20 καὶ ἀδυνάτως ὑπὲρ τοῦ ἀδελφοῦ καὶ ἐμαυτοῦ τὴν κατηγορίαν ποιήσωμαι · ὅμως δὲ πειράσομαι ὑμᾶς ἐξ ἀρχῆς
ὡς ἂν δύνωμαι δι᾽ ἐλαχίστων διδάξαι.

4 Οὑμὸς πατὴρ Κέφαλος ἐπείσθη μὲν ὑπὸ Περικλέους
εἰς ταύτην τὴν γῆν ἀφικέσθαι, ἔτη δὲ τριάκοντα ᾤκησε,
25 καὶ οὐδενὶ πώποτε οὔτε ἡμεῖς οὔτε ἐκεῖνος δίκην οὔτε
ἐδικασάμεθα οὔτε ἐφύγομεν, ἀλλ᾽ οὕτως ᾠκοῦμεν δημο-
κρατούμενοι, ὥστε μήτε εἰς τοὺς ἄλλους ἐξαμαρτάνειν

the Clerk of the Court had read Lysias's formal complaint, so that the speaker does not need to name the defendant at this point. — **κατ-έστην**: as the perfect of this verb is used as a present, " the aorist may take a perfect translation" (GS. 249) and govern a subordinate clause as a primary tense (GS. 252). — **τὴν κατηγορίαν ποιή-σωμαι**: cp. τοὺς λόγους ποιοῦμαι § 2. The Ms. reading is ποιήσο-μαι. For the question of mood involved see Crit. Note. — **δι᾽ ἐλα-χίστων**: the usual expression is διὰ βραχυτάτων, as in § 62, 16. 9, 24. 4. Cp. διὰ βραχέων ἐρῶ *I will tell in a few words*, 24. 5.

4. Κέφαλος: Introd. p. 9. — **ἐπείσθη**: a shrewd reference, before this jury of the restored democracy, to the close family connection of the complainant with the greatest democrat of the last generation. — **ᾤκησε**: cp. ᾠκοῦμεν below. Here, the aorist with a

'definite number' (GS. 243). Otherwise ᾤκησε would usually mean *settled* (inceptive aorist), in distinction from ᾤκει *lived*. — **οὔτε ἐδικασάμεθα οὔτε ἐφύγομεν**: as a student of rhetoric, and perhaps already a teacher of pleading, Lysias is liable to the suspicion which the common men of the jury have against the professional rhetorician ; he here forestalls this. Nor has his family been guilty of the prevalent sycophancy, nor of attempting to resist by litigation the claims of others. They have lived the quiet and careful life that befits a family who receive the hospitality of the city. As to the rights of metics in the courts see Introd. p. 44. — **ἐδικασάμεθα**: still another term for the *prosecution* of a case ; cp. on τοὺς κατηγοροῦν-τας § 2. — **μήτε . . . μήτε**: on the παρίσωσις see App. § 57. 2. — **ἐξα-μαρτάνειν**: in ἐδικασάμεθα and ἐφύγομεν (aorist) he denies every

5 μήτε ὑπὸ τῶν ἄλλων ἀδικεῖσθαι.   ἐπειδὴ δ' οἱ τριάκοντα
πονηροὶ καὶ συκοφάνται ὄντες εἰς τὴν ἀρχὴν κατέστη-
30 σαν, φάσκοντες χρῆναι τῶν ἀδίκων καθαρὰν ποιῆσαι
τὴν πόλιν καὶ τοὺς λοιποὺς πολίτας ἐπ' ἀρετὴν καὶ
δικαιοσύνην προτρέψαι, τοιαῦτα λέγοντες οὐ τοιαῦτα
ποιεῖν ἐτόλμων, ὡς ἐγὼ περὶ τῶν ἐμαυτοῦ πρῶτον εἰπὼν
6 καὶ περὶ τῶν ὑμετέρων ἀναμνῆσαι πειράσομαι.   Θέο-
35 γνις γὰρ καὶ Πείσων ἔλεγον ἐν τοῖς τριάκοντα περὶ τῶν

occurrence; in ἐξαμαρτάνειν and
ἀδικεῖσθαι (imperf.) he denies the
whole course of conduct; cp. on
ἐξαμαρτάνειν § 2.

5. φάσκοντες: *asserting*; the
common use of φάσκων in distinction from λέγων; the falsity of the
assertion is commonly implied. —
οὐ... ἐτόλμων: *they could not bring
themselves*. τολμᾶν is wicked daring (so in § 2) or good courage,
according to the context. The use
of the imperf. with οὐ adds to the
idea of resistance that is in the
word itself. "The negative imperfect commonly denotes resistance
to pressure or disappointment.
Simple negation is aoristic" (GS.
216).   So οὐδὲ ἐτυγχάνομεν § 20;
οὐδενὶ ἐτόλμα πείθεσθαι 32. 2: οὐκ
ἤθελε 32. 12.   For a little time
the Thirty did live up to their professions.   Aristotle says of them:
*At first, indeed, they behaved with
moderation towards the citizens
and pretended to administer the
state according to the ancient con-*

*stitution . . . and they destroyed
the professional accusers and those
mischievous and evil-minded persons who, to the great detriment
of the democracy, had attached
themselves to it in order to curry
favor with it.   With all of this
the city was much pleased, and
thought that the Thirty did it with
the best of motives.   But so soon
as they had got a firmer hold on
the city, they spared no class of
citizens, but put to death any persons who were eminent for wealth
or birth or character* (*Resp. Ath.*
35, Kenyon's tr.).   Xenophon gives
similar testimony, *Hell.* 2. 3. 12.

6. γάρ: explicative γάρ.   See
on 19. 12. — ἐν τοῖς τριάκοντα: ἐν
is the regular expression for *at a
meeting of*; so ἐν τοῖς Ἀμφικτύ-
οσι *at the meeting of the Amphic-
tyons*, Aes. 3. 114; ἐν τοῖς αὐτοῖς
δικασταῖς, *at a session of the same
court*, Ant. 6. 23.   Cp. ἐν τῇ βουλῇ
§ 77, ἐν τῷ δήμῳ 16. 20, ἐν τῇ
ἐκκλησίᾳ 19. 50.   The reference

μετοίκων, ὡς εἶέν τινες τῇ πολιτείᾳ ἀχθόμενοι· καλλί-
στην οὖν εἶναι πρόφασιν τιμωρεῖσθαι μὲν δοκεῖν, τῷ
δ' ἔργῳ χρηματίζεσθαι· πάντως δὲ τὴν μὲν πόλιν
7 πένεσθαι, τὴν δ' ἀρχὴν δεῖσθαι χρημάτων. καὶ τοὺς
40 ἀκούοντας οὐ χαλεπῶς ἔπειθον· ἀποκτιννύναι μὲν γὰρ
ἀνθρώπους περὶ οὐδενὸς ἡγοῦντο, λαμβάνειν δὲ χρήματα
περὶ πολλοῦ ἐποιοῦντο. ἔδοξεν οὖν αὐτοῖς δέκα συλλαβεῖν, τούτων δὲ δύο πένητας, ἵνα αὐτοῖς ᾖ πρὸς τοὺς
ἄλλους ἀπολογία, ὡς οὐ χρημάτων ἕνεκα ταῦτα πέπρακ-
45 ται, ἀλλὰ συμφέροντα τῇ πολιτείᾳ γεγένηται, ὥσπερ τι

here is to the discussion of the matter at a session of the Thirty by themselves, at their headquarters, the Tholus. From § 25 we conclude that the proposition was carried thence to the Senate and there discussed and acted upon. The Tholus, a building near the senate-house, was the headquarters and dining-hall of the Prytanes. It was thus the natural center of the administration of the Thirty, who used the subservient Senate to give a form of legality to their own acts. — δεῖσθαι χρημάτων : when the Thirty took control they found the treasury exhausted by the expenses of the Peloponnesian War. They had not only to provide for the ordinary expenses of the government, but to pay their Spartan garrison on the Acropolis. Xenophon says (*Hell.* 2. 3. 21) that the despoiling of the metics was to meet the latter expense.

7. ἀποκτιννύναι . . . ἐποιοῦντο : for the periodic form see App. § 57. 3. — ἔδοξεν : note that the preliminary process and the attitude of mind are expressed by the imperfs. ἔπειθον, ἡγοῦντο, ἐποιοῦντο ; the final decision, the "upshot" of it all, by the aorist ἔδοξεν. GS. 238. — δέκα : these were certainly the first arrests of metics by the Thirty. Xenophon says (*Hell.* 2. 3. 21) that each member of the Thirty was to arrest one metic ; this was probably on a later occasion. Diodorus says (14. 5. 6) that the Thirty executed the sixty richest foreigners ; this may be the whole number executed under their administration. — πρὸς τοὺς ἄλλους : *in the case of the rest* (of the ten metics). — ὡς οὐ κτέ. : on the παρί-σωσις see App. § 57. 2. — συμφέ-ροντα : predicate, in agreement with ταῦτα ; related to γεγένηται as χρημάτων ἕνεκα to πέπρακται.

8 τῶν ἄλλων εὐλόγως πεποιηκότες. διαλαβόντες δὲ τὰς
οἰκίας ἐβάδιζον · καὶ ἐμὲ μὲν ξένους ἑστιῶντα κατέλαβον, οὓς ἐξελάσαντες Πείσωνί με παραδιδόασιν · οἱ δὲ

— ὥσπερ κτλ.: (sarcastic) *as though
they had done any one of all their
other deeds on good grounds.* Thalheim separates ὥσπερ from πεποιηκότες, *conduct* (*as*) *shrewd as that
in any one of all their other
measures.* πεποιηκότες is placed
loosely in the nominative, its subject really being αὐτοῖς ; but αὐτοῖς
ᾗ ἀπολογία is in effect equal to
ἀπολογίαν ἔχωσιν.

8. ἐβάδιζον : *they set forth.*
The imperfect, as the tense that
presents an act as in progress, is
sometimes used to present the act
as it gets under way ; we see the
act in progress in its first stage,
the beginning of its evolution.
Some would name this the *ingressive imperfect* ; others, the *imperfect of evolution* (see *A.J.P.* XVI,
p. 150). Cp. ἐβάδιζον *I set forth*
1. 24, 1. 41 ; ἀλλ᾽ οἴκοθεν ἔχοντες
ἂν ἐβαδίζομεν *but we should have
started from home with them* 4. 7 ;
ἔφευγον *I set forth in flight* 12. 16
(so ἔφευγεν 12. 42) ; τὴν ἐκκλησίαν ἐποίουν *they proceeded to hold
the assembly* 12. 72 ; τὰ τείχη
κατέσκαπτον *they proceeded to
tear down the walls,* Xen. *Hell.*
2. 2. 23 ; εὐθὺς ἂν ἀπελογούμην *I
would at once proceed to my defense,* Dem. 18. 9 ; Xen. *Mem.*

1. 2. 16 εὐθὺς ἀποπηδήσαντε Σω-
κράτους ἐπραττέτην τὰ πολιτικά
*they instantly left Socrates with a
leap and proceeded to take active
part in politics.* For other examples with adverbs of rapidity
see GS. 206. The succession of
tenses in this whole narrative is
noteworthy. Great force is given
by the interweaving of imperfects
of vivid description (ἀπεγράφοντο,
ἠρώτων, ἔφασκεν, *etc.* GS. 207),
the aorists of summary statement
(κατέλαβον, εἶπον, ὡμολόγησε,
ἐκέλευσεν, *etc.*), and the numerous historical presents (παραδιδόασιν, ἀνοίγνυμι, εἰσέρχεται,
καλεῖ, *etc.*). — ἐμὲ μὲν κατέλαβον :
when μέν stands without a corresponding δέ a contrasted thought
is often latent. Here there is an
underlying thought of his brother's
fate. Cp. 19. 1, 19. 7, 32. 13, 32.
17. Cp. on 25. 16. Lysias was
arrested at his house in the Piraeus,
as we see by the fact that he sent
Archeneos εἰς ἄστυ (§ 16). This
entrance into Lysias's house was,
in spirit, a violation of the principle that a man's house is his
sanctuary, a principle as jealously
maintained in Athens as in modern states. But in form it was
legal, for Pison was executing a

ἄλλοι εἰς τὸ ἐργαστήριον ἐλθόντες τὰ ἀνδράποδα ἀπε-
50 γράφοντο. ἐγὼ δὲ Πείσωνα μὲν ἠρώτων εἰ βούλοιτό
9 με σῶσαι χρήματα λαβών· ὁ δ' ἔφασκεν, εἰ πολλὰ
εἴη. εἶπον οὖν ὅτι τάλαντον ἀργυρίου ἕτοιμος εἴην δοῦ-
ναι· ὁ δ' ὡμολόγησε ταῦτα ποιήσειν. ἠπιστάμην μὲν
οὖν ὅτι οὔτε θεοὺς οὔτ' ἀνθρώπους νομίζει, ὅμως δ' ἐκ
55 τῶν παρόντων ἐδόκει μοι ἀναγκαιότατον εἶναι πίστιν
10 παρ' αὐτοῦ λαβεῖν. ἐπειδὴ δὲ ὤμοσεν, ἐξώλειαν ἑαυτῷ
καὶ τοῖς παισὶν ἐπαρώμενος, λαβὼν τὸ τάλαντόν με
σώσειν, εἰσελθὼν εἰς τὸ δωμάτιον τὴν κιβωτὸν ἀνοί-
γνυμι· Πείσων δ' αἰσθόμενος εἰσέρχεται, καὶ ἰδὼν τὰ

decree of the supreme governing body, and at all times, even under the democracy, search of the house and arrest of a criminal were open to the proper officers acting under such a warrant. But this authority was outrageously abused by the Thirty. The patriot Thrasybulus reminds his followers of their sufferings under such treatment: δειπνοῦντες συνελαμβανόμεθα καὶ καθεύδοντες καὶ ἀγοράζοντες *we were seized at table, in bed, in the agora* (Xen. *Hell.* 2. 4. 14). — ἐργαστήριον : the shield factory. — ἀπεγράφοντο : the usual word for an inventory. For the causative middle see HA. 815 ; G. 1245 ; B. 505 ; Gl. 500 d.

9. .εἶπον οὖν, . . . ἠπιστάμην μὲν οὖν: *I said therefore,* . . . *now I knew.* The first οὖν is inferential, the second, transitional,

marking the passage from the narrative to the parenthetical remark. See on § 3 (B). — νομίζει : the ordinary word with θεούς (cp. Plato *Apol.* 26 c ταῦτα λέγω, ὡς τὸ παράπαν οὐ νομίζεις θεούς) ; but it has, as used here, so much of the idea of ' respect,' 'fear,' that the speaker can even add ἀνθρώπους. The retention of the indic. in νομίζει (ind. discourse with the secondary ἠπιστάμην) is a part of the increasing vividness with which Lysias recalls the events as his narrative advances, and which brings in the historical present (ἀνοίγνυμι) in the following sentence. — ἐκ τῶν παρόντων : ἐκ, because the circumstances are viewed as the *source* of the conviction.

10. σώσειν : tense, HA. 948 a ; G. 1286 ; B. 549. 2 ; Gl. 578.

60 ἐνόντα καλεῖ τῶν ὑπηρετῶν δύο, καὶ τὰ ἐν τῇ κιβωτῷ
11 λαβεῖν ἐκέλευσεν. ἐπειδὴ δὲ οὐχ ὅσον ὡμολόγησεν
εἶχεν, ὦ ἄνδρες δικασταί, ἀλλὰ τρία τάλαντα ἀργυρίου
καὶ τετρακοσίους κυζικηνοὺς καὶ ἑκατὸν δαρεικοὺς
καὶ φιάλας ἀργυρᾶς τέτταρας, ἐδεόμην αὐτοῦ ἐφόδιά μοι
65 δοῦναι· ὁ δ' ἀγαπήσειν με ἔφασκεν, εἰ τὸ σῶμα σώσω.
12 ἐξιοῦσι δ' ἐμοὶ καὶ Πείσωνι ἐπιτυγχάνει Μηλόβιός τε
καὶ Μνησιθείδης ἐκ τοῦ ἐργαστηρίου ἀπιόντες, καὶ
καταλαμβάνουσι πρὸς αὐταῖς ταῖς θύραις, καὶ ἐρωτῶσιν ὅποι βαδίζοιμεν· ὁ δ' ἔφασκεν εἰς τἀδελφοῦ τοῦ
70 ἐμοῦ, ἵνα καὶ τὰ ἐν ἐκείνῃ τῇ οἰκίᾳ σκέψηται. ἐκεῖνον

11. ὡμολόγησεν: sc. λαβεῖν, cp.
σῶσαι χρήματα λαβών § 8. — κυζικηνούς: sc. στατῆρας. For the
sums mentioned see App. § 61 f.
This was only the ready money
which Lysias happened to have in
his strong box; perhaps the ready
money of the shield manufactory.
In addition to this, Lysias lost his
house, his share in the stock and
tools in the shield factory, and his
share in the 120 slaves (§ 19).
Yet it would appear from the accounts of his later contributions to
the patriot cause that a considerable amount of his property escaped
the hands of the Thirty (see p. 20,
n. 1). — ἀγαπήσειν: the direct
form is ἀγαπήσεις, εἰ τὸ σῶμα σώσεις you may consider yourself
lucky, if you save your skin. The
curt sarcasm well expresses the
brutality of the whole proceeding.

ἀγαπήσεις is a 'jussive' future.
GS. 269; HA. 844; G. 1265; B.
583 n. 1.   For the mood of
σώσεις see HA. 899; G. 1405;
Gl. 648.

12. ἐπιτυγχάνει: the verb
agrees, as often, with the first of
the two noms.; but the two being
once expressed, the plural naturally
follows in ἀπιόντες, καταλαμβάνουσι, ἐρωτῶσιν. By the same
usage ἐξιοῦσι might have been
singular. — βαδίζοιμεν: optative
after ἐρωτῶσιν, a historical present. HA. 932. 2; G. 1268, 1487;
B. 517. 1, 581; Gl. 661. — εἰς τἀδελφοῦ . . . εἰς Δαμνίππου: the
Greek idiom is precisely the same
as the colloquial English. — σκέψηται: the same sarcastic tone as
in the preceding. The hearer
feels with what cruel unconcern
these robbers treated their victims.

μὲν οὖν ἐκέλευον βαδίζειν, ἐμὲ δὲ μεθ' αὐτῶν ἀκολου-
13 θεῖν εἰς Δαμνίππου. Πείσων δὲ προσελθὼν σιγᾶν μοι
παρεκελεύετο καὶ θαρρεῖν, ὡς ἥξων ἐκεῖσε. καταλαμ-
βάνομεν δὲ αὐτόθι Θέογνιν ἑτέρους φυλάττοντα· ᾧ
75 παραδόντες ἐμὲ πάλιν ᾤχοντο. ἐν τοιούτῳ δ' ὄντι μοι
κινδυνεύειν ἐδόκει, ὡς τοῦ γε ἀποθανεῖν ὑπάρχοντος
14 ἤδη. καλέσας δὲ Δάμνιππον λέγω πρὸς αὐτὸν τάδε,
" ἐπιτήδειος μέν μοι τυγχάνεις ὤν, ἥκω δ' εἰς τὴν σὴν
οἰκίαν, ἀδικῶ δ' οὐδέν, χρημάτων δ' ἕνεκα ἀπόλλυμαι.
80 σὺ οὖν ταῦτα πάσχοντί μοι πρόθυμον παράσχου τὴν

— **μὲν οὖν**: force, see on § 3. —
βαδίζειν: to go on his way, cp. on
ἐβάδιζον § 8.

13. σιγᾶν: Lysias would have
us suspect that Pison was planning to keep for himself the confiscated money. — **ὡς ἥξων ἐκεῖσε**:
'on the understanding that he
would come there'; for ὡς 'subjective' see on 16. 8. — **κινδυνεύειν
ἐδόκει, ὡς . . . ὑπάρχοντος**: it seemed
to me wise to make a venture, believing that death at any rate was
to be counted on already, i.e. whatever risks might be involved in
any attempt to escape, one risk at
least (γέ), and that the supreme
one, was already upon me (ὑπάρχοντος, see on ὑπάρχει § 23). κινδυνεύειν is usually to meet danger,
to be in danger, but it is used here
for ἀποκινδυνεύειν or παρακινδυ-
νεύειν = to take a risk; cp. 1. 45
ἂν . . . τοιοῦτον κίνδυνον ἐκινδύ-
νευον would I have taken such a

risk; 4. 17 ἀλλ' ἀπεκινδύνευον
τοῦτο but I took this risk.

14. Δάμνιππον: this is all that
we know of Damnippus; he was
evidently a trusted adherent of
the Thirty. — **ἀδικῶ**: I am guilty
(not I am doing wrong). A
present state or condition viewed
as the result of a past action is
usually represented in Greek, as
in English, by the perfect; but
certain words in Greek frequently
express this idea by the present:
A. Words of hearing and saying,
ἀκούω, πυνθάνομαι (12. 62), αἰσθά-
νομαι, γιγνώσκω, μανθάνω, λέγω.
B. Words of coming and going,
especially ἥκω and οἴχομαι, I am
come, I am gone (not I am on the
way). C. ἀδικῶ (12. 82, 25. 1,
25. 24), φεύγω (12. 57), νικῶ
(12. 36), κρατῶ, ἡττῶμαι, στέρο-
μαι (and all verbs of privation, GS.
204), and some others. Kühn.
§ 382. 4. — **ἀπόλλυμαι**: the action

σεαυτοῦ δύναμιν εἰς τὴν ἐμὴν σωτηρίαν." ὁ δ' ὑπέσχετο ταῦτα ποιήσειν. ἐδόκει δ' αὐτῷ βέλτιον εἶναι
πρὸς Θέογνιν μνησθῆναι· ἡγεῖτο γὰρ ἅπαν ποιήσειν
15 αὐτόν, εἴ τις ἀργύριον διδοίη. ἐκείνου δὲ διαλεγομένου
85 Θεόγνιδι (ἔμπειρος γὰρ ὢν ἐτύγχανον τῆς οἰκίας, καὶ
ἤδη ὅτι ἀμφίθυρος εἴη) ἐδόκει μοι ταύτῃ πειρᾶσθαι
σωθῆναι, ἐνθυμουμένῳ ὅτι, ἐὰν μὲν λάθω, σωθήσομαι,

is already under way, *I am being
destroyed.* The change to direct
discourse in the series of brief
clauses with the repeated "and"
reproduces the breathless earnestness and haste of the appeal. This
earnestness of feeling leads Lysias
into one of his rare personifica-
tions, that of δύναμιν by the personal epithet πρόθυμον; for other
examples see Introd. p. 25, n. 5. —
εἰς . . . σωτηρίαν: the purpose of
an act is that *toward which* the act
goes out; it may therefore be
expressed by each of the prepositions εἰς, πρός, and ἐπί with the
accus. But Lysias prefers εἰς,
using πρός in 19. 22 and 19. 61
only, and ἐπί in 19. 21 and 28. 14
only. For διά with acc. expressing purpose see on 32. 22, and for
ἐπί with dat. see on 12. 24. For
εἰς cp. 12. 18, 19. 39, 19. 55, 24. 10.
— **ὑπέσχετο ποιήσειν**: for the fut.
infin. see on σώσειν § 10. — **ἅπαν**:
anything. Cp. Demos. 18. 5,
πάντων μὲν γὰρ ἀποστερεῖσθαι λυ-
πηρόν ἐστι, *to be robbed of anything*

is *vexatious.* — **διδοίη,** *offer,* conative present, see on πυνθάνεσθαι
§ 2.

15. ἐνθυμουμένῳ κτλ. :
ἐδόκει μοι ταύτῃ πειρᾶσθαι σωθῆναι
       ἐνθυμουμένῳ ὅτι

1. { ἐὰν μὲν λάθω
    { σωθήσομαι

2. { ἐὰν δὲ ληφθῶ
    { ——

ἡγούμην
   (a)   εἰ εἴη πεπεισμένος
         ἀφεθήσεσθαι
   (b)   εἰ δὲ μή
         ἀποθανεῖσθαι

The irregularity in this otherwise
symmetrical sentence lies in the
fact that after the second main
protasis (ἐὰν δὲ ληφθῶ) the governing verb is repeated in new
form (ἡγούμην replacing ἐνθυμουμένῳ), which shifts the construction of the apodosis from the fut.
indic. of indir. disc. with ὅτι,
to the fut. infin. of indir. disc.
This insertion of ἡγούμην makes
the thought clearer to the listener
by separating the second princi-

ἐὰν δὲ ληφθῶ, ἡγούμην μέν, εἰ Θέογνις εἴη πεπεισμέ-
89 νος ὑπὸ τοῦ Δαμνίππου χρήματα λαβεῖν, οὐδὲν ἧττον
16 ἀφεθήσεσθαι, εἰ δὲ μή, ὁμοίως ἀποθανεῖσθαι. ταῦτα
διανοηθεὶς ἔφευγον, ἐκείνων ἐπὶ τῇ αὐλείῳ θύρᾳ τὴν
φυλακὴν ποιουμένων· τριῶν δὲ θυρῶν οὐσῶν, ἃς ἔδει
με διελθεῖν, ἅπασαι ἀνεῳγμέναι ἔτυχον. ἀφικόμενος
δὲ εἰς Ἀρχένεω τοῦ ναυκλήρου ἐκεῖνον πέμπω εἰς ἄστυ,

pal protasis from the subordinate ones that follow. This separation is further strengthened by shifting from the subj. in the leading pair of protases to the opt. of ind. disc. in the subordinate protasis. — ἡγούμην μέν: μέν is drawn to the leading verb from its natural position after εἰ. Such displacement of μέν throws emphasis upon the word that it follows. So in 16. 18. For corresponding displacement of δέ see on 16. 7. — εἰ δὲ μή: a stereotyped expression which may be used even when there is no place for the negative. Here with neg. force; so in 22. 6, 22. 21. Without neg. force, 12. 50.

16. ἔφευγον: *set forth.* The impf. pictures the flight in its beginning, where the aor. would merely state the fact of flight. See on ἐβάδιζον § 8. — αὐλείῳ θύρᾳ: defined by Harpocration (*s.v.* αὔλειος) as ἡ ἀπὸ τῆς ὁδοῦ πρώτη θύρα τῆς οἰκίας *the front door, street door.* The term ἀμφίθυρος (§ 15) must mean that the house

had a second outer door, though we have no knowledge of such an arrangement except from this passage. The third door through which Lysias passed may have opened through a garden wall into a back street. But we have no facts on which to base anything more than conjecture. For the plan of the Greek house see Gardner, "The Greek House," *Journal of Hellenic Studies,* 21 (1901), 293 ff.; Gulick, *Life of the Ancient Greeks,* p. 21 ff.; Gardner and Jevons, *Manual of Greek Antiquities,* p. 31 ff.; Smith, *Dic'y Greek and Roman Antiq.,* article "Domus." — εἰς ἄστυ: cp. the English "to town." Here ἄστυ is used as a proper name, the city in distinction from the Piraeus. Lysias's custom varies as to the use of the article with ἄστυ; cp. εἰς ἄστυ 13. 24, 32. 8; ἐν ἄστει 25. 1; but πρὸς τὸ ἄστυ 13. 80; εἰς τὸ ἄστυ 12. 54. Lysias sends Archeneos to the city as the speediest and

95 πευσόμενον περὶ τοῦ ἀδελφοῦ· ἥκων δὲ ἔλεγεν ὅτι Ἐρατοσθένης αὐτὸν ἐν τῇ ὁδῷ λαβὼν εἰς τὸ δεσμωτήριον
17 ἀπαγάγοι. καὶ ἐγὼ τοιαῦτα πεπυσμένος τῆς ἐπιούσης
νυκτὸς διέπλευσα Μέγαράδε. Πολεμάρχῳ δὲ παρήγ-
γειλαν οἱ τριάκοντα τοὐπ᾽ ἐκείνων εἰθισμένον παράγ-
100 γελμα, πίνειν κώνειον, πρὶν τὴν αἰτίαν εἰπεῖν δι᾽ ἥντινα
ἔμελλεν ἀποθανεῖσθαι· οὕτω πολλοῦ ἐδέησε κριθῆναι

surest means of learning whether his brother is under arrest, for he would be taken there by the arresting party. It does not imply that Polemarchus lived in the city rather than in the Piraeus.

17. **τοὐπ᾽ ἐκείνων**: ἐπί with gen. of a personal word = *in the time of.* So in 12. 42, 12. 65, 16. 3, 22. 9, 24. 25, 25. 21, 34. 4.—**πίνειν**: present tense, because this particular order is defined as an instance of the *customary* order. So Socrates's jailor says χαλεπαίνουσι καὶ καταρῶνται, ἐπειδὰν αὐτοῖς παραγγέλλω πίνειν τὸ φάρμακον *they are angry and curse me, when I give them the order to drink the drug* (Plato, *Phaedo* 116 c). — **πρὶν εἰπεῖν**: *before telling,* used loosely for *without telling;* cp. on 19. 7, πρὶν παραγενέσθαι. The English would allow the same loose expression, which comes from the underlying thought of the haste of the action. Aeschines uses πρίν in the same way in speaking of the crimes of the Thirty, πλείους

ἢ χιλίους καὶ πεντακοσίους τῶν πολιτῶν ἀκρίτους ἀπέκτειναν, πρὶν καὶ τὰς αἰτίας ἀκοῦσαι, ἐφ᾽ αἷς ἔμελλον ἀποθνῄσκειν, καὶ οὐδ᾽ ἐπὶ τὰς ταφὰς καὶ ἐκφορὰς τῶν τελευτησάντων εἴων τοὺς προσήκοντας παραγενέσθαι *more than 1500 of the citizens they put to death without trial, before they even heard the charges on which they were about to die, and they would not even allow the relatives to be present at their funerals or to follow them to their graves,* 3. 235. Cp. Ant. *Tetral.* A γ 2 φεύγοντες πρότερον ἢ ἀπέδυσαν *fleeing before they had time to strip them.* With the coming of the Thirty to power all legal protection of citizens was thrown aside. One of the most common charges against them is that they condemned citizens to death without a trial, whereas the right of every citizen to trial with full opportunity for defense was one of the fundamental principles of the democracy. This right was extended to metics also.

18 καὶ ἀπολογήσασθαι. καὶ ἐπειδὴ ἀπεφέρετο ἐκ τοῦ
δεσμωτηρίου τεθνεώς, τριῶν ἡμῖν οἰκιῶν οὐσῶν ἐξ οὐδεμιᾶς εἴασαν ἐξενεχθῆναι, ἀλλὰ κλεισίον μισθωσάμενοι
105 προὔθεντο αὐτόν. καὶ πολλῶν ὄντων ἱματίων αἰτοῦσιν
οὐδὲν ἔδοσαν εἰς τὴν ταφήν, ἀλλὰ τῶν φίλων ὁ μὲν
ἱμάτιον, ὁ δὲ προσκεφάλαιον, ὁ δὲ ὅ τι ἕκαστος ἔτυχεν
19 ἔδωκεν εἰς τὴν ἐκείνου ταφήν. καὶ ἔχοντες μὲν ἑπτακο-
σίας ἀσπίδας τῶν ἡμετέρων, ἔχοντες δὲ ἀργύριον καὶ
110 χρυσίον τοσοῦτον, χαλκὸν δὲ καὶ κόσμον καὶ ἔπιπλα καὶ
ἱμάτια γυναικεῖα ὅσα οὐδεπώποτε ᾤοντο κτήσεσθαι,
καὶ ἀνδράποδα εἴκοσι καὶ ἑκατόν, ὧν τὰ μὲν βέλτιστα
ἔλαβον, τὰ δὲ λοιπὰ εἰς τὸ δημόσιον ἀπέδοσαν, εἰς
τοσαύτην ἀπληστίαν καὶ αἰσχροκέρδειαν ἀφίκοντο καὶ

18. ἀπεφέρετο: not ἐκφέρετο,
because ἐκφέρειν is the usual word
for the orderly funeral ceremony
(cp. ἐξενεχθῆναι below). — οὐδεμιᾶς: while οὐδεμιᾶς depends on
ἐξενεχθῆναι, the negative part of
it goes over to εἴασαν; hence οὐ-,
not μη-. — κλεισίον: see L. & S.
κλισίον. That the form is κλεισ-
is determined by inscriptions. —
προὔθεντο: see the description of
funeral customs in Gulick, 292 ff. ;
Becker's *Charicles*, English ed.,
p. 383 ff. ; Gardner and Jevons,
Greek Antiquities, p. 360 ff. ;
Guhl and Koner, *Life of the
Greeks and Romans*, p. 289 ff.
— εἰς τὴν ταφήν: see on εἰς σωτηρίαν § 14.
19. On the πολυσύνδετον of

this section see App. § 58. 4. — τὸ
δημόσιον: L. & S. *s.v.* III. 3. —
ἀπέδοσαν: ἀπο- because the confiscated property belonged now to
the state. — ἀπληστίαν καὶ αἰσχροκέρδειαν: the doubling of words
merely for rhetorical effect is as
rare in the simple style of Lysias
as it is common in the rhetorical
style of Demosthenes ; see App.
§ 58. 2. — εἰς τοσαύτην . . . ἀφίκοντο: the ὥστε construction which
we expect after τοσαύτην is thrust
aside by the emphatic καὶ τοῦ
τρόπου τοῦ αὐτῶν ἀπόδειξιν ἐποιήσαντο. The whole force of the
long period is thus thrown upon
what is really the one emphatic
thought, that this act about to be
described exhibits the real char-

115 τοῦ τρόπου τοῦ αὐτῶν ἀπόδειξιν ἐποιήσαντο · τῆς γὰρ
Πολεμάρχου γυναικὸς χρυσοῦς ἑλικτῆρας, οὓς ἔχουσα
ἐτύγχανεν, ὅτε πρῶτον ἦλθεν εἰς τὴν οἰκίαν Μηλόβιος,
20 ἐκ τῶν ὤτων ἐξείλετο. καὶ οὐδὲ κατὰ τὸ ἐλάχιστον
μέρος τῆς οὐσίας ἐλέου παρ' αὐτῶν ἐτυγχάνομεν. ἀλλ'
120 οὕτως εἰς ἡμᾶς διὰ τὰ χρήματα ἐξημάρτανον, ὥσπερ ἂν
ἕτεροι μεγάλων ἀδικημάτων ὀργὴν ἔχοντες, οὐ τούτων
ἀξίους γε ὄντας τῇ πόλει, ἀλλὰ πάσας μὲν τὰς χορη-

acter of the men. With this idea fresh in the minds of the hearers, and their attention sharpened by the interruption in the narrative, Lysias at last gives the fact for which they are waiting, in the more independent form of the clause with γάρ. — **γάρ**: explicative γάρ, see on 19. 12. — **ὅτε πρῶτον**: *as soon as* (for the different meaning of ὅτε τὸ πρῶτον see Crit. Note). — **Μηλόβιος**: Melobius was one of the party that went to Lysias's house, drove out his guests, and put him under arrest (§§ 8 and 12).

20. **ἐτυγχάνομεν**: the negative imperfect of " disappointment "; see on ἐτόλμων § 5. — **διὰ τὰ χρήματα**: the whole preceding narrative has laid all stress upon the fact that this was outright robbery — murder for money, not a political arrest and assassination. An honorable revolution might necessitate the summary execution of some political opponents, but this

act was robbery and murder. The defendant stands under the protection of the feeling that there should be a general amnesty for political offenses. Lysias is shrewdly bringing every fact to the point that Eratosthenes and his companions had used politics merely as a means for personal enrichment. If this is so, they should be treated like robbers, not like reconciled political opponents. — **ὥσπερ ἂν ἕτεροι**: sc. ἐξαμάρτοιεν or ἐξήμαρτον. HA. 905 ; G. 1313 ; B. 616. 4 ; Gl. 656 b (the protasis here is ἔχοντες, giving therefore ὥσπερ ἂν for ὥσπερ ἂν εἰ of the grammars). — **τούτων**: *this treatment.* — **πόλει**: the dative of the one " in relation to whom " οὐκ ἀξίους is true. HA. 771 ; G. 1172. 1 ; B. 382, 2d example ; Gl. 523 a, 5th example. — **χορηγίας**: for the nature and extent of such services see Gulick, p. 62. For the relation of metics to public burdens cp. p. 9, and see Gardner

γίας χορηγήσαντας, πολλὰς δ᾽ εἰσφορὰς εἰσενεγκόντας,
κοσμίους δ᾽ ἡμᾶς αὐτοὺς παρέχοντας καὶ πᾶν τὸ προσ-
125 ταττόμενον ποιοῦντας, ἐχθρὸν δ᾽ οὐδένα κεκτημένους,

and Jevons, *Greek Antiquities*, p. 455. Pleas for favor based on such services are a common-place of Athenian court speeches. Lysias himself gives a notable illustration in his twenty-first speech, see on 19. 43. — **χορηγήσαν-τας**: in sharp antithesis to ὄντας and with this modifying ἡμᾶς above; but the series of partici-ples, starting in this construction, is so far prolonged that the feeling of their grammatical connection with the preceding is lost, and the sentence is closed with em-phasis by bringing in a new inde-pendent verb, ἠξίωσαν; to the object of ἠξίωσαν the later partici-ples attach themselves by a slight anacoluthon. — **εἰσφοράς**: the εἰσ-φορά was a direct property tax levied upon members of the three upper property classes to meet extraordinary expenses of war. As the Peloponnesian War steadily exhausted the ordinary revenues of the state, the εἰσφορά became a frequent and pressing burden. — **κοσμίους**: by the close of the fifth century the abuses of democ-racy had become so notorious, and the trade of politics so corrupt, that ambition for political promi-nence had become cause for sus-

picion; yet the obligation of every citizen to take his place in the common life of the state was still a fundamental principle. Under these influences it was felt that the ideal citizen was the quiet, modest, law-abiding man, who neither sought political power nor neg-lected political obligations. Lysias defines the attitude of the ideal citizen in his twenty-first speech (§ 19): δέομαι οὖν ὑμῶν, ὦ ἄν-δρες δικασταί, . . . μὴ μόνον τῶν δημοσίων λῃτουργιῶν μεμνῆ-σθαι, ἀλλὰ τῶν ἰδίων ἐπιτηδευμάτων ἐνθυμεῖσθαι, ἡγουμένους ταύτην εἶναι τὴν λῃτουργίαν ἐπιπονωτάτην, διὰ τέλους τὸν πάντα χρόνον κόσ-μιον εἶναι καὶ σώφρονα καὶ μήθ᾽ ὑφ᾽ ἡδονῆς ἡττηθῆναι μήθ᾽ ὑπὸ κέρδους ἐπαρθῆναι, ἀλλὰ τοιοῦτον παρασχεῖν ἑαυτὸν ὥστε μηδένα τῶν πολιτῶν μήτε μέμψασθαι μήτε δίκην τολμῆσαι προσκαλέσασθαι *I ask you, gentlemen of the jury, not only to remember my public ser-vices, but to consider my personal habits, thinking that this is the most difficult public service, to be from first to last always an orderly man, and discreet, to be neither conquered by pleasure nor carried away by gain, and to show one's self such a man that no citizen*

πολλοὺς δ' 'Αθηναίων ἐκ τῶν πολεμίων λυσαμένους
τοιούτων ἠξίωσαν, οὐχ ὁμοίως μετοικοῦντας ὥσπερ αὐτοὶ
21 ἐπολιτεύοντο.   οὗτοι γὰρ πολλοὺς μὲν τῶν πολιτῶν εἰς
τοὺς πολεμίους ἐξήλασαν, πολλοὺς δ' ἀδίκως ἀποκτεί-
130 ναντες ἀτάφους ἐποίησαν, πολλοὺς δ' ἐπιτίμους ὄντας
ἀτίμους κατέστησαν, πολλῶν δὲ θυγατέρας μελλούσας
22 ἐκδίδοσθαι ἐκώλυσαν.   Καὶ εἰς τοσοῦτόν εἰσι τόλμης

*will complain of him nor dare
summon him into court.* Cp.
Dem. 18. 308 ἔστι γάρ, ἔστιν
ἡσυχία δικαία καὶ συμφέρουσα τῇ
πόλει, ἣν οἱ πολλοὶ τῶν πολιτῶν
ὑμεῖς ἁπλῶς ἄγετε *there is, there
is a quiet that is right and useful
to the state, which you the majority
of the citizens keep in sincerity.*
The attitude that was thus honored
in the citizen was even more to
be demanded of the metic. — λυσαμένους: causative mid. See on
ἀπεγράφοντο § 8. — οὐχ ὁμοίως . . .
ἐπολιτεύοντο: *not such metics as
they were citizens.* The restrained
simplicity of the under-statement
(*Miosis*) is stronger than the
strongest terms could make it.
    21. οὗτοι: cp. on αὐτοῖς § 1.
The Thirty are now so definitely
before the minds of the hearers
that οὗτοι becomes the natural expression, and with the Thirty are
associated in οὗτοι those who support Eratosthenes in this trial.
For the periodic form of the sentence see App. § 46. — εἰς τοὺς

πολεμίους: the rhetorical period
which is to contrast the conduct
of the Thirty with that of Lysias
and his family gains emphasis by
having its opening colon in verbal
antithesis to the last colon of the
preceding series: πολλοὺς δ' 'Αθηναίων ἐκ τῶν πολεμίων λυσαμένους
vs. πολλοὺς μὲν τῶν πολιτῶν
εἰς τοὺς πολεμίους ἐξήλασαν. —
ἀτίμους: the technical term for
men under ἀτιμία, the complete or
partial deprivation of privileges of
citizenship, inflicted by the courts
as a penalty for crime. See Gulick, p. 61. — θυγατέρας: the dowry
was so important in marriages of
well-to-do Athenians that the
seizure of the fathers' property by
the Thirty destroyed the hopes of
marriage for many girls of good
family. The lot of the Athenian
wife was narrow and poor enough;
to the unmarried woman no respectable career was open. — ἐκώλυσαν: every verb in the series of
aorists ἐξήλασαν . . . ἐποίησαν . . .
κατέστησαν . . . ἐκώλυσαν ex-

ἀφιγμένοι ὥσθ' ἥκουσιν ἀπολογησόμενοι, καὶ λέγουσιν
ὡς οὐδὲν κακὸν οὐδ' αἰσχρὸν εἰργασμένοι εἰσίν. ἐγὼ
135 δ' ἐβουλόμην ἂν αὐτοὺς ἀληθῆ λέγειν· μετῆν γὰρ ἂν
23 καὶ ἐμοὶ τούτου τἀγαθοῦ οὐκ ἐλάχιστον μέρος. νῦν
δὲ οὔτε πρὸς τὴν πόλιν αὐτοῖς τοιαῦτα ὑπάρχει οὔτε
πρὸς ἐμέ· τὸν ἀδελφὸν γάρ μου, ὥσπερ καὶ πρότερον

presses a 'repeated past action';
the study of such a series will help
to correct the notion that the
aorist is confined to 'single' or
'simple' actions. These 'complexive' aorists (GS. 243) sum up
the whole career of the Thirty.
On the ὁμοιοτέλευτον see App.
§ 57. 4.

22. κακόν, αἰσχρόν: on the
συνωνυμία see App. § 58. 2. — εἰργασμένοι εἰσίν: when any aspect
of a past action brings it up into
immediate relation to the present,
the whole idea of *past action in
present relation* is usually expressed by the perfect. In the
case of passive forms, the *resulting condition* is the usual present
aspect which causes the perfect to
be used; in the case of active and
deponent verbs among the most
common aspects are *credit, guilt,
responsibility*; εἰργάσαντο *they did
the deed*; εἰργασμένοι εἰσί *they
have done the deed*, with the underlying idea in Greek as in English,
*they are responsible for the deed,
they are guilty of the deed*. Cp.
πέπρακται § 7, εἰργασμένοις § 33,

πεποιήκασιν § 89, καταψηφισμένους
ἔσεσθαι § 100. — ἐβουλόμην ἄν : imperf. indic. of a *hopeless wish* (=
vellem), GS. 367 (cp. 398) ; B.
588 n. ; Gl. 461 d. The "potential indic." of G. 1339 and GMT.
246.

23. τοιαῦτα : *i.e.* ὡς οὐδὲν κακὸν
. . . εἰργασμένοι εἰσίν. — ὑπάρχει :
In our eight speeches note the following uses of ὑπάρχειν : A. In the
original sense, *to begin*, 24. 18 τοὺς
ὑπάρξαντας *those who began it*.
B. Of what *exists*, or *is true* ; fact
in distinction from claim or false-
hood, 12. 1, 12. 23, 12. 70, 34. 6.
C. Of what exists or is true *to
start with*, 12. 97, 19. 29, 25. 6,
34. 3, 34. 8. D. Of what is now
so sure that it is *to be counted
upon* (whether for good or ill),
12. 13, 19. 11, 19. 20, 25. 4. E. Of
what *is ready*, 12. 72. F. τὰ
ὑπάρχοντα = *property* (= what one
has to start with), 31. 18 τούτους
ἀφῃρεῖτο τὰ ὑπάρχοντα *these he
robbed of their property*. In 32.
28 τὰ ὑπάρχοντα = *capital*, in distinction from interest. — καὶ πρότερον : see on καὶ ἡμῶν 19. 2 (C).

εἶπον, Ἐρατοσθένης ἀπέκτεινεν, οὔτε αὐτὸς ἰδίᾳ ἀδικού-
140 μενος οὔτε εἰς τὴν πόλιν ὁρῶν ἐξαμαρτάνοντα, ἀλλὰ τῇ
ἑαυτοῦ παρανομίᾳ προθύμως ἐξυπηρετῶν.

24 Ἀναβιβασάμενος δ᾽ αὐτὸν βούλομαι ἐρέσθαι, ὦ ἄνδρες δικασταί. τοιαύτην γὰρ γνώμην ἔχω· ἐπὶ μὲν τῇ
τούτου ὠφελείᾳ καὶ πρὸς ἕτερον περὶ τούτου διαλέγε-
145 σθαι ἀσεβὲς εἶναι νομίζω, ἐπὶ δὲ τῇ τούτου βλάβῃ καὶ
πρὸς αὐτὸν τοῦτον ὅσιον καὶ εὐσεβές. ἀνάβηθι οὖν
μοι καὶ ἀπόκριναι, ὅ τι ἄν σε ἐρωτῶ.

25 Ἀπήγαγες Πολέμαρχον ἢ οὔ; Τὰ ὑπὸ τῶν ἀρχόν-

— τῇ ἑαυτοῦ παρανομίᾳ: a personification (rare in Lysias) like
that of δύναμιν § 14, and better
suited to the tone of its passage.
See Introd. p. 25, n. 5. — ἐξ-υπηρε-
τῶν: *serving to the end.*

24. ἐρέσθαι: for the formal
questioning of an opponent in
court see App. § 20. — ἐπὶ ὠφελείᾳ: ἐπί with the dative properly
denotes the ground of an act,
that upon which it rests (cp.
on 32. 17); but often the ultimate
ground of an act is its purpose,
hence the use of ἐπί with the dat.,
instead of the phrases enumerated
on εἰς σωτηρίαν § 14. So ἐπὶ τῇ
βλάβῃ § 48; ἐπ᾽ ὀλέθρῳ § 60. In
13. 20 ground and purpose are
coupled: οὐκ ἐπ᾽ εὐνοίᾳ τῇ ὑμετέρᾳ
ἀλλ᾽ ἐπὶ καταλύσει τοῦ δήμου τοῦ
ὑμετέρου *not from good will to you,
but for the destruction of your democracy.* — διαλέγεσθαι: the cere-

monial impurity of a murderer was
so great that the accused was,
after indictment, forbidden entrance to the sanctuaries or the
Agora while awaiting trial. The
trial itself was held in the open
air, in order, as Antiphon tells us
(5. 11), "that the jurors might not
come into the same inclosure with
those whose hands were defiled,
nor the prosecutor come under the
same roof with the murderer." —
καὶ πρὸς αὐτὸν τοῦτον: *even (to
talk) with him himself.* So καὶ
πρὸς ἕτερον above. — ἀνάβηθι: to
the platform for witnesses. See
App. § 20. — ὅσιον καὶ εὐσεβές:
for the συνωνυμία see App. § 58. 2.
The amplified expression gives
dignity and force to the final
colon of the period. — μοι: case,
HA. 767; G. 1165, cp. 1167;
B. 377-378; Gl. 523 a, first
example.

τῶν προσταχθέντα δεδιὼς ἐποίουν. Ἦσθα δ' ἐν τῷ
150 βουλευτηρίῳ, ὅτε οἱ λόγοι ἐγίγνοντο περὶ ἡμῶν;
Ἦ. Πότερον συνηγόρευες τοῖς κελεύουσιν ἀποκτεῖναι ἢ
ἀντέλεγες; Ἀντέλεγον, ἵνα μὴ ἀποθάνητε. Ἡγούμενος ἡμᾶς ἄδικα πάσχειν ἢ δίκαια; Ἄδικα.

26 Εἶτ', ὦ σχετλιώτατε πάντων, ἀντέλεγες μὲν ἵνα
155 σώσειας, συνελάμβανες δὲ ἵνα ἀποκτείνειας; καὶ ὅτε
μὲν τὸ πλῆθος ἦν ὑμῶν κύριον τῆς σωτηρίας τῆς ἡμετέρας, ἀντιλέγειν φῇς τοῖς βουλομένοις ἡμᾶς ἀπολέσαι,
ἐπειδὴ δὲ ἐπὶ σοὶ μόνῳ ἐγένετο καὶ σῶσαι Πολέμαρχον
καὶ μή, εἰς τὸ δεσμωτήριον ἀπήγαγες; εἶθ' ὅτι μέν,

25. ἐποίουν : *I was doing.*
When the motive of an act is the
chief object of thought, the act
itself is naturally viewed in its
progress, hence the change from
the aor. ἀπήγαγες to (δεδιὼς) ἐποίουν. Cp. §§ 26, 27, 90; 19. 59,
22. 3, 22. 11, 22. 12, 25. 13. The
following imperfects (ἐγίγνοντο,
συνηγόρευες, ἀντέλεγες, ἀντέλεγον) represent vividly the progress
of the discussion (cp. the similar
imperfects in § 8 ff.). In § 26 the
motive is again the chief thought
in ἀντέλεγες and συνελάμβανες.
As Lysias passes to the consum-
mation of the whole, he returns to
the aorist, ἀπήγαγες, ἀπέκτεινας.
— βουλευτηρίῳ: for the relation
of this discussion to the discussion
among the Thirty by themselves,
see on ἐν τοῖς τριάκοντα § 6. Under the Thirty the popular courts

had been abolished and their functions transferred to the Senate, a
body entirely subservient to the
will of the Thirty.

26. On Lysias's use of rhetorical questions see App. § 59. 1. —
εἶτα: Lysias has εἶτα in the following uses: A. = *again, secondly*;
but ἔπειτα is his usual word for
this. See 19. 15. B. = *then*,
i.e. *under those circumstances*. See
19. 51. C. Meaning as under B,
but in a question implying indignation or astonishment. With our
passage compare 34. 6. — ἀντιλέγειν: pres. infin. in ind. disc. representing the impf. of the direct. HA.
853 a; G. 1285. 1; B. 551; Gl.
577 a; GMT. 119; GS. 327. So
εἶναι 12. 49; πράττειν 12. 63; ἔχειν
32. 20. — ἐπὶ σοί: *in your power.*
Cp. ἐπί in § 33, 22. 17. — καὶ σῶσαι
. . . καὶ μή: *both . . . and*, where

160 ὡς φῄς, ἀντειπὼν οὐδὲν ὠφέλησας, ἀξιοῖς χρηστὸς νομίζεσθαι, ὅτι δὲ συλλαβὼν ἀπέκτεινας, οὐκ οἴει δεῖν ἐμοὶ
καὶ τουτοισὶ δοῦναι δίκην ;

27   Καὶ μὴν οὐδὲ τοῦτο εἰκὸς αὐτῷ πιστεύειν, εἴπερ
ἀληθῆ λέγει φάσκων ἀντειπεῖν, ὡς αὐτῷ προσετάχθη.
165 οὐ γὰρ δήπου ἐν τοῖς μετοίκοις πίστιν παρ᾽ αὐτοῦ
ἐλάμβανον. ἔπειτα τῷ ἧττον εἰκὸς ἦν προσταχθῆναι
ἢ ὅστις ἀντειπών γε ἐτύγχανε καὶ γνώμην ἀποδεδειγμένος ; τίνα γὰρ εἰκὸς ἦν ἧττον ταῦτα ὑπηρετῆσαι ἢ

the English, less logically, has *or*.
Cp. 27. 3 ὁπόταν ἐν χρήμασιν ᾖ καὶ
σωθῆναι τῇ πόλει καὶ μή *when the
safety or destruction of the city
depends upon money*.

27. εἴπερ ἀληθῆ λέγει: *if he is
speaking the truth* (though I deny
that he is). εἴπερ gives emphasis;
it is oftenest, though not always,
used (A) where there is an implied denial or doubt of the truth
of the statement, §§ 32, 48; 16. 8,
22. 12, 25. 5; or (B) with implied
protest against the fact stated,
§ 29. — **ὡς προσετάχθη**: in apposition with τοῦτο. — **ἐν τοῖς μετοίκοις**: cp. Isoc. *Panegyr.* 85 ἐπεδείξαντο δὲ τὰς αὐτῶν εὐψυχίας
. . . ἐν τοῖς ὑπὸ Δαρείου πεμφθεῖ-
σιν *they exhibited their bravery in
the case of those who were sent by
Darius*. — **πίστιν ἐλάμβανον**: Eratosthenes may claim that his colleagues, suspicious of his loyalty
to them, forced him to make this
arrest in order to implicate him so

deeply in their crimes that he could
not withdraw (we have Plato's testimony, *Apol.* 32 c, that they used
this means to hold men who were
not of their own number). Lysias
replies that for such a purpose they
would have sent him to arrest some
one more important and conspicuous than a mere metic. That such
a claim by Eratosthenes will be
insincere is implied in the ironical
δήπου. For the force of πίστιν
cp. § 9; there the 'guaranty' lay
in the oath; here it would be in
the act. — **ἐλάμβανον**: tense, see
on ἐποίουν § 25. — **εἰκὸς ἦν**: for
the non-use of ἄν see HA. 897;
G. 1400. 1; B. 567; Gl. 460; GMT.
415–417; GS. 363. — **ἀντειπών,
ἀποδεδειγμένος**: the opposition and
the expression of opinion were
both past with reference to ἐτύγχανε, but the opinion expressed
remained as a basis for the action
of his colleagues, hence the change
to the perfect. ὅστις ἀντιλέγων

28 τὸν ἀντειπόντα οἷς ἐκεῖνοι ἐβούλοντο πραχθῆναι ; Ἔτι
170 δὲ τοῖς μὲν ἄλλοις Ἀθηναίοις ἱκανή μοι δοκεῖ πρόφασις
εἶναι τῶν γεγενημένων εἰς τοὺς τριάκοντα ἀναφέρειν τὴν
αἰτίαν· αὐτοὺς δὲ τοὺς τριάκοντα, ἐὰν εἰς σφᾶς αὐτοὺς
29 ἀναφέρωσι, πῶς ὑμᾶς εἰκὸς ἀποδέχεσθαι ; εἰ μὲν γάρ
τις ἦν ἐν τῇ πόλει ἀρχὴ ἰσχυροτέρα αὐτῆς, ὑφ᾽ ἧς αὐτῷ
175 προσετάττετο παρὰ τὸ δίκαιον ἀνθρώπους ἀπολλύναι,
ἴσως ἂν εἰκότως αὐτῷ συγγνώμην εἴχετε· νῦν δὲ παρὰ
τοῦ ποτε καὶ λήψεσθε δίκην, εἴπερ ἐξέσται τοῖς τριάκοντα λέγειν ὅτι τὰ ὑπὸ τῶν τριάκοντα προσταχθέντα

(pres.) ἐτύγχανε would mean *who happened to be opposing*. GMT. 144, 146. ἀποφαίνεσθαι is the more common word with γνώμην. In such expressions γνώμη has become so fused with the verb that it seldom takes the article even when *the* opinion expressed is specifically given in the following clause; cp. 31. 6 γνώμῃ δὲ χρῶνται ὡς πᾶσα γῆ πατρὶς αὐτοῖς ἐστιν ἐν ᾗ ἂν τὰ ἐπιτήδεια ἔχωσιν *who hold the opinion that every land that feeds them is their fatherland*; so Xen. *Anab.* 5. 5. 3 ἀπεδείξαντο . . . γνώμην ὅτι κτλ.

28. ἔτι : *again*, introducing the third point in the argument, as ἔπειτα introduced the second.

29. αὐτῆς : *itself*, HA. 680. 3 ; G. 990; B. 475. 2 n.; Gl. 558.— προσετάττετο : for the assimilation

of tense to that of ἦν see HA. 919 b; G. 1440; GMT. 559.— νῦν δέ: cp. § 23. — παρὰ τοῦ ποτε καὶ λήψεσθε δίκην: *whom in the world WILL you punish ?* καί is used as an emphatic particle in questions, implying the inability of the speaker to answer his own question, or his impatience at the circumstances that raise the question. Its only English equivalent is a peculiar emphasis. Cp. 24. 12, 24. 23. — ποτέ: the tone given by καί is further strengthened by ποτέ; the indefinite word of time gives the idea of utter loss for an answer. In English we prefer the indefinite expression of place, *in the world*. Cp. § 34 and 32. 12. — εἴπερ: *if it is actually going to be permitted*. See on § 27.— ἐξέσται: a monitory protasis (see on § 35) made still more emphatic by the intensive -περ.

30 ἐποίουν; Καὶ μὲν δὴ οὐκ ἐν τῇ οἰκίᾳ ἀλλ' ἐν τῇ ὁδῷ,
180 σῴζειν τε αὐτὸν καὶ τὰ τούτοις ἐψηφισμένα παρόν,
συλλαβὼν ἀπήγαγεν. ὑμεῖς δὲ πᾶσιν ὀργίζεσθε, ὅσοι
εἰς τὰς οἰκίας ἦλθον τὰς ὑμετέρας ζήτησιν ποιούμενοι
31 ἢ ὑμῶν ἢ τῶν ὑμετέρων τινός. καίτοι εἰ χρὴ τοῖς διὰ
τὴν ἑαυτῶν σωτηρίαν ἑτέρους ἀπολέσασι συγγνώμην
185 ἔχειν, ἐκείνοις ἂν δικαιότερον ἔχοιτε· κίνδυνος γὰρ ἦν
πεμφθεῖσι μὴ ἐλθεῖν καὶ καταλαβοῦσιν ἐξάρνοις γενέσθαι. τῷ δὲ Ἐρατοσθένει ἐξῆν εἰπεῖν ὅτι οὐκ ἀπήντη-
σεν, ἔπειτα ὅτι οὐκ εἶδεν· ταῦτα γὰρ οὔτ' ἔλεγχον οὔτε

30. **καὶ μὲν δή**: in this combination μέν has the affirmative force
of its stronger form μήν. Where
the main statement or argument
has been concluded the combination καὶ μὲν δή often introduces
another, less important, but confirmatory, statement. So in §§ 35,
49, 89; 22. 19, 22. 21, 25. 17. —
σῴζειν: precisely fitted to govern
αὐτόν only, but with slight extension of meaning made to govern
τὰ ἐψηφισμένα also. It was possible for Eratosthenes, not finding
Polemarchus at home, to pretend
that he did not see him in the
street, and so "keep" him safe,
and at the same time "keep" the
commands of the Thirty. — **σῴζειν
τε**: unusual position of τε, as
though καὶ σῴζειν were to follow;
cp. Isae. 2. 1 βοηθεῖν τε τῷ πατρὶ
καὶ ἐμαυτῷ *both to help my father
and myself*, for *to help both my*

father and myself. — **παρόν**: HA.
973; G. 1569; B. 658; Gl. 591.
— **πᾶσιν**: referring not only to
members of the Thirty, but to
many honorable citizens whom
they forced to do work of this
kind, and for whom some excuse might be offered; cp. on
§ 27.

31. **ἐξάρνοις**: pred. of γενέσθαι,
assimilated to the dat. pronoun
understood with κίνδυνος ἦν; see
on λέγοντι § 1. — **τῷ δὲ Ἐρατοσθένει**: Lysias seldom uses the
article with the names of parties
to a suit. Here the antithesis to
ἐκείνοις accounts for its use. —
ἐξῆν εἰπεῖν: *he could have said*
(cp. παρόν, § 30). For non-use
of ἄν see on εἰκὸς ἦν § 27. We
have the same omission in οἷόν
τ' εἶναι below, and in χρῆν § 32.
— **ἔλεγχον, βάσανον**: for the συνωνυμία see App. § 58. 2.

189 βάσανον εἶχεν, ὥστε μηδ' ὑπὸ τῶν ἐχθρῶν βουλομένων
32 οἷόν τ' εἶναι ἐξελεγχθῆναι. χρῆν δέ σε, ὦ Ἐρατόσθενες,
εἴπερ ἦσθα χρηστός, πολὺ μᾶλλον τοῖς μέλλουσιν ἀδίκως ἀποθανεῖσθαι μηνυτὴν γενέσθαι ἢ τοὺς ἀδίκως
ἀπολουμένους συλλαμβάνειν· νῦν δέ σου τὰ ἔργα
194 φανερὰ γεγένηται οὐχ ὡς ἀνιωμένου ἀλλ' ὡς ἡδομένου
33 τοῖς γιγνομένοις, ὥστε τούσδε ἐκ τῶν ἔργων χρὴ μᾶλλον ἢ ἐκ τῶν λόγων τὴν ψῆφον φέρειν, ἃ ἴσασι γεγενημένα τῶν τότε λεγομένων τεκμήρια λαμβάνοντας, ἐπειδὴ
μάρτυρας περὶ αὐτῶν οὐχ οἷόν τε παρασχέσθαι. οὐ
γὰρ μόνον ἡμῖν παρεῖναι οὐκ ἐξῆν, ἀλλ' οὐδὲ παρ'

32. For the use of antithesis in this section and the next see App. § 57. 1. — εἴπερ : force, see on § 27. — μηνυτήν : usually in bad sense, 'informer,' but here and in § 48 in good sense. — συλλαμβάνειν : present tense of a course of conduct. — ἀνιωμένου . . . ἡδομένου : present in form, impf. in force. Cp. §§ 42, 50, 51, 99; 16. 5, 16. 6. See HA. 856 a; G. 1289; B. 542. 1; GMT. 140; GS. 337. Cp. on ἀντιλέγειν § 26. On the rhetorical form see App. § 58. 5.

33. τῶν λεγομένων : connect with τεκμήρια. — οὐ γὰρ μόνον κτλ. : on the periodic structure see App. § 54. — ἡμῖν : thrust between οὐ μόνον and παρεῖναι to throw emphasis upon the latter. Hyperbaton, the interruption of the natural order of words, arrests the attention, and thus throws the attention, and thus throws

emphasis sometimes upon the inserted word, sometimes upon one or both of the words that it has crowded apart. Cp. εἴησαν § 82; νῦν § 94; ὑπ' ἐμοῦ 16. 8; τινές 19. 52; μοι 24. 1; ὑμῖν and ἔχειν 24. 21; τοῖς ἅπασι 24. 22; ὑμῖν 24. 27; ἀεί 25. 25; οὕτως 32. 13. — παρεῖναι : the secrecy of the meetings of the Thirty was in evil contrast with the openness of proceedings in the democratic assemblies. Yet even under the democracy the Senate might hold secret sessions on special occasions. Lysias indulges in a grim pun in παρ-εῖναι, παρ' αὐτοῖς εἶναι, even bringing in an uncommon expression for the sake of it. See App. § 58. 5. — παρ' αὐτοῖς : at our own homes, or in our own land. Cp. chez nous, apud nos. Cp. παρὰ τοῖς ἄλλοις 24. 20. For the Greek for to one's

200 αὐτοῖς εἶναι, ὥστ' ἐπὶ τούτοις ἐστὶ πάντα τὰ κακὰ
εἰργασμένοις τὴν πόλιν πάντα τἀγαθὰ περὶ αὑτῶν
34 λέγειν. τοῦτο μέντοι οὐ φεύγω, ἀλλ' ὁμολογῶ σοι,
εἰ βούλει, ἀντειπεῖν. θαυμάζω δὲ τί ἄν ποτ' ἐποίησας συνειπών, ὁπότε ἀντειπεῖν φάσκων ἀπέκτεινας
205 Πολέμαρχον.

Φέρε δή, τί ἄν εἰ καὶ ἀδελφοὶ ὄντες ἐτυγχάνετε αὐτοῦ
ἢ καὶ ὑεῖς; ἀπεψηφίσασθε; δεῖ γάρ, ὦ ἄνδρες δικασταί, Ἐρατοσθένην δυοῖν θάτερον ἀποδεῖξαι, ἢ ὡς οὐκ
ἀπήγαγεν αὐτόν, ἢ ὡς δικαίως τοῦτ' ἔπραξεν. οὗτος
210 δὲ ὡμολόγηκεν ἀδίκως συλλαβεῖν, ὥστε ῥᾳδίαν ὑμῖν
35 τὴν διαψήφισιν περὶ αὐτοῦ πεποίηκε. Καὶ μὲν δὴ
πολλοὶ καὶ τῶν ἀστῶν καὶ τῶν ξένων ἥκουσιν εἰσόμενοι
τίνα γνώμην περὶ τούτων ἕξετε. ὧν οἱ μὲν ὑμέτεροι

home see on 16. 4. For παρά
with dat. = *under one's care* see
on 19. 22.— **αὐτοῖς**: for ἡμῖν αὐτοῖς HA. 686 a; G. 995; B. 471,
n. 1.— **ἐπὶ τούτοις**: see on ἐπὶ σοί
§ 26.— **πάντα τὰ κακά**: *all possible injuries ;* the article is less
often used in this expression.—
εἰργασμένοις: tense, see on § 22.

34. **τί ἄν ποτ' ἐποίησας**: *what
in the world you would have done.*
For ποτέ see on § 29.— **φάσκων**:
see on φάσκοντες § 5.— **δή**: see
on 25. 9 A.—**τί ἄν εἰ**: the Greek
hearer was no more conscious of
the loss of a verb here than we
are with our own "what if." The
ἄν serves its own phrase and
also the following ἀπεψηφίσα-

σθε.— **καὶ ἀδελφοί . . . καὶ ὑεῖς**:
καί (= *even*) is not here to be
connected with εἰ. Cp. on 19. 18.
— **αὐτοῦ**: Eratosthenes. — **ὑεῖς**:
the ι of υἱός disappeared in Attic
writers of the fourth century, and
largely in Attic prose writers even
in the fifth. Declension, HA. 216.
19; G. 291. 35; B. 115. 25; Gl.
142. 9.— **ἀπεψηφίσασθε**: on this
rare use of the aorist see Crit.
Note.

35. **καὶ μὲν δή**: force, see on
§ 30.— **ἀστῶν**: distinguish from
πολιτῶν, L. & S. *s.v.* ἀστός. The
word is chosen here as suggesting those of the πολῖται who
supported the Thirty and were
known as οἱ ἐξ ἄστεως.— **οἱ μὲν**

ὄντες πολῖται μαθόντες ἀπίασιν πότερον δίκην δώσου-
215 σιν ὧν ἂν ἐξαμάρτωσιν, ἢ πράξαντες μὲν ὧν ἐφίενται
τύραννοι τῆς πόλεως ἔσονται, δυστυχήσαντες δὲ τὸ
ἴσον ὑμῖν ἕξουσιν· ὅσοι δὲ ξένοι ἐπιδημοῦσιν, εἴσονται
πότερον ἀδίκως τοὺς τριάκοντα ἐκκηρύττουσιν ἐκ τῶν
πόλεων ἢ δικαίως. εἰ γὰρ δὴ αὐτοὶ οἱ κακῶς πεπονθότες
220 λαβόντες ἀφήσουσιν, ἦ που σφᾶς γ᾽ αὐτοὺς ἡγήσον-
36 ται περιέργους ὑπὲρ ὑμῶν τηρουμένους. οὐκ οὖν δεινὸν

κτλ.: the scheme of the sentence
is:

οἱ μὲν . . . μαθόντες ἀπίασιν
πότερον δίκην δώσουσιν

ὧν { ἢ { πράξαντες μὲν . . .
ἔσονται
δυστυχήσαντες δὲ . . .
ἕξουσιν

ὅσοι δὲ ξένοι ἐπιδημοῦσιν
εἴσονται

πότερον ἀδίκως . . . ἐκκηρύττουσιν
ἢ δικαίως

— **ὧν** (before ἄν) : assimilated from
cognate accus. to case of omitted
antecedent, HA. 996 a. 2 ; G. 1032 ;
B. 484. 1, 486; Gl. 614. For **ὧν**
ἐφίενται (without assimilation) see
HA. 739, 996 a. 1 ; G. 1099, 1033 ;
B. 356; Gl. 510 d. — **ἐξαμάρτωσιν** :
indefinite, hypothetical sins of
the future (general future supposition) ; ἐφίενται (indic.), the definite, known aims of the present.
— **δή** : force, see on 25. 9 (B). —
ἀφήσουσιν : a monitory protasis.
For the future indic. in minatory

and monitory conditions see
GMT. 447 n. 1; G. 1405; Gl.
648 b. So in §§ 29, 74, 85, 90 ;
22. 17, 34. 6. — **τηρουμένους** : see
Crit. Note. We infer that some
of the states friendly to Athens
had made formal proclamation
excluding members of the late
oligarchy from taking refuge with
them. While Eleusis had been
set apart as an asylum for the
Thirty and their supporters, it is
not unlikely that some, fearing that
the democracy would not keep its
promise of immunity, sought refuge
in other states.

36. οὖν: for οὖν as a particle
of emphasis see on 19. 7 (A). —
δεινὸν εἰ: the thought as it lies in
Lysias's mind at the beginning is
οὐ δεινόν ἐστι

εἰ { τοὺς μὲν στρατηγούς . . . θανάτῳ ἐζημιώσατε
τούτους δέ . . . οὐ κολάσεσθε ;

but as he comes to the climax the
thought οὐκ οὖν δεινὸν is too re-
mote, and he turns to a stronger,

εἰ τοὺς μὲν στρατηγούς, οἳ ἐνίκων ναυμαχοῦντες,
ὅτε διὰ χειμῶνα οὐχ οἷοί τ᾽ ἔφασαν εἶναι τοὺς ἐκ τῆς
θαλάττης ἀνελέσθαι, θανάτῳ ἐζημιώσατε, ἡγούμενοι

more passionate form in the direct
appeal οὐκ ἄρα χρὴ . . . κολάζεσθαι; this leaves τούτους without
government, and the introductory
εἰ, which was brought in by the
expected οὐ κολάσεσθε, apparently,
but only apparently, stands in the
place of ὅτι. — ἐνίκων: tense, see
on ἀδικῶ § 14. — τοὺς ἐκ τῆς
θαλάττης: in speaking of the same
event Plato uses τοὺς ἐκ τῆς
ναυμαχίας (Apol. 32 b); con-
structio praegnans, τοὺς ἐκ τῆς
θαλάττης standing both for τοὺς
ἐν τῇ θαλάττῃ, and ἐκ τῆς θαλάττης (with ἀνελέσθαι). HA. 788 a;
G. 1225; B. 398 n. 3. — θανάτῳ
ἐζημιώσατε: in the summer of 406
the Athenian fleet under Conon
was shut up in the harbor of
Mytilene by the Lacedaemonians.
Desperate efforts were made for
their rescue; a new fleet was
hastily equipped and manned by
a general call to arms. Seldom
had an expedition enlisted so
many citizens of every class. The
new fleet met the enemy off the Arginusae islands, and, in the greatest
naval battle ever fought between
Greek fleets, won a glorious victory. The generals, wishing to
push on in pursuit of the enemy,
detailed forty-seven ships under

subordinate officers to rescue the
Athenian wounded from the wreck-
age. A sudden storm made both
pursuit and rescue impossible, and
more than 4000 men, probably
half of them Athenian citizens,
were lost. The blow fell upon so
many homes in Athens that public
indignation against the generals
passed all bounds, and the generals were condemned to death.
Not only was the sentence in
itself unjust, but it was carried by
a vote against the accused in a
body, in violation of the law's
guaranty of a separate vote upon
the case of every accused citizen.
A reaction in feeling followed, a
part of the general reaction against
the abuses of the democracy.
That the popular repentance was
not as general or as permanent as
it ought to have been is clear
from the fact that now, three years
after the event, Lysias dares appeal to this precedent as ground
for righteous severity in the present case; he is evidently not afraid
that it will be a warning to them
to beware of overseverity when
acting under passion. Yet he
shows his consciousness that he is
on dangerous ground, for he takes
pains to state the defense of the

225 χρῆναι τῇ τῶν τεθνεώτων ἀρετῇ παρ' ἐκείνων δίκην
λαβεῖν, τούτους δέ, οἳ ἰδιῶται μὲν ὄντες καθ' ὅσον ἐδύναντο ἐποίησαν ἡττηθῆναι ναυμαχοῦντας, ἐπειδὴ δὲ εἰς
τὴν ἀρχὴν κατέστησαν, ὁμολογοῦσιν ἑκόντες πολλοὺς
τῶν πολιτῶν ἀκρίτους ἀποκτιννύναι, οὐκ ἄρα χρὴ αὐ-
230 τοὺς καὶ τοὺς παῖδας ὑφ' ὑμῶν ταῖς ἐσχάταις ζημίαις
κολάζεσθαι ;

37 Ἐγὼ τοίνυν, ὦ ἄνδρες δικασταί, ἠξίουν ἱκανὰ εἶναι
τὰ κατηγορημένα · μέχρι γὰρ τούτου νομίζω χρῆναι

generals and the ground on which it was overruled. — **τῇ ἀρετῇ**: for Lysias's rare use of personification see Introd. p. 25, n. 5. — **ἰδιῶται . . . ἐποίησαν ἡττηθῆναι**: Lysias appeals confidently to the popular suspicion that the oligarchical clubs were in negotiation with the Spartans during the last years of the war, and that the catastrophe at Aegospotami was a piece of sheer treachery carried out under their plans. The mismanagement there was so notorious that we are not surprised at the suspicion, though it is doubtful whether there was real cause for it. The suspicion was greatly increased by the fact that one general slipped away unharmed, while another was released by the Spartans, although all the other Athenian prisoners were put to death. — **καὶ τοὺς παῖδας**: an exaggeration, as it is in § 83, where he says that the death of these men and that

of their children would not be sufficient punishment for them. No one ever seriously proposed at Athens to put sons to death for their fathers' crimes, but lesser penalties were put upon them; loss of civil rights (ἀτιμία) was often visited upon the sons of a man condemned, and the common penalty of death and confiscation of property brought heavy suffering to the family (so in the case of the family for which Lysias pleads in Speech XIX). Yet even here the treatment was not inhuman; Demosthenes says (27. 65), "Even when you condemn any one, you do not take away everything, but you are merciful to wife or children, and leave some part for them."

37. **τοίνυν**: force, see on 16. 7. — **ἠξίουν κτλ**.: ἄξιον ἦν ἱκανὰ εἶναι τὰ κατηγορημένα would mean, *the charges ought to be sufficient*; but in order to add to this the idea

κατηγορεῖν, ἕως ἂν θανάτου δόξῃ τῷ φεύγοντι ἄξια
235 εἰργάσθαι. ταύτην γὰρ ἐσχάτην δίκην δυνάμεθα παρ'
αὐτῶν λαβεῖν. ὥστ' οὐκ οἶδ' ὅ τι δεῖ πολλὰ κατηγορεῖν τοιούτων ἀνδρῶν, οἳ οὐδ' ἂν ὑπὲρ ἑνὸς ἑκάστου
τῶν πεπραγμένων δὶς ἀποθανόντες δίκην δοῦναι ἀξίαν
239 δύναιντο.

38 Οὐ γὰρ δὴ οὐδὲ τοῦτο αὐτῷ προσήκει ποιῆσαι,
ὅπερ ἐν τῇδε τῇ πόλει εἰθισμένον ἐστί, πρὸς μὲν
τὰ κατηγορημένα μηδὲν ἀπολογεῖσθαι, περὶ δὲ σφῶν
αὐτῶν ἕτερα λέγοντες ἐνίοτε ἐξαπατῶσιν, ὑμῖν ἀποδει-

"I think," the Greek substitutes for ἄξιον ἦν (*ought*) the verb ἀξιόω (*I think . . . ought*), putting it in the mood and tense proper to ἄξιον ἦν; we translate, then, *I think the charges ought to be sufficient*. For non-use of ἄν see on εἰκὸς ἦν § 27. — τῷ φεύγοντι: dat. of agent with εἰργάσθαι. — ταύτην: the neut. pronoun is assimilated in gender to its predicate appositive (δίκην) as always in Lysias. Cp. 16. 6, 24. 10, 25. 13, 25. 23, 25. 28. See GS. 127; B. 465. — αὐτῶν: plural because of the plurality implied in the indefinite τῷ φεύγοντι, to which it refers. — οὐκ οἶδ' ὅ τι: the τί (adverbial acc.) of the direct question becomes ὅ τι of the indirect. HA. 719 c, 700; G. 1060, 1013; B. 336, 490; Gl. 540, 621. — ὑπέρ: see on 25. 5. — ἑνός: the word adds emphasis to the individuality in ἑκάστου, *each*

one. The speech against Ergocles (XXVIII) opens with words similar to these: τὰ μὲν κατηγορημένα οὕτως ἐστὶ πολλὰ καὶ δεινά, ὦ ἄνδρες Ἀθηναῖοι, ὥστε οὐκ ἄν μοι δοκεῖ δύνασθαι Ἐργοκλῆς ὑπὲρ ἑνὸς ἑκάστου τῶν πεπραγμένων αὐτῷ πολλάκις ἀποθανὼν δοῦναι δίκην ἀξίαν τῷ ὑμετέρῳ πλήθει *the charges are so many and so grave, Athenians, that it does not seem to me that Ergocles, though he should die many deaths for each one of his deeds, could pay sufficient penalty to you the people*.

38. γάρ: force, as noted on 16. 10. — δή: force, see on 25. 9 (B). — οὐ . . . οὐδέ: for the double negative see on 16. 10. — ἐξαπατῶ-σιν: a change from the infin. construction begun in ἀπολογεῖσθαι to the independent indicative; the anacoluthon makes it possible to present the long and detailed

κνύντες ὡς στρατιῶται ἀγαθοί εἰσιν, ἢ ὡς πολλὰς τῶν
245 πολεμίων ναῦς ἔλαβον τριηραρχήσαντες, ἢ ὡς πόλεις
39 πολεμίας οὔσας φίλας ἐποίησαν· ἐπεὶ κελεύετε αὐτὸν
ἀποδεῖξαι ὅπου τοσούτους τῶν πολεμίων ἀπέκτειναν
ὅσους τῶν πολιτῶν, ἢ ναῦς ὅπου τοσαύτας ἔλαβον ὅσας
249 αὐτοὶ παρέδοσαν, ἢ πόλιν ἥντινα τοιαύτην προσεκτή-
40 σαντο οἵαν τὴν ὑμετέραν κατεδουλώσαντο. ἀλλὰ γὰρ

thought of the second member in
a simpler and more direct form.
— **τριηραρχήσαντες** : note that the
time of this aorist partic. is coincident with that of the leading
verb, ἔλαβον. " The action of the
aorist participle is ordinarily prior,
but it may be coincident, so especially when the leading verb is
aorist or future," GS. 339. Cp.
HA. 856 b; G. 1290; B. 543, 545.
— **φίλας**: φιλίας is more common ;
but cp. Dem. 19. 137 Ἀμφίπολιν
. . . ἢν τότε σύμμαχον αὐτοῦ καὶ
φίλην ἔγραψεν (*enrolled*) ; Dem.
20. 59 καὶ παρασχόντες φίλην ὑμῖν
τὴν αὐτῶν πατρίδα; Isoc. 16. 21
πόλεις . . . φίλας ὑμῖν ἐποίησε.

39. For the use of antithesis
in this section and the next see
App. § 57. 1. — **ἐπεί**: introducing
the reason for the statement above,
οὐ προσήκει ; *for tell him to show*
is here only a more emphatic way
of saying, " for he could not show."
— **ὅσους**: for the number see note
on § 17. — **ναῦς ὅπου**: the first
ὅπου had its natural place at the
beginning of its clause, but the

second ὅπου and the corresponding ἥντινα of the third question
are displaced to give emphasis of
position to ναῦς and πόλιν. — **παρέδοσαν** : though the ships were
all lost before the establishment
of the Thirty, the oligarchical
leaders were commonly charged
with having betrayed the fleet at
Aegospotami (cp. on § 36), and
were held responsible for the terms
of the final surrender, which included the surrender of all but
twelve of the war-ships that remained (Xen. *Hell.* 2. 2. 20, Andoc.
3. 12). — **οἵαν** : the use of this
relative adjective where the English has only ' *as* ' enables the
Greek to use a more compact
expression.

40. ἀλλὰ γάρ κτλ. : *but in fact
they seized so many arms of the
enemy* (and only so many) *as they
took from you ; they captured such
walls* (and only such) *as the walls
of their country, which they dis-
mantled ; i.e.* you, their fellow-
citizens, are the only enemy that
they ever faced. — **ἀλλὰ γάρ**: see

ὅπλα τῶν πολεμίων τοσαῦτα ἐσκύλευσαν ὅσα περ ὑμῶν
ἀφείλοντο, ἀλλὰ τείχη τοιαῦτα εἷλον οἷα τῆς ἑαυτῶν
πατρίδος κατέσκαψαν· οἵτινες καὶ τὰ περὶ τὴν Ἀττι-
κὴν φρούρια καθεῖλον, καὶ ὑμῖν ἐδήλωσαν ὅτι οὐδὲ τὸν
255 Πειραιᾶ Λακεδαιμονίων προσταττόντων περιεῖλον, ἀλλ᾽
ὅτι ἑαυτοῖς τὴν ἀρχὴν οὕτω βεβαιοτέραν ἐνόμιζον εἶναι.
41　Πολλάκις οὖν ἐθαύμασα τῆς τόλμης τῶν λεγόντων

HA. 1050. 4 d; Gl. 672 d. In
ἀλλὰ γάρ the original confirmatory
force of γάρ is preserved (see on
19. 12) ; it is not *for*, but *surely,
certainly, in fact*. It is often
better left untranslated in English. We are not to assume an
ellipsis and γάρ in the causal sense
but this is so, for. An emphatic
but is natural in closing the discussion of a point; ἀλλὰ γάρ is
often so used. Cp. § 99; 22. 11,
24. 14, 24. 21, 25. 17, 34. 10. —
ὑμῶν: possess. gen. in the series
ὑμετέραν . . . τῶν πολεμίων . . .
ὑμῶν . . . τῆς ἑαυτῶν πατρίδος. —
ἀφείλοντο: for the seizure of the
arms of all citizens outside the
3000 supporters of the Thirty, see
Xen. *Hell.* 2. 3. 20. This meant
more than the crippling of the
power of the people to resist. It
was a keen personal affront to
every man, for the lance and
shield of the Athenian hoplite
were an outward sign of his political and social rank. Lycurgus
speaks of them (76) as ἱερὰ ὅπλα.
The seizure of these arms, which

many of the citizens had carried
through all the years of the Peloponnesian War, was one of the
most outrageous acts of the Thirty.
— οἵτινες: the simple relative οἵ
is replaced by the indefinite rel.
in a *characterizing* clause. ὅς
specifies; ὅσπερ specifies and
identifies, laying stress upon the
identity (cp. 22. 15, 24. 21, 25. 20,
25. 22, 25. 31, 32. 15, 34. 1, 34. 5) ;
while ὅστις often characterizes, =
the sort of man who. "With ὅστις
you relegate the man to the class
of people who do that sort of
thing; with ὅς γε you have in
mind only the man himself and
his deed" (Forman, *Selections
from Plato*, p. 450). Cp. § 84,
25. 17, 25. 18, 25. 23. — φρούρια:
we have no other knowledge of
this treacherous recall of frontier
garrisons.

41. ἐθαύμασα . . . ὅταν ἐνθυμηθῶ: for the tense of ἐθαύμασα
see on κατέστην § 3. As the aor.
expresses here a repeated action
it properly stands as apodosis of
the general protasis ὅταν ἐνθυμηθῶ.

ὑπὲρ αὐτοῦ, πλὴν ὅταν ἐνθυμηθῶ ὅτι τῶν αὐτῶν ἐστιν
259 αὐτούς τε πάντα τὰ κακὰ ἐργάζεσθαι καὶ τοὺς τοιούτους
42 ἐπαινεῖν. οὐ γὰρ νῦν πρῶτον τῷ ὑμετέρῳ πλήθει τὰ
ἐναντία ἔπραξεν, ἀλλὰ καὶ ἐπὶ τῶν τετρακοσίων ἐν τῷ
στρατοπέδῳ ὀλιγαρχίαν καθιστὰς ἔφευγεν ἐξ Ἑλλη-
σπόντου τριήραρχος καταλιπὼν τὴν ναῦν, μετὰ Ἰατρο-
κλέους καὶ ἑτέρων, ὧν τὰ ὀνόματα οὐδὲν δέομαι λέγειν.
265 ἀφικόμενος δὲ δεῦρο τἀναντία τοῖς βουλομένοις δημοκρατίαν εἶναι ἔπραττε. καὶ τούτων μάρτυρας ὑμῖν
παρέξομαι.

ΜΑΡΤΥΡΕΣ

43 Τὸν μὲν τοίνυν μεταξὺ βίον αὐτοῦ παρήσω· ἐπειδὴ
δὲ ἡ ναυμαχία καὶ ἡ συμφορὰ τῇ πόλει ἐγένετο, δημο-

— τῶν αὐτῶν : a pred. gen. is often
used to denote one whose *nature
it is* to do the act expressed by
an accompanying infin. HA.
732 c. — πάντα τὰ κακά: as in
§ 33. — τοὺς τοιούτους : *i.e.* τοὺς
πάντα τὰ κακὰ ἐργαζομένους.
42. τῷ ὑμετέρῳ πλήθει : the
common term for the democratic
body of citizens in distinction from
the oligarchical faction. — ἐπί :
force, see on § 17. The time is
here to be taken broadly, including
the months of preparation. — τῶν
τετρακοσίων : see Introd. p. 35.
— καθιστάς : conative imperf. of
an act preliminary to the main
verb ἔφευγεν. See on ἀνιωμένου
§ 32. — ἔφευγεν : imperf. of the
beginning of the flight (see on
ἐβάδιζον § 8), the end of which

is expressed by ἀφικόμενος. We
must conclude that while the
leaders of the movement were
working at Athens and among the
allied cities (Thuc. 8. 64. 1), Eratosthenes was coöperating with
them in the fleet on the Hellespont,
which had headquarters at Ses-
tos. — καταλιπών : and so guilty
of desertion, for the trierarch was
required to serve in person as
commander of his ship (for some
exceptions see on 19. 62). — Ἰατρο-
κλέους : otherwise unknown. —
ΜΑΡΤΥΡΕΣ : the clerk of the court
here reads the depositions of witnesses, the witnesses themselves
only acknowledging the written
testimony as theirs. App. § 20.
43. τοίνυν : see on 16. 7 (D). —
μεταξύ : *i.e.* from 412/11-405 B.C.

₂₇₀ κρατίας ἔτι οὔσης, ὅθεν τῆς στάσεως ἦρξαν, πέντε
ἄνδρες ἔφοροι κατέστησαν ὑπὸ τῶν καλουμένων ἑταί-
ρων, συναγωγεῖς μὲν τῶν πολιτῶν, ἄρχοντες δὲ τῶν
συνωμοτῶν, ἐναντία δὲ τῷ ὑμετέρῳ πλήθει πράττον-
44 τες · ὧν Ἐρατοσθένης καὶ Κριτίας ἦσαν. οὗτοι δὲ

— ἡ ναυμαχία : the addition of ἡ
συμφορά makes clear what battle
is meant. Lysias elsewhere calls
it ἡ τελευταία ναυμαχία (18. 4,
21. 9), ἡ ναυμαχία ἡ ἐν Ἑλλησπόντῳ (19. 16), ἡ ἐν Ἑλλησπόντῳ
συμφορά (16. 4). — ὅθεν : the
antecedent of ὅθεν is here, as often
with ὅθεν, the whole following
clause. Here this position serves
the periodic form by avoiding any
interruption in the close succession : πέντε ἄνδρες ἔφοροι κατέ-
στησαν . . . | συναγωγεῖς μὲν τῶν
πολιτῶν | ἄρχοντες δὲ τῶν συνω-
μοτῶν | ἐναντία δὲ . . . πράττοντες.
— ἔφοροι : a central committee, in
control of the political machine.
As the leaders of the pro-Spartan
party, they were well named after
the Spartan Ephors. The steps
recounted here were the preliminary, secret steps taken to organize
the anti-democratic citizens, pre-
paratory to the open attempt to
set aside again the democratic
constitution. The organization
was effected through the league
of secret oligarchical clubs, ἑταιρεῖαι ; see Introd. p. 37. — κατέστησαν : the passive force of this

intrans. act. form justifies the
agent construction with ὑπό ; cp.
the trans. κατέστησαν § 21. —
Κριτίας : the secret oligarchical
clubs had played a large part in
the revolution of 411 B.C., and
had probably continued after the
overthrow of the Four Hundred.
When Lysander received the surrender of the city (April, 404),
former members and supporters
of the Four Hundred who had
been in exile entered the city with
him ; among these was Critias.
It is probable that it was these
returned exiles, who felt themselves unsafe under the democracy,
who put new energy into the
" clubs " and organized their new
central committee (ἔφοροι). The
fact that it was not one of their
faction, but Theramenes, to whom
were intrusted the final negotiations with Sparta as to terms
of surrender, confirms the supposition that their activity was after
the surrender and the return of
the oligarchical exiles. Lysias
chooses here to represent it as
before the surrender, in order to
give the impression that Eratos-

275 φυλάρχους τε ἐπὶ τὰς φυλὰς κατέστησαν, καὶ ὅ τι
δέοι χειροτονεῖσθαι καὶ οὕστινας χρείη ἄρχειν παρήγγελλον, καὶ εἴ τι ἄλλο πράττειν βούλοιντο, κύριοι
ἦσαν· οὕτως οὐχ ὑπὸ τῶν πολεμίων μόνον ἀλλὰ καὶ
ὑπὸ τούτων πολιτῶν ὄντων ἐπεβουλεύεσθε ὅπως μήτ᾽
280 ἀγαθὸν μηδὲν ψηφιεῖσθε πολλῶν τε ἐνδεεῖς ἔσεσθε.
45 τοῦτο γὰρ καλῶς ἠπίσταντο, ὅτι ἄλλως μὲν οὐχ οἷοί
τε ἔσονται περιγενέσθαι, κακῶς δὲ πραττόντων δυνή-
σονται· καὶ ὑμᾶς ἡγοῦντο τῶν παρόντων κακῶν
284 ἐπιθυμοῦντας ἀπαλλαγῆναι περὶ τῶν μελλόντων οὐκ

thenes sought his own safety in the fall of the city (cp. §§ 44–45). We cannot determine whether Lysias is right in charging Eratosthenes with having been one of the ἔφοροι. He does not claim to have any proof except what his witnesses swear they have heard Eratosthenes say. The probability is against Lysias's claim, for Eratosthenes was certainly the close political adherent of Theramenes, and Theramenes did not belong to the inner faction of the ἑταιρεῖαι (see the explicit statement of Arist. *Resp. Ath.* 34. 3, confirmed by Lys. 12. 76). It is very strange, moreover, that if Eratosthenes was so prominent in the first stage of the movement, we have no mention of any activity on his part in the accounts given by Xenophon and Aristotle.

44. φυλάρχους, φυλάς: the ten phylae were the first political subdivisions of the citizen body. These φύλαρχοι were well planned as 'district leaders' to pass the orders of the five chiefs on to the club members in their several phylae. The name φύλαρχοι is borrowed from that of the commanders of the cavalry, the favorite military department in aristocratic circles. — **παρήγγελλον** : Lysias purposely uses the common term for passing the orders of a military commander down the line. — **ψηφιεῖσθε** : mood, HA. 885 a; G. 1372; B. 593; Gl. 638 a.

45. πραττόντων : *sc.* ὑμῶν. HA. 972 a; G. 1568; B. 657 n. 1; Gl. 590 a. — **τῶν παρόντων κακῶν** : the hearers would naturally understand this as referring to the hard pressure of famine before the surrender; see on Κριτίας § 43.

46 ἐνθυμήσεσθαι. ὡς τοίνυν τῶν ἐφόρων ἐγένετο, μάρτυρας ὑμῖν παρέξομαι, οὐ τοὺς τότε συμπράττοντας (οὐ
γὰρ ἂν δυναίμην), ἀλλὰ τοὺς αὐτοῦ Ἐρατοσθένους ἀκού-
47 σαντας. καίτοι κἀκεῖνοι εἰ ἐσωφρόνουν κατεμαρτύρουν
ἂν αὐτῶν, καὶ τοὺς διδασκάλους τῶν σφετέρων ἁμαρτη-
290 μάτων σφόδρ᾽ ἂν ἐκόλαζον, καὶ τοὺς ὅρκους, εἰ ἐσωφρόνουν, οὐκ ἂν ἐπὶ μὲν τοῖς τῶν πολιτῶν κακοῖς πιστοὺς
ἐνόμιζον, ἐπὶ δὲ τοῖς τῆς πόλεως ἀγαθοῖς ῥᾳδίως παρέβαινον. πρὸς μὲν οὖν τούτους τοσαῦτα λέγω, τοὺς δὲ
294 μάρτυράς μοι κάλει. Καὶ ὑμεῖς ἀνάβητε.

ΜΑΡΤΥΡΕΣ

48 Τῶν μὲν μαρτύρων ἀκηκόατε. τὸ δὲ τελευταῖον εἰς
τὴν ἀρχὴν καταστὰς ἀγαθοῦ μὲν οὐδενὸς μετέσχεν,

47. τοὺς ὅρκους : they would
not, if they were wise, hold invio-
lable the initiation oaths of their
political clubs, while lightly vio-
lating the oath of loyalty which
they had taken as Ephebi entering
on citizenship. τοὺς ὅρκους includes both oaths. The construction is —

εἰ ἐσωφρόνουν
οὐκ ἂν $\begin{cases} ἐπὶ μὲν \ldots ἐνόμιζον \\ ἐπὶ δὲ \ldots παρέβαινον \end{cases}$

The English construction would
put "would not" with only one
of the clauses, and express the
other by "while" with a participle.
The Greek gives the sharper
antithesis and so expresses the

thought more precisely. — πρός :
see on 32. 19, Crit. Note. — μὲν
οὖν : force, see on 12. 3 (C). —
κάλει : addressed to the court crier
(κῆρυξ). — ἀνάβητε : i.e. to the
platform, to acknowledge their
written testimony. (See App.
§ 20.)

48. ἀκηκόατε : the testimony is
before you. As commonly with
the perfect the emphasis is not
on the past action (the hearing),
but on the present result. — τὴν
ἀρχήν : Wilamowitz (Arist. u.
Athen. II. 219) calls attention to
this expression as supporting the
theory that Eratosthenes is under-
going δοκιμασία for his office, not
being tried for murder (cp. Introd.

ἄλλων δὲ πολλῶν. καίτοι εἴπερ ἦν ἀνὴρ ἀγαθός, ἐχρῆν
αὐτὸν πρῶτον μὲν μὴ παρανόμως ἄρχειν, ἔπειτα τῇ
βουλῇ μηνυτὴν γίγνεσθαι περὶ τῶν εἰσαγγελιῶν ἀπα-
300 σῶν, ὅτι ψευδεῖς εἶεν, καὶ Βάτραχος καὶ Αἰσχυλίδης οὐ
τἀληθῆ μηνύουσιν, ἀλλὰ τὰ ὑπὸ τῶν τριάκοντα πλα-
σθέντα εἰσαγγέλλουσι, συγκείμενα ἐπὶ τῇ τῶν πολιτῶν

p. 44). — **ἄλλων πολλῶν**: for κα-κῶν πολλῶν. Such euphemism is common in referring to troubles and disasters. To use it of Eratosthenes's crimes gives a fine touch of irony. — **εἴπερ** : see on § 27. — **ἐχρῆν**: χρή (§§ 31, 33) is a feminine noun, with ἐστί supplied. χρῆν (§ 32) is for χρὴ ἦν, so having an augment in ἦν. The other imperf. form, ἐχρῆν, somewhat less frequent than χρῆν, is made by the mistaken addition of another augment to the form χρῆν; hence its peculiar accent. On the possibility of ἄν here with ἐχρῆν see Crit. Note. — **αὐτόν**: intensive. — **μηνυτήν**: as in § 32. — **γίγνεσθαι** : present, of a series of informations ; in § 32 χρῆν . . . μηνυτὴν γενέσθαι (aorist) refers to a specific case. — **εἰσαγγελιῶν**: in the process called εἰσαγγελία the Thirty found a legal name for their illegal acts. The εἰσαγγελία under the democracy was a process by which any citizen could file information before the Senate, and secure more summary action than through the ordinary course of

law ; but the accused had opportunity for defense before the Senate, and, in the more serious cases, before the Ecclesia or a law court which had final jurisdiction. Under the Thirty the accused lost these privileges of defense. — **Βάτραχος**: one of the most notorious of the informers ; although protected from legal prosecution under the terms of the amnesty, he did not venture to return to Athens ([Lys.] 6. 45). Of Aeschylides we know only that Lysias selects him as a worthy mate for Batrachus. — **εἶεν** . . . **μηνύουσιν** : the choice between opt. of ind. disc. and the mood of the direct depends so entirely on the momentary feeling of the speaker that it is. not strange that as Lysias proceeds to give the details of what Eratosthenes should have said, he passes over to the mood of the direct discourse ; see GMT. 670. — **συγκείμενα**: used as pass. of συντίθημι, here in its bad sense, *concocted*. — **ἐπί** : force, see on § 24.

49 βλάβῃ. καὶ μὲν δή, ὦ ἄνδρες δικασταί, ὅσοι κακόνοι
ἦσαν τῷ ὑμετέρῳ πλήθει, οὐδὲν ἔλαττον εἶχον σιω-
305 πῶντες· ἕτεροι γὰρ ἦσαν οἱ λέγοντες καὶ πράττοντες
ὧν οὐχ οἷόν τ᾽ ἦν μείζω κακὰ γενέσθαι τῇ πόλει.
ὁπόσοι δ᾽ εὖνοί φασιν εἶναι, πῶς οὐκ ἐνταῦθα ἔδειξαν, αὐτοί τε τὰ βέλτιστα λέγοντες καὶ τοὺς ἐξαμαρ-
309 τάνοντας ἀποτρέποντες;

50 Ἴσως δ᾽ ἂν ἔχοι εἰπεῖν ὅτι ἐδεδοίκει, καὶ ὑμῶν τοῦτο
ἐνίοις ἱκανὸν ἔσται. ὅπως τοίνυν μὴ φανήσεται ἐν τῷ
λόγῳ τοῖς τριάκοντα ἐναντιούμενος· εἰ δὲ μή, ἐνταυθοῖ

---

49. καὶ μὲν δή: force, see on
§ 30. — **σιωπῶντες**: Eratosthenes
cannot claim that silence in this
crisis showed disapproval; such
men " were none the worse off for
their silence," for there were other
conspirators whose function it was
to speak and act, and the silent
men shared their evil gains. Outspoken opposition was the only
proof of patriotism in those times.
— **ὧν οὐχ κτλ.**: *than which no
greater evils could have come to
the city*. The case of ὧν is governed by μείζω; its antecedent is
the omitted object of λέγοντες and
πράττοντες. — **εἶναι**: tense, see on
ἀντιλέγειν § 26. — **ἀποτρέποντες**:
conative present. See on πυνθάνεσθαι § 2.

50. ὅπως . . . **φανήσεται**: a
colloquial expression of warning,
HA. 886; G. 1352: B. 583 n. 3;
Gl. 638. b; GMT. 271. — **τοίνυν**:

force, see on 16. 7 (A). — **ἐν τῷ
λόγῳ**: *in his speech*. Lysias fore-
sees that Eratosthenes will lay
great stress upon the fact that he
belonged to the faction of Theramenes, the man who lost his life
in trying to check the abuses of
Critias and the extreme oligarchs.
Eratosthenes will certainly claim
that he joined Theramenes in opposing the crimes of his colleagues.
Lysias shrewdly tries to forestall
this plea by claiming that if Eratosthenes was strong enough ever
to oppose, his failure to oppose in
cases like those just mentioned in
§ 48 must have been due to his
approval of what was being done.
— **ἐναντιούμενος**: tense, see on
ἀνιωμένου § 32. — **εἰ δὲ μή**: *otherwise*; the expression became a
formula, not necessarily negative.
— **ἐνταυθοῖ**: the -ι is the locative
ending, as in οἴκοι, πέδοι; so

δῆλος ἔσται ὅτι ἐκεῖνά τε αὐτῷ ἤρεσκε, καὶ τοσοῦτον
ἐδύνατο ὥστε ἐναντιούμενος μηδὲν κακὸν παθεῖν ὑπ'
315 αὐτῶν. χρῆν δ' αὐτὸν ὑπὲρ τῆς ὑμετέρας σωτηρίας
ταύτην τὴν προθυμίαν ἔχειν, ἀλλὰ μὴ ὑπὲρ Θηραμένους, ὃς εἰς ὑμᾶς πολλὰ ἐξήμαρτεν. ἀλλ' οὗτος τὴν
51 μὲν πόλιν ἐχθρὰν ἐνόμιζεν εἶναι, τοὺς δ' ὑμετέρους
ἐχθροὺς φίλους, ὡς ἀμφότερα ταῦτα ἐγὼ πολλοῖς
320 τεκμηρίοις παραστήσω, καὶ τὰς πρὸς ἀλλήλους δια-
φορὰς οὐχ ὑπὲρ ὑμῶν ἀλλ' ὑπὲρ ἑαυτῶν γιγνομένας,
ὁπότεροι τὰ πράγματα πράξουσι καὶ τῆς πόλεως

Ἰσθμοῖ, Μεγαροῖ; cp. on 19. 28 and
63. — δῆλος : with ὅτι we usually
find the impersonal δῆλον ; with the
personal form a participle usually
follows ; cp. § 90 δῆλοι ἔσεσθε ὡς
ὀργιζόμενοι, and 24. 3 δῆλός ἐστι
φθονῶν. — ἐκεῖνα : the εἰσαγγελίαι
of § 48. — εἰς : force, see on πρός
32. 19, Crit. Note.

51. παραστήσω : this verb, introduced in a parenthetical clause,
becomes for the remainder of
the sentence the governing verb,
throwing γιγνομένας out of the indic. (it should be coördinate with
ἐνόμιζεν) into the partic. of ind.
disc. — πρός : see on 32. 19, Crit.
Note. — γιγνομένας : tense, see on
ἀνιωμένου § 32. — ὁπότεροι : which
faction, that of Theramenes or
that of Critias. Isocrates, writing
a quarter of a century after the
events discussed here, contrasts
the spirit of the parties of later

times with that of the parties in
the time of the Persian wars. He
says of the men of the earlier time
(4. 79) : οὕτω δὲ πολιτικῶς εἶχον,
ὥστε καὶ τὰς στάσεις ἐποιοῦντο
πρὸς ἀλλήλους, οὐχ ὁπότεροι τοὺς
ἑτέρους ἀπολέσαντες τῶν λοιπῶν
ἄρξουσιν, ἀλλ' ὁπότεροι φθήσονται
τὴν πόλιν ἀγαθόν τι ποιήσαντες ·
καὶ τὰς ἑταιρείας συνῆγον οὐχ ὑπὲρ
τῶν ἰδίᾳ συμφερόντων ἀλλ' ἐπὶ τῃ
τοῦ πλήθους ὠφελείᾳ they were
so public spirited that even their
party struggles were not to see
which party could destroy the other
and rule the rest, but which could
be the first to do the state some service. And their secret clubs they
formed, not for their private interests, but for the service of the
state. Isocrates found warrant for
this view in Herodotus, who represents Aristides as beginning his
night interview with his party op-

52 ἄρξουσιν. εἰ γὰρ ὑπὲρ τῶν ἀδικουμένων ἐστασίαζον,
ποῦ κάλλιον ἦν ἀνδρὶ ἄρχοντι, ἢ Θρασυβούλου Φυλὴν
325 κατειληφότος, τότε ἐπιδείξασθαι τὴν αὑτοῦ εὔνοιαν· ὁ
δ' ἀντὶ τοῦ ἐπαγγείλασθαί τι ἢ πρᾶξαι ἀγαθὸν πρὸς
τοὺς ἐπὶ Φυλῇ, ἐλθὼν μετὰ τῶν συναρχόντων εἰς Σαλαμῖνα καὶ Ἐλευσῖνάδε τριακοσίους τῶν πολιτῶν ἀπήγαγεν εἰς τὸ δεσμωτήριον, καὶ μιᾷ ψήφῳ αὐτῶν ἀπάντων
330 θάνατον κατεψηφίσατο.

53 Ἐπειδὴ δὲ εἰς τὸν Πειραιᾶ ἤλθομεν καὶ αἱ ταραχαὶ
γεγενημέναι ἦσαν καὶ περὶ τῶν διαλλαγῶν οἱ λόγοι

ponent, Themistocles, before the
battle of Salamis with these words
(8. 79): ἡμέας στασιάζειν χρεόν
ἐστι εἰ ἐν τεῷ ἄλλῳ καιρῷ καὶ δὴ
καὶ ἐν τῷδε περὶ τοῦ ὁκότερος
ἡμέων πλέω ἀγαθὰ τὴν πατρίδα
ἐργάσεται *Now, if ever, we must
vie one with the other to see which
one of us will do his country the
greater service.*

52. κάλλιον ἦν: for non-use
of ἄν see on εἰκὸς ἦν § 27. —
Φυλήν: for the event see Chron.
App. Phyle lay high up on the
pass across Mt. Parnes (hence
τοὺς ἐπὶ Φυλῇ). — **Σαλαμῖνα καὶ
Ἐλευσῖνάδε** : see Chron. App.,
and the full account of the arrest
of the Eleusinians given by Xenophon, who was probably one of
the cavalry who executed it (*Hell.*
2. 4. 8–10). — **μιᾷ ψήφῳ**: these
were Athenian citizens, entitled
each to a separate verdict in any
trial ; cp. on § 36.

53. ἤλθομεν : Lysias implies
that he himself was with the exiles
(see Introd. p. 20). He would
be safe in returning from Megara
as soon as Thrasybulus seized
Munychia. — **ταραχαί**: in speaking to a jury made up of men from
both sides, Lysias wisely uses a
mild term for events which included months of armed hostility
and one desperate battle, in which
the leader of the Thirty was killed.
— **οἱ λόγοι**: immediately after the
battle at the Piraeus there was
friendly conference between the
troops while under truce for bury-
ing the dead. Xenophon (*Hell.*
2. 4. 20 ff.) gives the earnest appeal
of one of the exiles. But the more
formal negotiations began after
the arrival of the Spartan king,
Pausanias. — **ἐπειδὴ ἤλθομεν . . .
γεγενημέναι ἦσαν . . . ἐγίγνοντο**:
this combination of tenses is noteworthy (GS. 264): *after our ar-*

ἐγίγνοντο, πολλὰς ἑκάτεροι ἐλπίδας εἴχομεν πρὸς ἀλλήλους διαλλαγήσεσθαι, ὡς ἀμφότεροι ἔδειξαν. οἱ μὲν
335 γὰρ ἐκ Πειραιῶς κρείττους ὄντες εἴασαν αὐτοὺς ἀπελ-
54 θεῖν· οἱ δὲ εἰς τὸ ἄστυ ἐλθόντες τοὺς μὲν τριάκοντα
ἐξέβαλον πλὴν Φείδωνος καὶ Ἐρατοσθένους, ἄρχοντας
δὲ τοὺς ἐκείνοις ἐχθίστους εἵλοντο, ἡγούμενοι δικαίως
339 ἂν ὑπὸ τῶν αὐτῶν τούς τε τριάκοντα μισεῖσθαι καὶ

rival . . . after the completion . . .
during-the discussions. ἐπειδή usually takes the aor., forming the
equivalent of the Eng. plup.; when
it has the plup., it is to lay stress
upon the completion of the action
(as here) or upon its abiding
result; with the imperf. it represents the action as under way.
— ἑκάτεροι . . . εἴχομεν: definite
recognition of the fact that on
the jury are members of both
parties. — ἔδειξαν: the text is uncertain (see Crit. Note), but the
change to the third person is not
strange, as the division into the
two parties immediately follows.
The exiles showed their hope of
reconciliation by letting the van-
quished return unmolested to the
city; the city party showed their
like hope by deposing their war
leaders. — κρείττους : another in-
tentionally mild term for the vic-
tors in a hard battle.

54. ἐξέβαλον: the Thirty were
probably not formally banished;
but, deposed from office, only the

least compromised among them
could safely remain, as the peace
party was apparently coming into
control. Cp. Xen. *Hell.* 2. 4.
23 f. καὶ τὸ τελευταῖον ἐψηφίσαντο
ἐκείνους μὲν καταπαῦσαι, ἄλλους
δὲ ἑλέσθαι. καὶ εἵλοντο δέκα, ἕνα
ἀπὸ φυλῆς. καὶ οἱ μὲν τριάκοντα
Ἐλευσῖνάδε ἀπῆλθον *And finally
they voted to depose them and elect
others. And they elected ten, one
from each phyle. And the Thirty
went to Eleusis*; Arist. *Resp. Ath.*
38. 1 τοὺς μὲν τριάκοντα κατέλυ-
σαν, αἱροῦνται δὲ δέκα τῶν πολιτῶν
αὐτοκράτορας ἐπὶ τὴν τοῦ πολέ-
μου κατάλυσιν *They deposed the
Thirty, and they elect ten citizens,
with full power, to put a stop to
the war.* — Ἐρατοσθένους : Eratosthenes was not one of the new
board. The fact that he dared to
remain in the city is a strong argument in his favor, which Lysias tries
to counteract by throwing upon
him the odium of connection with
Phidon. — ἐκείνοις : the Thirty as
represented by the war faction. —

55 τοὺς ἐν Πειραιεῖ φιλεῖσθαι. τούτων τοίνυν Φείδων γενόμενος καὶ Ἱπποκλῆς καὶ Ἐπιχάρης ὁ Λαμπτρεὺς καὶ
ἕτεροι οἱ δοκοῦντες εἶναι ἐναντιώτατοι Χαρικλεῖ καὶ
Κριτίᾳ καὶ τῇ ἐκείνων ἑταιρείᾳ, ἐπειδὴ αὐτοὶ εἰς τὴν
344 ἀρχὴν κατέστησαν, πολὺ μείζω στάσιν καὶ πόλεμον
56 ἐπὶ τοὺς ἐν Πειραιεῖ τοῖς ἐξ ἄστεως ἐποίησαν· ᾧ καὶ
φανερῶς ἐπεδείξαντο ὅτι οὐχ ὑπὲρ τῶν ἐν Πειραιεῖ
οὐδ' ὑπὲρ τῶν ἀδίκως ἀπολλυμένων ἐστασίαζον, οὐδ' οἱ
τεθνεῶτες αὐτοὺς ἐλύπουν οὐδ' οἱ μέλλοντες ἀποθανεῖ-
349 σθαι, ἀλλ' οἱ μεῖζον δυνάμενοι καὶ θᾶττον πλουτοῦντες.
57 λαβόντες γὰρ τὰς ἀρχὰς καὶ τὴν πόλιν ἀμφοτέροις ἐπο-

μισεῖσθαι, φιλεῖσθαι: on the rhetorical form see App. § 57. 3.

55. Ἐπιχάρης ὁ Λαμπτρεύς:
Andocides describes an Epichares
as a sycophant under the democracy, a tool of the Thirty, and a
member of the Senate under
them (Andoc. 1. 95, 99). — Χαρικλεῖ: Xenophon (*Mem.* 1. 2. 31)
and Aristotle (*Pol.* 1305ᵇ 25) speak
of him as a leader of the extreme
faction. — τῇ ἐκείνων ἑταιρείᾳ: the
"club" element formed only a
part of the Thirty. There was a
large conservative element in the
city who were dismayed at seeing
the radicals with Critias in control; they now took the lead, but
were again disappointed in that
the new board of Ten fell under
control of men who were in full
sympathy with the Thirty at Eleusis, actively coöperated with them,

and continued their war policy. It
was an instance, not infrequent in
modern times, of the better element in a city rising up under
a sudden impulse and apparently
overthrowing a political machine,
only to find the machine still in
control after the excitement was
over. — στάσιν καὶ πόλεμον: on
the συνωνυμία see App. § 58. 2.
— ἐπί: see on πρός 32. 19, Crit.
Note.

56. ἐστασίαζον, ἐλύπουν: progressive imperfects of acts previous to ἐπεδείξαντο. The simple
Eng. plup. secures the expression
of the preliminary time (not expressed in the Greek) at the
sacrifice of the expression of the
progressive quality of the act; but
the Eng. forms "had been quar-
reling," "had been troubling"
combine both ideas.

λέμουν, τοῖς τε τριάκοντα πάντα κακὰ εἰργασμένοις καὶ
ὑμῖν πάντα κακὰ πεπονθόσι. καίτοι τοῦτο πᾶσι δῆλον
ἦν, ὅτι εἰ μὲν ἐκεῖνοι δικαίως ἔφευγον, ὑμεῖς ἀδίκως,
εἰ δ᾽ ὑμεῖς δικαίως, οἱ τριάκοντα ἀδίκως· οὐ γὰρ δὴ
355 ἑτέρων ἔργων αἰτίαν λαβόντες ἐκ τῆς πόλεως ἐξέπεσον,
58 ἀλλὰ τούτων. ὥστε σφόδρα χρὴ ὀργίζεσθαι, ὅτι Φείδων αἱρεθεὶς ὑμᾶς διαλλάξαι καὶ καταγαγεῖν τῶν αὐτῶν
ἔργων Ἐρατοσθένει μετεῖχε καὶ τῇ αὐτῇ γνώμῃ τοὺς
μὲν κρείττους αὐτῶν δι᾽ ὑμᾶς κακῶς ποιεῖν ἕτοιμος ἦν,

57. **τοῖς τε τριάκοντα**: here, as
in the statement that the city party
"expelled" the Thirty, Lysias exaggerates. The Ten, so far from
making war on the Thirty at
Eleusis, joined them in asking
help from Sparta against the democrats. In answer to their common request, Lysander came up
to Eleusis and there raised a mercenary force, directly protecting
the Thirty. Xenophon says (*Hell.*
2. 4. 29), οἱ δ᾽ ἐν τῷ ἄστει πάλιν
αὖ μέγα ἐφρόνουν ἐπὶ τῷ Λυσάνδρῳ
*the city party were again greatly
encouraged by Lysander's action.*
Indeed, Lysias himself ascribes to
Phidon the securing of this very
force which Lysander organized
at Eleusis (§ 59). — **πάντα κακά**:
but in § 33 πάντα τὰ κακά. — **ὑμῖν**,
ὑμεῖς: the democratic exiles. So
large a portion of the jury were
of the party of the Piraeus that
Lysias speaks as though all were.
The other element in the jury were

not at all offended at being included among the 'patriots.' —
ἔφευγον: *were in exile*; see on
ἀδικῶ § 14. — **δή** : see on 25. 9
(B). — **αἰτίαν λαβόντες**: αἰτίαν λαβεῖν and αἰτίαν σχεῖν (ingressive
aorists) = *to incur a charge*: αἰτίαν
ἔχειν = *to be under a charge* (cp.
22. 18 πολλῶν ἤδη ἐχόντων ταύτην
τὴν αἰτίαν). — **ἐξέπεσον**: used as
passive of ἐξέβαλον (§ 54), HA.
820; G. 1241; B. 513; Gl. 499 a.
58. **ὀργίζεσθαι ὅτι** : see on
§ 80. — **διαλλάξαι**: a true dative
infinitive, HA. 951; G. 1532; B.
640; Gl. 565. — **καταγαγεῖν**: again
he speaks as though all the jury
were of the Piraeus party. — **τῇ**
αὐτῇ γνώμῃ: *i.e.* the same as that
of Eratosthenes. — **τοὺς μὲν κρείτ-**
τους: their colleagues among the
Thirty. — **δι᾽ ὑμᾶς**: *through your
means*. For διά with acc. see on
§ 87. The Thirty were deposed
by the city party, but it was in the
interest of reconciliation, and so

360 ὑμῖν δὲ ἀδίκως φεύγουσιν οὐκ ἠθέλησεν ἀποδοῦναι τὴν
πόλιν, ἀλλ' ἐλθὼν εἰς Λακεδαίμονα ἔπειθεν αὐτοὺς στρατεύεσθαι, διαβάλλων ὅτι Βοιωτῶν ἡ πόλις ἔσται, καὶ
59 ἄλλα λέγων οἷς ᾤετο πείσειν μάλιστα. οὐ δυνάμενος
δὲ τούτων τυχεῖν, εἴτε καὶ τῶν ἱερῶν ἐμποδὼν ὄντων εἴτε
365 καὶ αὐτῶν οὐ βουλομένων, ἑκατὸν τάλαντα ἐδανείσατο, ἵνα ἔχοι ἐπικούρους μισθοῦσθαι, καὶ Λύσανδρον
ἄρχοντα ᾐτήσατο, εὐνούστατον μὲν ὄντα τῇ ὀλιγαρχίᾳ,
κακονούστατον δὲ τῇ πόλει, μισοῦντα δὲ μάλιστα τοὺς
60 ἐν Πειραιεῖ. μισθωσάμενοι δὲ πάντας ἀνθρώπους ἐπ'
370 ὀλέθρῳ τῆς πόλεως, καὶ πόλεις ὅλας ἐπάγοντες, καὶ
τελευτῶντες Λακεδαιμονίους καὶ τῶν συμμάχων ὁπόσους
ἐδύναντο πεῖσαι, οὐ διαλλάξαι ἀλλ' ἀπολέσαι παρε-

it was done "thanks to" the exiles.
The speaker strains the facts for
the sake of his neat antithesis:
δι' ὑμᾶς κακῶς ποιεῖν ἕτοιμος ἦν,
ὑμῖν δὲ . . . ἀποδοῦναι τὴν πόλιν.
— ἔπειθεν : conative impf. HA.
832 ; G. 1255 ; B. 527 ; Gl. 459 a ;
GMT. 36 ; GS. 213. Cp. 19. 22.
— Βοιωτῶν : the exiles gathered at
Thebes before they seized Phyle,
and were hospitably received there.

59. εἴτε καὶ . . . εἴτε καί : the
correlation of the two clauses is
emphasized by adding καί . . . καί
to εἴτε . . . εἴτε. — ἱερῶν : an allu-
sion to the well-known superstition
of the Spartans. Lysias may have
in mind the Carnean festival (Aug.-
Sept.), which made the Spartans
too late for the glories of Mara-

thon (Herod. 6. 106). — αὐτῶν :
intensive. — εὐνούστατον, κακονούστατον : on the παρονομασία see
App. § 58. 5.

60. μισθωσάμενοι : the mercenary force raised by Lysander at
Eleusis ; it supported the Thirty as
much as the Ten ; Lysias chooses
to misrepresent their relation. Cp.
on § 57. — ἐπ' ὀλέθρῳ : a substantive purpose construction. See on
§ 24. — πόλεις ὅλας : a great exaggeration. The only "cities" which
sent out troops were those which
later joined Pausanias, and these
are included in τῶν συμμάχων of
the next line. — οὐ διαλλάξαι : inserted to keep the jury intent upon
the central thought that in all this
Phidon and Eratosthenes were

σκευάζοντο τὴν πόλιν, εἰ μὴ δι' ἄνδρας ἀγαθούς, οἷς
374 ὑμεῖς δηλώσατε παρὰ τῶν ἐχθρῶν δίκην λαβόντες, ὅτι
61 καὶ ἐκείνοις χάριν ἀποδώσετε. ταῦτα δὲ ἐπίστασθε
μὲν καὶ αὐτοί, καὶ οὐκ οἶδ' ὅ τι δεῖ μάρτυρας παρασχέ-
σθαι· ὅμως δέ· ἐγώ τε γὰρ δέομαι ἀναπαύσασθαι,
ὑμῶν τ' ἐνίοις ἥδιον ὡς πλείστων τοὺς αὐτοὺς λόγους
379 ἀκούειν.

ΜΑΡΤΥΡΕΣ

62　Φέρε δὴ καὶ περὶ Θηραμένους ὡς ἂν δύνωμαι διὰ
βραχυτάτων διδάξω. δέομαι δ' ὑμῶν ἀκοῦσαι ὑπέρ τ'

betraying their trust and belying
their own professions. Note that
while the infin. (not in ind.
disc.) regularly takes μή, a negatived infin. standing in parenthetical antithesis takes οὐ. — εἰ μὴ δι'
ἄνδρας ἀγαθούς : *but for good men.*
For διά with acc. see on § 87.
εἰ μὴ διά became a fixed formula,
like Eng. "but for" (cp. on εἰ
δὲ μή § 50). The phrase throws
its force back upon ἀπολέσαι only
(not upon παρεσκευάζοντο). There
underlies it the thought that the
action ἀπολέσαι did not come to
pass, and it states whom we have
to thank for it, HA. 905. 2 ; G.
1414. 1 ; B. 616. 2 ; Gl. 656 a. The
"good men" to whom, above all
others, the exiles owed their rescue from an apparently hopeless
situation were the Spartan king,
Pausanias, and others of the anti-
Lysander faction in Sparta. Lysias
shrewdly hints to the jury that in

punishing the men who were responsible for Lysander's efforts at
Eleusis in support of the Thirty and
the Ten, they will please the present Spartan administration. — οἷς
ὑμεῖς δηλώσατε : the Eng. requires
"must" in place of the simpler
Greek imperative in a relative
clause ; cp. ὥστε with the impv., 16.
8 N. — ἐκείνοις : the "good men."

61. οὐκ οἶδ' ὅ τι : see on § 37
and Crit. Note. — δέομαι ἀναπαύσασθαι : hardly the real reason ; he
had ' rested ' a few moments before
(§§ 42, 47) ; but by seeming indifferent to the testimony, he gives to
his statements an air of certainty
as needing no proof. In fact, he
knows that they are full of exaggeration. What his witnesses proved
we cannot say : certainly not that
Eratosthenes was responsible for
the policy of Phidon and the Ten.

62. δή : cf. § 34 and see on
25. 9 (A). — διδάξω : " The sub-

ἐμαυτοῦ καὶ τῆς πόλεως. καὶ μηδενὶ τοῦτο παραστῇ,
ὡς Ἐρατοσθένους κινδυνεύοντος Θηραμένους κατηγορῶ.
384 πυνθάνομαι γὰρ ταῦτα ἀπολογήσεσθαι αὐτόν, ὅτι
63 ἐκείνῳ φίλος ἦν καὶ τῶν αὐτῶν ἔργων μετεῖχε. καίτοι
σφόδρ' ἂν αὐτὸν οἶμαι μετὰ Θεμιστοκλέους πολιτευό-
μενον προσποιεῖσθαι πράττειν ὅπως οἰκοδομηθήσεται
τὰ τείχη, ὁπότε καὶ μετὰ Θηραμένους ὅπως καθαιρεθή-
σεται. οὐ γάρ μοι δοκοῦσιν ἴσου ἄξιοι γεγενῆσθαι· ὁ
390 μὲν γὰρ Λακεδαιμονίων ἀκόντων ᾠκοδόμησεν αὐτά,

junctive is used as the imperative
of the first person, positive and
negative. The negative particle
is μή. The first person singular
is less common than the plural,
and is usually preceded by φέρε,
instead of which Homer uses ἄγε,"
GS. 373 f. Cp. HA. 866. 1 ; G.
1344–5 ; B. 585 ; Gl. 472. — Θηραμένους : for the bearing of this
discussion of Theramenes's career
see Introd. pp. 54–56. — ὡς . . .
κατηγορῶ : 'Let not the thought
occur to you that I am accusing
Theramenes when it is Eratosthenes who is on trial. I am,
indeed, accusing Theramenes, but
as a part of my prosecution
of Eratosthenes, for he will try
to win your favor by claiming to
have been a friend and supporter
of Theramenes.' — πυνθάνομαι :
tense, see on ἀδικῶ § 14.

63. The thought is : That citizen must indeed be in desperate

straits and in sore need of reha-
bilitation who seeks to make himself more respectable by claiming
connection with the man who destroyed our walls. 'If Eratosthenes is so eager to claim connection
with Theramenes, who destroyed
the walls, how eagerly he would
have claimed connection with
Themistocles, who built them, if
he had but lived in his time!' —
σφόδρ' ἄν : emphatic position,
widely separated from the verb
(προσποιεῖσθαι) ; for ἄν see HA.
964 b ; G. 1308 ; B. 647 ; Gl. 579.
— πράττειν : tense, see on ἀντιλέγειν § 26. — ὁπότε καί : when
actually. — μετὰ Θηραμένους : sc.
πολιτευόμενος προσποιεῖται πράττειν. — ὁ μὲν . . . οὗτος δέ : a shrewd
device for throwing contempt on
the modern 'patriot.' For Theramenes's responsibility for the
destruction of the walls see on
§ 68.

64 οὗτος δὲ τοὺς πολίτας ἐξαπατήσας καθεῖλε. περιέστη-
κεν οὖν τῇ πόλει τοὐναντίον ἢ ὡς εἰκὸς ἦν. ἄξιον μὲν
γὰρ ἦν καὶ τοὺς φίλους τοὺς Θηραμένους προσαπολω-
λέναι, πλὴν εἴ τις ἐτύγχανεν ἐκείνῳ τἀναντία πράττων·
395 νῦν δὲ ὁρῶ τάς τε ἀπολογίας εἰς ἐκεῖνον ἀναφερομένας,
τούς τ᾽ ἐκείνῳ συνόντας τιμᾶσθαι πειρωμένους, ὥσπερ
πολλῶν ἀγαθῶν αἰτίου ἀλλ᾽ οὐ μεγάλων κακῶν γεγε-
65 νημένου. ὃς πρῶτον μὲν τῆς προτέρας ὀλιγαρχίας
αἰτιώτατος ἐγένετο, πείσας ὑμᾶς τὴν ἐπὶ τῶν τετρακο-

64. τοὐναντίον: subject of περι-
έστηκεν; so Thuc. 6. 24. 2 τοὐναντίον περιέστη αὐτῷ. A more
common construction is that of
Dem. 25. 12 φοβοῦμαι μὴ τὸ
πρᾶγμ᾽ εἰς τοὐναντίον περιστῇ. —
τοὐναντίον ἢ ὡς: ἐναντίος is treated
as a comparative, and may be followed (1) by ἤ, (2) by the less
common comparative connective
ἢ ὡς, or (3) by the gen. without
ἤ. (1) § 2, τοὐναντίον . . . ἢ ἐν
τῷ πρὸ τοῦ χρόνῳ (2) Herod.
1. 22 ἤκουε τοῦ κήρυκος . . . τοὺς
ἐναντίους λόγους ἢ ὡς αὐτὸς κατε-
δόκεε *he heard from the herald
words the opposite of what he had
expected*. (3) Dem. 19. 329 δέ-
δοικα μὴ τοὐναντίον οὗ βούλομαι
ποιῶ *I fear I may do the opposite
of what I wish*. For ἢ ὡς with
other comparative words cp. Xen.
Anab. 1. 5. 8 θᾶττον ἢ ὥς τις ἂν
ᾤετο *more quickly than one would
have thought*. Dem. 6. 11 ἔστι
γὰρ μείζω τὰ κείνων ἔργα, ἢ ὡς τῷ

λόγῳ τις ἂν εἴποι *their deeds are
greater than one could tell*. —
ἀλλ᾽ οὐ: ὥσπερ is not treated as
conditional, and takes the neg. οὐ,
HA. 978. a; G. 1576; B. 656 n.;
Gl. 593 d; GMT. 867. See on
25. 23. — **γεγενημένου**: see on πραττόντων § 45.

65. αἰτιώτατος: Thucydides
says (8. 68) that Antiphon was
the moving spirit in planning the
revolution of 411 B.C., that Pisander was the most prominent man
in its execution, and Phrynichus
the most daring; but he adds, καὶ
Θηραμένης ὁ τοῦ Ἅγνωνος ἐν τοῖς
ξυγκαταλύουσι τὸν δῆμον πρῶτος
ἦν, ἀνὴρ οὔτε εἰπεῖν οὔτε γνῶναι
ἀδύνατος *and Theramenes, the son
of Hagnon, was a prime mover
in the abolition of the democracy,
a man not without ability as a
speaker and thinker*. Aristotle
says (*Resp. Ath*. 32. 2) ἡ μὲν οὖν
ὀλιγαρχία τοῦτον κατέστη τὸν τρόπον, . . . αἰτίων μάλιστα γενο-

400 σίων πολιτείαν ἐλέσθαι. καὶ ὁ μὲν πατὴρ αὐτοῦ τῶν
προβούλων ὢν ταῦτ᾽ ἔπραττεν, αὐτὸς δὲ δοκῶν εὐνού-
στατος εἶναι τοῖς πράγμασι στρατηγὸς ὑπ᾽ αὐτῶν
66 ἡρέθη. καὶ ἕως μὲν ἐτιμᾶτο, πιστὸν ἑαυτὸν τῇ πολιτείᾳ
παρεῖχεν· ἐπειδὴ δὲ Πείσανδρον μὲν καὶ Κάλλαισχρον
405 καὶ ἑτέρους ἑώρα προτέρους αὐτοῦ γιγνομένους, τὸ δὲ

μένων Πεισάνδρου καὶ Ἀντιφῶντος
καὶ Θηραμένους, ἀνδρῶν καὶ γεγενημένων εὖ, καὶ συνέσει καὶ γνώμῃ δοκούντων διαφέρειν *so the oligarchy
was thus established* . . . *the men
most responsible being Pisander
and Antiphon and Theramenes,
men of good birth and of eminent
reputation for ability and judgment*. Lysias exaggerates somewhat by failing to mention the
two who shared the leadership
with Theramenes, but he charges
Theramenes with little more than
do Thucydides and Aristotle, who
are friendly to him.— ἐπὶ τῶν
τετρακοσίων : for ἐπί, see on § 17.
— προβούλων : see Chron. App.,
413 B.C. ; cp. Thuc. 8. 1. 3,
67. 1 ; Arist. *Resp. Ath.* 29. 2.
Membership in this board was an
honor, in view of the emergency
which the πρόβουλοι were elected
to meet. Some of them, like
Hagnon, actively favored the
change in government ; others
assented to it reluctantly, as being
the only possible course. Aristotle's Rhetoric (3. 18) preserves

an anecdote of Sophocles (probably the poet) which illustrates the
attitude of men of this second
class : Σοφοκλῆς ἐρωτώμενος ὑπὸ
Πεισάνδρου εἰ ἔδοξεν αὐτῷ ὥσπερ
καὶ τοῖς ἄλλοις προβούλοις, κατα-
στῆσαι τοὺς τετρακοσίους, ἔφη·
τί δέ; οὐ πονηρά σοι ταῦτα ἐδόκει εἶναι; ἔφη· οὐκοῦν σὺ ταῦτα
ἔπραξας τὰ πονηρά; ναὶ ἔφη· οὐ
γὰρ ἦν ἄλλα βελτίω Sophocles,
*when asked by Pisander whether
he, like the other Probouloi, ap-
proved of the establishment of
the Four Hundred, said, " Yes."
" But what ? Did that not seem
to you a bad business ? " " Yes,"
said he. " Then did you take
part in that 'bad business' ? "
" Yes," said he, " for there was
nothing better to do."* — τοῖς πράγμασι : *to the government* ; see
on 16. 3. — ὑπ᾽ αὐτῶν : *i.e.* τῶν
τετρακοσίων.

66. τῇ πολιτείᾳ : *to the administration.*— ἐπειδή : for ἐπειδή with
imperf., see on ἐγίγνοντο, § 53.
— Κάλλαισχρον : his son Critias
became the head of the second

ὑμέτερον πλῆθος οὐκέτι βουλόμενον τούτων ἀκροᾶσθαι,
τότ' ἤδη διά τε τὸν πρὸς ἐκείνους φθόνον καὶ τὸ παρ'
67 ὑμῶν δέος μετέσχε τῶν Ἀριστοκράτους ἔργων. βουλόμενος δὲ τῷ ὑμετέρῳ πλήθει δοκεῖν πιστὸς εἶναι
410 Ἀντιφῶντα καὶ Ἀρχεπτόλεμον φιλτάτους ὄντας αὐτῷ
κατηγορῶν ἀπέκτεινεν, εἰς τοσοῦτον δὲ κακίας ἦλθεν,
ὥστε ἅμα μὲν διὰ τὴν πρὸς ἐκείνους πίστιν ὑμᾶς κατεδουλώσατο, διὰ δὲ τὴν πρὸς ὑμᾶς τοὺς φίλους ἀπώλεσε.

oligarchy seven years later. — **οὐκέτι**: the people had been persuaded to accept the new form of
government in the hope of ending
the war through Alcibiades with
Persian support; this hope had
now failed, Introd. p. 36. — **ἤδη**:
strengthening τότε, *then, and not
till then*. So in 25. 22. — **τε**: for
position see on § 30. — **τὸν πρὸς
ἐκείνους φθόνον . . . τὸ παρ' ὑμῶν
δέος**: the active emotion, *envy*,
takes πρός with accus. of the object
toward which the envy is directed;
the passive emotion, *fear*, takes
παρά with the gen. of the source
from which the emotion springs.
The objective gen. is oftener used
with δέος, but the prepositional
phrase is more explicit and stands
in better parallelism with πρὸς ἐκείνους. — **μετέσχε**: ingressive aorist
(see on μετέσχον, 16. 3); cp. the
imperf. in §§ 58 and 62. — **Ἀριστοκράτους**: a man of prominent
family, who had done the city

good service during the war. He
was put to death in 406 B.C. with
other generals after the battle of
Arginusae. His association with
Theramenes in deposing the Four
Hundred is confirmed by Aristotle, *Resp. Ath.* 33. 2 αἰτιώτατοι
δ' ἐγένοντο τῆς καταλύσεως Ἀρι-
στοκράτης καὶ Θηραμένης. So
Thuc. 8. 89. 2.

67. τῷ ὑμετέρῳ πλήθει: cp.
§ 66 and see on § 42. — **Ἀντιφῶντα**: see on § 65. — **Ἀρχεπτόλεμον**: he had worked for peace
with Sparta earlier in the war
(Ar. *Equ.* 794). After the deposition of the Four Hundred, Antiphon and Archeptolemus were put
to death on the charge of having
plotted with others of the oligarchs to betray· the city to
Sparta. Theramenes was at the
head of the government, under a
moderate constitution, from September, 411, to about July, 410
(see Introd. p. 55).

68 τιμώμενος δὲ καὶ τῶν μεγίστων ἀξιούμενος, αὐτὸς ἐπαγ-
415 γειλάμενος σώσειν τὴν πόλιν αὐτὸς ἀπώλεσε, φάσκων
πρᾶγμα ηὑρηκέναι μέγα καὶ πολλοῦ ἄξιον. ὑπέσχετο
δὲ εἰρήνην ποιήσειν μήτε ὅμηρα δοὺς μήτε τὰ τείχη
καθελὼν μήτε τὰς ναῦς παραδούς· ταῦτα δὲ εἰπεῖν
419 μὲν οὐδενὶ ἠθέλησεν, ἐκέλευσε δὲ αὐτῷ πιστεύειν.

68. The following events belong to the time (404 B.C.) after
the complete restoration of the
democracy, when the administration had passed from Theramenes
and the moderate aristocrats into
the hands of Cleophon and other
popular leaders. Under their mismanagement came the disaster at
Aegospotami, the siege of the
city, and the unsuccessful attempts to obtain from Sparta
moderate terms of peace. In that
crisis Theramenes came forward
and offered to go to Lysander
(see Introd. p. 37). — αὐτός: *of
his own accord.* Greatly strengthened by repetition (ἐπαναφορά,
App. § 57. 5) with ἀπώλεσε. —
μέγα, πολλοῦ ἄξιον: on the συνωνυμία, see App. § 58. 2. — ὑπέσχετο
δέ: after a general statement (here
φάσκων . . . ηὑρηκέναι) the particular explanation is often introduced by a neutral δέ, which has
lost all adversative force. The
English, and usually the Greek,
more logically uses " for," as giving the grounds for the general
statement. Cp. on γάρ explicative,

19. 12. — ὑπέσχετο: Xenophon
says (*Hell.* 2. 2. 14 ff.) that the
Spartans had already announced
the destruction of ten stadia of
the Long Walls as a condition of
peace, and that what Theramenes
offered to do was to find out from
Lysander whether this was intended as a preliminary to the
enslavement of the city, or only
as a means of guaranteeing their
faithful obedience to the other
terms of peace. After remaining
three months with Lysander he
returned to Athens with the report that Lysander had no power
in the matter, and that it must be
determined by the government at
Sparta. Theramenes was then
sent to Sparta with nine others to
negotiate peace. Lysias represents
all this as one mission, and as
the work of Theramenes alone;
the whole impression given is purposely misleading. — μήτε, μήτε:
μή instead of οὐ with the participles because they depend on
ποιήσειν, which, if negatived,
would take μή. HA. 1024 (last
line); G. 1496; B. 549. 2.   A

69 ὑμεῖς δέ, ὦ ἄνδρες Ἀθηναῖοι, πραττούσης μὲν τῆς ἐν
Ἀρείῳ πάγῳ βουλῆς σωτήρια, ἀντιλεγόντων δὲ πολλῶν Θηραμένει, εἰδότες δὲ ὅτι οἱ μὲν ἄλλοι ἄνθρωποι
τῶν πολεμίων ἕνεκα τἀπόρρητα ποιοῦνται, ἐκεῖνος δ᾽ ἐν
τοῖς αὑτοῦ πολίταις οὐκ ἠθέλησεν εἰπεῖν ταῦθ᾽ ἃ πρὸς
425 τοὺς πολεμίους ἔμελλεν ἐρεῖν, ὅμως ἐπετρέψατε αὐτῷ
πατρίδα καὶ παῖδας καὶ γυναῖκας καὶ ὑμᾶς αὐτούς.
70 ὁ δὲ ὧν μὲν ὑπέσχετο οὐδὲν ἔπραξεν, οὕτως δὲ ἐνετεθύμητο ὡς χρὴ μικρὰν καὶ ἀσθενῆ γενέσθαι τὴν πόλιν,

participle takes μή (A) when it is
equivalent to a protasis (this includes "generic" expressions, see
on 25. 1). So in 12. 85, 19. 29,
19. 53, 25. 34. (B) when it depends
on a verb which.has μή or would
have it if negatived. So in 19.
33, 19. 37, 19. 51, 24. 18, 24. 26,
25. 4, 25. 22, 32. 18.

69.

πραττούσης μὲν ... βουλῆς ⎫
ἀντιλεγόντων δὲ πολλῶν ⎪
εἰδότες δὲ ὅτι {οἱ μὲν ἄλλοι ... ⎬
{ἐκεῖνος δὲ ... ⎪
ὑμεῖς ... ἐπετρέψατε. ⎭

The use of μέν ... δέ ... δέ is
due to the fact that while εἰδότες
is not correlative in form with the
two other participles, it is in
thought. We find similar construction in 19. 23, 19. 26, 25. 31.
— σωτήρια : we have no other
knowledge of these measures.
Ordinarily the Areopagus had no
jurisdiction in political or military
affairs, but this crisis was so

extreme, involving the very existence of the city, that extraordinary action by the Areopagus
is not unlikely. — ἀντιλεγόντων :
see Introd. p. 37. — τἀπόρρητα
ποιοῦνται : keep state secrets. —
αὐτῷ : on the first mission, that
to Lysander, Theramenes went
alone, but had no authority to negotiate ; on the second, he had
authority, but it was shared with
nine fellow-ambassadors. Lysias
purposely represents it as resting
entirely with him. — γυναῖκας : the
article is often omitted with words
of family relationship (definite by
their own force), especially where
several are joined ; cp. the Eng.
omission of the possessive pronoun in the same expressions ;
both languages extend the construction to 'fatherland.'
70. οὕτως ἐνετεθύμητο : he was
so convinced ; the plup. to express
mental attitude where the impf.
would express mental action. Cp.

ὥστε περὶ ὧν οὐδεὶς πώποτε οὔτε τῶν πολεμίων ἐμνήσθη
430 οὔτε τῶν πολιτῶν ἤλπισε, ταῦθ' ὑμᾶς ἔπεισε πρᾶξαι,
οὐχ ὑπὸ Λακεδαιμονίων ἀναγκαζόμενος, ἀλλ' αὐτὸς
ἐκείνοις ἐπαγγελλόμενος, τοῦ τε Πειραιῶς τὰ τείχη
περιελεῖν καὶ τὴν ὑπάρχουσαν πολιτείαν καταλῦσαι, εὖ
434 εἰδὼς ὅτι, εἰ μὴ πασῶν τῶν ἐλπίδων ἀποστερήσεσθε,
71 ταχεῖαν παρ' αὐτοῦ τὴν τιμωρίαν κομιεῖσθε. καὶ τὸ

on καταπεφρόνηκεν § 84. — ἤλπισε :
ἐλπίζω has strictly only the idea
of expectation ; hope (its usual
force) or fear is determined by the
context. — ἔπεισε : *i.e.* in the assembly which received and acted upon
the report of the ten ambassadors
on the day after their return
(Xen. *Hell.* 2. 2. 22). — αὐτός : as
in § 68. — Πειραιῶς : the demand
made on the first embassy was for
the destruction of ten stadia of the
Long Walls. The new demand
was probably caused in part by
exasperation at the stubborn refusal of ˙Athens to accept unexpectedly mild terms, and in part
by Sparta's finding it necessary
to compromise with some of her
own leading allies, who demanded
the annihilation of the city. —
— πολιτείαν καταλῦσαι : it is
almost certain that the change
of government was agreed upon
between Sparta and Theramenes
and his friends before the surrender ; but it is not likely that it
was one of the formal conditions

of peace openly proposed to the
people and ratified by them. It
is not included in the terms given
by Xenophon (*Hell.* 2. 2. 20) and
Andocides (3. 12). Aristotle
(*Resp. Ath.* 34. 3) regards it as
one of the actual conditions ; so
Diodorus (14. 3. 2). The expression of Lysias himself in 13. 14
ὀνόματι μὲν εἰρήνην λεγομένην, τῷ
δ' ἔργῳ τὴν δημοκρατίαν καταλυο-
μένην implies that the change of
government was not in the *nominal* terms of peace. — ἀποστερήσεσθε : voice, HA. 496 ; G. 1248 ;
B. 514–15 ; Gl. 393. — τιμωρίαν :
Lysias is claiming that Theramenes sought to destroy the inde-
pendence of the city from fear that
if the people should be left free to
act their pleasure, they would
inflict extreme punishment upon
him. But punishment for what ?
He was under no accusation and
in no danger. In the period immediately after the fall of the Four
Hundred, when some of his colleagues were executed and others

τελευταῖον, ὦ ἄνδρες δικασταί, οὐ πρότερον εἴασε τὴν
ἐκκλησίαν γενέσθαι, ἕως ὁ ὡμολογημένος ὑπ᾽ ἐκείνων
καιρὸς ἐπιμελῶς ὑπ᾽ αὐτοῦ ἐτηρήθη, καὶ μετεπέμψατο
139 μὲν τὰς μετὰ Λυσάνδρου ναῦς ἐκ Σάμου, ἐπεδήμησε δὲ
72 τὸ τῶν πολεμίων στρατόπεδον. τότε δὲ τούτων ὑπαρ-

banished, he retained the confidence of the people and was for a time at the head of the new administration. In the years that followed (410–404), when the extreme democracy had returned to the fullest power, still no attack was made upon him. Had he been able to secure moderate terms from Sparta, he would have been the most popular man in the city.

71. ἐκκλησίαν: Lysias, having shown that Theramenes carried the proposition for surrender in the assembly on the day after his return from Sparta, turns now to the discussion of his efforts in a later assembly, called to discuss a change of government. He expects his hearers to understand by the words τὸ τελευταῖον that he is passing to this later and final act. To hearers familiar with the events, less than two years past, this was probably clear; by us the words τὴν ἐκκλησίαν are liable at first to be understood as referring to the assembly of which he has just been speaking; but six lines below he makes all clear by adding the phrase περὶ τῆς πολιτείας.

This explicit statement should acquit Lysias of the charge brought by recent critics (ep. Meyer, Gesch. des Alterthums IV. 666) that he is purposely confusing the two assemblies. — οὐ πρότερον . . . ἕως: the ordinary construction is either οὐ πρότερον . . . πρίν or οὐ . . . ἕως; here the two are combined, as in 25. 26. — ἐκείνων: the Spartans. — ἐκ Σάμου: see Chron. App. Diodorus says (14. 3. 4–5) that Lysander had just taken Samos and that he came to the Piraeus with 100 ships. But Xenophon (Hell. 2. 3. 7) says that on the surrender of Samos Lysander dissolved the Lacedaemonian fleet, and gives the impression that he sailed directly from Samos home. It is probable then that his visit to Athens was during the siege of Samos, with only a part of his fleet, and that he returned to Samos to complete the siege. — τὸ στρατόπεδον: the large Peloponnesian army which Pausanias brought up to Athens after Aegospotami, and which encamped in the Academy with Agis's troops from Decelea, was soon dismissed,

χόντων, καὶ παρόντος Λυσάνδρου καὶ Φιλοχάρους καὶ
Μιλτιάδου, περὶ τῆς πολιτείας τὴν ἐκκλησίαν ἐποίουν,
ἵνα μήτε ῥήτωρ αὐτοῖς μηδεὶς ἐναντιοῖτο μηδὲ δι-
444 απειλοῖτο ὑμεῖς τε μὴ τὰ τῇ πόλει συμφέροντα ἕλοι-
73 σθε, ἀλλὰ τἀκείνοις δοκοῦντα ψηφίσαισθε. ἀναστὰς
δὲ Θηραμένης ἐκέλευσεν ὑμᾶς τριάκοντα ἀνδράσιν
ἐπιτρέψαι τὴν πόλιν καὶ τῇ πολιτείᾳ χρῆσθαι ἣν Δρακοντίδης ἀπέφαινεν. ὑμεῖς δ' ὅμως καὶ οὕτω διακεί-

Lysander being left to carry on the
winter siege with his fleet (Diodor.
13. 107. 3); but a Spartan land
force probably remained to co-
operate with Lysander, and even
after the surrender it would naturally be retained till the Athenians
had completed the stipulated destruction of their walls, the work
of several months.

72. ὑπαρχόντων: force, see on
ὑπάρχει § 23. — **Φιλοχάρους, Μιλτιάδου**: the names are Attic; we
can only conjecture that they were
prominent men of the oligarchical
party. — **ἐποίουν**: tense, see on
ἐβάδιζον § 8. — **ῥήτωρ**: the term
for one who addresses the popular
assembly. The ῥήτωρ may or
may not have the technical training of the rhetoricians. The power
possessed by one who could move
the assembly tended to develop a
class of professional ῥήτορες. —
τε: correlative with μήτε, and used
instead of a second μήτε, so that
it may connect the preceding with

both the negative ἕλοισθε and the
positive ψηφίσαισθε, —

$$
\tilde{\iota}\nu\alpha
\begin{cases}
\mu\acute{\eta}\tau\epsilon\ \dot{\rho}\acute{\eta}\tau\omega\rho
\begin{cases}
\dot{\epsilon}\nu\alpha\nu\tau\iota o\hat{\iota}\tau o \\
\mu\eta\delta\grave{\epsilon} \\
\delta\iota\alpha\pi\epsilon\iota\lambda o\hat{\iota}\tau o
\end{cases} \\
\dot{\upsilon}\mu\epsilon\hat{\iota}\varsigma\ \tau\epsilon
\begin{cases}
\mu\grave{\eta}\ \check{\epsilon}\lambda o\iota\sigma\theta\epsilon \\
\dot{\alpha}\lambda\lambda\grave{\alpha} \\
\psi\eta\phi\acute{\iota}\sigma\alpha\iota\sigma\theta\epsilon
\end{cases}
\end{cases}
$$

73. Δρακοντίδης: confirmed by
Arist. *Resp. Ath.* 34. 3. He was
appointed one of the Thirty. —
ἀπέφαινεν: the word would be
used properly of the publication
of a scheme of government by a
lawgiver, or of the 'report' of a
commission appointed to frame
laws; Lysias uses it with the sarcastic implication that this was
not a proposition for the people to
discuss, but a ready-made scheme
thrust upon them. There is no
real inconsistency between the
statement of Lysias that Dracontides presented a form of government (πολιτείαν ἀπέφαινεν) and
that of Xenophon (*Hell.* 2. 3. 11)
that the Thirty were appointed to

μενοι ἐθορυβεῖτε ὡς οὐ ποιήσοντες ταῦτα· ἐγιγνώσκετε
450 γὰρ ὅτι περὶ δουλείας καὶ ἐλευθερίας ἐν ἐκείνῃ τῇ ἡμέρᾳ
74 ἠκκλησιάζετε. Θηραμένης δέ, ὦ ἄνδρες δικασταί, (καὶ
τούτων ὑμᾶς αὐτοὺς μάρτυρας παρέξομαι) εἶπεν ὅτι
οὐδὲν αὐτῷ μέλοι τοῦ ὑμετέρου θορύβου, ἐπειδὴ πολλοὺς μὲν Ἀθηναίων εἰδείη τοὺς τὰ ὅμοια πράττοντας
455 αὐτῷ, δοκοῦντα δὲ Λυσάνδρῳ καὶ Λακεδαιμονίοις λέγοι.
μετ᾽ ἐκεῖνον δὲ Λύσανδρος ἀναστὰς ἄλλα τε πολλὰ εἶπε
καὶ ὅτι παρασπόνδους ὑμᾶς ἔχοι, καὶ ὅτι οὐ περὶ πολιτείας ὑμῖν ἔσται ἀλλὰ περὶ σωτηρίας, εἰ μὴ ποιήσεθ᾽
75 ἃ Θηραμένης κελεύει. τῶν δ᾽ ἐν τῇ ἐκκλησίᾳ ὅσοι
460 ἄνδρες ἀγαθοὶ ἦσαν, γνόντες τὴν παρασκευὴν καὶ τὴν
ἀνάγκην, οἱ μὲν αὐτοῦ μένοντες ἡσυχίαν ἦγον, οἱ δὲ
ᾤχοντο ἀπιόντες, τοῦτο γοῦν σφίσιν αὐτοῖς συνειδότες,

frame a constitution (συγγράψαι νόμους). Dracontides doubtless presented the general plan, and the Thirty were chosen to draft a constitution which should carry it out in detail. — ὡς : for the usual force of ὡς with a partic. see on 16. 8. But sometimes, as here and in § 90 and 32. 23, it gives to the partic. nearly the same force of ind. disc. which ὡς so often gives to the indic. HA. 978; G. 1593. 1 ; B. 661 N. 4; Gl. 594; GMT. 919. — ἠκκλησιάζετε : for the form of augment see Crit. Note. The addition of ἐν ἐκείνῃ τῇ ἡμέρᾳ has led editors to the rejection of ἐκκλησιάζετε, the Mss. reading (present, normal ind. disc. con-

struction). For the rare impf. see GMT. 674. 2; HA. 936; G. 1489. 1.

74. πολλούς : emphatic predicate of τοὺς πράττοντας. — παρασπόνδους : Diodorus (14. 3. 6) and Plutarch (*Lysander* 15) say that the Athenians had not completed the demolition of their walls within the appointed time. — ἔσται . . . ποιήσεθ᾽ . . . κελεύει : for mood see Crit. Note and on ἀφήσουσιν § 35.

75. γνόντες : ingressive aor., see on μετέσχον 16. 3. — αὐτοῦ : the adverb. — ᾤχοντο ἀπιόντες : ᾤχοντο, *were gone*, is more summary than ἀπῆλθον; ᾤχοντο ἀπιόντες is more summary still, *went straight off*.

ὅτι οὐδὲν κακὸν τῇ πόλει ἐψηφίσαντο · ὀλίγοι δέ τινες
464 καὶ πονηροὶ καὶ κακῶς βουλευόμενοι τὰ προσταχθέντα
76 ἐχειροτόνησαν. παρήγγελτο γὰρ αὐτοῖς δέκα μὲν οὓς
Θηραμένης ἀπέδειξε χειροτονῆσαι, δέκα δὲ οὓς οἱ καθε-
στηκότες ἔφοροι κελεύοιεν, δέκα δ' ἐκ τῶν παρόντων ·
οὕτω γὰρ τὴν ὑμετέραν ἀσθένειαν ἑώρων καὶ τὴν αὐτῶν
469 δύναμιν ἠπίσταντο, ὥστε πρότερον ᾔδεσαν τὰ μέλ-
77 λοντα ἐν τῇ ἐκκλησίᾳ πραχθήσεσθαι. ταῦτα δὲ οὐκ
ἐμοὶ δεῖ πιστεῦσαι, ἀλλὰ ἐκείνῳ · πάντα γὰρ τὰ ὑπ'
ἐμοῦ εἰρημένα ἐν τῇ βουλῇ ἀπολογούμενος ἔλεγεν,

76. The scheme was carried out by means of the political machinery described in detail in § 44. — δέκα: it is evident that the Board of Thirty was the result of a union between the aristocratic club element represented by Critias and the moderate aristocrats led by Theramenes, with the addition of a third group to give nominal representation to the democratic masses (cp. Aristotle's explicit statement as to the two aristocratic groups, *Resp. Ath.* 34. 3). Theramenes was at first the strongest man in the plot because of his personal connection with Lysander. This compromise in the formation of the new administration explains the fact of the almost immediate outbreak of dissension within its own ranks. — ἀπέδειξε . . . κελεύοιεν: Theramenes had doubtless designated his ten candidates before the preliminary club meetings were held; at these meetings the district leaders appear to have said to the members, naming two groups of ten men each, "Vote for these ten men whom Theramenes has designated (ἀπέδειξε), and for the following ten whom our chiefs, the Ephors, order you (κελεύουσιν) to vote for." ἀπέδειξε remains unchanged according to the regular principle that dependent *secondary* tenses of the indicative do not become opt. in ind. disc., HA. 935 b, c; G. 1497. 2, 1499; B. 675. 1, 3; GMT. 689. 3, cp. 695 I, last paragraph. — ἐκ τῶν παρόντων: *i.e.* from the citizens at large; a mere pretense of representation of a popular body.

77. ἀπολογούμενος: Xenophon (*Hell.* 2. 3. 35–49) gives at some length the speech of Theramenes

ὀνειδίζων μὲν τοῖς φεύγουσιν, ὅτι δι' αὐτὸν κατέλθοιεν,
οὐδὲν φροντιζόντων Λακεδαιμονίων, ὀνειδίζων δὲ τοῖς τῆς
475 πολιτείας μετέχουσιν, ὅτι πάντων τῶν πεπραγμένων τοῖς
εἰρημένοις τρόποις ὑπ' ἐμοῦ αὐτὸς αἴτιος γεγενημένος
τοιούτων τυγχάνοι, πολλὰς πίστεις αὐτοῖς ἔργῳ δεδω-
78 κὼς καὶ παρ' ἐκείνων ὅρκους εἰληφώς. καὶ τοσούτων
καὶ ἑτέρων κακῶν καὶ αἰσχρῶν καὶ πάλαι καὶ νεωστὶ
480 καὶ μικρῶν καὶ μεγάλων αἰτίου γεγενημένου τολμήσουσιν αὐτοὺς φίλους ὄντας ἀποφαίνειν, οὐχ ὑπὲρ ὑμῶν
ἀποθανόντος Θηραμένους ἀλλ' ὑπὲρ τῆς αὐτοῦ πονη-

when accused by Critias before the Senate; but it is probably Xenophon's own defense of his former party chief rather than a literal report of the speech delivered. There is in it no reference to the points which Lysias mentions here. — ὀνειδίζων, ὀνειδίζων: on the ἐπαναφορά see App. § 57. 5. — δι' αὐτόν: *they had him to thank for their return*. See on § 87. — κατέλθοιεν: see note on Κριτίας § 43. The return of the aristocrats who had been banished after the overthrow of the Four Hundred was one of the terms of the peace which Theramenes and his fellow-ambassadors negotiated with Sparta. The Spartans were probably not as indifferent to this as Lysias would have us believe. The best guaranty of the continuance of Athens under Spartan hegemony lay in the repression of the democracy. The-

ramenes and his friends saw in this fact their own opportunity. — ὑπ' ἐμοῦ: emphasis is given by the variation from the normal position (cp. τὰ ὑπ' ἐμοῦ εἰρημένα five lines above). The central point of the argument is, "Theramenes's speech agrees with *my* account." — πίστεις: L. & S. *s.v.* II. — ἐκείνων: referring to the same persons as αὐτοῖς in the preceding line. When two clauses or phrases are sharply contrasted, ἐκεῖνος often takes the place of αὐτός in one of them. Cp. 14. 28 οὐχ ὡς ἀδελφὸν αὐτῆς, ἀλλ' ὡς ἄνδρα ἐκείνης *not as her brother, but as her husband*; Plato, *Euthyphro* 14 d αἰτεῖν τε φῂς αὐτοὺς καὶ διδόναι ἐκείνοις *do you say that we ask of them (the gods) and give to them?*

78. On the striking πολυσύν-δετον of the opening words see App. § 58. 4. — ὑπὲρ . . . πονηρίας: ' he was serving — not the people,

ρίας, καὶ δικαίως μὲν ἐν ὀλιγαρχίᾳ δίκην δόντος, ἤδη
γὰρ αὐτὴν κατέλυσε· δικαίως δ' ἂν ἐν δημοκρατίᾳ, δὶς
485 γὰρ ὑμᾶς κατεδουλώσατο, τῶν μὲν παρόντων καταφρονῶν, τῶν δὲ ἀπόντων ἐπιθυμῶν, καὶ τῷ καλλίστῳ ὀνόματι χρώμενος δεινοτάτων ἔργων διδάσκαλος καταστάς.

79 Περὶ μὲν τοίνυν Θηραμένους ἱκανά μοί ἐστι τὰ κατη-
γορημένα· ἥκει δ' ὑμῖν ἐκεῖνος ὁ καιρός, ἐν ᾧ δεῖ
490 συγγνώμην καὶ ἔλεον μὴ εἶναι ἐν ταῖς ὑμετέραις γνώ-
μαις, ἀλλὰ παρὰ Ἐρατοσθένους καὶ τῶν τούτου συναρχόντων δίκην λαβεῖν, μηδὲ μαχομένους μὲν κρείττους
εἶναι τῶν πολεμίων, ψηφιζομένους δὲ ἥττους τῶν ἐχθρῶν.

but his own base nature'; ὑπέρ
gives a touch of personification
that we should not have in ἕνεκα.
Cp. on ὑπό § 3. — κατέλυσε: for
force of the tense see Crit. Note.
— δικαίως δ' ἄν: ἄν in this connection marks the thought as
'contrary to fact' (δόντος being
supplied from the preceding).
HA. 987 (b) ; G. 1308. 2 ;
B. 662, 606 ; Gl. 595. The
thought is that had the Thirty
not put Theramenes to death the
restored democracy would justly
have done it. On the ἐπαναφορά
of δικαίως, δικαίως see App. § 57. 5.
Cp. ὀνειδίζων, ὀνειδίζων § 77. —
παρόντων . . . ἀπόντων: to de-
spise what one has and to covet
what one has not was a proverbial
mark of the restless and discon-
tented man, the man who did not
submit to the decrees of the gods

as fixing his lot in life, and who
failed of the due measure of self-
control. On the rhetorical form
of the clauses see App. § 57. 3.
— ὀνόματι: the name of restoration of the government to the
form of the ancestral limited democracy. — δεινοτάτων : outrageous, a stronger word than
αἴσχιστος, the ordinary opposite
of κάλλιστος.

79. ἐκεῖνος : used rather than
οὗτος, as suggesting "that time"
for which they had long been
hoping. — τούτου : note that συναρχόντων has become so fully sub-
stantivized as to take the gen.
instead of the dat. proper to it as
a participle. So τοὺς συνάρχοντας
αὐτοῦ § 87. GS. 39; HA. 966 a ;
B. 650 n. 1. — συναρχόντων: see
Introd. p. 44, note 3. — ἐχθρῶν:
since the amnesty the Thirty are

80 μηδ' ὧν φασι μέλλειν πράξειν πλείω χάριν αὐτοῖς
495 ἴστε, ἢ ὧν ἐποίησαν ὀργίζεσθε· μηδ' ἀποῦσι μὲν
τοῖς τριάκοντα ἐπιβουλεύετε, παρόντας δ' ἀφῆτε· μηδὲ
τῆς τύχης, ἢ τούτους παρέδωκε τῇ πόλει, κάκιον ὑμεῖς
ὑμῖν αὐτοῖς βοηθήσητε.

81 Κατηγόρηται μὲν Ἐρατοσθένους καὶ τῶν τούτου φίλων,

no longer πολέμιοι, but in the
feeling of their former victims
they will always be ἐχθροί.

80. ὀργίζεσθε : ὧν is assimilated
to the case of the (omitted) antecedent. Cp. on § 35. Lysias's constructions with ὀργίζεσθαι are the
following : (A) the person against
whom the anger is felt is always
in the dat., 16. 17, 22. 2, 25. 1,
and often. (B) the occasion of
the anger is expressed by (1) gen.
with ὑπέρ, 12. 2 ; (2) gen. with
ἀντί, 12. 96 ; (3) dat. with ἐπί,
14. 13, 28. 2, 32. 21 ; (4) acc. with
διά, 21. 9, 30. 13 ; (5) dat. without prep., 12. 90, 20. 1 ; (6) gen.
without prep., 12. 80, 27. 11, 31.
11 (in the first two the gen.
is connected with another gen.
clause) ; (7) a ὅτι clause, 1. 15,
12. 58, 14. 20. — ἀποῦσι : the
Thirty had withdrawn to Eleusis ;
the people were by no means
sure that they could be safely
allowed to hold that place permanently. In fact two years later
Athens came to armed conflict
with the aristocrats at Eleusis,
and brought that city back under

the Athenian government. — ἐπιβουλεύετε, ἀφῆτε : the English
idiom does not here allow the
use of coördinate clauses corresponding to the Greek (cp. on
§ 47 ἐνόμιζον . . . παρέβαινον) ;
the Greek yields the sharper
antithesis. For change of mood
and tense from ὀργίζεσθε . . .
ἐπιβουλεύετε to ἀφῆτε . . . βοηθήσητε see HA. 874 a ; G. 1346 ;
B. 584 ; Gl. 485.

81. κατηγόρηται : § 79 marks
the close of the attack on the
memory of Theramenes, and § 81
the close of the attack on the
career of Eratosthenes and the
whole moderate party. — τούτου :
used of one's opponent present in
court, as in § 79, Ἐρατοσθένους
καὶ τῶν τούτου συναρχόντων. The
English admits only the colorless
"his" (αὐτοῦ). Cp. § 84, 24. 3,
25. 3, 25. 24, 25. 33, 34. 1, 34. 6. —
φίλων : Theramenes, Phidon, and
the others whom he has attacked ;
to be distinguished from the
friends who will plead for Eratosthenes in court (τῶν συνερούντων) ;
the attack upon them comes in

500 οἷς τὰς ἀπολογίας ἀνοίσει καὶ μεθ' ὧν αὐτῷ ταῦτα
πέπρακται. ὁ μέντοι ἀγὼν οὐκ ἐξ ἴσου τῇ πόλει καὶ
'Ερατοσθένει· οὗτος μὲν γὰρ κατήγορος καὶ δικαστὴς
ὁ αὐτὸς ἦν τῶν κρινομένων, ἡμεῖς δὲ νυνὶ εἰς κατη-
82 γορίαν καὶ ἀπολογίαν καθέσταμεν. καὶ οὗτοι μὲν τοὺς
505 οὐδὲν ἀδικοῦντας ἀκρίτους ἀπέκτειναν, ὑμεῖς δὲ τοὺς
ἀπολέσαντας τὴν πόλιν κατὰ τὸν νόμον ἀξιοῦτε κρίνειν,
παρ' ὧν οὐδ' ἂν παρανόμως βουλόμενοι δίκην λαμβάνειν
ἀξίαν τῶν ἀδικημάτων ὧν τὴν πόλιν ἠδικήκασι λάβοιτε.
509 τί γὰρ ἂν παθόντες δίκην τὴν ἀξίαν εἴησαν τῶν ἔργων
83 δεδωκότες ; πότερον εἰ αὐτοὺς ἀποκτείναιτε καὶ τοὺς
παῖδας αὐτῶν, ἱκανὴν ἂν τοῦ φόνου δίκην λάβοιμεν, ὧν
οὗτοι πατέρας καὶ ὑεῖς καὶ ἀδελφοὺς ἀκρίτους ἀπέκτειναν ; ἀλλὰ γὰρ εἰ τὰ χρήματα τὰ φανερὰ δημεύσαιτε,
514 καλῶς ἂν ἔχοι ἢ τῇ πόλει, ἧς οὗτοι πολλὰ εἰλήφασιν, ἢ
84 τοῖς ἰδιώταις, ὧν τὰς οἰκίας ἐξεπόρθησαν ; ἐπειδὴ τοίνυν

§ 86. — οἷς . . . ἀνοίσει : an unusual construction for the regular
one of § 64.
82. ἀδικοῦντας : tense, see on
ἀδικῶ § 14. — ἀκρίτους : cp. on
§ 17. — ἀξιοῦτε : L. & S. s.v.
III. 2. — δίκην τὴν ἀξίαν : "the
substantive takes no article before
it, when it would have none if the
attributive were dropped," HA.
668 a ; cp. B. 452. — δίκην . . .
δεδωκότες : the unusual position of
words throughout gives emphasis ;
see on ἡμῖν § 33.
83. παῖδας : cp. on καὶ τοὺς
παῖδας § 36. — λάβοιμεν : note the

change to the first person. The
jury alone could put them to death,
but Lysias would share in this
requital for wrongs suffered. — ὧν :
the antec. is the subject of λάβοιμεν. — ὑεῖς : form, see on § 34.
— ἀλλὰ γάρ : emphatic γάρ really,
possibly (see on § 40) ; connect
with καλῶς ἂν ἔχοι. — τὰ φανερά :
it is assumed that they have put
all their other property out of
reach. — ἧς. ὧν : possessive gen.
— εἰλήφασιν : the perfect implies
that they still have their ill-gotten
gains in their possession.
84. τοίνυν : force, see on 16.

πάντα ποιοῦντες δίκην παρ᾽ αὐτῶν τὴν ἀξίαν οὐκ ἂν
δύναισθε λαβεῖν, πῶς οὐκ αἰσχρὸν ὑμῖν καὶ ἡντινοῦν
ἀπολιπεῖν, ἥντινά τις βούλοιτο παρὰ τούτων λαμβάνειν;

520 Πᾶν δ᾽ ἄν μοι δοκεῖ τολμῆσαι, ὅστις νυνὶ οὐχ ἑτέρων
ὄντων τῶν δικαστῶν ἀλλ᾽ αὐτῶν τῶν κακῶς πεπονθότων,
ἥκει ἀπολογησόμενος πρὸς αὐτοὺς τοὺς μάρτυρας τῆς
τούτου πονηρίας· τοσοῦτον ἢ ὑμῶν καταπεφρόνηκεν ἢ
85 ἑτέροις πεπίστευκεν. ὧν ἀμφοτέρων ἄξιον ἐπιμεληθῆ-
525 ναι, ἐνθυμουμένους ὅτι οὔτ᾽ ἂν ἐκεῖνα ἐδύναντο ποιεῖν

7 (A). — ἡντινοῦν: sc. δίκην. For
the force of -ουν see HA. 285;
G. 432. 1; B. 151 n.; Gl. 221 c.
— βούλοιτο: opt. in protasis, the
apodosis πῶς οὐκ αἰσχρὸν . . .
ἀπολιπεῖν being nearly equivalent
to πῶς οὐκ αἰσχρῶς ἂν ἀπολίποιτε.
GMT. 555. — ἄν: see on § 1. —
ὅστις: the ὅστις of a 'characterizing clause,' see on § 40. As the sentence advances the speaker passes
from the general word ὅστις to
the particular τούτου. For τούτου
rather than ἑαυτοῦ see on τούτου
§ 81. — ἥκει ἀπολογησόμενος: this
implies that Eratosthenes has
come into court of his own free
will. It is therefore a very strong
argument for the theory that this
is a case of accounting, not
a prosecution for murder. Cp.
Introd. p. 44. — τοσοῦτον: for the
asyndeton cp. Crit. Note on
εἴργασται § 1. — καταπεφρόνηκεν,

πεπίστευκεν: perfect to denote a
permanent attitude of mind where
the present would denote a present
mental action (cp. καταφρονῶν
§ 78; the distinction is one of
emphasis). Lysias nowhere else
uses the perf. active of either of
these verbs. Cp. ἐνετεθύμητο § 70;
Dinarch. 1. 104 σὺ δ᾽ οὕτω σφόδρα
πεπίστευκας τοῖς σεαυτοῦ λόγοις
καὶ καταπεφρόνηκας τῆς τούτων
εὐηθείας *you have such confidence in your own eloquence and
such contempt for the honesty
of these citizens*; Lycurg. 68 καὶ
οὕτως ἐστὶν ἀνόητος καὶ παντά-
πασιν ὑμῶν καταπεφρονηκώς *he
is so foolish and so full of contempt for you*; Isoc. 4. 136
δικαίως ἁπάντων ἡμῶν καταπεφρονηκώς.

85. ἀμφοτέρων: their scorn of
you and their trust in others; but
what follows deals with the second

μὴ ἑτέρων συμπραττόντων, οὔτ᾽ ἂν νῦν ἐπεχείρησαν
ἐλθεῖν μὴ ὑπὸ τῶν αὐτῶν οἰόμενοι σωθήσεσθαι, οἳ οὐ
τούτοις ἥκουσι βοηθήσοντες, ἀλλὰ ἡγούμενοι πολλὴν
ἄδειαν σφίσιν ἔσεσθαι καὶ τοῦ λοιποῦ ποιεῖν ὅ τι ἂν
530 βούλωνται, εἰ τοὺς μεγίστων κακῶν αἰτίους λαβόντες
86 ἀφήσετε. Ἀλλὰ καὶ τῶν συνερούντων αὐτοῖς ἄξιον
θαυμάζειν, πότερον ὡς καλοὶ κἀγαθοὶ αἰτήσονται, τὴν
αὐτῶν ἀρετὴν πλείονος ἀξίαν ἀποφαίνοντες τῆς τούτων
πονηρίας · ἐβουλόμην μέντ᾽ ἂν αὐτοὺς οὕτω προθύμους
535 εἶναι σῴζειν τὴν πόλιν, ὥσπερ οὗτοι ἀπολλύναι · ἢ
ὡς δεινοὶ λέγειν ἀπολογήσονται καὶ τὰ τούτων ἔργα
πολλοῦ ἄξια ἀποφανοῦσιν. ἀλλ᾽ οὐχ ὑπὲρ ὑμῶν οὐδεὶς
αὐτῶν οὐδὲ τὰ δίκαια πώποτε ἐπεχείρησεν εἰπεῖν.

87 Ἀλλὰ τοὺς μάρτυρας ἄξιον ἰδεῖν, οἳ τούτοις μαρτυ-
540 ροῦντες αὐτῶν κατηγοροῦσι, σφόδρα ἐπιλήσμονας καὶ

---

idea only. — μὴ ἑτέρων συμπραττόντων : μή in protasis, see on § 68
(A). — τοῦ λοιποῦ ποιεῖν : the
fuller and more regular construction is that of 30. 34 ἄδειαν εἰς τὸν
λοιπὸν χρόνον λήψεσθαι τοῦ ποιεῖν
ὅ τι ἂν βούλωνται. For case of
λοιποῦ see HA. 759; G. 1136;
B. 359; Gl. 515. — ἀφήσετε : mood
and tense, see on ἀφήσουσιν § 35.

86. ἄξιον θαυμάζειν

   { πότερον ὡς καλοὶ . . .
       αἰτήσονται
       ἢ ὡς δεινοὶ . . . ἀπο-
       λογήσονται.

The two halves of the double question are widely separated by the

insertion of the parenthetical sentence ἐβουλόμην . . . ἀπολλύναι.
— ἐβουλόμην ἄν : cp. on § 22.
— σῴζειν, ἀπολλύναι : conative
presents, see on πυνθάνεσθαι § 2.
— δεινοὶ λέγειν : a common characterization of the sophists and of
the rising profession of pleaders,
voicing the popular suspicion of
their power; cp. Plato, *Apol.* 17 a
ἔλεγον ὡς χρὴ ὑμᾶς εὐλαβεῖσθαι
μὴ ὑπ᾽ ἐμοῦ ἐξαπατηθῆτε ὡς δεινοῦ
ὄντος λέγειν *they said that you
must be on your guard against
being deceived by me, on the
ground that I am an eloquent
speaker.*

εὐήθεις νομίζοντες ὑμᾶς εἶναι, εἰ διὰ μὲν τοῦ ὑμετέρου
πλήθους ἀδεῶς ἡγοῦνται τοὺς τριάκοντα σώσειν, διὰ δὲ
Ἐρατοσθένην καὶ τοὺς συνάρχοντας αὐτοῦ δεινὸν ἦν καὶ
88 τῶν τεθνεώτων ἐπ᾽ ἐκφορὰν ἐλθεῖν. καίτοι οὗτοι μὲν
545 σωθέντες πάλιν ἂν δύναιντο τὴν πόλιν ἀπολέσαι· ἐκεῖνοι δέ, οὓς οὗτοι ἀπώλεσαν, τελευτήσαντες τὸν βίον
πέρας ἔχουσι τῆς τῶν ἐχθρῶν τιμωρίας. οὐκ οὖν δεινὸν
εἰ τῶν μὲν ἀδίκως τεθνεώτων οἱ φίλοι συναπώλλυντο,
αὐτοῖς δὲ τοῖς τὴν πόλιν ἀπολέσασιν — ἦ που ἐπ᾽

87. **εὐήθεις**: for the change of
this word from an originally good
meaning (εὖ, ἦθος) cp. the history of Eng. *simple* and *silly*. —
διὰ πλήθους, διὰ Ἐρατοσθένην: note
the change from gen. to accus.
with διά. ὑπό with the gen. denotes the voluntary agent *by whom*
an act is performed. διά with the
gen. denotes the *mediator* (GS.
163) *through* whose voluntary action an effect is produced. διά
with the acc. denotes the person
through whom an effect is produced without implying that it
was directly intended by him, the
person *thanks to whom* something
comes about. "When διά with
gen. is used the agency is pur-
poseful, when διά with acc. is used
it is accidental" (Gildersleeve,
A.J.P. XI. 372). For διά with
gen. cp. § 92, 32. 27; διά with
acc. §§ 58, 60, 77; 25. 6, 25. 27,
25. 29, 25. 30, 25. 32. For combination of the two see 25. 33.

— **πλήθους**: cp. §§ 42, 66, 67. —
δέ: substitute Eng. *while*; as in
§§ 47 and 80 the Eng. idiom
does not allow the coördinate
clauses. — **αὐτοῦ**: for the case see
on τούτου § 79.

88. 'Extreme severity against
the Thirty is necessary, for they,
if permitted to live, will endanger
the state, whereas their severity
in dishonoring the dead bodies
of their victims was wanton bar-
barity.' — **ἔχουσι**: we should expect εἶχον, but Lysias neglects
precision of connection in the
pressure of his feeling that vengeance for his brother and the rest
can come only through the fidelity
of their friends *now*. — **ἐχθρῶν**:
obj. gen. — **συναπώλλυντο**: *were
in danger of dying with them*,
impf. of an *expected* action, B. 527;
GS. 213. So ἐγίγνετο 25. 10,
ἀπεστερούμην 25. 13. — **ἦ που κτλ.**:
Lysias started to say, "Is it not
then outrageous, if the friends of

550 ἐκφορὰν πολλοὶ ἥξουσιν, ὁπότε βοηθεῖν τοσοῦτοι παρα-
89 σκευάζονται. καὶ μὲν δὴ πολὺ ῥᾷον ἡγοῦμαι εἶναι ὑπὲρ
ὧν ὑμεῖς ἐπάσχετε ἀντειπεῖν, ἢ ὑπὲρ ὧν οὗτοι πεποιήκασιν ἀπολογήσασθαι. καίτοι λέγουσιν ὡς Ἐρατοσθένει ἐλάχιστα τῶν τριάκοντα κακὰ εἴργασται, καὶ διὰ
555 τοῦτο αὐτὸν ἀξιοῦσι σωθῆναι · ὅτι δὲ τῶν ἄλλων Ἑλλήνων πλεῖστα εἰς ὑμᾶς ἐξημάρτηκεν, οὐκ οἴονται χρῆναι
90 αὐτὸν ἀπολέσθαι; ὑμεῖς δὲ δείξετε ἥντινα γνώμην
ἔχετε περὶ τῶν πραγμάτων. εἰ μὲν γὰρ τούτου καταψηφιεῖσθε, δῆλοι ἔσεσθε ὡς ὀργιζόμενοι τοῖς πεπραγ-
560 μένοις · εἰ δὲ ἀποψηφιεῖσθε, ὀφθήσεσθε τῶν αὐτῶν
ἔργων ἐπιθυμηταὶ τούτοις ὄντες, καὶ οὐχ ἕξετε λέγειν

those who were unjustly put to death were in danger of perishing with them, while (δέ) to the very men who destroyed the city so many are preparing to bring aid?" But instead of following out the second half of the sentence he interrupts it with a bitterly sarcastic exclamation, and from that point abandons the connection with the original principal clause, οὐκ οὖν δεινόν: Aye, doubtless many will come to their funeral, when so many are preparing to bring them aid. — ἐπ' ἐκφοράν: a grim reminder to the defense, that there is no doubt whatever as to the coming verdict.

89. καὶ μὲν δή: force, see on § 30. — εἶναι: the direct discourse would have πολὺ ῥᾷον ἦν . . . ἀντειπεῖν ἢ (ἐστί) ἀπολογήσασθαι

it were much easier to accuse than (it is) to defend. For ἦν without ἄν see on εἰκὸς ἦν § 27. — ὑπὲρ ὧν: cp. on ὧν § 35. On ὑπέρ see on 25. 5. — πεποιήκασιν: tense, see on εἰργασμένοι εἰσίν § 22. — τῶν ἄλλων Ἑ. πλεῖστα: strictly it should be τῶν ἄλλων Ἑλλήνων πλείω, but such looseness of expression with the superlative is not infrequent, and is here caused by the parallelism with ἐλάχιστα τῶν τριάκοντα. — εἰς ὑμᾶς: force, see on πρός 32. 19, Crit. Note.

90. καταψηφιεῖσθε: monitory protasis, see on ἀφήσουσιν § 35. — ὡς: an uncommon use with δῆλος and the partic. of ind. disc. (see on § 73); cp. Xen. Anab. I. 5. 9 δῆλος ἦν Κῦρος ὡς σπεύδων it was evident that Cyrus was hastening. — τοῖς πεπραγμένοις:

124 ΛΥΣΙΟΥ

91 ὅτι τὰ ὑπὸ τῶν τριάκοντα προσταχθέντα ἐποιεῖτε· νυνὶ
μὲν γὰρ οὐδεὶς ὑμᾶς ἀναγκάζει παρὰ τὴν ὑμετέραν
γνώμην ψηφίζεσθαι. ὥστε συμβουλεύω μὴ τούτων
565 ἀποψηφισαμένους ὑμῶν αὐτῶν καταψηφίσασθαι. μηδ'
οἴεσθε κρύβδην εἶναι τὴν ψῆφον· φανερὰν γὰρ τῇ
πόλει τὴν ὑμετέραν γνώμην ποιήσετε.

92 Βούλομαι δὲ ὀλίγα ἑκατέρους ἀναμνήσας καταβαίνειν, τούς τε ἐξ ἄστεως καὶ τοὺς ἐκ Πειραιῶς, ἵνα τὰς
570 ὑμῖν διὰ τούτων γεγενημένας συμφορὰς παραδείγματα
ἔχοντες τὴν ψῆφον φέρητε. καὶ πρῶτον μὲν ὅσοι ἐξ
ἄστεώς ἐστε, σκέψασθε ὅτι ὑπὸ τούτων οὕτω σφόδρα
ἤρχεσθε, ὥστε ἀδελφοῖς καὶ ὑέσι καὶ πολίταις ἠναγκά-
ζεσθε πολεμεῖν τοιοῦτον πόλεμον, ἐν ᾧ ἡττηθέντες μὲν
575 τοῖς νικήσασι τὸ ἴσον ἔχετε, νικήσαντες δ' ἂν τούτοις

case, see on ὀργίζεσθε § 80. —
προσταχθέντα: a side thrust at
Eratosthenes's excuse, § 25. —
ἐποιεῖτε: tense, see on ἐποίουν
§ 25.
91. μηδ' οἴεσθε: *nor think*,
"*The ballot is secret.*" The ballot
of the individual juror will be
secret, but the jurors are not to
be influenced by that fact, for if
the secret ballot acquits Eratosthenes, it will be clear that the members of the city party have so voted,
and are therefore still hostile to
the democracy. The negative μηδ'
οἴεσθε does not imply the untruth
of κρύβδην εἶναι, as it would in
an ordinary connection. Precisely
similar is the use of the negative

in μηδενὶ τοῦτο παραστῇ, ὡς . . .
κατηγορῶ § 62.
92. καταβαίνειν: *i.e.* from the
speaker's platform. — διὰ τούτων:
force, see on διὰ πλήθους § 87. —
τὴν ψῆφον φέρητε: by position and
construction this is the leading
phrase as compared with τὰς συμφορὰς . . . ἔχοντες, but subordinate in thought. The dropping
of emphasis in delivery would give
to it its real subordination; it may
well be made subord. in trans.:
*that you may have the misfortunes
. . . as warnings, as you cast your
vote.* — ἐν ᾧ: the main clause of
result has the construction οὕτω
. . . ὥστε, the subordinate one,
τοιοῦτον ἐν ᾧ.

93 ἐδουλεύετε. καὶ τοὺς ἰδίους οἴκους οὗτοι μὲν ἐκ τῶν
πραγμάτων μεγάλους ἐκτήσαντο, ὑμεῖς δὲ διὰ τὸν πρὸς
ἀλλήλους πόλεμον ἐλάττους ἔχετε· συνωφελεῖσθαι μὲν
γὰρ ὑμᾶς οὐκ ἠξίουν, συνδιαβάλλεσθαι δ' ἠνάγκαζον,
580 εἰς τοσοῦτον ὑπεροψίας ἐλθόντες ὥστε οὐ τῶν ἀγαθῶν
κοινούμενοι πιστοὺς ὑμᾶς ἐκτῶντο, ἀλλὰ τῶν ὀνειδῶν
94 μεταδιδόντες εὔνους ᾤοντο εἶναι. ἀνθ' ὧν ὑμεῖς νῦν
ἐν τῷ θαρραλέῳ ὄντες, καθ' ὅσον δύνασθε, καὶ ὑπὲρ
ὑμῶν αὐτῶν καὶ ὑπὲρ τῶν ἐκ Πειραιῶς τιμωρήσασθε,
585 ἐνθυμηθέντες μὲν ὅτι ὑπὸ τούτων πονηροτάτων ὄντων
ἤρχεσθε, ἐνθυμηθέντες δὲ ὅτι μετ' ἀνδρῶν νῦν ἀρίστων πολιτεύεσθε καὶ τοῖς πολεμίοις μάχεσθε καὶ
περὶ τῆς πόλεως βουλεύεσθε, ἀναμνησθέντες δὲ τῶν

93. For the use of antithesis
in this section see App. § 57. 1.
— οἴκους: Xenophon sums up a
discussion on the meaning of οἶκος
in these words, οἶκος δ' ἡμῖν ἐφαί-
νετο ὅπερ κτῆσις ἡ σύμπασα we
agreed that οἶκος is the same as
one's whole property (Oeconom.
6. 4). — τοὺς ἰδίους οἴκους . . . μεγάλους ἐκτήσαντο: the Greek con-
denses into the one expression
the thoughts expressed by the two
Eng. sentences, "They acquired
great estates" and "They made
their own estates great." — ἐκ τῶν
πραγμάτων: from their political
activity, see on 16. 3. — πρός : see
32. 19, Crit. Note. — ἐκτῶντο : conative impf., see on ἔπειθεν § 58. —
ἀλλὰ . . . ᾤοντο εἶναι: but they

thought you were satisfied if they
let you share the blame.

94. νῦν ἐν τῷ θαρραλέῳ: implying that under the Thirty they had
acted from fear. — ἐνθυμηθέντες, ἐνθυμηθέντες: on the ἐπαναφορά see
App. § 57. 5. — νῦν ἀρίστων: νῦν
with πολιτεύεσθε ; the reversal of
the ordinary position, ἀρίστων νῦν,
throws strong emphasis upon both
words ; see on ἡμῖν § 33. — πολεμίοις: 'you now fight against the
enemy, no longer against your fellow-citizens.' Not that Athens
was at war at this time, but that
the former supporters of the Thirty
are now back in normal relations ;
their wars are now against the
public enemies, no longer against
brothers and sons and fellow-

ἐπικούρων, οὓς οὗτοι φύλακας τῆς σφετέρας ἀρχῆς καὶ
590 τῆς ὑμετέρας δουλείας εἰς τὴν ἀκρόπολιν κατέστησαν.
95 καὶ πρὸς ὑμᾶς μὲν ἔτι πολλῶν ὄντων εἰπεῖν τοσαῦτα λέγω.
ὅσοι δ' ἐκ Πειραιῶς ἐστε, πρῶτον μὲν τῶν ὅπλων ἀναμνήσθητε, ὅτι πολλὰς μάχας ἐν τῇ ἀλλοτρίᾳ μαχεσάμενοι
οὐχ ὑπὸ τῶν πολεμίων ἀλλ' ὑπὸ τούτων εἰρήνης οὔσης
595 ἀφῃρέθητε τὰ ὅπλα, ἔπειθ' ὅτι ἐξεκηρύχθητε μὲν ἐκ τῆς
πόλεως, ἣν ὑμῖν οἱ πατέρες παρέδοσαν, φεύγοντας δὲ
96 ὑμᾶς ἐκ τῶν πόλεων ἐξῃτοῦντο. ἀνθ' ὧν ὀργίσθητε μὲν
ὥσπερ ὅτ' ἐφεύγετε, ἀναμνήσθητε δὲ καὶ τῶν ἄλλων
κακῶν ἃ πεπόνθατε ὑπ' αὐτῶν, οἳ τοὺς μὲν ἐκ τῆς

citizens (§ 92). — ἐπικούρων : the
Spartan garrison under Callibius
(see Chron. App.). Lysias represents the calling in of foreign
troops as a sign that the Thirty
distrusted their own supporters.

95. τῶν ὅπλων : brought out of
the ὅτι clause into immediate connection with ἀναμνήσθητε (*pro-
lepsis*) ; its repetition in the ὅτι
clause is unusual, but is justified
by the length of the intervening expression and by the emphasis that
rests upon the words ἀφῃρέθητε
τὰ ὅπλα. — ἀλλοτρίᾳ : L. & S. *s.v.*
II. 2. — ἐκ τῆς πόλεως : strictly
speaking ἐκ τοῦ ἄστεως only (προ-
εἶπον μὲν τοῖς ἔξω τοῦ καταλόγου
μὴ εἰσιέναι εἰς τὸ ἄστυ, Xen. *Hell.*
2. 4. 1). The term πόλις would
include the Piraeus, but very many
of the exiles feared to remain

there ; Lysias's statement is therefore little beyond the fact. — ἐκ
τῶν πόλεων : the cities of the Peloponnesian alliance, the demand
being made by Sparta, the supporter of the Thirty. But not
all these cities obeyed. Thebes
became the chief rallying point
of the exiles. When Lacedaemonian ambassadors demanded of
Argos the surrender of certain of
the fugitives, the Argives gave the
embassy till sunset to leave the
country (Dem. 15. 22) ; exiles
were also harbored at Megara
(Xen. *Hell.* 2. 4. 1) and at Chal-
cis (Lys. 24. 25). — ἐξῃτοῦντο : the
imperf. of the repeated and inef-
fectual action ; cp. the aorists ἀφῃρέθητε, ἐξεκηρύχθητε, of summary,
consummated actions.

96. ἀνθ' ὧν : see on ὀργίζεσθε

600 ἀγορᾶς τοὺς δ' ἐκ τῶν ἱερῶν συναρπάζοντες βιαίως
ἀπέκτειναν, τοὺς δὲ ἀπὸ τέκνων καὶ γονέων καὶ γυναι-
κῶν ἀφέλκοντες φονέας αὐτῶν ἠνάγκασαν γενέσθαι
καὶ οὐδὲ ταφῆς τῆς νομιζομένης εἴασαν τυχεῖν, ἡγού-
604 μενοι τὴν αὐτῶν ἀρχὴν βεβαιοτέραν εἶναι τῆς παρὰ τῶν
97 θεῶν τιμωρίας. ὅσοι δὲ τὸν θάνατον διέφυγον, πολλα-
χοῦ κινδυνεύσαντες καὶ εἰς πολλὰς πόλεις πλανηθέντες
καὶ πανταχόθεν ἐκκηρυττόμενοι, ἐνδεεῖς ὄντες τῶν ἐπι-
τηδείων, οἱ μὲν ἐν πολεμίᾳ τῇ πατρίδι τοὺς παῖδας
καταλιπόντες, οἱ δ' ἐν ξένῃ γῇ, πολλῶν ἐναντιουμένων
610 ἤλθετε εἰς τὸν Πειραιᾶ. πολλῶν δὲ καὶ μεγάλων κινδύνων ὑπαρξάντων ἄνδρες ἀγαθοὶ γενόμενοι τοὺς μὲν
98 ἠλευθερώσατε, τοὺς δ' εἰς τὴν πατρίδα κατηγάγετε. εἰ
δὲ ἐδυστυχήσατε καὶ τούτων ἡμάρτετε, αὐτοὶ μὲν ἂν
δείσαντες ἐφεύγετε μὴ πάθητε τοιαῦτα οἷα καὶ πρό-
615 τερον, καὶ οὔτ' ἂν ἱερὰ οὔτε βωμοὶ ὑμᾶς ἀδικουμένους

§ 80. — ἱερῶν: cp. § 98. — φονέας
αὐτῶν . . . ταφῆς: as in the case
of Polemarchus. — τῆς νομιζομένης:
for position see on τὴν ἀξίαν
§ 82.

97. πολεμίᾳ: the Greek predicate position provides a more
compact expression than is possible in Eng.; see on ἐκτήσαντο
§ 93, and cp. Xen. Anab. I. 3. 14
ἡγεμόνα αἰτεῖν Κῦρον ὅστις διὰ
φιλίας τῆς χώρας ἀπάξει. — ἤλθετε:
the sentence began with διέφυγον,
but as it develops the speaker
passes over unconsciously to the
second person. — ὑπαρξάντων:

force, see on ὑπάρχει § 23. — τοὺς
μέν: the children left at Athens.

98. τούτων: the safe return
and the rescue of their children.
— ἐφεύγετε: the time may be present or past (HA. 895 and 895 a;
G. 1397; B. 606; Gl. 649), you
would now be in exile, or you
would have gone into exile (cp.
ἔφευγον § 16); the second trans.
is better, for οὔτ' ἂν ἱερὰ . . . ὠφέλησαν (aor.) must be past. — μὴ
πάθητε: connect with δείσαντες;
a negative purpose after ἐφεύγετε
would in Lysias have ἵνα μή
(GMT. 315 n. 1). — καὶ πρότε-

διὰ τοὺς τούτων τρόπους ὠφέλησαν, ἃ καὶ τοῖς ἀδικοῦσι
σωτήρια γίγνεται· οἱ δὲ παῖδες ὑμῶν, ὅσοι μὲν ἐνθάδε
ἦσαν, ὑπὸ τούτων ἂν ὑβρίζοντο, οἱ δ' ἐπὶ ξένης μικρῶν
ἂν ἕνεκα συμβολαίων ἐδούλευον ἐρημίᾳ τῶν ἐπικουρη-
620 σόντων.

99   Ἀλλὰ γὰρ οὐ τὰ μέλλοντα ἔσεσθαι βούλομαι λέγειν,
τὰ πραχθέντα ὑπὸ τούτων οὐ δυνάμενος εἰπεῖν. οὐδὲ
γὰρ ἑνὸς κατηγόρου οὐδὲ δυοῖν ἔργον ἐστίν, ἀλλὰ
πολλῶν. ὅμως δὲ τῆς ἐμῆς προθυμίας οὐδὲν ἐλλέ-
625 λειπται, ὑπέρ τε τῶν ἱερῶν, ἃ οὗτοι τὰ μὲν ἀπέδοντο τὰ
δ' εἰσιόντες ἐμίαινον, ὑπέρ τε τῆς πόλεως, ἣν μικρὰν
ἐποίουν, ὑπέρ τε τῶν νεωρίων, ἃ καθεῖλον, καὶ ὑπὲρ τῶν

ρον: for καί in a comparison see
on 19. 2. — διὰ τρόπους: connect
with οὔτε ὠφέλησαν. — ἅ: agreement, HA. 628; G. 1021 (a); B.
463; Gl. 613 a. — ὑβρίζοντο . . .
ἐδούλευον: of present time. — ἕνεκα:
on the position of ἕνεκα see on 19.
17. — συμβολαίων: *loans*. How far
slavery for debt existed in other
states is uncertain; in Athens it
had not existed since Solon's re-
forms. Perhaps the term ἐδούλευον is used only as a strong
expression for forced labor of a
debtor unable to meet his note by
money payment.

    99. ἀλλὰ γάρ: force, see on
§ 40. — τὰ μέλλοντα: = ἃ ἔμελλεν.
For the non-use of ἄν see G. 1402.
3; B. 567. 1. On the tense see on
ἀνιωμένου § 32. — λέγειν . . . εἰπεῖν:
continuative present, complexive

aorist. — τέ, τέ, τέ, καί: on the
πολυσύνδετον see App. § 58. 4. —
τὰ μέν: not the temples, but probably treasures from the temples,
and especially tracts of land belonging to their endowments,
ordinarily rented to private persons for the benefit of the temple
funds. — ἐμίαινον: the Thirty were
so steeped in guilt that their very
entrance into a temple was a pol-
lution to it. — νεωρίων: the entire
loss of the fleet at the close of
the Peloponnesian War had left
the dockyards and naval arsenal
empty. It was the plan of Sparta
and her Athenian supporters to
see to it that the fleet should never
be restored. This was the more
acceptable to the Thirty as the
fleet had always been the center
of democratic power. We are not

τεθνεώτων, οἷς ὑμεῖς, ἐπειδὴ ζῶσιν ἐπαμῦναι οὐκ ἐδύ-
100 νασθε, ἀποθανοῦσι βοηθήσατε. οἶμαι δ' αὐτοὺς ἡμῶν
630 τε ἀκροᾶσθαι καὶ ὑμᾶς εἴσεσθαι τὴν ψῆφον φέροντας,
ἡγουμένους, ὅσοι μὲν ἂν τούτων ἀποψηφίσησθε, αὐτῶν
θάνατον κατεψηφισμένους ἔσεσθαι, ὅσοι δ' ἂν παρὰ
τούτων δίκην λάβωσιν, ὑπὲρ αὐτῶν τὰς τιμωρίας πεποιη-
μένους.

635 Παύσομαι κατηγορῶν. ἀκηκόατε, ἑωράκατε, πεπόνθατε, — ἔχετε· δικάζετε.

surprised, then, to read in Isocrates (7. 66) that the dockyards,
which had cost not less than
1000 t., were sold by the Thirty
for 3 t. to be broken up. But
apparently the work of destruction was not completed, for four
years after the Thirty Lysias (30.
22) speaks of the dockyards as
then falling into decay.

100. ὑμᾶς εἴσεσθαι τὴν ψῆφον
φέροντας : this would ordinarily
mean, "*will know that you cast
your vote*," an impossible meaning
here. The parallelism with ἡμῶν
τε ἀκροᾶσθαι, together with proper
division of phrases in delivery,
makes the meaning clear :
*I think they hear us, and will take
knowledge of you, as you cast your
vote*; see G. 1582–3. For the ingressive meaning of εἴσεσθαι cp.
27. 7 ἤκουσι δὲ πάντες οἱ τὰ τῆς
πόλεως πράττοντες οὐχ ἡμῶν ἀκρο-
ασόμενοι, ἀλλ' ὑμᾶς εἰσόμενοι ἥντινα γνώμην περὶ τῶν ἀδικούντων

ἔξετε *all who are active in politics
have come, not to hear us, but to
take knowledge of you, what view
you are going to hold about the
guilty.* — κατεψηφισμένους ἔσεσθαι :
tense, future *responsibility* ; cp. on
εἰργασμένοι εἰσίν § 22. — τὰς τιμωρίας: the penalty due. This passage
is of great interest as bearing on
the question of the belief of the
common people, in distinction from
that of the poets and philosophers,
as to the condition of the dead.
Lysias assumes that the jurymen
believe in the conscious existence
of the dead, and their knowledge
of what is being done in this world
for or against them. An appeal
of this sort is not uncommon in
Athenian pleas, but in all other
instances is qualified by some expression which implies that such
knowledge on the part of the
dead is only a possibility. — On
the remarkable ἀσύνδετον in the
final sentence see App. § 58. 3.

The Speech for Mantitheus

INTRODUCTION

LYSIAS wrote this speech for Mantitheus,[1] a young man who, as a candidate for office, probably that of senator, was to appear before the outgoing Senate to pass his scrutiny (δοκιμασία).[2]

The charge was brought against Mantitheus that he had been a member of the cavalry which had supported the Thirty, and that he was therefore not a fit candidate for office.

The following facts as to cavalry service in Athens will make clear the point of this attack, and the bearing of the argument in reply.

Before the Peloponnesian War Athens had made very little use of cavalry, but from the beginning of that war to the close of the next century a force of a thousand horsemen was maintained.[3]

---

[1] We know the name only from the title handed down in the Mss. In § 13 we find one Orthobulus having charge of the cavalry list of the speaker's tribe. On a fragment of an Attic treaty, probably of the year 378 B.C., an Orthobulus of the deme Ceramicus is named as one of an embassy to Byzantium. If this is the Orthobulus of § 13, that fact determines the tribe of Mantitheus, for Ceramicus belonged to Acamantis (Köhler, *Hermes*, V. 11).

[2] See p. 253 N. 2. The office must have been that of senator or archon, for these offices only were subject to δοκιμασία by the Senate (Arist. *Resp. Ath.* 45. 3). In § 8, where Mantitheus cites precedents, he speaks of senators, generals, and hipparchs, but not of archons. Nor is there any reference to special duties involved in the office sought, or to the second δοκιμασία, which would follow before a law court if the office were an archonship (Arist. *ibid.* 55. 2).

[3] These ἱππεῖς are not to be confused with the ἱππεῖς who formed the second property class of Athenian citizens. The name as applied to the

This force was made up from members of the first two property classes, selected by a board of ten Commissioners (καταλογεῖς), who were appointed annually.[1] Cavalrymen on the new list, who had served the year before, might be excused by the Senate upon their taking oath that they were physically incapable of serving longer. Newly enrolled members who refused to serve could be compelled to do so through legal proceedings. But the service was popular, and it is probable that a large part of the men of one year were glad to be enrolled for the next, and that many young men stood ready to fill vacancies.[2] The new members were obliged to pass their δοκιμασία before the Senate.[3]

The cavalryman furnished his own horse, and in time of peace kept it in his own stable, but both in peace and in war he received a fixed sum for its keeping. He also received from the state, on entrance into the corps, a sum of money (κατάστασις) for an outfit.[4]

The cavalry not only served in war but played an important part in the festal processions of the city. It was a matter of pride to appear there·with spirited and finely trained horses, with brilliant equipment, and with perfect training in maneuvers. The frieze of the Parthenon preserves in idealized form the beauty of such a troop of cavalry in the Panathenaic festival.

An enrolment which thus offered opportunity for display in time of peace, and a less dangerous and less irksome form of service in war, attracted the more ambitious and proud young men of the aristocracy. As the feeling against the radical democracy steadily strengthened during the Peloponnesian War it found strong sup-

political division was an inheritance from a very early time when probably the aristocracy were all ἱππεῖς. In the historic time membership in the *political* division was purely a matter of property rating.

[1] Arist. *Resp. Ath.* 49. 2. But see on § 13.

[2] See Xenophon, *Hipparchicus*, 1. 11 f.

[3] Arist. *l.c.* Lys. 14. 8, τοῦ νόμου κελεύοντος ἐάν τις ἀδοκίμαστος ἱππεύῃ, ἄτιμον εἶναι. Cp. 16. 13.

[4] What the outfit included we learn from Xenophon's list in his pamphlet, *De Re Equestri*, 12. 1–12.

port in this aristocratic corps, and when at last the Thirty gained control of the city they depended largely for their military strength upon this well trained and equipped body of cavalry, coöperating with the Spartan garrison.   When the returning exiles seized Phyle the cavalry went out with the garrison to attack them,[1] and two squadrons of the cavalry were left to guard the frontier.[2] At a later date the cavalry were drawn up outside the gate at Eleusis as the citizens were treacherously led out and seized, and they took the captives to Athens to their death.[3]   Later they took part in the unsuccessful assault on Munychia.[4]   When the Thirty were replaced by the Ten, the cavalry still supported the city party, guarding the circuit of the walls by night, and skirmishing against the Piraeus troops by day.[5]   Finally they were with the Spartans under Pausanias in their attack on the exiles at the Piraeus.[6]   From first to last they fought stubbornly to maintain the power of the oligarchy, and were the objects of the bitter hatred of the exiles.[7]

The cavalry were, of course, included in the amnesty, but we learn from our speech (§ 6) that a vote was passed requiring every cavalryman to pay back into the treasury the sum which he had received for his outfit (κατάστασις).   The full purpose of this action is not clear.   The motive may have been to raise

---

[1] Xen. *Hell.* 2. 4. 2.   [2] *Ibid.* 2. 4. 4.   [3] *Ibid.* 2. 4. 8.
[4] *Ibid.* 2. 4. 10.   [5] *Ibid.* 2. 4. 24, 26.   [6] *Ibid.* 2. 4. 31.

[7] Xenophon was probably a member of the cavalry during this whole period. The fact of the suspicion under which he was sure to stand with the democracy in consequence of this service may well have been a strong motive in determining him to join his friend Proxenus in the expedition with Cyrus. He gives a striking testimony to the hatred of the democracy toward the cavalry corps in his statement that when, four years after the Return, the Spartans called upon Athens to furnish cavalry to help in the campaign in Asia Minor, the Athenians sent them three hundred of those who had served as cavalrymen under the Thirty, νομίζοντες κέρδος τῷ δήμῳ, εἰ ἀποδημοῖεν καὶ ἐναπόλοιντο *thinking it a good thing for the Demos if they should go abroad and die there* (*Hell.* 3. 1. 4), a statement which betrays Xenophon's own feeling toward the people.

money for the empty treasury by putting this indirect tax upon the rich aristocrats, without a technical violation of the terms of the amnesty ; but some consider this only a part of a wider decree dissolving the whole corps.[1]

As public life settled back into the old channels after the Return, individuals from among these former cavalrymen of the Thirty began to come forward in political life and even to offer themselves as candidates for office. It must have seemed to many of the returned exiles that the men who had so actively supported the lost cause ought to be more than content with permission to live retired lives as private citizens, and that for them to come forward now, seeking public office or any political influence whatever, was the height of presumption, and more than was ever intended, morally, at least, by the amnesty.[2]

Such, then, was the state of feeling when Mantitheus presented himself for the δοκιμασία.

The senatorship was open to all citizens who had reached the age of thirty years. Fifty seats belonged to each of the ten phylae, and were distributed among the several demes according to their population. The lot was drawn in early spring among the members of the deme who offered themselves as candidates. The year of service for the new Senate began on the 14th of Scirophorion (two weeks before the close of the civil year, July–August).

The list of senators for the new year having been thus drawn up, the outgoing Senate passed upon the qualifications of each candidate. This scrutiny (δοκιμασία) did not cover questions as to technical knowledge of the duties to be performed, but only questions of good character and citizenship. Aristotle gives the following description of the examination of candidates for the

---

[1] We find the statement in Harpocration (*s.v.* κατάστασις) that the κατάστασις was always paid back to the treasury when a cavalryman retired from service. If this is true, the decree that all now repay their κατάστασις is doubtless a part of a decree dissolving the force ; but the statement in Harpocration may be based only on a misunderstanding of the present case.

[2] For Lysias's position on this question, see Introd. pp. 40–42.

archonship, which probably did not differ materially from the examination for the senatorship : "When they are examined, they are asked, first, ' Who is your father, and of what deme?   Who is your father's·father?   Who is your mother?   Who is your mother's father, and of what deme?'   Then the candidate is asked whether he has an ancestral Apollo and a household Zeus, and where their sanctuaries are ; next, if he possesses a family tomb, and where ; then, if he treats his parents well, and pays his taxes, and has served on the required military expeditions.[1]   When the examiner has put these questions, he proceeds, ' Call the witnesses to these facts ' ; and when the candidate has produced his witnesses, he next asks, ' Does any one wish to make any accusation against this man?'" (*Resp. Ath.*, ch. 55, Kenyon's trans.).

We conclude, then, that when at the hearing before the Senate the presiding officer asked the final question, some member of the outgoing Senate, or some private citizen, presented the formal objection that Mantitheus had served in the cavalry under the Thirty.   The candidate must now have been given time to prepare a defense, so that we must assume that the charge was laid over for a later meeting of the Senate.   Mantitheus then went to Lysias, who had in the past ten years won a reputation as a writer of court speeches, and employed him to compose a speech.

The lawyer could not appear in the Senate to plead for his client, but the young man was obliged, according to the custom both of court and Senate, to deliver his own plea.

The problem for Lysias was, then, to learn whether the charge was true, and if true whether it formed a valid ground for his client's exclusion, and to determine what pleas could be presented to offset the charge.   Moreover, Lysias had to bear in mind the fact that the speech was to be spoken by the young man himself. The more the writer could adapt the tone of the speech and the

[1] The question as to taxes would hardly be asked of candidates for a senatorship, for this was open to men of the lowest property class, who were not subject to taxation.

nature of the plea to the personality of his client, the less artificial would the plea appear, and the more effective would it be. He had, in short, to write the speech which the young man would himself have written if he had possessed Lysias's knowledge of law and politics, and Lysias's training in argumentation.

As the advocate went over the facts with his client, it appeared that the complainants did not attempt to cite any instance when Mantitheus had served with the cavalry, but had based their whole attack upon the fact that his name was found in the official list. The first business of the defense was, therefore, to throw discredit on this list. But if that should not convince the Senate, it remained still to show that service in the cavalry of the Thirty had not been interpreted as excluding a man from holding office under the restored democracy, if he was otherwise uncompromised. So much the lawyer could furnish for the defense. But Lysias knew the Athenian audience too well to suppose that plausible proof or valid proof would carry the case. He knew that their verdict would be determined more by their feelings than their judgment, and as he talked with his young client he saw that the man's own personality would be his best defense ; that after the briefest argument on the technical charge the best possible course would be to let the young man talk in the most frank way of his own attitude and conduct. For he was a type of the best citizen, frank, enthusiastic, eager to serve the state, personally brave in danger, " the first to take the field and the last to return " ; he had shown his devotion to the restored democracy by the most honorable military service ; he had only to tell his story to the jury as he told it to Lysias to win their confidence. And so Lysias let him tell his story. Few speech writers would have been able to compose a speech which would let the man speak in his own hearty, unconscious way, and yet would present each fact in the most telling form. " Youth is confident and talkative, it lays stress upon details, it overestimates the importance of what it has itself experienced and accomplished. In Mantitheus these qualities seem to have been especially marked. In his interviews with his lawyer they would not have failed to manifest themselves."[1] Lysias's mastery of simple, clear language, of brief expression, of vivid narration, was precisely what was needed in preparing a speech which should seem the natural expression of his client's own qualities.[2]

The date of the speech is between 394 and 389 B.C. It cannot have been written before 394, for § 15 speaks of events of that year. It can hardly have been written after 388, because in that year Thrasybulus died, while the sportive way in which he is spoken of in § 15, and the use of the perfect tense in ὠνειδικότος in that passage, almost compel the inference that he was living when the speech was delivered. The reference (§ 18) to other military services than those of § 15 makes it likely that the speech falls a considerable time after 394. It was certainly after the tide of popular feeling had begun to turn from Thrasybulus (see on § 15).

OUTLINE

I. Προοίμιον, *Exordium* (with first Πρόθεσις), §§ 1–3.

I am confident in my innocence (§§ 1–2); I shall prove that I have shown more than passive loyalty to the Democracy; but first I shall prove that I did not serve in the cavalry of the Thirty (Πρόθεσις), (§ 3).

II. Πίστεις, *Argumentatio*, §§ 4–8.

Answer to the immediate charge.

A. Proof that I could not have been in the cavalry, §§ 4–5.

B. Invalidation of the official cavalry roll.

1. It has been found unreliable in other cases, § 6.

2. My name is not in the reliable roll of the phylarchs, §§ 6–7.

C. Even had I served, precedent is in favor of my admission to office, § 8.

---

[1] Bruns, *Literarisches Porträt*, p. 448.

[2] In this speech Lysias was evidently concerned only for securing a verdict for his client. The argument is entirely personal. The great issues involved in the question of the interpretation of the amnesty are not discussed.

III. Second Πρόθεσις, *Propositio*, § 9.

A plea in δοκιμασία should include review of the whole life : such a review I will give.

IV. Διήγησις, *Narratio*, §§ 10–18.

A. My family relations, § 10.

B. My social relations, §§ 11–12.

C. My military record :

1. The expedition to Haliartus, §§ 13–14.

2. The expedition to Corinth, §§ 15–17.

3. Other military service, § 18.

V. Λύσις, *Refutatio*, §§ 18–21.

A. Answer to prejudice arising from my personal appearance and bearing, §§ 18–19.

B. Answer to the charge of forwardness in taking part in public life, §§ 20–21.

COMMENTS ON ARGUMENT AND STYLE

I. Προοίμιον, *Exordium*, §§ 1–3.

The opening words strike the note of confidence that is to pervade the speech.

An important point in any good proem is its power to catch the attention of the hearer ; to this end a bright paradox is an excellent means. So the attention of any senator who was expecting to hear the usual complaint against the malice of the prosecution is pleasantly quickened by the opening remark that the speaker is almost grateful to them.

The formal scheme of the rhetoricians for the framework of a speech prescribed, as the second or third division, a πρόθεσις (*propositio*), a formal statement of what the speaker proposes to prove. But here Lysias weaves his πρόθεσις into the proem so naturally and closely that we can hardly draw the line between them ; § 3 begins as part of the proem, but its last sentence is in the full form of πρόθεσις.

The proem is free from rhetorical embellishment. The language is dignified and forcible, but entirely natural.

II. Πίστεις, *Argumentatio*, §§ 4–8.

A. §§ 4–5. The argument that the Thirty would not have received so late a comer into their service is weak. The time when the exiles were moving down upon the Piraeus was just the time when the Thirty were glad of help. The fact that Mantitheus chose this time to return to the city, and that he was admitted by the administration, looks as though he was avowedly on their side. From what we see later of the enthusiastic eagerness of the young man to be at the front in time of danger, it is hard to believe that, returning to Athens as the crisis was approaching, he took sides with neither party.

B. §§ 6–7. The argument from the double lists is stronger, but it is impossible to say how strong. If the testimony presented at the close of § 8 included testimony from the phylarchs that his name was not on their lists, it would be almost convincing. But it is not quite certain that the absence of the name from the list of those who received the cavalry outfit proves that he was not in the service during the last weeks. May not some have furnished their own outfit in those times of great financial need on the part of the administration, and would this not be particularly likely in the case of a late comer and well-to-do volunteer like Mantitheus? The most surprising thing is that neither the prosecution nor the defense seems to have produced the testimony of the officers under whom Mantitheus would have served.

C. § 8. The third argument would be conclusive if we could count upon consistent action by the Athenian courts or Senate. The amnesty, if followed in good faith, ought to have precluded even the raising of the question of excluding a former member of the cavalry from the Senate. But the fact that Lysias does not dare let the case rest upon this one argument and that he passes over it quickly, shows how unreliable he felt the temper of the people to be.

The language is as simple and direct as that of the proem. There is nothing to suggest to the hearer that Mantitheus is speaking words other than his own.

III. Second Πρόθεσις, *Propositio*, § 9.

Lysias now prepares the way for his main defense, the presentation of the young man in his own frank, enthusiastic personality.

IV. Διήγησις, *Narratio*, §§ 10–18.

For this broader phase of the defense Lysias turns to narrative. There are three ways of using narrative as a part of a plea : the speaker may give his full narrative and then argue the conclusions to be drawn from it ;[1] or he may narrate step by step, and at each step argue as to the conclusion to be drawn from a particular incident ;[2] or he may give the full narrative without argument or comment, trusting to the power of the narrative itself to make its own argument. This last and most artistic form Lysias chooses for Mantitheus, making only the slightest comment on the bearing of the several statements. As Mantitheus proceeds with his story the senators see in him the generous brother, the temperate and orderly young man in a social circle inclined to intemperance and folly, the eager young soldier, seeking out the post of danger, and generous in sharing his means with his poorer comrades. If a little too eager in putting himself forward, and a little too confident in telling of his own achievements, yet he has only the amiable faults of youth. It needed no argument to convince the hearers that such a man as that, and with such a record of chivalrous service to the restored democracy, was not a dangerous man to sit in their Senate. Lysias leaves the simple, clear account to make its own impression.

V. Λύσις, *Refutatio*, §§ 18–21.

In a strict sense all that a defendant says in his argument is in the nature of a " refutation " of the charges ; but the term λύσις

[1] So in Lys. XII, the narrative of the abuse of Lysias and his family.
[2] So in Lys. XII, the discussion of the career of Theramenes (see p. 56).

applies also to the answer to attacks of the other side subordinate to the main attack. Lysias knows that two such minor attacks are likely to be .made ; one, that the defendant belongs to the long-haired, swaggering Laconizers, the other that he is a forward and conceited aspirant for political preferment. Lightly and modestly Mantitheus answers both, without attempting to deny that he has given some occasion for such an impression. Then, with a word of compliment to the senators, quite unexpectedly, without summing up or final plea or peroration of any kind, he steps down.

This omission of the usual appeal to the feelings of the hearers is quite in keeping with the confident tone of the whole speech. The omission of the peroration is also wise from the rhetorical point of view. Throughout the speech Lysias has repressed everything that could suggest artificial or studied speech ; it is in keeping with this that he omits that part of the plea in which rhetorical art was usually most displayed.

The language of sections IV and V preserves the simplicity of the earlier sections. We notice only a tendency to use larger and more rounded sentences in the main narrative, §§ 13–17, giving a compactness and force that are less often found in narrative style.[1] There is also a considerable use of antithetic cola [2] in this part of the plea, but hardly more than is natural in any earnest speech.

No speech of Lysias offered a better opportunity for his peculiar skill in fitting the speech to the man ($\dot{\eta}\theta o\pi o\iota\acute{\iota}a$) ;[3] having decided to let the case depend chiefly on the impression which Mantitheus's personality ($\mathring{\eta}\theta o\varsigma$) would make upon the hearers, he developed every thought and expression which would reveal this, and suppressed every other.

It is noticeable that there is no counter-attack on the prosecution, no denunciation of those who, according to his claim, must

---

[1] On this type of sentence structure see App. § 51.

[2] For the term 'colon' see App. § 44.

[3] On the meaning of $\dot{\eta}\theta o\pi o\iota\acute{\iota}a$ see Introd. p. 28.

have maliciously inserted his name in the list of the cavalry. Here, too, he is a gentleman and speaks like one. He says plainly that the motive in this complaint is personal injury to himself (§ 1), and speaks of the complainants as enemies of his (τῶν ἐχθρῶν, § 3), but that is all. Lysias always refrains from abuse and scurrilous language, but he knows how, on occasion, to attack his opponent (cp. p. 31) ; in this speech he refrains from it altogether.

XVI

ΕΝ ΒΟΥΛΗΙ
ΜΑΝΤΙΘΕΩΙ ΔΟΚΙΜΑΖΟΜΕΝΩΙ ΑΠΟΛΟΓΙΑ

1 Εἰ μὴ συνῄδη, ὦ βουλή, τοῖς κατηγόροις βουλομένοις
ἐκ παντὸς τρόπου κακῶς ἐμὲ ποιεῖν, πολλὴν ἂν αὐτοῖς
χάριν εἶχον ταύτης τῆς κατηγορίας· ἡγοῦμαι γὰρ τοῖς
ἀδίκως διαβεβλημένοις τούτους εἶναι μεγίστων ἀγαθῶν
5 αἰτίους, οἵτινες ἂν αὐτοὺς ἀναγκάζωσιν εἰς ἔλεγχον
2 τῶν αὐτοῖς βεβιωμένων καταστῆναι. ἐγὼ γὰρ οὕτω
σφόδρα ἐμαυτῷ πιστεύω, ὥστ᾽ ἐλπίζω καὶ εἴ τις πρός
με τυγχάνει ἀηδῶς διακείμενος, ἐπειδὰν ἐμοῦ λέγοντος
ἀκούσῃ περὶ τῶν πεπραγμένων, μεταμελήσειν αὐτῷ
10 καὶ πολὺ βελτίω με εἰς τὸν λοιπὸν χρόνον ἡγήσεσθαι.
3 ἀξιῶ δέ, ὦ βουλή, ἐὰν μὲν τοῦτο μόνον ὑμῖν ἐπιδείξω,

---

1. **συνῄδη**: the older Attic form
is *ᾔδη*, contracted from *ᾔδεα* (used
by Homer). The later *ᾔδειν* became the usual form in the fourth
century B.C. — **τοῖς κατηγόροις βουλομένοις**: as *οἶδα* takes the accusa-
tive participial construction in
indirect discourse, so *σύνοιδα* takes
the dative. — **οἵτινες** : see on 12.
40. — **εἰς ἔλεγχον κτλ.** : *to present
themselves for an investigation of
their life.* — **τῶν βεβιωμένων**: cp.

Dem. 18. 265 ἐξέτασον τοίνυν παρ᾽
ἄλληλα τὰ σοὶ κἀμοὶ βεβιωμένα
*examine side by side your life and
mine.*

2. **καὶ εἰ**: *even if.* So 19. 3,
19. 37, 19. 59, 34. 8. *καὶ εἰ* represents a statement as an extreme
supposition, or as the utmost that
can be assumed, or as improbable.
But *εἰ καί* represents the statement as something that, while not
disputed, is of little importance

ὡς εὔνους εἰμὶ τοῖς καθεστηκόσι πράγμασι καὶ ὡς
ἠνάγκασμαι τῶν αὐτῶν κινδύνων μετέχειν ὑμῖν, μηδέν
πώ μοι πλέον εἶναι· ἐὰν δὲ φαίνωμαι καὶ περὶ τὰ
15 ἄλλα μετρίως βεβιωκὼς καὶ πολὺ παρὰ τὴν δόξαν καὶ
παρὰ τοὺς λόγους τοὺς τῶν ἐχθρῶν, δέομαι ὑμῶν ἐμὲ
μὲν δοκιμάζειν, τούτους δὲ ἡγεῖσθαι χείρους εἶναι.

for the matter at issue, or as something that is waived aside ; so in
19. 1, 32. 11.

3. τοῖς καθεστηκόσι πράγμασι :
to the existing government, viz.
the democracy. τὰ πράγματα is
often used of *the government,* as
here, and in 12. 65, 25. 3, 25. 8,
25. 10, 25. 12. But also in the
sense of *administration of public
affairs, political control* ; so in
12. 93, 25. 14, 25. 18, 25. 23.—
ἠνάγκασμαι : see on εἰργασμένοι
εἰσίν 12. 22. — **τῶν αὐτῶν κινδύνων :**
not the dangers of the exile under
the Thirty, to which citizens so
proudly referred in these times, but
dangers in the Corinthian War,
where Mantitheus has served the
restored democracy and thereby
shown his loyalty to it. — **μηδέν
κτλ.** : *not yet do I claim any advantage for myself,* viz. until I
have shown more than this, I
make no plea for special consideration from you. — **πλέον :** *more*
than if I did not have such conduct to my credit. — **καὶ περὶ τὰ
ἄλλα :** *in all other relations also.*
— **μετρίως βεβιωκώς :** an expression

which comes from the heart of
Greek ideals of life. The Greek,
and especially the Athenian, demanded avoidance of extremes as
a fundamental principle in ethics,
precisely as in literature and art.
Asceticism was as far from the
ideal as drunkenness, officious-
ness as little worthy of praise as
indifference. The words μετρίως
βεβιωκώς express this ideal life
both in private and public relations. μηδὲν ἄγαν is the ancient
proverbial expression of the same
standard, σωφροσύνη its abstract
name. In Athenian public life the
doctrine of democratic equality
strengthened this principle. Especially was this quality demanded
of the rich or gifted man, who
could easily show insolence toward
common men. Cp. Taylor, *Ancient
Ideals,* I. 202 ff. — **δέομαι :** he had
said, " *I do not claim* " ; by a
neat turn he now uses the modest
" *I beg* " (δέομαι). — **δοκιμάζειν :**
in the technical sense ; see In-
trod. p. 133. — **χείρους :** *i.e.* to hold
them in less esteem than in the
past. So the plaintiff in the

πρῶτον δὲ ἀποδείξω ὡς οὐχ ἵππευον ἐπὶ τῶν τριάκοντα,
19 οὐδὲ μετέσχον τῆς τότε πολιτείας.

4 Ἡμᾶς γὰρ ὁ πατὴρ πρὸ τῆς ἐν Ἑλλησπόντῳ συμφορᾶς ὡς Σάτυρον τὸν ἐν τῷ Πόντῳ διαιτησομένους
ἐξέπεμψε, καὶ οὔτε τῶν τειχῶν καθαιρουμένων ἐπεδημοῦμεν οὔτε μεθισταμένης τῆς πολιτείας, ἀλλ᾽ ἦλθο-

speech against Diogiton tells
the jury, in case he shall fail to
prove his charges, to hold him
and his associates in less esteem
for all future time (ἡμᾶς δὲ εἰς τὸν
λοιπὸν χρόνον ἡγεῖσθαι χείρους
εἶναι 32. 3). — ἐπί: force, see on
12. 17. — μετέσχον : ingressive
aorist, *received a share*. HA.
841 ; G. 1260; B. 529; Gl. 464;
GMT. 55 ; GS. 239. Cp. μετέσχε
12. 66, μετέσχον 25. 18, γνόντες
12. 75, ἀθυμῆσαι 24. 7, ὠργίσθημεν 32. 21.

4. γάρ: explicative γάρ, see
on 19. 12. — τῆς συμφορᾶς : the
battle of Aegospotami. Cp.
on 12. 43. — ὡς : Lysias uses ὡς
oftener than any other word for
" to " with personal words after
verbs of motion. (He always uses
it when the idea of going to one's
house or shop is clearly added to
that of going to the man.) Cp.
19. 22, 19. 23, 24. 19, 24. 20.
παρά is used in this way only in
1. 15, 1. 35, 3. 8. πρός only in
32. 10 (twice), 32. 14, 1. 16, 1. 19,
4. 7, 7. 2, Fr. 1. 1. — Σάτυρον :
In a speech of Isocrates, de-

livered about this time, we read
(17. 57) that Satyrus, and his
father before him, had always
given trade preference to the Athenians, that they had furnished cargoes of grain for Athenian ships
when others had to go away empty,
and that as judges in civil suits
they had given Athenian litigants
more than justice. Cp. Hicks and
Hill, *Greek Historical Inscriptions*, 269 ff. — Πόντῳ : otherwise
called τὸ κοινὸν τῶν Βοσπορανῶν,
a Greek colony in the Taurian
Chersonese (Crimea). Its chief
city was Panticapeum (modern
Kertch). It stood in close trade
relations with Athens, furnishing
cargoes of grain and salt fish,
and of the hides and other raw
products of the interior. — καθαιρουμένων : the demolition of the
walls, begun in a spectacular way
by Lysander (Xen. *Hell*. 2. 2. 23),
but left to the Athenians themselves to complete, continued for
some time, being probably still un-
finished when Lysander returned
to Athens from Samos to set up
the oligarchy (cp. on 12. 74). —

24 μὲν πρὶν τοὺς ἀπὸ Φυλῆς εἰς τὸν Πειραιᾶ κατελθεῖν
5 πρότερον πένθ' ἡμέραις. καίτοι οὔτε ἡμᾶς εἰκὸς ἦν
εἰς τοιοῦτον καιρὸν ἀφιγμένους ἐπιθυμεῖν μετέχειν τῶν
ἀλλοτρίων κινδύνων, οὔτ' ἐκεῖνοι φαίνονται τοιαύτην
γνώμην ἔχοντες ὥστε καὶ τοῖς ἀποδημοῦσι καὶ μηδὲν
ἐξαμαρτάνουσι μεταδιδόναι τῆς πολιτείας, ἀλλὰ μᾶλ-
30 λον ἠτίμαζον καὶ τοὺς συγκαταλύσαντας τὸν δῆμον.
6 Ἔπειτα δὲ ἐκ μὲν τοῦ σανιδίου τοὺς ἱππεύσαντας
σκοπεῖν εὔηθές ἐστιν· ἐν τούτῳ γὰρ πολλοὶ μὲν τῶν

κατελθεῖν: the compound is doubly fitting as applied to the 'coming down' from their hill fort, Phyle (see on 12. 52), and the 'coming back' from exile, for which it is the regular expression (cp. § 6; so 25. 29 φεύγοντες μὲν . . . κατελθόντες δέ). — **πένθ' ἡμέραις**: in emphatic position and drawing πρότερον with it from its natural position before πρίν.

5. εἰκός: for the prominence of the argument from 'probability' (εἰκός) in the teaching of the current rhetoric, see Introd. p. 14. — **εἰς**: this is the only place where Lysias uses εἰς καιρόν for the ordinary ἐν καιρῷ (cp. 30. 14 ἐν τοιούτῳ καιρῷ); the accus. with εἰς represents the act as breaking into the time. — **μετέχειν**: compare the tense with that of μετέσχον § 3. — **ἔχοντες**: impf. with reference to φαίνονται; so ἀποδημοῦσι and ἐξαμαρτάνουσι impf. with reference to μεταδιδόναι. See on

ἀνιωμένου 12. 32. — **ἠτίμαζον**: i.e. visited them with ἀτιμία; impf. referring to the general policy of the ruling faction of the Thirty.

6. σανιδίου: a wooden tablet with whitened surface, used for public documents which were not of sufficient importance to be inscribed on stone. The prosecution had probably obtained from the official archives the list of cavalrymen called out for service under the Thirty. Some men whose names were in such a list may have been out of the city, others excused from serving (cp. Arist. *Resp. Ath.* 49. 2), and under the great pressure of the final conflict, others, not originally drawn for the service, are likely to have been accepted. We need not assume any tampering with the list to account for the statement that it was not reliable. — **εὔηθες**: meaning, cp. on 12. 87.

ὁμολογούντων ἱππεύειν οὐκ ἔνεισιν, ἔνιοι δὲ τῶν ἀποδημούντων ἐγγεγραμμένοι εἰσίν. ἐκεῖνος δ' ἐστὶν
35 ἔλεγχος μέγιστος· ἐπειδὴ γὰρ κατήλθετε, ἐψηφίσασθε τοὺς φυλάρχους ἀπενεγκεῖν τοὺς ἱππεύσαντας,
7 ἵνα τὰς καταστάσεις ἀναπράξητε παρ' αὐτῶν. ἐμὲ
τοίνυν οὐδεὶς ἂν ἀποδείξειεν οὔτ' ἀπενεχθέντα ὑπὸ τῶν

— ἱππεύειν, ἀποδημούντων : tense,
see on ἀνιωμένου 12. 32. — ἐκεῖνος
. . . μέγιστος : *but the greatest
proof lies in another fact* (not
in this (τοῦτο) worthless list).
Although the pronoun refers to
what immediately follows and to
what is nearest in thought, the
fact of its sharp contrast brings in
ἐκεῖνος in place of ὅδε. For gender see on ταύτην 12. 37. — φυλάρχους : one phylarch was elected
annually from each of the ten
phylae as commander of its cavalry contingent. The whole force
was under the command of two
hipparchs. The phylarchs here
referred to are the new board,
elected after the return of the exiles. — ἀπενεγκεῖν τοὺς ἱππεύσαντας : *make a return of the names
of those who joined the cavalry*
(under the Thirty). — καταστάσεις : see Introd. p. 131. — ἀναπράξητε : mood, HA. 881 a ; G.
1369; B. 590, 674; Gl. 642 a.
For the usage of Lysias and others
in the choice between subj. and
opt. in final clauses after a secondary tense, see GMT. 320 n. 1.

7. τοίνυν : this particle is a
compound of τοί (locative of
the demonstrative τό), and νῦν
in its weakened form νύν, as a
particle of transition. The τοί
was a weaker equivalent of the
Homeric τῷ = *in that case, therefore.* τοίνυν thus receives illative
force (= *therefore*) from its first
member, and transitional force
from its second. In its common
use sometimes one prevails, sometimes the other, but for the strictly
illative use Lysias commonly prefers οὖν. His uses of τοίνυν are
these : (A) As an illative particle
= οὖν *therefore*, 12. 50, 12. 84,
19. 38, 19. 51, 24. 3, 24. 7, 24. 26,
25. 20, 25. 23. (B) As a weak
illative, marking the close of an
argument, or in turning to testimony, or in commenting on it,
12. 37, 12. 46, 12. 79, 16. 9, 19. 23,
and often. (C) With slight illative
force, after the statement of a
general fact or principle, τοίνυν
introduces the individual instance
to which the principle is applied,
19. 57, 19. 60, 25. 11, 25. 12.
(D) As a mere particle of transi-

φυλάρχων οὔτε παραδοθέντα τοῖς συνδίκοις ὡς κατά-
40 στασιν παραλαβόντα. καίτοι πᾶσι ῥᾴδιον τοῦτο
γνῶναι, ὅτι ἀναγκαῖον ἦν τοῖς φυλάρχοις, εἰ μὴ ἀποδείξειαν τοὺς ἔχοντας τὰς καταστάσεις, αὐτοῖς ζημιοῦ-
σθαι. ὥστε πολὺ ἂν δικαιότερον ἐκείνοις τοῖς γράμμασιν ἢ τούτοις πιστεύοιτε· ἐκ μὲν γὰρ τούτων ῥᾴδιον
45 ἦν ἐξαλειφθῆναι τῷ βουλομένῳ, ἐν ἐκείνοις δὲ τοὺς

tion (= μὲν οὖν) marking the next
step in the argument, or the next
detail in the narrative = *again*,
further, now; so in our passage,
and in 12. 43, 12. 55, 16. 12,
16. 14, 16. 15, 16. 18, 19. 15,
19. 59, 25. 15, and very often.
— παραδοθέντα : by the Senate. —
τοῖς συνδίκοις: after the restoration of the democracy it was
found that there were many claims
of individuals for the restoration
of property that had been seized
by the oligarchy in the name of
the state, and many others for the
recovery of state property that had
come into the possession of individuals. To investigate these
claims, and to preside in civil suits
arising from them, special commissioners, called σύνδικοι, were
appointed. The recovery of state
funds paid to the cavalry properly
fell to them. — ἀναγκαῖον : *inevitable.* — ἀποδείξειαν: opt. because it
is the indir. expression of the past
thought in the minds of the phylarchs (ἐὰν μὴ ἀποδείξωμεν). HA.

937 ; G. 1502. 2 ; B. 677 ; GMT.
696. — ἐκείνοις τοῖς γράμμασιν : the
lists reported by the phylarchs.
— τούτοις : the lists presented in
court from the archives (either the
originals or certified copies). The
argument is, 'The absence of my
name from the phylarchs' lists is
conclusive, for a name could not
fail there, as it might so easily in
the complainants' list.' The usual
explanation of the possibility of
erasure from the state list is that
it was kept posted in a public
place. But if erasure had been
so easy, few names would have
remained on the bulletin boards
after the Return. The possibility
of erasure lay in the possibility
of securing the connivance of
the keepers of the records. —
ἐν ἐκείνοις δέ: the placing of δέ
after ἐκείνοις (cp. ἐκ μέν just
before) throws emphasis on
ἐκείνοις. So in § 10 ; 24. 4, 25.
22. For similar displacement
of μέν see on 12. 15. — τοὺς
ἱππεύσαντας : cp. the construc-

ἱππεύσαντας ἀναγκαῖον ἦν ὑπὸ τῶν φυλάρχων ἀπε-
8 νεχθῆναι. Ἔτι δέ, ὦ βουλή, εἴπερ ἵππευσα, οὐκ ἂν
ἦ ἔξαρνος ὡς δεινόν τι πεποιηκώς, ἀλλ᾽ ἠξίουν, ἀπο-
δείξας ὡς οὐδεὶς ὑπ᾽ ἐμοῦ τῶν πολιτῶν κακῶς πέπονθε,
50 δοκιμάζεσθαι. ὁρῶ δὲ καὶ ὑμᾶς ταύτῃ τῇ γνώμῃ
χρωμένους, καὶ πολλοὺς μὲν τῶν τότε ἱππευσάντων
βουλεύοντας, πολλοὺς δ᾽ αὐτῶν στρατηγοὺς καὶ ἱππάρ-
χους κεχειροτονημένους. ὥστε μηδὲν δι᾽ ἄλλο με

tion with that of τοῖς φυλάρχοις
above.

8. ἔτι : *furthermore*, cp. ἔπειτα
§ 6. — εἴπερ : see on 12. 27. — ἄν :
with both ἦ and ἠξίουν. — ἦ : the
older Attic form is ἦ, contracted
from ἦα (used by Homer) ; the
later form ἦν was beginning to
appear in literature late in the
fifth century ; cp. ἤδη and ᾔδειν
(§ 1, N.). — ὡς . . . πεποιηκώς : with a participle ὡς has
"subjective" force. The idea expressed by the participle is represented as lying in the mind of
some person, as something which
appears to him to be true, or something which he assumes to be true.
It may or may not be true in fact,
and the writer may or may not
believe in it ; subjective ὡς does
not, like the English *as if*, imply
untruth. Cp. on 12. 13. So
12. 2, 16. 14, 22. 5, 24. 13,
25. 13. — πεποιηκώς, πέπονθε : perf.
because the question is as to
the speaker's credit or guilt. See

on εἰργασμένοι εἰσίν 12. 22. —
ἠξίουν : *I would claim as my right*.
Cp. ἀξιῶ § 3. — ὑπ᾽ ἐμοῦ : for position see on ἡμῖν 12. 33. — πολλούς,
πολλούς : on the ἐπαναφορά see
App. § 57. 5. — βουλεύοντας : in
the technical sense of membership in the βουλή. — κεχειροτονημένους : the Athenians did not
venture to make universal their
general principle of appointment
to office by lot. The lot applied
to officials whose work did not
absolutely demand political or
military experience or technical
knowledge. But they elected all
higher military officers, the chief
treasury officials, the officers who
superintended the training of the
cadets, and a few others whose
work needed special knowledge
or experience. — ὥστε μηδὲν . . .
ἡγεῖσθε : *so that you must not suppose*. ὥστε with the imperative
gives closer connection than the
illative οὖν. Cp. the imperative in
relative clauses, 12. 60 N. — μηδέν :

ἡγεῖσθε ταύτην ποιεῖσθαι τὴν ἀπολογίαν, ἢ ὅτι περι-
55 φανῶς ἐτόλμησάν μου καταψεύσασθαι. Ἀνάβηθι δέ
μοι καὶ μαρτύρησον.

ΜΑΡΤΥΡΙΑ

9 Περὶ μὲν τοίνυν αὐτῆς τῆς αἰτίας οὐκ οἶδ' ὅ τι δεῖ
πλείω λέγειν· δοκεῖ δέ μοι, ὦ βουλή, ἐν μὲν τοῖς
ἄλλοις ἀγῶσι περὶ αὐτῶν μόνων τῶν κατηγορημένων
60 προσήκειν ἀπολογεῖσθαι, ἐν δὲ ταῖς δοκιμασίαις δίκαιον εἶναι παντὸς τοῦ βίου λόγον διδόναι. δέομαι
οὖν ὑμῶν μετ' εὐνοίας ἀκροάσασθαί μου. ποιήσομαι
δὲ τὴν ἀπολογίαν ὡς ἂν δύνωμαι διὰ βραχυτάτων.

10 Ἐγὼ γὰρ πρῶτον μὲν οὐσίας μοι οὐ πολλῆς κατα-
65 λειφθείσης διὰ τὰς συμφορὰς καὶ τὰς τοῦ πατρὸς καὶ
τὰς τῆς πόλεως, δύο μὲν ἀδελφὰς ἐξέδωκα ἐπιδοὺς
τριάκοντα μνᾶς ἑκατέρᾳ, πρὸς τὸν ἀδελφὸν δ' οὕτως
ἐνειμάμην ὥστ' ἐκεῖνον πλέον ὁμολογεῖν ἔχειν ἐμοῦ
τῶν πατρῴων, καὶ πρὸς τοὺς ἄλλους ἅπαντας οὕτως

the negative would be οὐδέν (infin.
in ind. disc.) but for the effect of
the imperative.

9. τοίνυν: force, see on § 7 (B).
— παντὸς τοῦ βίου: on this plea
see Introd. p. 135. — διὰ βραχυτάτων: see on δι' ἐλαχίστων
12. 3.

10. γάρ: here explicative γάρ
introduces a new point in the discussion, without any preceding
general statement; see on 19. 12.
— ἐξέδωκα: if a father left both
sons and daughters, the sons only

inherited the property, but with it
they inherited the father's obligation for the support of the daughters and for proper dowry for their
marriage. — τριάκοντα μνᾶς: in
court speeches we have numerous
references to dowries; from these it
appears that thirty minae was an
average sum in a family of moderate means. The rich Diogiton
provided that his widow should
have twice this amount if she
married again (32. 6). — ἀδελφὸν
δέ: for position of δέ see on § 7.

70 βεβίωκα ὥστε μηδεπώποτέ μοι μηδὲ πρὸς ἕνα μηδὲν
11 ἔγκλημα γενέσθαι. καὶ τὰ μὲν ἴδια οὕτως διῴκηκα·
περὶ δὲ τῶν κοινῶν μοι μέγιστον ἡγοῦμαι τεκμήριον
εἶναι τῆς ἐμῆς ἐπιεικείας, ὅτι τῶν νεωτέρων ὅσοι περὶ
κύβους ἢ πότους ἢ τὰς τοιαύτας ἀκολασίας τυγχά-

— μηδεπώποτε ... μηδὲ ... μηδέν:
HA. 1030; G. 1619; B. 433; Gl.
487. The Greek, unlike the English, recognized the value of the
instinctive tendency to pile up
negatives for emphatic denial, and
made the usage normal, under restrictions which avoided confusion.
Morgan's translation gives an excellent equivalent under the limitations of English usage: "There
has never been any ground of complaint at all against me on the
part of a single solitary man."
— μηδὲ πρὸς ἕνα: stronger than
μηδένα by bringing ἕνα into sharp
relief. πρὸς ἕνα is not strictly
equal to a prep. with the genitive,
complaint coming *from* one, but
has originally the meaning *in
my relation toward* as in πρὸς
τὸν ἀδελφόν and πρὸς τοὺς ἄλλους
just above. This peculiar use
of πρός arises from the fact
that with words of friendship,
agreement, hostility, complaint,
and the like, we may think
of the friendship, hostility, *etc.*,
as coming to us in our *relation
toward a person* (πρός τινα), as
well as coming to us *from a per-*

son (παρά τινος). For other examples see 32. 2; 10. 23 τίνος
ὄντος ἐμοὶ πρὸς ὑμᾶς ἐγκλήματος
*on the ground of what complaint
from you against me?* So Thuc.
5. 105. 1 πρὸς τὸ θεῖον εὐμενείας
favor from heaven; Isoc. 7. 8
τῆς ἔχθρας τῆς πρὸς βασιλέα *the
hostility of the king*; Dem. 18. 36
τὴν μὲν ἀπέχθειαν τὴν πρὸς Θη-
βαίους καὶ Θετταλοὺς τῇ πόλει
γενέσθαι *the hatred of the Thebans
and Thessalians came to the city.*
11. ἴδια ... κοινῶν: under
κοινῶν Mantitheus includes all
conduct that touches the public,
not merely his political relations.
— κύβους: gambling with dice was
common. The son of Alcibiades
was alleged to have lost his property at dice (κατακυβεύσας τὰ
ὄντα 14. 27). The aged Isocrates
includes it in his list of the em-
ployments of the young men of
the times as contrasted with the
earnest pursuits of the youths
of Marathonian Athens: *The
young men did not waste their
time in the gambling halls, nor
among the flute girls, nor in company of the sort in which they*

75 νουσι τὰς διατριβὰς ποιούμενοι, πάντας αὐτοὺς ὄψεσθέ
μοι διαφόρους ὄντας, καὶ πλεῖστα τούτους περὶ ἐμοῦ
λογοποιοῦντας καὶ ψευδομένους. καίτοι δῆλον ὅτι, εἰ
τῶν αὐτῶν ἐπεθυμοῦμεν, οὐκ ἂν τοιαύτην γνώμην εἶχον
12 περὶ ἐμοῦ. ἔτι δ᾽, ὦ βουλή, οὐδεὶς ἂν ἀποδεῖξαι περὶ
80 ἐμοῦ δύναιτο οὔτε δίκην αἰσχρὰν οὔτε γραφὴν οὔτε
εἰσαγγελίαν γεγενημένην· καίτοι ἑτέρους ὁρᾶτε πολλάκις εἰς τοιούτους ἀγῶνας καθεστηκότας. πρὸς τοίνυν
τὰς στρατείας καὶ τοὺς κινδύνους τοὺς πρὸς τοὺς πολε-
13 μίους σκέψασθε οἷον ἐμαυτὸν παρέχω τῇ πόλει. πρῶ-
85 τον μὲν γάρ, ὅτε τὴν συμμαχίαν ἐποιήσασθε πρὸς

now spend their days, but they at-
tended to the business appointed
to them, admiring and emulating
their superiors in these employ-
ments. *And they so shunned
the Agora that if they did have to
pass through it, they were seen to
do it with great modesty and pro-
priety. . . . But as for eating
or drinking in a tavern, not even
a respectable slave would have
ventured to do that* (7. 48, 49).
— πάντας αὐτούς : οὗτος is the
usual word for taking up the
relative pronoun and carrying it
into the antecedent clause, when
the relative clause has preceded
(οὗτος *analeptic*) ; but here the
weaker αὐτούς takes the place of
τούτους in order that the whole
stress may fall upon πάντας. In
the next clause the pronoun becomes emphatic, and the stronger

τούτους appears ; cp. 25. 11 and
note.

12. ἔτι : cp. ἔτι § 8 and ἔπειτα
§ 6. — δίκην, γραφήν, εἰσαγγελίαν :
δίκη is a civil suit, γραφή a criminal indictment, εἰσαγγελία a summary criminal prosecution (cp. on
12. 48). Mantitheus does not, as
Lysias himself does in the twelfth
speech (§ 4), claim to have kept
entirely out of the courts, but only
that there has been no litigation
that reflected upon his character.
— τοίνυν : *further*, introducing the
next detail in the argument ; cp. ἔτι
above, and see on § 7, τοίνυν (D).
— πρός (line 83) : see on 19. 20.

13. πρῶτον μέν : correl. with
μετὰ ταῦτα τοίνυν § 15. — τὴν συμμαχίαν : When, in 395 B.C., the
Spartans were fully engaged in
their contest against Persia on the
coast of Asia Minor, Thebes saw

Βοιωτοὺς καὶ εἰς Ἁλίαρτον ἔδει βοηθεῖν, ὑπὸ Ὀρθοβούλου κατειλεγμένος ἱππεύειν, ἐπειδὴ πάντας ἐώρων
τοῖς μὲν ἱππεύουσιν ἀσφάλειαν εἶναι δεῖν νομίζοντας,
τοῖς δ᾽ ὁπλίταις κίνδυνον ἡγουμένους, ἑτέρων ἀνα-
90 βάντων ἐπὶ τοὺς ἵππους ἀδοκιμάστων παρὰ τὸν νόμον
ἐγὼ προσελθὼν εἶπον τῷ Ὀρθοβούλῳ ἐξαλεῖψαί με ἐκ

the possibility of becoming the center of a coalition against Sparta. Athens was ready to grasp any opportunity to weaken Sparta, and the veterans of the democratic exile were grateful for the help which they had received at Thebes when banished by the Thirty acting with the support of Sparta. The advance of two Spartan armies upon Boeotia led to an urgent call for help from Athens. The response of Athens was the first step in her reëntrance into Hellenic affairs after her entire prostration. — **πρὸς Βοιωτούς**: on omission of the article see Crit. Note. — **Ἁλίαρτον**: Haliartus was the Boeotian city immediately threatened by Lysander's army. Before the Athenian contingent arrived the Spartans had been defeated and Lysander killed (Chron. App.) — **ἐπειδὴ πάντας κτλ.**: *when I saw that all believed the cavalry were likely to be safe.* The Athenians never lost their dread of the Spartan hoplites. — **εἶναι δεῖν**: here used of what 'ought' from the nature of the case to follow. —

ἀδοκιμάστων: without passing the scrutiny of the Senate. See Introd. p. 131. Shortly before this Lysias had written two speeches for clients who prosecuted the son of Alcibiades for just this conduct at this time. — **Ὀρθοβούλῳ**: if the method of making up the cavalry roll described by Aristotle (Introd. p. 131) was in use as early as this, — and the reference to the *dokimasia* of the cavalry supports this view, — Orthobulus must have been the *καταλογεύς* of Mantitheus's tribe (ὑπὸ Ὀρθοβούλου κατειλεγμένος) and unable to erase a name, now that the lists had been passed on by the Senate and handed over to the cavalry commanders. Perhaps Mantitheus appealed to him to secure the change by special act of the Senate. But it is possible that the method of Aristotle's time was not yet in use, and that at this earlier time the phylarchs drew up the lists and had power to excuse members, even after *dokimasia* by the Senate. On this supposition Orthobulus was

τοῦ καταλόγου, ἡγούμενος αἰσχρὸν εἶναι τοῦ πλήθους
μέλλοντος κινδυνεύειν ἄδειαν ἐμαυτῷ παρασκευάσαντα
94 στρατεύεσθαι. Καί μοι ἀνάβηθι, Ὀρθόβουλε.

ΜΑΡΤΥΡΙΑ

14 Συλλεγέντων τοίνυν τῶν δημοτῶν πρὸ τῆς ἐξόδου,
εἰδὼς αὐτῶν ἐνίους πολίτας μὲν χρηστοὺς ὄντας καὶ
προθύμους, ἐφοδίων δὲ ἀποροῦντας, εἶπον ὅτι χρὴ τοὺς
ἔχοντας παρέχειν τὰ ἐπιτήδεια τοῖς ἀπόρως διακει-
μένοις. καὶ οὐ μόνον τοῦτο συνεβούλευον τοῖς ἄλλοις,
100 ἀλλὰ καὶ αὐτὸς ἔδωκα δυοῖν ἀνδροῖν τριάκοντα δραχμὰς
ἑκατέρῳ, οὐχ ὡς πολλὰ κεκτημένος, ἀλλ᾽ ἵνα παράδειγμα
τοῦτο τοῖς ἄλλοις γένηται. Καί μοι ἀνάβητε.

the phylarch of Mantitheus's tribe.
See Introd. p. 130.

14. τῶν δημοτῶν: the contingent
from a deme was one of the units
of which the levy from the tribe
was made up. Fellow-demesmen
were neighbors and knew one
another's circumstances. — **ἐφοδίων**: the state allowed an average
of two obols a day as pay to the
hoplite, and two obols for food;
the four obols were about what an
unskilled laborer would earn at
home. A poor man who had to
support his family at home on this
pay might well need help. Cp.
App. § 63 f. Under the earlier
military organization only members
of the three higher property classes
served as hoplites, the men of the

lowest class, the Thetes, serving
only as light-armed troops, or as
rowers in the fleet. But at the
time of the Sicilian Expedition the
hoplites had been so reduced in
number by pestilence and war
that Thetes were called in to arm
as hoplites and serve as fighting
men on ship-board (ἐπιβάται τῶν
νεῶν Thuc. 6. 43). From that
time on they were used for similar
service. We do not know how far
they were called upon for hoplite
service on land. Cp. Gulick, *The
Life of the Ancient Greeks*, 190 ff. —
τριάκοντα δραχμάς: as much as the
man would receive from the state
for service of a month and a half.
— **ἑκατέρῳ**: HA. 624 d; G. 914;
B. 319. — **ὡς**: force, see on § 8.

ΜΑΡΤΥΡΕΣ

15 Μετὰ ταῦτα τοίνυν, ὦ βουλή, εἰς Κόρινθον ἐξόδου
γενομένης καὶ πάντων προειδότων ὅτι δεήσει κινδυνεύειν,
105 ἑτέρων ἀναδυομένων ἐγὼ διεπραξάμην ὥστε τῆς πρώτης
τεταγμένος μάχεσθαι τοῖς πολεμίοις· καὶ μάλιστα τῆς
ἡμετέρας φυλῆς δυστυχησάσης, καὶ πλείστων ἐναποθανόντων, ὕστερος ἀνεχώρησα τοῦ σεμνοῦ Στειριῶς

15. **μετὰ ταῦτα**: the battle of
Haliartus was in the autumn of
395, the expedition to Corinth in the
following spring or early summer.
The victory at Haliartus brought
Corinth into the anti-Spartan alliance of Athens and Thebes, and
in the next summer the allies attempted to hold the Isthmus of
Corinth against the advance of a
large Peloponnesian army. The
armies met at the north of the
stream Nemea, on the coast a
little west of Corinth. Never before had so large forces of Greeks
met in battle. The Athenian hoplites were in the most dangerous
position, for they stood opposed
to the Spartans, and in such way
that the Spartans could easily
outflank them if the Athenians
kept connection with the rest of
the army. The Athenians were
defeated with heavy loss. This
led to the defeat of the whole
army of the allies, and they were
forced to retreat upon Corinth
(Xen. *Hell.* 4. 2. 9-23). — **τῆς**

πρώτης: *sc.* τάξεως. Case, HA.
732 a; G. 1096, 1094. 7; B. 355. 2;
Gl. 508. — **μάλιστα . . . δυστυχησάσης**: therefore probably on the
left wing, which was overlapped
by the Spartan right. — **ἐναποθανόντων**: ἐν = 'therein,' ἐν ταύτῃ
τῇ δυστυχίᾳ. — **σεμνοῦ**: a word
properly of good meaning, but
often used as here in a sarcastic
sense. The σεμνὸς ἀνήρ is the
man who 'takes himself seriously.'
For the relation of this slur on
Thrasybulus to the question of
the date of this speech, see Introd. p. 136. Thrasybulus was at
first the idol of the people under
the restored democracy; but his
moderate and conservative policy,
sternly opposed to every violation
of the amnesty and every indul-
gence of revenge, grew vexatious
to the more radical element. Only
an inflexible will could keep back
the crowd from acts which would
reopen the old controversies and
endanger the democracy itself.
It is not strange that they came to

16 τοῦ πᾶσιν ἀνθρώποις δειλίαν ὠνειδικότος. καὶ οὐ
110 πολλαῖς ἡμέραις ὕστερον μετὰ ταῦτα ἐν Κορίνθῳ
χωρίων ἰσχυρῶν κατειλημμένων, ὥστε τοὺς πολεμίους
μὴ δύνασθαι προσιέναι, Ἀγησιλάου δ' εἰς τὴν Βοιω-
τίαν ἐμβαλόντος ψηφισαμένων τῶν ἀρχόντων ἀποχωρίσαι τάξεις αἵτινες βοηθήσουσι, φοβουμένων ἁπάντων
115 (εἰκότως, ὦ βουλή· δεινὸν γὰρ ἦν ἀγαπητῶς ὀλίγῳ
πρότερον σεσωμένους ἐφ' ἕτερον κίνδυνον ἰέναι) προσελθὼν ἐγὼ τὸν ταξίαρχον ἐκέλευον ἀκληρωτὶ τὴν

feel that he was self-willed and that 'he despised the people' (αὐθάδης, ὑπερόπτης τοῦ δήμου, Schol. Ar. *Eccl.* 203). The defeat of the expedition to Corinth in 394 was a blow to his reputation. Then came Conon with his foreign fleet and Persian subsidies (see XIX. Introd. p. 160) and in the full tide of enthusiasm for the new navy and its commander the people forgot their allegiance to Thrasybulus. It is significant that Lysias dares to sneer at him in a speech before a body largely made up of democrats of the Return. — Στειριῶς : Thrasybulus was of the deme Stiria. — ὠνειδικότος : the perfect would not be used if Thrasybulus were now dead ; nor would Lysias be likely to speak of him in this jesting tone. He evidently refers to some well-known speech of his.

16. χωρίων ἰσχυρῶν: the occupation of these posts held back the great Peloponnesian army from

crossing the Isthmus and joining Agesilaus, who, recalled from Asia, and coming by the land route, was entering Boeotia from the north. — προσιέναι : see Crit. Note. — Ἀγησιλάου . . . ἐμβαλόντος : modifying ψηφισαμέων τῶν ἀρχόντων. — ἀποχωρίσαι : see Crit. Note. — τάξεις : not as in § 15 (τῆς πρώτης) of a line in battle, but the regular word for the contingent from a tribe. Its commander is the ταξίαρχος ; he corresponds to the φύλαρχος of the cavalry contingent. — βοηθήσουσι : for the relative clause of purpose see HA. 911 ; G. 1442 ; B. 591 ; Gl. 615. — ἀγαπητῶς : *barely*. The word has passed far from its original meaning : (1) *to one's satisfaction*, (2) *in a way with which one may well be satisfied* (cp. ἀγαπήσειν 12. 11), hence (3) *scarcely, barely*. — ἐκέλευον : had the request been granted we should expect to hear of Mantitheus's part in the Boeotian cam-

156 ΛΥΣΙΟΥ

17 ἡμετέραν τάξιν πέμπειν. ὥστ᾽ εἴ τινες ὑμῶν ὀργίζονται
τοῖς τὰ μὲν τῆς πόλεως ἀξιοῦσι πράττειν, ἐκ δὲ τῶν
120 κινδύνων ἀποδιδράσκουσιν, οὐκ ἂν δικαίως περὶ ἐμοῦ
τὴν γνώμην ταύτην ἔχοιεν· οὐ γὰρ μόνον τὰ προστατ-
τόμενα ἐποίουν προθύμως, ἀλλὰ καὶ κινδυνεύειν ἐτόλμων. καὶ ταῦτ᾽ ἐποίουν οὐχ ὡς οὐ δεινὸν ἡγούμενος
εἶναι Λακεδαιμονίοις μάχεσθαι, ἀλλ᾽ ἵνα, εἴ ποτε ἀδίκως
125 εἰς κίνδυνον καθισταίμην, διὰ ταῦτα βελτίων ὑφ᾽ ὑμῶν
νομιζόμενος ἁπάντων τῶν δικαίων τυγχάνοιμι. Καί
μοι ἀνάβητε τούτων μάρτυρες.

ΜΑΡΤΥΡΕΣ

18 Τῶν τοίνυν ἄλλων στρατειῶν καὶ φρουρῶν οὐδεμιᾶς
ἀπελείφθην πώποτε, ἀλλὰ πάντα τὸν χρόνον διατετέ-
130 λεκα μετὰ τῶν πρώτων μὲν τὰς ἐξόδους ποιούμενος,
μετὰ τῶν τελευταίων δὲ ἀναχωρῶν. καίτοι χρὴ τοὺς

paign with its great battle of Coro-
nea. We must conclude that his
comrades did not second his request.
17. ὥστ᾽ . . . **οὐκ ἂν δικαίως**
. . . **ἔχοιεν**: ὥστε here much like
ὥστε with impv., § 8 ; stronger
than οὖν. — **τοῖς** . . . **ἀξιοῦσι**: case,
see on ὀργίζεσθε 12. 80. — **ἵνα
κτλ.**: a neat turn of the thought;
the jury do not for a moment
understand him as really representing this as his motive. Cp.
the similar turn in 25. 13. — **βελτίων**: cp. on χείρους § 3. — **ἁπάντων τῶν δικαίων**: one of his
'rights' certainly is to hold office
like other citizens.

18. ἄλλων: as the expedition
to Haliartus was the first after the
Peloponnesian War, and the one
to Corinth the second, these other
expeditions and services in garrison must have been after 394.
The speech, then, could hardly
have been delivered before 392 ;
cf. Introd. p. 136. — **πώποτε**: very
emphatic by its position in its
own clause, and by the chiastic
arrangement with πάντα τὸν χρόνον. — **τῶν πρώτων μέν**: for the
position of μέν see on 12. 15. —
τοὺς . . . **πολιτευομένους**: the object of σκοπεῖν. — **ἐκ τῶν τοιούτων**:
ἐκ with the gen. to express the

φιλοτίμως καὶ κοσμίως πολιτευομένους ἐκ τῶν τοιούτων
σκοπεῖν, ἀλλ' οὐκ εἴ τις κομᾷ, διὰ τοῦτο μισεῖν· τὰ
μὲν γὰρ τοιαῦτα ἐπιτηδεύματα οὔτε τοὺς ἰδιώτας οὔτε
135 τὸ κοινὸν τῆς πόλεως βλάπτει, ἐκ δὲ τῶν κινδυνεύειν
ἐθελόντων πρὸς τοὺς πολεμίους ἅπαντες ὑμεῖς ὠφε-
19 λεῖσθε. ὥστε οὐκ ἄξιον ἀπ' ὄψεως, ὦ βουλή, οὔτε
φιλεῖν οὔτε μισεῖν οὐδένα, ἀλλ' ἐκ τῶν ἔργων σκοπεῖν·
πολλοὶ μὲν γὰρ μικρὸν διαλεγόμενοι καὶ κοσμίως

source from which the knowledge
must come. — κομᾷ: the Homeric
custom of wearing the hair long
(κάρη κομόωντες) prevailed always
at Sparta, but at Athens from
about the time of the Persian wars
only boys wore long hair. When
they became of age their hair was
cut as a sign of their entering into
manhood, and from that time on
they wore hair about as short as
modern custom prescribes; only
the athletes made a point of wearing it close-cut. Cp. Gulick, 175 ff.
But there was a certain aristocratic
set of young Spartomaniacs who
affected Spartan appearance along
with their pro-Spartan sentiments,
and who were proud of wearing
long hair, to the disgust of their
fellow-citizens. These were the
men who largely made up the
cavalry corps. Aristophanes in
the *Knights* (580) makes them
say to the people that they have
only one thing to ask, if ever
peace comes and they be free from

trouble: μὴ φθονεῖθ' ἡμῖν κομῶσι
μηδ' ἀπεστλεγγισμένοις *do not
begrudge us our long hair or our
shining skin.* The plain old
Strepsiades says of his spendthrift
son ὁ δὲ κόμην ἔχων ἱππάζεται
(Ar. *Clouds* 14). The extreme
Laconizers are thus described:
ἐλακωνομάνουν ἅπαντες ἄνθρωποι
τότε,
ἐκόμων, ἐπείνων, ἐρρύπων, ἐσωκρά-
των,
σκυτάλι' ἐφόρουν
*all men had Laconomania then;
they wore long hair, they starved
themselves, they went dirty, they
Socratized, they carried canes* (Ar.
Birds 1281). — ἐκ τῶν ἐθελόντων:
such men are the *source* of the
common good; *agency* would be
expressed by ὑπό.

19. πολλοί κτλ.: 'many who
have the voice and dress of quiet
gentlemen.' Cp. on μετρίως βεβιωκώς § 3. — μικρὸν διαλεγόμενοι:
a loud voice was by Athenian, even
more than by modern, standards

140 ἀμπεχόμενοι μεγάλων κακῶν αἴτιοι γεγόνασιν, ἕτεροι
δὲ τῶν τοιούτων ἀμελοῦντες πολλὰ κἀγαθὰ ὑμᾶς εἰσιν
εἰργασμένοι.

20 Ἤδη δέ τινων ᾐσθόμην, ὦ βουλή, καὶ διὰ ταῦτα
ἀχθομένων μοι, ὅτι νεώτερος ὢν ἐπεχείρησα λέγειν ἐν
145 τῷ δήμῳ. ἐγὼ δὲ τὸ μὲν πρῶτον ἠναγκάσθην ὑπὲρ
τῶν ἐμαυτοῦ πραγμάτων δημηγορῆσαι, ἔπειτα μέντοι
καὶ ἐμαυτῷ δοκῶ φιλοτιμότερον διατεθῆναι τοῦ δέον-
τος, ἅμα μὲν τῶν προγόνων ἐνθυμούμενος, ὅτι οὐδὲν

a mark either of ill-breeding or of
conceit. A client of Demosthenes
(37. 52) complains that his enemies
say of him, Νικόβουλος δ᾽ ἐπίφθονός
ἐστι, καὶ ταχέως βαδίζει, καὶ μέγα
φθέγγεται, καὶ βακτηρίαν φορεῖ
*Nicobulus is crabbed, and he walks
fast, and talks loud, and carries
a cane.* Mantitheus makes no
apology for his voice and manner,
which are quite in keeping with his
natural impulsiveness and his good
opinion of himself. — κοσμίως ἀμπεχόμενοι: the Athenian gentleman was as careful of his dress
as the Spartan was careless. Neg-
lect here was another affectation
of some of the young aristocrats.

20. ᾐσθόμην: empirical aorist.
"When the aorist has a temporal
adverb or a negative or a numeral
with it, it is best referred to the
same class with the English perfect of experience (empirical aorist)," GS. 259. With ἤδη as here
19. 4; with πολλάκις 19. 9; with

πολλάκις ἤδη 22. 16, 25. 28; with
πολλοί 19. 45; with πολλοὶ ἤδη
19. 51, 22. 18, 34. 10. — νεώτερος:
the young Athenian attained his
majority in his nineteenth year, but
for two years his service as cadet
in garrison (see Gulick 89 f.) almost necessarily precluded his
exercising the privileges of a citizen. From his twentieth year on
he might take any part in the
Ecclesia which his modesty permitted. — ὑπὲρ πραγμάτων: in § 10
Mantitheus connects the loss of
the family property with the disaster to the city and his father's
troubles; the relation to the foreign prince implies wide commer-
cial connections. Probably some
of Mantitheus's property claims
were affected by the early legisla-
tion after the Return. — τῶν προγόνων: proleptic with ἐνθυμούμενος,
HA. 878; B. 717. 18; or it may
be considered as modifying the
whole clause ὅτι . . . πέπαυνται. —

21 πέπαυνται τὰ τῆς πόλεως πράττοντες, ἅμα δὲ ὑμᾶς
150 ὁρῶν (τὰ γὰρ ἀληθῆ χρὴ λέγειν) τοὺς τοιούτους μόνους
πολλοῦ ἀξίους νομίζοντας εἶναι· ὥστε ὁρῶν ὑμᾶς ταύτην
τὴν γνώμην ἔχοντας τίς οὐκ ἂν ἐπαρθείη πράττειν καὶ
λέγειν ὑπὲρ τῆς πόλεως; ἔτι δὲ τί ἂν τοῖς τοιούτοις
ἄχθοισθε; οὐ γὰρ ἕτεροι περὶ αὐτῶν κριταί εἰσιν, ἀλλ᾽
155 ὑμεῖς.

ὅτι . . . πράττοντες: *that they have always been in public life.*

21. τοὺς τοιούτους: *i.e.* men who take a leading part in politics.
— τὰ γὰρ ἀληθῆ χρὴ λέγειν: why need Mantitheus apologize for his statement? The answer lies in the fact that the Athenian theory was that the ideal citizen was the quiet one (see on κοσμίους 12. 20); Mantitheus tells the senators that in practice the honors go to the men who put themselves forward.

The Speech on the Estate of Aristophanes

INTRODUCTION

THE events which led up to this speech began with the connection of two ambitious Athenians, Nicophemus and his son
Aristophanes, with the naval enterprises of Conon.

After the disaster at Aegospotami Conon, and probably Nicophemus with him, fearing to return to Athens, took refuge with
Evagoras, king of Salamis in Cyprus. Supported by Evagoras,
Conon passed into Persian service, and was enabled to bring to
Athens his Graeco-Persian fleet and Persian subsidies at the critical moment when, with Thebes, Corinth, and Argos, Athens was
again facing Sparta in war (the "Corinthian War," 395–386). In
the brief but brilliant career of Conon which followed, Nicophemus
had a share, and after Conon's death in Cyprus (about 390), he
remained there, the friend and helper of Evagoras.[1]

The attempts of Evagoras to gain control of all Cyprus brought
him into collision with Persia. Hard pressed to defend himself
against a threatened attack, he sent envoys to Athens proposing an
alliance and asking for ships and men (§ 21, Xen. *Hell.* 4. 8. 24).
Although the Athenians were receiving Persian support in their
war against Sparta, they took the doubtful step of securing Evagoras's support by voting the alliance and dispatching a squadron
of ten ships under Philocrates (390 B.C.). On the voyage they were
overtaken by a Spartan squadron and all were captured (Xen. *l.c.*).

---

[1] For Nicophemus's connection with Conon see, besides our speech, Diodor.
14. 81 (where Νικόδημον is probably a mistake of the MSS. for Νικόφημον)
and Xen. *Hell.* 4. 8. 8.

The threatened Persian attack on Evagoras was delayed, but in the spring of 387, in response to a second appeal, another fleet of ten ships, with eight hundred peltasts, was sent out from Athens under Chabrias (Xen. *Hell.* 5. 1. 10). With their help. Evagoras completed his conquest of Cyprus (Nepos, *Chabrias* 2. 2).

In the negotiations with Evagoras and the equipment of ships for him, a prominent part had been taken by a son of Nicophemus, Aristophanes, who had all the time made his home in Athens.

Aristophanes, in response to letters received from his father, did everything possible to secure favorable action by the state, made every effort to raise money to supplement the equipment of the fleet, and was sent as envoy, probably in advance of the fleet, to complete the negotiations with Evagoras.

It is uncertain whether these efforts were in connection with the first or the second expedition. We know only that sooner or later Aristophanes and Nicophemus fell under the gravest charges on the part of their countrymen, and that they were arrested and summarily executed. They were granted no opportunity for defense, their friends were not even allowed to see them after their arrest, and their bodies were not given to their family for burial (§ 7). Their property was declared confiscate, and so much of it as could be found was seized and sold.[1]

---

[1] Both time and place of these events are in dispute. The time reference in § 29 is too vague for any safe reckoning. Thalheim (with Frohberger and Fuhr) places the efforts of Nicophemus and Aristophanes to aid Evagoras in connection with the first expedition. He thinks that its total failure led to the fierce anger against its promoters ; that Nicophemus and Aristophanes, charged with ἀπάτη τοῦ δήμου, were brought back to Athens on a dispatch ship, and that they were put to death after a summary trial, in which they were refused the ordinary rights of defendants.

Blass (*Att. Bered.* I² 531) holds that the connection of Nicophemus and Aristophanes was with the second expedition ; that afterwards charges were brought against them in the Ecclesia, and that that body condemned them to death; that the penalty was executed in Cyprus by Chabrias.

In favor of the first expedition are the facts that Aristophanes went as envoy (§ 23), that in our speech there is no reference to an earlier expedition,

But the amount of property thus seized fell so far short of what they were supposed to have had, after their intimate connection with Conon and Evagoras, that it was suspected that a part was being concealed in the interest of the widow and children of Aristophanes. Suit was accordingly brought against the wife's father, now an old man of seventy years. His death before the time of trial threw the suit over to his son, who had now to defend the estate, and for whom Lysias wrote our speech.[1]

The prosecution demanded the seizure of the speaker's property to reimburse the treasury for that part of Aristophanes's estate supposed to have been concealed by the speaker's father.[2]

The date of the trial is 387, or very early in 386, for the generalship of Diotimus (388/7) is a recent event (§ 50), and the

and that the severity of treatment is best explained by the anger of the people at the failure of the first. This theory, too, gives room for some form of trial, which is implied in § 7, πρὶν παραγενέσθαι τινὰ αὐτοῖς ἐλεγχομένοις ὡς ἠδίκουν. The objection to the theory is the difficulty in believing that an Athenian citizen, brought to Athens under arrest, could have been treated with such disregard of all legal forms and privileges. But we know one case, just after the restoration of the democracy, in which a man was executed without trial (Arist. *Resp. Ath.* 40. 2), and we hear of such action being proposed in other cases in the period under discussion (Lys. 22. 2, 27. 8; Isoc. 17. 42).

Meyer (*Gesch. des Alt.* V. §§ 870 Anm., 873 Anm.) connects the efforts of Aristophanes with the first expedition, but thinks that the execution was in Cyprus after the arrival of the second.

The confiscation of the property seems to have been by separate action, for Harpocration (*s. v.* Χύτροι) has preserved the title of a speech of Lysias Κατ' Αἰσχίνου περὶ τῆς δημεύσεως τῶν 'Αριστοφάνους χρημάτων. (For the natural connection of Lysias with the fortunes of this family see on § 15.)

[1] The family connection is : —

The friend of Conon and Evagoras	The original defendant
Nicophemus	(unnamed) now dead

Aristophanes *m.* Daughter Son, the speaker (unnamed).

[2] Strictly speaking, the title of our speech, Περὶ τῶν 'Αριστοφάνους χρημάτων, as handed down by the Mss., is incorrect. The property now at stake is that of Aristophanes's brother-in-law.

Peace of Antalcidas (winter of 387/6 or spring of 386) is not yet concluded (the speaker is trierarch, § 62).

The events which led to this speech were connected with two dangerous tendencies in the political life of the fourth century, the enrichment of naval commanders through their office, and the hasty and unreasonable punishment of public officers in response to a fickle public sentiment.

Under the Athenian Empire the cost of the navy had been amply provided for from the ordinary revenues of the state ; the ships were built and furnished with the more important rigging ; the other expenses of equipment and repair were met by the trierarchs, while the pay of seamen and soldiers — some two hundred men to a trireme — was furnished from the state treasury. But after the Peloponnesian War had cut off all revenues from allies, it was only by the utmost exertions that sufficient ships could be built and equipped. The regular payment for the men — a sum ranging from $\frac{1}{2}$ t. to 1 t. a month for each trireme — was a burden for which the state could not adequately provide. The generals and trierarchs found themselves in constant difficulty with their men ; more and more they were forced to find money for their payment by the operations of the fleet itself. The first and most dangerous source of supply was the subsidy from Persian satraps or the princes of the Asiatic cities. Conon's fleet, which won the battle of Cnidus, was created and supported by Persian subsidies ; it was for a time so supported after it passed into the service of Athens. When the pay came from foreign sources, the generals could be under no such system of accurate accounting as when all funds came from the treasury of the state, while the relations with the foreign powers offered dangerous opportunities for personal corruption.

With the attempt to bring the island and coast cities back under Athenian rule, after the battle of Cnidus, payment from these cities was resumed, whether by way of a stated tax, or of penalty for resistance. From others forced contributions were exacted as the fleet cruised from city to city. The collection of most of these funds probably rested with the generals. Upon the restoration of Athenian control of the Hellespont (390–389) the tax on incoming and outgoing vessels was reimposed, and new opportunities were opened for favors between commanders and merchants. To these were added the opportunities for gifts and bribes from merchants whose ships had to have a convoy in these years when hostile fleets were constantly cruising in the Aegean.

Commanders of Athenian fleets, and even of single ships, were thus put into a position where they handled large sums of money, under circumstances in which there could be no efficient control by the home government, and which offered constant temptation to corruption. Nor was it always easy for an honest man to draw the line between bribes and legitimate gifts from rich patrons, like the Persian satraps and such princes as Evagoras.

It came to be expected during the Corinthian War (395–386) that the higher naval officers would enrich themselves. It is significant that in our speech it is assumed, without apology, that Conon and his associates were all the time building up their private fortunes (§§ 35–36).

The effect of all this was to undermine the confidence of the people in their naval officers. The first reverse was the signal for their enemies to come before the people with charges that they were betraying the state for money. Public opinion was quick to respond with the demand for punishment — usually the confiscation of their property, often banishment or death. And this tendency was increased by the desperate straits of the political leaders to find money for the treasury. The city was attempting to take her old place in international affairs, with no sufficient revenue ; the people saw in each new confiscation relief for the treasury. Men were even heard to plead in court for a conviction on the ground that only thus would the treasury have money to pay them for sitting on the case (Lys. 27. 1).

The case of Nicophemus and Aristophanes is but one among many between 388 and 386, when these prosecutions were at their height. It is disappointing to find that Lysias, the stout defender of justice in this suit, was, nevertheless, ready to use his pen on the side of confiscation and death when occasion offered. We have three speeches of his written about a year before the present one, in which he makes every appeal to the prejudice and suspicion of the masses. The following extracts will show the spirit in which public men and even friends of the great liberator, Thrasybulus, were attacked : [1]

From the Speech against Epicrates (27. 8–11) : " In my opinion, Athenians, if you should put these men to death without giving them trial or opportunity of defense, they could not be said to have perished ' without trial ' ($ἄκριτοι$), but rather to have received the justice that is their due. For those are not 'without trial ' upon whom you pass judgment with knowledge of their deeds, but rather those who, slandered by their enemies, in matters unknown to you, are deprived of a hearing. But the real accusers of these men now on trial are their own deeds, and we, the accusers, are but witnesses."

" These men in the war have, from your possessions, become rich out of poverty, and you, poor through them. But it is not the business of the leaders of the people in your misfortunes to lay hands on what is yours, but rather to give their own to you. But we have come to such a state that men who, when we were at peace, were not even able to support themselves, are now paying income taxes and performing liturgies [2] and building fine houses. . . . And you are no longer angry at what they steal, but grateful for what you get, as though they were your paymasters, and not the thieves of your goods."

From the Speech against Ergocles (the friend of Thrasybulus) : " Why should you spare men when you see the fleets that they commanded scattering and going to pieces for lack of funds, and these men, who set sail poor and needy, so quickly become the

[1] Thrasybulus himself was under summons to return home on such a charge when death released him from the undeserved disgrace.

[2] Thus their very services to the state are made ground of accusation. See p. 30.

richest of all the citizens " (§ 2). And yet Lysias knew, when he wrote these words, that few fleets in all the history of the city had done grander service than had this, under the defendants, with Thrasybulus ! He says further of these officers, " They enrich themselves and hate you, and they are preparing no longer to obey you, but to rule you, and fearing because of their ill-gotten gains, they are ready to seize strongholds, and to set up an oligarchy, and to do everything to keep you in extreme daily peril " (28. 7). " I beg you to come to your own relief, and much rather to punish the guilty than pity those who are keeping what belongs to the city. For the fines that they will pay will be no money of theirs, — they will simply restore to you your own " (29. 8).

If, in the speech for the defense on the Property of Aristophanes, Lysias found himself working against an unreasoning and lawless public sentiment, he could make no complaint, for he had helped to create it. The speech is full of incidental interest for its glimpses of the more personal affairs of famous men, but its greatest value is for the intimate knowledge which, with the speeches of the earlier group, it gives of the demoralized condition of the democracy.

OUTLINE

I. Προοίμιον, *Exordium*, §§ 1–11.

Plea for kindly and just hearing on the ground of the disadvantages (*a*) of any inexperienced defendant, (*b*) of the defense in this particular case.

II. Πίστεις, *Argumentatio*, §§ 12–54.

The narrative (Διήγησις) is interwoven with the argument.

Argument against the probability (εἰκός) that the speaker's father had any of Aristophanes's property in his possession.

A. The original marriage connection with the family of Nicophemus was not made for the sake of money, §§ 12–17.

1. Narrative showing motive for the marriage, §§ 12–13.

2. Narrative supporting the first, by describing the other marriages of the family, §§ 14–17.

B. Aristophanes would not have left his property in the hands of a man whose tastes were so unlike his own as were those of his father-in-law, §§ 18–20.

C. Aristophanes had no property to leave when he set out for Cyprus, §§ 21–27.

1. Proved by his great exertions to borrow money, §§ 21–24.

2. Proved by his inability to loan money on the royal vase, §§ 25–27.

3. Proved by his borrowing table furnishings, § 27.

D. Answer to the common belief that Aristophanes must have had more property than the officers have found, §§ 28–54.

1. Argument from the shortness of time in which Aristophanes could have acquired property, and his heavy expenses, §§ 28–29.

2. Argument from the meager personal property even of old wealthy families, § 30.

3. Argument from the extraordinary care of the family in turning over Aristophanes's house uninjured to the state, § 31.

4. Argument from the willingness to take oath that all the property has been given up, § 32.

Brief Digression (Παρέκβασις). Description of the extreme hardships that threaten the defendant, § 33.

5. Argument from the unexpectedly small estate of Conon, and its proportion to what the state has obtained from that of Aristophanes, §§ 34–44.

6. Argument from the liability to error in the popular estimate of the estates of public men, §§ 45–52.

(1) The cases of Ischomachus (§ 46), Stephanus (§ 46), Nicias (§ 47), Alcibiades (§ 52), Callias (§ 48), Cleophon (§ 48).

(2) The cause of this error, § 49.

(3) The case of Diotimus, §§ 50–51.

Brief Digression (Παρέκβασις). Appeal based on the last argument, §§ 53–54.

III. Ἐπίλογος, *Peroratio*, §§ 55–64.

A. Ἀνακεφαλαίωσις, *Enumeratio*.

Brief recapitulation of the main argument, § 55.

B. Appeal to the feelings of the jury, §§ 55–64.

1. The exemplary life of the speaker, § 55.

2. The father's unselfish character as seen in his public services, §§ 56–63.

3. Final appeal, § 64.

COMMENTS ON ARGUMENT AND STYLE

I. Προοίμιον, §§ 1–11.

No other proem of Lysias is so long or developed in such detail. The reason is to be found in the fact that the speaker is addressing a jury who are thoroughly prejudiced against his case. Nicophemus and Aristophanes are believed to have been guilty of the gravest crimes, and now the defendant is believed to be concealing their property to the damage of the state. The prosecution have said everything possible to intensify this feeling.

The proem falls into two parts, one (§§ 1–6) general, the other (§§ 7–11) based on the facts peculiar to this case. It is surprising to find that for the first part Lysias has taken a ready-made proem from some book on rhetoric, and used it with slight changes. We discover this fact by comparing §§ 1–6 with the proem of Andocides's speech *On the Mysteries*, delivered twelve years earlier, and the proem of Isocrates's speech Περὶ Ἀντιδόσεως (XV), published thirty-four years after that of Lysias. Andocides has divided the section, inserting a passage applicable to his peculiar case, but the two parts agree closely with Lysias's proem. Isocrates has used a small part of the same material, but much more freely, changing the order and the phraseology, and amplifying the selected parts to fit his own style. The following text gives a comparative view of the proems of Andocides and Lysias : —

ANDOCIDES I	LYSIAS XIX
1. Τὴν μὲν παρασκευήν, ὦ ἄνδρες,	**2.** τὴν μὲν οὖν παρασκευὴν
καὶ τὴν προθυμίαν τῶν ἐχθρῶν τῶν ἐμῶν, ὥστε με κακῶς ποιεῖν ἐκ παντὸς τρόπου καὶ δικαίως καὶ ἀδίκως, ἐξ ἀρχῆς ἐπειδὴ τάχιστα ἀφικόμην εἰς τὴν πόλιν ταυτηνί,	καὶ τὴν προθυμίαν τῶν ἐχθρῶν
σχεδόν τι πάντες ἐπίστασθε,	ὁρᾶτε,
καὶ οὐδὲν δεῖ περὶ τούτων πολλοὺς λόγους ποιεῖσθαι·	καὶ οὐδὲν δεῖ περὶ τούτων λέγειν·
	τὴν δ᾽ ἐμὴν ἀπειρίαν πάντες ἴσασιν, ὅσοι ἐμὲ γιγνώσκουσιν.
ἐγὼ δέ, ὦ ἄνδρες, δεήσομαι ὑμῶν δίκαια καὶ ὑμῖν τε ῥᾴδια χαρίζεσθαι καὶ ἐμοὶ ἄξια πολλοῦ τυχεῖν παρ᾽ ὑμῶν.	αἰτήσομαι οὖν ὑμᾶς δίκαια καὶ ῥᾴδια χαρίσασθαι,
Here follow four paragraphs applicable to this particular case. The general proem is resumed at § **6** :	
αἰτοῦμαι οὖν ὑμᾶς, ὦ ἄνδρες, εὔνοιαν πλείω παρασχέσθαι ἐμοὶ τῷ ἀπολογουμένῳ ἢ τοῖς κατηγόροις, εἰδότες ὅτι κἂν ἐξ ἴσου ἀκροᾶσθε, ἀνάγκη τὸν ἀπολογούμενον	ἄνευ ὀργῆς καὶ ἡμῶν ἀκοῦσαι, ὥσπερ καὶ τῶν κατηγόρων.
ἔλαττον ἔχειν.	**3.** ἀνάγκη γὰρ τὸν ἀπολογούμενον, κἂν ἐξ ἴσου ἀκροᾶσθε, ἔλαττον ἔχειν.
οἱ μὲν γὰρ ἐκ πολλοῦ χρόνου ἐπιβουλεύσαντες καὶ συνθέντες, αὐτοὶ ἄνευ κινδύνων ὄντες, τὴν κατηγορίαν ἐποιήσαντο, ἐγὼ δὲ μετὰ δέους καὶ κινδύνου καὶ διαβολῆς τῆς μεγίστης τὴν ἀπολογίαν ποιοῦμαι.	οἱ μὲν γὰρ ἐκ πολλοῦ χρόνου ἐπιβουλεύοντες, αὐτοὶ ἄνευ κινδύνων ὄντες, τὴν κατηγορίαν ἐποιήσαντο, ἡμεῖς δὲ ἀγωνιζόμεθα μετὰ δέους καὶ διαβολῆς καὶ κινδύνου τοῦ μεγίστου.

ANDOCIDES I	LYSIAS XIX

εἰκὸς οὖν ὑμᾶς ἐστιν εὔνοιαν πλείω παρασχέσθαι ἐμοὶ ἢ τοῖς κατηγόροις.

εἰκὸς οὖν ὑμᾶς εὔνοιαν πλείω ἔχειν τοῖς ἀπολογουμένοις.

4. οἶμαι γὰρ πάντας ὑμᾶς εἰδέναι

7. ἔτι δὲ καὶ τόδε ἐνθυμητέον, ὅτι πολλοὶ ἤδη πολλὰ καὶ δεινὰ κατηγορήσαντες παραχρῆμα ἐξηλέγχθησαν ψευδόμενοι οὕτω φανερῶς, ὥστε

ὅτι πολλοὶ ἤδη πολλὰ καὶ δεινὰ καπηγορήσαντες παραχρῆμα ἐξηλέγχθησαν ψευδόμενοι οὕτω φανερῶς, ὥστε ὑπὸ πάντων τῶν παραγενομένων μισηθέντες ἀπελθεῖν·

ὑμᾶς πολὺ ἂν ἥδιον δίκην λαβεῖν παρὰ τῶν κατηγόρων ἢ παρὰ τῶν κατηγορουμένων· (Cp. Isoc. 15. 19.)

οἱ δ᾽ αὖ, μαρτυρήσαντες τὰ ψευδῆ καὶ ἀδίκως ἀνθρώπους ἀπολέσαντες, ἑάλωσαν παρ᾽ ὑμῖν ψευδομαρτυριῶν, ἡνίκ᾽ οὐδὲν ἦν ἔτι πλέον τοῖς πεπονθόσιν.

οἱ δ᾽ αὖ μαρτυρήσαντες τὰ ψευδῆ καὶ ἀδίκως ἀπολέσαντες ἀνθρώπους ἑάλωσαν, ἡνίκα οὐδὲν ἦν πλέον τοῖς πεπονθόσιν.

ὁπότ᾽ οὖν ἤδη πολλὰ τοιαῦτα γεγένηται,

5. ὅτ᾽ οὖν τοιαῦτα πολλὰ γεγένηται, ὡς ἐγὼ ἀκούω,

εἰκὸς ὑμᾶς ἐστι

εἰκὸς ὑμᾶς, ὦ ἄνδρες δικασταί,

μήπω τοὺς τῶν κατηγόρων ‹λόγους πιστοὺς ἡγεῖσθαι.

μήπω τοὺς τῶν κατηγόρων λόγους ἡγεῖσθαι πιττούς, πρὶν ἂν καὶ ἡμεῖς εἴπωμεν (cp. Isoc. 15. 17).

εἰ μὲν γὰρ δεινὰ κατηγόρηται ἢ μή, οἷόν τε γνῶναι ἐκ τῶν τοῦ κατηγόρου λόγων· εἰ δὲ ἀληθῆ ταῦτά ἐστιν ἢ ψευδῆ, οὐχ οἷόν τε ὑμᾶς

ANDOCIDES I

πρότερον εἰδέναι πρὶν ἂν καὶ ἐμοῦ
ἀκούσητε ἀπολογουμένου (cp.
Isoc. 15. 17).

LYSIAS XIX

ἀκούω γὰρ ἔγωγε, καὶ ὑμῶν δὲ τοὺς
πολλοὺς οἶμαι εἰδέναι, ὅτι πάντων
δεινότατόν ἐστι διαβολή.
Cp. Isoc. 15. 18 ὡς ἔστι μέγιστον κακὸν διαβολή· Lysias
goes on to illustrate the statement, while Isocrates amplifies it.

An examination of the matter common to the two writers shows
that the borrowed proem was composed as a model for the opening of a defense ; it was a plea for a kindly hearing on the ground
(1) that any defendant is at a disadvantage (Andoc. and Lysias) ;
(2) that oftentimes accusations have sooner or later been found
to be false (Andoc., Lysias, Isoc.) ; (3) that the truth or falsity of
charges can be learned only by hearing both sides (Andoc., Isoc.) ;
(4) that slander is dangerous (Lysias, Isocrates).[1]

In the parts where the three writers use common matter, Isocrates agrees with Andocides rather than with Lysias ; we may conclude that Lysias has changed the original more than Andocides has.
Lysias's form is in general shorter and simpler. There is also an
occasional happy variation of a word, or of a tense, or of word order :

ANDOCIDES	LYSIAS
πολλοὺς λόγους ποιεῖσθαι, § 1,	λέγειν, § 2.
δεήσομαι, § 1,	αἰτήσομαι, § 2.
χαρίζεσθαι, § 1,	χαρίσασθαι, § 2.
ἐπιβουλεύσαντες, § 6,	ἐπιβουλεύοντες, § 3.
τὴν ἀπολογίαν ποιοῦμαι, § 6,	ἀγωνιζόμεθα, § 3.
εἰκός ἐστιν, §§ 6, 7,	εἰκός, §§ 3, 5.
ὁπότε, § 7,	ὅτε, § 5.
πιστοὺς ἡγεῖσθαι, § 7,	ἡγεῖσθαι πιστούς, § 5.

[1] Blass, arguing from certain phrases of Andocides, attributes the original
proem to Antiphon, *Att. Bered.* I.² 115.

Especially interesting are Lysias's additions designed to serve the ἦθος of his client, who carefully preserves throughout the speech the attitude of a man inexperienced in public life; in § 4 Lysias says, οἶμαι πάντας ὑμᾶς εἰδέναι, where Andocides *bids them consider;* in § 5 Lysias inserts ὡς ἐγὼ ἀκούω and ἀκούω γὰρ ἔγωγε, a disclaimer of making statements on his own authority. He also substitutes the simple expression πρὶν ἂν καὶ ἡμεῖς εἴπωμεν, § 5, for the artificial antithesis of Andocides, § 7.

This is the only case in Lysias's works in which we can discover the use of such a stock proem. We know that the publication of such ready-made proems and epilogues was common. The first rhetoricians gave great attention to these parts of the speech, and gave to them especial ornamentation both of thought and phraseology. It was possible to compose them in such general terms that any one of them would fit a large class of cases. We hear of such collections by Thrasymachus, Antiphon, and Critias, and the Mss. of Demosthenes have preserved to us a large collection of proems of his composition, five of which we find actually used in extant speeches of his.

The second part of our proem (§§ 7–11) is an appeal for kindly hearing, based on the peculiar hardships of the speaker. For the closing words of this, Lysias goes again to his stock proem, as we see by comparing them with later words of Andocides:

ANDOCIDES, § 9	LYSIAS, § 11
τάδε δὲ ὑμῶν δέομαι, μετ' εὐνοίας μου τὴν ἀκρόασιν τῆς ἀπολογίας ποιήσασθαι, καὶ μήτε μοι ἀντιδίκους καταστῆναι μήτε ὑπονοεῖν τὰ λεγόμενα μήτε ῥήματα θηρεύειν, ἀκροασαμένους δὲ διὰ τέλους τῆς ἀπολογίας τότε ἤδη ψηφίζεσθαι τοῦτο ὅ τι ἂν ὑμῖν αὐτοῖς ἄριστον καὶ εὐορκότατον νομίζητε εἶναι.	δέομαι δ' ὑμῶν πάσῃ τέχνῃ καὶ μηχανῇ μετ' εὐνοίας ἀκροασαμένους ἡμῶν διὰ τέλους, ὅ τι ἂν ὑμῖν ἄριστον καὶ εὐορκότατον νομίζητε εἶναι, τοῦτο ψηφίσασθαι.

II. Πίστεις, *Argumentatio*, §§ 12–54.

Lysias omits the formal Πρόθεσις, and proceeds at once to the narrative (§ 12) that is to form the basis of his first argument.

His purpose is first to dispel the idea that the defendant's father had concealed any of the property. Apparently the prosecution had made no specific charges, and the refutation must rest entirely upon probabilities. He makes a plausible argument (*A* and *B*, §§ 12–20), but one which has less value for its own purpose than for giving such a picture of Aristophanes that the jury will be prepared for the next claim, and the one which forms the real foundation of the case, *i.e.* that Aristophanes had little property (*C*, §§ 21–27). The facts cited to prove this are pertinent and convincing. Yet Lysias knows how little weight such proof will have with a prejudiced jury. He therefore addresses himself to the removal of that prejudice by an elaborate argument (D, §§ 28–54), based partly on the facts of this case, and still more on the notorious instances of mistaken popular judgment in similar cases. It is an instance of the wisdom of the skilled pleader, who sees that logic is by no means sufficient with a popular jury, but that the appeal must take great account of prejudice.

III. Ἐπίλογος, *Peroratio*, §§ 55–64.

The recapitulation is of the briefest, covering only the central points of the positive argument, and is followed by an appeal to the jury, based on the good character of the defendant and his father, and their services to the city. But here Lysias turns from this use of the facts, so common in epilogues, and returns to argumentation, drawing from the facts of their life the conclusion of the improbability of the crime charged against them (the common argument *Probabile ex vita*). The final appeal is brief and simple.

The style of the whole speech is as simple as its framework. We can find hardly a trace of the artificial " figures " of rhetoric. Even antithesis, which Lysias often uses to excess, and nearly always in abundance, is almost excluded. The sentences are usually simple and non-periodic. In every particular Lysias has

fitted the speech to the man : the quiet, retiring, sincere gentleman. This adaptation of the language to the personality of the
speaker (ἦθος) is perfected by delicate touches here and there.
He reminds us of his inexperience in court, and of his fear under
the pressing danger (§§ 2, 3, 53). He avoids putting forward
his own knowledge or experience, but says, ὡς ἐγὼ ἀκούω, ἀκούω
γὰρ ἔγωγε (§ 5), ὡς ἐγὼ ἀκούω (§ 14), ὡς ἐγὼ ἀκήκοα (§ 19), ἀκήκοα
γὰρ ἔγωγε (§ 45), φασὶ δέ (§ 53). His only boasting is of the
quietness of his life, his filial obedience, and the good will of his
neighbors (all condensed into four lines, § 55). His public service as trierarch comes in only incidentally, as does the fact of
his scrupulous protection of the state's property confiscated unjustly. If we compare all this with the personality of Mantitheus
(see p. 135 f.), we see the grounds on which Lysias is regarded as a
master of ἠθοποιία. But here, as in other speeches (cp. p. 29),
other personalities beside those of the speaker are made to stand
out. We feel that we know Aristophanes : ambitious, restless,
hopeful, hurrying from one enterprise to another, eager to have a
part in large movements ; and clearest of all, the original defendant, the speaker's father : a gentleman of the old school ; arranging for his children marriages that should bring honor rather than
gold to the family, and connect them with old families and men
of character (§§ 12–17) ; the trusted friend of the great Conon
(§ 12) ; ready to loan all his ready money to help his son-in-law
in his enterprise (§ 22) ; bearing large burdens for the city beyond
the requirements of the law, yet seeking no office (§§ 56–58) ;
the generous friend and neighbor (§ 59) ; in a life of seventy years
free from all charge of love of money, and even in the year of
his death, in his old age, contributing to the city in the most
costly service (§ 62), and finally leaving the small fortune of two
talents. And this characterization of the man is the more telling
in that many of the particulars are brought out only incidentally.

But these personal portraitures are not simply works of art ;
they are vitally related to the plea itself. More powerful than any
argument of the speech is the feeling of the hearer that a man like

Aristophanes may well be believed to have died poor; that a man like the speaker is indeed to be pitied, forced into court to plead for all that he has, and by no possible fault of his own; and that a man like his father would never have committed the crime with which he was charged.[1]

And here lies much of the power of Lysias.   We often feel that his arguments are inconclusive; he fails to appeal strongly to the passions; in a case like this, where strong appeal might be made to our pity for the widow and little children, he seems cold. But the personality of the speaker and his friends is so real and their charm so irresistible, that at the close we find ourselves on their side.

[1] Cf. Bruns, *Literarisches Porträt*, pp. 466–467.

ΥΠΕΡ ΤΩΝ ΑΡΙΣΤΟΦΑΝΟΥΣ ΧΡΗΜΑΤΩΝ, ΠΡΟΣ ΤΟ ΔΗΜΟΣΙΟΝ

1 Πολλήν μοι ἀπορίαν παρέχει ὁ ἀγὼν οὑτοσί, ὦ
ἄνδρες δικασταί, ὅταν ἐνθυμηθῶ ὅτι, ἐὰν ἐγὼ μὲν μὴ
νῦν εὖ εἴπω, οὐ μόνον ἐγὼ ἀλλὰ καὶ ὁ πατὴρ δόξει
ἄδικος εἶναι καὶ τῶν ὄντων ἁπάντων στερήσομαι.
5 ἀνάγκη οὖν, εἰ καὶ μὴ δεινὸς πρὸς ταῦτα πέφυκα,
βοηθεῖν τῷ πατρὶ καὶ ἐμαυτῷ οὕτως ὅπως ἂν δύνωμαι.
2 τὴν μὲν οὖν παρασκευὴν καὶ τὴν προθυμίαν τῶν
ἐχθρῶν ὁρᾶτε, καὶ οὐδὲν δεῖ περὶ τούτων λέγειν·
τὴν δ' ἐμὴν ἀπειρίαν πάντες ἴσασιν, ὅσοι ἐμὲ γιγνώ-
10 σκουσιν. αἰτήσομαι οὖν ὑμᾶς δίκαια καὶ ῥᾴδια

ΠΡΟΣ ΤΟ ΔΗΜΟΣΙΟΝ: *in reply to the commonwealth.* A defendant pleads πρός τινα, a plaintiff brings suit and accusation κατά τινος (cp. ΚΑΤΑ ΔΙΟΓΕΙ-ΤΟΝΟΣ, the title of XXXII). In this case, while perhaps a private individual appears as plaintiff, it is only to prosecute the claim of the commonwealth to the property (see on § 64).

1. On the use of borrowed material in this proem see Introd. p. 168 ff. These parts are indicated in the text by spaced type.

— ἐγὼ μέν : the contrast (μέν) is in the underlying thought, "If I fail, there is no other man to save us." Cp. on ἐμὲ μέν 12. 8. — εἰ καί κτλ. : *however little gifted for this I am by nature.* See on καὶ εἰ 16. 2. — δεινός : see on δεινοὶ λέγειν 12. 86. — τῷ πατρί : the suit was brought against the father. In the interval before it came to trial he had died, and the son now had to defend his father's memory as well as his own inheritance (Introd. p. 162).

2. μὲν οὖν : see on 12. 3 (A).

χαρίσασθαι, ἄνευ ὀργῆς καὶ ἡμῶν ἀκοῦσαι, ὥσπερ
3 καὶ τῶν κατηγόρων. ἀνάγκη γὰρ τὸν ἀπολογού-
μενον, κἂν ἐξ ἴσου ἀκροᾶσθε, ἔλαττον ἔχειν. οἱ
μὲν γὰρ ἐκ πολλοῦ χρόνου ἐπιβουλεύοντες,
15 αὐτοὶ ἄνευ κινδύνων ὄντες, τὴν κατηγορίαν
ἐποιήσαντο, ἡμεῖς δὲ ἀγωνιζόμεθα μετὰ δέους
καὶ διαβολῆς καὶ κινδύνου τοῦ μεγίστου. εἰκὸς
οὖν ὑμᾶς εὔνοιαν πλείω ἔχειν τοῖς ἀπολογουμένοις.
4 οἶμαι γὰρ πάντας ὑμᾶς εἰδέναι ὅτι πολλοὶ ἤδη
20 πολλὰ καὶ δεινὰ κατηγορήσαντες παραχρῆμα
ἐξηλέγχθησαν ψευδόμενοι οὕτω φανερῶς, ὥστε
ὑπὸ πάντων τῶν παραγενομένων μισηθέντες ἀπελθεῖν·
οἱ δ' αὖ μαρτυρήσαντες τὰ ψευδῆ καὶ ἀδίκως
24 ἀπολέσαντες ἀνθρώπους ἑάλωσαν, ἡνίκα οὐδὲν

— καὶ ἡμῶν ... ὥσπερ καί: phrases
or clauses which contain or imply
a comparison often take καί in one
or both members to emphasize
their mutual relation. We can in
English use *also* in the first member only; the Greek oftener uses
it in the second : (A) καί in both
members ; here (Crit. N.) and § 36.
(B) καί in the first member, 24.
25. (C) καί in the second member, 12. 23, 12. 98, 19. 62, 22. 11,
24. 21, 34. 1. — ἀκοῦσαι : one
clause of the jurors' oath was
ἦ μὴν ὁμοίως ἀκροάσεσθαι τῶν
κατηγορούντων καὶ τῶν ἀπολογου-
μένων to give equal hearing to
prosecution and defense (Isoc.
15. 21).

3. κἄν: cp. εἰ καί § 1, and see
on καὶ εἰ 16. 2. — ἐξ ἴσου: cp. 12.
81. — ἐπιβουλεύοντες : tense, see on
ἀνιωμένου 12. 32. — μετὰ δέους:
μετά of manner. So in §§ 11
and 56. Cp. on § 14.
4. ἐξηλέγχθησαν : tense, see on
ᾐσθόμην 16. 20. — αὖ, ἡνίκα : Lysias
uses neither of these words elsewhere. Their use here, as that of
several other expressions in this
proem, betrays his use of borrowed
material (Introd. p. 168). — ἡνίκα
. . . πλέον: *when it was too late
to be of any use.* Cp. Antiphon
5. 95 τί ἔσται πλέον τῷ γε ἀποθα-
νόντι *what good will it do the
dead?* Cp. μηδέν . . . πλέον
16. 3.

5 ἦν πλέον τοῖς πεπονθόσιν. ὅτ᾽ οὖν τοιαῦτα
πολλὰ γεγένηται, ὡς ἐγὼ ἀκούω, εἰκὸς ὑμᾶς, ὦ
ἄνδρες δικασταί, μήπω τοὺς τῶν κατηγόρων
λόγους ἡγεῖσθαι πιστούς, πρὶν ἂν καὶ ἡμεῖς εἴπωμεν. ἀκούω γὰρ ἔγωγε, καὶ ὑμῶν δὲ τοὺς πολλοὺς
30 οἶμαι εἰδέναι, ὅτι πάντων δεινότατόν ἐστι διαβολή.
6 μάλιστα δὲ τοῦτο ἔχοι ἄν τις ἰδεῖν, ὅταν πολλοὶ ἐπὶ
τῇ αὐτῇ αἰτίᾳ εἰς ἀγῶνα καταστῶσιν. ὡς γὰρ ἐπὶ τὸ
πολὺ οἱ τελευταῖοι κρινόμενοι σῴζονται· πεπαυμένοι
γὰρ τῆς ὀργῆς αὐτῶν ἀκροᾶσθε, καὶ τοὺς ἐλέγχους
35 ἤδη ἐθέλοντες ἀποδέχεσθε.

7 Ἐνθυμεῖσθε οὖν ὅτι Νικόφημος καὶ Ἀριστοφάνης
ἄκριτοι ἀπέθανον, πρὶν παραγενέσθαι τινὰ αὐτοῖς

---

5. **ὅτε**: causal. — **ὡς ἐγὼ ἀκούω**: to give the impression that he has no personal experience of proceedings in the courts. So ἀκούω γὰρ ἔγωγε below. — **πάντων . . . διαβολή**: cp. Herod. 7. 10 διαβολὴ γάρ ἐστι δεινότατον κτλ. Isoc. 15. 18 ὡς ἔστι μέγιστον κακὸν διαβολή· τί γὰρ ἂν γένοιτο ταύτης κακουργότερον κτλ. Both Herodotus and Isocrates proceed to give a short disquisition on the evils of slander. Such neat characterizations by way of praise (ἐγκώμια) or blame (ψόγοι) were favorite exercises of the sophists and rhetoricians. — **δεινότατον**: a common Greek construction, but Lysias uses it in this passage only; HA. 617; G. 925; B. 423; Gl. 544.

6. **ὡς ἐπὶ τὸ πολύ**: *as a rule*. Lysias uses the expression here only.

7. **οὖν**: with transitional force. οὖν was originally a *confirmative* adverb, strengthening an assertion or question, in view of something just said. From this grew its use as a mere particle of transition, and its common post-Homeric use as an illative conjunction = *therefore*. Lysias has the three uses: (A) As a particle of emphasis, 12. 36, 14. 18, 1. 49. (B) As a particle of transition (Eng. *now*), 19. 7, 19. 22. For this he ordinarily uses μὲν οὖν or τοίνυν (see on 12. 3). (C) Illative = *therefore* 19. 1, 19. 2, 19. 3, and constantly. — **ἄκριτοι**: cp. on 12. 17. The

ἐλεγχομένοις ὡς ἠδίκουν. οὐδεὶς γὰρ οὐδ' εἶδεν ἐκείνους μετὰ τὴν σύλληψιν· οὐδὲ γὰρ θάψαι τὰ σώματ'
40 αὐτῶν ἀπέδοσαν, ἀλλ' οὕτω δεινὴ ἡ συμφορὰ γεγένηται
8 ὥστε πρὸς τοῖς ἄλλοις καὶ τούτου ἐστέρηνται. ἀλλὰ
ταῦτα μὲν ἐάσω· οὐδὲν γὰρ ἂν περαίνοιμι· πολὺ δὲ
ἀθλιώτεροι δοκοῦσί μοι οἱ παῖδες οἱ Ἀριστοφάνους·
οὐδένα γὰρ οὔτ' ἰδίᾳ οὔτε δημοσίᾳ ἠδικηκότες οὐ μόνον
45 τὰ πατρῷα ἀπολωλέκασι παρὰ τοὺς νόμους τοὺς ὑμετέρους, ἀλλὰ καὶ ἡ ὑπόλοιπος ἐλπὶς ἦν, ἀπὸ τῶν τοῦ
9 πάππου ἐκτραφῆναι, οὕτως ἐν δεινῷ καθέστηκεν. ἔτι
δ' ἡμεῖς ἐστερημένοι μὲν κηδεστῶν, ἐστερημένοι δὲ

word does not necessarily mean
"without trial," but may mean
without full process as guaranteed
by the constitution. — **πρὶν παραγενέσθαι κτλ.**: *before the arrival
of any one* (of their friends) *to hear
their examination*; or *without the
presence of any one* (of their
friends) *at their examination* (for
the second use of πρίν cp. πρὶν
εἰπεῖν 12. 17 in a similar connection). The first interpretation
would imply that the examination and execution took place in
Cyprus; the second implies nothing as to the place. In either case
the implication is that the men
had an examination of some sort.
See Introd. p. 161 N. 1. — **γεγένηται,
ἐστέρηνται**: perfect, because the
separate sad events of the past
(ἀπέθανον, εἶδεν, ἀπέδωκεν) are
now gathered up in the summary

συμφορά, and regarded as a standing illustration of the fact that
"slander is the worst of all things "
(§ 5).

8. ταῦτα μὲν ἐάσω: *this* (but
not the other abuses). See on ἐμὲ
μέν 12. 8. — **παρὰ τοὺς νόμους**: referring to the fact that Nicophemus
and Aristophanes were put to
death ἄκριτοι (§ 7). The confiscation of property was often added to
a death sentence. In this case it
appears that the confiscation was
by a separate decree; see Introd.
p. 161 N. 1. — **τοῦ πάππου**: their
mother's father, against whose
estate the present suit is brought.

9. ἡμεῖς: the widow of Aristophanes, her brother (the speaker),
and her sister (the wife of one
Philomelus, § 15). — **ἐστερημένοι**:
on the ἐπαναφορά, see App.
§ 57. 5. — **κηδεστῶν**: Aristophanes

τῆς προικός, παιδάρια δὲ τρία ἠναγκασμένοι τρέφειν,
50 προσέτι συκοφαντούμεθα καὶ κινδυνεύομεν περὶ ὧν οἱ
πρόγονοι ἡμῖν κατέλιπον κτησάμενοι ἐκ τοῦ δικαίου.
καίτοι, ὦ ἄνδρες δικασταί, ὁ ἐμὸς πατὴρ ἐν ἅπαντι
τῷ βίῳ πλείω εἰς τὴν πόλιν ἀνήλωσεν ἢ εἰς αὑτὸν καὶ
54 τοὺς οἰκείους, διπλάσια δὲ ἢ νῦν ἔστιν ἡμῖν, ὡς ἐγὼ
10 λογιζομένῳ αὐτῷ πολλάκις παρεγενόμην. μὴ οὖν προκαταγιγνώσκετε ἀδικίαν τοῦ εἰς αὑτὸν μὲν μικρὰ δαπανῶντος, ὑμῖν δὲ πολλὰ καθ᾽ ἕκαστον τὸν ἐνιαυτόν, ἀλλ᾽
ὅσοι καὶ τὰ πατρῷα καὶ ἐάν τί ποθεν ἄλλοθεν ἔχωσιν,
59 εἰς τὰς αἰσχίστας ἡδονὰς εἰθισμένοι εἰσὶν ἀναλίσκειν.
11 χαλεπὸν μὲν οὖν, ὦ ἄνδρες δικασταί, ἀπολογεῖσθαι

and Nicophemus.— **προικός**: the
dowry of forty minae (§ 15) which
the speaker's sister brought to
Aristophanes, and which should,
at his death, have been returned
to her father, ought now to be
available for her support and that
of her little children. In the confiscation of Aristophanes's property even this dowry had been
included; cp. on § 32, and on 12.
36.— **παιδάρια**: the diminutive
touches the sympathy of the jury.
— **ἐκ τοῦ δικαίου**: a common expression, arising from a deeper
thought than that of mere manner
(δικαίως); justice is thought of as
the source and starting point of
the prosperity. Cp. 24. 5 ἐκ τῆς
τέχνης εὐπορίαν.— **εἰς αὑτόν**: see
on εἰς τὰς ναῦς § 21 (C).— δι-
πλάσια: in § 59 the sum is reckoned

as 9⅜ t. The present estate is
therefore estimated at something
more than 4 t. See further on
§§ 61 and 62.— **ὡς . . . παρεγενόμην**: *as he often computed in my
presence*. Note that ὡς, while
serving to connect the whole
clause, modifies λογιζομένῳ only.
Cp. οἷς in 25. 27. On the tense
of παρεγενόμην see on ᾐσθόμην
16. 20.

10. **προκαταγιγνώσκετε**: προ-,
in advance, i.e. πρὶν ἂν καὶ ἡμεῖς
εἴπωμεν (§ 5).— **τοῦ δαπανῶντος**:
case, HA. 752 a; G. 1123; B. 370;
Gl. 514 a. For the tense of δαπανῶντος see on ἀνιωμένου 12. 32.—
εἰς αὑτόν, εἰς ἡδονάς: see on εἰς τὰς
ναῦς § 21 (C) and (B).— **ὑμῖν**:
for the construction see Crit.
Note.

11. **μὲν οὖν**: see on 12. 3 (A).

πρὸς δόξαν ἦν ἔνιοι ἔχουσι περὶ τῆς Νικοφήμου οὐσίας,
καὶ σπάνιν ἀργυρίου ἢ νῦν ἐστιν ἐν τῇ πόλει, καὶ τοῦ
ἀγῶνος πρὸς τὸ δημόσιον ὄντος· ὅμως δὲ καὶ τούτων
ὑπαρχόντων ῥᾳδίως γνώσεσθε ὅτι οὐκ ἀληθῆ ἐστι τὰ
65 κατηγορημένα. δέομαι δ᾽ ὑμῶν πάσῃ τέχνῃ καὶ μηχανῇ μετ᾽ εὐνοίας ἀκροασαμένους ἡμῶν διὰ
τέλους, ὅ τι ἂν ὑμῖν ἄριστον καὶ εὐορκότατον
νομίζητε εἶναι, τοῦτο ψηφίσασθαι.

12 Πρῶτον μὲν οὖν, ᾧ τρόπῳ κηδεσταὶ ἡμῖν ἐγένοντο,
70 διδάξω ὑμᾶς. στρατηγῶν γὰρ Κόνων περὶ Πελοπόν-

— πρὸς δόξαν . . . καὶ σπάνιν: the
general belief that Nicophemus
was a rich man, and the present
scarcity of money in the city treasury, are two facts which favor the
prosecution, and *in the face of
which* (πρός) the speaker must
make his defense. See Introd.
p. 164.— ὑπαρχόντων: force, see on
ὑπάρχει 12. 23. — πάσῃ τέχνῃ καὶ
μηχανῇ: a comparison with § 53
shows that these words are to be
connected with ἀκροασαμένους
ψηφίσασθαι, and not with δέομαι.
12. ᾧ τρόπῳ: the relative for
the indefinite relative, see on οὕς
25. 7. — γάρ: explicative γάρ.
The original use of γάρ (a combination of γέ and ἄρα) was that of
a confirmative adverb, giving a
tone of assurance. From its frequent use in clauses which, though
coördinate, really gave the ground
or cause of what preceded, was

developed its force as denoting
cause or reason. We see a clear
effect of this origin of causal γάρ
in the fact that even the fully developed γάρ clause is still treated
as coördinate, not subordinate as
in English (see on πολλῶν γὰρ
εὐπορήσειν § 25). Lysias has the
following uses: (A) γάρ confirmative (the original force), 26. 7
ἐγὼ μὲν γὰρ οὐκ ἂν οἶμαι *I certainly
think he would not*. (B) γάρ of
the cause or reason of an action,
or the reason of a statement; so
used constantly. (C) γάρ explicative. (1) The γάρ clause proceeds
to give in full what was promised
in a general statement, as in our
passage; so 12. 2, 12. 6, 12. 19, 12.
64, 16. 4, 16. 6, 16. 13, 19. 25, 19.
50, 19. 55, 24. 4, 32. 24. (2) Sometimes the γάρ clause introduces
a new point in the discussion
without any preceding general

νῆσον, τριηραρχήσαντι τῷ ἐμῷ πατρὶ πάλαι φίλος
γεγενημένος, ἐδεήθη δοῦναι τὴν ἐμὴν ἀδελφὴν αἰτοῦντι
13 τῷ ὑεῖ τῷ Νικοφήμου. ὁ δὲ ὁρῶν αὐτοὺς ὑπ' ἐκείνου
τε πεπιστευμένους γεγονότας τε ἐπιεικεῖς τῇ τε πόλει ἕν
75 γε τῷ τότε χρόνῳ ἀρέσκοντας, ἐπείσθη δοῦναι, οὐκ
εἰδὼς τὴν ἐσομένην διαβολήν, ἀλλ' ὅτε καὶ ὑμῶν ὁστισοῦν ἂν ἐκείνοις ἠξίωσε κηδεστὴς γενέσθαι, ἐπεὶ ὅτι
γε οὐ χρημάτων ἕνεκα, ῥᾴδιον γνῶναι ἐκ τοῦ βίου
14 παντὸς καὶ τῶν ἔργων τῶν τοῦ πατρός. ἐκεῖνος γὰρ
80 ὅτ' ἦν ἐν τῇ ἡλικίᾳ, παρὸν μετὰ πολλῶν χρημάτων
γῆμαι ἄλλην, τὴν ἐμὴν μητέρα ἔλαβεν οὐδὲν ἐπιφερομένην, ὅτι δὲ Ξενοφῶντος ἦν θυγάτηρ τοῦ Εὐριπίδου

statement, 12. 38, 16. 10, 19. 34. (D)
καὶ γάρ, see on 24. 3. (E) ἀλλὰ
γάρ, see on 12. 40. — Κόνων : see
Introd. p. 160. — περὶ Πελοπόννη-
σον : see Introd. p. 160 N. 1.—
τριηραρχήσαντι : on some earlier
occasion, before the close of the
Peloponnesian War. — ἀδελφήν :
this sister was at that time a widow,
having been the wife of Phaedrus
(§ 15). — ὑεῖ : Aristophanes. For
the form see on 12. 34.

13. ἔν γε : γε, emphasizing a
prepositional phrase, stands regularly after the preposition (so § 49,
ὑπό γε ἐκείνων). Note that γε three
lines below follows the conjunction, thus emphasizing the whole
clause rather than χρημάτων alone.
— τῷ τότε χρόνῳ : Lysias wisely
avoids discussing the question of

the guilt or innocence of the two
men, contenting himself with the
invidious word διαβολήν below. —
ἀλλ' ὅτε : but at a time when. —
ἂν ἠξίωσε : potential (hypothetical) indicative, HA. 858 ; G. 1335 ;
B. 565 ; Gl. 467 c ; GMT. 243–5,
GS. 430. Cp. §§ 18, 24, 42 ; 25.
12, 25. 27.

14. παρόν : see on 12. 30. —
μετά : μετά is commonly used with
gen. of personal words only. With
material words Lysias uses it only
here and in 4. 7, 32. 16, 34. 4, Fr.
50 (Bury, Class. Rev. 7. 395).—
οὐδὲν ἐπιφερομένην : in speaking of
the dowry a bride is said ἐπιφέ-
ρεσθαι, her father or guardian ἐπιδοῦναι (cp. § 15 ; 16. 10, 32. 6). —
Ξενοφῶντος : not the Xenophon
of the Anabasis (the son of

νέος, ὃς οὐ μόνον ἰδίᾳ χρηστὸς ἐδόκει εἶναι, ἀλλὰ καὶ
15 στρατηγεῖν αὐτὸν ἠξιώσατε, ὡς ἐγὼ ἀκούω. τὰς τοίνυν
85 ἐμὰς ἀδελφὰς ἐθελόντων τινῶν λαβεῖν ἀπροίκους πάνυ
πλουσίων οὐκ ἔδωκεν, ὅτι ἐδόκουν κάκιον γεγονέναι,
ἀλλὰ τὴν μὲν Φιλομήλῳ τῷ Παιανιεῖ, ὃν οἱ πολλοὶ
βελτίω ἡγοῦνται εἶναι ἢ πλουσιώτερον, τὴν δὲ πένητι

Gryllus), but a general in the Peloponnesian War, who with two colleagues received the surrender of Potidaea in 430/29, and died the next year in battle before Spartolus on the Chalcidic peninsula (Thuc. 2. 70, 79). The Euripides mentioned as his father was not the poet. — **αὐτόν**: for the difference between the Greek and the English idiom see on αὐτοῖς (before χάριν) 25. 11. — **ὡς ἐγὼ ἀκούω**: the speaker, in his character of the simple and modest citizen, would give the impression of not being exactly informed on matters of political history, and of not dwelling too much upon his maternal grandfather's honorable career. Cp. p. 174.

15. **πάνυ πλουσίων**: so this speaker says πολλὴν πάνυ (§ 16), πάνυ ἐπιθυμῇ (§ 30), πάνυ πολλά (§ 48), οὐ πάνυ θαυμάζω (§ 49). πάνυ appears nowhere else in Lysias except in 24. 15 and in the doubtful fragment 61. It would seem therefore that Lysias in talking with his client noticed the young man's fondness for this *very*,

and so gave a touch of naturalness to his speech by letting him use his favorite word repeatedly. Compare with this the fact that the intensive γε is used in this speech seven times, while in XII, written for his own delivery, Lysias uses it only three times, though that speech is a third longer. In XXXI, written for a client, γε appears eleven times, though the speech is only a third as long as XII. Our speech also contains three of the four instances of the emphatic ἀλλὰ μήν to be found in Lysias. Cp. on ἡγοῦμαι 25. 2. — **Φιλομήλῳ**: the family was old and honored. That Philomelus was not a poor man is evident from several inscriptions which preserve his name as trierarch. — **βελτίω ἢ πλουσιώτερον**: *more honorable than rich.* "When two adjectives or adverbs are compared ἤ is always used, and both stand in the comparative degree." B. 426 n. 3; cp. HA. 645. So in Latin: *verior quam gratior more true than agreeable,* Livy 22. 38. — **τὴν δέ**: see on ἀδελφήν § 12.

184 ΛΥΣΙΟΥ

γεγενημένῳ οὐ διὰ κακίαν, ἀδελφιδῷ δὲ ὄντι, Φαίδρῳ
90 τῷ Μυρρινουσίῳ, ἐπιδοὺς τετταράκοντα μνᾶς, κᾷτ᾽
16 Ἀριστοφάνει τὸ ἴσον. πρὸς δὲ τούτοις ἐμοὶ πολλὴν
ἐξὸν πάνυ προῖκα λαβεῖν ἐλάττω συνεβούλευσεν, ὥστε
εὖ εἰδέναι ὅτι κηδεσταῖς χρησοίμην κοσμίοις καὶ
σώφροσι. καὶ νῦν ἔχω γυναῖκα τὴν Κριτοδήμου θυγα-
95 τέρα τοῦ Ἀλωπεκῆθεν, ὃς ὑπὸ Λακεδαιμονίων ἀπέθανεν,
17 ὅτε ἡ ναυμαχία ἐγένετο ἡ ἐν Ἑλλησπόντῳ. καίτοι, ὦ
ἄνδρες δικασταί, ὅστις αὐτός τε ἄνευ χρημάτων ἔγημε
τοῖν τε θυγατέροιν πολὺ ἀργύριον ἐπέδωκε τῷ τε υἱεῖ
ὀλίγην προῖκα ἔλαβε, πῶς οὐκ εἰκὸς περὶ τούτου πι-

That this was the daughter who afterward became the wife of Aristophanes is clear from § 17, where we learn that there were only two daughters. — **Φαίδρῳ**: the Phaedrus whom we know through Plato as a young friend of Socrates (*Sympos.* 176 D), one of the group who listened to the Sophist Hippias (*Prot.* 315 C), and the friend and enthusiastic admirer of Lysias, delicately portrayed in Plato's *Phaedrus*. It was not strange that when the proposition was made to confiscate the property of Aristophanes (cp. p. 161 N. 1), his widow turned for help to the friend of her first husband, now at the height of his fame as an advocate, nor that when the present suit against her father's estate came on Lysias again wrote the defense. — **τετταράκοντα μνᾶς**: see on 16. 10.

— **κᾷτ᾽**: *i.e.* after the death of Phaedrus. For εἶτα see on 12. 26. — **Ἀριστοφάνει τὸ ἴσον**: = Ἀριστοφάνει ἔδωκεν, τὸ ἴσον ἐπιδούς. The dat. with ἐπιδούς would be used only of the name of the bride, as in § 17 τοῖν θυγατέροιν ἐπέδωκε.

16. **ἐξόν**: cp. παρόν § 14. — **ὥστε . . . εἰδέναι**: one of the less common expressions of purpose, representing it as the intended result, like the English "so as to"; HA. 953 a; G. 1452; B. 595 n.; Gl. 566 b. — **κοσμίοις**: see on κοσμίους 12. 20. — **ἀπέθανεν**: after the battle of Aegospotami the Spartans put to death their Athenian prisoners (Xen. *Hell.* 2. 1. 32), 3000 in number (Plut. *Lysander* XI). — **ἡ ναυμαχία**: see on 12. 43.

100 στεύειν ὡς οὐχ ἕνεκα χρημάτων τούτοις κηδεστὴς
ἐγένετο ;

18 Ἀλλὰ μὴν ὅ γε Ἀριστοφάνης ἤδη ἔχων τὴν γυναῖκα
ὅτι πολλοῖς ἂν μᾶλλον ἐχρῆτο ἢ τῷ ἐμῷ πατρί, ῥᾴδιον
γνῶναι. ἤ τε γὰρ ἡλικία πολὺ διάφορος, ἤ τε φύσις
105 ἔτι πλέον· ἐκείνῳ μὲν γὰρ ἀρκοῦν ἦν τὰ ἑαυτοῦ πράττειν, Ἀριστοφάνης δὲ οὐ μόνον τῶν ἰδίων ἀλλὰ καὶ
τῶν κοινῶν ἐβούλετο ἐπιμελεῖσθαι, καὶ εἴ τι ἦν αὐτῷ
19 ἀργύριον, ἀνήλωσεν ἐπιθυμῶν τιμᾶσθαι. γνώσεσθε
δὲ ὅτι ἀληθῆ λέγω ἐξ αὐτῶν ὧν ἐκεῖνος ἔπραττε.
110 πρῶτον μὲν γὰρ βουλομένου Κόνωνος πέμπειν τινὰ
εἰς Σικελίαν, ᾤχετο ὑποστὰς μετὰ Εὐνόμου, Διονυσίου

17. ἕνεκα χρημάτων: ἕνεκα is
regularly placed after its object.
Lysias places it before its object
in two other passages only, ἕνεκα
πόρνης ἀνθρώπου 4. 9, and ἕνεκα
χρημάτων 24. 2. It may also stand
after a modifier of the genitive, as in
7. 40 τούτου ἕνεκα τοῦ κινδύνου, and
12. 98 μικρῶν ἂν ἕνεκα συμβολαίων.

18. ἂν . . . ἐχρῆτο: potential
indic.; see on ἂν ἠξίωσε § 13. —
καὶ εἰ: accidental juxtaposition of
the particles (so in 25. 13, 32. 13),
not the καὶ εἰ of 16. 2. — ἀνήλωσεν: note that the condition and
conclusion are in the "particular"
form (the conclusion in the summary aorist), 'he spent the property that he had'; in the next
sentence the detailed description
of this conduct is introduced by
the imperfect ἔπραττε.

19. ᾤχετο ὑποστάς: he undertook (the service) and went. —
Εὐνόμου: Isocrates (15. 93, 94)
mentions Eunomus first in a
group of men who have been
followers of his "from youth to
old age," all of whom the city
had honored with golden crowns,
and who had spent of their private
fortunes generously for the city.
Xenophon's account (Hell. 5. 1. 5,
9) of his failure as a naval commander not long before this speech
was delivered gives a less favorable
impression of his ability; he was
easily entrapped by the Spartan
commander, and lost four of his
little fleet of thirteen ships. —
Διονυσίου: this is Sauppe's conjecture for Λυσίου of the Ms.; for
the important question as to Lysias
involved in this reading, see Crit.

φίλου ὄντος καὶ ξένου, τὸ πλῆθος τὸ ὑμέτερον πλεῖστα
ἀγαθὰ πεποιηκότος, ὡς ἐγὼ ἀκήκοα τῶν ἐν Πειραιεῖ
20 τῶν παραγενομένων. ἦσαν δ᾽ ἐλπίδες τοῦ πλοῦ πεῖσαι
115 Διονύσιον κηδεστὴν μὲν γενέσθαι Εὐαγόρᾳ, πολέμιον
δὲ Λακεδαιμονίοις, φίλον δὲ καὶ σύμμαχον τῇ πόλει
τῇ ὑμετέρᾳ. καὶ ταῦτ᾽ ἔπραττον πολλῶν κινδύνων
ὑπαρχόντων πρὸς τὴν θάλατταν καὶ τοὺς πολεμίους,
119 καὶ ἔπεισαν Διονύσιον μὴ πέμψαι τὰς τριήρεις ἃς
21 τότε παρεσκεύαστο Λακεδαιμονίοις. μετὰ δὲ ταῦτα
ἐπειδὴ οἱ πρέσβεις ἧκον ἐκ Κύπρου ἐπὶ τὴν βοήθειαν,
οὐδὲν ἐνέλιπε προθυμίας σπεύδων. ὑμεῖς δὲ δέκα

Note. Early in 393 a compli-
mentary decree had been passed
in honor of Dionysius and his
brothers (Köhler, *Hermes* III.
156 ff.). — τὸ πλῆθος : see on 12. 42.
— ὡς ἐγὼ ἀκήκοα: the same modest disclaimer of political knowledge as in § 14 ὡς ἐγὼ ἀκούω.
As the speaker is now a man of
thirty (§ 55), he was a boy of
fourteen at the time of the Return. — τῶν ἐν Πειραιεῖ : men of
the Piraeus party, *i.e.* the democrats ; cp. 12. 55.
   20. τοῦ πλοῦ : case, HA. 729 b ;
G. 1085. 2 ; B. 349. Here πεῖσαι
takes the place of the common
objective genitive with ἐλπίς ; cp.
§ 53 ἐλπὶς οὐδεμία σωτηρίας ; 25.
21 ἐλπίδας εἴχετε τῆς καθόδου. —
κηδεστήν : by marrying one of
the daughters of Evagoras. Dionysius was already living with

two wives, Doris, an Italian, and
Aristomache, a Syracusan (Diodor. 14. 44). In the choice of
both he had been governed by
political considerations. — ὑπαρχόντων : force, see on ὑπάρχει 12.
23. — πρὸς τὴν θάλατταν : probably it was a winter voyage. Lysias
always uses πρός and acc. with
κίνδυνος and κινδυνεύειν where the
English uses either *in the face of*
or *from*. So in 14. 15, 15. 12, 16.
12, 16. 18. — ἔπεισαν : with the mention of the difficulties under which
the ambassadors were laboring
during their mission we have the
imperfect, ἔπραττον, but the summary statement of the result is in
the aorist, ἔπεισαν. — παρεσκεύαστο : tense, see Crit. Note.
   21. οἱ πρέσβεις : for these
events see Introd. p. 160 f. — ἐπί:
one of Lysias's two instances of

τριήρεις αὐτοῖς ἔδοτε καὶ τἆλλα ἐψηφίσασθε, ἀργυρίου δ᾽ εἰς τὸν ἀπόστολον ἠπόρουν. ὀλίγα μὲν γὰρ
125 ἦλθον ἔχοντες χρήματα, πολλῶν δὲ προσεδεήθησαν·
οὐ γὰρ μόνον τοὺς εἰς τὰς ναῦς, ἀλλὰ καὶ πελταστὰς
22 ἐμισθώσαντο καὶ ὅπλα ἐπρίαντο. ᾿Αριστοφάνης οὖν
τῶν χρημάτων τὰ μὲν πλεῖστα αὐτὸς παρέσχεν· ἐπειδὴ
δὲ οὐχ ἱκανὰ ἦν, τοὺς φίλους ἔπειθε δεόμενος καὶ ἐγ-
130 γυώμενος, καὶ τοῦ ἀδελφοῦ τοῦ ὁμοπατρίου ἀποκειμέ-
νας παρ᾽ αὐτῷ τετταράκοντα μνᾶς ἀπορῶν κατεχρήσατο.
τῇ δὲ προτεραίᾳ ᾗ ἀνήγετο, εἰσελθὼν ὡς τὸν πατέρα
τὸν ἐμὸν ἐκέλευσε χρῆσαι ὅ τι εἴη ἀργύριον. προσδεῖν γὰρ ἔφη πρὸς τὸν μισθὸν τοῖς πελτασταῖς. ἦσαν

ἐπί with accus. to denote purpose ;
see on εἰς σωτηρίαν 12. 14. —
τἆλλα: the alliance of which this
expedition was the result (Xen.
Hell. 4. 8. 24). — ἠπόρουν: Athens
furnished ships equipped by her
own trierarchs (cp. § 25), but
Evagoras had probably counted
on her supplying crews and fight-
ing-men ; his ambassadors had
not brought money enough to
meet the unexpected expense of
hiring them. — εἰς τὰς ναῦς: from
the use of εἰς to denote local
destination comes its frequent use
to express figurative destination,
passing over to the full idea of
purpose (see on 12. 14). Closely
connected with the ideas of destination and of purpose is the
frequent use of εἰς governing the
name of the person or thing for

which or upon which expenditure
is made. (A) Figurative destination, this passage, εἰς τὸν ἀπόστολον above, and § 39. (B) Expenditure for or upon an object,
§§ 10, 25, 43; 32. 9, 32. 21, 32.
22. (C) Expenditure upon a person, §§ 9, 10, 56, 62; 25. 17,
32. 20.

22. οὖν: see on § 7 (B). —
ἔπειθε: conative impf., see on ἔπειθεν 12. 58 (contrast πεῖσαι and
ἔπεισαν § 20). That he succeeded
in part is evident from § 24. — τοῦ
ἀδελφοῦ τοῦ ὁμοπατρίου: *his half-
brother*. For the Greek for *own
brother* see 32. 4. — παρ᾽ αὐτῷ:
with him = in his care. So in
§§ 36, 48; 32. 16. — ὡς: see on
16. 4. — πρὸς τὸν μισθόν: πρός
rather than the usual εἰς, from the
influence of προς- in προσδεῖν.

135 δ' ἡμῖν ἔνδον ἑπτὰ μναῖ· ὁ δὲ καὶ ταύτας λαβὼν κατε-
23 χρήσατο. τίνα γὰρ οἴεσθε, ὦ ἄνδρες δικασταί, φιλό-
τιμον μὲν ὄντα, ἐπιστολῶν δ' αὐτῷ ἡκουσῶν παρὰ τοῦ
πατρὸς μηδενὸς ἀπορήσειν ἐκ Κύπρου, ἡρημένον δὲ
πρεσβευτὴν καὶ μέλλοντα πλεῖν ὡς Εὐαγόραν, ὑπο-
140 λιπέσθαι ἄν τι τῶν ὄντων, ἀλλ' οὐκ εἰ ἦν δυνατὸς
πάντα παρασχόντα χαρίσασθαι ἐκείνῳ ἐφ' ᾧ τε καὶ
κομίσασθαι μὴ ἐλάττω; Ὡς τοίνυν ταῦτ' ἐστὶν ἀληθῆ,
κάλει μοι Εὔνομον.

MARTYPIA

144 Κάλει μοι καὶ τοὺς ἄλλους μάρτυρας.

ΜΑΡΤΥΡΕΣ

24 Τῶν μὲν μαρτύρων ἀκούετε, οὐ μόνον ὅτι ἔχρησαν τὸ ἀργύριον ἐκείνου δεηθέντος, ἀλλὰ καὶ ὅτι

For the only other instance in Lysias of πρός in a purpose phrase see on § 61 and cp. on εἰς σωτηρίαν 12. 14.— ἔνδον: *in the house,* "*by us,*" cp. on § 47.

23. ὄντα, ἡκουσῶν: for correlation of gen. abs. with participles in other construction see on πρατ- τούσης κτλ. 12. 69.— πατρός: the father was in Cyprus with Evago- ras.— μηδενός: this form rather than οὐδενός from the idea of *promising* implied in ἐπιστολῶν. For the use of μή with fut. infin. with words of this class see HA. 1024 (last sentence) and 948 a; G. 1496 and 1286; B. 549. 2; Gl.

579 a.— ἀπορήσειν: Aristopha- nes's father assured him that on his arrival at Cyprus Evagoras would more than repay him for all advances that he might make for the equipment of the expedi- tion. — ἐκ Κύπρου: see Crit. Note. — ἄν: with both ὑπολιπέσθαι and χαρίσασθαι. The construction is that of ind. disc. for the potential indic. noted on ἂν ἠξίωσε § 13. — τῶν ὄντων, . . . πάντα: his own property, . . . all the cost of the expedition. — ἀλλ' οὐκ: *but (would) not rather.* — Εὔνομον: called to acknowledge his testi- mony as to the facts of §§ 19 and 20.

ἀπειλήφασιν· ἐκομίσθη γὰρ αὐτοῖς ἐπὶ τῆς τριή-
ρους.

'Ράδιον μὲν οὖν ἐκ τῶν εἰρημένων γνῶναι ὅτι τοιού-
150 των καιρῶν συμπεσόντων οὐδενὸς ἂν ἐφείσατο τῶν
25 ἑαυτοῦ· ὃ δὲ μέγιστον τεκμήριον· Δῆμος γὰρ ὁ
Πυριλάμπους, τριηραρχῶν εἰς Κύπρον, ἐδεήθη μου
προσελθεῖν αὐτῷ, λέγων ὅτι ἔλαβε μὲν σύμβολον

24. ἀπειλήφασιν: the perfect,
because the question at issue is
where the money now is which
Aristophanes is supposed to have
had at his death. The speaker
shows that this part of it *is now
back in the hands* of the men who
loaned it to him. — ἐπὶ τῆς τριή-
ρους: probably one of the two
state dispatch boats, the *Paralus*
or the *Salaminia*, was sent to
carry Aristophanes in advance of
the fleet on his mission to Cyprus,
and immediately brought back the
money from Evagoras with which
to repay the loans that had been
made in his service. — μὲν οὖν:
force, see on 12. 3 (C). — ἂν ἐφείσατο: cp. on ἂν ἠξίωσε § 13, and
ὑπολιπέσθαι ἄν § 23.

25. ὅ: the antecedent is the
γάρ clause. See on § 33, and cp.
32. 24. — Δῆμος: Aristophanes
speaks of this Demus as Δῆμος
καλός (*Wasps* 98). Plato has his
joke on the name when he says
that Callicles is lover of two at
once, τοῦ τε 'Αθηναίων δήμου καὶ

τοῦ Πυριλάμπους (*Gorg.* 481 D).
The father, Pyrilampus, was, according to Plato (*Charm.* 158 A),
among the most honored of all
who were sent from time to time
to negotiate with the king of Persia. It is probable that this gold
cup was given to him and inherited by Demus, together with his
father's ξενία. Such cups, doubtless bearing some royal sign, were
common gifts of the Great King,
intended to serve as a token of
his confidence in the bearer and
his desire that he be helped by
Persian officials in all the satrapies.
The possession of such a token
would be of especial value to Aristophanes on his mission to Asia.
— γάρ: γάρ explicative, see on
§ 12. — τριηραρχῶν: in the fleet
of ten triremes which was to follow
as soon as possible. We learn
from Xenophon (*Hell.* 4. 8. 24)
that the fleet was overtaken on
the voyage by the Spartans and
every trireme captured. — εἰς Κύπρον: εἰς of 'destination,' see on

παρὰ βασιλέως τοῦ μεγάλου φιάλην χρυσῆν, ὑποθή-
155 σει δὲ Ἀριστοφάνει λαβὼν ἑκκαίδεκα μνᾶς ἐπ' αὐτῇ,
ἵν' ἔχοι ἀναλίσκειν εἰς τὴν τριηραρχίαν· ἐπειδὴ δὲ
εἰς Κύπρον ἀφίκοιτο, λύσεσθαι ἀποδοὺς εἴκοσι μνᾶς·
πολλῶν γὰρ ἀγαθῶν καὶ ἄλλων χρημάτων εὐπορήσειν
26 διὰ τὸ σύμβολον ἐν πάσῃ τῇ ἠπείρῳ. Ἀριστοφάνης
160 τοίνυν ἀκούων μὲν ταῦτα Δήμου, δεομένου δ' ἐμοῦ,
μέλλων δ' ἄξειν τὸ χρυσίον, τέτταρας δὲ μνᾶς τόκον
λήψεσθαι, οὐκ ἔφη εἶναι, ἀλλ' ὤμνυε καὶ προσδεδανεῖσθαι τοῖς ξένοις ἄλλοθεν, ἐπειδὴ ἥδιστ' ἂν ἀνθρώπων ἄγειν τε εὐθὺς ἐκεῖνο τὸ σύμβολον καὶ χαρίσασθαι

εἰς τὰς ναῦς § 21. — ὑποθήσει
κτλ. : the text here is doubtful
(see Crit. Note), but the proposition of Demus certainly was that
Aristophanes loan him sixteen
minae to help him fit out his trireme, and take the cup as security.
The offer of 25 % on the short loan
was a tempting one (the ordinary
rate was 12 % to 18 % per annum).
— εἰς τὴν τριηραρχίαν : see on εἰς
τὰς ναῦς § 21 (Β). — πολλῶν γὰρ
εὐπορήσειν : the Greek does not
treat a γάρ clause as fully subordinate, hence the ind. disc. carries
the infin. construction to εὐπορήσειν. See on § 12.
   26. ἀκούων, δεομένου : cp. on
ὄντα, ἠκουσῶν § 23. — εἶναι :
= ἐξεῖναι. — καὶ προσδεδανεῖσθαι :
he had not only spent all of his
own money, but had also borrowed. For the middle see HA.

816. 7 ; G. 1245 ; B. 506. Cp.
ἐδανείσατο 12. 59.— τοῖς ξένοις :
the mercenaries mentioned in § 21.
— ἀνθρώπων : part. gen. with ἥδιστα, HA. 756, 755 b ; G. 1088 ;
B. 355. 1 ; Gl. 507 d. Cp. μόνος
ἀνθρώπων 24. 9. ἥδιστα, reënforced
by ἀνθρώπων (see L. & S. ἄνθρω-
πος 3 b) and followed by εὐθύς
instantly, emphasizes the eagerness with which Aristophanes
would have accepted the offer. —
ἂν ἄγειν καὶ χαρίσασθαι : for with
the utmost pleasure (he said) he
would instantly have taken that
security with him and have done
us the favor. For the occasional
use of the infin. in ind. disc. even
in a subordinate clause see HA.
947 a ; G. 1524 ; B. 671 n. ; GMT.
755. This is the only instance
of the construction in Lysias. The
direct form would be ἥδιστ' ἂν

27 ἡμῖν ἃ ἐδεόμεθα. ὡς δὲ ταῦτ' ἐστὶν ἀληθῆ, μάρτυρας
166 ὑμῖν παρέξομαι.

ΜΑΡΤΥΡΕΣ

Ὅτι μὲν τοίνυν οὐ κατέλιπεν Ἀριστοφάνης ἀργύριον
οὐδὲ χρυσίον, ῥᾴδιον γνῶναι ἐκ τῶν εἰρημένων καὶ
μεμαρτυρημένων· χαλκώματα δὲ σύμμεικτα οὐ πολλὰ
170 ἐκέκτητο, ἀλλὰ καὶ ὅθ' εἰστία τοὺς παρ' Εὐαγόρου
πρεσβεύοντας, αἰτησάμενος ἐχρήσατο. ἃ δὲ κατέλιπεν, ἀναγνώσεται ὑμῖν.

ΑΠΟΓΡΑΦΗ ΧΑΛΚΩΜΑΤΩΝ

28 Ἴσως ἐνίοις ὑμῶν, ὦ ἄνδρες δικασταί, δοκεῖ ὀλίγα
εἶναι· ἀλλ' ἐκεῖνο ἐνθυμεῖσθε, ὅτι πρὶν τὴν ναυμαχίαν

ἦγον τε . . . καὶ ἐχαρισάμην (if I had the money) *most gladly would I take this security with me and do you the favor.* For this rare use of the aorist indic. in an unreal apodosis belonging to time immediately future see 12. 34 Crit. Note. But another explanation is possible; it may be that the ἐπειδή clause is incorporated into the ind. disc. only so far as to throw its verbs into the infin., otherwise leaving the expression as it would be uttered by the *narrator*, not by the *original speaker*; the narrator would say ἥδιστ' ἂν ἦγέ τε . . . καὶ ἐχαρίσατο *most gladly would he have carried that security with him and have done us the favor.* In support of the second explanation is the ἐκεῖνο (which

implies the point of view of the narrator); cp. on ἠκκλησιάζετε 12. 73. For analogous cases of incomplete incorporation of subord. clauses in ind. disc. see GMT. 674. 2, 3.

27. σύμμεικτα: see L. & S. σύμμικτα; the spelling of the text is established by inscriptions.— αἰτησάμενος: cp. ᾐτημένους 24. 12.— ἀναγνώσεται: *sc.* ὁ γραμματεύς, GS. 72.

28. ὀλίγα: *i.e.* too small to be true. — πρίν . . . νικῆσαι: πρίν with infin. even though the principal clause is negative. "An infinitive with πρίν sometimes depends on a negative clause, where a finite mood might be allowed, because the temporal relation is still so prominent as to determine

175 νικῆσαι Κόνωνα, Ἀριστοφάνει γῇ μὲν οὐκ ἦν ἀλλ᾽ ἢ
χωρίδιον μικρὸν Ῥαμνοῦντι. ἐγένετο δ᾽ ἡ ναυμαχία
29 ἐπ᾽ Εὐβουλίδου ἄρχοντος. ἐν οὖν τέτταρσιν ἢ πέντε
ἔτεσι, πρότερον μὴ ὑπαρχούσης οὐσίας, χαλεπόν, ὦ
ἄνδρες δικασταί, τραγῳδοῖς τε δὶς χορηγῆσαι, ὑπὲρ
180 αὑτοῦ τε καὶ τοῦ πατρός, καὶ τρία ἔτη συνεχῶς τριηραρχῆσαι, εἰσφοράς τε πολλὰς εἰσενηνοχέναι, οἰκίαν
τε πεντήκοντα μνῶν πρίασθαι, γῆς τε πλέον ἢ τριακό-
σια πλέθρα κτήσασθαι· ἔτι δὲ πρὸς τούτοις οἴεσθε

the construction," GMT. 628, cp. 627. — **ναυμαχίαν**: the battle of Cnidus, 394 B.C. — **ἀλλ᾽ ἤ**: *except*. **Ῥαμνοῦντι**: a true locative, HA. 783 b ; G. 1197 ; B. 383 ; Gl. 527 a. Rhamnus was an Attic deme on the east coast, north of Marathon.

29. τέτταρσιν: between the battle of Cnidus (394) and the mission to Cyprus, see Introd. p. 161 N. 1. — **πρότερον μὴ ὑπαρχούσης οὐσίας**: *assuming that (μή) he had no property at the beginning*. See on ὑπάρχει 12. 23. For μή see on μήτε 12. 68 (A). — **τραγῳδοῖς**: see on 24. 9. — **χορηγῆσαι**: the sums spent in this and the other services are given in § 42. — **πατρός**: the father being absent on public service. — **συνεχῶς**: by law any one liturgy fell upon a citizen not oftener than every other year ; the trierarchy (at any rate in the middle of the fourth century), not oftener than one year in three (Isae. 7. 38). But public-spirited

citizens sometimes volunteered for continuous service (so the speaker of XXI says that he served as trierarch for a period of seven years (21. 2)). — **τριηραρχῆσαι**: note the 'complexive' aorist in this definite and summary statement of a "continued act"; see on ᾤκησε 12. 4. — **οἰκίαν**: that the house of a man reputed to be rich was worth only $900 is another indication of the simplicity of life in Athens (see on 32. 23) and of the great purchasing power of money there. — **γῆς**: the land cost (in round numbers) 250 minae (§ 42, land and house cost "more than 5 t." = 300 minae +). Reckoning the plethron as = .087 hekt. (Nissen), we have 65 acres at about $70 an acre. This is the only passage in Greek authors which, by giving both the contents and the price of a piece of land, enables us to reckon land value. As we know neither the situation

30 χρῆναι ἔπιπλα πολλὰ καταλελοιπέναι; ἀλλ' οὐδ' οἱ
185 πάλαι πλούσιοι δοκοῦντες εἶναι ἄξια λόγου ἔχοιεν ἂν
ἐξενεγκεῖν· ἐνίοτε γὰρ οὐκ ἔστιν, οὐδ' ἐάν τις πάνυ
ἐπιθυμῇ, πρίασθαι τοιαῦτα ἃ κτησαμένῳ εἰς τὸν λοιπὸν
31 χρόνον ἡδονὴν ἂν παρέχοι. ἀλλὰ τόδε σκοπεῖτε. τῶν
ἄλλων, ὅσων ἐδημεύσατε τὰ χρήματα, οὐχ ὅπως σκεύη
190 ἀπέδοσθε, ἀλλὰ καὶ αἱ θύραι ἀπὸ τῶν οἰκημάτων ἀφηρ-
πάσθησαν· ἡμεῖς δὲ ἤδη δεδημευμένων καὶ ἐξεληλυ-
θυίας τῆς ἐμῆς ἀδελφῆς φύλακα κατεστήσαμεν ἐν τῇ
ἐρήμῃ οἰκίᾳ, ἵνα μήτε θυρώματα μήτε ἀγγεῖα μήτε
ἄλλο μηδὲν ἀπόλοιτο. ἔπιπλα δὲ ἀπεφαίνετο πλεῖν ἢ
32 χιλίων δραχμῶν, ὅσα οὐδενὸς πώποτ' ἐλάβετε. πρὸς
196 δὲ τούτοις καὶ πρότερον πρὸς τοὺς συνδίκους καὶ νῦν

nor the nature of this land, even
this information is of little worth.
— **καταλελοιπέναι**: for the tense
cp. on ἀπειλήφασιν § 24.

30. **ἄξια λόγου**: *sc.* ἔπιπλα. —
ἐξενεγκεῖν: *to produce, exhibit*, as
evidence of wealth. — **ἐνίοτε γάρ
κτλ.**: 'even old and wealthy families are not always able to find in
the market personal ornaments
and house furnishings (all included in ἔπιπλα) that correspond
with their means and their tastes.'

31. **οὐχ ὅπως** (= οὐκ ἐρῶ ὅπως)
κτλ.: *not to speak of your selling
the furniture,* — *even the doors
had been stripped from the rooms,*
= *not only did you not sell the furniture* (that having been removed
before your officers could seize it),

*but even the doors had been stripped
from the rooms.* HA. 1035 a; G.
1504 (where the passage is mis-
translated after Reiske). — **δεδημευμένων**: *sc.* τῶν χρημάτων from
τὰ χρήματα above. — **ἀπεφαίνετο**;
i.e. when the officers made their
inventory. — **πλεῖν**: form, see on
32. 20. — **χιλίων δραχμῶν**: a further
indication of the simplicity of life
and the high purchasing power of
money. — **οὐδενός**: for the case cp.
on ὑμῶν 12. 40 and ἧς 12. 83.

32. **πρότερον**: in the preliminary steps of the case. — **συνδίκους**: see on 16. 7. We conclude
that this extraordinary commission
had been continued after the immediate occasion for its appointment was past, and that it now

ἐθέλομεν πίστιν δοῦναι, ἥτις ἐστὶ μεγίστη τοῖς ἀνθρώποις, μηδὲν ἔχειν τῶν Ἀριστοφάνους χρημάτων, ἐνοφείλεσθαι δὲ τὴν προῖκα τῆς ἀδελφῆς καὶ τὰς ἑπτὰ
200 μνᾶς, ἃς ᾤχετο λαβὼν παρὰ τοῦ πατρὸς τοῦ ἐμοῦ.
33 πῶς ἂν οὖν εἶεν ἄνθρωποι ἀθλιώτεροι, ἢ εἰ τὰ σφέτερ'
αὐτῶν ἀπολωλεκότες δοκοῖεν τἀκείνων ἔχειν; ὁ δὲ
πάντων δεινότατον, τὴν ἀδελφὴν ὑποδέξασθαι παιδία
ἔχουσαν πολλά, καὶ ταῦτα τρέφειν, μηδ' αὐτοὺς ἔχον-
205 τας μηδέν, ἐὰν ὑμεῖς τὰ ὄντ' ἀφέλησθε.
34   Φέρε πρὸς θεῶν Ὀλυμπίων· οὕτω γὰρ σκοπεῖτε, ὦ

had jurisdiction in cases of confiscation in general. The preliminary hearing and the presidency
at the trial would rest with these
σύνδικοι (see App. § 9). We find
no mention of such a board after
this date. — πίστιν: by the most
solemn oath. Cp. 12. 10, 32. 13.
— ἐνοφείλεσθαι: *rests as a claim*
(upon the confiscated property).
The dowry was never looked upon
as the absolute property of the
husband, but as held in trust for
the wife; it could not therefore
be confiscated with the husband's
estate; cp. on καὶ τοὺς παῖδας 12.
36, and see Gardner and Jevons,
Greek Antiquities, p. 555 ff. —
ἑπτὰ μνᾶς: the loan mentioned
in § 22.

33. ἐκείνων: Aristophanes and
his father. The speaker unconsciously passes from the hypothetical case (ἄνθρωποι) to his

own. — ὁ . . . δεινότατον: the construction is, ὁ δὲ πάντων δεινό-
τατον (ἐστίν) | (τοῦτ' ἔστιν) |
ὑποδέξασθαι καὶ τρέφειν. A simpler expression is that of Plato's
Apology 41 b καὶ δὴ τὸ μέγιστον
| (τοῦτ' ἔστιν) | ἐξετάζοντα διά-
γειν; less close is the connection
where the relative precedes a clause
with a finite verb, as in 32. 24 ὁ
δὲ πάντων δεινότατον (ἐστίν), ὦ
ἄνδρες δικασταί· οὗτος γὰρ . . .
λελόγισται. So in 19. 25. Cp.
HA. 1009 a. — παιδία πολλά: *a
lot of little children* is something
of an exaggeration for the παιδάρια
τρία of § 9. — μηδέ: see on μήτε
12. 68 (B).

34. πρὸς θεῶν Ὀλυμπίων: the
only form of oath used by Lysias,
and this only here and in § 54, and
in the earnest closing appeal to the
jury in 13. 95. This avoidance
of the common oaths of every-day

ἄνδρες δικασταί. εἴ τις ὑμῶν ἔτυχε δοὺς Τιμοθέῳ τῷ
Κόνωνος τὴν θυγατέρα ἢ τὴν ἀδελφήν, καὶ ἐκείνου
ἀποδημήσαντος καὶ ἐν διαβολῇ γενομένου ἐδημεύθη
210 ἡ οὐσία, καὶ μὴ ἐγένετο τῇ πόλει πραθέντων ἁπάντων
τέτταρα τάλαντα ἀργυρίου, διὰ τοῦτο ἠξιοῦτε ἂν τοὺς
κηδεστὰς τοὺς ἐκείνου καὶ τοὺς προσήκοντας ἀπολέσθαι, ὅτι οὐδὲ πολλοστὸν μέρος τῆς δόξης τῆς παρ᾽
35 ὑμῖν ἐφάνη τὰ χρήματα; ἀλλὰ μὴν τοῦτό γε πάντες
215 ἐπίστασθε Κόνωνα μὲν ἄρχοντα, Νικόφημον δὲ ποι-
οῦντα ὅ τι ἐκεῖνος προστάττοι. τῶν οὖν ὠφελειῶν
Κόνωνα εἰκὸς πολλοστὸν μέρος ἄλλῳ τινὶ μεταδιδόναι,
ὥστ᾽ εἰ οἴονται πολλὰ γενέσθαι Νικοφήμῳ, ὁμολογή-
36 σειαν ἂν τὰ Κόνωνος εἶναι πλεῖν ἢ δεκαπλάσια. ἔτι
220 δὲ φαίνονται οὐδὲν πώποτε διενεχθέντες, ὥστ᾽ εἰκὸς καὶ

impassioned speech is as fitting to
the calm and simple style of Lysias
as is their constant use to the
vehement style of Demosthenes.
— **γάρ**: force, see on § 12 (C) (2).
— **Τιμοθέῳ τῷ Κόνωνος**: Conon had
died in Cyprus not long before
this. Because of his services to
the king of Persia, and later to
Evagoras of Cyprus, he had been
believed to be enormously rich.
His son, Timotheus, was now
already well known in the city,
although he did not enter upon
his career of political leadership
until some years later. — **τέτταρα
τάλαντα**: we conclude that the sale
of Aristophanes's property had
yielded about this sum to the state.

— **ἀπολέσθαι**: financial 'ruin'; so
in § 45. — **ὅτι οὐδὲ πολλοστόν κτλ.** :
*because his property was found to
be not even the smallest part of
what you had supposed.* πολλοστὸν μέρος τῆς δόξης is perfectly
intelligible, if less logical than the
equivalent expression in § 39 πολλοστὸν μέρος ἦν τὰ χρήματα ὧν
ὑμεῖς προσεδοκᾶτε.

35. τοῦτο: the participial
phrases stand in apposition with
τοῦτο, an uncommon construction.
See Crit. Note. Cp. Xen. *Anab.*
7. 2. 4 ἔχαιρε ταῦτα ἀκούων διαφθει-
ρόμενον τὸ στράτευμα. — **τῶν ὠφελειῶν**: it is assumed as a matter
of course that the officers were
enriching themselves. See p. 164.

περὶ τῶν χρημάτων ταὐτὰ γνῶναι, ἱκανὰ μὲν ἐνθάδε
τῷ ὑεῖ ἑκάτερον καταλιπεῖν, τὰ δὲ ἄλλα παρ' αὐτοῖς
ἔχειν· ἦν γὰρ Κόνωνι μὲν ὑὸς ἐν Κύπρῳ καὶ γυνή,
Νικοφήμῳ δὲ γυνὴ καὶ θυγάτηρ, ἡγοῦντο δὲ καὶ τὰ
225 ἐκεῖ ὁμοίως σφίσιν εἶναι σᾶ ὥσπερ καὶ τὰ ἐνθάδε.
37 πρὸς δὲ τούτοις ἐνθυμεῖσθε ὅτι καὶ εἴ τις μὴ κτησά-
μενος ἀλλὰ παρὰ τοῦ πατρὸς παραλαβὼν τοῖς παισὶ
διένειμεν, οὐκ ἐλάχιστα ἂν αὐτῷ ὑπέλιπε· βούλονται
γὰρ πάντες ὑπὸ τῶν παίδων θεραπεύεσθαι ἔχοντες χρή-
230 ματα μᾶλλον ἢ ἐκείνων δεῖσθαι ἀποροῦντες.
38   Νῦν τοίνυν εἰ δημεύσαιτε τὰ τοῦ Τιμοθέου, — ὃ μὴ
γένοιτο, εἰ μή τι μέλλει μέγα ἀγαθὸν ἔσεσθαι τῇ πόλει
—, ἐλάττω δὲ ἐξ αὐτῶν λάβοιτ' ἢ ἃ ἐκ τῶν Ἀριστοφάνους
γεγένηται, τούτου ἕνεκα ἂν ἠξιοῦτε τοὺς ἀναγκαίους

36. **ταὐτὰ γνῶναι**: this 'common resolution' of Conon and Nicophemus is explained by the infin.
clauses, ἱκανὰ μὲν . . . καταλι-
πεῖν | τὰ δὲ ἄλλα παρ' αὐτοῖς ἔχειν.
— **ἐνθάδε** . . . **παρ' αὐτοῖς**: at Athens
. . . in Cyprus. — **καὶ τὰ ἐκεῖ** . . .
ὥσπερ καί: see on § 2 (A).
37. **καὶ εἴ τις κτλ.**: 'even a
father who held ancestral property,
and therefore regarded it as in
trust for his children, would not,
had he been in Nicophemus's place,
have turned over the larger part
in his own lifetime to his son ; still
less one who had acquired his
property by his own efforts, as
Nicophemus had. The fact, therefore, that little of Nicophemus's

property was found in Aristophanes's estate furnishes no ground
for suspicion.' On καὶ εἰ see on
16. 2. — **μή**: see on μήτε 12. 68 (B).
— **θεραπεύεσθαι**: a son whose father
still keeps the property in his own
control will presumably be most
attentive to him.
38. **εἰ μή τι κτλ.**: i.e. unless the
public good shall require it, as punishment for some crime on his part.
The sentiment is quite in keeping
with the deference which an Athenian pleader in court would show
toward the supreme interests and
will of the sovereign people. —
ἂν ἠξιοῦτε: the case which was
thought of at first as supposable
(εἰ δημεύσαιτε, λάβοιτε) is, as the

39 τοὺς ἐκείνου τὰ σφέτερ' αὐτῶν ἀπολέσαι; ἀλλ' οὐκ
236 εἰκός, ὦ ἄνδρες δικασταί· ὁ γὰρ Κόνωνος θάνατος
καὶ αἱ διαθῆκαι, ἃς διέθετο ἐν Κύπρῳ, σαφῶς ἐδήλωσαν ὅτι πολλοστὸν μέρος ἦν τὰ χρήματα ὧν ὑμεῖς
προσεδοκᾶτε· τῇ μὲν γὰρ Ἀθηνᾷ καθιέρωσεν εἰς
240 ἀναθήματα καὶ τῷ Ἀπόλλωνι εἰς Δελφοὺς πεντακισ-
40 χιλίους στατῆρας· τῷ δὲ ἀδελφιδῷ τῷ ἑαυτοῦ, ὃς
ἐφύλαττεν αὐτῷ καὶ ἐταμίευε πάντα τὰ ἐν Κύπρῳ, ἔδωκεν ὡς μυρίας δραχμάς, τῷ δὲ ἀδελφῷ τρία τάλαντα·
τὰ δὲ λοιπὰ τῷ υἱεῖ κατέλιπε, τάλαντα ἑπτακαίδεκα.
245 τούτων δὲ κεφάλαιον γίγνεται περὶ τετταράκοντα τά-
41 λαντα. καὶ οὐδενὶ οἷόν τε εἰπεῖν ὅτι διηρπάσθη ἢ
ὡς οὐ δικαίως ἀπεφάνθη· αὐτὸς γὰρ ἐν τῇ νόσῳ ὢν
εὖ φρονῶν διέθετο. Καί μοι κάλει τούτων μάρτυρας.

ΜΑΡΤΥΡΕΣ

sentence proceeds, treated as impossible (ἂν ἠξιοῦτε, the " contrary to fact" construction).

39. εἰκός: *sc.* ὑμᾶς τοῦτ' ἂν
ἀξιοῦν. — **εἰς:** see on εἰς τὰς ναῦς
§ 21 (A). — **ἀναθήματα:** votive
offerings to Athena, probably to
be placed on the Acropolis. Conon
had already dedicated a golden
crown in memory of the battle of
Cnidus, bearing the inscription
Κόνων ἀπὸ τῆς ναυμαχίας τῆς πρὸς
Λακεδαιμονίους (Dem. 22. 72).

40. τῷ υἱεῖ: Timotheus. What
provision was made for the son
of the Cyprian wife (§ 36), if he
was still living, does not appear.

Timotheus was already beginning
to set an example of greater luxury than that of the older generation. Aristophanes in the *Plutus*
(388 B. C.) speaks of his house as
a πύργος (v. 180).

41. ἐν τῇ νόσῳ . . . διέθετο:
important for our knowledge of
Conon's death (cp. διέθετο ἐν
Κύπρῳ § 39), for from a statement
of Isocrates (ἐπὶ θανάτῳ συλλαβεῖν 4. 154) we should naturally,
though not necessarily, infer that
Conon was put to death by the
Persians. — **εὖ φρονῶν:** a technical
term in Attic law, corresponding to
the English "being of sound mind."

42 Ἀλλὰ μὴν ὁστισοῦν, ὦ ἄνδρες δικασταί, πρὶν ἀμφό-
250 τερα δῆλα γενέσθαι, πολλοστὸν μέρος τὰ Νικοφήμου
τῶν Κόνωνος χρημάτων ᾠήθη ἂν εἶναι. Ἀριστοφάνης
τοίνυν γῆν μὲν καὶ οἰκίαν ἐκτήσατο πλεῖν ἢ πέντε
ταλάντων, κατεχορήγησε δὲ ὑπὲρ αὑτοῦ καὶ τοῦ πατρὸς
πεντακισχιλίας δραχμάς, τριηραρχῶν δὲ ἀνήλωσεν
43 ὀγδοήκοντα μνᾶς. εἰσενήνεκται δὲ ὑπὲρ ἀμφοτέρων
256 οὐκ ἔλαττον μνῶν τετταράκοντα. εἰς δὲ τὸν ἐπὶ Σικελίας πλοῦν ἀνήλωσεν ἑκατὸν μνᾶς. εἰς δὲ τὸν ἀπόστολον τῶν τριήρων, ὅτε οἱ Κύπριοι ἦλθον καὶ ἔδοτε αὐτοῖς
τὰς δέκα ναῦς, καὶ τῶν πελταστῶν τὴν μίσθωσιν καὶ
260 τῶν ὅπλων τὴν ὠνὴν παρέσχε τρισμυρίας δραχμάς.
καὶ τούτων κεφάλαιον πάντων γίγνεται μικροῦ λείπον-

---

42. The following details are valuable as showing something of the cost of public services rendered, partly voluntarily, and partly under compulsion, by the wealthy Athenians. The facts have been more briefly stated in § 29.— ᾠήθη ἄν: see on ἂν ἠξίωσε § 13.— γῆν, οἰκίαν: see on § 29.— κατε- χορήγησε: for force of κατα- see L. & S. *s.v. κατά*, E VI; here without any disparaging sense. Cp. English 'use up.' Cp. κατεχρή- σατο § 22.— πεντακισχιλίας δραχ- μάς: in his two services as cho- ragus. For full description of these duties see Haigh, *Attic The- atre* (2d ed.), p. 73 ff.; cp. Gulick, p. 62.— ὀγδοήκοντα μνᾶς: this was for a period of three years

(§ 29) = 26⅔ minae a year. The defendant in XXI reckons his expenditure for seven years as trierarch at 6 t. = 360 minae, an average of 51⅖ minae a year, about twice the sum given in our passage. We may reasonably assume that our speaker was συντριήραρχος, bearing only half of the expense. For the similar case of Diogiton, with an expenditure of 24 minae, see 32. 26, and note on 32. 24.

43. εἰσενήνεκται: in § 29 the occasions are spoken of as εἰσφο- ρὰς πολλάς. For the εἰσφορά see on 12. 20.— εἰς: see on εἰς τὰς ναῦς § 21 (B).— ἐπὶ Σικελίας: see § 19.— τῶν τριήρων: see § 21 ff. — λείποντος: impersonal; for the personal construc. see 32. 24 and 27.

44 τος πεντεκαίδεκα τάλαντα. ὥστε οὐκ ἂν εἰκότως ἡμᾶς
αἰτιάσαισθε, ἐπεὶ τῶν Κόνωνος, τῶν ὁμολογουμένων δικαίως ἀποφανθῆναι ὑπ' αὐτοῦ ἐκείνου, πολλαπλασίων
265 δοκούντων πλεῖν ἢ τρίτον μέρος φαίνεται τὰ 'Αριστοφά-

— πεντεκαίδεκα τάλαντα : of the
15 t. expended in the five or six
years in question, the speaker has
reckoned 5 t. for house and land,
and 10 t. for the various public services; of this sum 2⅝ t. was for
ordinary liturgies of a rich citizen
(service as choragus and trierarch)
and for direct war taxes — an
average of a little less than half
a talent a year. A still more
important source of information
as to the public services of rich
Athenian citizens is the account
which Lysias gives in XXI (§§ 1–5)
of the public expenditures of his
client for the first seven years
after he attained his majority; the
items are as follows : —

1st year.
Choragus (tragic chorus) 3000 dr.
Choragus (men's chorus) 2000
2d year.
Choragus (Pyrrhic) . . 800
Choragus (men's chorus) 5000
3d year.
Choragus (cyclic chorus) 300
7th year.
Gymnasiarch 1200
Choragus (boys' chorus) 1500+
Trierarch, 7 years . 6 t.
War tax 3000
War tax 4000
    Total . . . 9 t. 2800+ dr.

This gives an average contribution of about 1⅓ t. a year. But
these years were the final years of
the Peloponnesian War, when public burdens were extraordinarily
heavy; the same man gives smaller
sums for the time immediately
following. Moreover, the speaker
says that the law would have required of him less than one fourth
this amount. Unfortunately we
have neither in this case nor in
that of Aristophanes any knowledge of the total property or
income from which these contributions were made, so that we
have no sufficient basis for comparison with modern times. We
lack the same data in the case
of the speaker's father, whose
services of this kind amounted to
9 t. 2000 dr. in a period of fifty
years (§ 59). We know that at
his death the estate amounted to
between four and five talents (see
on § 9), but the son says that he
left ἐκ πολλῶν ὀλίγα, so that we
can form no safe estimate of the
father's property or income during
the years of his active life.

44. τρίτον μέρος: Conon's will
showed 40 t. (§ 40) ; the speaker

νους. καὶ οὐ προσλογιζόμεθα ὅσα αὐτὸς ἐν Κύπρῳ ἔσχε
Νικόφημος, οὔσης αὐτῷ ἐκεῖ γυναικὸς καὶ θυγατρός.

45 Ἐγὼ μὲν οὖν οὐκ ἀξιῶ, ὦ ἄνδρες δικασταί, οὕτω
πολλὰ καὶ μεγάλα τεκμήρια παρασχομένους ἡμᾶς
270 ἀπολέσθαι ἀδίκως. ἀκήκοα γὰρ ἔγωγε καὶ τοῦ πατρὸς
καὶ ἄλλων πρεσβυτέρων, ὅτι οὐ νῦν μόνον ἀλλὰ καὶ
ἐν τῷ ἔμπροσθεν χρόνῳ πολλῶν ἐψεύσθητε τῆς οὐσίας,
οἳ ζῶντες μὲν πλουτεῖν ἐδόκουν, ἀποθανόντες δὲ πολὺ
46 παρὰ τὴν δόξαν τὴν ὑμετέραν ἐφάνησαν. αὐτίκα
275 Ἰσχομάχῳ, ἕως ἔζη, πάντες ᾤοντο εἶναι πλεῖν ἢ ἑβδομήκοντα τάλαντα, ὡς ἐγὼ ἀκούω· ἐνειμάσθην δὲ τὼ
ὑεῖ οὐδὲ δέκα τάλαντα ἑκάτερος ἀποθανόντος. Στε-

has accounted for about 15 t. of the
property of Nicophemus and Aristophanes. — ἔσχε: *kept* (not ingressive, *got*).

45. ἐγὼ μέν: cp. on ἐμὲ μέν,
12. 8. — οὐκ ἀξιῶ: with ἀξιῶ and
an infinitive the negative (οὐ)
stands oftener with ἀξιῶ than
(μή) with the infinitive. — ἀπολέσθαι : see on § 34. — ἀκήκοα:
see on §§ 14 and 19. — ἐψεύσθητε: 'empirical' aorist, see on
ᾐσθόμην 16. 20. — οὐσίας : case
HA. 748; G. 1117; B. 362. 1 ;
Gl. 509 a. — πολὺ παρὰ τὴν δόξαν:
the phrase stands as predicate of
ἐφάνησαν, the indefinite participle
(ὄντες or οὐσίαν ἔχοντες) being
omitted. For the same phrase cp.
16. 3.

46. αὐτίκα: *for example*; so

in § 63. See L. & S. *s.v.* II.—
Ἰσχομάχῳ : Xenophon in his *Oeco-
nomicus* presents Ischomachus as
the ideal gentleman, citizen, and
man of affairs, and puts into his
mouth a detailed statement of the
principles and habits by which he
has attained the name of καλὸς
κἀγαθός. But Athenaeus (12.
537 c) cites a statement of Heraclides Ponticus that Ischomachus
lost his property at the hands of
a couple of parasites. It would
appear, therefore, that the later
life of Ischomachus did not justify
Xenophon's praise. — πλεῖν: for
the form see on 32. 20. — ἑβδομήκοντα τάλαντα : for the amount of
some Athenian fortunes see on
32. 23. — ὑεῖ: this form of the
nom. dual is established by Attic

φάνῳ δὲ τῷ Θάλλου ἐλέγετο εἶναι πλεῖν ἢ πεντήκοντα
τάλαντα, ἀποθανόντος δ' ἡ οὐσία ἐφάνη περὶ ἕνδεκα
47 τάλαντα. ὁ τοίνυν Νικίου οἶκος προσεδοκᾶτο εἶναι
281 οὐκ ἔλαττον ἢ ἑκατὸν ταλάντων, καὶ τούτων τὰ πολλὰ
ἔνδον· Νικήρατος δὲ ὅτ' ἀπέθνῃσκεν, ἀργύριον μὲν
ἢ χρυσίον οὐδ' αὐτὸς ἔφη καταλείπειν οὐδέν, ἀλλὰ
τὴν οὐσίαν ἣν κατέλιπε τῷ ὑεῖ, οὐ πλείονος ἀξία
52 ἐστὶν ἢ τεττάρων καὶ δέκα ταλάντων. ἔπειτ' οἴομαι
286 ὑμᾶς εἰδέναι ὅτι 'Αλκιβιάδης τέτταρα ἢ πέντε ἔτη

inscriptions. — **Στεφάνῳ** : otherwise
unknown to us. — **περὶ ἕνδεκα τάλαντα** : the phrase takes the place
of a predicate nominative with
ἐφάνη. A similar phrase may be
used as subject, as in 13. 8 εἰ
κατασκαφείη τῶν τειχῶν τῶν μα-
κρῶν ἐπὶ δέκα στάδια ἑκατέρου *if
of the long walls a space of ten
stadia each should be destroyed.*

47. τοίνυν : force, see on 16. 7
(D). — **Νικίου** : the conservative
statesman and general, who led
the ill-fated Sicilian expedition,
and was captured and put to death
by the Syracusans. Athenaeus
(VI. 272 c) calls him ὁ τῶν Ἑλλήνων ζάπλουτος Νικίας. Plutarch
says of him (*Nicias*, III) that
" he won the people by his services
as choragus and gymnasiarch and
other such ambitious expenditures,
surpassing in liberality and munifi-
cence all the men of former times,
as well as his own contemporaries."
— **ἔνδον** : used, as in § 22, of " ready

money," in distinction from loans,
real estate, etc. — **Νικήρατος** : of Ni-
ceratus, the son of Nicias, Lysias
says that, although like his father
an aristocrat, he was recognized as
dangerous to the party that over-
threw the democracy, and was put
to death by the Thirty. — **τὴν
οὐσίαν ἥν** : " inverse attraction "
is most common when the antecedent would be nom. or accus.,
least common when it would be
dat. Cp. Xen. *Anab.* 3. 1. 6 ἀνεῖ-
λεν αὐτῷ ὁ 'Απόλλων θεοῖς οἷς
ἔδει θύειν (θεοῖς for θεούς). HA.
1003; G. 1035; B. 484. 2; Gl.
613 c.

52. For the question of the
genuineness and position of this
paragraph, see Crit. Note. — **'Αλκιβιάδης** : Alcibiades was banished
in 415, and his property was confiscated. On his return to the city
in 408 (see Chron. App.), the state
gave him land to reimburse him
for the confiscated property (Isoc.

ἐφεξῆς ἐστρατήγει ἐπικρατῶν καὶ νενικηκὼς Λακεδαιμονίους, καὶ διπλάσια ἐκείνῳ ἠξίουν αἱ πόλεις διδόναι
ἢ ἄλλῳ τινὶ τῶν στρατηγῶν, ὥστ' ᾤοντο εἶναί τινες
290 αὐτῷ πλεῖν ἢ ἑκατὸν τάλαντα. ὁ δ' ἀποθανὼν ἐδήλω-
σεν ὅτι οὐκ ἀληθῆ ταῦτα ἦν· ἐλάττω γὰρ οὐσίαν
κατέλιπε τοῖς παισὶν ἢ αὐτὸς παρὰ τῶν ἐπιτροπευσάν-
48 των παρέλαβεν. Καλλίας τοίνυν ὁ Ἱππονίκου, ὅτε
νεωστὶ ἐτεθνήκει ὁ πατήρ, πλεῖστα τῶν Ἑλλήνων ἐδό-

16. 46). Upon the reversal of
sentiment toward him after the
disaster at Notium, he withdrew
to his possessions on the Thracian Chersonese, where he remained till after Aegospotami.
He then took refuge from the
Spartan power with the satrap
Pharnabazus. The Thirty passed
a decree of exile against him and
seized his land in Attica. At the
same time the Persians were persuaded, perhaps in part by the
Thirty, to put him to death. His
son returned from exile after the
deposition of the Thirty, and attempted to recover the land that
they had seized; in this he was
unsuccessful (Isoc. 16. 46). The
claim to this land, together with
the possessions in the Chersonese,
probably made up the inheritance
referred to in the text. — τέτταρα
ἢ πέντε: in the summer of 411 the
men of the fleet at Samos, refusing
to serve the Four Hundred, elected
Alcibiades general; he was in

power from that time until after
the battle of Notium (407). —
διδόναι: on these contributions
to commanders of fleets, see Introd. p. 163 f. — τινες: position, see
on ἡμῖν 12. 33. — παισίν: Alcibiades left two legitimate children,
a son and a daughter. — τῶν ἐπι-
τροπευσάντων: τοῦ δὲ Ἀλκιβιάδου
Περικλῆς καὶ Ἀρίφρων οἱ Ξανθίπ-
που, προσήκοντες (relatives) κατὰ
γένος, ἐπετρόπευον (Plut. Alcibiades, I).

48. Καλλίας ὁ Ἱππονίκου: the
foundation of the fortune of this
famous family is said to have been
laid by a Hipponicus, a friend of
Solon, who, learning from Solon
of his plan to relieve debtors without disturbing land titles, hastily
borrowed large sums of money
and invested in land (Plutarch,
Solon, XV). His nephew, Callias the first, was famous for his
wealth, his hatred of the Pisi-
stratidae, and his lavish expenditures (Herod. 6. 121). Callias's

295 κει κεκτῆσθαι, καὶ ὥς φασι, διακοσίων ταλάντων ἐτιμήσατο τὰ αὐτοῦ ὁ πάππος, τὸ δὲ τούτου νῦν τίμημα
οὐδὲ δυοῖν ταλάντοιν ἐστί. Κλεοφῶντα δὲ πάντες ἴστε,
ὅτι πολλὰ ἔτη διεχείρισε τὰ τῆς πόλεως πάντα καὶ
προσεδοκᾶτο πάνυ πολλὰ ἐκ τῆς ἀρχῆς ἔχειν· ἀπο-
300 θανόντος δ' αὐτοῦ οὐδαμοῦ δῆλα τὰ χρήματα, ἀλλὰ
καὶ οἱ προσήκοντες καὶ οἱ κηδεσταί, παρ' οἷς κατέλιπεν
49 ἄν, ὁμολογουμένως πένητές εἰσι. φαινόμεθα οὖν καὶ

son, Hipponicus the second, is said to have added to his inherited wealth the treasure of a Persian general, which had been left in his hands by an Eretrian (Athen. XII. 537). His son, Callias the second, the πάππος of our passage, was reputed to be the richest Athenian of his time. Hipponicus the third inherited this wealth. He had 600 slaves let out in the mines; he gave his daughter, on her marriage to Alcibiades, the unheard-of dowry of ten talents. His son, the Callias of our text, finally dissipated the family wealth. He affected the new learning, and we have in Plato's *Protagoras* (VI ff.) a humorous description of his house, infested by foreign sophists. His lavish expenditures upon flatterers and prostitutes still further wasted his property, and he died in actual want (Athen. *l.c.*): — **τοίνυν**: force as in § 47. — **ἐτιμήσατο, τίμημα**: the technical terms for *valuation*

in connection with assessment of taxes. But here they are used of the real value of the property, not of the 'assessed valuation.' (In determining the tax — at least after 378 — a certain fraction of the real valuation was taken as the 'assessed valuation,' and the tax levied upon that.) — **Κλεοφῶντα**: a typical demagogue, the leader of the extreme democrats in the last years of the Peloponnesian War. His chief services were in the department of finance, where he was successful under the greatest difficulties. He was violently and persistently opposed to any compromise with Sparta, and stood so in the way of the final surrender that, during the peace negotiations, his political opponents compassed his death upon a doubtful charge of desertion of post. — **προσήκοντες, κηδεσταί**: relatives by birth, connections by marriage.

τῶν ἀρχαιοπλούτων πολὺ ἐψευσμένοι καὶ τῶν νεωστὶ
ἐν δόξῃ γεγενημένων. αἴτιον δέ μοι δοκεῖ εἶναι, ὅτι
305 ῥᾳδίως τινὲς τολμῶσι λέγειν ὡς ὁ δεῖνα ἔχει τάλαντα
πολλὰ ἐκ τῆς ἀρχῆς. καὶ ὅσα μὲν περὶ τεθνεώτων
λέγουσιν, οὐ πάνυ θαυμάζω (οὐ γὰρ ὑπό γε ἐκείνων
ἐξελεγχθεῖεν ἄν), ἀλλ' ὅσα ζώντων ἐπιχειροῦσι κατα-
50 ψεύδεσθαι. αὐτοὶ γὰρ ἔναγχος ἠκούετε ἐν τῇ ἐκκλη-
310 σίᾳ, ὡς Διότιμος ἔχοι ταλάντοις τετταράκοντα πλείω
ἢ ὅσα αὐτὸς ὡμολόγει παρὰ τῶν ναυκλήρων καὶ ἐμ-
πόρων· καὶ ταῦτα, ἐπειδὴ ἦλθεν, ἐκείνου ἀπογράφοντος
καὶ χαλεπῶς φέροντος ὅτι ἀπὼν διεβάλλετο, οὐδεὶς
ἐξήλεγξε, δεομένης μὲν τῆς πόλεως χρημάτων, ἐθέλον-
51 τος δὲ ἐκείνου λογίσασθαι. ἐνθυμεῖσθε τοίνυν οἷον

49. τῶν ἀρχαιοπλούτων : for the
case see on οὐσίας § 45. — ἐκ τῆς
ἀρχῆς : as in the case on trial,
which turns upon the question
whether Nicophemus and Aristophanes had grown rich through
their naval service.

50. γάρ : explicative γάρ, see
on 19. 12. Here the γάρ clause
gives an instance illustrating a
general statement = Eng. *for instance.* — Διότιμος : in the last
campaign of the Corinthian War
(388/7) Diotimus and Iphicrates
commanded an Athenian fleet on
the Hellespont until forced back
by the Spartan Antalcidas (Xen.
Hell. 5. 1. 25 ff.). One duty of
the fleet was to convoy grain ships
coming from the Euxine. For

this service the merchants paid a
price to the treasury of the fleet,
and in addition they were likely
to make personal payments to the
commanders, in order to secure
prompt and efficient service.
Such gratuities opened the way
to serious abuse. — ταῦτα : connect
with ἐξήλεγξε. — ἀπογράφοντος :
Diotimus made haste to "hand
in his accounts" to the board of
auditors, not waiting for their
examination in regular course.
— διεβάλλετο : = Eng. pluperfect.
Whether a Greek subordinate
impf. represents an act in progress at the time of the leading
verb or before it, is determined
by the context only. Cp. on
12. 56.

316 ἂν ἐγένετο, εἰ Ἀθηναίων ἁπάντων ἀκηκοότων ὅτι τετταράκοντα τάλαντα ἔχοι Διότιμος, εἶτα ἔπαθέ τι πρὶν
καταπλεῦσαι δεῦρο. εἶτα οἱ προσήκοντες ἂν αὐτοῦ ἐν
κινδύνῳ ἦσαν τῷ μεγίστῳ, εἰ ἔδει αὐτοὺς πρὸς τοσαύ-
320 την διαβολὴν ἀπολογεῖσθαι, μὴ εἰδότας μηδὲν τῶν
πεπραγμένων. αἴτιοι οὖν εἰσι καὶ ὑμῖν πολλῶν ἤδη
ψευσθῆναι καὶ ἤδη ἀδίκως γέ τινας ἀπολέσθαι οἱ
ῥᾳδίως τολμῶντες ψεύδεσθαι καὶ συκοφαντεῖν ἀνθρώπους ἐπιθυμοῦντες.

53 Ὅτι μὲν οὖν καὶ ἐν τῷ ἔμπροσθεν χρόνῳ τοιαῦτα
326 ἐγίγνετο, ῥᾴδιον γνῶναι· φασὶ δὲ καὶ τοὺς ἀρίστους
καὶ σοφωτάτους μάλιστα ἐθέλειν μεταγιγνώσκειν. εἰ
οὖν δοκοῦμεν εἰκότα λέγειν καὶ ἱκανὰ τεκμήρια παρέ-
χεσθαι, ὦ ἄνδρες δικασταί, πάσῃ τέχνῃ καὶ μηχανῇ
330 ἐλεήσατε· ὡς ἡμεῖς τῆς μὲν διαβολῆς οὕτω μεγάλης
οὔσης ἀεὶ προσεδοκῶμεν κρατήσειν μετὰ τοῦ ἀληθοῦς·
ὑμῶν δὲ μηδενὶ τρόπῳ ἐθελησάντων πεισθῆναι οὐδ᾽
54 ἐλπὶς οὐδεμία σωτηρίας ἐδόκει ἡμῖν εἶναι. ἀλλὰ πρὸς
θεῶν Ὀλυμπίων, ὦ ἄνδρες δικασταί, βούλεσθε ἡμᾶς
335 δικαίως σῶσαι μᾶλλον ἢ ἀδίκως ἀπολέσαι, καὶ πιστεύετε τούτοις ἀληθῆ λέγειν, οἳ ἂν καὶ σιωπῶντες ἐν

---

51. ἔπαθε κτλ.: if some disaster
had prevented his return. πρίν
used loosely as in 12. 17. — μή :
see on μήτε 12. 68 (B). — ψευσθῆναι, ἀπολέσθαι : tense, see on
ἐψεύσθητε § 45.

53. μέν οὖν: force, see on
12. 3 C. — ἐγίγνετο : impf. because the argument turns on the
frequency of the occurrence. —

πάσῃ τέχνῃ καὶ μηχανῇ: see on
§ 11. — μηδενί : see on μήτε 12.
68 (A).

54. πρὸς θεῶν Ὀλυμπίων : see on
§ 34. — βούλεσθε : the positive and
active wish, in distinction from
mere willingness (cp. the neutral
ἐθελησάντων πεισθῆναι willing to be
persuaded § 53). — πιστεύετε τούτοις κτλ.: lit. trust them that they

ἅπαντι τῷ βίῳ παρέχωσι σώφρονας σφᾶς αὐτοὺς καὶ δικαίους.

55 Περὶ μὲν οὖν αὐτῆς τῆς γραφῆς, καὶ ᾧ τρόπῳ κηδε-
340 σταὶ ἡμῖν ἐγένοντο, καὶ ὅτι οὐκ ἐξῄρκει τὰ ἐκείνου εἰς
τὸν ἔκπλουν, ἀλλὰ καὶ ὡς ἄλλοθεν προσεδανείσατο,
ἀκηκόατε καὶ μεμαρτύρηται ὑμῖν· περὶ δ' ἐμαυτοῦ
βραχέα βούλομαι ὑμῖν εἰπεῖν. ἐγὼ γὰρ ἔτη γεγονὼς
ἤδη τριάκοντα οὔτε τῷ πατρὶ οὐδὲν πώποτε ἀντεῖπον,
345 οὔτε τῶν πολιτῶν οὐδείς μοι ἐνεκάλεσεν, ἐγγύς τε
οἰκῶν τῆς ἀγορᾶς οὔτε πρὸς δικαστηρίῳ οὔτε πρὸς

---

speak the truth. The subject of an infin. with πιστεύω is often thus drawn into immediate dependence upon πιστεύω. Cp. Andoc. I. 2 πιστεύσας μάλιστα μὲν τῷ δικαίῳ, ἔπειτα δὲ καὶ ὑμῖν γνώσεσθαι τὰ δίκαια *putting my trust first of all in the justice of my case, and then in you, that you will reach a just decision*; cp. the similar and common construction with οἶδα, as in § 48 Κλεοφῶντα δὲ πάντες ἴστε, ὅτι . . . διεχείρισε.

55. μὲν οὖν: as in § 53. On this recapitulation see Crit. Note. — εἰς τὸν ἔκπλουν: see on εἰς σωτηρίαν 12. 14. The structure of the negative sentence is: —

$$\begin{cases} \text{οὔτε ἀντεῖπον} \\ \text{οὔτε ἐνεκάλεσεν} \\ \text{ὤφθην τε } \begin{cases} \text{οὔτε πρός . . .} \\ \text{οὔτε πρός . . .} \end{cases} \end{cases}$$

— οὔτε ἀντεῖπον: Isocrates says (7. 49) of the young men of the

"good old times," ἀντειπεῖν δὲ τοῖς πρεσβυτέροις ἢ λοιδορήσασθαι δεινότερον ἐνόμιζον ἢ νῦν περὶ τοὺς γονέας ἐξαμαρτεῖν *to contradict their elders, or to speak impolitely to them, they considered worse than young men now consider ill-treatment of their parents*. Aristophanes's attack on Socrates in the *Clouds* gains much of its force in the picture of the son, corrupted and made impudent by his new learning, contradicting and correcting his old father. — οὐδείς μοι ἐνεκάλεσεν: cp. 12. 4. — ἀγορᾶς: the senate-house and several of the court rooms were on the Agora. Ordinary sessions of the Senate and all sessions of the courts were open to the public. The speaker in Isaeus's first speech (§ 1) prides himself upon the fact that he has never been in court, even as a listener.

βουλευτηρίῳ ὤφθην οὐδεπώποτε, πρὶν ταύτην τὴν συμ-
56 φορὰν γενέσθαι. περὶ μὲν οὖν ἐμαυτοῦ τοσαῦτα λέγω,
περὶ δὲ τοῦ πατρός, ἐπειδὴ ὥσπερ ἀδικοῦντος αἱ κατη-
350 γορίαι γεγένηνται, συγγνώμην ἔχετε, ἐὰν λέγω ἃ ἀνήλωσεν εἰς τὴν πόλιν καὶ εἰς τοὺς φίλους· οὐ γὰρ
φιλοτιμίας ἕνεκα ἀλλὰ τεκμήριον ποιούμενος ὅτι οὐ
τοῦ αὐτοῦ ἐστιν ἀνδρὸς ἄνευ ἀνάγκης τε πολλὰ ἀναλίσκειν καὶ μετὰ κινδύνου τοῦ μεγίστου ἐπιθυμῆ-
57 σαι ἔχειν τι τῶν κοινῶν. εἰσὶ δέ τινες οἱ προαναλί-
356 σκοντες μόνου τούτου ἕνεκα ἵνα ἄρχειν ὑφ᾽ ὑμῶν
ἀξιωθέντες διπλάσια κομίσωνται. ὁ τοίνυν ἐμὸς
πατὴρ ἄρχειν μὲν οὐδεπώποτε ἐπεθύμησε, τὰς δὲ
χορηγίας ἁπάσας κεχορήγηκε, τετριηράρχηκε δὲ
360 ἑπτάκις, εἰσφορὰς δὲ πολλὰς καὶ μεγάλας εἰσενή-

In the *Clouds* of Aristophanes
(991) the representative of the
old customs promises the youth
that he shall learn to hate the
Agora. Cp. on 16. 11.— πρὶν . . .
γενέσθαι: see on πρὶν . . . νικῆσαι
§ 28; "*until*" would serve with
πρὸς δικαστηρίῳ, but not with
βουλευτηρίῳ.

56. μὲν οὖν: as in §§ 53 and
55. — τοσαῦτα: *so much only*,
though here without the ἔτι πολλῶν ὄντων which made the meaning clear in 12. 95.— εἰς τὴν πόλιν:
see on εἰς τὰς ναῦς § 21 (C). —
ποιούμενος: *sc.* λέγω from the preceding sentence. — ἔχειν τι τῶν
κοινῶν: the charge, originally
brought against the speaker's

father, was that he was concealing property of his son-in-law,
Aristophanes, which belonged to
the state by the decree of confiscation.

57. προαναλίσκοντες : προ- *in
advance*; they treat their public
services as an investment. The
chief financial offices were elective.
See on 16. 8. — τοίνυν: force, see
on 16. 7 (C); but here the individual instance is cited as *in
contrast* with the general statement. — κεχορήγηκε : this and
the following perfects because
the present bearing of the acts
on the *credit* of the family
is the essential thought. See
on εἰργασμένοι εἰσίν 12. 22. —

νοχεν. ἵνα δὲ εἰδῆτε καὶ ὑμεῖς, καὶ καθ' ἑκάστην ἀναγνώ -εται.

ΛΗΙΤΟΥΡΓΙΑΙ

58 Ἀκούετε, ὦ ἄνδρες δικασταί, τὸ πλῆθος. πεντή-κοντα γὰρ ἔτη ἐστὶν ὅσα ὁ πατὴρ καὶ τοῖς χρήμασι
365 καὶ τῷ σώματι τῇ πόλει ἐλῃτούργει. ἐν οὖν τοσούτῳ χρόνῳ δοκοῦντά τι ἐξ ἀρχῆς ἔχειν οὐδεμίαν εἰκὸς δαπάνην πεφευγέναι. ὅμως δὲ καὶ μάρτυρας ὑμῖν παρέξομαι.

ΜΑΡΤΥΡΕΣ

59 Τούτων συμπάντων κεφάλαιόν ἐστιν ἐννέα τάλαντα
370 καὶ δισχίλιαι δραχμαί. ἔτι τοίνυν καὶ ἰδίᾳ τισὶ τῶν πολιτῶν ἀποροῦσι συνεξέδωκε θυγατέρας καὶ ἀδελφάς, τοὺς δ' ἐλύσατο ἐκ τῶν πολεμίων, τοῖς δ' εἰς ταφὴν

καὶ ὑμεῖς: you, as well as his family. — ἀναγνώσεται : as in § 27.

58. πεντήκοντα ἔτη: a young man who inherited property became subject to liturgies a year after he came of age (32. 24); the speaker's father died at the age of seventy (§ 60). — τῷ σώματι : by service as trierarch (§ 57) and as cavalryman (§ 63). — ἐλῃτούργει : impf. although with a definite number (which usually requires the aorist, GS. 208) because the emphasis is on the repetition of the act. Cf. on ᾤκησε 12. 4. — ἐν οὖν τοσούτῳ χρόνῳ κτλ.: *in so long a period therefore and having the*

reputation of being a man of property to start with (ἐξ ἀρχῆς), *it is reasonable to suppose that he avoided no expense, i.e.* it is safe to assume that the regular public services of a rich man were exacted of him.

59. ἔτι τοίνυν: force, see on 25. 15. — συνεξέδωκε: for the importance of the dowry see on 12. 21. — ἐλύσατο: voice, see on 12. 8. The custom of selling prisoners of war into slavery was so common that the family of any citizen serving in the field was liable to be called upon to buy back his freedom. The contribution of money to help poor fami-

παρέσχεν ἀργύριον.   καὶ ταῦτ᾽ ἐποίει ἡγούμενος εἶναι
ἀνδρὸς ἀγαθοῦ ὠφελεῖν τοὺς φίλους, καὶ εἰ μηδεὶς
375 μέλλοι εἴσεσθαι· νῦν δὲ πρέπον ἐστὶ καὶ ὑμᾶς ἀκοῦσαί
μου. Καί μοι κάλει τὸν καὶ τόν.

ΜΑΡΤΥΡΕΣ

60 Τῶν μὲν οὖν μαρτύρων ἀκηκόατε· ἐνθυμεῖσθε δὲ
ὅτι ὀλίγον μὲν χρόνον δύναιτ᾽ ἄν τις πλάσασθαι τὸν
τρόπον τὸν αὑτοῦ, ἐν ἑβδομήκοντα δὲ ἔτεσιν οὐδ᾽ ἂν
380 εἷς λάθοι πονηρὸς ὤν. τῷ τοίνυν πατρὶ τῷ ἐμῷ ἄλλα
μὲν ἄν τις ἔχοι ἐπικαλέσαι ἴσως, εἰς χρήματα δὲ οὐδεὶς
61 οὐδὲ τῶν ἐχθρῶν ἐτόλμησε πώποτε. οὔκουν ἄξιον τοῖς
τῶν κατηγόρων λόγοις πιστεῦσαι μᾶλλον ἢ τοῖς ἔργοις,
ἃ ἐπράχθη ἐν ἅπαντι τῷ βίῳ, καὶ τῷ χρόνῳ, ὃν ὑμεῖς

lies in such straits, as well as to dower their daughters, was as common as our custom of contributing to help them bury their dead. Men who sought political influence with the masses were especially liberal in these ways. Cp. Dem. 18. 268 οὔτ᾽ εἴ τινας ἐκ τῶν πολεμίων ἐλυσάμην, οὔτ᾽ εἴ τισιν θυγατέρας συνεξέδωκα. Even metics gladly shared in this service, cp. 12. 20. — ἐποίει: tense, see on ἐποίουν 12. 25.— καὶ εἰ: force, see on 16. 2.— καὶ ὑμᾶς: you, as well as the friends whom he helped; cp. καὶ ὑμεῖς § 57.— τὸν καὶ τόν: *one and another*, L. & S. *s.v.* A. VII. 2 ; cp. Demos. 9. 68 ἔδει γὰρ τὸ καὶ τὸ ποιῆσαι,

καὶ τὸ μὴ ποιῆσαι *we ought to have done this and that, and we ought not to have done the other*. Lysias purposely uses the vague expression as implying that he could find any number of witnesses. The clerk has in his hands the testimony, and the names of the witnesses who are to take the stand and acknowledge it ; see App. § 20.

60. μὲν οὖν: force, as §§ 53, 55, 56; see on 12. 3 C.— ἀκηκόατε: tense, see on 12. 48.— οὐδ᾽ ἂν εἷς: more emphatic than οὐδείς; cp. 24. 24 οὐδ᾽ ἂν εἷς ἀποδείξειεν. — εἷς: in the less usual sense *as regards*.

61. τοῖς λόγοις . . . τοῖς ἔργοις:

385 σαφέστατον ἔλεγχον τοῦ ἀληθοῦς νομίσατε. εἰ γὰρ
μὴ ἦν τοιοῦτος, οὐκ ἂν ἐκ πολλῶν ὀλίγα κατέλιπεν,
ἐπεὶ εἰ νῦν γε ἐξαπατηθείητε ὑπὸ τούτων καὶ δημεύσαιθ' ἡμῶν τὴν οὐσίαν, οὐδὲ δύο τάλαντα λάβοιτ' ἄν.
ὥστε οὐ μόνον πρὸς δόξαν ἀλλὰ καὶ εἰς χρημάτων
390 λόγον λυσιτελεῖ μᾶλλον ὑμῖν ἀποψηφίσασθαι· πολὺ
62 γὰρ πλείω ὠφεληθήσεσθ', ἐὰν ἡμεῖς ἔχωμεν. σκοπεῖτε
δὲ ἐκ τοῦ παρεληλυθότος χρόνου, ὅσα φαίνεται ἀνηλω-
μένα εἰς τὴν πόλιν· καὶ νῦν ἀπὸ τῶν ὑπολοίπων τριηραρχῶ μὲν ἐγώ, τριηραρχῶν δὲ ὁ πατὴρ ἀπέθανεν,

cp. 12. 33. — νομίσατε : on the
imperative in a relative clause
see on 12. 60. — δύο τάλαντα : the
property is over 4 t. (see on
§ 9) ; the speaker must assume
a shrinkage of one half by a
forced sale. — πρὸς δόξαν : for πρός
in a purpose phrase see on 12.
14. πρὸς δόξαν is a standing
phrase with other writers. — εἰς
χρημάτων λόγον : lit. *for reckoning of money* : we change the figurative preposition, and say '*from
the financial standpoint.*' — ἔχωμεν : the young man whose services have been described in the
note on § 43 makes the same plea
at greater length. He says (21.
13-14) : *You see, gentlemen of the
jury, how small is the income of
the state, and how what there is
is plundered by the office holders.
You may therefore well consider
the safest income of the state to be*

*the property of those who willingly
perform the liturgies. If, then,
you are wise, you will guard our
property no less than your own,
knowing that you will have the
use of all that is ours, in the
future as in the past. But I
think that you all know that I
shall be a much better adminis-
trator of mine for you than the men
who administer the city's property
for you. But if you make me a
poor man, you will wrong your-
selves, and others will divide this
among themselves, as they do the
rest.*

62. εἰς τὴν πόλιν : see on εἰς τὰς
ναῦς § 21 (C). — ἀπὸ τῶν ὑπολοίπων : the minimum of property
which subjected a citizen to the
liturgies was 3 t. (Isae. 3. 80). —
τριηραρχῶ : the necessity of appearing in court excuses the defendant
from the usual requirement of ser-

395 πειράσομαι δ', ὥσπερ καὶ ἐκεῖνον ἑώρων, ὀλίγα κατὰ
μικρὸν παρασκευάσασθαι εἰς τὰς κοινὰς ὠφελείας·
ὥστε τῷ τ' ἔργῳ τῇ πόλει ταῦτ' ἔσται, καὶ οὔτ' ἐγὼ
ἀφῃρημένος ἀδικεῖσθαι οἰήσομαι, ὑμῖν τε πλείους
63 οὕτως αἱ ὠφέλειαι ἢ εἰ δημεύσαιτε. πρὸς δὲ τούτοις
400 ἄξιον ἐνθυμηθῆναι οἵαν φύσιν εἶχεν ὁ πατήρ. ὅσα
γὰρ ἔξω τῶν ἀναγκαίων ἐπεθύμησεν ἀναλίσκειν πάντα
φανήσεται τοιαῦτα ὅθεν καὶ τῇ πόλει τιμὴ ἔμελλεν
ἔσεσθαι. αὐτίκα ὅτε ἵππευεν, οὐ μόνον ἵππους ἐκτήσατο λαμπροὺς ἀλλὰ καὶ ἀθληταῖς ἐνίκησεν Ἰσθμοῖ
405 καὶ Νεμέᾳ, ὥστε τὴν πόλιν κηρυχθῆναι καὶ αὐτὸν
64 στεφανωθῆναι. δέομαι οὖν ὑμῶν, ὦ ἄνδρες δικασταί,
καὶ τούτων καὶ τῶν ἄλλων μεμνημένους ἁπάντων τῶν
εἰρημένων βοηθεῖν ἡμῖν καὶ μὴ περιιδεῖν ὑπὸ τῶν

vice in person. (See on 12. 42.)
Moreover, if he was only συντριήραρχος, he would be required to
serve only half of the time. For
inference as to date of this speech
see p. 163. — ὀλίγα κατὰ μικρὸν
παρασκευάσασθαι: to provide a
modest amount, little by little.
A modest promise, in keeping
with the whole attitude of the
speaker.

63. τῶν ἀναγκαίων: as in 24.
10 and 16. — αὐτίκα: as in § 46.
— ἵππευεν: on enrolment in the
cavalry see XVI. Introd. p. 131. —
ἀθληταῖς: sc. ἵπποις. He was not
content with furnishing a cavalry
horse which would make a fine
appearance in the public proces-

sions, but he kept race horses
also to compete in the national
games. — Ἰσθμοῖ, Νεμέᾳ: for the
locative see HA. 220; G. 296;
B. 76. N.; Gl. 527 a. Cp. on
12. 50. — στεφανωθῆναι: the prize
at both of these games was a
wreath of parsley, which the victor
dedicated to the patron god of his
city.

64. ὑπὸ τῶν ἐχθρῶν: there is
nothing in the speech to show
whether the suit was instituted
by the σύνδικοι (see on § 32) or
by private citizens (see App. § 9);
but the speaker, like many speakers
in such suits, would have the jury
believe that private malice is back
of the prosecution. (If the first

ἐχθρῶν ἀναιρεθέντας. καὶ ταῦτα ποιοῦντες τά τε
410 δίκαια ψηφιεῖσθε καὶ ὑμῖν αὐτοῖς τὰ συμφέροντα.

part of § 2 were not from a ready-made proem, it would be conclusive proof that the attack was by private persons.) — **τά τε δίκαια ... καὶ τὰ συμφέροντα**: cp. the same appeal in 22. 22.

XXII

The Speech Against the Grain Dealers

INTRODUCTION

THIS speech was written for a senator who was leading the prosecution of certain retail grain dealers, on the charge that, by buying up a larger stock of grain than the law permitted, they had injured the importers, and raised the price of grain to the consumers. It was probably delivered early in 386.[1]

The successful expedition of Thrasybulus in 389/8 had brought the Hellespont under Athenian control, and thus secured the safety of the grain trade, which had been harassed by hostile fleets. But his death and the transfer of the command into less competent hands made the control of the Hellespont insecure again. At the same time the Spartans, having dislodged the Athenians from Aegina, were able constantly to endanger the grain ships at the home end of the route. The result was a period of unusual disturbance in the grain trade in the winter of 388/7.

The retail dealers (σιτοπῶλαι) were bidding one against another for the limited stock of grain in the hands of the importers, thus raising the price of bread.

One of the Commissioners of Grain now advised the retailers to form a combination to keep down the wholesale price. The importers had to sell; they were forbidden by law to store up

[1] The speech falls at a time when the acceptance of peace is in doubt (§ 14). The conspiracy fell in the winter before (§ 8). The air has been full of rumors of interference with the imports (§ 14). All of this fits the winter of 388/7 for the disturbance of trade, and the beginning of 386 for the speech, so closely that there can be little doubt of the dating.

more than one third of any cargo; two thirds had to be thrown upon the market immediately.[1] If, then, a sufficient combination could be made among the retail dealers, they could hold the price down effectively.

In accordance with this advice a ring was formed, but instead of passing the grain on to the consumers at a fair profit, the retailers used the low price to increase the stock of grain in their own storerooms, and put the retail price up according to the war rumors of the hour. The same practice was repeated in the following winter (§ 9).

When the facts of this combination became known, information (εἰσαγγελία) was lodged before the Prytanes, the business committee of the Senate, probably by some of the importers. The retail dealers had violated no law either in combining on the buying price, or (probably) in exacting an exorbitant profit on retail sales,[2] but there was a law which forbade any retailer to buy more than fifty baskets at any one time;[3] in their greed they had ignored this law, and through this it was possible to attack them.

When the Prytanes brought the complaint before the Senate, the senators were so aroused that some were ready to order the constables to arrest and execute the accused forthwith. But one of the senators, protesting against condemnation without trial, persuaded them to follow the legal procedure (§ 2). This would be for the Senate to give the accused a hearing, and if the charges were sustained, to pass the case on to a law court.[4]

The opinion of this senator prevailed, and at a subsequent

[1] See the quotation from Aristotle, below.

[2] See on § 8. The purpose of the law restricting the retailers to fifty baskets must have been to prevent their raising the retail price by cornering the market. But if the law fixed the retail price at a definite advance on the wholesale price, no accumulation of grain by the retailers could have raised it.

[3] §§ 5, 6.

[4] The Senate had final jurisdiction only in case of penalties not greater than a fine of 500 dr. ([Demos.] 47. 43); in all other judicial cases their findings had to be passed on to a law court for final action. Arist. *Resp. Ath.* 45. 1.

session of the Senate the dealers were examined. The senator by whose influence the orderly procedure had been adopted was the only one of the senators who at this session pressed the case against them (§ 3).[1] The Senate found the charges sustained, and sent the case to a court under the presidency of the Thesmothetae.[2]

The senator who had become so prominent in the prosecution felt obliged to carry the case through — otherwise he would have been believed to have been bought off by the "ring." He accordingly employed Lysias to prepare a speech for him to deliver in court.

A study of this case involves a knowledge of the Athenian laws relating to commerce.

The small area of the Attic territory in proportion to population, and the poor adaptedness of the soil to grain production as compared with that of olives and figs, left the people largely dependent upon foreign sources for their grain. More than half of the supply came from foreign ports; the greater part from the Hellespont and the Euxine.[3]

The development and protection of this trade and the control of the retail market were objects of especial care. In all the

[1] The threatening of suits against rich men had become so common on the part of professional blackmailers that reputable men were loath to have anything to do with a case like this (cp. § 1).

[2] For the course in such cases, see Arist. *Resp. Ath.* l.c.

[3] We have an inscription from Eleusis (CIA. II. 834 *b*) which gives the amount of barley and wheat received as the Eleusinian tax from Attica and the cleruchies, Salamis, Scyros, Lemnos, and Imbros, for the year 329/8 B.C. We know that this tax was one-sixth of one per cent on the whole production of barley, and one-twelfth of one per cent on the wheat (CIA. I. 27 *b*). From this it has been computed that the soil of Attica and the cleruchies gave the people of Attica for their own consumption in the following year about 600,000 med. of grain. A statement of Demosthenes (20. 31 f.) in 355 B.C. implies that the imports of grain at that time amounted to about 800,000 med. a year. While these data as to home and foreign grain are twenty-seven years apart, they may be taken as giving an approximate ratio for the two sources of supply. (See Meyer, *Forschungen zur alten Geschichte*, II. 190 ff.)

wars the control of the critical posts on the grain route was a constant aim ; colonies were sent out to points were they could both protect the route and become producers ; in time of war grain fleets were convoyed by triremes (cp. 19. 50). All export of grain from Attica was prohibited,[1] and no citizen or metic was allowed to carry grain from any source to any place save Attica,[2] or to lend money on grain cargoes destined to other ports.[3]

The importation was in the hands of wholesale dealers (ἔμπο-ροι) at the Piraeus. Their business, with that of the wholesale market in general, was under the control of a board of ten Superintendents of the Market ('Εμπορίου ἐπιμεληταί).

These officers kept records of all grain imported,[4] and enforced the law that of every cargo of grain two thirds must be taken from the Piraeus up to the city.[5]

The greater part of the grain thus passed at once into the hands of the retailers, but to prevent its accumulation in their storerooms and their consequent control of prices, it was provided by law, under penalty of death, that no retailer should buy more than fifty baskets at a time (§§ 5, 6).

---

[1] Scholium on Demos. 24. 136.

[2] [Demos.] 34. 37, 35. 50; Lycurg. 27.

[3] [Demos.] 35. 50 ff.

[4] Dem. 20. 32.

[5] Arist. *Resp. Ath.* 51. 4, ἐμπορίου δ' ἐπιμελητὰς δέκα κληροῦσιν· τούτοις δὲ προστέτακται τῶν τ' ἐμπορίων ἐπιμελεῖσθαι, καὶ τοῦ σίτου τοῦ καταπλέοντος εἰς τὸ σιτικὸν ἐμπόριον τὰ δύο μέρη τοὺς ἐμπόρους ἀναγκάζειν εἰς τὸ ἄστυ κομίζειν. This must mean that the importers at the Piraeus were obliged to sell immediately two thirds of every cargo to the retailers of the city proper (cp. Wilamowitz, *Aristoteles u. Athen*, I. 220 n. 68. Busolt, *Gr. Alter.*[2] p. 245). In this way the importers were allowed to hold enough in their warehouses to provide for emergencies, but prevented from holding back a stock sufficient to corner the market. The reading εἰς τὸ 'Αττικὸν ἐμπόριον in Harpocration *s.vv.* ἐπιμελητὴς ἐμπορίου (now corrected by the text of Arist.) led Boeckh to interpret this as meaning that of every cargo of grain brought by foreign merchants to the Piraeus only one third could be shipped on to other ports, a mistake which had become current in our handbooks before the discovery of Aristotle's treatise.

The whole retail grain trade was supervised by a board of Grain Commissioners ; of their appointment and duties we learn as follows from Aristotle (*Resp. Ath.* 51. 3) : —

"There were formerly ten σιτοφύλακες, appointed by lot, five for the Piraeus, and five for the city, but now there are twenty for the city, and fifteen for the Piraeus. They see, first, that the unground grain in the market is offered at a reasonable price (ὤνιος ἔσται δικαίως) ;[1] secondly, that the millers sell the barley meal at a price proportionate to that of barley, and that the bakers sell their loaves at a price proportionte to that of wheat, and of such weight as the commissioners may prescribe (for the law requires them to fix the weight)."

Thus the government followed the grain at every step from its reception in the Piraeus to the home of the consumer.

In special emergencies the people were not content with merely restrictive measures, but they elected a board of σιτῶναι to buy grain and sell it to the people at a reasonable price.[2] At the first meeting of the Ecclesia in every prytany a part of the routine business was the consideration of the grain supply.[3]

OUTLINE

I. Προοίμιον, *Exordium*, §§ 1–4.

Apology for appearing in the case, presented through brief narrative (Διήγησις) of the circumstances which connect the speaker with it.

II. Πρόθεσις, *Propositio*, §§ 5–7.

The general line of argument is indicated by the use of Ἐρώτησις (cp. 12. 24–25).

[1] For the question whether the ratio of the retail to the wholesale price was fixed by law, see on § 8.

[2] Boeckh, *Staatshaushaltung* I. 111 ; Dem. 18. 248 ; CIA. II. Nos. 335, 353.

[3] Arist. *Resp. Ath.* 43. 4.

III. Πίστεις, *Argumentatio*, §§ 8–21.

A. Answer to the claim that the defendants acted under direction of the Grain Commissioners, §§ 8–10.

1. The advice was by only one commissioner, and that only to stop their competition, not to corner the supply, §§ 8–9.

2. The advice was by a commissioner of last year; the prosecution is against acts of this year, § 9.

3. Should we grant that they acted under advice of the commissioners, our only conclusion must be that the commissioners ought to share their punishment, § 10.

B. Answer to the claim that the defendants acted for the purpose of keeping prices down, §§ 11–16.

1. This claim is inconsistent with the sudden and high rise of prices on the stock in their hands, §§ 11–12.

2. This claim is inconsistent with their manifest indifference to the good of the people when called upon to meet their share of the public burdens, § 13.

3. This claim is inconsistent with their notorious attempts to spread rumors of coming disaster, and their profits in your reverses, §§ 14–16.

C. An acquittal would be an affront to the importers, § 17.

D. Their acknowledgment of their violation of the law makes acquittal impossible, §§ 17–18.

E. The example of conviction is needed to keep this class of men in order in the future, §§ 19–20.

F. Refuse to pity them, but have sympathy rather with the citizens whom they have starved and the importers whom they have cheated, § 21.

IV. Ἐπίλογος, *Peroratio*, § 22.

Their guilt is notorious. Justice and cheaper food are the issues of your verdict.

COMMENTS ON ARGUMENT AND STYLE

The acknowledgment of the defendants that they had broken the letter of the law left for the prosecution only the task of breaking down the moral effect of their plea that they acted under direction of the Commissioners.   For this Lysias could count upon the common belief among the jury that the retailers were extortioners, and the popular indignation against anything that tended to raise the cost of food.   He skilfully throws upon this group of defendants the odium that belongs to their class.

The issue was so simple, the case so prejudiced in favor of the prosecution by the preliminary action of the Senate, and the odium of the act so certain, that Lysias was content to present every fact of the prosecution with the utmost simplicity and brevity.

The personality of the speaker does not appear, but the arguments are unanswerable, and the appeal to prejudice is shrewdly planned.

The language is as simple as the thought.   The speaker wishes to avoid every appearance of the professional prosecutor (§ 1) ; hence the language is free from all rhetorical artifice.   The final words reflect the spirit of the speech and the practical character of the man.

XXII

ΚΑΤΑ ΤΩΝ ΣΙΤΟΠΩΛΩΝ

1 Πολλοί μοι προσεληλύθασιν, ὦ ἄνδρες δικασταί,
θαυμάζοντες ὅτι ἐγὼ τῶν. σιτοπωλῶν ἐν τῇ βουλῇ
κατηγόρουν, καὶ λέγοντες ὅτι ὑμεῖς, εἰ ὡς μάλιστα
αὐτοὺς ἀδικεῖν ἡγεῖσθε, οὐδὲν ἧττον καὶ τοὺς περὶ
5 τούτων ποιουμένους τοὺς λόγους συκοφαντεῖν νομίζετε.
ὅθεν οὖν ἠνάγκασμαι κατηγορεῖν αὐτῶν, περὶ τούτων
πρῶτον εἰπεῖν βούλομαι.

2 Ἐπειδὴ γὰρ οἱ πρυτάνεις ἀπέδοσαν εἰς τὴν βουλὴν
περὶ αὐτῶν, οὕτως ὠργίσθησαν αὐτοῖς, ὥστε ἔλεγόν

---

1. **ἐν τῇ βουλῇ**: see Introd.
p. 214. — **καί** (before τούς): *also*.
The common idea of guilt in ἀδικεῖν and συκοφαντεῖν leads to the
use of καί. 'However guilty you
believe the dealers to be, you none
the less think that those also who
prosecute them are guilty—of sycophancy.' — **ποιουμένους τοὺς λόγους**:
cp. on 12. 2. — **συκοφαντεῖν**: an
indication of the extent to which
blackmail had gone in the hands of
the petty lawyers and politicians.
— **ὅθεν**: the antecedent is τούτων.

2. **οἱ πρυτάνεις**: as the executive committee of the Senate, the
Prytanes received the complaint

and laid it before the Senate.
Who the complainants were does
not appear. It is likely that they
were importers, for their interests
are urged in § 17. After the charge
was once taken over by the Senate
and the case sent on to court, these
complainants had no further official connection with it. — **ἀπέδοσαν**: the technical term for
reference of business to the body
to which it belongs (cp. the use
of the same word for payment of
a debt), L. & S. *s.v.* I. 2 b. So
Isoc. 18. 6 ἐκεῖνοι (the Ten) δ' εἰς
τὴν βουλὴν περὶ αὐτῶν ἀπέδοσαν.
— **αὐτοῖς**: case, see on ὀργίζεσθε

10 τινες τῶν ῥητόρων ὡς ἀκρίτους αὐτοὺς χρὴ τοῖς ἕνδεκα
παραδοῦναι θανάτῳ ζημιῶσαι. ἡγούμενος δὲ ἐγὼ
δεινὸν εἶναι τοιαῦτα ἐθίζεσθαι ποιεῖν τὴν βουλήν,
ἀναστὰς εἶπον ὅτι μοι δοκοίη κρίνειν τοὺς σιτοπώλας
κατὰ τὸν νόμον, νομίζων, εἰ μέν εἰσιν ἄξια θανάτου
15 εἰργασμένοι, ὑμᾶς οὐδὲν ἧττον ἡμῶν γνώσεσθαι τὰ
δίκαια, εἰ δὲ μηδὲν ἀδικοῦσιν, οὐ δεῖν αὐτοὺς ἀκρίτους
3 ἀπολωλέναι. πεισθείσης δὲ τῆς βουλῆς ταῦτα, διαβάλλειν ἐπεχείρουν με λέγοντες ὡς ἐγὼ σωτηρίας ἕνεκα
τῆς τῶν σιτοπωλῶν τοὺς λόγους τούτους ἐποιούμην.
20 πρὸς μὲν οὖν τὴν βουλήν, ὅτ᾽ ἦν αὐτοῖς ἡ κρίσις, ἔργῳ
ἀπελογησάμην· τῶν γὰρ ἄλλων ἡσυχίαν ἀγόντων
ἀναστὰς αὐτῶν κατηγόρουν, καὶ πᾶσι φανερὸν ἐποίησα
ὅτι οὐχ ὑπὲρ τούτων ἔλεγον, ἀλλὰ τοῖς νόμοις τοῖς

12. 80. — ἀκρίτους : see on 12. 17.
Note that metics are assumed here
to have the same right to trial as
citizens. — τοῖς ἕνδεκα : the board
of ten Constables and their clerk,
who had charge of prisons, executions, and the more important
arrests. To be distinguished from
the corps of 1200 public slaves
who made up the city police. —
ζημιῶσαι : cp. Arist. *Resp. Ath.*
29. 4 παραδοῦναι τοῖς ἕνδεκα θανάτῳ ζημιῶσαι. For the (dative)
infin. see HA. 951 ; G. 1532. 1 ;
B. 592 ; Gl. 565 ; GMT. 772 (a).
— ἐθίζεσθαι : the implication seems
to be that such customs of illegal
condemnation are already creeping
in. Cp. XIX. Introd. p. 161 N. 1.—

ἡμῶν : the Senate.—ἀκρίτους ἀπολωλέναι : the thought of the proposal
to put them to death without a
trial is so prominently in mind
that ἀκρίτους is used even in the
second half of the alternative,
where it strictly has no place : the
innocent ought not to be put to
death at all — tried or untried.

3. ἐπεχείρουν : *i.e.* after the session of the Senate. — ἐποιούμην :
i.e. at the recent session. Tense,
see on ἐποίουν 12. 25, and on 12. 56
and 19. 50.—ἡ κρίσις : at the second
session of the Senate, when they
decided whether to try the case
themselves or refer it to a jury. —
ἔργῳ ἀπελογησάμην : *I answered
the charge by my action.* — ἔλεγον,

4 κειμένοις ἐβοήθουν. ἠρξάμην μὲν οὖν τούτων ἕνεκα,
25 δεδιὼς τὰς αἰτίας· αἰσχρὸν δ' ἡγοῦμαι πρότερον παύσασθαι, πρὶν ἂν ὑμεῖς περὶ αὐτῶν ὅ τι ἂν βούλησθε
ψηφίσησθε.

5 Καὶ πρῶτον μὲν ἀνάβητε. εἰπὲ σὺ ἐμοί, μέτοικος
εἶ ; Ναί. Μετοικεῖς δὲ πότερον ὡς πεισόμενος τοῖς
30 νόμοις τοῖς τῆς πόλεως, ἢ ὡς ποιήσων ὅ τι ἂν βούλῃ ;
Ὡς πεισόμενος. Ἄλλο τι οὖν ἢ ἀξιοῖς ἀποθανεῖν, εἴ
τι πεποίηκας παρὰ τοὺς νόμους, ἐφ' οἷς θάνατος ἡ
ζημία ; Ἔγωγε. Ἀπόκριναι δή μοι, εἰ ὁμολογεῖς
πλείω σῖτον συμπρίασθαι πεντήκοντα φορμῶν, ὧν ὁ
35 νόμος ἐξεῖναι κελεύει. Ἐγὼ τῶν ἀρχόντων κελευόντων
συνεπριάμην.

ἐβοήθουν : i.e. on the first occasion. Trans. by Eng. plup. like ἐποιούμην above.

4. ἠρξάμην : i.e. at the second session, ἡ κρίσις § 3. — μὲν οὖν : force, see on 12. 3 C. — τὰς αἰτίας : the charges described in § 3 (διαβάλλειν . . . λέγοντες κτλ.). — πρίν : the governing clause is positive in form only, it has therefore the effect of a negative, HA. 924 A ; G. 1470 (last sentence) ; B. 627 ; Gl. 644 d ; GMT. 647.

5. On the ἐρώτησις cp. on 12. 24. — σύ : the speaker calls the whole group of defendants to the stand, but addresses one (perhaps the leader of the "ring") as their representative. — ὡς : force, see on 16. 8. — ἄλλο τι . . . ἤ : G. 1604 ; HA. 1015 b. — οἷς : the antecedent

is the indefinite idea implied in τι ; *any of the crimes for which death is the penalty.* — δή : see on 25. 9 (A). — συμπρίασθαι : *bought up :* the συν- implies the buying from various sources, not the combining with other buyers. In this case the buyers did combine to hold the price down, but the charge is that the individual retailer bought more than the law allowed. — φορμῶν : the word means a basket ; but as to how much the standard grain basket held we have no knowledge whatever. — ἀρχόντων : the σιτοφύλακες. For the attempt of the accused to defend himself by his answer, while admitting an apparent violation of the law, cp. 12. 25 τὰ ὑπὸ τῶν ἀρχόντων προσταχθέντα δεδιὼς ἐποίουν.

6 Ἐὰν μὲν τοίνυν ἀποδείξῃ, ὦ ἄνδρες δικασταί, ὡς
ἔστι νόμος ὃς κελεύει τοὺς σιτοπώλας συνωνεῖσθαι τὸν
σῖτον, ἐὰν οἱ ἄρχοντες κελεύωσιν, ἀποψηφίσασθε· εἰ
40 δὲ μή, δίκαιον ὑμᾶς καταψηφίσασθαι. ἡμεῖς γὰρ ὑμῖν
παρεσχόμεθα τὸν νόμον, ὃς ἀπαγορεύει μηδένα τῶν ἐν
τῇ πόλει πλείω σῖτον πεντήκοντα φορμῶν συνωνεῖσθαι·

7 Χρῆν μὲν τοίνυν, ὦ ἄνδρες δικασταί, ἱκανὴν εἶναι
ταύτην τὴν κατηγορίαν, ἐπειδὴ οὗτος μὲν ὁμολογεῖ
45 συμπρίασθαι, ὁ δὲ νόμος ἀπαγορεύων φαίνεται, ὑμεῖς
δὲ κατὰ τοὺς νόμους ὀμωμόκατε ψηφιεῖσθαι· ὅμως δ'
ἵνα πεισθῆτε ὅτι καὶ κατὰ τῶν ἀρχόντων ψεύδονται,
8 ἀνάγκη διὰ μακροτέρων εἰπεῖν περὶ αὐτῶν. ἐπειδὴ γὰρ
οὗτοι τὴν αἰτίαν εἰς ἐκείνους ἀνέφερον, παρακαλέσαντες
50 τοὺς ἄρχοντας ἠρωτῶμεν. καὶ οἱ μὲν τέτταρες οὐδὲν
ἔφασαν εἰδέναι τοῦ πράγματος, Ἄνυτος δ' ἔλεγεν ὡς
τοῦ προτέρου χειμῶνος, ἐπειδὴ τίμιος ἦν ὁ σῖτος, τούτων ὑπερβαλλόντων ἀλλήλους καὶ πρὸς σφᾶς αὐτοὺς

---

6. τοίνυν: force, see on 16. 7
(B). — εἰ δὲ μή: see on 12. 15. —
ἡμεῖς: the Senate. They would
send down to the court the facts
found in their investigation, the
laws involved, and their own conclusion. — μηδένα: HA. 1029; G.
1615; B. 434; Gl. 572.

7. ἀπαγορεύων φαίνεται: dis-
tinguish from ἀπαγορεύειν φαίνεται.
HA. 986; G. 1592. 1; B. 660. 1 n.;
Gl. 585 a.

8. ἠρωτῶμεν: at the hearing
held by the Senate (ἡ κρίσις § 3).
— οἱ μὲν τέτταρες: cp. on τὰς

ὀκτώ 32. 21. — Ἄνυτος : it is
uncertain whether this was the
Anytus who shared in the prosecution of Socrates. That Anytus,
a rich tanner, was a leading
democrat, associated with Thrasybulus in the Return. Cp. Isoc.
18. 23 Θρασύβουλος καὶ Ἄνυτος μέγιστον μὲν δυνάμενοι τῶν ἐν
τῇ πόλει (c. 399 B.C.). This activity in protecting the poor man's
food supply would be quite in
keeping with his democratic rôle.
— πρὸς σφᾶς αὐτούς : the reflexive
for the reciprocal pronoun (HA.

μαχομένων συμβουλεύσειεν αὐτοῖς παύσασθαι φιλονι-
55 κοῦσιν, ἡγούμενος συμφέρειν ὑμῖν τοῖς παρὰ τούτων
ὠνουμένοις ὡς ἀξιώτατον τούτους πρίασθαι· δεῖν γὰρ
9 αὐτοὺς ὀβολῷ μόνον πωλεῖν τιμιώτερον. ὡς τοίνυν οὐ

686 b; G. 996; B. 471 n. 2), a use
common in Attic prose; in Lysias
confined to this passage and 14. 42.
For πρός see on 32. 19, Crit. Note.
— μαχομένων: on the metaphorical language, see Introd. p. 25
n. 5. — παύσασθαι φιλονικοῦσιν:
cp. on παύσασθαι λέγοντι 12. 1. —
ἀξιώτατον: L. & S., ἄξιος I. 3 b;
cp. a. — δεῖν γάρ κτλ. : *for they had
to sell at an advance of not more
than an obol* (on the medimnus).
This gives the reason for Anytus's
belief that by the plan proposed
the people would get cheap grain:
the retailers are to combine to
keep down the wholesale price,
and then they in turn 'must' sell
at an advance of not more than
an obol. But why 'must' they?
Two interpretations are possible:
(1) It may be that there was a
law forbidding retailers of grain
to sell for more than an obol per
medimnus above the wholesale
price (*i.e.* the wholesale price at
the time of the sale). Such a
law would neither be difficult of
execution nor inconsistent with
the conduct reviewed in this
speech. The wholesale price day
by day was matter of common

knowledge, and the sales of retailers could easily be followed,
for it was in the interest of the
purchasers to report any overcharge. A case like that mentioned in § 12 is not inconsistent
with this, for a rise of a drachma
in the wholesale price would carry
with it the same rise in the retail
price. But we should suppose,
if there had been such a law, that
the violation of it would have been
one of the facts brought out in
the cross-questioning of § 5; there
the case seems to rest on the violation of the law restricting quantity. The statement of Aristotle
is not definite: οὗτοι (*sc.* οἱ σιτοφύλακες) δ' ἐπιμελοῦνται, πρῶτον
μὲν ὅπως ὁ ἐν ἀγορᾷ σῖτος ἀργὸς
ὤνιος ἔσται δικαίως *Resp. Ath.* 51.
3. See also p. 214 n. 2. (2) The
restriction of an obol's advance
may have been laid by Anytus
himself. He may have said to
the retailers (though he now
denies it) that he would over-
look their violation of the law as
to quantity on condition that they
confine themselves to a profit of
an obol per medimnus, so that the
outcome should be cheaper grain.

συμπριαμένους καταθέσθαι ἐκέλευεν αὐτούς, ἀλλὰ μὴ
ἀλλήλοις ἀντωνεῖσθαι συνεβούλευεν, αὐτὸν ὑμῖν Ἄνυ-
60 τον μάρτυρα παρέξομαι·

MAPTYPIA

Καὶ ὡς οὗτος μὲν ἐπὶ τῆς προτέρας βουλῆς τούτους
εἶπε τοὺς λόγους, οὗτοι δὲ τῆτες συνωνούμενοι φαίνονται.

MAPTYPIA

10   Ὅτι μὲν τοίνυν οὐχ ὑπὸ τῶν ἀρχόντων κελευσθέντες
65 συνεπρίαντο τὸν σῖτον, ἀκηκόατε· ἡγοῦμαι δ', ἐὰν ὡς
μάλιστα περὶ τούτων ἀληθῆ λέγωσιν, οὐχ ὑπὲρ αὐτῶν
αὐτοὺς ἀπολογήσεσθαι, ἀλλὰ τούτων κατηγορήσειν·
περὶ γὰρ ὧν εἰσι νόμοι διαρρήδην γεγραμμένοι, πῶς
οὐ χρὴ διδόναι δίκην καὶ τοὺς μὴ πειθομένους καὶ τοὺς
70 κελεύοντας τούτοις τἀναντία πράττειν ;

11   Ἀλλὰ γάρ, ὦ ἄνδρες δικασταί, οἴομαι αὐτοὺς ἐπὶ
μὲν τοῦτον τὸν λόγον οὐ τρέψεσθαι· ἴσως δ' ἐροῦσιν,
ὥσπερ καὶ ἐν τῇ βουλῇ, ὡς ἐπ' εὐνοίᾳ τῆς πόλεως

9. καὶ ὡς . . . εἶπε: for the
connection see Crit. Note.—ἐπὶ
τῆς προτέρας βουλῆς: for ἐπί see
on 12. 17. The claim that they
had an understanding with the
commissioner of last year might
have had weight in connection
with the acts of last year; but
the defendants are accused of acts
of the present year, and by the
Senate of the present year.—

συνωνούμενοι: tense, see on ἀνιωμένου 12. 32. For participle with
φαίνομαι see on § 7.

10. ὡς μάλιστα: cp. § 1.—ἀπολογήσεσθαι: the plea of the defendants will amount to an accusation
of the commissioners (τούτων), not
to a justification of themselves.

11. ἀλλὰ γάρ: force, see on
12. 40. — ἐπὶ λόγον: see Crit. Note.
— ὥσπερ καί: for καί in compari-

συνεωνοῦντο τὸν σῖτον, ἵν᾽ ὡς ἀξιώτατον ὑμῖν πωλοῖεν.
75 μέγιστον δ᾽ ὑμῖν ἐρῶ καὶ περιφανέστατον τεκμήριον
12 ὅτι ψεύδονται· ἐχρῆν γὰρ αὐτούς, εἴπερ ὑμῶν ἕνεκα
ἔπραττον ταῦτα, φαίνεσθαι τῆς αὐτῆς τιμῆς πολλὰς
ἡμέρας πωλοῦντας, ἕως ὁ συνεωνημένος αὐτοὺς ἐπέ-
λιπε· νῦν δ᾽ ἐνίοτε τῆς αὐτῆς ἡμέρας ἐπώλουν δραχμῇ
80 τιμιώτερον, ὥσπερ κατὰ μέδιμνον συνωνούμενοι. καὶ
13 τούτων ὑμᾶς μάρτυρας παρέχομαι. δεινὸν δέ μοι δοκεῖ
εἶναι, εἰ ὅταν μὲν εἰσφορὰν εἰσενεγκεῖν δέῃ, ἣν πάντες
εἴσεσθαι μέλλουσιν, οὐκ ἐθέλουσιν, ἀλλὰ πενίαν προ-
φασίζονται, ἐφ᾽ οἷς δὲ θάνατός ἐστιν ἡ ζημία καὶ
85 λαθεῖν αὐτοῖς συνέφερε, ταῦτα ἐπ᾽ εὐνοίᾳ φασὶ τῇ
ὑμετέρᾳ παρανομῆσαι. καίτοι πάντες ἐπίστασθε ὅτι
τούτοις ἥκιστα προσήκει τοιούτους ποιεῖσθαι λόγους.
14 τἀναντία γὰρ αὐτοῖς καὶ τοῖς ἄλλοις συμφέρει· τότε

sons see on 19. 2. — συνεωνοῦντο : tense, see on ἐποίουν 12. 25.

12. ἐχρῆν : form, cp. χρῆν § 7, and see on 12. 48. — εἴπερ : see on 12. 27. — ἕως ἐπέλιπε : the construction of an unfulfilled condition, GMT. 613. 2 ; note that ἐχρῆν = an apodosis with ἄν (see on εἰκὸς ἦν 12. 27).

13. εἰσφοράν : cp. on 12. 20. ' It is outrageous for these dealers to pretend that they have been willing to risk death in order to do the people a secret kindness, when we all know that when there is occasion to help the people by the payment of war taxes, of which the people

will know and for which they will be grateful, these same men make every effort to avoid the payment.' — εἰ . . . οὐκ ἐθέλουσιν : after expressions of wonder, delight, etc., a clause is sometimes treated as a real protasis (εἰ, neg. μή), sometimes as semi-causal (εἰ, neg. οὐ), and sometimes as an object clause stating the fact wondered at (ὅτι, neg. οὐ). — οἷς : for omission of the pronoun with λαθεῖν see on αὐτοῖς 25. 11. — ὑμετέρᾳ : = obj. gen. ὑμῶν. HA. 694; G. 999. — τοιούτους λόγους : i.e. that they rejoice in the prosperity of the citizens and labor for it.

γὰρ πλεῖστα κερδαίνουσιν, ὅταν κακοῦ τινος ἀπαγ-
90 γελθέντος τῇ πόλει τίμιον τὸν σῖτον πωλῶσιν. οὕτω
δ᾽ ἄσμενοι τὰς συμφορὰς τὰς ὑμετέρας ὁρῶσιν, ὥστε
τὰς μὲν πρότεροι τῶν ἄλλων πυνθάνονται, τὰς δ᾽ αὐτοὶ
λογοποιοῦσιν, ἢ τὰς ναῦς διεφθάρθαι τὰς ἐν τῷ Πόντῳ,
ἢ ὑπὸ Λακεδαιμονίων ἐκπλεούσας συνειλῆφθαι, ἢ τὰ
95 ἐμπόρια κεκλῇσθαι, ἢ τὰς σπονδὰς μέλλειν ἀπορρη-
15 θήσεσθαι, καὶ εἰς τοῦτ᾽ ἔχθρας ἐληλύθασιν, ὥστ᾽ ἐν
τοῖς αὐτοῖς καιροῖς ἐπιβουλεύουσιν ἡμῖν, ἐν οἷσπερ οἱ
πολέμιοι. ὅταν γὰρ μάλιστα σίτου τυγχάνητε δεό-
μενοι, ἀναρπάζουσιν οὗτοι καὶ οὐκ ἐθέλουσι πωλεῖν,
100 ἵνα μὴ περὶ τῆς τιμῆς διαφερώμεθα, ἀλλ᾽ ἀγαπῶμεν
ἐὰν ὁποσουτινοσοῦν πριάμενοι παρ᾽ αὐτῶν ἀπέλθωμεν.
ὥστ᾽ ἐνίοτε εἰρήνης οὔσης ὑπὸ τούτων πολιορκού-
16 μεθα. οὕτω δὲ πάλαι περὶ τῆς τούτων πανουργίας
καὶ κακονοίας ἡ πόλις ἔγνωκεν, ὥστ᾽ ἐπὶ μὲν τοῖς
105 ἄλλοις ὠνίοις ἅπασι τοὺς ἀγορανόμους φύλακας
κατεστήσατε, ἐπὶ δὲ ταύτῃ μόνῃ τῇ τέχνῃ χωρὶς
σιτοφύλακας ἀποκληροῦτε· καὶ πολλάκις ἤδη παρ᾽

---

14. λογοποιοῦσιν: cp. 16. 11.
— ἤ, ἤ, κτλ.: on the πολυσύνδετον
see App. § 58. 4.— ἐκπλεούσας: *i.e.*
out of the Hellespont. — κεκλῇσθαι: *are blockaded.*— ἀπορρηθή-
σεσθαι: L. & S. ἀπεῖπον IV. For
the conclusion as to date based on
this passage see Introd. p. 213 n. 1.

15. ἀγαπῶμεν: force, see on
ἀγαπήσειν 12. 11. Cp. on 16. 16.
— πολιορκούμεθα: on the metaphor see Introd. p. 25 n. 5.

16. πανουργίας, κακονο!ας: on
the συνωνυμία see App. § 58. 2. —
τοὺς ἀγορανόμους: they had the
general supervision of the markets,
issued trade licenses, guarded the
purity of the wares and the fresh-
ness of perishable food products,
and served as arbiters in disputes
between buyer and seller. A
board of five served for the city
and five for the Piraeus. — τέχνη:
the term includes "trade," as well

ἐκείνων πολιτῶν ὄντων δίκην τὴν μεγίστην ἐλάβετε,
ὅτι οὐχ οἷοί τ' ἦσαν τῆς τούτων πονηρίας ἐπικρα-
110 τῆσαι. καίτοι τί χρὴ αὐτοὺς τοὺς ἀδικοῦντας ὑφ'
ὑμῶν πάσχειν, ὁπότε καὶ τοὺς οὐ δυναμένους φυλάττειν ἀποκτείνετε;

17 Ἐνθυμεῖσθαι δὲ χρὴ ὅτι ἀδύνατον ὑμῖν ἐστιν ἀπο-
ψηφίσασθαι. εἰ γὰρ ἀπογνώσεσθε ὁμολογούντων αὐ-
115 τῶν ἐπὶ τοὺς ἐμπόρους συνίστασθαι, δόξεθ' ὑμεῖς
ἐπιβουλεύειν τοῖς εἰσπλέουσιν. εἰ μὲν γὰρ ἄλλην τινὰ
ἀπολογίαν ἐποιοῦντο, οὐδεὶς ἂν εἶχε τοῖς ἀποψηφισα-
μένοις ἐπιτιμᾶν· ἐφ' ὑμῖν γὰρ ὁποτέροις βούλεσθε
πιστεύειν· νῦν δὲ πῶς οὐ δεινὰ ἂν δόξαιτε ποιεῖν,
120 εἰ τοὺς ὁμολογοῦντας παρανομεῖν ἀζημίους ἀφήσετε;

18 ἀναμνήσθητε δέ, ὦ ἄνδρες δικασταί, ὅτι πολλῶν ἤδη
ἐχόντων ταύτην τὴν αἰτίαν, ἀμφισβητούντων καὶ μάρτυρας παρεχομένων, θάνατον κατέγνωτε, πιστοτέρους
ἡγησάμενοι τοὺς τῶν κατηγόρων λόγους. καίτοι πῶς
125 ἂν οὐ θαυμαστὸν εἴη, εἰ περὶ τῶν αὐτῶν ἁμαρτημάτων
δικάζοντες μᾶλλον ἐπιθυμεῖτε παρὰ τῶν ἀρνουμένων
19 δίκην λαμβάνειν; Καὶ μὲν δή, ὦ ἄνδρες δικασταί,

---

as "the trades," cp. 24. 19 f. —
πολιτῶν ὄντων: the defendants are
metics. — **δίκην τὴν μεγίστην**: for
the order see on δίκην τὴν ἀξίαν
12. 82. — **ἐλάβετε**: tense, see on
ᾐσθόμην 16. 20. — **φυλάττειν**: to
protect you.

17. **ἀπογνώσεσθε**: mood (cp. εἰ
ἀφήσετε below), see on ἀφήσουσιν
12. 35. — **ἐπί**: see on πρός 32. 19,
Crit. Note, C, 4. — **τοῖς εἰσπλέουσιν**:

= τοῖς ἐμπόροις the importers.
Here probably comes out the real
influence that lies behind this
prosecution, see Introd. p. 214.
— **ἐφ' ὑμῖν**: see on ἐπὶ σοί 12.
26.

18. **κατέγνωτε**: tense, see on
ᾐσθόμην 16. 20. — **εἰ ἐπιθυμεῖτε**:
for the mixed form of prot. and
apod. cp. § 17.

19. **καὶ μὲν δή**: force, see on

πᾶσιν ἡγοῦμαι φανερὸν εἶναι ὅτι οἱ περὶ τῶν τοιούτων
ἀγῶνες κοινότατοι τυγχάνουσιν ὄντες τοῖς ἐν τῇ πόλει,
130 ὥστε πεύσονται ἥντινα γνώμην περὶ αὐτῶν ἔχετε, ἡγούμενοι, ἐὰν μὲν θάνατον τούτων καταγνῶτε, κοσμιωτέ-
ρους ἔσεσθαι τοὺς λοιπούς· ἐὰν δ' ἀζημίους ἀφῆτε,
πολλὴν ἄδειαν αὐτοῖς ἐψηφισμένοι ἔσεσθε ποιεῖν ὅ τι
20 ἂν βούλωνται. χρὴ δέ, ὦ ἄνδρες δικασταί, μὴ μόνον
135 τῶν παρεληλυθότων ἕνεκα αὐτοὺς κολάζειν, ἀλλὰ καὶ
παραδείγματος ἕνεκα τῶν μελλόντων ἔσεσθαι· οὕτω
γὰρ ἔσονται μόγις ἀνεκτοί. ἐνθυμεῖσθε δὲ ὅτι ἐκ
ταύτης τῆς τέχνης πλεῖστοι περὶ τοῦ σώματός εἰσιν
ἠγωνισμένοι· καὶ οὕτω μεγάλα ἐξ αὐτῆς ὠφελοῦνται,
140 ὥστε μᾶλλον αἱροῦνται καθ' ἑκάστην ἡμέραν περὶ τῆς
ψυχῆς κινδυνεύειν ἢ παύσασθαι παρ' ὑμῶν ἀδίκως
21 κερδαίνοντες. καὶ μὲν δὴ οὐδ' ἐὰν ἀντιβολῶσιν ὑμᾶς
καὶ ἱκετεύωσι, δικαίως ἂν αὐτοὺς ἐλεήσαιτε, ἀλλὰ πολὺ
μᾶλλον τῶν τε πολιτῶν οἳ διὰ τὴν τούτων πονηρίαν
145 ἀπέθνησκον, καὶ τοὺς ἐμπόρους ἐφ' οὓς οὗτοι συνέστη-

---

12. 30.— κοινότατοι: *of the widest
interest*. The price of flour touched
every home.— ἄδειαν ποιεῖν: cp.
on τοῦ λοιποῦ ποιεῖν 12. 85.—
ἐψηφισμένοι ἔσεσθε: the abiding
result is the emphatic thought;
they will have standing immunity.

20. μόγις ἀνεκτοί: *barely en-
durable*. Cp. Thuc. 6. 23. 1 μόλις
οὕτως οἷοί τε ἐσόμεθα *in that case
we shall be barely able.*— περὶ τοῦ
σώματος: *for their lives.* The
same idea is expressed just below
by περὶ τῆς ψυχῆς. The Greek

idea of death as the separation
of ψυχή from σῶμα makes the two
expressions equivalent.

21. ἐὰν ἀντιβολῶσιν, ἂν ἐλεήσαιτε: cp. on εἰ ἐπιθυμεῖτε § 18.
On the συνωνυμία in ἀντιβολῶσιν
and ἱκετεύωσι see App. § 58. 2.—
τῶν πολιτῶν: part. gen. with the
omitted antec. of οἵ.— ἀπέθνησκον:
referring to δίκην τὴν μεγίστην,
inflicted on some of the σιτοφύλακες for failure to check the
abuses of the retailers, § 16.—
ἐφ' οὕς: see on πρός 32. 19, Crit.

σαν· οἷς ὑμεῖς χαριεῖσθε καὶ προθυμοτέρους ποιήσετε, δίκην παρὰ τούτων λαμβάνοντες. εἰ δὲ μή, τίν' αὐτοὺς οἴεσθε γνώμην ἕξειν, ἐπειδὰν πύθωνται ὅτι τῶν καπήλων, οἳ τοῖς εἰσπλέουσιν ὡμολόγησαν ἐπιβουλεύειν, 150 ἀπεψηφίσασθε;

22 Οὐκ οἶδ' ὅ τι δεῖ πλείω λέγειν· περὶ μὲν γὰρ τῶν ἄλλων τῶν ἀδικούντων, ὅτου δικάζονται δεῖ παρὰ τῶν κατηγόρων πυθέσθαι, τὴν δὲ τούτων πονηρίαν ἅπαντες ἐπίστασθε. ἐὰν οὖν τούτων καταψηφίσησθε, 155 τά τε δίκαια ποιήσετε καὶ ἀξιώτερον τὸν σῖτον ὠνήσεσθε· εἰ δὲ μή, τιμιώτερον.

Note, C, 4. — **οἷς**: for omission of the pronoun with ποιήσετε, which requires the accus., see on § 13.

22. **ὅτου**: *i.e. on what charge.*

The Speech for the Cripple

INTRODUCTION

LYSIAS wrote this speech in support of the plea of a crippled artisan for the retention of his name on the list of disabled paupers who received a dole of an obol a day from the public treasury.

In earlier times poor-relief by the state had been confined to the families that had become dependent through war.[1] But during the terrible hardships of the last years of the Peloponnesian War it became necessary to support large numbers of citizens, whose means of livelihood had been cut off by the war, and who, with their families, were shut up in the city. An allowance of two obols a day from the treasury was all that saved many people from starvation during the last third of the war.[2]

We infer from our speech, supplemented by the later testimony of Aristotle, that with the return of peace the state still gave poor-relief to the disabled (§ 4), without restricting it to veterans or the families of men who had fallen in war, but at the rate of only one obol a day (§§ 13, 26).[3]

---

[1] A system of military pensions for men who had been disabled, and for the sons and dependent parents of men who had died, goes back to the time of Solon and Pisistratus: the soldiers' pension under Pisistratus, after the example of Solon in the case of a single disabled veteran (Heraclides, cited by Plutarch, *Solon*, 31); support and education of sons, introduced by Solon (Diogenes Laert. I. 55). The pension of dependent parents (Plato, *Menex.* 248 E) presumably goes back to the same time.

[2] Arist. *Resp. Ath.* 28. 3; Wilamowitz, *Aristoteles u. Athen*, II, 212 ff.

[3] If the relief at issue in our speech had been granted on the ground of military service, that point would be brought out in the plea.

So many families had lost everything in the war and the sub-sequent exile under the Thirty that such general relief must have been necessary ; and we may well believe that the impoverished condition of the treasury made it necessary to cut the sum down to one obol.

The Senate now had control of the distribution, passing annually upon the list of beneficiaries (§ 26).[1] The year's allowance seems to have been given in ten payments.[2]

Subsequently the relief was raised to two obols. For the time of Aristotle we have the following specific statement : " The Senate examines the disabled (τοὺς ἀδυνάτους) also. For there is a law which requires that those whose property is of less value than three minae, and who are so disabled in body as not to be able to do any work, be examined by the Senate and granted support at public cost to the amount of two obols daily to each. They have a paymaster, appointed by lot."   (*Resp. Ath.* 49. 4.)[3]

The case with which our speech is concerned arose at the time of the annual scrutiny of the list. Remonstrance was formally made against the continuance (§§ 7, 26) of the name of a certain elderly cripple (§ 7), who had a shop near the Agora (§ 20).

---

[1] There is nothing in the words τὸ παρὰ τῆς πόλεως ἀργύριον (§ 4) to warrant the conclusion that the original grant to each individual was made by the Ecclesia. In § 22 the reference is to the act of the Ecclesia in establishing the system, not in making the individual award.

[2] Aeschin. I. 104 τὸν τῆς πρυτανείας μισθόν.

[3] Harpocration, *s.v.* ἀδύνατοι, cites a statement of Philochorus that the payment was 9 dr. per month. Reckoning the "month" as a prytany, we have $1\frac{1}{2}$ obols daily. The sum would naturally vary with changes in cost of living and with the financial ability of the state. A statement in the scholium on Aeschin. I. 103, that the sum was three obols, is probably due to a confusion of the relief payment with the daily pay of the juror.

It is to be remembered that the jury pay, available to all who cared to sit in court (see App. § 6), and the pay for sitting in the Ecclesia offered no small relief to the poor citizens. There were, moreover, Benevolent Orders, the members of which received help in emergencies from the funds of the fraternity (Boeckh, *Staatshaushaltung*, I. 312). For the aid often given by wealthy citizens, see on 19. 59.

The Senate, having heard the remonstrance, appointed a hearing, at which the cripple would have opportunity to defend his claim.

Thus far the facts are clear from references in our speech; but beyond this we can only conjecture the course of events.

From the tone of the speech we may assume that the remonstrant is a man of character and property, quite in earnest in his efforts for reform, and quite out of touch with the average, easygoing senator whom the lot has sent up to represent the people. The old cripple is all that is charged — a lusty rascal, a "character" about the Agora, and the delight of the young men of the sporting set, who make his shop their resort.

When the news comes to the shop that the "reformer" is after the old man, the young fellows — half in sport and half in earnest — crowd around him protesting that he is being abused, and assuring him that he shall have the best legal talent in the city for his defense.

Lysias is called in and enters heartily into the fun. At the time of the scrutiny of the list the remonstrant publicly stated the grounds of his objection, so that the defense is able to anticipate the line of attack. And now a speech is to be fitted to this defendant; it must be full of his homely wit and sarcasm, and full of coarse abuse of the "reformer." And, as a piece of literary fun, an air of learning and a flavor of rhetoric must pervade the whole speech, and make it a parody on the oratory of the day.

And so the speech was written, and the old rascal committed it to memory, and spoke it off before the Senate with due solemnity, — with what result we do not know, but it would be a most un-Athenian Senate which would fail to cap the hour's fun with a jolly vote of confidence in the pauper, and a defeat for the aristocratic enemy of the poor.

Of the date of the speech we can say only that it is some time after the rule of the Thirty.[1]

[1] Long enough after to give point to the parody on current pleas (§ 25), in which the attitude of a man toward the people in their exile had become a stock argument.

Some critics have held that this speech is only a bit of literary sport, and for an imaginary case.[1] Such rhetorical exercises were common enough among the writers of the time. The reason for so regarding the speech for the cripple is the feeling that the subject-matter is too unimportant, and the tone of the speech too comic, to have received the attention of the Senate. But the obol-case, small as it was, did rest with the Senate (Aristotle, *l.c.*), and the comic tone may well have been the only tone that would fit the man.

The ascription of the speech to Lysias seems to have been questioned in antiquity,[2] and has recently been vigorously attacked by Bruns.[3] The first objection raised by Bruns is that the tone and extent of the attack on the complainant are at variance with Lysias's uniform calmness and restraint in attack ; Lysias's defendants confine their attacks on the prosecutors to their acts in the case itself, and are far from giving a general characterization of the men ; the extent of the attack is always well proportioned to the gravity of the case. But in our speech we have a bitter and scornful attack on the whole character of the opponent, and it is as vehement as though the issue were some great thing — not an obol a day. Bruns sees a second violation of the Lysian manner in the failure of the defendant to press the real points at issue — his physical disability and his poverty — and the comical pose in which he is made to give, instead of argument, a picture of himself. Bruns's arguments serve to emphasize more sharply than had been done before the peculiarities of the speech, and they are conclusive against any view of it as a sober defense ; but they do not meet the theory that the speech is a humorous parody, written for the actual use of a notoriously odd character, for whom there

---

[1] Boeckh, *ibid.*, p. 309. A παίγνιον like the little *Encomium on Helen*, ascribed (probably correctly) to Gorgias, the author of which closes with the words, ἐβουλήθην γράψαι τὸν λόγον, Ἑλένης μὲν ἐγκώμιον, ἐμὸν δὲ παίγνιον.

[2] *Harp. s.v.* ἀδύνατοι : ἔστι δὲ καὶ λόγος τις, ὡς λέγεται, Λυσίου περὶ τοῦ ἀδυνάτου (Ed. Dindorf; Bekker reads ὡς Λυσίου).

[3] *Literarisches Porträt*, pp. 461–463.

was really no plea except his own comical personality. The definiteness of this personality, as it stands out in the speech, must always be the strongest argument for ascribing the work to the master of ἠθοποιία.

OUTLINE

I. Προοίμιον, *Exordium*, §§ 1–3.
The satisfaction of the speaker in having an opportunity to give an account of his life.
The envy that has led to this case.

II. Πρόθεσις, *Propositio*, §§ 4–5.
Outline of the complaint.
Introduction to *Narratio*.

III. Διήγησις, *Narratio*, § 6.
Description of his needy condition.

IV. Παρέκβασις, *Egressio*, §§ 7–9.
Appeal for justice and mercy, based on the *Narratio*, §§ 7, 8.
The insincerity of the complainant, § 9.

V. Πίστεις, *Argumentatio*, §§ 10–20.
   A. Answer to the argument based on his horseback riding, §§ 10–12.
   B. Answer to the claim that he is able to earn a living, §§ 13–14.
   C. Answer to the charge that he is immoral and insolent, §§ 15–18.
   D. Answer to the charge that his shop is the resort of the idle and dissolute, §§ 19–20.

VI. Ἐπίλογος, *Peroratio*, §§ 21–27.
   A. Appeal to the sympathy of the senators, §§ 21–23.
   B. Appeal based on his past life, §§ 24, 25 (the plea based on the *probabile ex vita*).
   C. Final appeal, §§ 26, 27.

COMMENTS ON ARGUMENT AND STYLE

In all criticism both of the matter and form of this speech we must bear in mind the large element of parody. Some of the arguments are purposely irrelevant, some of the expressions are purposely rhetorical.

I. Προοίμιον, *Exordium*, §§ 1–3.

The opening words of the speech for Mantitheus (XVI) show how neatly the old cripple is here imitating a stock form of introduction for a speech in δοκιμασία. This is, indeed, his δοκιμασία, for the office of — state pauper. The absurd humor of the rest of the proem puts the hearers into the right mood for appreciating the burlesque defense that is to follow.

The proem was the part of the speech on which the Gorgian school lavished their most artificial tricks of poetic word and form. It is a neat turn that Lysias gives in letting the illiterate old cripple close his proem with a couple of periods in the full Gorgian style : —

> καὶ γὰρ οἶμαι δεῖν, ὦ βουλή,
> τὰ τοῦ σώματος δυστυχήματα
> τοῖς τῆς ψυχῆς ἐπιτηδεύμασιν [1] ἰᾶσθαι · [2]
> καλῶς.
>
> εἰ γὰρ ἐξ ἴσου τῇ συμφορᾷ
> καὶ τὴν διάνοιαν ἕξω
> καὶ τὸν ἄλλον βίον διάξω,
> τί τούτου διοίσω ;
>
> περὶ μὲν τούτων τοσαῦτά μοι εἰρήσθω. [3]

II. Πρόθεσις, *Propositio*, §§ 4–5.

The outline of the complaint is probably an absurd travesty on it. We may suppose that the complainant had called attention

---

[1] On the παρονομασία see App. § 58. 5.
[2] On the metaphor see Introd. p. 25, n. 5.
[3] On the ὁμοιοτέλευτον see App. § 57. 4.

to the horseback riding, something that only the richer citizens could afford, as indicating that the cripple had rich friends who could and would support him ; the cripple pretends that the argument was that he was physically sound enough to jump onto a horse and ride it !

The complainant had doubtless charged against the character of the cripple that his shop was a gaming place for young spendthrifts ; the cripple represents the complaint as being that the income from his trade is so great that he is able to hold his own among men whose expenditures are most lavish.

III. Διήγησις, *Narratio*, § 6.

The simple description of his sad plight has its touch of fun in the implication that the old pauper still hopes for children and a slave (οὔπω εἰσίν, οὔπω δύναμαι κτήσασθαι).

IV. Παρέκβασις, *Egressio*, §§ 7–9.

The *Narratio* is used[1] as basis for an immediate appeal, instead of being followed directly by the arguments. Here, again, the style becomes rhetorical, in the conspicuous use of pairs of coördinate cola (see App. § 57. 3) : —

> μὴ τοίνυν, ἐπειδή γε ἔστιν, ὦ βουλή,
> σῶσαί με δικαίως,
> ἀπολέσητε ἀδίκως ·
> μηδὲ ἃ νεωτέρῳ καὶ μᾶλλον ἐρρωμένῳ ὄντι ἔδοτε
> πρεσβύτερον καὶ ἀσθενέστερον γιγνόμενον ἀφέλησθε. § 7.

V. Πίστεις, *Argumentatio*, §§ 10–20.

In the argument we have a combination of parody on stock arguments, and witty, shrewd turns of defense and attack. There is no sound proof of either poverty or incapacity to earn support — probably because there could be none. Lysias gives a shining example of his ability to meet the common definition of the rhetorician's task, τὸν ἥττω λόγον κρείττω ποιεῖν.

[1] So in 12. 20–23; see p. 50.

The argument from "probability" had been especially developed by Gorgias. It is with a fine sense of humor that Lysias makes the old man pass in §§ 16–18, where this comes forward, from the simple style of speech to the epideictic form, the utterance of wise observations on human nature, expressed in stilted, antithetic periods. Every sentence of §§ 16–18 falls into this formal, rhetorical mold ; *e.g.* :

> οὐ γὰρ τοὺς πενομένους
> καὶ λίαν ἀπόρως διακειμένους
> ὑβρίζειν εἰκός
> ἀλλὰ τοὺς πολλῷ πλείω τῶν ἀναγκαίων κεκτημένους.[1]
>
> οὐδὲ τοὺς ἀδυνάτους τοῖς σώμασιν ὄντας
> ἀλλὰ τοὺς μάλιστα πιστεύοντας ταῖς αὑτῶν ῥώμαις ·
>
> οὐδὲ τοὺς ἤδη προβεβηκότας τῇ ἡλικίᾳ
> ἀλλὰ τοὺς ἔτι νέους καὶ νέαις ταῖς διανοίαις χρωμένους.

VI. Ἐπίλογος, *Peroratio*, §§ 21–27.

The parody on the common pleas of the day is carried out in the absurd appeal based on the past life of the speaker : he has been no sycophant ; he, the cripple, has not been violent ; he, the pauper, refrained from sharing in the government of the aristocratic Thirty !

The closing words thrust again at the would-be reformer.

---

[1] On the ὁμοιοτέλευτον see App. § 57. 4.

XXIV

ΠΕΡΙ ΤΟΥ ΜΗ ΔΙΔΟΣΘΑΙ ΤΩΙ ΑΔΥΝΑΤΩΙ ΑΡΓΥΡΙΟΝ

1 Οὐ πολλοῦ δέω χάριν ἔχειν, ὦ βουλή, τῷ κατηγόρῳ,
ὅτι μοι παρεσκεύασε τὸν ἀγῶνα τουτονί. πρότερον
γὰρ οὐκ ἔχων πρόφασιν ἐφ᾽ ἧς τοῦ βίου λόγον δοίην,
νυνὶ διὰ τοῦτον εἴληφα. καὶ πειράσομαι τῷ λόγῳ
5 τοῦτον μὲν ἐπιδεῖξαι ψευδόμενον, ἐμαυτὸν δὲ βεβιωκότα
μέχρι τῆσδε τῆς ἡμέρας ἐπαίνου μᾶλλον ἄξιον ἢ
φθόνου· διὰ γὰρ οὐδὲν ἄλλο μοι δοκεῖ παρασκευάσαι
2 τόνδε μοι τὸν κίνδυνον οὗτος ἢ διὰ φθόνον. καίτοι
ὅστις τούτοις φθονεῖ οὓς οἱ ἄλλοι ἐλεοῦσι, τίνος ἂν
10 ὑμῖν ὁ τοιοῦτος ἀποσχέσθαι δοκεῖ πονηρίας; εἰ μὲν

---

1. **οὐ πολλοῦ**: μικροῦ or ὀλίγου
is the usual word with δέω, cp. 12.
17 οὕτω πολλοῦ ἐδέησε. — **ἐφ᾽ ἧς**:
for the usual ἐφ᾽ ᾗ to denote the
ground of an action (see on 32.
17). — **δοίην**: the mood is best
understood by comparison with a
construction like that of 32. 20
οὐκ ἔχων ὅποι τρέψειε τὰ χρήματα
as he was at a loss where to enter
the sums (expended). οὐκ ἔχων
is there equivalent to οὐκ εἰδώς,
or ἀπορῶν, and so takes the opt.
of ind. question. The direct form

would be the deliberative subjv.,
ποῖ τρέψω; In our passage we
have an extension of that usage,
for here οὐκ ἔχων has as its object, not an interrogative clause,
but the antecedent of a relative
clause. The idea of perplexity
which underlies both sentences
explains their common construction. — **ἄξιον**: see Crit. Note. —
τόνδε μοι: for position see on ἡμῖν
12. 33.

2. **ἄν**: see on 12. 1. — **πονηρίας**: doubly emphasized by its

239

γὰρ ἕνεκα χρημάτων με συκοφαντεῖ— · εἰ δ' ὡς ἐχθρὸν
ἑαυτοῦ με τιμωρεῖται, ψεύδεται · διὰ γὰρ τὴν πονηρίαν
αὐτοῦ οὔτε φίλῳ οὔτε ἐχθρῷ πώποτε ἐχρησάμην αὐτῷ.
3 ἤδη τοίνυν, ὦ βουλή, δῆλός ἐστι φθονῶν, ὅτι τοιαύτῃ
15 κεχρημένος συμφορᾷ τούτου βελτίων εἰμὶ πολίτης. καὶ
γὰρ οἶμαι δεῖν, ὦ βουλή, τὰ τοῦ σώματος δυστυχήματα
τοῖς τῆς ψυχῆς ἐπιτηδεύμασιν ἰᾶσθαι · καλῶς. εἰ γὰρ
ἐξ ἴσου τῇ συμφορᾷ καὶ τὴν διάνοιαν ἔξω καὶ τὸν
19 ἄλλον βίον διάξω, τί τούτου διοίσω;
4   Περὶ μὲν οὖν τούτων τοσαῦτά μοι εἰρήσθω · ὑπὲρ ὧν
δέ μοι προσήκει λέγειν, ὡς ἂν οἷός τ' ὦ διὰ βραχυτάτων ἐρῶ. φησὶ γὰρ ὁ κατήγορος οὐ δικαίως με λαμβάνειν τὸ παρὰ τῆς πόλεως ἀργύριον · καὶ γὰρ τῷ

wide separation from τίνος and by
its position at the end of the sentence. — ἕνεκα : for the unusual
position see on 19. 17. — συκοφαντεῖ : the cripple's look and gesture
call out a burst of laughter from
the hearers which makes an apodosis quite unnecessary.

   3. τούτου : see on 12. 81. —
καὶ γάρ : for the original force of
γάρ see on 19. 12. καὶ γάρ varies
in force according as the particles
are fused or retain their separate
force. The following include all
instances in our eight speeches :
(A) καὶ γάρ = emphatic γάρ for.
So in our passage. (B) Each
particle preserves its own force :
(1) γάρ = for, καί emphatic 24.8 ;
cp. 3. 43 καὶ γὰρ δεινὸν ἂν εἴη for it
would be a shame indeed. (2) γάρ

= for, καί correlative with a following καί, 24. 4. — καλῶς : and a
noble thought it is. — ἐξ ἴσου κτλ. :
i.e. I shall be as lame in principle
and conduct as he is. — καὶ τὴν
διάνοιαν : καί of comparison. See
on 19. 2.

   4. μὲν οὖν : force, see on 12.
3 C. — ὑπέρ : here and in § 21 =
περί, a usage that became common
with the later orators, especially
Demosthenes and Aeschines ; note
that in both passages Lysias sets
it over against a περί phrase. For
other uses of ὑπέρ see on 25. 5. —
ὧν δέ : for position of δέ see on
16. 7. — οἷός τ' ὦ : see Crit. Note.
— διὰ βραχυτάτων : see on δι' ἐλα-
χίστων 12. 3. — γάρ (after φησί) :
force, see on 19. 12 (C) (1). — καὶ
γάρ : see on § 3 (B) (2).

σώματι δύνασθαι καὶ οὐκ εἶναι τῶν ἀδυνάτων, καὶ
25 τέχνην ἐπίστασθαι τοιαύτην ὥστε καὶ ἄνευ τοῦ διδο-
5 μένου τούτου ζῆν. καὶ τεκμηρίοις χρῆται τῆς μὲν τοῦ
σώματος ῥώμης, ὅτι ἐπὶ τοὺς ἵππους ἀναβαίνω, τῆς δ'
ἐν τῇ τέχνῃ εὐπορίας, ὅτι δύναμαι συνεῖναι δυναμένοις
ἀνθρώποις ἀναλίσκειν. τὴν μὲν οὖν ἐκ τῆς τέχνης
30 εὐπορίαν καὶ τὸν ἄλλον τὸν ἐμὸν βίον, οἷος τυγχάνει,
πάντας ὑμᾶς οἴομαι γιγνώσκειν· ὅμως δὲ κἀγὼ διὰ
6 βραχέων ἐρῶ. ἐμοὶ γὰρ ὁ μὲν πατὴρ κατέλιπεν οὐδέν,
τὴν δὲ μητέρα τελευτήσασαν πέπαυμαι τρέφων τρίτον
ἔτος τουτί, παῖδες δέ μοι οὔπω εἰσὶν οἵ με θεραπεύ-
35 σουσι. τέχνην δὲ κέκτημαι βραχέα δυναμένην ὠφελεῖν, ἣν αὐτὸς μὲν ἤδη χαλεπῶς ἐργάζομαι, τὸν

---

5. On this travesty on the
complainant's speech see Introd.
p 236. — τοὺς ἵππους: for the article
see HA. 659; G. 950; B. 448.
τοὺς ἵππους ἀναβαίνει, *he rides
horseback*, takes the article as
regularly as does the English
"He plays the flute." Cp. 16. 13.
— ἐν τῇ τέχνῃ . . . ἐκ τῆς τέχνης :
we may think of the εὐπορία of a
workman as *lying in* (ἐν) his trade,
or as *coming from* (ἐκ) it. — τυγχάνει: the only instance in Lysias
of the omission of ὤν with τυγχάνει.

6. τρίτον ἔτος τουτί: for the
omission of the article where the
noun has both a demonstrative
and a numeral cp. Aeschin. 2. 149
συνεχῶς ἔτος ἤδη τουτὶ τρίτον

στρατηγῶν; Dem. 8. 2 ἑνδέκατον
μῆνα τουτονί. For the case see
HA. 721; G. 1063. — οὔπω : he
is already getting to be an old
man (πρεσβύτερον καὶ ἀσθενέστερον γιγνόμενον § 7) ; the jest is
as obvious as that in οὔπω δύναμαι
κτήσασθαι below. — θεραπεύσουσι :
for mood and tense see on βοηθήσουσι 16. 16. — τέχνην : he gives
no hint as to what his trade is.
He has a shop (§ 20), and his
lameness does not entirely inca-
pacitate him for his work (χαλεπῶς ἐργάζομαι § 6). Perhaps the
restriction in force in Aristotle's
time (Introd. p. 232), confining the
poor-relief to those so disabled
ὥστε μὴ δύνασθαι μηδὲν ἔργον
ἐργάζεσθαι, was not yet in force.

διαδεξόμενον δ' αὐτὴν οὔπω δύναμαι κτήσασθαι. πρό-
σοδος δέ μοι οὐκ ἔστιν ἄλλη πλὴν ταύτης, ἣν ἂν ἀφέ-
39 λησθέ με, κινδυνεύσαιμ' ἂν ὑπὸ τῇ δυσχερεστάτῃ
7 γενέσθαι τύχῃ. μὴ τοίνυν, ἐπειδή γε ἔστιν, ὦ βουλή,
σῶσαί με δικαίως, ἀπολέσητε ἀδίκως· μηδὲ ἃ νεωτέρῳ
καὶ μᾶλλον ἐρρωμένῳ ὄντι ἔδοτε, πρεσβύτερον καὶ
ἀσθενέστερον γιγνόμενον ἀφέλησθε· μηδὲ πρότερον
καὶ περὶ τοὺς οὐδὲν ἔχοντας κακὸν ἐλεημονέστατοι
45 δοκοῦντες εἶναι νυνὶ διὰ τοῦτον τοὺς καὶ τοῖς ἐχθροῖς
ἐλεεινοὺς ὄντας ἀγρίως ἀποδέξησθε· μηδ' ἐμὲ τολμή-
σαντες ἀδικῆσαι καὶ τοὺς ἄλλους τοὺς ὁμοίως ἐμοὶ
8 διακειμένους ἀθυμῆσαι ποιήσητε. καὶ γὰρ ἂν ἄτοπον
εἴη, ὦ βουλή, εἰ ὅτε μὲν ἁπλῆ μοι ἦν ἡ συμφορά, τότε
50 μὲν φαινοίμην λαμβάνων τὸ ἀργύριον τοῦτο, νῦν δ'
ἐπειδὴ καὶ γῆρας καὶ νόσοι καὶ τὰ τούτοις ἑπόμενα
9 κακὰ προσγίγνεταί μοι, τότε ἀφαιρεθείην. δοκεῖ δέ

— **κτήσασθαι**: the greater part of the skilled labor of the city was done by slaves, sometimes working in their owner's shop (cp. 12. 8), oftener let out to manufacturers. — **ἂν ἀφέλησθε . . . κινδυνεύσαιμ' ἄν**: mood, HA. 901 a; G. 1421. 2; B. 612. 1. — **ὑπὸ τύχῃ**: a slight personification of τύχη (cp. § 10). ὑπό with dat. is the regular expression for subjection under a *person*.

7. **δικαίως, ἀδίκως**: on the παρονομασία see App. § 58. 5. — **ἐρρωμένῳ** : the passage of the partic. into the complete adj. construction (pred. with ὄντι) is

helped here by its coördination with νεωτέρῳ. — **δοκοῦντες** : tense, see on ἀνιωμένου 12. 32. — **καί** (before τοὺς ἄλλους) : *also*. — **ἀθυμῆσαι** : ingressive aorist, see on μετέσχον 16. 3.

8. **καὶ γάρ**: *for indeed*, see on § 3 (B) (1). —

ὅτε μὲν ἦν | τότε μὲν φαινοίμην ||
νῦν δέ
ἐπειδὴ προσγιγν. | τότε ἀφαιρεθείην.
The antithesis is emphasized by using μέν in both cola of the first member. In the second member νῦν δέ is the real correlative of τότε μὲν (φαινοίμην), but is re-

μοι τῆς πενίας τῆς ἐμῆς τὸ μέγεθος ὁ κατήγορος ἂν
ἐπιδεῖξαι σαφέστατα μόνος ἀνθρώπων. εἰ γὰρ ἐγὼ
55 κατασταθεὶς χορηγὸς τραγῳδοῖς προκαλεσαίμην αὐτὸν
εἰς ἀντίδοσιν, δεκάκις ἂν ἕλοιτο χορηγῆσαι μᾶλλον ἢ
ἀντιδοῦναι ἅπαξ. καίτοι πῶς οὐ δεινόν ἐστι νῦν μὲν
κατηγορεῖν ὡς διὰ πολλὴν εὐπορίαν ἐξ ἴσου δύναμαι
συνεῖναι τοῖς πλουσιωτάτοις, εἰ δὲ ὧν ἐγὼ λέγω τύχοι
60 τι γενόμενον, ὁμολογεῖν ἂν με τοιοῦτον εἶναι καὶ ἔτι
πονηρότερον ;

10   Περὶ δὲ τῆς ἐμῆς ἱππικῆς, ἧς οὗτος ἐτόλμησε μνησθῆναι πρὸς ὑμᾶς, οὔτε τὴν τύχην δείσας οὔτε ὑμᾶς

enforced by the second τότε, which
gives a more perfect verbal balance
than a repetition of νῦν would have
given. Note that the first τότε is
to be taken strictly with λαμβάνων
only, for φαινοίμην refers to that
hypothetical *future* time when the
Senate may have refused him his
obol. On the tense of λαμβάνων
see on ἀνιωμένου 12. 32.

9. ἄν: cp. § 2 and see on 12. 1.
— σαφέστατα μόνος : a combination of two ideas, σαφέστατα ἀνθρώπων and μόνος ἀνθρώπων. So
Cicero, *Prov. Consul.* 12, *unus
omnium nequissimus.* — καταστα-
θείς: cp. διδάσκαλος καταστάς 12.
78. Lysias uses the aor. pass.
form only here and in 13. 35. It
is very rare in other prose writers.
— χορηγός: next to the trierarchy
the most costly of the liturgies;
see on 19. 43. — τραγῳδοῖς: L. &

S. *s.v.* I. 2. Case, HA. 767 ; G.
1165 ; B. 378 ; Gl. 523. Cp. 21. 2
ἀνδράσι χορηγῶν εἰς Διονύσια. —
ἀντίδοσιν : if A. was appointed for
a liturgy, but claimed that B., as
being richer than himself, should
have been called upon first, he
might demand of B. that he assume the burden or else exchange
property with him. If B. refused,
the courts decided which must
perform the liturgy. See Smith,
Dict. Antiq. s.v. — χορηγῆσαι:
tense, cp. on ᾤκησε 12. 4. — τοιοῦτον, πονηρότερον : 'that I am as
badly off as I claim to be, and
even worse.' πονηρότερον covers
both his physical and financial
wretchedness, both of which the
complainant disputes.

10. On the following argument
see Introd. p. 237. — τὴν τύχην
δείσας : τύχη is substituted here

αἰσχυνθείς, οὐ πολὺς ὁ λόγος. ἐγὼ γάρ, ὦ βουλή,
65 πάντας τοὺς ἔχοντάς τι δυστύχημα τοῦτ᾽ οἶμαι ζητεῖν
καὶ τοῦτο φιλοσοφεῖν, ὅπως ὡς ἀλυπότατα μεταχειριοῦν-
ται τὸ συμβεβηκὸς πάθος· ὧν εἷς ἐγώ. καὶ περιπε-
πτωκὼς τοιαύτῃ συμφορᾷ ταύτην ἐμαυτῷ ῥᾳστώνην
69 ἐξηῦρον εἰς τὰς ὁδοὺς τὰς μακροτέρας τῶν ἀναγκαίων.
11 ὃ δὲ μέγιστον, ὦ βουλή, τεκμήριον ὅτι διὰ τὴν συμφορὰν ἀλλ᾽ οὐ διὰ τὴν ὕβριν, ὡς οὗτός φησιν, ἐπὶ τοὺς
ἵππους ἀναβαίνω· εἰ γὰρ ἐκεκτήμην οὐσίαν, ἐπ᾽ ἀσ-
τράβης ἂν ὠχούμην, ἀλλ᾽ οὐκ ἐπὶ τοὺς ἀλλοτρίους

for τοὺς θεούς in the common formula for "fear of the gods and shame before men"; cp. 32. 13 εἰ μηδένα ἀνθρώπων ᾐσχύνου, τοὺς θεοὺς ἐχρῆν σε . . . δεδιέναι. Here τύχη is fitting as being that divine power which is particularly concerned in reversals of life, and may any day make a cripple and a beggar of the now prosperous complainant. The Greek conception of τύχη, while sometimes not passing beyond mere "chance," is usually that of an active power, and there is a strong tendency to personify it, making it coördinate with Providence, as Lysias distinctly does where he says (13. 63) ἡ δὲ τύχη καὶ ὁ δαίμων περιεποίησε but fortune and Providence saved them. The cripple's idea is expressed in Isocrates's warning (1. 29) μηδενὶ συμφορὰν ὀνειδίσῃς· κοινὴ γὰρ ἡ

τύχη καὶ τὸ μέλλον ἀόρατον revile no man for his misfortune, for fortune is common to all and the future unseen. — ζητεῖν, φιλοσο-φεῖν: on the συνωνυμία see App. § 58. 2. — ὧν εἷς ἐγώ: the emphasis upon the pronoun in this formula causes the frequent omission of the copula, even of the first and second persons, which in other connections is rarely omitted. — ταύτην: gender, see on 12. 37. — εἷς: see on εἰς σωτηρίαν 12. 14. — τῶν ἀναγκαίων: partitive, for the longer trips among those that I have to make; or perhaps = ἢ τὰς ἀναγκαίας ordinary trips, i.e. trips for the everyday necessities.

11. ὃ . . . τεκμήριον: cp. on 32. 24. — τὴν ὕβριν: the insolence charged by the complainant. — ἀσ-τράβης: a soft saddle with a back, for women and invalids. — ἄν:

ἵππους ἀνέβαινον · νυνὶ δ᾽ ἐπειδὴ τοιοῦτον οὐ δύναμαι
75 κτήσασθαι, τοῖς ἀλλοτρίοις ἵπποις ἀναγκάζομαι χρῆ-
12 σθαι πολλάκις. καίτοι πῶς οὐκ ἄτοπόν ἐστιν, ὦ βουλή,
τοῦτον ἂν αὐτόν, εἰ μὲν ἐπ᾽ ἀστράβης ὀχούμενον ἑώρα
με, σιωπᾶν (τί γὰρ ἂν καὶ ἔλεγεν;), ὅτι δ᾽ ἐπὶ τοὺς
ἠτημένους ἵππους ἀναβαίνω, πειρᾶσθαι πείθειν ὑμᾶς ὡς
80 δυνατός εἰμι; καὶ ὅτι μὲν δυοῖν βακτηρίαιν χρῶμαι,
τῶν ἄλλων μιᾷ χρωμένων, μὴ κατηγορεῖν ὡς καὶ τοῦτο
τῶν δυναμένων ἐστίν · ὅτι δ᾽ ἐπὶ τοὺς ἵππους ἀναβαίνω,
τεκμηρίῳ χρῆσθαι πρὸς ὑμᾶς ὡς εἰμὶ τῶν δυναμένων;
84 οἷς ἐγὼ διὰ τὴν αὐτὴν αἰτίαν ἀμφοτέροις χρῶμαι.

13 Τοσοῦτον δὲ διενήνοχεν ἀναισχυντίᾳ τῶν ἁπάντων
ἀνθρώπων, ὥστε ὑμᾶς πειρᾶται πείθειν, τοσούτους
ὄντας εἷς ὤν, ὡς οὐκ εἰμὶ τῶν ἀδυνάτων ἐγώ. καίτοι εἰ
τοῦτο πείσει τινὰς ὑμῶν, ὦ βουλή, τί με κωλύει κληροῦσθαι τῶν ἐννέα ἀρχόντων, καὶ ὑμᾶς ἐμοῦ μὲν ἀφελέ-

with both ὠχούμην and ἀνέβαινον,
cp. 16. 8.

12. καὶ ἔλεγεν. for the force
of καί see on 12. 29. — ἠτημένους:
borrowed. — τῶν δυναμένων: case,
cp. on τῶν αὐτῶν 12. 41.

13. εἰ . . . πείσει: the thought
is not that if the complainant *shall*
persuade, etc., then nothing *will*
hinder, but that if the jury is now
so disposed that the complainant
is going to persuade them, nothing
now hinders. See HA. 893 c;
G. 1391 ; B. 602 n. 2 ; Gl. 648 a ;
GMT. 407 ; but here it is not the
" present intention or necessity "

that is involved, but the present
prospect, due to the attitude of the
hearers. — κωλύει: no formal action had ever opened the archonship to members of the fourth
property class, as it had been
opened to those of the third class
in the fifth century ; but in practice the restriction was ignored.
The cripple's ineligibility was
therefore due to his physical im-
perfection, which rendered him
unfit for the priestly functions
involved in the archonship. — ἀρχόντων: case, see on τῶν ὁπλιτῶν
32. 5. — ἐμοῦ ἀφελέσθαι, τὸν αὐτὸν

90 σθαι τὸν ὀβολὸν ὡς ὑγιαίνοντος, τούτῳ δὲ ψηφίσασθαι
πάντας ὡς ἀναπήρῳ; οὐ γὰρ δήπου τὸν αὐτὸν ὑμεῖς
μὲν ὡς δυνάμενον ἀφαιρήσεσθε τὸ διδόμενον, οἱ δὲ
θεσμοθέται ὡς ἀδύνατον ὄντα κληροῦσθαι κωλύσουσιν.
14 ἀλλὰ γὰρ οὔτε ὑμεῖς τούτῳ τὴν αὐτὴν ἔχετε γνώμην,
95 οὔθ᾽ οὗτος ὑμῖν· εὖ ποιῶν. ὁ μὲν γὰρ ὥσπερ ἐπικλή-

ἀφαιρήσεσθε: case, HA. 724,
748 a; G. 1069, 1118; B. 340, 362;
Gl. 535, 509 a. — ὡς: force, see on
16. 8. — ψηφίσασθαι πάντας (cp.
πείσει τινάς above) : · it will be as
easy. for all (πάντας) to see a cripple in him, as for any (τινάς) to
see a sound man in me.' Forman
(Class. Rev. 10. 105) calls attention to the fact that no one of
Lysias's speakers but the cripple
uses πᾶς in the order, noun (or pronoun) + verb + πᾶς. He thinks
it may well be a touch of Ethopoiia
to catch this trick of the old man's
speech as he does in §§ 13, 14,
19, 21, 27. — θεσμοθέται : cp. Crit.
Note. Of the nine archons the
first three (Βασιλεύς, Πολέμαρχος,
Ἄρχων) had individual departments of administration; the six
others formed one board under the
name Θεσμοθέται. Their chief
work was the supervision of the
law courts (see App. § 5); to this
was added the drawing of the lot
for those officers who were not
elected by vote. Cf. Gulick, p. 301 f.

14. ἀλλὰ γάρ: for this use in
concluding a discussion see on 12.

40. — τούτῳ: drawn from its usual
position after τὴν αὐτήν to stand
close against its contrasted word :
ὑμεῖς τούτῳ | οὗτος ὑμῖν. — οὔθ᾽
οὗτος ὑμῖν : " The drastic tautology
of the two disjunctive members,
You do not think as he does, and
he does not think as you do, and
that is a right good thing, fits the
comic coloring of the passage"
(Frb.) ; cp. Crit. Note. — εὖ ποιῶν :
while grammatically εὖ ποιῶν is
connected with the second clause
only, its force extends over both.
It is a stereotyped expression, fortunately, thank heaven. Its formal
use went so far that Demosthenes
could say (23. 143), τοῦτο . . ., εὖ
ποιοῦν, οὐ συνέβη this, fortunately,
did not happen. — ὥσπερ ἐπικλή
ρου: on the simile and the personification, see Introd. p. 25, N. 5.
The point is that when by the
absence of sons an estate fell to a
daughter, the nearest male heir
could demand the hand of the
heiress in marriage, even to the
extent of taking her from her husband, if she was already married.
The provision was made in order

ρου τῆς συμφορᾶς οὔσης ἀμφισβητήσων ἥκει καὶ
πειρᾶται πείθειν ὑμᾶς ὡς οὐκ εἰμὶ τοιοῦτος οἷον ὑμεῖς
ὁρᾶτε πάντες· ὑμεῖς δὲ (ὃ τῶν εὖ φρονούντων ἔργον
ἐστί) μᾶλλον πιστεύετε τοῖς ὑμετέροις αὐτῶν ὀφθαλμοῖς
100 ἢ τοῖς τούτου λόγοις.

15 Λέγει δ' ὡς ὑβριστής εἰμι καὶ βίαιος καὶ λίαν ἀσελγῶς διακείμενος, ὥσπερ εἰ φοβερῶς ὀνομάσειε, μέλλων
ἀληθῆ λέγειν, ἀλλ' οὐκ, ἐὰν πάνυ πραόνως, ταῦτα ποιήσων. ἐγὼ δ' ὑμᾶς, ὦ βουλή, σαφῶς οἶμαι δεῖν διαγι-
105 γνώσκειν οἷς τ' ἐγχωρεῖ τῶν ἀνθρώπων ὑβρισταῖς εἶναι

16 καὶ οἷς οὐ προσήκει. οὐ γὰρ τοὺς πενομένους καὶ λίαν
ἀπόρως διακειμένους ὑβρίζειν εἰκός, ἀλλὰ τοὺς πολλῷ
πλείω τῶν ἀναγκαίων κεκτημένους· οὐδὲ τοὺς ἀδυνάτους τοῖς σώμασιν ὄντας, ἀλλὰ τοὺς μάλιστα πιστεύον-
110 τας ταῖς αὐτῶν ῥώμαις· οὐδὲ τοὺς ἤδη προβεβηκότας

to keep the property in the family (cp. on 32. 4). The cripple says that the complainant looks upon his misfortune as an heiress, and is trying to get possession of her inheritance of an obol a day. It is the best of the joke to represent the complainant as trying to get the cripple's obol for himself.

15. **φοβερῶς ὀνομάσειε** : 'he knows his claims to be false, so he tries to frighten you by calling me ὑβριστής, βίαιος, ἀσελγῶς διακείμενος.' — **μέλλων λέγειν, ταῦτα ποιήσων** : an instance of the use of the periphrastic future (*going to*) parallel with the simple future,

GS. 274. Note that the form of the apodoses corresponds to only one of the protases, and that too the one the verb of which is unexpressed (ἐὰν πάνυ πραόνως). — **πάνυ** : see on 19. 15. — **πραόνως** : for πράως ; used in only one other passage in Attic Greek (Aristoph. *Frogs*, 856). Probably used here to give a stilted tone to the cripple's "philosophy." — **οἷς** : see on οὕς 25. 7 ; cp. ᾧ τρόπῳ 19. 12. — **προσήκει** : force as in 25. 7 ; cp. εἰκός following.

16. **πολλῷ** : so in 17. 6 (πολλῷ πλέον) and 29. 8 (πολλῷ πλείω) ; elsewhere in Lysias, πολύ.

τῇ ἡλικίᾳ, ἀλλὰ τοὺς ἔτι νέους καὶ νέαις ταῖς διανοίαις
17 χρωμένους. οἱ μὲν γὰρ πλούσιοι τοῖς χρήμασιν ἐξω-
νοῦνται τοὺς κινδύνους, οἱ δὲ πένητες ὑπὸ τῆς παρούσης
ἀπορίας σωφρονεῖν ἀναγκάζονται· καὶ οἱ μὲν νέοι συγ-
115 γνώμης ἀξιοῦνται τυγχάνειν παρὰ τῶν πρεσβυτέρων,
τοῖς δὲ πρεσβυτέροις ἐξαμαρτάνουσιν ὁμοίως ἐπιτιμῶ-
18 σιν ἀμφότεροι· καὶ τοῖς μὲν ἰσχυροῖς ἐγχωρεῖ μηδὲν
αὐτοῖς πάσχουσιν οὓς ἂν βουληθῶσιν ὑβρίζειν, τοῖς
δὲ ἀσθενέσιν οὐκ ἔστιν οὔτε ὑβριζομένοις ἀμύνεσθαι
120 τοὺς ὑπάρξαντας οὔτε ὑβρίζειν βουλομένοις περιγίγνεσθαι τῶν ἀδικουμένων. ὥστε μοι δοκεῖ ὁ κατήγορος
εἰπεῖν περὶ τῆς ἐμῆς ὕβρεως οὐ σπουδάζων, ἀλλὰ
παίζων, οὐδ' ὑμᾶς πεῖσαι βουλόμενος ὡς εἰμὶ τοιοῦτος,
124 ἀλλ' ἐμὲ κωμῳδεῖν βουλόμενος, ὥσπερ τι καλὸν ποιῶν.
19 Ἔτι δὲ καὶ συλλέγεσθαί φησιν ἀνθρώπους ὡς ἐμὲ
πονηροὺς καὶ πολλούς, οἳ τὰ μὲν ἑαυτῶν ἀνηλώκασι,
τοῖς δὲ τὰ σφέτερα σῴζειν βουλομένοις ἐπιβουλεύουσιν. ὑμεῖς δὲ ἐνθυμήθητε πάντες ὅτι ταῦτα λέγων
οὐδὲν ἐμοῦ κατηγορεῖ μᾶλλον ἢ τῶν ἄλλων ὅσοι τέχνας
130 ἔχουσιν, οὐδὲ τῶν ὡς ἐμὲ εἰσιόντων μᾶλλον ἢ τῶν ὡς
20 τοὺς ἄλλους δημιουργούς. ἕκαστος γὰρ ὑμῶν εἴθισται
προσφοιτᾶν ὁ μὲν πρὸς μυροπώλιον, ὁ δὲ πρὸς κου-

---

17. ὑπὸ ἀπορίας : see on ὑπὸ
τῶν γεγενημένων 12. 3. — ἀμφότεροι : both young and old.

18. μηδέν : see on μήτε 12. 68
(B). — τοὺς ὑπάρξαντας : force, see
on ὑπάρχει 12. 23 A.

19. ὡς : see on 16. 4. — πολλούς : made emphatic by reversal

of the usual order, πολλοὺς καὶ
πονηρούς.

20. προσφοιτᾶν : an indication
of the simplicity of Athenian life.
In the capital city the barber's shop
and the cobbler's shop are the club-
houses of men of leisure as in the
modern country village. That no

ρεῖον, ὁ δὲ πρὸς σκυτοτομεῖον, ὁ δ' ὅποι ἂν τύχῃ, καὶ
πλεῖστοι μὲν ὡς τοὺς ἐγγυτάτω τῆς ἀγορᾶς κατεσκευ-
135 ασμένους, ἐλάχιστοι δὲ ὡς τοὺς πλεῖστον ἀπέχοντας
αὐτῆς· ὥστ' εἴ τις ὑμῶν πονηρίαν καταγνώσεται τῶν
ὡς ἐμὲ εἰσιόντων, δῆλον ὅτι καὶ τῶν παρὰ τοῖς ἄλλοις
διατριβόντων· εἰ δὲ κἀκείνων, ἁπάντων Ἀθηναίων·
ἅπαντες γὰρ εἴθισθε προσφοιτᾶν καὶ διατρίβειν ἀμου-
140 γέπου.

21 Ἀλλὰ γὰρ οὐκ οἶδ' ὅ τι δεῖ λίαν με ἀκριβῶς ἀπολο-
γούμενον πρὸς ἓν ἕκαστον ὑμῖν τῶν εἰρημένων ἐνοχλεῖν

reproach was involved in frequenting such places is clear from the fact that Demosthenes thinks it a good point to make with a jury that the man whom he is attacking (25. 52) does not frequent the shops : *He shares no man's affection or companionship; . . . nor does he resort to any of these barbers' shops or perfumers' shops in the city, nor any other shops — not one. But he is implacable, restless, unsocial, with no feeling of gratitude or friendship or anything else that a right-minded man feels.* These ancient assemblies, like their modern counterparts, "saved the country," — with words, — as Isocrates tells us (7. 15): *Which* (the constitution) *now become corrupted troubles us not, nor do we take thought how we may restore it; but we sit in the shops and find fault with the state of the country,*

and say that never in all the history of the democracy were we worse governed, — while in action, and in the principles that we cherish, we are better content with it than with the constitution that our fathers left us. — ὅποι ἂν τύχῃ : sc. προσφοιτῶν; cp. 12. 18.— ἀγορᾶς : on life about the Agora, see Gulick, p. 40 ff.— καταγνώσεται : with gen. and acc. HA. 752 a; G. 1123 (cp. 1121); B. 370; Gl. 514 a. — παρὰ τοῖς ἄλλοις: see on παρ' αὐτοῖς 12. 33.— ἀμουγέπου : see Crit. Note. ἀμου- is of the same origin as οὐδαμοῦ, ἀμόθεν, Eng. *some* (A.S. *sum*, Goth. *sums*) ; the Eng. has preserved the original meaning. Lysias has ἀμωσγέπως in 13. 7.

21. ἀλλὰ γάρ: in transition; see on 12. 40. — ὑμῖν: the interruption of the normal order πρὸς ἓν ἕκαστον τῶν εἰρημέων by ὑμῖν

πλείω χρόνον. εἰ γὰρ ὑπὲρ τῶν μεγίστων εἴρηκα, τί
δεῖ περὶ τῶν φαύλων ὁμοίως τούτῳ σπουδάζειν; ἐγὼ
145 δ᾽ ὑμῶν, ὦ βουλή, δέομαι πάντων τὴν αὐτὴν ἔχειν περὶ
22 ἐμοῦ διάνοιαν, ἥνπερ καὶ πρότερον· καὶ μὴ οὗ μόνου
μεταλαβεῖν ἔδωκεν ἡ τύχη μοι τῶν ἐν τῇ πατρίδι, τούτου διὰ τουτονὶ ἀποστερήσητέ με· μηδ᾽ ἃ πάλαι κοινῇ
πάντες ἔδοτέ μοι, νῦν οὗτος εἷς ὢν πείσῃ πάλιν ὑμᾶς
150 ἀφελέσθαι. ἐπειδὴ γάρ, ὦ βουλή, τῶν μεγίστων ἀρχῶν
ὁ δαίμων ἀπεστέρησεν ἡμᾶς, ἡ πόλις ἡμῖν ἐψηφίσατο
τοῦτο τὸ ἀργύριον, ἡγουμένη κοινὰς εἶναι τὰς τύχας
23 τοῖς ἅπασι καὶ τῶν κακῶν καὶ τῶν ἀγαθῶν. πῶς οὖν
οὐκ ἂν δειλαιότατος εἴην, εἰ τῶν μὲν καλλίστων καὶ
155 μεγίστων διὰ τὴν συμφορὰν ἀπεστερημένος εἴην, ἃ δ᾽
ἡ πόλις ἔδωκε προνοηθεῖσα τῶν οὕτως διακειμένων,
διὰ τὸν κατήγορον ἀφαιρεθείην; μηδαμῶς, ὦ βουλή,
ταύτῃ θῆσθε τὴν ψῆφον. διὰ τί γὰρ ἂν καὶ τύχοιμι

throws strong emphasis upon ἓν
ἕκαστον. Cp. τὴν αὐτήν . . . διάνοιαν below, and τὰς τύχας . . .
καὶ τῶν κακῶν καὶ τῶν ἀγαθῶν § 22 ;
cp. on ἡμῖν 12. 33.— ὑπὲρ τῶν
μεγίστων, περὶ τῶν φαύλων : for
ὑπέρ = περί see on § 4. It is
fully in the spirit of parody that
the cripple treats the complainant's sound arguments as "trivial"
and his own nonsense as "most
weighty."— ἥνπερ : see on οἵτινες
12. 40.— καὶ πρότερον : for καί in
comparisons see on 19. 2.

22. ἡ τύχη : note that ὁ δαίμων
is used below of the same power ;
cp. on § 10.— ἐψηφίσατο : i.e. by

the law which established poor-
relief in general. The award to
individuals would seem from this
speech to have rested with the
Senate ; the veto on any case was
certainly theirs.

23. δειλαιότατος : another touch
of fine phraseology in the cripple's
mouth ; the word is common only
in poetry.— καλλίστων καὶ μεγίστων : on the συνωνυμία see App.
58. 2. — διὰ τὸν κατήγορον : the
direct agents of the deprivation
would be the senators, but the
cripple would have the complainant
to 'thank for it.' See on 12. 87.—
καὶ τύχοιμι : for καί see on 12. 29.

24 τοιούτων ὑμῶν; πότερον ὅτι δι' ἐμέ τις εἰς ἀγῶνα
160 πώποτε καταστὰς ἀπώλεσε τὴν οὐσίαν; ἀλλ' οὐδ' ἂν
εἷς ἀποδείξειεν. ἀλλ' ὅτι πολυπράγμων εἰμὶ καὶ θρασὺς
καὶ φιλαπεχθήμων; ἀλλ' οὐ τοιαύταις ἀφορμαῖς τοῦ
25 βίου τυγχάνω χρώμενος. ἀλλ' ὅτι λίαν ὑβριστὴς
καὶ βίαιος; ἀλλ' οὐδ' ἂν αὐτὸς φήσειεν, εἰ μὴ βού-
165 λοιτο καὶ τοῦτο ψεύδεσθαι τοῖς ἄλλοις ὁμοίως. ἀλλ'
ὅτι ἐπὶ τῶν τριάκοντα γενόμενος ἐν δυνάμει κακῶς
ἐποίησα πολλοὺς τῶν πολιτῶν; ἀλλὰ μετὰ τοῦ ὑμετέρου πλήθους ἔφυγον εἰς Χαλκίδα, καὶ ἐξόν μοι μετ'
169 ἐκείνων ἀδεῶς πολιτεύεσθαι, μεθ' ὑμῶν εἱλόμην κινδυ-
26 νεύειν ἀποδημῶν. μὴ τοίνυν, ὦ βουλή, μηδὲν ἡμαρτη-
κὼς ὁμοίων ὑμῶν τύχοιμι τοῖς πολλὰ ἠδικηκόσιν, ἀλλὰ

24. 'I am no sycophant, as are
so many.' For the element of
parody in this appeal see Introd.
p. 238. — οὐδ' ἂν εἷς: stronger
than οὐδεὶς ἄν; see on 19. 60. —
ἀλλ' οὐ τοιαύταις κτλ.: *but fortune
has not given me the use of such
resources for a livelihood* (for she
has made me weak and dependent on the favor of others, cp. §
18). ἀφορμή originally = *starting
point*, then *resource*; in war, *base
of operations*; in finance, *capital*.
25. φήσειεν: if the speaker were
thinking of the particular assertion to this effect which the complainant had made (λέγει δ' ὡς
ὑβριστής εἰμι καὶ βίαιος καὶ λίαν
ἀσελγῶς διακείμενος § 15), we
should have ἔφη; but he is think-

ing of any such possible assertion
on his part in the same general way
in which he thinks of οὐδ' ἂν εἷς
ἀποδείξειε above. — καὶ τοῦτο: see
on καὶ ἡμῶν 19. 2. — ἐπὶ τῶν τριάκοντα: for ἐπί see on 12. 17. —
πλήθους: see on 12. 42.
26. τοίνυν: force, see on 16.
7 (A). — μηδέν: see on μήτε
12. 68 (B). — ἡμαρτηκώς: tense,
see on εἰργασμένοι εἰσίν 12. 22. —
ὁμοίων . . . τοῖς πολλὰ ἠδικηκόσιν:
as it stands the comparison seems
to be between ὑμῶν and τοῖς
ἠδικηκόσιν, but of course the
meaning is μὴ ὁμοίων ὑμῶν τύχοιμι
οἵων ὑμῶν τυγχάνουσιν οἱ πολλὰ
ἠδικηκότες. This looseness of expression in comparisons is common, resulting from an attempt at

τὴν αὐτὴν ψῆφον θέσθε περὶ ἐμοῦ ταῖς ἄλλαις βουλαῖς, ἀναμνησθέντες ὅτι οὔτε χρήματα διαχειρίσας τῆς πό-λεως δίδωμι λόγον αὐτῶν, οὔτε ἀρχὴν ἄρξας οὐδεμίαν 175 εὐθύνας ὑπέχω νῦν αὐτῆς, ἀλλὰ περὶ ὀβολοῦ μόνον ποι-27 οῦμαι τοὺς λόγους. καὶ οὕτως ὑμεῖς μὲν τὰ δίκαια γνώ-σεσθε πάντες, ἐγὼ δὲ τούτων ὑμῖν τυχὼν ἕξω τὴν χάριν, οὗτος δὲ τοῦ λοιποῦ μαθήσεται μὴ τοῖς ἀσθενεστέροις ἐπιβουλεύειν ἀλλὰ τῶν ὁμοίων αὐτῷ περιγίγνεσθαι.

brevity. Cp. Iliad I. 163 οὐ μὲν σοί ποτε ἴσον ἔχω γέρας. — ποιοῦ-μαι τοὺς λόγους : cp. on 12. 2.

27. τούτων ὑμῖν τυχὼν ἕξω : for

position of ὑμῖν cp. on ὑμῖν § 21, and see on ἡμῖν 12. 33. — ἐπιβου-λεύειν, περιγίγνεσθαι : present tense, of a practice, course of conduct.

Defense Against the Charge of Having Supported the Government of the Thirty

INTRODUCTION

THIS speech was written for a citizen who had been one of the Three Thousand admitted by the Thirty to a nominal share in their government. The speaker has now, under the restored democracy, been chosen (by vote or lot) to some office.[1]

At the δοκιμασία[2] his eligibility is challenged on the ground that he was a supporter of the Thirty. The complainants have brought no charge of specific acts, basing their attack upon the principle that former members of the oligarchical party (οἱ ἐξ ἄστεως) cannot be trusted in office under the democracy. The defense must attack this principle, and it is this fact which raises the speech above the plane of personal questions, and makes it one of the most interesting documents in the history of the period immediately after the Return.

---

[1] The title of the speech in the Mss. is Δήμου καταλύσεως ἀπολογία, but that is probably only an ancient editor's inference from the general character of the speech. It can hardly have been a defense against an indictment for treason, for the speaker nowhere expresses apprehension of any result save deprivation of some of the rights of a citizen (see §§ 3, 4, 23), and § 14 implies that he is pleading for an honor, not for safety (ὑφ' ὑμῶν νυνὶ τιμᾶσθαι δίκαιός εἰμι).

[2] All officials were required to submit to a formal scrutiny (δοκιμασία) before entering upon office. Except in the case of Archons and Senators this was conducted by a law court. Senators were examined by the outgoing Senate ; Archons appeared first before the Senate, then before a law court. See p. 133 f., and Gilbert, p. 218 ff. ; Gardner and Jevons, p. 465.

The oath of amnesty [1] provided for the exclusion from the city of certain specified leaders of the oligarchy; to all other citizens it guaranteed oblivion of the past (τῶν δὲ παρεληλυθότων μηδενὶ πρὸς μεδένα μνησικακεῖν ἐξεῖναι). Under any fair interpretation of this agreement the former supporters of the Thirty, even senators, office-holders, and soldiers under them, were perfectly eligible to office under the restored democracy. But to keep their pledges in the full spirit of them proved to be a severe test of the self-control of the party of the Return.[2]

The wiser democratic leaders fully recognized the critical nature of the situation. An attempt by one of the returned exiles to violate the agreement and take vengeance on one of the city party was met by the summary seizure of the complainant and his execution by the Senate without trial.[3] This made it clear that there was to be no policy of bloody reprisals; but the feeling of hostility remained.

Then, less than three years after the Return, came the attempt of the survivors of the Thirty, settled at Eleusis, to organize an attack by force. The prompt march of the citizen forces, together with their treacherous seizure of the oligarchical leaders, soon put down the movement. But now more than ever it seemed to the democratic masses intolerable that members of the city party should have equal privileges with themselves. Their spokesmen began to say that the aristocrats might consider the people generous indeed in allowing their former enemies to vote in the Ecclesia and to sit on juries; that to ask for more than this was an impertinence (Lys. 26. 2, 3).

Those who had been conspicuous supporters of the Thirty, or personally connected with their crimes of bloodshed and robbery, naturally refrained from thrusting themselves into prominence; indeed, few of these had probably remained in the city. But the first test came when men whose support of the Thirty had been only passive, and against whose personal character no charge

---

[1] Arist. *Resp. Ath.* ch. 39.   [2] Cp. XVI Introd. p. 133.
[3] Arist. *Resp. Ath.* 40, 2.

could be raised, ventured to become candidates for office. Their δοκιμασία gave opportunity for attack by personal enemies, by political blackmailers, or by politicians who were posing as jealous guardians of the democracy.

This speech was written by Lysias for one of the first cases of this sort, — it may have been the very first. The issue was vital. If a man like the speaker, of proved ability and personal character, untainted by crime under all the opportunities offered during the rule of the Thirty, was now to be excluded from office, the reconciliation must soon break down.

The date of the speech cannot be earlier than 400 B.C., nor can it be much later.[1]

OUTLINE

I. Προοίμιον, *Exordium*, §§ 1–6.

It is pardonable in you to feel resentment toward all who remained in the city under the Thirty, but it is amazing that my accusers try to persuade you to make no distinctions among us.

I will show that their charges against me are false.

Their conduct is consistent with their character ; yours should be for the protection of the innocent and for the good of the state.

[1] The new officials took their seats in midsummer; their δοκιμασία occurred shortly before. The siege of Eleusis is already past (§ 9); this fell in the archonship which closed July, 400 (ἐπὶ Ξ[εναι]νέτου ἄρχοντος Arist. *Resp. Ath.* 40. 4). The speech cannot be placed much later than 400, for the speaker, with all his pleas based on his good conduct before and during the rule of the Thirty, says nothing of his conduct since the Return (October, 403), nor does he cite cases of other men of his party holding office. Moreover, his warnings show that there are fugitives of the oligarchical party who still hope for a reaction and a counter blow against the democracy, and who are not yet sure what will be the treatment of the former supporters of the Thirty (§ 23), while in § 27 he speaks of the democracy not as established, but as *in process of being established* (δημοκρατία γίγνεται). A longer time would seem to be implied in the charges against the sycophants (ταχέως μὲν ἐκ πενήτων πλούσιοι γεγένηνται, πολλὰς δὲ ἀρχὰς ἄρχοντες οὐδεμιᾶς εὐθύνην διδόασιν), were these not stock charges, hardly to be taken seriously.

In return for my positive services to the state I ask only what you give to the merely harmless citizen.

My accusers try to lay upon me the crimes of the Thirty because they can find nothing wrong in my own conduct.

II. Πρόθεσις, *Propositio*, § 7.

It is unreasonable to suppose that I am hostile to the democracy (the πρόθεσις is incomplete, stating only the first of the arguments that are to follow).

III. Πίστεις, *Argumentatio*, §§ 8–28. (The πίστεις form the λύσις of the charges.)

A. The proposed refusal of office would be unjust to me, for I was never disaffected toward the democracy, §§ 8–18.

B. The policy of refusal would be unwise for you, §§ 19–28.

IV. Παρέκβασις, *Egressio*, §§ 29–34.

The complainants are unworthy of your confidence.

V. Ἐπίλογος, *Peroratio*. (The peroration probably began with § 35 ; it is lost by the mutilation of the Ms.)

COMMENTS ON ARGUMENT AND STYLE

I. Προοίμιον, *Exordium*, §§ 1–6.

The opening words, like those of the defense of Mantitheus, give at once the impression of conscious innocence, but with this we have here a more indignant tone of protest against the action of the complainants, and an earnest tone of warning to the jury. From the first the tone is less that of one pleading for favor than of one who identifies his interest with theirs and earnestly counsels them.

The sentences are long and dignified. Only after the proem is well under way is there any touch of artificial rhetoric.

II. Πρόθεσις, *Propositio*, § 7.

A speech for the defense need not open with a statement of the case, — the speech of the prosecution has already given that,

— but the defendant will naturally give at the beginning some statement of his line of argument. Lysias chooses to state here only his first point. When, in § 19, he passes on to his second argument, he does it without any πρόθεσις.

III. Πίστεις, *Argumentatio*, §§ 8–28.

A. §§ 8–18. The speaker cannot deny the fact that he remained in the city under the Thirty ; he must therefore deny the significance of the fact. The argument is surprising ; in the most blunt way he asserts that men follow self-interest in their attitude toward one form of government or another. He gives the jury to understand that he remained in the city under the Thirty because it was for his personal safety and for the safety of his property that he do so ; but he claims that it would have been still more to his personal advantage that the Thirty had never been established, and shows that support of the restored democracy is altogether to his personal advantage. He frankly tells the jury to assume that he acts from an enlightened self-interest, and demonstrates that on that assumption he will be a reliable supporter of their government.

The cool frankness with which he waives aside all claim of sentimental patriotism, ascribes his services to the earlier democracy to the desire to stand well with the people (§§ 12–18), admits that he submitted to the oligarchy, and asks the jury to estimate his relations to the new government purely on the basis of his personal interests, must have been refreshing to a jury weary of hearing pious protestations of loyalty and sacrifice for the sacred democracy. If their first thought was that they were dealing with a shameless egoist, their later feeling must have been that this was an outspoken man, who dared express his opinions frankly ; and then — who could deny the force of his arguments?

Not only is the argument as a whole novel and vigorous, but here and there Lysias gives a bright and unexpected turn to the subordinate parts. In the summary as to the speaker's conduct under the oligarchy he makes neat use of the dilemma : If the

Thirty offered him the chance to share their power and he refused, that shows that he was no friend to them; if the Thirty did not offer it, that shows that they were no friends to him (§ 14). Again, in § 17 he makes the keen plea that a man who kept his hands clean in times when there was every encouragement to wrong-doing can be counted on to be a law-abiding citizen under the present settled government.

The dignified language of the proem is continued throughout this argument. The sentences are in rounded, periodic form, with much of antithesis, which reaches its height in § 18 : —

ἡγοῦμαι δέ, ὦ ἄνδρες δικασταί
οὐκ ἂν δικαίως ὑμᾶς μισεῖν τοὺς ἐν τῇ ὀλιγαρχίᾳ μηδὲν πεπονθότας κακόν
ἐξὸν ὀργίζεσθαι τοῖς εἰς τὸ πλῆθος ἐξημαρτηκόσιν

οὐδὲ τοὺς μὴ φυγόντας ἐχθροὺς νομίζειν
ἀλλὰ τοὺς ὑμᾶς ἐκβαλόντας

οὐδὲ τοὺς προθυμουμένους τὰ ἑαυτῶν σῶσαι
ἀλλὰ τοὺς τὰ τῶν ἄλλων ἀφῃρημένους

οὐδὲ οἳ τῆς σφετέρας αὐτῶν σωτηρίας ἕνεκα ἔμειναν ἐν τῷ ἄστει
ἀλλ' οἵτινες ἑτέρους ἀπολέσαι βουλόμενοι μετέσχον τῶν πραγμάτων.

III. *B*. §§ 19–28. The speaker now assumes the part of political adviser. Entirely without passion, with the tone of one whose chief thought is for the good of the city, he analyzes the political situation, showing how essential it is that the restored democracy unite all citizens in its support, and how dangerous a course it would be to alienate from the new government the supporters of the oligarchy.

This is a strange tone for a defendant, that of political instruction and warning. But it was true to the situation. And such a plea was the more effective as coming from a speaker who had no sentimental illusions as to either form of government, but who argued purely on grounds of ordinary prudence.

The language becomes still more elevated with the increasing dignity and earnestness of the thought, almost reaching the epideictic style.

IV. Παρέκβασις, *Egressio*, §§ 29–34.

A counter attack on the prosecution is a natural and a common part of a plea for the defense. It usually falls, as here, between the argument in rebuttal and the epilogue.

The attack here is direct and forcible. It is ingenious in showing that the principle that underlies the complaint is precisely the principle that governed the Thirty — a point already made in another connection (§ 20) ; it includes the stock charge against the professional politicians, — that they are getting rich from their trade ; and it brings out distinctly the most serious charge, that they are fomenting discord in a community only just reunited.

The tone of the attack is severe and earnest, but always dignified. There is no display of personal passion. The speaker stands above petty recriminations, and in a most convincing way exposes the conduct of a group of small politicians who were coming to the front on false claims of service in the late civil war, and who were destined to succeed before long in discrediting and thrusting aside the great patriots of the Return.

In style of speech this attack keeps up the strong sentence structure, but the prevailing antitheses become sharper and clearer, particularly in the summary attack of § 30. In § 31 we have a period of the most artificial type, ἐκεῖνοι μὲν ὀλιγαρχίας οὔσης κτλ. : see App. § 57. 7.

In §§ 23 and 24 there is rhetorical play on the sound of words, not ill-fitted to the scornful tone of the attack ; see App. § 58. 5.

V. Ἐπίλογος, *Peroratio*, §§ 35–.

The epilogue ordinarily follows the Παρέκβασις, and the closing sentence of § 34 seems to form the transition from the attack on the prosecution to the prayer to the jury. There is therefore little doubt that the epilogue begins with § 35, and probably little of the speech has been lost by the mutilation of the Ms.

One who has read this speech comes to the close with a definite impression of the personality of the speaker. He is no enthusiast, he has no political sentiment; as a result of his observations of men he has reached the conclusion that all political attachments are determined by personal advantage, — and he is not afraid to express his opinion. This same analysis he brings to the discussion of party policy. He makes no appeal to the honor or generosity of the democratic jury, but with the utmost calmness and penetration he shows them that it is for the interest of their party to approve his candidacy.

We receive the impression that we are listening to a man of experience, of sharp observation of men, and of a personal dignity that forbids equally appeal to the sympathy of the jury and violent invective against his enemies.

The view that the speech embodies a true portrait of the client is most clearly expressed in the following words of Bruns.[1] In the conversation between lawyer and client " the talk would soon pass from personal matters to questions of political principles. The keen lawyer, who had himself had an eventful political experience, would be impressed by his client's views — mature and free from all illusions. The coolness with which he explained all political attachments on the ground of personal interest had its effect upon Lysias, and he counted upon its having its effect upon others. He therefore built up his defense on this idea. He believed that the good impression which he had himself received from the straightforward tone of the speaker — free from all personal small talk,[2] would not fail in the case of other listeners. And so in his treatment of the case, perhaps at the express request of the speaker, he let him pass quickly from his own person to general questions."

The style is noticeably more rhetorical than is usual with Lysias. In the more elevated parts his usual simplicity of sentence structure gives way to strong periods, with abundant antithesis and parallelism.

[1] *Literarisches Porträt*, p. 451.

[2] The speech for Mantitheus (XVI) offers a marked contrast in this respect. The young cavalryman is full of talk of his own achievements.

XXV

ΔΗΜΟΤ ΚΑΤΑΛΤΣΕΩΣ ΑΠΟΛΟΓΙΑ

1 Ὑμῖν μὲν πολλὴν συγγνώμην ἔχω, ὦ ἄνδρες δικασταί,
ἀκούουσι τοιούτων λόγων καὶ ἀναμιμνησκομένοις τῶν
γεγενημένων, ὁμοίως ἅπασιν ὀργίζεσθαι τοῖς ἐν ἄστει
μείνασι· τῶν δὲ κατηγόρων θαυμάζω, οἳ ἀμελοῦντες
5 τῶν οἰκείων τῶν ἀλλοτρίων ἐπιμελοῦνται, καὶ σαφῶς
εἰδότες τοὺς μηδὲν ἀδικοῦντας καὶ τοὺς πολλὰ ἐξη-
μαρτηκότας ζητοῦσι κερδαίνειν ἢ ὑμᾶς πείθειν περὶ
2 ἁπάντων ἡμῶν τὴν γνώμην ταύτην ἔχειν. εἰ μὲν οὖν
οἴονται ὅσα ὑπὸ τῶν τριάκοντα γεγένηται τῇ πόλει
10 ἐμοῦ κατηγορηκέναι, ἀδυνάτους αὐτοὺς ἡγοῦμαι λέγειν·

1. τοῖς μείνασι: case, see on
ὀργίζεσθε 12. 80. — ἄστει : for non-
use of the article see on 12. 16. —
μηδέν: when a participle or adjective with the article is equivalent
to an indefinite relative clause, it
takes μή as its negative, as such
a clause would do (μή in protasis). Such expressions refer to
a *class* of persons or things, and
this neg. may be called "μή generic." — ἀδικοῦντας, ἐξημαρτηκό-
τας : note the coupling of pres. and
perf. participles ; see on ἀδικῶ
12. 14, and for the perf. (of
"guilt ") see on εἰργασμένοι εἰσίν

12. 22. — κερδαίνειν : for interpretation see Crit. Note. — ταύτην :
the opinion urged by the complainants, and implied in ὀργίζεσθαι.

2. ἡγοῦμαι : this word expresses a more definite and mature conviction than οἴομαι (οἶμαι)
or νομίζω. It is significant that
this experienced and confident
speaker uses ἡγοῦμαι eight times
(§§ 2, 5, 6, 7, 11, 17, 18, 29) in
the eight (Teubner) pages, and
nowhere says νομίζω or οἴομαι.
The thirteenth speech shows a
like fondness for οἶμαι (fourteen

οὐδὲ γὰρ πολλοστὸν μέρος τῶν ἐκείνοις πεπραγμένων
εἰρήκασιν· εἰ δὲ ὡς ἐμοί τι προσῆκον περὶ αὐτῶν
ποιοῦνται τοὺς λόγους, ἀποδείξω τούτους μὲν ἅπαντα
14 ψευδομένους, ἐμαυτὸν δὲ τοιοῦτον ὄντα οἷόσπερ ἂν τῶν
3 ἐκ Πειραιῶς ὁ βέλτιστος ἐν ἄστει μείνας ἐγένετο. δέομαι δ᾽ ὑμῶν, ὦ ἄνδρες δικασταί, μὴ τὴν αὐτὴν γνώμην
ἔχειν τοῖς συκοφάνταις. τούτων μὲν γὰρ ἔργον ἐστὶ
καὶ τοὺς μηδὲν ἡμαρτηκότας εἰς αἰτίαν καθιστάναι, ἐκ
τούτων γὰρ ἂν μάλιστα χρηματίζοιντο· ὑμέτερον δὲ

occurrences in the twenty-one pages), but with the other words for " I think " used twice each. It is possible that in talking with his client Lysias noticed a fondness for this ἡγοῦμαι, and so gave a natural tone to the speech by its repeated use. Cp. on 19. 15. — ὡς ἐμοί . . . αὐτῶν: on the assumption that any charge against them involves me. — τοὺς λόγους: cp. on 12. 2. — τούτους: see on τούτου 12. 81. — ἐμαυτὸν δὲ τοιοῦτον ὄντα: the antithesis with τούτους μέν . . . ψευδομένους causes this construction instead of the more common nominative (τοιοῦτος ὤν); cp. § 4 ἀποφήνω . . . αἴτιος γεγενημένος. — ἐν ἄστει μείνας: had he remained in the city.

3. τούτων μέν: τούτων rather than αὐτῶν because these complainants are the particular sycophants whom he is attacking. For the greater precision of Greek as compared with Eng. in such use

of pronouns cp. on 12. 81, 84. — χρηματίζοιντο: blackmail by the threat of bringing innocent men before the courts on trumped-up charges was the regular work of the "sycophants." The quiet and orderly citizen was often ready to avoid both the reproach and the annoyance of a lawsuit by money payment. Xenophon tells how, by advice of Socrates, Crito finally supported a lawyer of his own to silence these fellows by counter attacks (Mem. 2. 9). The defendant for whom Isocrates wrote the speech against Callimachus tells how Callimachus began by telling in the streets and the shops that he had been wronged by the defendant; how then the defendant's friends came to him and advised him to buy Callimachus off, cautioning him that, however confident he was in the justice of his case, he must remember that many things in court turn out con-

20 τοῖς μηδὲν ἀδικοῦσιν ἐξ ἴσου τῆς πολιτείας μεταδιδόναι, οὕτω γὰρ ἂν τοῖς καθεστηκόσι πράγμασι πλεί-
4 στους συμμάχους ἔχοιτε. ἀξιῶ δέ, ὦ ἄνδρες δικασταί,
ἐὰν ἀποφήνω συμφορᾶς μὲν μηδεμιᾶς αἴτιος γεγενημένος, πολλὰ δὲ κἀγαθὰ εἰργασμένος τὴν πόλιν καὶ τῷ
25 σώματι καὶ τοῖς χρήμασι, ταῦτα γοῦν μοι παρ᾽ ὑμῶν
ὑπάρχειν, ὧν οὐ μόνον τοὺς εὖ πεποιηκότας ἀλλὰ καὶ
5 τοὺς μηδὲν ἀδικοῦντας τυγχάνειν δίκαιόν ἐστι. μέγα
μὲν οὖν ἡγοῦμαί μοι τεκμήριον εἶναι, ὅτι, εἴπερ ἐδύναντο οἱ κατήγοροι ἰδίᾳ με ἀδικοῦντα ἐξελέγξαι, οὐκ
30 ἂν τὰ τῶν τριάκοντα ἁμαρτήματα ἐμοῦ κατηγόρουν,
οὐδ᾽ ἂν ᾤοντο χρῆναι ὑπὲρ τῶν ἐκείνοις πεπραγμένων
ἑτέρους διαβάλλειν, ἀλλ᾽ αὐτοὺς τοὺς ἀδικοῦντας τιμω-
ρεῖσθαι· νῦν δὲ νομίζουσι τὴν πρὸς ἐκείνους ὀργὴν
34 ἱκανὴν εἶναι καὶ τοὺς μηδὲν κακὸν εἰργασμένους ἀπο-
6 λέσαι. ἐγὼ δὲ οὐχ ἡγοῦμαι δίκαιον εἶναι οὔτε εἴ τινες

trary to expectation, that verdicts
are more a matter of chance than of
justice, and that it is wise by paying
a small sum to be freed from great
accusations and the possibility of
great pecuniary losses (Isoc. 18.
9 f.). — **καθεστηκόσι πράγμασι** :
the established order = the existing
government. See on 16. 3.

4. μηδεμιᾶς : see on **μήτε** 12.
68 (B). — **αἴτιος γεγενημένος** : cp.
on ἐμαυτόν § 2 ; HA. 981 ; G.
1588 ; B. 661 ; Gl. 587. — **ὑπάρχειν** : *I may count upon.* See on
ὑπάρχει 12. 23.

5. τεκμήριον : predicate of the

ὅτι clause : *I hold the fact that,*
etc., . . . *to be a great proof in*
my favor. — **εἴπερ** : see on 12. 27.
— **ἰδίᾳ με ἀδικοῦντα** : *crimes of my*
own. — **ἁμαρτήματα, ἐμοῦ** : construction, see on καταγνώσεται 24.
20. — **ὑπέρ** : while ὑπέρ usually = *in*
behalf of, it is often used to give
the *ground* of a feeling or action,
especially with words of *thanking,*
praising, accusing, punishing, de-
fending, and the like. Cp. 12. 37,
12. 89, 25. 19. For ὑπέρ = περί
see on 24. 4. — **μηδέν** : see on § 1.

6. ἐγὼ δέ κτλ. : the normal construction would be as follows : —

τῇ πόλει πολλῶν ἀγαθῶν αἴτιοι γεγένηνται, ἄλλους
τινὰς ὑπὲρ τούτων τιμὴν ἢ χάριν κομίσασθαι παρ᾽
ὑμῶν, οὔτ᾽ εἴ τινες πολλὰ κακὰ εἰργασμένοι εἰσίν,
εἰκότως ἂν δι᾽ ἐκείνους τοὺς μηδὲν ἀδικοῦντας ὀνείδους
40 καὶ διαβολῆς τυγχάνειν· ἱκανοὶ γὰρ οἱ ὑπάρχοντες
ἐχθροὶ τῇ πόλει καὶ μέγα κέρδος νομίζοντες εἶναι
τοὺς ἀδίκως ἐν ταῖς διαβολαῖς καθεστηκότας.

7 Πειράσομαι δ᾽ ὑμᾶς διδάξαι, οὓς ἡγοῦμαι τῶν πολιτῶν προσήκειν ὀλιγαρχίας ἐπιθυμεῖν καὶ οὓς δημοκρα-
45 τίας. ἐκ τούτου γὰρ καὶ ὑμεῖς γνώσεσθε, κἀγὼ περὶ
ἐμαυτοῦ τὴν ἀπολογίαν ποιήσομαι, ἀποφαίνων ὡς οὔτε
ἐξ ὧν ἐν δημοκρατίᾳ οὔτε ἐξ ὧν ἐν ὀλιγαρχίᾳ πεποίηκα,
οὐδέν μοι προσῆκον κακόνουν εἶναι τῷ πλήθει τῷ ὑμε-
8 τέρῳ. πρῶτον μὲν οὖν ἐνθυμηθῆναι χρὴ ὅτι οὐδείς
50 ἐστιν ἀνθρώπων φύσει οὔτε ὀλιγαρχικὸς οὔτε δημο-

ἐγὼ δὲ οὐχ ἡγοῦμαι δίκαιον εἶναι
  οὔτε . . . κομίσασθαι
  οὔτε . . . τυγχάνειν.
But as the sentence develops
Lysias breaks the regular order
by adding to the thought of the
injustice the further thought of
unwisdom, leaving the broken
construction
ἐγὼ δὲ οὐχ ἡγοῦμαι
  δίκαιον εἶναι οὔτε . . . κομίσασθαι
  αὖτ᾽ εἰκότως ἂν τυγχάνειν.
— ἄν: see on 12. 1; cp. 24. 2,
24. 9. — δι᾽ ἐκείνους: for διά with
acc. see on 12. 87. — ἱκανοί κτλ.:
*for the city has enemies enough
already, and men enough who
think that those who stand*

*under false accusation are a
great gain to themselves*, viz.
'the city has enemies enough
already, and every false accusation
helps them by adding to their
number.'

7. οὕς: the rel. for the usual
indef. rel. in an indirect question.
Cp. 19. 12, 24. 15; HA. 1011 a;
G. 1600; B. 490; Gl. 621 a. —
προσήκειν: = εἰκὸς εἶναι. The dat.
with προσήκειν is more common
than the accus.; cp. § 11 προσήκειν αὐτοῖς ἐπιθυμεῖν; 12. 38
τοῦτο αὐτῷ προσήκει ποιῆσαι.
— οὐδέν: adverbial. — προσῆκον:
sc. ἐστί. — τῷ πλήθει: cp. on 12.
42.

κρατικός, ἀλλ' ἥτις ἂν ἑκάστῳ πολιτεία συμφέρῃ, ταύτην προθυμεῖται καθεστάναι· ὥστε οὐκ ἐλάχιστον ἐν
ὑμῖν ἐστι μέρος ὡς πλείστους ἐπιθυμεῖν τῶν παρόντων νυνὶ πραγμάτων. καὶ ταῦτα ὅτι οὕτως ἔχει, οὐ
55 χαλεπῶς ἐκ τῶν πρότερον γεγενημένων μαθήσεσθε.
9 σκέψασθε γάρ, ὦ ἄνδρες δικασταί, τοὺς προστάντας
ἀμφοτέρων τῶν πολιτειῶν, ὁσάκις δὴ μετεβάλοντο.
οὐ Φρύνιχος μὲν καὶ Πείσανδρος καὶ οἱ μετ' ἐκείνων

8. ὥστε οὐκ ἐλάχιστον κτλ.:
'So that in no small degree it is
in your power to secure for the
present government a great number of zealous supporters.' This
is quite aside from the argument,
a parenthetical reminder to the
jury that their action to-day will
have an important effect upon the
support of the new government. —
ἐλάχιστον: made emphatic by its
wide separation from its noun,
μέρος. Note that the English
idiom requires here the positive,
in no small degree, for the Greek
superlative. — μέρος : case, HA.
719; G. 1060; B. 336; Gl. 540.
— τῶν παρόντων νυνὶ πραγμάτων :
cp. τοῖς καθεστηκόσι πράγμασι § 3,
and see on 16. 3.

9. δή : Lysias seldom uses δή.
In the eight speeches of this volume there are seven instances of
καὶ μὲν δή (see on 12. 30) and
only eight of δή in other connections. Lysias's sparing use of
this vivid and emphatic particle

is quite in keeping with the simplicity and moderation of his style
(cp. on πάνυ 19. 15). The instances of δή are the following:
(A) To emphasize a preceding
word, 12. 34, 12. 62, 22. 5, all with
imperatives, a common usage;
34. 1 τότε δή. (B) To emphasize the whole statement, 12. 35,
12. 38, 12. 57. (C) To mark a
fact as a familiar one, 25. 9; this
usage is in other writers especially
common with relatives. — Φρύνιχος : a man of the common people,
commander in chief of the fleet.
He was at first strongly opposed
to the oligarchs, but becoming
involved in political intrigues he
found that his personal safety lay
in going over to Pisander. He
became one of the most unscrupulous of the oligarchs, and was
murdered in the Agora after the
reaction against the extreme oligarchs had set in. — Πείσανδρος :
he, too, was at first a prominent
democrat, and one of the chief

δημαγωγοί, ἐπειδὴ πολλὰ εἰς ὑμᾶς ἐξήμαρτον, τὰς
60 περὶ τούτων δείσαντες τιμωρίας τὴν προτέραν ὀλιγαρχίαν κατέστησαν, πολλοὶ δὲ τῶν τετρακοσίων μετὰ τῶν
ἐκ Πειραιῶς συγκατῆλθον, ἔνιοι δὲ τῶν ἐκείνους ἐκβα-
λόντων αὐτοὶ αὖθις τῶν τριάκοντα ἐγένοντο· εἰσὶ δὲ
64 οἵτινες τῶν Ἐλευσῖνάδε ἀπογραψαμένων, ἐξελθόντες
10 μεθ' ὑμῶν, ἐπολιόρκουν τοὺς μεθ' αὐτῶν. οὔκουν χαλεπὸν γνῶναι, ὦ ἄνδρες δικασταί, ὅτι οὐ περὶ πολιτείας

movers in the hue and cry raised over the mutilation of the Hermae as being the work of anti-democratic conspirators. He became the chief executive among those who planned and established the government of the Four Hundred. See Chron. App. 412 B.C. — **δημα-γωγοί**: *democratic leaders.* — **εἰς**: see on 32. 19, Crit. Note, πρός (C) 6. — **ἔνιοι**: the mention of names of those involved in the so recent revolutions is avoided. Under ἔνιοι all must think first of Theramenes, to whose faction the speaker probably belonged. — **ἐκεί-νους**: strictly only the extreme faction of the Four Hundred, expelled by the moderates under lead of Theramenes. See Chron. App. Sept. 411 B.C. — **τῶν Ἐλευσῖνάδε ἀπογραψαμένων**: the amnesty provided that any partisans of the Thirty who desired to settle with them in Eleusis should be permitted to do so within twenty days, on condition of enrolling their

names within ten days (Xen. *Hell.* 2. 4. 38, Arist. *Resp. Ath.* 39. 4). From our passage it appears that some who enrolled their names under the first fear of vengeance from the democracy became convinced of their safety in the city and did not withdraw. — **τοὺς μεθ' αὐτῶν**: viz. those who had formerly been with themselves in the city party. Xenophon gives a very brief account of this siege (*Hell.* 2. 4. 43); he says: "*Afterward they* (the Athenians), *hearing that those at Eleusis were hiring mercenaries, went out against them with all the citizen forces. They killed their generals, who had come into a conference with them, and sent friends and relatives to the others, and persuaded them to a reconciliation.*" Aristotle (*Resp. Ath.* 40. 4) places this event in the third year after the withdrawal to Eleusis (401/0 B.C.). For the bearing of this on the date of our speech see Introd. p. 255 n. 1.

εἰσὶν αἱ πρὸς ἀλλήλους διαφοραί, ἀλλὰ περὶ τῶν ἰδίᾳ
συμφερόντων ἑκάστῳ. ὑμᾶς οὖν χρὴ ἐκ τούτων δοκιμάζειν τοὺς πολίτας, σκοποῦντας μὲν ὅπως ἦσαν ἐν τῇ
70 δημοκρατίᾳ πεπολιτευμένοι, ζητοῦντας δὲ εἴ τις αὐτοῖς
ἐγίγνετο ὠφέλεια τῶν πραγμάτων μεταπεσόντων· οὕτως
γὰρ ἂν δικαιοτάτην τὴν κρίσιν περὶ αὐτῶν ποιοῖσθε.

11 ἐγὼ τοίνυν ἡγοῦμαι, ὅσοι μὲν ἐν τῇ δημοκρατίᾳ ἄτιμοι
ἦσαν ἢ τῶν ὄντων ἀπεστερημένοι ἢ ἄλλη τινὶ συμφορᾷ
75 τοιαύτῃ κεχρημένοι, προσήκειν αὐτοῖς ἑτέρας ἐπιθυμεῖν
πολιτείας, ἐλπίζοντας τὴν μεταβολὴν ὠφέλειάν τινα
αὐτοῖς ἔσεσθαι· ὅσοι δὲ τὸν δῆμον πολλὰ κἀγαθὰ
εἰργασμένοι εἰσί, κακὸν δὲ μηδὲν πώποτε, ὀφείλεται
δὲ αὐτοῖς χάριν κομίσασθαι παρ᾽ ὑμῶν μᾶλλον ἢ
80 δοῦναι δίκην τῶν πεπραγμένων, οὐκ ἄξιον τὰς περὶ

---

10. **πρός**: see on 32. 19 Crit.
Note. — **ἐκ τούτων**: *on this basis.*
— **δοκιμάζειν**: probably here in the
technical sense, L. & S. *s.v.* II. 2.
— **ἐν τῇ δημοκρατίᾳ**: the (definite)
democracy which preceded the
rule of the Thirty; cp. *ἐν δημοκρατίᾳ* § 7, where the less specific
reference causes the omission of
the article. — **ἐγίγνετο**: *was coming,*
impf. of an expected event; see
on *συναπώλλυντο* 12. 88. — **τῶν
πραγμάτων**: force, see on 16. 3.

11. **ἄτιμοι**: see on 12. 21. —
ἀπεστερημένοι: the tense implies
both the past ill-treatment and the
abiding resentment resulting from
it. — **προσήκειν**: tense, cp. on *ἀντιλέγειν* 12. 26. For force and

construction see on § 7. — **αὐτοῖς**
(before ἑτέρας) : instead of οὗτος
analeptic (see on *πάντας αὐτούς* 16.
11). The desire to throw the stress
upon *προσήκειν* causes the use of
the less emphatic **αὐτοῖς**. In the
contrasted and emphatic form
below we have *τούτων* (τὰς περὶ
τούτων). — **αὐτοῖς** (before χάριν) :
to whom. In a coördinate relative
clause the Eng. repeats the relative, while the Greek usually carries the idea along by a personal
or demons. pronoun, especially if
the case changes; HA. 1005; G.
1040; Gl. 615 a. So in 19. 14.
But sometimes the pronoun is
omitted in the second clause, as
in 22. 13 and 21; HA. 1005; G.

τούτων ἀποδέχεσθαι διαβολάς, οὐδ' ἐὰν πάντες οἱ τὰ
τῆς πόλεως πράττοντες ὀλιγαρχικοὺς αὐτοὺς φάσκωσιν
εἶναι.

12 Ἐμοὶ τοίνυν, ὦ ἄνδρες δικασταί, οὔτ' ἰδίᾳ οὔτε
85 δημοσίᾳ συμφορὰ ἐν ἐκείνῳ τῷ χρόνῳ οὐδεμία πώποτε
ἐγένετο, ἀνθ' ἧς τινος ἂν προθυμούμενος τῶν παρόντων
κακῶν ἀπαλλαγῆναι ἑτέρων ἐπεθύμουν πραγμάτων.
τετριηράρχηκα μὲν γὰρ πεντάκις, τετράκις δὲ νεναυμάχηκα, καὶ εἰσφορὰς ἐν τῷ πολέμῳ πολλὰς εἰσενή-
90 νοχα, καὶ τᾶλλα λελῃτούργηκα οὐδενὸς χεῖρον τῶν
13 πολιτῶν. καίτοι διὰ τοῦτο πλείω τῶν ὑπὸ τῆς πόλεως
προσταττομένων ἐδαπανώμην, ἵνα καὶ βελτίων ὑφ' ὑμῶν
νομιζοίμην, καὶ εἴ πού μοί τις συμφορὰ γένοιτο, ἄμεινον ἀγωνιζοίμην. ὧν ἐν τῇ ὀλιγαρχίᾳ ἁπάντων ἀπε-
95 στερούμην· οὐ γὰρ τοὺς τῷ πλήθει ἀγαθοῦ τινος
αἰτίους γεγενημένους χάριτος παρ' αὐτῶν ἠξίουν τυγχάνειν, ἀλλὰ τοὺς πλεῖστα κακὰ ὑμᾶς εἰργασμένους εἰς

1041; B. 487. For an instance
of both constructions in the same
sentence see 32. 27 and note.

12. ἑτέρων πραγμάτων: cp. ἑτέρας πολιτείας § 11. The more
common expression is νεώτερα
πράγματα (res novae). Cp. on
16. 3. — ἂν ἐπεθύμουν: force, see
on ἂν ἠξίωσε 19. 13. — τετριηράρχηκα: perf. of "credit," see on
εἰργασμένοι εἰσίν 12. 22. The
logical connection would lead us
to expect the pluperfect in this and
the following verbs, for the argument is that he had these services

to his credit at the time when the
revolution was under discussion;
but all the time the speaker has
also in mind the fact that he has
these things to his credit now, an
argument for a favorable verdict
now; so he half unconsciously
uses the less logical perfect. —
νεναυμάχηκα: see Crit. Note. —
λελῃτούργηκα: for such services
see on 19. 43.

13. ἐδαπανώμην: tense, see on
ἐποίουν 12. 25. — καὶ εἰ: see on 19.
18. — ἀγωνιζοίμην: viz. when involved in a case at law. — ἀπεστε-

τὰς τιμὰς καθίστασαν, ὡς ταύτην παρ' ἡμῶν πίστιν
εἰληφότες. ἃ χρὴ πάντας ἐνθυμουμένους μὴ τοῖς τού-
100 των λόγοις πιστεύειν, ἀλλὰ ἐκ τῶν ἔργων σκοπεῖν ἃ
14 ἑκάστῳ τυγχάνει πεπραγμένα. ἐγὼ γάρ, ὦ ἄνδρες
δικασταί, οὔτε τῶν τετρακοσίων ἐγενόμην· ἢ τῶν κατηγόρων ὁ βουλόμενος παρελθὼν ἐλεγξάτω· οὐ τοίνυν
οὐδ' ἐπειδὴ οἱ τριάκοντα κατέστησαν, οὐδείς με ἀπο-
105 δείξει οὔτε βουλεύσαντα οὔτε ἀρχὴν οὐδεμίαν ἄρξαντα.
καίτοι εἰ μὲν ἐξόν μοι ἄρχειν μὴ ἐβουλόμην, ὑφ' ὑμῶν
νυνὶ τιμᾶσθαι δίκαιός εἰμι· εἰ δὲ οἱ τότε δυνάμενοι μὴ
ἠξίουν μοι μεταδιδόναι τῶν πραγμάτων, πῶς ἂν φανε-
ρώτερον ἢ οὕτως ψευδομένους ἀποδείξαιμι τοὺς κατη-
110 γόρους;

15 Ἔτι τοίνυν, ὦ ἄνδρες δικασταί, καὶ ἐκ τῶν ἄλλων
τῶν ἐμοὶ πεπραγμένων ἄξιον σκέψασθαι. ἐγὼ γὰρ
τοιοῦτον ἐμαυτὸν ἐν ταῖς τῆς πόλεως συμφοραῖς παρέσχον ὥστε, εἰ πάντες τὴν αὐτὴν γνώμην ἔσχον ἐμοί,
115 μηδένα ἂν ὑμῶν μηδεμιᾷ χρήσασθαι συμφορᾷ. ὑπ'

ρούμην: tense, cp. on ἐγίγνετο § 10.
— ὡς: force, see on 16. 8. — ταύτην: i.e. πλεῖστα κακὰ ὑμᾶς εἰργάσθαι. For the fact cp. 12. 27 and
93. For the gender see on ταύτην
12. 37. — παρ' ἡμῶν: the people
who remained in the city. — τῶν
ἔργων: the deeds of each individual, contrasted with the words
of these complainants.
    14. παρελθών: the technical
word for coming forward to the
speaker's platform. — οὐ τοίνυν

οὐδ': corresponding, with slight
anacoluthon, to οὔτε above. —
βουλεύσαντα: in technical sense,
L. & S. s.v. III. — ἐξόν: see on
παρόν 12. 30. — δίκαιος: personal
construction, HA. 944; G. 1527;
B. 641; Gl. 565 a. — τῶν πραγμάτων: force, see on 16. 3.
    15. ἔτι τοίνυν: the τοίνυν of
transition (see on 16. 7 (D)) is
here strengthened by the more
specific ἔτι; so in 19. 59, 32. 14.
— παρέσχον: cp. 12. 20 κοσμίους δ'

ἐμοῦ γὰρ ἐν τῇ ὀλιγαρχίᾳ οὔτε ἀπαχθεὶς οὐδεὶς φανήσεται, οὔτε τῶν ἐχθρῶν οὐδεὶς τετιμωρημένος, οὔτε
16 τῶν φίλων εὖ πεπονθώς. (καὶ τοῦτο μὲν οὐκ ἄξιον
θαυμάζειν· εὖ μὲν γὰρ ποιεῖν ἐν ἐκείνῳ τῷ χρόνῳ
120 χαλεπὸν ἦν, ἐξαμαρτάνειν δὲ τῷ βουλομένῳ ῥᾴδιον.)
οὐ τοίνυν οὐδ' εἰς τὸν κατάλογον Ἀθηναίων καταλέξας

ἡμᾶς αὐτοὺς παρέχοντας. — ἀπα-
χθείς: a technical term. The ἀπα-
γωγή was, under the democracy,
a summary process for the arrest
and punishment of one caught in
a criminal act of the grosser sort.
It became a convenient form of
law under which the Thirty could
cover their arrests and executions;
cp. the case of Polemarchus, 12.
25, and cp. on εἰσαγγελιῶν 12. 48.

16. τοῦτο μέν: viz. οὐδένα τῶν
φίλων εὖ πεπονθέναι. While μέν
without a correlative usually suggests an unexpressed contrast (see
on 12. 8) it sometimes, as here,
becomes a mere particle of emphasis. The speaker sees that in
saying that he had helped no
friend, he may meet the retort,
"Were you then so contemptible
a coward as to refuse to help your
friends in such troublous times?"
He guards against this by the
parenthetical statement. — τὸν
κατάλογον: we hear of two "lists"
drawn up under the Thirty; one
was the list of 3000 who were
nominally to enjoy political rights
(Xen. Hell. 2. 3. 18), the other a

proscription list known to us only
by two statements of Isocrates.
The speaker in the case against
Callimachus, referring to the time
of the Thirty, says, "It will be
made clear that I have brought
upon no citizen loss of money, or
peril of life; nor erased his name
from those who held political
rights, and enrolled him in the
list with Lysander (18. 16). In
another plea (21. 2) Isocrates
makes the speaker say of his
friend Nicias, that after the establishment of the Thirty his enemies
erased his name from those who
held political rights and enrolled
him in the list with Lysander
(τὸν μετὰ Λυσάνδρου κατάλογον).
This is doubtless the list referred
to in our passage. Why it was
called the "Lysander list" we can
only conjecture; it would be natural that on the drawing up of
such a list Lysander would cause
the insertion of the names of
those who had most persistently
held out against reconciliation
with Sparta. The existence of
such a list gave opportunity for

οὐδένα φανήσομαι, οὐδὲ δίαιταν καταδιαιτησάμενος
οὐδενός, οὐδὲ πλουσιώτερος ἐκ τῶν ὑμετέρων γεγονὼς
συμφορῶν. καίτοι εἰ τοῖς τῶν γεγενημένων κακῶν
125 αἰτίοις ὀργίζεσθε, εἰκὸς καὶ τοὺς μηδὲν ἡμαρτηκότας
17 βελτίους ὑφ᾽ ὑμῶν νομίζεσθαι. καὶ μὲν δή, ὦ ἄνδρες
δικασταί, μεγίστην ἡγοῦμαι περὶ ἐμαυτοῦ τῇ δημοκρατίᾳ πίστιν δεδωκέναι. ὅστις γὰρ τότε οὐδὲν ἐξήμαρτον
οὕτω πολλῆς δεδομένης ἐξουσίας, ἦ που νῦν σφόδρα
130 προθυμηθήσομαι χρηστὸς εἶναι, εὖ εἰδὼς ὅτι, ἐὰν
ἀδικῶ, παραχρῆμα δώσω δίκην. ἀλλὰ γὰρ τοιαύτην
διὰ τέλους γνώμην ἔχω, ὥστε ἐν ὀλιγαρχίᾳ μὲν μὴ
ἐπιθυμεῖν τῶν ἀλλοτρίων, ἐν δημοκρατίᾳ δὲ τὰ ὄντα
134 προθύμως εἰς ὑμᾶς ἀναλίσκειν.

satisfying private enmities, as is clear from the case of Nicias. — **Ἀθηναίων** : connect with οὐδένα. — **δίαιταν** : a provision of the Athenian system sent a large class of cases to official arbitrators ; see App. § 29. It is not likely that official arbitrators were a part of the system of the Thirty, as the popular courts themselves were abolished. The reference is probably to private arbitration. The custom of thus settling cases out of court was always common. — **καταδιαιτησάμενος** : *procuring an unfavorable verdict* ; the active would be used of rendering a verdict.

17. **πίστιν δεδωκέναι** : cp. 12. 27 οὐ γάρ . . . πίστιν παρ᾽ αὐτοῦ ἐλάμβανον. Perfect tense because

the emphasis is quite as much on the fact that the jury *now have* the evidence as upon his *having given* it. — Cp. on ἀκηκόατε 12. 48. — **ὅστις** : here preferred to ὅς, because the emphasis is on the characteristic of the man (see on οἵτινες 12. 40), not his identity. By the personal inflection of the verb the Greek combines two ideas that are expressed less simply in Eng. by *I, a man who.* — **ἦ που** : these particles, giving emphasis to an apodosis (as in 12. 88), are often strengthened as here by σφόδρα, or as in 12. 35 by γε. — **ἀλλὰ γάρ** : for this use in concluding a discussion see on 12. 40. — **εἰς ὑμᾶς** : see on εἰς τὰς ναῦς 19. 21 (C).

18 Ἡγοῦμαι δέ, ὦ ἄνδρες δικασταί, οὐκ ἂν δικαίως
ὑμᾶς μισεῖν τοὺς ἐν τῇ ὀλιγαρχίᾳ μηδὲν πεπονθότας
κακόν, ἐξὸν ὀργίζεσθαι τοῖς εἰς τὸ πλῆθος ἐξημαρτηκόσιν, οὐδὲ τοὺς μὴ φυγόντας ἐχθροὺς νομίζειν, ἀλλὰ
τοὺς ὑμᾶς ἐκβαλόντας, οὐδὲ τοὺς προθυμουμένους τὰ
140 ἑαυτῶν σῶσαι, ἀλλὰ τοὺς τὰ τῶν ἄλλων ἀφῃρημένους,
οὐδὲ οἳ τῆς σφετέρας αὐτῶν σωτηρίας ἕνεκα ἔμειναν
ἐν τῷ ἄστει, ἀλλ᾽ οἵτινες ἑτέρους ἀπολέσαι βουλόμενοι
μετέσχον τῶν πραγμάτων. εἰ δὲ οἴεσθε χρῆναι, οὓς
ἐκεῖνοι παρέλιπον ἀδικοῦντες, ὑμεῖς ἀπολέσαι, οὐδεὶς
145 τῶν πολιτῶν ὑπολειφθήσεται.

19 Σκοπεῖν δὲ χρὴ καὶ ἐκ τῶνδε, ὦ ἄνδρες δικασταί.
πάντες γὰρ ἐπίστασθε ὅτι ἐν τῇ προτέρᾳ δημοκρατίᾳ
τῶν τὰ τῆς πόλεως πραττόντων πολλοὶ μὲν τὰ δημόσια
ἔκλεπτον, ἔνιοι δ᾽ ἐπὶ τοῖς ὑμετέροις ἐδωροδόκουν, οἱ

18. For the repeated use of
antithesis in this section see App.
§ 57. 1. — ἄν: cp. § 6, and see on
12. 1. — ἐν τῷ ἄστει: for the article
see on 12. 16. — οἵτινες: cp. on
ὅστις § 17. Here the characteristic of the men as a class is
the emphatic thought; cp. οἵ of
the preceding clause. — μετέσχον:
tense, see on μετέσχον 16. 3. —
ὑμεῖς: assimilated in case to the
subject of the leading verb.

19. ἔκλεπτον: the stealing of
the politicians was as common a
theme in ancient, as in modern,
times. Athenian politicians seem
to have been notoriously open to
the charge, if we may trust Chiriso-

phus's joke in reminding Xenophon
of the abilities of his countrymen:
κἀγὼ ὑμᾶς τοὺς Ἀθηναίους ἀκούω
δεινοὺς εἶναι κλέπτειν τὰ δημόσια,
καὶ μάλα ὄντος δεινοῦ τοῦ κινδύνου
τῷ κλέπτοντι, καὶ τοὺς κρατίστους
μέντοι μάλιστα, εἴπερ ὑμῖν οἱ κρά-
τιστοι ἄρχειν ἀξιοῦνται, Xen. Anab.
4. 6. 16. — ἐπὶ τοῖς ὑμετέροις:
against your interests. More
clearly stated in Din. 2. 26 δῶρα
δεχόμενον ἐπὶ τοῖς τῆς πατρίδος
συμφέρουσιν taking bribes against
the interests of his country. ἐπί
with dat. in hostile sense is not
common (see on 32. 19, Crit.
Note); it is oftenest used of bribery, but occasionally in other con-

150 δὲ συκοφαντοῦντες τοὺς συμμάχους ἀφίστασαν. καὶ
εἰ μὲν οἱ τριάκοντα τούτους μόνους ἐτιμωροῦντο, ἄνδρας
ἀγαθοὺς καὶ ὑμεῖς ἂν αὐτοὺς ἡγεῖσθε· νῦν δέ, ὅτε ὑπὲρ
τῶν ἐκείνοις ἡμαρτημένων τὸ πλῆθος κακῶς ποιεῖν
ἠξίουν, ἠγανακτεῖτε, ἡγούμενοι δεινὸν εἶναι τὰ τῶν
155 ὀλίγων ἀδικήματα πάσῃ τῇ πόλει κοινὰ γίγνεσθαι.
20 οὐ τοίνυν ἄξιον χρῆσθαι τούτοις, οἷς ἐκείνους ἑωρᾶτε
ἐξαμαρτάνοντας, οὐδὲ ἃ πάσχοντες ἄδικα ἐνομίζετε
πάσχειν, ὅταν ἑτέρους ποιῆτε, δίκαια ἡγεῖσθαι, ἀλλὰ
τὴν αὐτὴν κατελθόντες περὶ ἡμῶν γνώμην ἔχετε, ἥνπερ
160 φεύγοντες περὶ ὑμῶν αὐτῶν εἴχετε· ἐκ τούτων γὰρ καὶ
ὁμόνοιαν πλείστην ποιήσετε, καὶ ἡ πόλις ἔσται μεγίστη, καὶ τοῖς ἐχθροῖς ἀνιαρότατα ψηφιεῖσθε.

nections from Homer down. Cp.
Thuc. 1. 102 τὴν γενομένην ἐπὶ τῷ
Μήδῳ ξυμμαχίαν *the alliance that
had been made against the Mede.*
— ἀφίστασαν: one of the chief
causes of the break up of the
Athenian empire was the requirement that a large class of cases
at law arising in the allied cities
be tried at Athens by Athenian
courts. The loss of time, the
expense of travel, and the uncertainty of justice before a foreign
jury were so great that the sycophant found a rich field here. A
wealthy foreigner could afford to
pay liberally to buy off a threatened prosecution. Under honest
administration the system would
have been burdensome to the
allies; under the actual abuses it

became intolerable. — ἄνδρας ἀγαθούς: this was the case at first; see
on 12. 5. — ὑπέρ: force, see on § 5.
— κοινά: viz. a common charge.

20. οἷς: neuter, obj. of ἐξαμαρτάνοντας, but assimilated in case
to its antec. τούτοις. — οὐδὲ ἃ πάσχοντες κτλ.: *nor treatment which,
when you received it, you considered to be unjust treatment.* ἄδικα
is obj. of πάσχειν. — κατελθόντες:
force, see on 16. 4. Cp. κατιέναι
§ 22. — ἔχετε: in passing to the
positive half of the sentence,
Lysias shifts from the mild ἄξιον
construction to the earnest imperative. On the rhetorical form,
ἔχετε, εἴχετε, see App. § 57. 6. —
ἥνπερ: see on οἵτινες 12. 40. —
ἐχθροῖς: the enemies of the democracy, some of whom were now

21 Ἐνθυμηθῆναι δὲ χρή, ὦ ἄνδρες δικασταί, καὶ τῶν
ἐπὶ τῶν τριάκοντα γεγενημένων, ἵνα τὰ τῶν ἐχθρῶν
165 ἁμαρτήματα ἄμεινον ὑμᾶς ποιήσῃ περὶ τῶν ὑμετέρων
αὐτῶν βουλεύσασθαι. ὅτε μὲν γὰρ ἀκούοιτε τοὺς ἐν
ἄστε τὴν αὐτὴν γνώμην ἔχειν, μικρὰς ἐλπίδας εἴχετε
τῆς καθόδου, ἡγούμενοι τὴν ἡμετέραν ὁμόνοιαν μέ-
22 γιϲ ον κακὸν εἶναι τῇ ὑμετέρᾳ φυγῇ· ἐπειδὴ δὲ πυν-
170 θ(οισθε τοὺς μὲν τρισχιλίους στασιάζοντας, τοὺς
ἄλλους δὲ πολίτας ἐκ τοῦ ἄστεως ἐκκεκηρυγμένους,
τοὺς δὲ τριάκοντα μὴ τὴν αὐτὴν γνώμην ἔχοντας,
πλείους δὲ ὄντας τοὺς ὑπὲρ ὑμῶν δεδιότας ἢ τοὺς ὑμῖν
πολεμοῦντας, τότ᾽ ἤδη καὶ κατιέναι προσεδοκᾶτε καὶ
175 παρὰ τῶν ἐχθρῶν λήψεσθαι δίκην. ταῦτα γὰρ τοῖς
θεοῖς ηὔχεσθε, ἅπερ ἐκείνους ἑωρᾶτε ποιοῦντας, ἡγούμενοι διὰ τὴν τῶν τριάκοντα πονηρίαν πολὺ μᾶλλον
σωθήσεσθαι ἢ διὰ τὴν τῶν φευγόντων δύναμιν κατιέ-

in exile, others protected by the
amnesty.

21. ἐπί: force, see on 12. 17.
— **ὅτε ἀκούοιτε, ἐπειδὴ πυνθάνοισθε**
(§ 22): in both instances the reference is to the repeated rumors
that came from the city. HA.
914 B (2); G. 1431. 2; B. 625;
Gl. 616 b; GMT. 532. — **φυγῇ**:
best taken in the (rare) collective
sense = *you, the exiles.* So Xen.
Hell. 5. 2. 9 κατάγειν ἐβούλοντο
τὴν φυγήν. Cp. τὴν ἀρχήν = *the
administration* Lys. 12. 6. For
the argument, cp. the plea of
Theramenes to the same effect,
Xen. *Hell.* 2. 3. 44.

22. τρισχιλίους: see on § 16.
— **στασιάζοντας**: the execution of
Theramenes marked the beginning
of open division, which culminated
after the battle at Munychia in the
deposition of the Thirty and the
appointment of the Ten; see
Chron. App. — **τοὺς ἄλλους δέ**: the
displacement of δέ throws emphasis upon ἄλλους. See on 16. 7.
— **ἐκκεκηρυγμένους**: cp. 12. 95. —
μὴ ἔχοντας: μή because ἔχοντας
depends on a verb in protasis;
see on μήτε 12. 68 (B). — **τότ᾽ ἤδη**:
see on 12. 66. — **ἅπερ**: cp. ἥνπερ
§ 20 and see on οἵτινες 12. 40. —
κατιέναι (after δύναμιν): note that

23 ναι.   χρὴ τοίνυν, ὦ ἄνδρες δικασταί, τοῖς πρότερον
180 γεγενημένοις παραδείγμασι χρωμένους βουλεύεσθαι
περὶ τῶν μελλόντων ἔσεσθαι, καὶ τούτους ἡγεῖσθαι
δημοτικωτάτους, οἵτινες ὁμονοεῖν ὑμᾶς βουλόμενοι τοῖς
ὅρκοις καὶ ταῖς συνθήκαις ἐμμένουσι, νομίζοντες καὶ
τῆς πόλεως ταύτην ἱκανωτάτην εἶναι σωτηρίαν καὶ
185 τῶν ἐχθρῶν μεγίστην τιμωρίαν· οὐδὲν γὰρ ἂν εἴη
αὐτοῖς τούτων χαλεπώτερον, ἢ πυνθάνεσθαι μὲν ἡμᾶς
μετέχοντας τῶν πραγμάτων, αἰσθάνεσθαι δὲ οὕτως
διακειμένους τοὺς πολίτας ὥσπερ μηδενὸς ἐγκλήματος
24 πρὸς ἀλλήλους γεγενημένου.   χρὴ δὲ εἰδέναι, ὦ ἄνδρες
190 δικασταί, ὅτι οἱ φεύγοντες τῶν ἄλλων πολιτῶν ὡς
πλείστους καὶ διαβεβλῆσθαι καὶ ἠτιμῶσθαι βούλονται,
ἐλπίζοντες τοὺς ὑφ᾽ ὑμῶν ἀδικουμένους ἑαυτοῖς ἔσεσθαι

the present form is coördinate
with the fut. σωθήσεσθαι, HA.
828 a; G. 1257; B. 524 N.;
Gl. 385 b. The verb is unnecessary here, for the διά phrases
might both be attached to σωθήσεσθαι; but Lysias is fond of
balanced cola ending with words
in similar construction (see App.
57. 3).

23. οἵτινες: see on 12. 40. —
ταύτην: gender, see on ταύτην
12. 37. — **σωτηρίαν . . . τιμωρίαν**:
for the παρονομασία see App.
§ 58. 5. — **ἤ**: the idea compared
is anticipated, without effect upon
its construction, by the comparative gen. τούτων. This construction is found from Homer down.

— **ἡμᾶς**: former members of the
Three Thousand. — **οὕτως διακειμένους κτλ.**: writing at a later date
Isocrates says (18. 46), ἐπειδὴ δὲ
τὰς πίστεις ἀλλήλοις ἔδομεν εἰς
ταὐτὸν συνελθόντες, οὕτω καλῶς
καὶ κοινῶς πολιτευόμεθα, ὥσπερ οὐδεμιᾶς ἡμῖν συμφορᾶς γεγενημένης.
Note that Isocrates uses οὐδεμιᾶς,
the regular negative after ὥσπερ
(see on ἀλλ᾽ οὐ 12. 64), while
Lysias has μηδενός. The μη-
is due to the governing verb
(infin.). — **πρός**: see on 32. 19
Crit. Note.

24. οἱ φεύγοντες: see on τοῖς
ἐχθροῖς § 20; cp. ἐχθρῶν § 23. —
ἠτιμῶσθαι: in technical sense, see
on 12. 21. — **ἀδικουμένους**: tense,

συμμάχους, τοὺς δὲ συκοφάντας εὐδοκιμεῖν δέξαιντ' ἂν
παρ' ὑμῖν καὶ μέγα δύνασθαι ἐν τῇ πόλει · τὴν γὰρ
195 τούτων πονηρίαν ἑαυτῶν ἡγοῦνται σωτηρίαν.

25 Ἄξιον δὲ μνησθῆναι καὶ τῶν μετὰ τοὺς τετρακοσίους
πραγμάτων · εὖ γὰρ εἴσεσθε ὅτι, ἃ μὲν οὗτοι συμβουλεύουσιν, οὐδεπώποτε ὑμῖν ἐλυσιτέλησεν, ἃ δ' ἐγὼ
παραινῶ, ἀμφοτέραις ἀεὶ ταῖς πολιτείαις συμφέρει.
200 ὥστε γὰρ Ἐπιγένην καὶ Δημοφάνην καὶ Κλεισθένην
ἰδίᾳ μὲν καρπωσαμένους τὰς τῆς πόλεως συμφοράς,
26 δημοσίᾳ δὲ ὄντας μεγίστων κακῶν αἰτίους. ἐνίων μὲν
γὰρ ἔπεισαν ὑμᾶς ἀκρίτων θάνατον καταψηφίσασθαι,
πολλῶν δὲ ἀδίκως δημεῦσαι τὰς οὐσίας, τοὺς δ' ἐξελά-

see on ἀδικῶ 12. 14. — **δέξαιντ' ἄν:**
would prefer, a meaning which
comes from a shortening of the
phrase μᾶλλον δέχεσθαι ἤ. Cp.
§ 32 δέξαιντ' ἄν . . . μᾶλλον ἤ. —
τούτων: cp. on τούτων 12. 81.—
πονηρίαν, σωτηρίαν: for the παρονομασία see App. 58. 5.

25. μετὰ τοὺς τετρακοσίους: the
fall of the Four Hundred was
followed by a brief compromise
administration under Theramenes
and the moderates (see Chron.
App. 411/10), but this gave way
to full democracy, under which a
violent reaction set in against all
who had had a share in the oligarchical movement. It went so
far that the men who had remained
in the city and served in the forces
under the Four Hundred were put
under a form of ἀτιμία which ex-

cluded them from the Senate and
from the privilege of speaking in
the Ecclesia (Andoc. 1. 75).—
ἃ μὲν οὗτοι συμβουλεύουσιν: from
these words, and ὥστε οὐκ ἄξιον
κτλ. § 27, it is probable that Epigenes, Demophanes, and Clisthenes were the complainants (οὗτοι)
in this case. Epigenes was the
mover of the resolution (409 B.C.)
by which the work on the Erechtheum was resumed (*C.I.A.* I.
322), a measure perhaps designed
to give relief to the unemployed.
See Crit. Note. — **ἀεί:** position,
see on ἡμῖν 12. 33. — **καρπωσαμένους:** for the metaphor see Introd.
p. 25, N. 5. — **ὄντας:** for the impf.
(note its coördination with καρπωσαμένους) see on ἀνιωμένους 12. 32.

26. ἀκρίτων: cp. on 12. 17. —
δημεῦσαι: confiscation of prop-

205 σαι καὶ ἀτιμῶσαι τῶν πολιτῶν· τοιοῦτοι γὰρ ἦσαν
ὥστε τοὺς μὲν ἡμαρτηκότας ἀργύριον λαμβάνοντες
ἀφιέναι, τοὺς δὲ μηδὲν ἠδικηκότας εἰς ὑμᾶς εἰσιόντες
ἀπολλύναι. καὶ οὐ πρότερον ἐπαύσαντο, ἕως τὴν μὲν
209 πόλιν εἰς στάσεις καὶ τὰς μεγίστας συμφορὰς κατέ-
27 στησαν, αὐτοὶ δ' ἐκ πενήτων πλούσιοι ἐγένοντο. ὑμεῖς
δὲ οὕτως διετέθητε ὥστε τοὺς μὲν φεύγοντας κατεδέ-
ξασθε, τοὺς δ' ἀτίμους ἐπιτίμους ἐποιήσατε, τοῖς δ'
ἄλλοις περὶ ὁμονοίας ὅρκους ὤμνυτε· τελευτῶντες δὲ

erty as a punishment for political offenses (cp. on 19. 8) had
come down from early times. The
custom offered to the demagogues
and 'sycophants' a ready field
for personal enrichment through
blackmail, and for securing popularity by bringing the property of
rich men into the treasury. — ἀτιμῶσαι: see on ἠτιμῶσθαι § 24. —
τῶν πολιτῶν: the position gives
the greatest emphasis possible. —
ὥστε ἀφιέναι: the emphasis is not
so much on what they did as on
the character revealed by it. HA.
927; G. 1450; B. 595; Gl. 639;
cp. the opening sentence of § 27.
— οὐ πρότερον ἕως: see on 12. 71.
— στάσεις: the divisions that culminated in the revolution of the
Thirty.

27. τοὺς μὲν φεύγοντας κτλ.:
we learn from Andocides (1. 73,
76) that after Aegospotami and
the beginning of the siege by the

Lacedaemonians, the Athenians
took special action for the reconciliation of factions. They voted
to restore civic rights to those who
were under ἀτιμία (τοὺς ἀτίμους
ἐπιτίμους ποιῆσαι), and to give
mutual pledges of agreement between factions (πίστιν ἀλλήλοις
περὶ ὁμονοίας δοῦναι ἐν ἀκροπόλει).
But he says (1. 80) that the exiles
were not at this time recalled.
The return of the exiles (those
banished after the fall of the Four
Hundred) both Andocides (1. 80)
and Xenophon (Hell. 2. 2. 23)
place after the surrender. Lysias
distorts the facts for the sake of
his argument, representing the
recall of the oligarchical exiles,
which was really forced upon the
city by Sparta, as a voluntary act
connected with the reconciliation
of parties before the surrender. —
τελευτῶντες: force, HA. 968 a; G.
1564; B. 653 N. 2; Gl. 583 a.

ἥδιον ἂν τοὺς ἐν τῇ δημοκρατίᾳ συκοφαντοῦντας ἐτι-
215 μωρήσασθε ἢ τοὺς ἄρξαντας ἐν τῇ ὀλιγαρχίᾳ. καὶ
εἰκότως, ὦ ἄνδρες δικασταί· πᾶσι γὰρ ἤδη φανερόν
ἐστιν ὅτι διὰ τοὺς μὲν ἀδίκως πολιτευομένους ἐν τῇ
ὀλιγαρχίᾳ δημοκρατία γίγνεται, διὰ δὲ τοὺς ἐν τῇ
δημοκρατίᾳ συκοφαντοῦντας ὀλιγαρχία δὶς κατέστη.
220 ὥστε οὐκ ἄξιον τούτοις πολλάκις χρῆσθαι συμβούλοις,
οἷς οὐδὲ ἅπαξ ἐλυσιτέλησε πειθομένοις.

28   Σκέψασθαι δὲ χρὴ ὅτι καὶ τῶν ἐκ Πειραιῶς οἱ μεγί-

— **ἥδιον**: see the testimony of
Aristotle, quoted on 12. 5.— **ἂν
ἐτιμωρήσασθε**: see on ἂν ἠξίωσε
19. 13.— **τῇ ὀλιγαρχίᾳ**: the Four
Hundred.— **διὰ τούς κτλ.**: see on
διὰ πλήθους 12. 87. The democracy
is being established *in consequence
of* the action of the wicked rulers
of the oligarchy, but by no means
by their desire.— **δημοκρατία γίγνεται**: the speaker does not consider the work as yet completed.
— **τούτοις**: the complainants and
the whole class of men, present
and past, which they represent;
cp. on § 25.— **πειθομένοις**: in
agreement with ὑμῖν understood,
and governing οἷς.

28. **οἱ ἔχοντες . . . διεκελεύσαντο**: their foremost leader,
Thrasybulus, above all. Xenophon (*Hell.* 2. 4. 42) quotes these
words from the speech of Thrasybulus in the assembly after the
Return: οὐ μέντοι γε ὑμᾶς, ὦ
ἄνδρες, ἀξιῶ ἐγὼ ὧν ὀμωμόκατε

παραβῆναι οὐδέν, ἀλλὰ καὶ τοῦτο
πρὸς τοῖς ἄλλοις καλοῖς ἐπιδεῖξαι,
ὅτι καὶ εὔορκοι καὶ ὅσιοί ἐστε *but
I would not have you, fellow-citizens, in any way violate your oaths,
but rather show this in addition
to your other noble deeds, that you
are reverent and faithful to your
pledges.* Isocrates some time later
testifies to the self-restraint of
Thrasybulus and Anytus: Θρασύβουλος καὶ Ἄνυτος μέγιστον μὲν
δυνάμενοι τῶν ἐν τῇ πόλει, πολλῶν
δ᾽ ἀπεστερημένοι χρημάτων, εἰδότες
δὲ τοὺς ἀπογράψαντας, ὅμως οὐ
τολμῶσιν αὐτοῖς δίκας λαγχάνειν
οὐδὲ μνησικακεῖν *Thrasybulus and
Anytus, who are the most powerful
men in the city, and have been
robbed of great possessions, though
they know who confiscated them,
nevertheless are unwilling to bring
suit or cherish anger* (18. 23). Archinus, a third democratic leader,
when one of the returned exiles
attempted to violate the amnesty

στην δόξαν ἔχοντες καὶ μάλιστα κεκινδυνευκότες καὶ
πλεῖστα ὑμᾶς ἀγαθὰ εἰργασμένοι πολλάκις ἤδη τῷ
225 ὑμετέρῳ πλήθει διεκελεύσαντο τοῖς ὅρκοις καὶ ταῖς
συνθήκαις ἐμμένειν, ἡγούμενοι ταύτην δημοκρατίας
εἶναι φυλακήν· τοῖς μὲν γὰρ ἐξ ἄστεως ὑπὲρ τῶν
παρεληλυθότων ἄδειαν ποιήσειν, τοῖς δ᾽ ἐκ Πειραιῶς
229 οὕτως πλεῖστον ἂν χρόνον τὴν πολιτείαν παραμεῖναι.
29 οἷς ὑμεῖς πολὺ ἂν δικαιότερον πιστεύοιτε ἢ τούτοις,
οἳ φεύγοντες μὲν δι᾽ ἑτέρους ἐσώθησαν, κατελθόντες
δὲ συκοφαντεῖν ἐπιχειροῦσιν. ἡγοῦμαι δέ, ὦ ἄνδρες
δικασταί, τοὺς μὲν τὴν αὐτὴν γνώμην ἔχοντας ἐμοὶ
τῶν ἐν ἄστει μεινάντων φανεροὺς γεγενῆσθαι καὶ ἐν
235 ὀλιγαρχίᾳ καὶ ἐν δημοκρατίᾳ, ὁποῖοί τινές εἰσι πολῖ-
30 ται· τούτων δ᾽ ἄξιον θαυμάζειν, ὅ τι ἂν ἐποίησαν, εἴ
τις αὐτοὺς εἴασε τῶν τριάκοντα γενέσθαι, οἳ νῦν δημοκρατίας οὔσης ταὐτὰ ἐκείνοις πράττουσι, καὶ ταχέως
μὲν ἐκ πενήτων πλούσιοι γεγένηνται, πολλὰς δὲ ἀρχὰς

(μνησικακεῖν), carried through the
Senate his condemnation to death
without trial, as an example to all
citizens who might be tempted to
violate the oaths of reconciliation
(Arist. *Resp. Ath.* 40. 2). — κεκινδυνευκότες : tense, see on εἰργασμένοι εἰσίν 12. 22. — διεκελεύσαντο :
tense, see on ἠσθόμην 16. 20. —
ὑπέρ : as words of penalty and
punishment take ὑπέρ (see on § 5),
it is natural that the same word
stand with ἄδειαν, a negative of
penalty. — ἂν παραμεῖναι : cp. §§ 6,
18 ; see on 12. 1.

29. δι᾽ ἑτέρους : *through* others,
though not by their direct intention, hence acc. ; see on 12. 87. —
γνώμην : the political principle defined at the end of § 17. — ὀλιγαρχίᾳ : for omission of the article
cp. on § 10.

30. πλούσιοι : this is a stock
charge of the orators against their
opponents, and not to be taken
very seriously. Lysias has already
represented these men as having
become ἐκ πενήτων πλούσιοι (§ 26)
before the time of the Thirty.
Now they have done it again !

240 ἄρχοντες οὐδεμιᾶς εὐθύνην διδόασιν, ἀλλ᾽ ἀντὶ μὲν
ὁμονοίας ὑποψίαν πρὸς ἀλλήλους πεποιήκασιν, ἀντὶ
δὲ εἰρήνης πόλεμον κατηγγέλκασι, διὰ τούτους δὲ
31 ἄπιστοι τοῖς Ἕλλησι γεγενήμεθα. καὶ τοσούτων
κακῶν καὶ ἑτέρων πολλῶν ὄντες αἴτιοι, καὶ οὐδὲν δια-
245 φέροντες τῶν τριάκοντα πλὴν ὅτι ἐκεῖνοι μὲν ὀλιγαρχίας οὔσης ἐπεθύμουν ὧνπερ οὗτοι, οὗτοι δὲ καὶ
δημοκρατίας τῶν αὐτῶν ὧνπερ ἐκεῖνοι, ὅμως οἴονται
χρῆναι οὕτως ῥᾳδίως ὃν ἂν βούλωνται κακῶς ποιεῖν,

— **εὐθύνην**: possibly an Athenian official did sometimes avoid the required εὔθυναι, but it could only be by unusually efficient party machinery or through an overriding personality (like that of Alcibiades), for the legal system of accounting was most minute. It included audit by independent boards, and offered the utmost freedom of complaint to all citizens. Charges like the present one are on a par with the general charges of thievery and rapid enrichment; without the specification of cases they are of little value. Every Athenian official was required every prytany (every thirty-five days) to submit an account of his receipts and expenditures to a board of ten auditors, selected by lot from the Senate. At the close of his term of office he was also required to present complete accounts to another board; see Introd. p. 44. —

πόλεμον: the feeling had been so excited as to lead to the siege of the remnant of the Thirty at Eleusis; but from Xenophon's account it appears that it was the action of the exiles themselves which led to this. Lysias is either misrepresenting the cause of the expedition to Eleusis or greatly exaggerating the extent of the existing ill-feeling at home. — **διά**: see on 12. 87. — **τούτους**: for the change from the relative see on αὐτοῖς § 11. — **ἄπιστοι**: the failure to abide by the terms of the amnesty, which allowed the Thirty to hold Eleusis, and the treacherous seizure of their leaders, may well have produced this effect.

31. For the rhetorical ἐπαναστροφή and κύκλος see App. § 57. 7 f. — **ὧνπερ**: see on οἵτινες 12. 40. — **δημοκρατίας**: sc. οὔσης. — **χρῆναι**: 'they actually regard this conduct as a duty; they pose as righteous men punishing the un-

249 ὥσπερ τῶν μὲν ἄλλων ἀδικούντων, ἄριστοι δὲ ἄνδρες
32 αὐτοὶ γεγενημένοι. (καὶ τούτων μὲν οὐκ ἄξιον θαυμάζειν, ὑμῶν δέ, ὅτι οἴεσθε μὲν δημοκρατίαν εἶναι,
γίγνεται δὲ ὅ τι ἂν οὗτοι βούλωνται, καὶ δίκην διδόασιν οὐχ οἱ τὸ ὑμέτερον πλῆθος ἀδικοῦντες, ἀλλ'
οἱ τὰ σφέτερα αὐτῶν μὴ διδόντες.) καὶ δέξαιντ' ἂν
255 μικρὰν εἶναι τὴν πόλιν μᾶλλον ἢ δι' ἄλλους μεγάλην
33 καὶ ἐλευθέραν, ἡγούμενοι νῦν μὲν διὰ τοὺς ἐκ Πειραιῶς κινδύνους αὐτοῖς ἐξεῖναι ποιεῖν ὅ τι ἂν βούλωνται, ἐὰν δ' ὕστερον ὑμῖν δι' ἑτέρους σωτήρια
γένηται, τούτους μὲν πεπαύσεσθαι, ἐκείνους δὲ μεῖζον
260 δυνήσεσθαι· ὥστε οἱ τοιοῦτοι πάντες ἐμποδών εἰσιν,
34 ἐάν τι δι' ἄλλων ἀγαθὸν ὑμῖν φαίνηται. τοῦτο μὲν
οὖν οὐ χαλεπὸν τῷ βουλομένῳ κατανοῆσαι· αὐτοί τε

---

righteous.'— ἄριστοι δὲ γεγενημένοι: for correlation of gen. abs.
with participles in other construction see on πραττούσης 12. 69.

32. ὅ τι ἂν βούλωνται : 'you
have exchanged the tyranny of
the Thirty for the tyranny of a
group of sycophants, who override
the first principles of democracy.'
— μὴ διδόντες : viz. whoever will not
buy off the sycophants. μή generic,
see on μηδέν § 1. — δέξαιντ' ἂν : see
on § 24. — μικράν : cp. the same
charge against Theramenes, 12. 70.

33. ἐκ Πειραιῶς : see Crit. Note.
The Piraeus was the starting point
of the dangerous undertaking. —
τούτους μέν . . . ἐκείνους δέ : these
sycophants (τούτους) now hold

undisputed lead, on the ground
of the dangers which they met in
helping to secure the return. They
think that if, in the new situation,
other men shall come forward and
benefit the state, the leadership
will pass to these others (ἐκείνους) ;
they therefore try to discredit men
like the speaker who seek honestly and unselfishly to serve the
state. For τούτους cp. on τούτου
12. 81.— δι' ἄλλων (cp. δι' ἑτέρους
above) : see on 12. 87.

34. αὐτοί τε γάρ κτλ. : the structure is

$$\gamma\acute{\alpha}\rho \begin{cases} \alpha\mathring{\upsilon}\tau o\acute{\iota} \ \tau\epsilon \begin{cases} o\mathring{\upsilon}\kappa \ \mathring{\epsilon}\pi\iota\theta\upsilon\mu o\mathring{\upsilon}\sigma\iota \\ \mathring{\alpha}\lambda\lambda' \ \alpha\mathring{\iota}\sigma\chi\acute{\upsilon}\nu o\nu\tau\alpha\iota \end{cases} \\ \mathring{\upsilon}\mu\epsilon\mathring{\iota}\varsigma \ \tau\epsilon \begin{cases} \tau\grave{\alpha} \ \mu\grave{\epsilon}\nu \ \mathring{o}\rho\mathring{\alpha}\tau\epsilon \\ \tau\grave{\alpha} \ \delta' \ \mathring{\alpha}\kappa o\acute{\upsilon}\epsilon\tau\epsilon \end{cases} \end{cases}$$

γὰρ οὐκ ἐπιθυμοῦσι λανθάνειν, ἀλλ' αἰσχύνονται μὴ
δοκοῦντες εἶναι πονηροί, ὑμεῖς τε τὰ μὲν αὐτοὶ ὁρᾶτε
265 τὰ δ' ἑτέρων πολλῶν ἀκούετε. ἡμεῖς δέ, ὦ ἄνδρες
δικασταί, δίκαιον μὲν ἡγούμεθ' εἶναι πρὸς πάντας
ὑμᾶς τοὺς πολίτας ταῖς συνθήκαις καὶ τοῖς ὅρκοις
35 ἐμμένειν, ὅμως δέ, ὅταν μὲν ἴδωμεν τοὺς τῶν κακῶν
αἰτίους δίκην διδόντας, τῶν τότε περὶ ὑμᾶς γεγενη-
270 μένων μεμνημένοι συγγνώμην ἔχομεν, ὅταν δὲ φανε-
ροὶ γένησθε τοὺς μηδὲν αἰτίους ἐξ ἴσου τοῖς ἀδικοῦσι
τιμωρούμενοι, τῇ αὐτῇ ψήφῳ πάντας ἡμᾶς εἰς ὑποψίαν
καταστήσετε. . . .

— μὴ δοκοῦντες: see on μήτε 12.
68 (A). — ἡμεῖς: we of the city
party. — ὑμᾶς: the subject of ἐμμένειν, thrust between πάντας and
its substantive (πολίτας) to emphasize πάντας.   See on ἡμῖν
12. 33.

35. δίκην διδόντας: the seizure

and execution of the leaders at
Eleusis was a violation of the
amnesty, though done under great
provocation. We have record of
no other instance, though Isocrates says (18. 2) that such attempts
were made, and that a special law
was passed to prevent them.

XXXII

The Speech Against Diogiton

INTRODUCTION

DIODOTUS, a wealthy Athenian merchant, married the daughter of his brother, Diogiton. Of this marriage a daughter and two sons were born. Diogiton was thus their uncle on the father's side, and their grandfather on the mother's side.

The father, Diodotus, was called upon in 410 B.C.[1] to join the expedition of Thrasyllus to the coast of Asia Minor, and was killed in the attack on Ephesus (§§ 4–7). Before leaving home he had made a will in which he provided for his sons, and bequeathed to his wife his personal valuables and one talent as dowry in case of her remarriage, and to his daughter one talent as dowry (§ 6).

Diodotus left the will with his brother, Diogiton, and a copy of it with his wife (§ 7).

We have no full inventory of the property, but the plaintiff claims that it included the following sums:

Left on deposit with Diogiton (§§ 5, 13),	5 t.
Invested in a loan on bottomry (§§ 6, 14),	7 t. 4000 dr.
Due in the Chersonese (§ 6),	2000 dr.
Left with his wife (§ 6) and turned over by her to	
Diogiton on the death of her husband (§ 15),	
20 minae =	2000 dr.
30 Cyzicene staters[2] =	840 dr.
A mortgage on real estate (§ 15), 100 minae =	1 t. 4000 dr.
Total,	15 t. 840 dr.

[1] For the date see Chron. App.

[2] The value of the Cyzicene stater is not entirely fixed. See App. § 62.

283

To this are to be added valuable house furnishings (§ 15).[1]

On the death of Diodotus, Diogiton became the guardian of his widowed daughter and her three children. For a time he concealed from them the fact of Diodotus's death, and under the pretext that certain documents were needed for conducting his brother's business, he obtained from his daughter the sealed package of papers that had been left with her (§ 7). After the death of Diodotus became known to her, the widow turned over to Diogiton whatever property was in her possession, to be administered for the family (§ 15).

Diogiton, as guardian of his widowed daughter, arranged a second marriage for her with one Hegemon (§ 12), but gave a sixth less dowry than the will prescribed (§ 8). In due time he arranged a marriage for his granddaughter also (§ 2) ; there is no claim that he gave with her less than the dowry required by the will.[2]

For eight years Diogiton supported the boys from the income of the estate, but when the elder came of age, he called them to him and told them that their father had left for them only 2840 dr.,[3] and that this had all been expended for their support ; that already he had himself paid out much for them, and that the elder must now take care of himself (§ 9).

The boys, who had supposed that they were to come into a large fortune, at once appealed to their mother, and she hastened to her daughter's husband, as the only representative of the family who might secure justice from her father. But all appeals to Diogiton and all attempts at settlement through family friends

[1] The above reckoning assumes that the 2000 dr. of § 15 are the same as the claim of 2000 dr. in the Chersonese (§ 6); but it is quite possible that this is another investment.

[2] It would seem that the daughter was married not long before the trial, for in the estimate of reasonable expense for the children the speaker includes provision for the daughter and her maid for the full eight years (§ 28).

[3] This was the sum which their mother had turned over to Diogiton in cash, and which he could not deny having received.

were in vain, and the case was brought to court (§§ 10–12). The elder son was the plaintiff, and the daughter's husband, as his συνήγορος, made the main plea for him[1] by delivering this speech, prepared by Lysias.

In the preparation of his defense Diogiton saw that he could not maintain his original claim that he had received only 2840 dr. for the boys. The mother had documentary proof of his having received one sum of 7 t. 4000 dr. (§ 14), and Diogiton now acknowledged in his sworn answer that he had received that sum, but he submitted detailed accounts purporting to show that it had all been used for the family (§§ 20, 28).[2]

The date of this speech is determined by the fact that Diodotus died in 410 B.C. (§ 5), and that the boys were under Diogiton's guardianship eight years (§ 29). It is not likely that a suit involving the whole family fortune would be long delayed, so that the trial must be put in 402/1 B.C. or very soon thereafter.

This speech is not contained in our MSS. of Lysias, but the part which we have is preserved in the treatise of Dionysius of Halicarnassus, *On the Ancient Orators*.[3] After a discussion of the peculiarities of Lysias's style, Dionysius transcribes this speech, with comments after each rhetorical subdivision ; unfortunately he does not give the last part of the proof or the epilogue.

[1] See App. § 17.

[2] It is not clear just how much Diogiton did acknowledge. If he did not retract his first statement, the 2840 dr. must be added to the 7 t. 4000 dr. And then there remains the question whether he included in these sums the money paid in the two dowries. Lysias says in § 20 that Diogiton in his reckoning claimed to have spent the 7 t. 4000 dr. for the two boys and their sister; but it is possible that the mother's and the sister's dowries were reckoned in this total in Diogiton's account.

If we had the documents which were presented in court and the complete speech of Lysias, these points, which seem in our fragment strangely confused, would probably be made clear.

[3] Dionysius was a student and teacher of literature who came to Rome in 30 B.C. He taught Rhetoric both by lectures and by published treatises, and published a History of Rome from the earliest times to the beginning of the

OUTLINE

I. Προοίμιον, *Exordium*, §§ 1–3.

Apology for bringing a family dispute into the courts.

Justification of the speaker's appearance in the case, after earnest efforts to effect a private settlement.

General πρόθεσις : the speaker will show that these plaintiffs have been worse abused by their grandfather than any one ever was even by men not related.

II. Διήγησις, *Narratio*, §§ 4–18.

The marriage of Diodotus to his niece, the daughter of Diogiton. Diodotus's departure for the wars and his provision for his family. His death, and the conduct of Diogiton thereafter. The action of Diogiton when the eldest son came of age. Protests of the family and their attempts to secure justice out of court. The mother's plea to her father and its effect on the hearers.

III. Particular πρόθεσις, *Propositio*, §§ 18, 19.

The call for witnesses for the speaker, and the request to the jury to examine the accounts of the defendant.

IV. Πίστεις, *Argumentatio*, §§ 20– .

A. Examination of the items charged against the sum which Diogiton admits that he received.

B. Argument that the sum received was much larger than Diogiton admits (this argument is not preserved ; see p. 290).

Dionysius has not preserved the epilogue.

Punic Wars. He was an enthusiastic student of classical Greek oratory, and devoted himself to the attempt to revive its pure standards as against the degenerate rhetoric of the later times. He published a treatise on Lysias, Isocrates, and Isaeus, as a part of a work on *The Ancient Orators ;* a second part was to treat of Demosthenes, Hyperides, and Aeschines, but it is uncertain whether it was ever written.

COMMENTS ON ARGUMENT AND STYLE

I. Προοίμιον, *Exordium*, §§ 1–3.

The Greek rhetoricians, and the Romans after them, prescribed three ends to be sought in a proem : the gaining of the good will of the hearers, instructing them as to the case in hand and its proposed treatment, and arousing their attention (εὔνοια, εὐμάθεια, πρόσεξις).

Dionysius [1] in his criticism of the proem of this speech evidently has this definition in mind. He says that in the case of a suit against members of one's own family the rhetoricians are agreed that the plaintiff must above all things else guard against prejudice on the part of the jury in the suspicion that he is following an unworthy and litigious course. The plaintiff must show that the wrongs which he is attacking are unendurable ; that he is pleading in behalf of other members of the family nearer to him and dependent upon him for securing redress ; that it would be wicked for him to refuse his aid. He must show further that he has made every attempt to settle the case out of court.

This first quality of the ideal proem, adaptedness to secure the good will of the jury by the means indicated, Dionysius finds in full in our proem.

The second purpose of a proem, the clear instruction of the jury as to the case in hand, Dionysius finds equally well fulfilled. The proem includes a virtual πρόθεσις, which gives all the information that is needed for the understanding of what follows.

The third aim of a proem, the quickening of attention, Dionysius says is to be reached by surprising or even paradoxical statements, and by direct appeal to the jury. These things, too, Dionysius assures us that he finds in this proem, but to the modern reader it seems that his wish to find here all the elements of the ideal proem must have been father to the thought ; for there is certainly no touch of the novel or surprising or paradoxical in thought. Some others of Lysias's proems have these character-

[1] *Lysias*, § 24.

istics in a marked degree, but not this one. There is a direct prayer to the jury, but that is brief and not very impressive.

The language of the proem, like that of Lysias's proems in general, is for the most part periodic. A larger group of thoughts is brought together under a single sentence structure both in § 1 and in §§ 2–3 than is usual with Lysias. The impression is one of dignity and earnestness. There is no rhetorical embellishment either in grouping of cola or in play on words or phrases.

II. Διήγησις, *Narratio*, §§ 4–18.

Dionysius gives no comment on this "narrative," but before quoting this speech he had summed up his views of Lysias's excellence in each part of a speech. He there spoke as follows of his powers in narration (§ 18) : "In narration, which in my opinion demands the utmost wisdom and attention, I consider him unquestionably the greatest of all orators, and I declare him to be the measure and standard (ὅρον τε καὶ κανόνα). And I believe that the treatises on the theory of rhetoric which contain anything valuable on the subject of 'narration' have derived their inspiration and their precepts from no source more than from the works of Lysias. For his narratives excel in conciseness and clearness. No others are so charming and persuasive. They convince you before you are aware, so that it is not easy to find any narrative as a whole, or any part of one, that is false or unconvincing. Such persuasion and charm are in his speech, and so completely do the hearers forget to ask whether it is true or fictitious."

This enthusiasm of Dionysius for Lysias's narratives is justified, and in no case more fully than in that of the narrative under discussion. This, like the great narrative of the arrest in XII, and the even greater narrative in I — an honest husband's story of the seduction of his young wife by an aristocrat — has the persuasive power of simple and clear speech. But in this narrative there is a stroke of genius that places it above even the other two. This is the introduction of the mother's plea in her own words. The mother could not plead in court, but by picturing the scene in the family council Lysias carries the jurors in imagination to that room where a woman pleads with her father, protesting against the unnatural greed that has robbed his own grandsons, and begging him to do simple justice to her children. As the jurors heard how the hearers of that plea arose and left the room, silent and in tears, there was little need for argument.

Here, again, Lysias secures his result by the simplest means. As he talked in his office with his clients and heard their story of the family meeting, and how the mother of the boys had pleaded with her father, he had the insight to see that the central point of the prosecution should be to make the jury see this case as the mother saw it. Her view of it moved him, and he knew it would move the jury. His work was to take this narrative from the lips of his clients, to preserve its naturalness and simplicity, to suppress non-essentials, and to bring out the points of real power, condensing and clarifying all. The result was a work of art perfect in the concealment of art.

The language is, as in Lysias's narratives generally, of the simplest form. For the most part the sentences are short. When they are expanded, it is by a series of simple coördinate cola, binding the thoughts without making the whole complex. So the long narrative sentence of § 5. The long sentence of § 10 is a typical example of the running, in distinction from the periodic, structure.[1] But, as often in Lysias, the simple narrative is concluded by a strong, amplified sentence, in full periodic form (see App. § 44) : —

§ 18.   τότε μὲν οὖν, ὦ ἄνδρες δικασταί
          πολλῶν καὶ δεινῶν ὑπὸ τῆς γυναικὸς ῥηθέντων
       οὕτω διετέθημεν πάντες οἱ παρόντες
          ὑπὸ τῶν τούτῳ πεπραγμένων
          καὶ τῶν λόγων τῶν ἐκείνης

[1] See App. § 42.

ὁρῶντες μὲν τοὺς παῖδας
   οἷα ἦσαν πεπονθότες
ἀναμιμνῃσκόμενοι δὲ τοῦ ἀποθανόντος
   ὡς ἀνάξιον τῆς οὐσίας τὸν ἐπίτροπον κατέλιπεν
ἐνθυμούμενοι δὲ ὡς χαλεπὸν ἐξευρεῖν
   ὅτῳ χρὴ περὶ τῶν ἑαυτοῦ πιστεῦσαι

ὥστε, ὦ ἄνδρες δικασταί,
μηδένα τῶν παρόντων δύνασθαι φθέγξασθαι
ἀλλὰ καὶ δακρύοντας μὴ ἧττον τῶν πεπονθότων
ἀπιόντας οἴχεσθαι σιωπῇ.

III. Πρόθεσις, *Propositio*, §§ 18, 19.

A brief πρόθεσις introduces the affidavits of witnesses and the discussion of the guardian's accounts as filed with the court.

IV. Πίστεις, *Argumentatio*.

We know from Dionysius[1] that the argument on the accounts submitted by Diogiton fell into two parts: *A*, Discussion of the use that Diogiton claims to have made of the property which he admits he has received from the estate; *B*, Proof that he has received a much larger sum than he admits. The second part is not included in what is preserved.

The examination of the alleged expenditures is sharp and clear. The overcharge seems written on the face of every item, and the series culminates in a case of the most shameless fraud (§§ 26, 27). The most striking characteristic of this convincing argument is the Lysian brevity. Out of an accounting of eight years Lysias selects a very few typical items, makes the most of them in a brief, cutting comment, and then passes on before the hearers are wearied with the discussion of details.

The language is in short and rounded periods. Vigor and terseness prevail in it all, and there is an occasional sharpening of expression by rhetorical device. Antitheses are common as in

[1] *Lysias*, § 26.

all vigorous speech of Lysias, and some are heightened by rhyming of the final words of cola (ὁμοιοτέλευτον, see App. 57. 4).

§ 19. ἵνα τοὺς μὲν νεανίσκους διὰ τὸ μέγεθος τῶν συμφορῶν ἐλεήσητε, τοῦτον δ' ἄπασι τοῖς πολίταις ἄξιον ὀργῆς ἡγήσησθε.

§ 25.   καίτοι εἰ μὲν τὰς ζημίας τούτων ἀποδείξει
    τὰ δὲ σωθέντα τῶν χρημάτων αὐτὸς ἕξει
   ὅποι μὲν ἀνήλωται τὰ χρήματα
   οὐ χαλεπῶς εἰς τὸν λόγον ἐγγράψει
   ῥαδίως δὲ ἐκ τῶν ἀλλοτρίων αὐτὸς πλουτήσει.

The word play (παρονομασία, App. § 58. 5) in § 22, a turn of speech rare in Lysias, but a favorite with the rhetoricians, is fitted to the sarcastic tone : —

ἵνα γράμματα αὐτοῖς ἀντὶ τῶν χρημάτων ἀποδείξειεν.

The personification in § 23, a figure equally rare in Lysias (Introd. p. 25. n. 5), is in the same sarcastic tone : —

ἡγούμενος δεῖν τὴν αὐτοῦ πονηρίαν κληρονόμον εἶναι τῶν τοῦ τεθνεῶτος χρημάτων.

§ 24 offers a striking instance of Lysias's power of condensation. Each of the four brief phrases adds an incriminating feature of the action : —

οὗτος δὲ πάππος ὢν | παρὰ τοὺς νόμους | τῆς ἑαυτοῦ τριηραρχίας | παρὰ τῶν θυγατριδῶν | τὸ ἥμισυ πράττεται.

Of ἠθοποιία in the ordinary sense, the nice fitting of thought and speech to the personality of the speaker, so that the individuality of the man stands out in his plea, there is nothing here. The speaker might be any Athenian gentleman ; we get no impression of his age or temperament or character.

Some see definite ἠθοποιία in the mother's speech, but it is rather the ἦθος of womanhood and motherhood than of this particular mother.

But there is another form of portraiture, closely allied to ἠθοποιία,[1] the picturing of the character, not of the speaker, but of

[1] See Introd. p. 29.

his opponent.   We have certainly a personal portrait of Diogiton, and this by the simple recital of his words and conduct.   There is no piling up of opprobrious epithets.   By his own conduct greed is shown to have been the one principle of his life, from the time when he married his daughter to his brother to keep hold of his increasing property, to the day when, with hollow professions of regret and with shameless lies, he turned his grandsons out of doors.

XXXII

ΚΑΤΑ ΔΙΟΓΕΙΤΟΝΟΣ

1 Εἰ μὲν μὴ μεγάλα ἦν τὰ διαφέροντα, ὦ ἄνδρες δικασταί, οὐκ ἄν ποτε εἰς ὑμᾶς εἰσελθεῖν τούτους εἴασα,
νομίζων αἴσχιστον εἶναι πρὸς τοὺς οἰκείους διαφέρε-
σθαι, εἰδώς τε ὅτι οὐ μόνον οἱ ἀδικοῦντες χείρους ὑμῖν
5 εἶναι δοκοῦσιν, ἀλλὰ καὶ οἴτινες ἂν ἔλαττον ὑπὸ τῶν
προσηκόντων ἔχοντες ἀνέχεσθαι μὴ δύνωνται· ἐπειδὴ
μέντοι, ὦ ἄνδρες δικασταί, πολλῶν χρημάτων ἀπεστέρηνται, καὶ πολλὰ καὶ δεινὰ πεπονθότες ὑφ᾽ ὧν ἥκιστα
9 ἐχρῆν ἐπ᾽ ἐμὲ κηδεστὴν ὄντα κατέφυγον, ἀνάγκη μοι

1. τὰ διαφέροντα: ἐμοὶ διαφέ-
ρει = *it matters to me, I have
something at stake*, hence τὰ διαφέ-
ροντα=*the issues at stake.* — εἰσελθεῖν: a technical term; cp. 25. 26
εἰς ὑμᾶς εἰσιόντες. — τούτους: the
usual word for either plaintiff or
defendant; here the elder son,
who has only recently come of
age, is technically the only plaintiff, but his younger brother is
equally interested in the suit, and
is doubtless present. — πρός: see
on § 19 Crit. Note. — τε: the simple τε (without καί or a correl. τε)
is very rarely used in prose to connect single words; its use to connect clauses (as here) is common
in Herod. and Thuc., less common in Xen., and rare in the
orators (Kühn. II. ii. p. 242). Cp.
§ 22, and 1. 17, 13. 1, 31. 2. It
is Lysias's one bit of old-fashioned
syntax. See Introd. p. 25. —
ἔλαττον ἔχοντες: *being worsted,
injured.* For connection with
ὑπό see on κατέστησαν 12. 43. —
ἐχρῆν: for the form see on 12. 48.
For force see on εἰκὸς ἦν 12. 27. —
κηδεστήν: *affinis,* any connection
by marriage. By the context here
of a brother-in-law; in § 5 of
a father-in-law. Cp. on 19. 48. —
κατέφυγον: the perfect might have

2 γεγένηται εἰπεῖν ὑπὲρ αὐτῶν. ἔχω δὲ τούτων μὲν ἀδελφήν, Διογείτονος δὲ θυγατριδῆν, καὶ πολλὰ δεηθεὶς
ἀμφοτέρων τὸ μὲν πρῶτον ἔπεισα τοῖς φίλοις ἐπιτρέψαι
δίαιταν, περὶ πολλοῦ ποιούμενος τὰ τούτων πράγματα
μηδένα τῶν ἄλλων εἰδέναι· ἐπειδὴ δὲ Διογείτων ἃ φανε-
15 ρῶς ἔχων ἐξηλέγχετο, περὶ τούτων οὐδενὶ τῶν αὐτοῦ
φίλων ἐτόλμα πείθεσθαι, ἀλλ' ἐβουλήθη καὶ φεύγειν
δίκας καὶ μὴ οὔσας διώκειν καὶ ὑπομεῖναι τοὺς ἐσχά-

been used as in the corresponding clause (ἀπεστέρηνται), but their appeal to the speaker was something so striking and definite, and stands so vividly in his mind, that he uses the aorist (of the definite act) rather than the perfect (of the present situation).

2. δεηθείς: passive in form only, L. & S. *s.v.* II. 2; HA. 497; G. 444; B. 158. 3; Gl. 394. — **ἐπιτρέψαι δίαιταν**: a technical term, cp. [Dem.] 59. 45 συνῆγον αὐτοὺς οἱ ἐπιτήδειοι καὶ ἔπεισαν δίαιταν ἐπιτρέψαι αὐτοῖς *their friends brought them together and persuaded them to submit to their arbitration.* — **πράγματα**: L. & S. *s.v.* III. 5. — **ἃ ἐξηλέγχετο, περὶ τούτων**: the position of the rel. clause before its antecedent makes it emphatic. The prosecution had indisputable proof as to a part of the estate; Diogiton was not willing to yield even as to this. — **ἐτόλμα**: force as in 12. 5; cp. ἐβουλήθη in the following clause.

— **καὶ φεύγειν δίκας καὶ μὴ οὔσας διώκειν**: the present infinitives and the plurals (δίκας . . . οὔσας) refer not to any particular movement of Diogiton, but to his determination to avail himself of all the 'twists and turns of the law.' φεύγειν δίκας is the usual term for defending suits. μὴ οὔσας διώκειν, *to prosecute suits to set aside default,* refers to one of the tricks for gaining time. If a party to a suit failed to appear at the time set for trial, he lost his case by default; such a case in the courts was called ἡ ἔρημος δίκη; if it was before a board of arbitrators it was also called ἡ μὴ οὖσα δίκη. But one who had thus lost a case by default might, within a specified time, appeal for a hearing on the ground that there was sufficient reason for his non-appearance: in this case he was said τὴν ἔρημον (δίκην) ἀντιλαχεῖν or τὴν μὴ οὖσαν (δίκην) ἀντιλαχεῖν. — **τοὺς ἐσχάτους κινδύνους**: an exagger-

τοὺς κινδύνους μᾶλλον ἢ τὰ δίκαια ποιήσας ἀπηλλάχθαι
3 τῶν πρὸς τούτους ἐγκλημάτων, ὑμῶν δέομαι, ἐὰν μὲν
20 ἀποδείξω οὕτως αἰσχρῶς αὐτοὺς ἐπιτετροπευμένους ὑπὸ
τοῦ πάππου ὡς οὐδεὶς πώποτε ὑπὸ τῶν μηδὲν προσηκόντων ἐν τῇ πόλει, βοηθεῖν αὐτοῖς τὰ δίκαια, εἰ δὲ μή,
τούτῳ μὲν ἅπαντα πιστεύειν, ἡμᾶς δὲ εἰς τὸν λοιπὸν
χρόνον ἡγεῖσθαι χείρους εἶναι. ἐξ ἀρχῆς δ' ὑμᾶς περὶ
25 αὐτῶν διδάξαι πειράσομαι.

4 Ἀδελφοὶ ἦσαν, ὦ ἄνδρες δικασταί, Διόδοτος καὶ
Διογείτων ὁμοπάτριοι καὶ ὁμομήτριοι, καὶ τὴν μὲν
ἀφανῆ οὐσίαν ἐνείμαντο, τῆς δὲ φανερᾶς ἐκοινώνουν.
ἐργασαμένου δὲ Διοδότου κατ' ἐμπορίαν πολλὰ χρή-
30 ματα πείθει αὐτὸν Διογείτων λαβεῖν τὴν ἑαυτοῦ θυγα-

ated statement; at the most the
penalty would be only the restoration of the sum found to have
been taken, and a fine of one
sixth of that amount; still the
public disgrace must be counted
among the 'dangers.'— πρὸς τούτους: force, see on 16. 10.

3. ἐπιτετροπευμένους: perf. because the guilt of the guardian is
the fact that is discussed. See on
εἰργασμένοι εἰσίν 12. 22. — βοηθεῖν
αὐτοῖς τὰ δίκαια: a common condensed expression; τὰ δίκαια
(their rights) is the acc. of effect
(HA. 714; G. 1055. 1; B. 333-4;
Gl. 536. b); to aid them their
rights = to aid them in obtain-
ing their rights. — χείρους: see on
16. 3.

4. ἀφανῆ, φανερᾶς: in general
= personal property, real estate;
cash, investments, and credits are
always οὐσία ἀφανής; houses and
lands are οὐσία φανερά; the application of the terms to other property is variable, as they are not
sharply defined legal terms. —
θυγατέρα: Greek marriages were
regularly arranged by parents and
guardians; naturally the property
relations of the contract were a
prominent consideration. Out of
this grew the tendency to encour-
age marriage between near relatives (cp. Lysias's own marriage,
Introd. p. 23) in order to keep
the family property intact.   A
man might even marry his half-
sister if she was of a different

τέρα, ἥπερ ἦν αὐτῷ μόνη· καὶ γίγνονται αὐτῷ ὑεῖ
5 δύο καὶ θυγάτηρ. χρόνῳ δὲ ὕστερον καταλεγεὶς Διόδοτος μετὰ Θρασύλλου τῶν ὁπλιτῶν, καλέσας τὴν
ἑαυτοῦ γυναῖκα, ἀδελφιδῆν οὖσαν, καὶ τὸν ἐκείνης
35 μὲν πατέρα, αὐτοῦ δὲ κηδεστὴν καὶ ἀδελφόν, πάππον
δὲ τῶν παιδίων καὶ θεῖον, ἡγούμενος διὰ ταύτας τὰς
ἀναγκαιότητας οὐδενὶ μᾶλλον προσήκειν δικαίῳ περὶ
τοὺς αὐτοῦ παῖδας γενέσθαι, διαθήκην αὐτῷ δίδωσι
6 καὶ πέντε τάλαντα ἀργυρίου παρακαταθήκην· ναυτικὰ

mother. — **ὑεῖ**: form, see on 12. 34.

5. καταλεγείς: the names of all citizens liable to military service (men between eighteen and sixty years of age) were kept publicly posted in an official list. When troops were to be called into service a special decree of the Ecclesia determined the ages within which the draft should be made. Out of these available names the military authorities selected as many as were needed for the immediate emergency, and posted a list, which became the official roll. Such a list is here referred to. — **Θρασύλλου**: 410 B.C. See Chron. App. While Alcibiades was operating on the Hellespont, Thrasyllus was sent out to the coast of Asia Minor, with a force of 1000 hoplites, 100 cavalry, and 50 triremes (Xen. *Hell.* 1. 1. 34). Xenophon, who was one of these cavalrymen, has left a detailed

account of the preliminary skirmishes of the expedition, and of their severe defeat before Ephesus (*Hell.* 1. 2. 1–9). Thrasyllus was an efficient and popular general, an opponent of the Four Hundred, and closely associated with Thrasybulus. It is a wise thought to let the jury know that the father of the plaintiff lost his life under their popular general. — **τῶν ὁπλιτῶν**: case, HA. 732; G. 1095; B. 355. 2; Gl. 508. Cp. *τῶν ἀρχόντων* 24. 13. — **ἐκείνης**: in contrast with *αὐτοῦ* below. Cp. on *ἐκείνων* 12. 77. — **κηδεστήν**: cp. on § 1. — **δικαίῳ**: agreement, cp. on *λέγοντι* 12. 1. — **παρακαταθήκην**: *i.e.* in trust for his family, and in case of his death to be disposed of according to the will.

6. For the value of the sums mentioned see App. § 61. — **ναυτικά**: in the great extension of Athenian trade in the fifth century there grew up a carefully guarded

40 δὲ ἀπέδειξεν ἐκδεδομένα ἑπτὰ τάλαντα καὶ τετταράκοντα μνᾶς . . ., δισχιλίας δὲ ὀφειλομένας ἐν Χερ-
ρονήσῳ. ἐπέσκηψε δέ, ἐάν τι πάθῃ, τάλαντον μὲν
ἐπιδοῦναι τῇ γυναικὶ καὶ τὰ ἐν τῷ δωματίῳ δοῦναι,
τάλαντον δὲ τῇ θυγατρί. κατέλιπε δὲ καὶ εἴκοσι
45 μνᾶς τῇ γυναικὶ καὶ τριάκοντα στατῆρας Κυζικηνούς.
7 ταῦτα δὲ πράξας καὶ οἴκοι ἀντίγραφα καταλιπὼν ᾤχετο
στρατευσόμενος μετὰ Θρασύλλου. ἀποθανόντος δὲ
ἐκείνου ἐν Ἐφέσῳ Διογείτων τὴν μὲν θυγατέρα ἔκρυπτε
τὸν θάνατον τοῦ ἀνδρός, . . . καὶ τὰ γράμματα λαμ-

system of loans on vessels or their
cargoes. There was no system
of maritime insurance, while the
primitive means of navigation,
the prevalence of piracy, and the
frequent dangers by war made
the risks greater than in modern
times. Accordingly the rates of
interest were high; 12 per cent
was common, and the rate sometimes went above 30 per cent.
The papers in each case specified
definitely the limits of place and
time within which the voyage was
to be made. In this period of the
war the dangers were particularly
great. — μνᾶς . . . : editors assume
a *lacuna* here, for in § 15 we find
that the family claimed an item of
100 minae on a real estate mort-
gage. The 2000 dr. of § 15 may
be the 2000 dr. loaned in the
Chersonese (§ 6). — δισχιλίας : sc.
δραχμάς, which is often omitted

with numbers. — ἐπιδοῦναι : as
dowry (cp. on 16. 10 and 19. 14) ;
δοῦναι, a personal gift. — τὰ ἐν τῷ
δωματίῳ : cp. 12. 10. — τῇ θυγατρί :
i.e. as dowry on her marriage. —
κατέλιπε : not to be understood
of the will ; he 'left' this sum in
cash with his wife on his departure ; after his death she turned it
over to her father (§ 15).

7. ἀντίγραφα : the plural is generally used of a single 'copy,'
probably from the connection with
τὰ γράμματα, but the singular oc-
curs, as in Andoc. 1. 76, Demos.
36. 7. The original will was left
with Diogiton (§ 5) ; the copy
was left at Diodotus's own house,
probably sealed up with the other
papers (§ 7). — ἔκρυπτε : impf. of
an attempted action (which succeeded for a time). — ἀνδρός . . . .
see Crit. Note. There is force in
Thalheim's conjecture that the

50 βάνει ἃ κατέλιπε σεσημασμένα, φάσκων τὰ ναυτικὰ
χρήματα δεῖν ἐκ τούτων τῶν γραμματείων κομίσασθαι.
8 ἐπειδὴ δὲ χρόνῳ ἐδήλωσε τὸν θάνατον αὐτοῖς καὶ
ἐποίησαν τὰ νομιζόμενα, τὸν μὲν πρῶτον ἐνιαυτὸν ἐν
Πειραιεῖ διῃτῶντο· ἅπαντα γὰρ αὐτοῦ κατελέλειπτο
55 τὰ ἐπιτήδεια· ἐκείνων δὲ ἐπιλειπόντων τοὺς μὲν παῖδας
εἰς ἄστυ ἀναπέμπει, τὴν δὲ μητέρα αὐτῶν ἐκδίδωσιν
ἐπιδοὺς πεντακισχιλίας δραχμάς, χιλίαις ἔλαττον ὧν
9 ὁ ἀνὴρ αὐτῆς ἔδωκεν. ὀγδόῳ δ᾽ ἔτει δοκιμασθέντος

lost words are τὰ δ᾽ ἀντίγραφα,
for that assumption explains the
fact that the speaker makes no
use of a copy of the will in his
plea. — τὰ γράμματα : the notes for
the several loans.

8. τὰ νομιζόμενα : Xenophon
says that those who died fighting
before Ephesus were buried at
Notium (*Hell.* I. 2. II). The
' rites ' here referred to were probably in connection with the dedi-
cation of a cenotaph at Athens
(the μνῆμα of § 21), according to
a common custom. — ἐν Πειραιεῖ
διῃτῶντο : they 'lived on ' at the
Piraeus, where the father had naturally fixed his residence because
of his foreign trade. At the end
of the year the boys were sent to
their grandfather's house in the
city in the deme Collytus (§ 14);
they afterward removed with his
family to another house (τὴν Φαίδρου οἰκίαν § 14) ; apparently the
heirs claim that the last house

was purchased with money of the
estate, for when the grandfather
proposes to send them out to care
for themselves, their mother says
he is casting them ἐκ τῆς οἰκίας
τῆς αὐτῶν (§ 16). — αὐτοῦ : the
adverb. — ἐπιλειπόντων : note the
force of the present, as compared
with κατελέλειπτο above. — εἰς
ἄστυ : see on 12. 16. — ἐκδίδωσιν :
Diogiton became the head of the
family, as the oldest son was a
minor ; it rested with him therefore
to arrange the second marriage ;
we learn the name of the husband
from § 12. — πεντακισχιλίας : cp.
on 16. 10. The amount, though
not niggardly, is small for a wealthy
family.

9. δοκιμασθέντος : on a fixed day
of each year (perhaps in July at
the beginning of the civil year)
all young men who had passed
their eighteenth birthday in the
twelve months preceding were entitled to enrollment in the citizens'

μετὰ ταῦτα τοῦ πρεσβυτέρου τοῖν μειρακίοιν, καλέσας
60 αὐτοὺς εἶπε Διογείτων, ὅτι καταλίποι αὐτοῖς ὁ πατὴρ
εἴκοσι μνᾶς ἀργυρίου καὶ τριάκοντα στατῆρας. " ἐγὼ
οὖν πολλὰ τῶν ἐμαυτοῦ δεδαπάνηκα εἰς τὴν ὑμετέραν
τροφήν. καὶ ἕως μὲν εἶχον, οὐδέν μοι διέφερεν· νυνὶ
δὲ καὶ αὐτὸς ἀπόρως διάκειμαι. σὺ οὖν, ἐπειδὴ δεδο-
65 κίμασαι καὶ ἀνὴρ γεγένησαι, σκόπει αὐτὸς ἤδη πόθεν
10 ἕξεις τὰ ἐπιτήδεια." ταῦτ' ἀκούσαντες ἐκπεπληγμένοι
καὶ δακρύοντες ᾤχοντο πρὸς τὴν μητέρα, καὶ παραλα-
βόντες ἐκείνην ἧκον πρὸς ἐμέ, οἰκτρῶς ὑπὸ τοῦ πάθους
διακείμενοι καὶ ἀθλίως ἐκπεπτωκότες, κλάοντες καὶ
70 παρακαλοῦντές με μὴ περιιδεῖν αὐτοὺς ἀποστερηθέντας
τῶν πατρῴων μηδ' εἰς πτωχείαν καταστάντας, ὑβρισμέ-
νους ὑφ' ὧν ἥκιστα ἐχρῆν, ἀλλὰ βοηθῆσαι καὶ τῆς
11 ἀδελφῆς ἕνεκα καὶ σφῶν αὐτῶν. πολλὰ ἂν εἴη λέγειν,

list (the modern check list). But
to guard this enrollment it was
provided that the candidate must
secure the approval of the assembled citizens of his deme, and the
ratification of their act by the Senate. This δοκιμασία was intended
to guarantee the candidate's having reached the full age, and his
being of pure, free Athenian birth.
With this enrollment the young
man passed from under control of
his father or guardian and assumed all rights and obligations
of citizenship so far as they were
compatible with the special duties
of his two years of service in the
cadet corps, which immediately

followed (see on 16. 20). If he
had been under guardianship, his
property was now turned over to
him, with accounts of its management. — εἰς . . . τροφήν: see on
εἰς τὰς ναῦς 19. 21 (B).

10. πρός: Lysias seldom uses
πρός in this way; cp. § 14 πρὸς
αὐτήν, and see on ὡς 16. 4. —
ὑπό: force, see on 12. 3. — ἐκπεπτωκότες: ἐκπίπτω is the regular
passive of ἐκβάλλω expel: cp. ἐκβάλλειν . . . ἐκ τῆς οἰκίας § 16,
and see on ἐξέπεσον 12. 57.

11. Asyndeton between sentences (as rare in Greek as it is
common in English) draws attention to the second sentence. Here

ὅσον πένθος ἐν τῇ ἐμῇ οἰκίᾳ ἦν ἐν ἐκείνῳ τῷ χρόνῳ.
75 τελευτῶσα δὲ ἡ μήτηρ αὐτῶν ἠντεβόλει με καὶ ἱκέτευε
συναγαγεῖν αὐτῆς τὸν πατέρα καὶ τοὺς φίλους, εἰποῦσα
ὅτι, εἰ καὶ μὴ πρότερον εἴθισται λέγειν ἐν ἀνδράσι, τὸ
μέγεθος αὐτὴν ἀναγκάσει τῶν συμφορῶν περὶ τῶν σφε-
12 τέρων κακῶν δηλῶσαι πάντα πρὸς ἡμᾶς. ἐλθὼν δ' ἐγὼ
80 ἠγανάκτουν μὲν πρὸς Ἡγήμονα τὸν ἔχοντα τὴν τούτου
θυγατέρα, λόγους δ' ἐποιούμην πρὸς τοὺς ἄλλους ἐπιτη-
δείους, ἠξίουν δὲ τοῦτον εἰς ἔλεγχον ἰέναι περὶ τῶν
πραγμάτων. Διογείτων δὲ τὸ μὲν πρῶτον οὐκ ἤθελε,
τελευτῶν δὲ ὑπὸ τῶν φίλων ἠναγκάσθη. ἐπειδὴ δὲ
85 συνήλθομεν, ἤρετο αὐτὸν ἡ γυνή, τίνα ποτὲ ψυχὴν
ἔχων ἀξιοῖ περὶ τῶν παίδων τοιαύτῃ γνώμῃ χρῆσθαι,
" ἀδελφὸς μὲν ὢν τοῦ πατρὸς αὐτῶν, πατὴρ δ' ἐμός,
13 θεῖος δὲ αὐτοῖς καὶ πάππος. καὶ εἰ μηδένα ἀνθρώπων ᾐσχύνου, τοὺς θεοὺς ἐχρῆν σε " φησί " δεδιέναι ·
90 ὃς ἔλαβες μέν, ὅτ' ἐκεῖνος ἐξέπλει, πέντε τάλαντα παρ'
αὐτοῦ παρακαταθήκην. καὶ περὶ τούτων ἐγὼ ἐθέλω

it gives a touch of deeper feeling.
— ἠντεβόλει: for the double augment see HA. 361 a; G. 544.
On the συνωνυμία see App. § 58. 2.
— εἰ καί: force, see on 16. 2. —
λέγειν: to talk; cp. different force
of the present above, πολλὰ ἂν εἴη
λέγειν to recount. — ἐν ἀνδράσι: for
the seclusion of Athenian women
see Gardner and Jevons, 342 ff.;
Becker, Charicles (Eng. trans.),
462 ff.; Gulick, 30 f., 119 ff.

12. Ἡγήμονα: see Introd. p.

284. — λόγους δ' ἐποιούμην: see on
12. 2. — ἠξίουν: as in 16. 8. — εἰς
ἔλεγχον ἰέναι: see on 16. 1. — οὐκ
ἤθελε: impf. of persistent refusal,
'resistance to pressure'; see on
ἐτόλμων 12. 5. — τίνα ποτὲ ψυχήν:
what possible heart, cp. on ποτέ
12. 29. — ἀξιοῖ: the ind. disc.
passes over quickly to the direct
in πατὴρ δ' ἐμός.

13. καὶ εἰ: see on 19. 18. —
ἔλαβες μέν: who certainly received
(whatever became of it). See on

τοὺς παῖδας παραστησαμένη καὶ τούτους καὶ τοὺς
ὕστερον ἐμαυτῇ γενομένους ὀμόσαι ὅπου ἂν οὗτος
λέγῃ. καίτοι οὐχ οὕτως ἐγώ εἰμι ἀθλία, οὐδ' οὕτω
95 περὶ πολλοῦ ποιοῦμαι χρήματα, ὥστ' ἐπιορκήσασα
κατὰ τῶν παίδων τῶν ἐμαυτῆς τὸν βίον καταβαλεῖν,
14 ἀδίκως δὲ ἀφελέσθαι τὴν τοῦ πατρὸς οὐσίαν·" ἔτι
τοίνυν ἐξήλεγχεν αὐτὴ ἑπτὰ τάλαντα κεκομισμένον
ναυτικὰ καὶ τετρακισχιλίας δραχμάς, καὶ τούτων τὰ
100 γράμματα ἀπέδειξεν· ἐν γὰρ τῇ ἐξοικίσει, ὅτ' ἐκ Κολλυτοῦ ἐξῳκίζετο εἰς τὴν Φαίδρου οἰκίαν, τοὺς παῖδας
ἐπιτυχόντας ἐκβεβλημένῳ βιβλίῳ ἐνεγκεῖν πρὸς αὐτήν.
15 ἀπέφηνε δ' αὐτὸν ἑκατὸν μνᾶς κεκομισμένον ἐγγείῳ ἐπὶ
τόκῳ δεδανεισμένας, καὶ ἑτέρας δισχιλίας δραχμὰς
105 καὶ ἔπιπλα πολλοῦ ἄξια· φοιτᾶν δὲ καὶ σῖτον αὐτοῖς

ἐμὲ μέν 12. 8. — τοὺς ὕστερον: by
her marriage with Hegemon. —
ὀμόσαι: for a parent to swear before an altar with the hand on the
head of a child was to stake upon
the truth of the oath what one
held most dear. The penalty
would be the death of the child.
See Crit. Note, and cp. Pison's
oath 12. 10. — ὅπου: i.e. at any
shrine, however sacred. — οὗτος:
the woman now turns appealingly
to her friends. — οὕτως: position,
see on ἡμῖν 12. 33. — κατὰ τῶν
παίδων: see on πρός 32. 19, Crit.
Note. — τοῦ πατρός: my father's.

14. ἔτι τοίνυν: force, see on
25. 15. — τὰ γράμματα: the entries
in the old memorandum or account book which the boys had
found, and of which their mother
had retained possession. The original 'writings' which secured the
loans had been carried off by
Diogiton with the other sealed
papers (§ 7). — Κολλυτοῦ: a deme
lying just north of the Acropolis.
We conclude from a statement of
Plutarch that it was a favorite
residential quarter (Plut. de Exil.
6 οὐδὲ γὰρ Ἀθηναῖοι πάντες κα-
τοικοῦσι Κολλυτόν). — οἰκίαν: see
on § 8. — ἐνεγκεῖν: in indir. disc.
loosely dependent on the idea of
saying implied in ἐξήλεγχεν.

15. ἐγγείῳ ἐπὶ τόκῳ: on a mort-
gage on real estate. — ἔπιπλα: cp.
12. 19. — φοιτᾶν: of a regular

ἐκ Χερρονήσου καθ᾽ ἕκαστον ἐνιαυτόν. "ἔπειτα σὺ
ἐτόλμησας" ἔφη "εἰπεῖν, ἔχων τοσαῦτα χρήματα, ὡς
δισχιλίας δραχμὰς ὁ τούτων πατὴρ κατέλιπε καὶ τριά-
109 κοντα στατῆρας, ἅπερ ἐμοὶ καταλειφθέντα ἐκείνου
16 τελευτήσαντος ἐγώ σοι ἔδωκα; καὶ ἐκβάλλειν τούτους
ἠξίωκας θυγατριδοῦς ὄντας ἐκ τῆς οἰκίας τῆς αὐτῶν
ἐν τριβωνίοις, ἀνυποδήτους, οὐ μετὰ ἀκολούθου, οὐ
μετὰ στρωμάτων, οὐ μετὰ ἱματίων, οὐ μετὰ τῶν ἐπί-
114 πλων ἃ ὁ πατὴρ αὐτοῖς κατέλιπεν, οὐδὲ μετὰ τῶν
17 παρακαταθηκῶν ἃς ἐκεῖνος παρὰ σοὶ κατέθετο. καὶ

coming. As we read of a claim of a claim of 2000 dr. in the Chersonese (§ 6), we may perhaps assume that this grain was sent annually as payment of the interest. — ἔπειτα: εἶτα is the more common word to introduce an indignant comment upon conduct as related to a preceding statement (as in 12. 26), then, in view of all that. — δισχιλίας δραχμάς κτλ.: Diogiton at first acknowledged only the money which his daughter had herself turned over to him as head of the family. — ἅπερ: force, see on οἵτινες 12. 40.

16. ἐκβάλλειν: tense, see Crit. Note. — τούτους: it was to the oldest boy only that the grand-father had said that he must shift for himself; though he says that they are living on his generosity, he does not intimate that the younger brother must go now.

But the family naturally take it as the casting out of both. — τῆς αὐτῶν: see on § 8. — ἐν τριβωνίοις, ἀνυποδήτους: in rags, barefoot. — οὐ μετά: on the ἐπανα-φορά see App. § 57. 5, and on the ἀσύνδετον, App. § 58. 3. — ἀκολού-θου: a man of ordinary standing was expected to have a slave at-tendant as he went about his busi-ness. Even the schoolboy had his παιδαγωγός. Among the in-equalities that are to be abolished in the reformed society of Aris-tophanes's Ecclesiazusae (v. 593) is the undemocratic state of things by which, while one citizen has many slaves, another has not even a personal attendant (ἀνδραπόδοις τὸν μὲν χρῆσθαι πολλοῖς τὸν δ᾽ οὐδ᾽ ἀκολούθῳ). Cp. Gulick, 66 ff. — μετὰ στρωμάτων: see on μετά 19. 14. — παρὰ σοί: see on παρ᾽ αὐτῷ 19. 22.

νῦν τοὺς μὲν ἐκ τῆς μητρυιᾶς τῆς ἐμῆς παιδεύεις ἐν
πολλοῖς χρήμασιν εὐδαίμονας ὄντας· καὶ ταῦτα μὲν
καλῶς ποιεῖς· τοὺς δ᾽ ἐμοὺς ἀδικεῖς, οὓς ἀτίμους ἐκ
τῆς οἰκίας ἐκβαλὼν ἀντὶ πλουσίων πτωχοὺς ἀποδεῖξαι
120 προθυμῇ. καὶ ἐπὶ τοιούτοις ἔργοις οὔτε τοὺς θεοὺς
φοβῇ, οὔτε ἐμὲ τὴν συνειδυῖαν αἰσχύνῃ, οὔτε τοῦ
ἀδελφοῦ μέμνησαι, ἀλλὰ πάντας ἡμᾶς περὶ ἐλάττονος
18 ποιῇ χρημάτων." τότε μὲν οὖν, ὦ ἄνδρες δικασταί,
πολλῶν καὶ δεινῶν ὑπὸ τῆς γυναικὸς ῥηθέντων οὕτω
125 διετέθημεν πάντες οἱ παρόντες ὑπὸ τῶν τούτῳ πεπραγμένων καὶ τῶν λόγων τῶν ἐκείνης, ὁρῶντες μὲν τοὺς
παῖδας, οἷα ἦσαν πεπονθότες, ἀναμιμνῃσκόμενοι δὲ
τοῦ ἀποθανόντος, ὡς ἀνάξιον τῆς οὐσίας τὸν ἐπίτρο-

17. **ταῦτα μέν**: contrast with
her censure of his other conduct
is implied. See on **ἐμὲ μέν** 12. 8.
— **ἀποδεῖξαι**: often nearly equal
to **ποιῆσαι**; here it combines the
idea of *making* the children beg-
gars with that of *exhibiting* their
sad condition to the world. —
προθυμῇ: in the course of the
fourth century B.C. writers probably used the endings -η and -ει
with equal freedom; in the fifth -η
is to be assumed. Lysias belongs
so far to the earlier generation
that he is more likely to have used
the older form exclusively. — **ἐπὶ
τοιούτοις ἔργοις**: a natural development from **ἐπί** local is the use of
ἐπί with the dat. in a figurative
sense to give the *ground* of an

action or feeling. So **ἐφ᾽ ᾧ** § 21 ;
cp. 14. 35 **ἐπὶ τῇ τοῦ πατρὸς πονη-
ρίᾳ φιλοτιμεῖται** *he is proud of
his father's wickedness*. For the
development of this into the purpose construction see on 12. 24.
For **ἐπί** with gen. see on 24. 1. —
πάντας ἡμᾶς . . . χρημάτων: the
position brings the contrast into
relief and leaves **χρημάτων** as the
last word of the mother's indignant complaint.

18. **μὲν οὖν**: see on 12. 3 (B).
— **ὑπό** : force, see on 12. 3. — **ὡς
ἀνάξιον . . . τὸν ἐπίτροπον κατέλιπεν**: the Greek combines the two
idioms of English " how unworthy
a guardian he had left," and " how
unworthy the guardian whom he
had left." — **τῆς οὐσίας** : connect

πον κατέλιπεν, ἐνθυμούμενοι δὲ ὡς χαλεπὸν ἐξευρεῖν
130 ὅτῳ χρὴ περὶ τῶν ἑαυτοῦ πιστεῦσαι, ὥστε, ὦ ἄνδρες
δικασταί, μηδένα τῶν παρόντων δύνασθαι φθέγξασθαι,
ἀλλὰ καὶ δακρύοντας μὴ ἧττον τῶν πεπονθότων ἀπιόντας οἴχεσθαι σιωπῇ.
134 Πρῶτον μὲν οὖν τούτων ἀνάβητέ μοι μάρτυρες.

ΜΑΡΤΥΡΕΣ

with ἐπίτροπον. — ἑαυτοῦ : referring
to the indef. subject of πιστεῦσαι,
*how hard it is to find a man in whom
one may safely put confidence as
regards his property, i.e.* to whom
one may safely intrust his property.
— φθέγξασθαι : the strongest possible word = *to utter a sound,* cp.
Dem. 18. 199 εἰ γὰρ . . . σὺ προὔλε-
γες καὶ διεμαρτύρου βοῶν καὶ κεκρα-
γώς, ὃς οὐδ' ἐφθέγξω *for even if
you had foretold and protested with
shouts and cries, you who did not
even open your mouth.* — μὴ ἧττον :
cp. on μήτε 12. 68 (B). — οἴχεσθαι : the subject is πάντας, supplied from the connection with
μηδένα δύνασθαι. — σιωπῇ : an
instance of the force that may
lie in the final word of a sentence ;
cp. χρημάτων § 17.

A review of the tenses used
in this whole section, §§ 10–18, is
instructive as bearing on the use
of historical present, impf., aorist,
and plupf. in narrative and description :

The preliminary narrative :
ᾤχοντο, ἧκον § 10, impf. with plupf.
force.
ἠντεβόλει, ἱκέτευε § 11, descriptive
impf. (GS. 207) with added idea
of persistence.
ἠγανάκτουν § 12, descriptive impf.
ἐποιούμην, ἠξίουν descriptive
impf. with added idea of
repetition.
οὐκ ἤθελε impf. with negative, 'resistance to pressure' (GS. 216).
ἠναγκάσθη aor. of 'attainment'
(GS. 214).
The main narrative :
ἤρετο narrative aor. (GS. 238).
φησί § 13, histor. pres. ; the scene
becomes most vivid, with direct
quotation.
ἐξήλεγχεν § 14, descriptive impf.,
the general statement.
ἀπέδειξεν § 14, ἀπέφηνε § 15, narrative aor.
ἔφη neutral (one form for impf.
and aor.).
διετέθημεν § 18, aor., the "upshot" of it all (GS. 238).

19 Ἀξιῶ τοίνυν, ὦ ἄνδρες δικασταί, τῷ λογισμῷ προσέχειν τὸν νοῦν, ἵνα τοὺς μὲν νεανίσκους διὰ τὸ μέγεθος
τῶν συμφορῶν ἐλεήσητε, τοῦτον δ' ἅπασι τοῖς πολίταις
ἄξιον ὀργῆς ἡγήσησθε. εἰς τοσαύτην γὰρ ὑποψίαν
Διογείτων πάντας ἀνθρώπους πρὸς ἀλλήλους καθίστη-
140 σιν, ὥστε μήτε ζῶντας μήτε ἀποθνῄσκοντας μηδὲν
μᾶλλον τοῖς οἰκειοτάτοις ἢ τοῖς ἐχθίστοις πιστεύειν·
20 ὃς ἐτόλμησε τῶν μὲν ἔξαρνος γενέσθαι, τὰ δὲ τελευτῶν
ὁμολογήσας ἔχειν, εἰς δύο παῖδας καὶ ἀδελφὴν λῆμμα
καὶ ἀνάλωμα ἐν ὀκτὼ ἔτεσιν ἑπτὰ τάλαντα ἀργυρίου
145 καὶ τετρακισχιλίας δραχμὰς ἀποδεῖξαι. καὶ εἰς τοῦτο
ἦλθεν ἀναισχυντίας, ὥστε οὐκ ἔχων ὅποι τρέψειε τὰ
χρήματα, εἰς ὄψον μὲν δυοῖν παιδίοιν καὶ ἀδελφῇ πέντε
ὀβολοὺς τῆς ἡμέρας ἐλογίζετο, εἰς ὑποδήματα δὲ καὶ
εἰς γναφεῖον καὶ εἰς κουρέως κατὰ μῆνα οὐκ ἦν αὐτῷ

19. τῷ λογισμῷ : the statement
of accounts filed with the court
by Diogiton. — πολίταις : construction, L. & S. ἄξιος II. 2 b. —
πρὸς ἀλλήλους : for πρός see Crit.
Note.

20. τελευτῶν : cp. §§ 11, 12. —
ἔχειν : tense, see on ἀντιλέγειν
12. 26. — εἰς δύο παῖδας : see on
εἰς τὰς ναῦς 19. 21 (C). — ἑπτὰ
τάλαντα . . . καὶ τεττρα. δρ. : see
Crit. Note. This, the sum proved
by the book that the boys found,
is what Diogiton admits that he
had for the use of the children.
It does not appear what claim he
made as to the money for the
dowries of the widow and daugh-

ter. See Introd. p. 285 N. 2. — τρέψειε : i.e. under what items to
distribute so much as he claims
to have spent. Mood, HA. 932.
2 (2); G. 1490; B. 673 last paragraph; Gl. 661; GMT. 677. For
an important extension of this
construction see on δοίην 24. 1. —
ὄψον : the term covers all that is
eaten except bread, viz. meat, fish,
vegetables, relishes, and desserts.
Cp. Gulick, p. 144 ff. Xenophon
tells some bright anecdotes of
Socrates on the relation of bread
to ὄψον, Mem. 3. 14. 1–7. Cp.
Plato, Republic, II. 372. — εἰς
γναφεῖον : under this item is
included the whole expense for

150 οὐδὲ κατ᾽ ἐνιαυτὸν γεγραμμένα, συλλήβδην δὲ παντὸς
21 τοῦ χρόνου πλεῖν ἢ τάλαντον ἀργυρίου. εἰς δὲ τὸ
μνῆμα τοῦ πατρὸς οὐκ ἀναλώσας πέντε καὶ εἴκοσι
μνᾶς ἐκ πεντακισχιλίων δραχμῶν, τὸ μὲν ἥμισυ αὐτῷ
τίθησι, τὸ δὲ τούτοις λελόγισται. εἰς Διονύσια τοίνυν,
155 ὦ ἄνδρες δικασταί, (οὐκ ἄτοπον γάρ μοι δοκεῖ καὶ
περὶ τούτου μνησθῆναι) ἐκκαίδεκα δραχμῶν ἀπέφηνεν

clothing. Originally the γναφεύς only dressed and whitened the cloth that came from the home looms; then he added the work of a laundry; to this was again added the full business of the modern tailor and dealer in clothing (so we read in Aristoph. *Eccl.* 408 ff., the "most democratic" proposal that on the approach of cold weather the fullers give a cloak to every citizen who needs one). Cp. Gulick, p. 229. Still, much of the work, both of weaving and making of clothing, was done by the slaves of a household. — εἰς κουρέως : *sc.* ἐργαστήριον. At "the barber's" one not only had the hair dressed, but bought the oil and ointments that were regularly used at the bath. — παντὸς τοῦ χρόνου : note the various constructions for time in this section : τελευτῶν, ἐν ὀκτὼ ἔτεσιν, τῆς ἡμέρας, κατὰ μῆνα, παντὸς τοῦ χρόνου. — πλεῖν : a shortened form of πλεῖον. See Crit. Note; cp. 19. 31, 19. 46.

21. εἰς : see on εἰς τὰς ναῦς 19. 21 (B). — μνῆμα : see on § 8. The Athenian tombs and monuments were among the finest products of Greek art. There was a tendency to extravagant outlay, but in most artistic form. The expense was great as compared with the expenditure for the living. We know of sums ranging from 3 minae to 2 talents. For full description and illustration see Percy Gardner's *Sculptured Tombs of Hellas.* Cp. Gulick, 297 ff. — τὸ μὲν ἥμισυ : *i.e.* half of the 5000 dr., the pretended cost. His brother thus receives a very creditable monument, charged entirely to the estate. — εἰς Διονύσια : Lysias uses names of festivals without the article; so Eng. "for Christmas," "for Easter."—ἐκκαίδεκα δραχμῶν : the price is perhaps unreasonable (see App. § 64), though not so if this particular festival fell in one of the last years of the war; but the thing that hurts is that the children are charged with half the

ἐωνημένον ἀρνίον, καὶ τούτων τὰς ὀκτὼ δραχμὰς ἐλογίζετο τοῖς παισίν· ἐφ᾽ ᾧ ἡμεῖς οὐχ ἥκιστα ὠργίσθημεν.
οὕτως, ὦ ἄνδρες, ἐν ταῖς μεγάλαις ζημίαις ἐνίοτε οὐχ
160 ἧττον τὰ μικρὰ λυπεῖ τοὺς ἀδικουμένους· λίαν γὰρ
φανερὰν τὴν πονηρίαν τῶν ἀδικούντων ἐπιδείκνυσιν.
22 εἰς τοίνυν τὰς ἄλλας ἑορτὰς καὶ θυσίας ἐλογίσατο
αὐτοῖς πλεῖν ἢ τετρακισχιλίας δραχμὰς ἀνηλωμένας,
ἕτερά τε παμπληθῆ, ἃ πρὸς τὸ κεφάλαιον συνελογίζετο,
165 ὥσπερ διὰ τοῦτο ἐπίτροπος τῶν παιδίων καταλειφθείς,
ἵνα γράμματα αὐτοῖς ἀντὶ τῶν χρημάτων ἀποδείξειεν
καὶ πενεστάτους ἀντὶ πλουσίων ἀποφήνειε, καὶ ἵνα,
εἰ μέν τις αὐτοῖς πατρικὸς ἐχθρὸς ἦν, ἐκείνου μὲν
169 ἐπιλάθωνται, τῷ δ᾽ ἐπιτρόπῳ τῶν πατρῴων ἀπεστερη-
23 μένοι πολεμῶσι. καίτοι εἰ ἐβούλετο δίκαιος εἶναι περὶ
τοὺς παῖδας, ἐξῆν αὐτῷ, κατὰ τοὺς νόμους οἳ κεῖνται

expense of the family thanksgiving
festival by their own grandfather.
— τὰς ὀκτώ: the numeral as such
would not take the article, but
there goes with it here the idea
of "*the half*"; HA. 664 a; G.
948 a. — ἐφ᾽ ᾧ: force, see on ἐπί
§ 17, and on ὀργίζεσθε 12. 80. —
ὠργίσθημεν: ingressive aor., see on
μετέσχον 16. 3. — οὕτως: see 12. 1
Crit. Note.

22. εἰς: see on § 21. — τε: cp.
on § 1. — πρὸς τὸ κεφάλαιον: *for
his total.* — συνελογίζετο: be gathered up (σύν) and reckoned in. —
διὰ τοῦτο, ἵνα: the purpose of an
act is its "final cause," hence it is
not strange that sometimes the

common purpose phrase, εἰς with
acc. (see on 12. 14), is replaced
by the causal phrase διά with acc.;
here the purpose idea is fully developed by the ἵνα clause. So in
1. 35 διὰ τοῦτο, ἵνα κτλ. — γράμματα, χρημάτων: for the play on
sound see App. § 58. 5. — εἰ μέν,
ἐκείνου μέν: for the repetition of
μέν cp. on 24. 8. — ἐπιλάθωνται,
πολεμῶσι: for the change from the
preceding optatives, and the consequent gain in vividness of the
presentation of the purpose, see
GMT. 321. πολεμῶσι, present of
a state of war. For the metaphorical use see Introd. p. 25, N. 5.

23. κατὰ τοὺς νόμους: in such

περὶ τῶν ὀρφανῶν καὶ τοῖς ἀδυνάτοις τῶν ἐπιτρόπων
καὶ τοῖς δυναμένοις, μισθῶσαι τὸν οἶκον ἀπηλλαγμένον
πολλῶν πραγμάτων, ἢ γῆν πριάμενον ἐκ τῶν προσιόν-
175 των τοὺς παῖδας τρέφειν· καὶ ὁπότερα τούτων ἐποίησεν,
οὐδενὸς ἂν ἧττον Ἀθηναίων πλούσιοι ἦσαν. νῦν δέ
μοι δοκεῖ οὐδεπώποτε διανοηθῆναι ὡς φανερὰν κατα-

case the first Archon, the state guardian of orphans, offered the lease of the entire property at public auction, taking security from the lessee. Such property often yielded more than 12 per cent interest. — τοῖς ἀδυνάτοις: guardians *disabled* from managing the property by reason either of ill health or of business cares. — πραγμάτων: force as in § 2. — ἐποίησεν: mood and tense HA. 915; G. 1433; B. 622. — οὐδενὸς ἂν ἧττον: cp. οὐδενὸς χεῖρον τῶν πολιτῶν 25. 12. The statement that the boys would have been as rich as any boys in the city (having about 12 t. after the payment of expenses for the eight years and of dowries for mother and sister) seems reasonable from what we know of Athenian fortunes. The war and the internal political troubles had impoverished the older rich families, and had pressed even harder upon the merchants, whose foreign trade had been destroyed, while their public burdens were enormous. The fabulously rich men of the older generation, Nicias and Callias, were popularly supposed to have had fortunes of 100 and 200 talents. But a man who had 8 to 10 talents at the close of the Peloponnesian War was a rich man. In comparing these with modern fortunes we must remember that property yielded from three to four times as much interest as now, that the price of living and of labor was very low (see App. § 63 ff.), and above all that the habits of life were simple. Demosthenes's father was a rich man, having property about equal to that in question here (about $15,000), but his house was estimated as worth only $540 (cp. on 19. 29). It was only after Alexander's conquests had brought Oriental ideas of luxury and the means to grow rich by conquest and by trade on a large scale, that the Greek family needed very much money to be "rich." Cp. on 19. 42 ff. — νῦν δέ μοι κτλ.: *but the fact is, as it seems to me, that he never for a moment proposed to make public the amount*

στήσων τὴν οὐσίαν, ἀλλ᾽ ὡς αὐτὸς ἕξων τὰ τούτων,
179 ἡγούμενος δεῖν τὴν αὐτοῦ πονηρίαν κληρονόμον εἶναι
24 τῶν τοῦ τεθνεῶτος χρημάτων. ὃ δὲ πάντων δεινότατον,
ὦ ἄνδρες δικασταί· οὗτος γὰρ συντριηραρχῶν ᾿Αλέξιδι
τῷ ᾿Αριστοδίκου, φάσκων δυοῖν δεούσας πεντήκοντα
μνᾶς ἐκείνῳ συμβαλέσθαι, τὸ ἥμισυ τούτοις ὀρφανοῖς
οὖσι λελόγισται, οὓς ἡ πόλις οὐ μόνον παῖδας ὄντας
185 ἀτελεῖς ἐποίησεν, ἀλλὰ καὶ ἐπειδὰν δοκιμασθῶσιν ἐνιαυτὸν ἀφῆκεν ἁπασῶν τῶν λητουργιῶν. οὗτος δὲ
πάππος ὢν παρὰ τοὺς νόμους τῆς ἑαυτοῦ τριηραρχίας
25 παρὰ τῶν θυγατριδῶν τὸ ἥμισυ πράττεται. καὶ ἀπο-
πέμψας εἰς τὸν ᾿Αδρίαν ὁλκάδα δυοῖν ταλάντοιν, ὅτε
190 μὲν ἀπέστελλεν, ἔλεγε πρὸς τὴν μητέρα αὐτῶν ὅτι τῶν

of the estate (as he must have done if he had made the public loan through the Archon or invested it in real estate). φανεράν has the double suggestion of property revealed and of visible property, i.e. real estate. διανοέομαι with ὡς and partic. of ind. disc. for infin. is rare ; cp. on ὡς 12. 73. — πονηρίαν κληρονόμον: for the personification see Introd. p. 25, N. 5.

24. ὅ: the antecedent is the following sentence ; cp. on ὅ ... δεινότατον 19. 33. — γάρ: force, see on 19. 12 (C) (1). — συντριηραρχῶν: in the last years of the Peloponnesian War, because of the long-continued demand for service and the decline in wealth, it became

necessary to assign two men to the burden that one had carried before. For the cost of the trierarchy see on 19. 42. — δοκιμασθῶσιν : see on § 9. — πράττεται : see L. & S. s.v. V. 2. Present tense : he is doing it now by trying to persuade the court to accept the accounting.

25. ᾿Αδρίαν: a notoriously dangerous voyage. Lysias says of a rascal at the Piraeus that his neighbors would rather take a voyage to the Adriatic than lend him money (Frag. 1. 4). — ταλάντοιν: i.e. with a cargo of that value. — ὅτε μὲν ἀπέστελλεν, ἐπειδὴ δὲ ἐσώθη: note ὅτε with the impf. for the contemporary, ἐπειδή with the aor. for the preliminary, act

παίδων ὁ κίνδυνος εἴη, ἐπειδὴ δὲ ἐσώθη καὶ ἐδιπλασί-
ασεν, αὐτοῦ τὴν ἐμπορίαν ἔφασκεν εἶναι. καίτοι εἰ
μὲν τὰς ζημίας τούτων ἀποδείξει, τὰ δὲ σωθέντα τῶν
χρημάτων αὐτὸς ἕξει, ὅποι μὲν ἀνήλωται τὰ χρήματα
195 οὐ χαλεπῶς εἰς τὸν λόγον ἐγγράψει, ῥᾳδίως δὲ ἐκ τῶν
26 ἀλλοτρίων αὐτὸς πλουτήσει. καθ' ἕκαστον μὲν οὖν,
ὦ ἄνδρες δικασταί, πολὺ ἂν ἔργον εἴη πρὸς ὑμᾶς
λογίζεσθαι· ἐπειδὴ δὲ μόλις παρ' αὐτοῦ παρέλαβον
τὰ γράμματα, μάρτυρας ἔχων ἠρώτων Ἀριστόδικον
200 τὸν ἀδελφὸν τὸν Ἀλέξιδος (αὐτὸς γὰρ ἐτύγχανε τετε-
λευτηκώς), εἰ ὁ λόγος αὐτῷ εἴη ὁ τῆς τριηραρχίας· ὁ
δὲ ἔφασκεν εἶναι, καὶ ἐλθόντες οἴκαδε ηὕρομεν Διογεί-
τονα τέτταρας καὶ εἴκοσι μνᾶς ἐκείνῳ συμβεβλημένον
27 εἰς τὴν τριηραρχίαν. οὗτος δὲ ἐπέδειξε δυοῖν δεούσας
205 πεντήκοντα μνᾶς ἀνηλωκέναι, ὥστε τούτοις λελογίσθαι
ὅσονπερ ὅλον τὸ ἀνάλωμα αὐτῷ γεγένηται. καίτοι τί
αὐτὸν οἴεσθε πεποιηκέναι περὶ ὧν αὐτῷ οὐδεὶς σύνοιδεν

(see on 12. 53). — τούτων : pred.
possess. — ὅποι : *under what head*
(in the account) as in § 20 ὅποι
τρέψειε τὰ χρήματα. — τὸν λόγον :
= τῷ λογισμῷ of § 19 and τὰ
γράμματα of § 26. — ἐγγράψει : its
object is the clause ὅποι . . . χρήματα.

26. καθ' ἕκαστον : cp. κατὰ μῆνα
§ 20. — πολὺ ἂν ἔργον εἴη . . .
λογίζεσθαι : cp. the rare, condensed
expression of § 11 πολλὰ ἂν εἴη
λέγειν.

27. ὅσονπερ : cp. on οἵτινες 12.
40. — περὶ ὧν αὐτῷ κτλ. : *as to*

those matters the knowledge of
which no one shares with him, but
which he handled all alone. The
object of σύνοιδεν is assimilated to
the case of its omitted antecedent
(gen. with περί), and the object
of διεχείριζεν is to be supplied from
ὧν. Immediately following is an
instance of the carrying forward
of the relative idea by the demonstrative,

ἃ δὲ ἑτέρων ἐπράχθη
καὶ οὐ χαλεπὸν ἦν
περὶ τούτων πυθέσθαι.

For the omission of the second
relative, or the substitution of a

ἀλλ' αὐτὸς μόνος διεχείριζεν, ὃς ἃ δι' ἑτέρων ἐπράχθη
καὶ οὐ χαλεπὸν ἦν περὶ τούτων πυθέσθαι, ἐτόλμησε
210 ψευσάμενος τέτταρσι καὶ εἴκοσι μναῖς τοὺς αὐτοῦ
θυγατριδοῦς ζημιῶσαι; Καί μοι ἀνάβητε τούτων μάρτυρες.

MΑΡΤΥΡΕΣ

28   Τῶν μὲν μαρτύρων ἀκηκόατε, ὦ ἄνδρες δικασταί·
ἐγὼ δ' ὅσα τελευτῶν ὡμολόγησεν ἔχειν αὐτὸς χρήματα,
215 ἑπτὰ τάλαντα καὶ τετταράκοντα μνᾶς, ἐκ τούτων αὐτῷ
λογιοῦμαι, πρόσοδον μὲν οὐδεμίαν ἀποφαίνων, ἀπὸ δὲ
τῶν ὑπαρχόντων ἀναλίσκων, καὶ θήσω ὅσον οὐδεὶς
πώποτ' ἐν τῇ πόλει, εἰς δύο παῖδας καὶ ἀδελφὴν καὶ
παιδαγωγὸν καὶ θεράπαιναν χιλίας δραχμὰς ἑκάστου
220 ἐνιαυτοῦ, μικρῷ ἔλαττον ἢ τρεῖς δραχμὰς τῆς ἡμέρας·

personal or demonstrative pronoun for 'it, see on 25. 11. — **δι' ἑτέρων** : see on διὰ πλήθους 12. 87.

28. ἀκηκόατε : tense, see on 12. 48. — **τελευτῶν** : cp. on § 20. — **ὡμολόγησεν** : see on § 20. — **πρόσο- δον, τῶν ὑπαρχόντων** : *interest, cap- ital* ; see on ὑπάρχει 12. 23. The estate would have yielded 12 per cent, enough to support the family and add a good sum to the capital yearly. — **θήσω** : cp. τίθησι § 21. — **παιδαγωγόν** : a family slave who cared for the boys at home and on their way to and from school ; see Gulick, p. 77. — **θεράπαιναν** : the sister's attendant. — **χιλίας δραχμάς** : this statement is of value in estimating the relative

cost of living in Athens and in modern cities. But in such esti- mates we must bear in mind the greater simplicity of dress, the small use of meat, and the low price of labor. (Cp. on § 23.) The eight years covered by this guardianship included six years of the war, culminating in actual famine before the surrender. The estimate is for the children of a rich family, and covers both food and clothing. Thirty years later we find the young Demosthenes with his mother and sister supported from the father's estate at a cost of 7 minae (= 700 dr.) per year (this probably included the board and clothing of personal servants).

29 ἐν ὀκτὼ αὗται ἔτεσι γίγνονται ὀκτακισχίλιαι δραχμαί,
καὶ ἀποδείκνυνται ἐξ τάλαντα περιόντα καὶ εἴκοσι
μναῖ. οὐ γὰρ ἂν δύναιτο ἀποδεῖξαι οὔθ᾽ ὑπὸ λῃστῶν
ἀπολωλεκὼς οὔτε ζημίαν εἰληφὼς οὔτε χρήσταις ἀπο-
225 δεδωκώς. . . .

29. **περιόντα**: in the absence of the full account (λογισμός) which was before the jury (§ 19) we can form no safe estimate of what surplus really should have been found. Cp. Introd. p. 285 N. 2.

The Speech on the Constitution

INTRODUCTION

THIS speech was written immediately after the return of the democratic exiles from the Piraeus, for a citizen to deliver in opposition to a motion that under the restored democracy the franchise be restricted to holders of real estate and to men of pure Athenian descent.[1]

By the amnesty effected under the mediation of the Spartan king, Pausanias, the two opposing parties were now reunited. The past was to be forgotten, the exiles restored to their homes, and the orderly life of the city taken up again. Pending the election of officers and the establishment of courts, a provisional administration was set up by the election of twenty men as a governing board, doubtless made up of ten from each party (Andoc. 1. 81).

The first question to be settled, before senators or other officers could be chosen or courts put into operation, was that of the franchise. Should citizenship with full political rights be open to all Athenian men as before the oligarchical revolution, or should it be restricted according to the understanding with Sparta the year before in connection with the surrender?[2]

[1] The first restriction only is mentioned by Dionysius in his introduction, but the second is implied in οὔτε γένει ἀπελαυνόμενος § 3 ; it was far less important than the first.

[2] Usener (*Jahrb.* 1873, p. 164 ff.) holds that the men of the lowest class were not admitted to the first deliberations after the Return, but that the restriction of the franchise which had been legally adopted in connection with the establishment of the Thirty was considered as still in force. He holds that the question now under discussion was that of the continuance of

It might well be presumed that the restoration of the demo-cratic constitution would be considered an affront to Sparta, and it is possible that the Spartans had made definite statements to this effect.[1] Moreover, the large body of conservatives who had, both in the revolution of 411 and in that of 404, sought to exclude the lowest class from political privileges, feared now more than ever to see the Demos brought back to power, embittered as the democratic exiles were by their sufferings and flushed with success. Who could guarantee the loyalty of the Demos to the terms of the amnesty, when once demagogue and sycophant should resume their trade?

This, too, seemed to be a good opportunity to clear the voting lists of many names of men of doubtful descent, who had been admitted to citizenship in recent years because of the great losses

this restriction, and that the assembly for which the speech of Lysias was written included only the men of the upper classes. Usener finds support for this view in the fact that the appeal in our speech is constantly to the men of property, and, by supplying πόλιν with τὴν ὑμετέραν, § 5, he obtains explicit confirmation of the statement that on their return the Demos did not take part in the administration (αὐτὸς δὲ ταύτης οὐκ ἐτόλμησε μετασχεῖν). Wilamo-witz (*Aristoteles u. Athen*, II, p. 225 ff.) finds confirmation of Usener's view in the statement of Aristotle (*Resp. Ath.* 39. 6) that under the amnesty the former officials of the city party were to give their accounting before the citizens whose names were on the assessors' lists (τοῖς τὰ τιμήματα παρεχομέ-νοις), *i.e.* the men of the upper classes ; from this he concludes that this body formed the citizen body during the interval between the Return and the settlement of the permanent form of government. But the very fact that the amnesty provides that only property holders shall audit the accounts of offi-cers of the city party implies that the government in general is to be in the hands of the whole people. Nor does the theory of the exclusion of the Thetes from the suffrage accord with the address of Thrasybulus immediately after the return, when he reminds the members of the city party that they are being handed over like muzzled dogs to the Demos (Xen. *Hell.* 2. 4. 41). In our speech of Lysias the appeal is certainly to the property holders, but that is natural in any case, for the result will turn on their action. For the position against Usener, see Blass, p. 449 ff. ; Meyer, *Forschungen zur alten Geschichte*, II, p. 177, n. 1.

[1] Cp. § 6.

of citizens by war, but who were really ineligible under the constitution. For, since the amendment of Pericles in 451/0 B.C., those who could not show pure Athenian descent through both parents had been by law excluded from citizenship. Not only was it thought wise now to clear the lists of such names, but it was evident that the practically obsolete law must be revived to guard against the incoming of many new applicants, sons of Athenians who had until recently lived among the tributary states of the empire. These citizens had married foreign wives, and now many of them with their families were returning to Athens, bringing with them the question of admitting their half-Athenian sons to citizenship.[1]

The two proposals were formally brought before the people by motion of Phormisius. He had been a well-known soldier in the war,[2] and was one of the leading supporters of Theramenes.[3] The death of his party chief and the suppression of the moderate aristocrats by Critias drove him over to the democrats, and he shared their exile and return.[4] It was natural that upon the reorganization of the democracy he should attempt to embody in the new constitution the principle for which Theramenes had always stood, a moderate limitation of the franchise. But his well-known record as a supporter of one faction of the oligarchs gave point to the charge that he was still an oligarch at heart, and had joined the democrats at the Piraeus only to secure his own safety (§ 2).[5]

[1] Schaefer, *Demosthenes*, I.² 139.

[2] Aristophanes makes sport of Phormisius's hairy face and military bearing (*Frogs*, 965 f., 405 B.C.); he calls him *a trumpeting-whiskered-lancer, a gnashing-pinebender*.

[3] Arist. *Resp. Ath.* 34. 3.   [4] § 2 of our speech, Dionysius, *Lysias*, § 32.

[5] Of the later fortunes of Phormisius we know only that he was a prominent member of an unsuccessful embassy to Susa just before the Peace of Antalcidas (the poet Plato, Πρέσβεις, Fr. 119–121, Kock), and that he in some way escaped the condemnation that befell a part of the embassy on their return (Dem. 19. 277), for we hear of him as one of the Athenians who in 379 gave active support to the Theban exiles in recovering their city from the Spartan garrison (Din. 1. 38).

To his proposal the democratic leaders of the Return were opposed. They insisted on the political rights of their poorer comrades, and some were ready even to grant citizenship to metics and slaves who had shared their dangers.

The outcome was the defeat of Phormisius's motion, and the reënactment of the old Solonian constitution as a temporary form of government. To a special commission, acting with the Senate, was intrusted the preparation and adoption of such amendments as they might judge to be necessary to adapt it to present conditions.[1] The conservatives were probably placated by the terms of the enactment, which read: ἔδοξε τῷ δήμῳ, Τεισαμενὸς εἶπε, πολιτεύεσθαι ᾿Αθηναίους κατὰ τὰ πάτρια, νόμοις δὲ χρῆσθαι τοῖς Σόλωνος, καὶ μέτροις καὶ σταθμοῖς, χρῆσθαι δὲ καὶ τοῖς Δράκοντος θεσμοῖς, οἷσπερ ἐχρώμεθα ἐν τῷ πρόσθεν χρόνῳ (Andoc. 1. 83). This, if taken literally, would mean that, while the franchise was to be open to all classes, and all would have seats on the juries, the other political privileges of the lower classes, which had grown into the constitution since Solon's time, would be cut off, and a really conservative democracy would result. This may have been the effect during the short time occupied by the Constitutional Commission in making the revision, but when their work was completed it was found that the Periclean type of democracy, and not the Solonian, was the result.

One part of Phormisius's proposal was, however, renewed in the same year, when Aristophon carried a motion that the sons of foreign mothers be excluded from the franchise; but this action was too sweeping, and it was soon so modified by the resolution of Nicomenes that the exclusion was not retroactive, but applied only to sons born after 403.[2]

Not content with defeating the essential provisions of Phormisius's motion, the democrats two years later carried a motion

[1] That our speech was not written for delivery before the commission is clear from the fact that the address is not to senators but to citizens (§§ 1, 3, 9, 11), and that the appeal is not to men acting for others, but for themselves.

[2] Schaefer, *Demosthenes*, I.[2] 138 ff.

of Thrasybulus that the franchise be extended to all who had
shared in the Return from the Piraeus.   But one of their own
leaders, Archinus, succeeded in annulling it in the courts as un-
constitutional.[1]   But, as a compromise, citizenship was granted to
the little group of foreigners who had stood with the first small
band of exiles at Phyle.[2]

COMMENTS ON ARGUMENT AND STYLE

This speech of Lysias is of especial interest as being his earliest
extant speech, and perhaps the first that he wrote for a client.
It is, moreover, the only extant speech of his composed for delivery before the Ecclesia.   We owe its preservation to Dionysius
of Halicarnassus, who incorporated it in his treatise on Lysias,[3] as
an example of his style.

It is generally assumed that the speech as preserved by Dionysius is only a fragment.   While it is complete in thought, and
while §§ 10–11 would form a fitting peroration, yet the speech

[1] See Introd. p. 21.

[2] A part of the original record of this act was discovered on the Acropolis
in 1884.   It contains also a mutilated list of the metics who received citizenship, a group of humble laboring men; among them are "Chaeredemus the
farmer, Leptines the cook, Demetrius the carpenter, Euphorion the muleteer,
Hegesias the gardener, Sosias the fuller," and others of like occupation, while
among these good Greek names stands Bendiphanes, a name to shock the
blue-blooded Athenian who should find it on the check-list of his tribe.   It is
probable that this decree was moved by Archinus, who was the mover of the
decree bestowing honors upon the citizens of the Phyle band (Aeschin. 3. 187,
190), and who would naturally, after defeating the more generous proposal
of Thrasybulus, be the man to present the alternative proposition.   The
decree for the metics of Phyle was passed in 401/0 (Koerte, *MAI.* XXV,
p. 394, against von Prott, *ibid.* p. 37) and its natural connection with the
motion of Thrasybulus warrants Meyer (*Gesch. d. Alt.* V. 222) in carrying that
motion over to the same year, against the corrupt account of the biographers
of Lysias, who place it immediately after the Return (ἐπ᾽ ἀναρχίας τῆς πρὸ
Εὐκλείδου, Ps.-Plut. 835 F).   For other considerations in favor of this date see
Meyer, *l.c.*

[3] See p. 285, n. 3.

seems too brief for the occasion. Neither of the two other speeches preserved by Dionysius is given in full, and it is probable that he took this part from the beginning of a longer speech. Appeals to members of the former city party and to the class in danger of disfranchisement may have followed.

The uncertainty as to the relation of the extant fragment to the whole speech makes it impossible to determine the relations of its subdivisions, or to judge of its effectiveness. The plan of this part is simple : to appeal to the great middle class, men who have shared in the exile and the Return, and to convince them that the loss of the support of the non-landholding citizens will be more dangerous to the restored democracy than the chance of offending Sparta by failing to meet her wishes as to the revision of the constitution. The event proved the soundness of the argument. Sparta did not interfere (see on § 6), and the democracy was soon called upon to take up arms again against the oligarchs at Eleusis.

In the composition of the speech two facts are significant : first, the meaning is not always clear. One must read and reread before being sure of the meaning of some sentences, and some are capable of widely differing interpretations ; much is left to be supplied between the lines. The brevity is like Lysias, but not the obscurity. Second, there is a marked rhetorical coloring in the whole. The tricks of the current rhetoric are conspicuous — repeated antithesis and balance of cola, the rhyming of successive cola, and play on the sound of words. We may probably see in these features evidence of immaturity in practical oratory. Up to this time Lysias had written only for exhibition and for hearers who cared more for novelty of expression than clearness of thought. The language of this first public speech is not clear enough for argument in the Ecclesia, and it has too many marks of the rhetorician to be put into the mouth of a client.

How soon and how thoroughly Lysias corrected both faults, we see in the speech against Diogiton (written a year or two later) and that for Mantitheus (some ten years later).

The more noteworthy rhetorical expressions are the following:

§ 4. ὧν ὑμεῖς ἀντεχόμενοι βεβαίως δημοκρατήσεσθε
τῶν δὲ ἐχθρῶν πλέον ἐπικρατήσετε
ὠφελιμώτεροι δὲ τοῖς συμμάχοις ἔσεσθε.

πολλοὺς μὲν αὐτῶν ἀποθανόντας
πολλοὺς δ᾽ ἐκ τῆς πόλεως ἐκπεσόντας.[1]

§ 5. οὐδὲ τοὺς λόγους πιστοτέρους τῶν ἔργων
οὐδὲ τὰ μέλλοντα τῶν γεγενημένων νομιεῖτε.

οἳ τῷ μὲν λόγῳ τῷ δήμῳ πολεμοῦσι
τῷ δὲ ἔργῳ τῶν ὑμετέρων ἐπιθυμοῦσιν.

§ 11. ὅτε μὲν ἐφεύγομεν ·
ἐμαχόμεθα Λακεδαιμονίοις
ἵνα κατέλθωμεν
κατελθόντες δὲ φευξόμεθα
ἵνα μὴ μαχώμεθα.

The last period is quoted in Aristotle, *Rhetoric*, 2. 23, as follows:

εἰ φεύγοντες μὲν ἐμαχόμεθα ὅπως κατέλθωμεν
κατελθόντες δὲ φευξόμεθα ὅπως μὴ μαχώμεθα.

The rhetoricians have evidently worked over the period to make it even more formal.   See App. § 57. 7.

[1] On the παρομοίωσις and ἐπαναφορά see App. § 57. 3, 5.

ΠΕΡΙ ΤΟΥ ΜΗ ΚΑΤΑΛΥΣΑΙ ΤΗΝ ΠΑΤΡΙΟΝ ΠΟΛΙΤΕΙΑΝ ΑΘΗΝΗΣΙ

1 Ὅτε ἐνομίζομεν, ὦ ἄνδρες Ἀθηναῖοι, τὰς γεγενημένας συμφορὰς ἱκανὰ μνημεῖα τῇ πόλει καταλελεῖφθαι,
ὥστε μηδ' ἂν τοὺς ἐπιγιγνομένους ἑτέρας πολιτείας ἐπιθυμεῖν, τότε δὴ οὗτοι τοὺς κακῶς πεπονθότας καὶ ἀμφο-
5 τέρων πεπειραμένους ἐξαπατῆσαι ζητοῦσι τοῖς αὐτοῖς
2 ψηφίσμασιν, οἷσπερ καὶ πρότερον δὶς ἤδη. καὶ τούτων μὲν οὐ θαυμάζω, ὑμῶν δὲ τῶν ἀκροωμένων, ὅτι
πάντων ἐστὲ ἐπιλησμονέστατοι ἢ πάσχειν ἑτοιμότατοι
κακῶς ὑπὸ τοιούτων ἀνδρῶν, οἳ τῇ μὲν τύχῃ τῶν Πει-

1. **ἄν**: see on 12. 1. — **πολιτείας**: *polity, form of government*;
cp. on § 3. — **δή**: force, see on 25.
9 (A). — **οὗτοι**: Phormisius and
his supporters; see Introd. p. 315.
— **ἀμφοτέρων**: both constitutions,
democratic and oligarchical. — **οἷσπερ**: see on οἵτινες 12. 40. — **καὶ
πρότερον**: for καί in comparisons
see on 19. 2 (C). — **δὶς ἤδη**: one
of the first steps in the institution
of the oligarchies of the Four
Hundred and of the Thirty was
the exclusion of the masses from
political rights.

2. **ὑμῶν**: the appeal throughout
the speech is to the members of
the upper classes. They form a
large majority of a full ecclesia,
and their vote will decide the
question. Some of them have
been supporters of the Thirty,
others have just returned with
Thrasybulus from exile. (On the
number of the Thetes see on § 4.)
— **Πειραιοῖ**: locative, HA. 220;
G. 296; B. 76 N.; Gl. 527. Cp.
on 12. 50. For the connection
of Phormisius with the party of
the Piraeus see Introd. p. 315.

10 ραιοῖ πραγμάτων μετέσχον, τῇ δὲ γνώμῃ τῶν ἐξ
ἄστεως. καίτοι τί ἔδει φεύγοντας κατελθεῖν, εἰ χειρο-
3 τονοῦντες ὑμᾶς αὐτοὺς καταδουλώσεσθε; ἐγὼ μὲν οὖν,
ὦ ἄνδρες Ἀθηναῖοι, οὔτε οὐσίᾳ τῆς πολιτείας οὔτε γένει
ἀπελαυνόμενος, ἀλλ' ἀμφότερα τῶν ἀντιλεγόντων πρό-
15 τερος ὤν, ἡγοῦμαι ταύτην μόνην σωτηρίαν εἶναι τῇ
πόλει, ἄπασιν Ἀθηναίοις τῆς πολιτείας μετεῖναι, ἐπεὶ
ὅτε καὶ τὰ τείχη καὶ τὰς ναῦς καὶ χρήματα καὶ συμμάχους ἐκεκτήμεθα, οὐχ ὅπως τινὰ Ἀθηναῖον ἀπώσομεν
διενοούμεθα, ἀλλὰ καὶ Εὐβοεῦσιν ἐπιγαμίαν ἐποιού-
20 μεθα· νῦν δὲ καὶ τοὺς ὑπάρχοντας πολίτας ἀπελῶμεν;
4 οὔκ, ἐὰν ἔμοιγε πείθησθε, οὐδὲ μετὰ τῶν τειχῶν καὶ
ταῦτα ἡμῶν αὐτῶν περιαιρησόμεθα, ὁπλίτας πολλοὺς

— κατελθεῖν: force, see on 16. 4.
— καταδουλώσεσθε : future tense
of an action intended, proposed
(= μέλλω with infin.). See on
εἰ πείσει 24. 13.

3. πολιτείας: *citizenship*. See
Crit. Note. — γένει : see Introd.
p. 314 f. — Εὐβοεῦσιν ἐπιγαμίαν : as
a mark of especial gratitude or
friendship Athens sometimes con-
ferred upon individual foreigners,
and even upon cities, the privileges of intermarriage (ἐπιγαμία),
acquisition of real estate in Attica
(ἔγκτησις γῆς καὶ οἰκίας, cp. p. 10,
N. 1), and exemption from the
metics' tax (ἀτέλεια, cp. p. 9).
Close connection with Euboea was
always of the utmost importance
to Athens. The ἐπιγαμία not

only bound the states together,
but enabled the Athenian cle-
ruchs, who were settled there in
large numbers, to intermarry with
their neighbors. The sons of
such marriage had full Athenian
citizenship. — ὑπάρχοντας : force,
see on ὑπάρχει 12. 23.

4. μετὰ τῶν τειχῶν : the Long
Walls had been torn down the
year before under the terms of
the surrender. For μετά see on
19. 14. — περιαιρησόμεθα : Lysias
assumes that if the masses are
disfranchised they can no longer
be called out with the citizen
troops. Deprived of their rights
in the state, they could not be
trusted to fight for it. — ὁπλίτας,
ἱππέας, τοξότας : the regular hop-

καὶ ἱππέας καὶ τοξότας· ὧν ὑμεῖς ἀντεχόμενοι βεβαίως
δημοκρατήσεσθε, τῶν δὲ ἐχθρῶν πλέον ἐπικρατήσετε,
25 ὠφελιμώτεροι δὲ τοῖς συμμάχοις ἔσεσθε· ἐπίστασθε
γὰρ τὰ ἐν ταῖς ἐφ᾽ ἡμῶν ὀλιγαρχίαις γεγενημένα καὶ
οὐ τοὺς γῆν κεκτημένους ἔχοντας τὴν πόλιν, ἀλλὰ
πολλοὺς μὲν αὐτῶν ἀποθανόντας, πολλοὺς δ᾽ ἐκ τῆς

lites and horsemen were of the higher property classes, and would not be affected by this change. But under the pressure of the long war the state had come to make considerable use of the Thetes beyond their regular service as rowers of the triremes (see on 16. 14). With the annihilation of the navy the work as rowers had ceased, so Lysias naturally speaks only of their other service. Perhaps he has in mind also the fact that many members of the classes that regularly furnished hoplites and horsemen are now by loss of property reduced to the class of Thetes. Dionysius says (*Lysias*, § 32) that about 5000 men would have been excluded from citizenship by this motion. The number of Thetes at the beginning of the Peloponnesian War is estimated at about 20,000 (Meyer, *Forschungen zur alten Geschichte* II. 168 ff.). The greatest losses of life in the war fell upon them through their service in the fleet. — δημοκρατήσε-

σθε: the oligarchy had but just been put down ; some of its leaders and many of its supporters were now settled at Eleusis ; the future of the democracy was still matter of anxiety (cp. 12. 35, spoken soon after). — τῶν ἐχθρῶν : the exiled oligarchs. — τοῖς συμμάχοις : the Spartans. One of the conditions of surrender was alliance with Sparta (τὸν αὐτὸν ἐχθρὸν καὶ φίλον νομίζοντας Λακεδαιμονίοις ἔπεσθαι καὶ κατὰ γῆν καὶ κατὰ θάλατταν ὅποι ἂν ἡγῶνται Xen. *Hell*. 2. 2. 20). It had been urged that the proposed measure must be passed to please the Spartans. Lysias says that a united people will be a more useful ally. — ἐφ᾽ ἡμῶν : see on 12. 17. — οὐ τοὺς γῆν κτλ. : 'the advocates of the measure urge you to intrust your welfare to the holders of real estate ; but experience has proved that against the oligarchs, your past and present enemies, the landholders are powerless ; it is only the strength of the Demos that can protect you.'

5 πόλεως ἐκπεσόντας, οὓς ὁ δῆμος καταγαγὼν ὑμῖν
30 μὲν τὴν ὑμετέραν ἀπέδωκεν, αὐτὸς δὲ ταύτης οὐκ ἐτόλμησε μετασχεῖν. ὥστ᾽, ἐὰν ἔμοιγε πείθησθε, οὐ τοὺς
εὐεργέτας, καθὸ δύνασθε, τῆς πατρίδος ἀποστερήσετε,
οὐδὲ τοὺς λόγους πιστοτέρους τῶν ἔργων οὐδὲ τὰ μέλλοντα τῶν γεγενημένων νομιεῖτε, ἄλλως τε καὶ μεμνη-
35 μένοι τῶν περὶ τῆς ὀλιγαρχίας μαχομένων, οἳ τῷ μὲν
λόγῳ τῷ δήμῳ πολεμοῦσι, τῷ δὲ ἔργῳ τῶν ὑμετέρων
ἐπιθυμοῦσιν· ἅπερ κτήσονται, ὅταν ὑμᾶς ἐρήμους συμμάχων λάβωσιν.

6 Εἶτα τοιούτων ἡμῖν ὑπαρχόντων ἐρωτῶσι τίς ἔσται
40 σωτηρία τῇ πόλει, εἰ μὴ ποιήσομεν ἃ Λακεδαιμόνιοι

5. **ἐκπεσόντας**: see on *ἐξέπεσον*
12. 57.— **καταγαγών**: cp. on *κατελθεῖν* 16. 4.— **τὴν ὑμετέραν**: *sc.*
γῆν. Much property had been
confiscated by the Thirty, much
abandoned in the flight of the
owners. The restored Demos put
the owners back into possession,
and made no attempt at a distribution of land among themselves. For a different interpretation, by supplying *πόλιν* with *τὴν*
ὑμετέραν (from *ἔχοντας τὴν πόλιν*
above) see Introd. p. 313 N. 2.—
αὐτὸς δὲ . . . οὐκ ἐτόλμησε: *while*
themselves not venturing. An
English speaker would use the
logical subordination for this
clause; see on 12. 47.— **τὰ μέλλοντα**: *sc.* πιστότερα. — **ἐπιθυμοῦσιν**: the facts justify this charge.

The Thirty had not been content
with robbing metics, but had made
themselves feared and hated by
the citizen property owners.—
ὑμᾶς: the men of the upper classes,
the holders of property.

6. **εἶτα**: see on 12. 26 (C).— **τοιούτων ἡμῖν ὑπαρχόντων**: force, see
on *ὑπάρχει* 12. 23.— **ποιήσομεν**:
'monitory,' see on *ἀφήσουσιν* 12.
35. — **κελεύουσιν**: see Introd. p.
314. The event showed that the
Spartan insistence upon dictating
in the internal affairs of Athens
had been due to the personal influence of Lysander. With his
fall from power this policy was
abandoned, and the restored Athenian democracy was left undis-
turbed. — **τούτους εἰπεῖν ἀξιῶ**: *I call
upon them to tell.* τούτους, the

κελεύουσιν; ἐγὼ δὲ τούτους εἰπεῖν ἀξιῶ, τίς τῷ πλήθει
περιγενήσεται, εἰ ποιήσομεν ἃ ἐκεῖνοι προστάττουσιν;
εἰ δὲ μή, πολὺ κάλλιον μαχομένοις ἀποθνήσκειν ἢ
7 φανερῶς ἡμῶν αὐτῶν θάνατον καταψηφίσασθαι. ἡγοῦ-
45 μαι γάρ, ἐὰν μὲν πείσω, ἀμφοτέροις κοινὸν εἶναι τὸν
κίνδυνον· ὁρῶ δὲ καὶ Ἀργείους καὶ Μαντινέας τὴν
αὐτὴν ἔχοντας γνώμην τὴν αὐτῶν οἰκοῦντας, τοὺς μὲν

regular word for the opponents in
court or debate ; see on τούτου 12.
81. — τίς : sc. σωτηρία. — τῷ πλήθει : force, see on 12. 42. — ἐκεῖνοι :
the Spartans. — εἰ δὲ μή κτλ. :
'*but if they cannot tell that, it is
much better for us to die fighting
than to condemn ourselves to certain death.*'

7. ἡγοῦμαι κτλ. : the proposal
of Phormisius involves extreme
danger to one part (τῷ πλήθει)
of the state ; the speaker admits
that his own policy also involves
danger, but he holds that it is the
more honorable course (κάλλιον),
because both parties in the state
(ἀμφοτέροις) will share the danger.
— ὁρῶ δέ κτλ. : he has said, "It is
better to die fighting"; but now
he shows that, after all, there is
no likelihood of things coming
to that pass. The example of the
Argives and Mantineans shows
that a people weaker than Sparta
may venture to administer their
own affairs, knowing that Sparta
will not take the risk of losing
what she has in the hopeless

attempt to enslave a determined
people. Argos never followed the
lead of Sparta except under compulsion, or by the action of her
own oligarchical faction, which
sought supremacy by Spartan support. In 418 Argos was forced
into alliance with Sparta, and an
oligarchical government was set
up. But in the next year a successful democratic reaction carried
the state over to the Athenian
alliance, and with more or less of
vigor it supported Athens throughout the war. Mantinea, which
had joined Argos against Sparta,
was like her forced by the events
of 418 to return to the Spartan
alliance, and remained nominally
under Sparta's lead throughout
the war. But she maintained her
democratic constitution, and gave
only indifferent support to the
Spartans. — τὴν αὐτὴν ἔχοντας γνώμην : '*although maintaining the
same policy* that I advise,' *i.e.*
that of refusing to abandon democratic government at Spartan dictation. — τὴν αὐτῶν οἰκοῦντας :

ὁμόρους ὄντας Λακεδαιμονίοις, τοὺς δὲ ἐγγὺς οἰκοῦντας,
49 καὶ τοὺς μὲν οὐδὲν ἡμῶν πλείους, τοὺς δὲ οὐδὲ τρισχι-
8 λίους ὄντας. ἴσασι γὰρ ὅτι, κἂν πολλάκις εἰς τὴν τούτων ἐμβάλλωσι, πολλάκις αὐτοῖς ἀπαντήσονται ὅπλα
λαβόντες, ὥστε οὐ καλὸς αὐτοῖς ὁ κίνδυνος δοκεῖ εἶναι,
ἐὰν μὲν νικήσωσι, τούτους μὴ καταδουλώσασθαί γε,
ἐὰν δὲ ἡττηθῶσι, σφᾶς αὐτοὺς τῶν ὑπαρχόντων ἀγαθῶν
55 ἀποστερῆσαι· ὅσῳ δ' ἂν ἄμεινον πράττωσι, τοσούτῳ
9 ἧττον ἐπιθυμοῦσι κινδυνεύειν. εἴχομεν δέ, ὦ ἄνδρες
Ἀθηναῖοι, καὶ ἡμεῖς ταύτην τὴν γνώμην, ὅτε τῶν Ἑλλήνων ἤρχομεν, καὶ ἐδοκοῦμεν καλῶς βουλεύεσθαι περι-
ορῶντες μὲν τὴν χώραν τεμνομένην, οὐ νομίζοντες δὲ
60 χρῆναι περὶ αὐτῆς διαμάχεσθαι· ἄξιον γὰρ ἦν ὀλίγων
ἀμελοῦντας πολλῶν ἀγαθῶν φείσασθαι. νῦν δέ, ἐπεὶ
ἐκείνων μὲν ἁπάντων μάχῃ ἐστερήμεθα, ἡ δὲ πατρὶς

holding their own territory, i.e. against any attempt of Sparta to dislodge them as dangerous neighbors.

8. ἴσασι: sc. Λακεδαιμόνιοι, see Crit. Note. — **κἂν πολλάκις κτλ.**: even if they invade them again and again. In fact, they have ceased invading. For καὶ εἰ see on 16. 2. — **πολλάκις, πολλάκις**: on the ἐπαναφορά see App. § 57. 5. — **τούτων**: the Argives and Mantineans.— **ὥστε . . . δοκεῖ εἶναι**: so that the risk seems to them (the Spartans) to be inglorious. If the Spartans conquer, they know that they will not succeed in enslaving the Argives and Mantineans, for

both peoples always rise up again after their defeats, as stubborn as ever. It is not worth while, then, for the Spartans to risk serious losses of their own for the slight gain of an incomplete subjugation of their neighbors. — **τῶν ὑπαρχόντων**: see on ὑπάρχει 12. 23.

9. τὴν χώραν τεμνομένην: according to the advice of Pericles at the opening of the Peloponnesian War, to allow the Spartans to ravage Attica rather than risk defeat on land, where Athens was weak, and to consider the maintenance of her empire by sea so great an issue as to make the losses of orchards and houses

ἡμῖν λέλειπται, ἴσμεν ὅτι ὁ κίνδυνος οὗτος μόνος ἔχει
10 τὰς ἐλπίδας τῆς σωτηρίας. ἀλλὰ γὰρ χρὴ ἀναμνη-
65 σθέντας ὅτι ἤδη καὶ ἑτέροις ἀδικουμένοις βοηθήσαντες
ἐν τῇ ἀλλοτρίᾳ πολλὰ τρόπαια τῶν πολεμίων ἐστή-
σαμεν, ἄνδρας ἀγαθοὺς περὶ τῆς πατρίδος καὶ ἡμῶν
αὐτῶν γίγνεσθαι, πιστεύοντας μὲν τοῖς θεοῖς ἐλπίζον-
69 τας δ' ἔτι τὸ δίκαιον μετὰ τῶν ἀδικουμένων ἔσεσθαι.
11 δεινὸν γὰρ ἂν εἴη, ὦ ἄνδρες Ἀθηναῖοι, εἰ, ὅτε μὲν
ἐφεύγομεν, ἐμαχόμεθα Λακεδαιμονίοις, ἵνα κατέλθωμεν,
κατελθόντες δὲ φευξόμεθα, ἵνα μὴ μαχώμεθα. οὐκ
οὖν αἰσχρὸν εἰ εἰς τοῦτο κακίας ἥξομεν, ὥστε οἱ μὲν
πρόγονοι καὶ ὑπὲρ τῆς τῶν ἄλλων ἐλευθερίας διεκινδύ-
75 νευον, ὑμεῖς δὲ οὐδὲ ὑπὲρ τῆς ὑμετέρας αὐτῶν τολμᾶτε
πολεμεῖν; . . .

trifling in comparison (Thuc. 2. 62). — **ὁ κίνδυνος οὗτος** : *this risk:* 'only by taking the risk of ignoring Sparta's dictation, and keeping a united people, can we hope to maintain ourselves against the attempts of the exiled oligarchs.'

10. **ἀλλὰ γάρ**: force, see on 12. 40. — **ἀλλοτρίᾳ**: *sc. γῇ.* — **ἐστή- σαμεν**: empirical aorist, see on

ᾐσθόμην 16. 20. — **τὸ δίκαιον . . . ἔσεσθαι**: *justice will be with the victims of injustice*. But the text is doubtful, see Crit. Note.

11. **ὥστε οἱ μὲν πρόγονοι**: *that, while our fathers*. On the Greek preference for coördination of antithetic clauses cp. on § 5 and on 12. 47. For the rhetorical ἐπανα- στροφή and κύκλος in this section see App. § 57. 7, 8.

Appendix

I. CHRONOLOGICAL OUTLINE

[In this chronological outline the sole purpose is to furnish a table of reference for the events involved in the speeches of Lysias that are contained in this volume. Some events that are otherwise of little importance are included because necessary to an understanding of the speeches.

For the dating of the speeches, see Blass, p. 647. For Speeches I, IV, V, and XXIII not even approximate dates can be given. For the outline of events from 413 to 404 B.C. I have followed Busolt, III, ii, p. xxxi ff. For the period after 404, Meyer and Beloch. For 410–403 cp. Boerner, *De Rebus a Graecis inde ab Anno 410 usque ad Annum 403 A. Chr. N. gestis Quaestiones Historicae*, Göttingen, 1894. For 408–380 cp. Judeich, *Kleinasiatische Studien*, Marburg, 1892.]

I. Events before the Revolution of the Four Hundred.

413 B.C. *September*. Defeat of the Athenian expedition to Sicily.

Appointment of ten Πρόβουλοι by the Athenians as an extraordinary Committee of Safety, taking over a part of the work of the democratic Senate.

412 Rapid defection of Athenian allies. Sparta assured of active support of Syracuse and of Persia. Seat of war transferred to subject states of the Aegean.

Lysias and Polemarchus are banished from Thurii.

November–December. The Athenian Pisander heads a movement among trierarchs of the fleet to win the Persian support away from Sparta through intercession of Alcibiades. This service of Alcibiades is conditioned on a change in Athenian government by limiting the democracy.

December. Pisander is sent to Athens with a committee from the leaders of the fleet to propose the change in constitution.

411 *January*. The Ecclesia reluctantly approves the plan, and appoints Pisander and ten others to treat with Alcibiades and Tissaphernes.

Pisander perfects the organization of the oligarchical clubs in the city to prepare for the revolution.

Pisander and the other commissioners return to the fleet. They fail in their negotiations with Alcibiades and Tissaphernes. Unable to retreat safely from the revolutionary movement, Pisander with five of the commissioners returns to Athens to complete the work.

May. The oligarchical clubs with Lysander finish their preparations.

June. The revolution is consummated by the establishment of the provisional government of the Four Hundred in place of the democratic Senate, the restriction of the franchise to a body of not less than five thousand property holders, and the adoption of temporary and permanent constitutions. The Four Hundred are for the time being in absolute control.

Lysias and Polemarchus return to Athens.

II. The Rule of the Four Hundred, June to September, 411 B.C.

The men of the fleet at Samos refuse to submit to the Four Hundred, organize themselves as the sovereign democracy, elect generals of their own, and call Alcibiades to the chief command.

The Four Hundred negotiate for peace with Sparta, and plan for the complete control of the harbor.

Growing opposition between the extreme oligarchs, led by Antiphon, and the moderate oligarchs, led by Aristocrates and Theramenes. The moderates demand that the five thousand citizens be designated. They hope for reconciliation with Alcibiades and the men of the fleet.

September. The approach of a Lacedaemonian fleet and the loss of Euboea bring the reaction to a head. The people, led by Theramenes, depose the Four Hundred and place the government in the hands of 'all citizens who can furnish arms.' This moderate restriction of the franchise is known to be acceptable to Alcibiades and the fleet.

III. The Rule of the Moderate Aristocracy, led by Theramenes, 411–410 B.C.

The new government carries out the reconciliation with Alcibiades and the fleet.

Some of the extreme oligarchs flee to the Spartan camp. Antiphon and two others are executed as traitors, Theramenes taking an active part in their prosecution.

Many less prominent oligarchs are punished with **fine or** otherwise.

The new administration is strengthened by a naval victory off Cynossema on the Hellespont (*Sept.*) and another at Abydus (*Nov.*).

410 *Early Spring.* Alcibiades wins the great victory of Cyzicus, capturing the whole Peloponnesian fleet. Regains control of the grain route.

May–June. Thrasyllus sails from Athens with reënforcements of ships and men for Alcibiades; he suffers a severe defeat in an attack on Ephesus.[1]

The moderate restrictions of the compromise constitution are removed, and democracy is fully restored without violence (before the beginning of the new civil year, July 13).

IV. The Rule of the Radical Democracy after the First Restoration, 410–404 B.C.

Cleophon, the popular leader, provides for the masses by daily donations and by employment on public works.

The "sycophants" resume their trade, and vigorous attacks are made in the courts against the lesser supporters of the Four Hundred.

409 Beginning of friendly relations with Evagoras, tyrant of Salamis in Cyprus.

Winter (409/8). Alcibiades takes Byzantium.

408 *June.* Alcibiades returns to Athens. He is received with extraordinary honors, and is given practical control of the administration.

407 The Athenian defeat at Notium leads to the deposition of Alcibiades. Conon succeeds him in chief command.

406 *June.* Great efforts to equip a fleet to rescue Conon, blockaded in the harbor of Mytilene.

July–August. Athens wins a victory at Arginusae, but loses some four thousand men by the storm.

Autumn. Condemnation and execution of the generals of Arginusae.

---

[1] Grote and Beloch place the expedition of Thrasyllus in 409 and the return of Alcibiades in 407. Beloch places the battle of Notium in 406. For a summary of this much-disputed question, see Busolt, III. ii. 1529.

Peace proposals of the Spartans are rejected under influence of Cleophon.

405 *September*.   Lysander seizes the Athenian fleet at Aegospotami.
Conon takes refuge with Evagoras.

Late Autumn.   Beginning of the siege of Athens.

Ambassadors sent to Agis to treat for peace.   Then, by his direction, sent to Lacedaemonia.   Their proposals refused, and other conditions laid down.

404 *January*.   Theramenes sent to Lysander to learn the real purpose of Sparta.   He uses the opportunity to mature plans for Lysander's help in overthrowing the democracy and restoring the banished oligarchs.   He stays with Lysander three months.

The aristocrats come into control, and secure the death of Cleophon.

April.   Theramenes, at the head of an embassy of ten, is sent to Sparta with full powers to negotiate peace.

Lysander takes possession of Athens, and begins the demolition of the walls (about April 25).

Lysander besieges Samos.

The two aristocratic factions, led respectively by Critias and Theramenes, together mature plans for the overthrow of the democracy.

Early Summer (?).   The oligarchy of the Thirty is set up by the help of Lysander.[1]

V. The Rule of the Thirty and their Successors, 404–403 B.C.

1. ADMINISTRATION OF THE THIRTY.

The Thirty receive a Spartan garrison under Callibius.[2]

Execution of prominent democratic leaders.

Death of Polemarchus and flight of Lysias.

Three thousand admitted to nominal political rights.   All others are disarmed.

Growing disagreement between the extreme and moderate factions of the Thirty.   Theramenes is put to death by influence of Critias.

All men outside the three thousand are forced to leave the city.

[1] For the month, see Meyer, V. 19 Anm.   So Beloch, II. 109 Anm.; Boerner (p. 71), Sept.; Judeich (p. 28 Anm.), late summer.

[2] On the order of events, see Meyer, V. 23 Anm.

Early Winter. Thrasybulus with about seventy exiles seizes Phyle.

403 The Thirty provide a place of ultimate refuge for themselves by seizing Eleusis. They put to death three hundred citizens of Eleusis and Salamis.

Early Spring. Thrasybulus with his force, now increased to one thousand, moves down to Munychia. He repels the attack of the Thirty. Critias is killed in battle.

The three thousand depose the Thirty, nearly all of whom retire to Eleusis. A Board of Ten succeeds them.

2. ADMINISTRATION OF THE TEN.

The Ten prosecute the war against the exiled democrats, instead of seeking reconciliation. They coöperate with the Thirty at Eleusis in securing help from Sparta. Sparta grants a loan of 100 t., with which Lysander raises a mercenary force at Eleusis. A Spartan fleet blockades the Piraeus.

Pausanias follows with Spartan troops, and effects a reconciliation between the oligarchs and the exiles.[1]

October 4. Formal entry of the democratic exiles into the city.
Lysias returns with the exiles.

VI. The Rule of the Democracy after the Second Restoration, 403–.

1. TEMPORARY ADMINISTRATION BY A COMMISSION OF TWENTY.

Rejection of motion of Phormisius to limit the franchise to holders of real estate.

Lysias, Speech XXXIV, *On the Constitution.*

Reëstablishment of Senate and courts. Arrangements for the revision of the Solonian Constitution.

Lysias, Speech XII, *Against Eratosthenes* (possibly a little later than this).

2. ADMINISTRATION BY THE REGULAR OFFICERS OF THE DEMOCRACY.

402 (?) Lysias, Speech XXIV, *For the Cripple* (some time after 403).

Lysias, Speech XXXII, *Against Diogiton*, and XXI, *Defense on Charge of Bribery* (402/1).

---

[1] Aristotle (*Resp. Ath.* 38. 3) says that this reconciliation took place under a second Board of Ten. Xenophon says nothing of a second Board. For the argument in favor of Xenophon's account, see Meyer, V. 39 Anm.

401 Expedition of Cyrus.

> The exiled oligarchs at Eleusis surrender.

> Failure of Thrasybulus's proposal to extend the franchise to all who helped in the Return. *Lysias thus fails to secure Athenian citizenship.* (See p. 317.)

400 Sparta enters upon war with Persia for control of the Greek cities of the eastern Aegean.

> Lysias, Speech XXV, *Defense of a Supporter of the Thirty* (*c.* 400).

399 Trial and execution of Socrates.

> Lysias, Speech XXX, *Against Nicomachus* (399/8).

398 Lysias, Speech XXXI, *Against Philon* (*c.* 398). Speech XIII, *Against Agoratus* (398 or later).

397 Conon appointed admiral of a Persian fleet.

> Lysias, Speech XVII, *On the Property of Eraton.*

396 Lysias, Speech XVIII, *On the Confiscation of the Property of Eucrates* (*c.* 396).

395 Beginning of war between Sparta and Thebes. Athenian troops help win Theban victory at Haliartus. Euboea, Corinth, and Argos join the anti-Spartan alliance. This begins the CORINTHIAN WAR (395–386).

> Lysias, Speech VII, *On the Sacred Olive* (395 or later). Speech XIV, *Against Alcibiades* (395/4).

394 Beginning of rebuilding of the Piraeus walls.

> *July.* Athenians and allies defeated at Nemea.

> Conon and Pharnabazus win decisive naval victory for Persia against Sparta at Cnidus. Greeks of the eastern Aegean revolt from Sparta.

> Agesilaus wins indecisive victory at Coronea.

393 Conon and Pharnabazus cruise along the coast of Peloponnesus; join delegates of the Athenian alliance at Corinth.

> Conon comes to Athens with his fleet, and helps complete the walls. Great honors to Conon and his patron, Evagoras.

> Conon tries through Aristophanes and Eunomus to turn Dionysius from support of Sparta by proposing a marriage connection with Evagoras.

> Sparta tries through Antalcidas to turn Persia from the support of Athens.

> Lysias, Speech XVI, *For Mantitheus* (394–388).

392 Conon arrested at Sardis by the Persian satrap. Escapes to Cyprus, where he dies not long after.

> Lysias, Speech III, *Against Simon* (*c.* 392).

390 Evagoras appeals to Athens for help against Persia. Aristophanes is sent to complete negotiations. Philocrates sails for Cyprus with ten ships; fleet is captured by the Spartans.

389 Thrasybulus regains control of Thracian coast and the Hellespont, and of many coast and island cities.

> Lysias, Speech XXVII, *Against Epicrates* (*c.* 389).

388 Popular feeling turns against Thrasybulus and his colleagues. Suspicion that they are enriching themselves. Recall is ordered, but Thrasybulus dies before it can be executed.[1]

> Spartan Antalcidas wins active support of Dionysius, and goes to Persia to negotiate for withdrawal of Persian support from Athens.

> Lysias, Speech XXXIII, *The Olympic Speech*. Speeches XXVIII[2] and XXIX, *Against Ergocles, Against Philocrates* (comrades of Thrasybulus).

387 Ill success of Athenian fleets on the Hellespont and on the home coast.

> High price of grain at Athens because of uncertainty of control of Hellespont.

> Second expedition to help Evagoras; Chabrias in command.

> Spartans gain control of the Hellespont, and are even raiding the Attic coast.

> Lysias, Speech XIX, *On the Property of Aristophanes* (387 or early in 386).

386 Lysias, Speech XXII, *Against the Grain Dealers*.

> *Winter or Spring.* Final ratification of the Peace of Antalcidas by the Greek States.[3]

384/3 Lysias, Speech X, *Against Theomnestus*.

382 Outbreak of War between Sparta and Thebes.

> Lysias, Speech XXVI, *Against Evander*.

380 The last known speech of Lysias, *For Pherenicus*.

> *The death of Lysias is probably to be placed soon after this.*

---

[1] Beloch, *Attische Politik*, 355.

[2] Blass, 389 B.C. The date depends on that of the recall of Thrasybulus.

[3] On the date, see Swoboda, *MAI.* VII. 180 ff.

II. ATHENIAN LEGAL PROCEDURE

[The following account is in general based on Lipsius's revision of Meier and
Schömann, *Der Attische Process*, and his revision of Schömann, *Griechische Alter-
thümer*. The conditions described are those of the early part of the fourth century B.C., the time of Lysias's professional activity.]

CONSTITUTION OF THE COURTS

1. Athenian legal practice divided cases into three classes: (1) cases
of homicide, (2) public cases other than those of homicide, (3) private
cases. The separation of homicide from other cases was a survival of
the ancient view of bloodshed as primarily a sin against the gods, to be
atoned for both by criminal penalties and ceremonial cleansing.

2. The ancient court of Areopagus, composed of the ex-archons,
sitting under the presidency of the Ἄρχων βασιλεύς, the religious head
of the state, had sole jurisdiction in cases of premeditated homicide.[1]
The other forms of homicide were tried by the Ephetae, a special court
of fifty-one members selected by lot from the noblest families, sitting
under the same presidency.

3. Public cases (δίκαι δημόσιαι), other than those of homicide, included all cases in which the issue directly concerned the state, either
alone or in common with an individual. Here belonged prosecutions
for such offenses against the state as treason, bribery, desertion, im-
piety, and suits involving claims to public property; here, too, fell the
numerous suits to test the legality of acts of the Ecclesia (γραφαὶ παρανόμων), the examination before a jury required of every public officer
before taking up his office (δοκιμασία), and his examination at the close
of his term of office (εὔθυναι). Public cases were tried before the
heliastic courts.

4. Private cases were those in which the issue directly concerned
individuals only, the state having no other interest than the preservation of the general order and the protection of individual rights.
Here belonged suits concerning contracts and property; all cases
concerning wills and inheritances, prosecution for damage in case of
assault or slander, and for restitution in case of theft or fraud. Private
cases came before the same courts as public cases, but the preliminary
steps were different.[2]

---

[1] Arson also fell under their jurisdiction.   [2] See §§ 27–29.

5. The presidency of the various courts involved the reception of the complaints and documents necessary to the institution of a suit, the conduct of preliminary hearings, the presidency over the court at the time of the jury trial, and provision for the execution of the penalty in case of conviction. This presidency was assigned upon the principle that every official of the state should hold the presidency of the court in any case arising within the domain of his own office. Thus a case involving the claims of the state against a trierarch would be tried under the presidency of the Naval Board; cases arising from family relations were tried under the presidency of the First Archon; the Ἄρχων πολέμαρχος presided in cases concerning foreigners; the six lower archons, the Θεσμοθέται, presided in a large body of cases which did not fall within the field of other magistrates or boards.

6. All cases except those of homicide were tried before large juries, made up from a body of citizens drawn by lot from voluntary candidates for jury service for the year. The total number of these annual jurymen was, in theory, 6000, enough to provide ten sections of 500 men each, and to leave 1000 men to fill vacancies. But with the loss of population caused by the Peloponnesian War it became impossible to keep the number full. Under these conditions any citizen who chose to offer his name was sure of a place; he might even be enrolled as a regular member of one section and a substitute member of one or more sections besides, thus helping to fill out the scant number of jurymen, and earning his juror's wages on days when his service was not required in his own section.

7. Any citizen over thirty years of age, who was possessed of full civic rights, was eligible for jury service. The jurymen all took a solemn oath at the beginning of their year of office, and were then liable to be called on at any time for service in court. In the time of Lysias there was not such a pressure of legal business as in the Periclean period, when the Athenian courts were crowded with cases from the league cities, but a juror was probably in actual service more than half of the time. He might serve on year after year, and thus the service might become the regular employment of men who were quite content with small pay for light work, and of old men whose days of physical labor were over. From the time of Pericles the pay of the juryman was an obol for each day of actual service, until Cleon raised it to three obols, about the wages of an unskilled laborer.

8. The whole body of jurymen was divided into ten sections, and on the morning of each court day the Thesmothetae drew lots to determine what sections, or parts of sections, should sit for that day in the court rooms in different parts of the city. The number of men assigned to any case was determined by the nature of the case. A less important private suit had the smallest jury, 200 men; other private suits required 400; the ordinary number for public suits was 500, but in more important cases two or more sections were united, so that we read of juries of 1000, 1500, 2000, 2500,[1] and even of a case where the whole panel of 6000 sat as one jury.[2]

Procedure in Public Suits

9. The institution of a private suit depended, of course, upon the initiative of one of the parties directly concerned. In public cases suit might be instituted in two ways. First, it was the duty of any public officer who became cognizant of a violation of law in the department under his control to prosecute the offender.[3] Secondly, any private citizen holding full civil rights was equally at liberty to bring any public case before the courts and to prosecute it to the end. To guard against malicious or hasty prosecution, however, it was provided that one who brought such a suit and then presented so weak a case that he failed to receive one fifth of the votes of the jury, must pay a fine of 1000 dr., and was thereafter disqualified from bringing a similar suit (partial $\dot{a}\tau\iota\mu\acute{\iota}a$).[4]

10. As the first step in the introduction of a public suit, the plaintiff had to summon the defendant to appear at a stated time before the magistrate under whose jurisdiction the trial would fall. This summons was served in person and before witnesses ($\kappa\lambda\eta\tau\hat{\eta}\rho\epsilon\varsigma$).[5]

[1] To the round numbers given one man was added in each case to avoid a tie, making juries of 201, 501, *etc.*   [2] Andoc. I. 17.

[3] When a notorious crime had been committed, the Ecclesia sometimes appointed a special commission to investigate the case and prosecute the offender in the courts. There were no standing prosecuting attorneys as in our system.

[4] In many private suits the plaintiff who did not win one fifth of the votes had to pay to the defendant one sixth of the sum for which he sued ($\dot{\epsilon}\pi\omega\beta\epsilon\lambda\acute{\iota}a$, *i.e.* one obol in every drachma).

[5] It was not customary to arrest the accused and confine him while awaiting trial, except in a special class of crimes, prosecuted by special and more summary procedures, called $\dot{a}\pi\alpha\gamma\omega\gamma\acute{\eta}$, $\dot{\epsilon}\phi\acute{\eta}\gamma\eta\sigma\iota\varsigma$, and $\check{\epsilon}\nu\delta\epsilon\iota\xi\iota\varsigma$; even then the defendant was released if he could furnish sufficient security for his appearance in court.

11. The second step was the appearance of the two parties before the magistrate on the day designated in the summons. If the magistrate accepted the case as falling within his jurisdiction, he received from the plaintiff a written statement of the charge, and from the defendant his written denial, and then appointed a day for a preliminary hearing of the case. He then published the accusation by posting it in a public place.

12. The third step was the preliminary hearing (ἀνάκρισις) before the same magistrate. The defendant might now take exception to the jurisdiction of the magistrate or to the technical form of the accusation, and in some cases this exception had to be tried as a separate case in court before the original case could proceed. If the defendant accepted the jurisdiction of the magistrate and the form of the charge, each party was required to take oath, the plaintiff to the truth of his accusation, the defendant to the truth of his denial. Each was also required to produce all the evidence which he wished to use at the coming jury trial. This evidence might include copies of the laws involved, documents of all kinds, such as contracts, wills, letters, and the testimony of witnesses. This testimony might consist of attested affidavits of witnesses necessarily absent, or of the statements of witnesses present at the hearing; but in the latter case the testimony was usually written down before the hearing, so that at the time of the hearing the witnesses had only to assent to the record of their testimony as correct. Usually each party administered an oath to the witnesses of the other party.

13. Many cases involved the testimony of slaves. This evidence was held valid only when given under torture, on the supposition that the desire for release from the torture on the one side would counterbalance the natural desire of the slave to testify according to his master's orders on the other. A party to a suit either challenged his opponent to submit his slaves or offered his own slaves. This testimony was taken in the presence of witnesses, usually previous to the ἀνάκρισις, and presented to the magistrate in writing with the other documents. The torture was conducted by the litigants themselves or by men agreed upon by them, or in some cases by public slaves. The point to which the torture should be carried was previously agreed upon by the litigants.

14. At the conclusion of the ἀνάκρισις the magistrate sealed up all documents, including all the testimony, in two urns, one for each side, and kept them in his custody until the trial. No other testimony could be presented at the coming trial.[1]

15. The fourth step in the case was the trial before a jury, under the presidency of the magistrate before whom the preliminary hearing had been held. On the morning of the appointed day the Thesmothetae, meeting at the central court house, assigned by lot to this magistrate a court house, and a section of jurymen sufficient for the hearing of the appointed case.

16. The court room had wooden seats for the jurors, provision for listeners outside the railing which shut in the jurors' seats, and four platforms. The presiding magistrate occupied one platform, a second served as speaker's platform, while plaintiff and defendant had each a platform for his own seat and those of his immediate friends.

17. Proceedings opened with libation and prayer by the herald of the court. The clerk then read the charge as sworn to by the plaintiff at the ἀνάκρισις, and the corresponding answer of the defendant. The plaintiff then took the speaker's platform and proceeded to argue his case. The law required every man to deliver his plea in person. If he had not the ability to compose a speech for himself, he could employ a professional speech writer (λογογράφος) to write it for him ; he then committed the speech to memory and delivered it as his own. By the time of Lysias's professional activity such employment of a λογογράφος had become the common custom. Further, if no objection was raised by the jurors, the speaker might, at the conclusion of his own speech, call upon one or more of his friends to address the jury in his behalf. These συνήγοροι might present aspects of the case not taken up by the first speaker, and might be men of greater ability as speakers ; but they made it clear to the jury that they were impelled entirely by personal friendship to the one party, or personal hostility to the other ; a speech by a hired advocate was not tolerated. But very often these speeches of the συνήγοροι were also written by professional speech writers and delivered from memory.

18. At the conclusion of the speech or speeches for the prosecution the defendant followed under the same conditions. No opportunity for speeches in rebuttal was given except in the case of certain private suits.

[1] A rare exception was where at the trial one party challenged the other, in the presence of the jury, to present some piece of evidence, and the challenge was accepted.

19. The whole trial was concluded in one day, and in certain classes of important cases a fixed time, measured by the clepsydra, was at the beginning of the trial assigned to each side.

20. As a plea proceeded, the speaker called upon the clerk of the court from time to time to read the documents filed at the $\dot{a}\nu\dot{a}\kappa\rho\iota\sigma\iota\varsigma$.[1] When testimony was read, the witness mounted the speaker's $\beta\hat{\eta}\mu a$ and assented to the testimony as correct, — in some cases he read it aloud himself, — but he was not allowed to give new testimony, nor might he be cross-questioned. Each litigant might, however, call his opponent to the platform and cross-question him in the presence of the jury, and the law required him to answer. In the hands of a trained speaker this became a powerful weapon.[2]

21. It was customary for the defendant to make an earnest appeal, in the last part of his speech, to the emotions of the jurors, by reciting the sufferings that threatened him, and by presenting in court dependent relatives, — wife, children, aged parents, — who would suffer with him. Another form of supplication was the appeal to the presence in court of prominent and popular public men, as indorsing the speaker's plea.

22. At the close of the speeches there was no exposition of the law by the presiding magistrate, nor was there any opportunity for the jurymen to consult one with another, but the herald of the court called upon them to come forward to the platform immediately and deposit their votes.

23. On the platform stood two urns, one of bronze, the other of wood. Each juryman received two small bronze disks ($\psi\hat{\eta}\phi o\iota$), one pierced by a solid axis, the other by a hollow one. The disk with solid axis was a vote for the defendant, the other for the plaintiff. As each juryman passed before the two urns, he threw into the bronze urn the disk which represented his vote, and threw the discarded vote into the wooden urn. As one held the disks with the ends of the axis between thumb and finger, it was impossible for even the nearest bystander to see which vote he put into the bronze urn; the secrecy of the vote was thus fully protected. The voting finished, the bronze urn was emptied

---

[1] When $\lambda o\gamma o\gamma\rho\dot{a}\phi o\iota$ published their speeches as literary productions they usually omitted these documents, merely indicating the points at which they were presented.

[2] So Lysias, 12. 25, 22. 5. Cp. Socrates's cross-questioning of Meletus in Plato's *Apology*, 24 c ff.

upon a stone table, the solid and perforated votes sorted and counted, and the result announced by the presiding magistrate, and recorded by the clerk.

24. In many cases the penalty to follow conviction was prescribed by law (ἀγῶνες ἀτίμητοι); but in other cases (ἀγῶνες τιμητοί), if the jury voted for conviction, they then listened to a further argument from the prosecution, proposing a certain penalty, and then to one from the defense, proposing a milder one. They then had to vote again to determine which of the two penalties proposed should be inflicted.

25. From a verdict once rendered by a heliastic court there was no appeal; there was no provision for arguing "exceptions" taken during the trial, and usually no possibility of securing a second trial.[1]

26. The penalty was immediately executed: if death, by the Eleven (the chief constables); if loss of property, by the civil officers of the deme or by the Eleven; if a fine, by the collectors of the treasury to which the fine would be paid. Imprisonment was not used as a penalty, but only as a means for securing the presence of a criminal in court in certain cases (see § 10, n. 5), or as temporary confinement until the payment of a fine, or until the execution of a man condemned to death.

Procedure in Private Suits

27. The early stages of a private suit differed in important particulars from those just described as belonging to public suits. Private suits as a whole fell under the jurisdiction of a board of forty justices, selected by lot and serving in groups of four, one group for each tribe.[2]

28. The first step in a private suit was, like that in a public suit, the formal summons of the defendant; but the second step carried the case, not to a civil magistrate, but to the group of four justices who represented the tribe of the defendant. In petty cases, involving not

[1] A defeated litigant might, however, bring suit on the ground that false testimony had been given against him.

[2] Several large classes of private cases, in which it was necessary to expedite proceedings, were grouped as "month cases" (δίκαι ἔμμηνοι), under the jurisdiction of a separate board of five εἰσαγωγεῖς, who carried them through the jury courts to a decision within a period of one month. In cases involving not more than ten drachmas the εἰσαγωγεῖς themselves gave final decision, without a jury trial. These cases were for the most part concerned with business and banking.

more than ten drachmas, the decision of the four justices was final. If the sum was greater, they turned the case over to a public arbitrator (διαιτητής).

29. The justices selected this arbitrator by lot from a large board of public arbitrators, who were liable to service for the year. This board consisted of all citizens who were in their sixtieth year, and who had thus just completed the forty-one years in which a citizen was liable to military service.[1] To one of these elderly men the four justices turned over the private case, and after one or more formal hearings, at which testimony for both sides was produced, he gave his decision. If both parties accepted this decision, the case was ended. But either party had the right of appeal to a jury court. In case of such appeal the arbitrator sealed up all documents, including copies of all the evidence, in two urns, and handed them over to the board of four justices from whom he had received the case.[2] This board now resumed charge of the case, received from the Thesmothetae a jury for its hearing, and presided at the trial, taking in every respect the place held by the magistrate in a public suit.

30. In comparing the Athenian legal system with our own, we are first of all impressed with the absence of a trained judiciary, standing between the executive officers and the citizen. The men who conducted all hearings and presided at all jury trials were ordinary citizens, selected usually by lot, and having no professional knowledge of the law. Their short term of office precluded the practical knowledge that might have come by experience. The control exercised by our judges — men of thorough legal learning and years of experience in the courts, and holding their office for a long term — was entirely unknown to the

[1] The names of these men for any year were readily obtainable from the citizen rolls. The young men who reached their majority in any year were enrolled as one group, forming a standing group for military purposes. The men of such a group all completed their last year of liability to military service together, and together passed on as the board of public arbitrators for the ensuing year. The total number, as well as the proportion from any one tribe, would, of course, vary from year to year. For the year 325/4 B.C. we have a list of one hundred and three names of arbitrators, "crowned" by the people. See Sandys on Aristotle, *Resp. Ath.* 53. 4.

[2] The hearing before the arbitrator in a private suit thus became in case of appeal what the ἀνάκρισις was in a public suit.

Athenian system. There was no impartial presiding judge to expound the law and to explain to the jury the bearing of facts on technical points. The jury were at the mercy of the shrewd pleas of the speech writers.

31. Nor was there, as in our system, the possibility of appeal in the larger cases from the verdict of the jury court to the decision of a body of expert and impartial judges. At no stage could the honest litigant depend upon the protection given by legal knowledge.

32. Nor was the composition of the jury itself such as to inspire great respect for its decisions. Its large size did guard against the danger of individual bribery, but it gave to the body the faults and dangers inherent in any large assembly. This was especially true in public cases, where not less than five hundred men sat as one jury. In such a body the feeling of individual responsibility is weakened, and the contagious emotions of the crowd have full sway. But this was not the worst. The Athenian jury was far from being representative of the best intelligence and character of the city. Service was voluntary, and the pay was that of ordinary unskilled labor. The inevitable result was that the annual jury panel was filled up with men to whom the day offered no more rewarding occupation — the small politicians, the idle, the poor and enfeebled old men. The sturdy farmers from the country could not afford to take up such service, still less the successful men of the city demes. And there was no possibility of bettering this in any individual case. The more critical the suit, the larger the crowd that was called in to decide it. In our own system a great constitutional case comes before a board of expert justices, qualified by the ripest legal experience and the highest character. In Athens such a case would have been judged by increasing an incompetent jury of five hundred by a thousand or two thousand men of no greater wisdom or experience. To appreciate conditions in Athens we have only to imagine all the legal business of Boston or Chicago settled by jury courts made up by lot from native-born citizens, offering themselves for service at a dollar and a half a day, and presided over by men from the various executive boards of the city.

33. The lack of judicial control and the low type of jury service had its inevitable effect on the style of pleading followed by the λογο-γράφοι. It was useless to attempt any argument that involved long and close reasoning, or minute and careful attention to legal provisions. The argument that served best with such a court was the one that most flattered their self-esteem, most shrewdly appealed to their prejudices, and most vigorously stirred their sympathies and passions. The profession of law was, in the time of Lysias, gradually developing out of that of the rhetorician; even in the next generation rhetorical skill formed a larger part of the equipment of the legal speech writer than knowledge of the law. Some men there were who were learned in the law, but the mass of the λογογράφοι were rather rhetoricians than lawyers.

34. Such a system of courts furnished a rich field for the "sycophants." When one of these professional haranguers, trained in the plausible rhetorical art, popular with the masses, and skilled in moving their emotions, threatened a quiet, law-abiding, wealthy citizen with a lawsuit, the citizen might well think twice before deciding to trust to the protection of the courts; to buy off the prosecutor was the simpler and safer way.

35. We must remember also that the Athenian jury courts had the widest possible jurisdiction. Through a γραφὴ παρανόμων the validity of every resolution of Senate and Ecclesia might be submitted to a jury. Every official had to pass his approval (δοκιμασία) in a jury court before entering upon office, and his record as an official was reviewed by another jury at the close of the year (εὔθυναι). The jury system was rightly looked upon as the very heart of the democratic constitution. Here the sovereign people exercised their real power, and here they displayed their real weakness.

36. The Athenian legal system shows endless ingenuity in all the petty details, — the complicated allotment of jurors to their sections and court rooms, the orderly and secret ballots, the distribution of cases among magistrates, — but its fundamental principle, that voluntary, underpaid, and unskilled courts could safely be intrusted with the greatest public and private interests, was a mistake. It is not strange that from such an Athenian system the Roman and the modern world, while inheriting magnificent specimens of legal rhetoric, received no speeches which are of permanent value as legal arguments, and no commanding legal precedents.

III. RHETORICAL TERMS

A. The Three Types of Prose Composition

37. I. ὁ ἁδρὸς χαρακτήρ, *genus grande atque robustum,* The Grand Style. Thucydides.

II. ὁ ἰσχνὸς χαρακτήρ, *genus subtile,* The Plain Style. Lysias.

III. ὁ μέσος χαρακτήρ, *genus medium,* The Intermediate Style (Mixed Style). Thrasymachus, Isocrates, Plato.

The Greek rhetoricians, beginning probably with Antisthenes, a contemporary of Lysias,[1] distinguished three great types, χαρακτῆρες, of prose composition.[2]

38. They found in Thucydides the perfection of the grand style. Dionysius thus sums up his characteristics:[3] "In fine, there are four 'instruments,' so to say, of the style of Thucydides — the artificial character of the vocabulary, the variety of the constructions, the roughness of the harmony, the speed of the narrative. Its 'colours' are solidity, pungency, condensation, austerity, gravity, terrible vehemence, and, above all, his power of stirring the emotions."

39. Lysias was the representative of the plain style. Its basis was the adaptation of the language of daily life to literary effects. The master of this style depends upon common words, avoiding archaic and poetic diction; he refrains from the formation of new compounds

---

[1] Volkmann (*Rhetorik der Griechen und Römer,* 532 ff.) traces the development of the theories and classification of "Styles" in the Greek and Roman schools. He shows that the division into three styles was the original one, and that other divisions were modifications of it.

[2] Dionysius uses χαρακτῆρες as his precise technical term; but in discussing each χαρακτήρ, *style,* he often uses for it the more general term λέξις, *language.* Jebb's note, *Attic Orators,* I. 21, which says that the three λέξεις distinguished in Dionysius's essay on Demosthenes, cc. 1–3, refer "to the choice of words" is not justified. In those chapters λέξις is used for the more precise χαρακτῆρες; that it is not limited to the "choice of words" appears in the subsequent chapters; *e.g.* the λέξις of Isocrates it is said (*Demosthenes,* c. 4) that it borrows Gorgias's antitheses and pairs of equal cola, gives excessive attention to rhythm and the avoidance of hiatus; and strives at unbroken periodic flow. All of these things are beyond the mere choice of words. For the relation of the three ἁρμονίαι of Jebb's note to the χαρακτῆρες, see Volkmann, 545–7.

[3] Dionysius, *Second Letter to Ammaeus,* 793, Roberts's translation.

and from the use of metaphor and simile; he perfects a simple and yet strong and rounded sentence structure, and his language flows on smoothly and rapidly, without appearance of effort for rhythmical effect.

40. Isocrates was the representative of the third style, the intermediate type. His style showed a union of the best qualities of the other two.[1] He has the purity and precision of diction of the plain style, and for the most part he avoids metaphorical language. But with the simplicity and persuasiveness of the plain style he combines the dignity and grandeur and eloquence of the grand style.

41. So long as Thucydides, Lysias, and Isocrates were the greatest of prose writers these three " styles " served the purpose of classification; but when the critics were confronted with the problem of defining and classifying the oratory of Demosthenes, they saw the inadequacy of the old formulae. Demosthenes could be classed neither with Thucydides nor Lysias nor Isocrates. If he were placed with Isocrates as a representative of the intermediate style, the term would become so inclusive as to break down by its vagueness, and he could certainly be placed with neither of the extremes. The critics solved this problem of classification in two ways: some, like Demetrius,[2] added a fourth style, χαρακτὴρ δεινός, *the powerful style*. This new "style" was a recognition of the fact that the real characteristic of Demosthenes's oratory was not any mingling of grand and simple language, but a great *power* which moved men. Other critics, like Dionysius, made no attempt to remodel the old system of classification, or to find a place for Demosthenes within it. They preferred rather to treat the style of Demosthenes as something outside and above the three older types; a style which gathered up into itself the virtues of all, and so was superior to all, a δεινότης, *power*, of which the three χαρακτῆρες became the instruments.[3]

B. Running Style and Periodic Style

42. I. ἡ εἰρομένη λέξις.

II. ἡ κατεστραμμένη λέξις = ἡ ἐν περιόδοις.

Thrasymachus, a contemporary of Lysias,[4] was the first to teach

[1] Dionysius, *Demosthenes*, c. 4.   [2] Περὶ ἑρμηνείας, §§ 36, 240 ff.

[3] Dionysius's whole essay on Demosthenes is founded on this idea. For the whole discussion as outlined above, see Volkmann, 537 ff.

[4] See Introd. p. 16 f.

the distinction between the loose, running form of speech, and the compact, periodic form, and he first developed the periodic form as a distinct artistic type.[1] None of the definitions of Thrasymachus have come down to us, but Aristotle in the next generation gives in his *Rhetoric* (3. 9) a discussion of the periodic style, which probably represents the developed theory of Thrasymachus, and which has remained the fundamental exposition of periodic theory for both ancient and modern times.[2] Aristotle calls the running style ἡ εἰρομένη λέξις, *the strung style*. The separate thoughts are strung along one after another like beads ; the first gives no suggestion that the second is coming, nor the second that a third is to follow ; the series may stop at any point, or it may go on indefinitely.

43. Good examples of the running style, λέξις εἰρομένη, are the following :

12. 9 ὁ δ' ἔφασκεν

εἰ πολλὰ εἴη.

εἶπον οὖν ὅτι τάλαντον ἀργυρίου ἕτοιμος εἴην δοῦναι ·

ὁ δ' ὡμολόγησε ταῦτα ποιήσειν.

He said yes,

if it was a large sum.

I said therefore that I was ready to give a talent of silver.

And he agreed to do it.

12. 14 ὁ δ' ὑπέσχετο ταῦτα ποιήσειν.

ἐδόκει δ' αὐτῷ βέλτιον εἶναι πρὸς Θέογνιν μνησθῆναι ·

ἡγεῖτο γὰρ ἅπαν ποιήσειν αὐτόν

εἴ τις ἀργύριον διδοίη.

[1] Writers before Thrasymachus had used periodic structure freely, but Thrasymachus was the first to make it a matter of conscious study. Here, as in almost all matters of rhetoric, we must distinguish between the forms which the practical speakers instinctively shaped for themselves, and the names and theories which the rhetoricians afterward applied to them. The testimony as to Thrasymachus is that of Suidas, *s.v.* Θρασύμαχος, and of Theophrastus, cited by Dionysius, *Lysias*, c. 6.

[2] The rhetorical treatise Περὶ Ἑρμηνείας, which bears the name of Demetrius, but is of unknown authorship, presents the Aristotelian theory as still further developed by the later rhetoricians. Roberts's edition (*Demetrius on Style*, Cambridge, 1902), with its admirable translation, commentary, and glossary of technical terms, makes this treatise available as the best starting point for the study of the theory of Greek prose style.

And he promised to do this.
  But it seemed to him to be better to speak to Theognis,
    for he thought he would do anything,
    if one should give him money.

In these passages we have a complete thought at the end of each
clause, and nothing suggests that another clause is to follow, nor when
we reach the end of the passage is there anything to give the feeling
that the separate thoughts have now rounded out one larger, compre-
hensive idea. It is to be noted that the running style is not made up
simply of a succession of "and" clauses; the second passage above
shows how subordinate clauses, like those of cause or condition, may
fit into the running style by being placed after the principal clause of
the sentence.

44. In the periodic style, λέξις κατεστραμμένη, the separate thoughts
are so drawn together and compacted that they form parts of larger
expressions, each group gathering the separate parts into a rounded,
definite whole. As we hear the first thought, we anticipate another to
correspond to it, or to complete its meaning; we cannot dismiss the
first until the second and all that follow have been taken up with it;
and when we hear the last, we have the feeling that the whole thought
is now rounded out and complete. Such an expression the rhetoricians
call a *period*, and its constituent parts — often, but not always, identical
with the clauses of a sentence — they call *cola*.

45. Typical periods are the following:

> 12. 7 ἀποκτιννύναι μὲν γὰρ ἀνθρώπους περὶ οὐδενὸς ἡγοῦντο
>   λαμβάνειν δὲ χρήματα περὶ πολλοῦ ἐποιοῦντο.
>   *To kill men they regarded as naught,*
>   *but to get money they held as of great importance.*

The μέν in the first colon (with the emphatic ἀποκτιννύναι) leads us to
expect a colon to balance it;[1] we foresee the antithesis, and only when
we have heard the corresponding member do we feel that the thought
is rounded out. The first colon is like one arc of a circle, which
implies one or more other arcs; or, to use the simile that underlies
the·Greek names, the first member is like the section of the race course
out to the turning post; this section implies and demands the corre-

---

[1] Like the periodic effect of μέν . . . δέ is that of οὔτε . . . οὔτε, and the
other correlative particles. Cp. 12. 4 μήτε εἰς κτλ.

sponding section (κῶλον), from the post back to the starting point, to complete the full circuit (περί-οδος).[1]

Antithesis of cola is the foundation of a large proportion of the more studied periods in Lysias. The earliest writers, especially Antiphon, had reveled in antitheses; the other school, the Gorgian, unlike them in many respects, had carried antithetic structure even further. Lysias, even in his plainest style, followed the custom of his time, and made frequent use of antithetic periods. His more elevated passages are full of them.

46. But a second type of period rests upon mere parallelism of cola. When successive cola are parallel both in form and thought, we feel, as the series proceeds, that each is part of a larger unity, and so receive, at least in some degree, the effect of a period. Such a period is less perfect, for often we do not at the end of each colon feel that the thought is incomplete and so demand another colon to round it out; but the group as a whole does give the impression of periodic unity. Such a period we have in 12. 21 :

οὗτοι γὰρ

πολλοὺς μὲν τῶν πολιτῶν εἰς τοὺς πολεμίους ἐξήλασαν
πολλοὺς δ' ἀδίκως ἀποκτείναντες ἀτάφους ἐποίησαν
πολλοὺς δ' ἐπιτίμους ὄντας ἀτίμους κατέστησαν
πολλῶν δὲ θυγατέρας μελλούσας ἐκδίδοσθαι ἐκώλυσαν.

For they drove many of the citizens into hostile lands,
and many they unjustly killed and robbed of funeral rites,
and many who had been citizens they deprived of citizenship,
and the daughters of many they prevented as they were on the point
of marriage.

In the English we lose much of the periodic effect in losing the similarity of sound at the beginning and end of the cola, which in the Greek added to the unity produced by the parallelism of thought and construction, and by the uniform length of the cola.

47. A third basis of periodic structure is the impression of unity produced by expressing the subordinate thoughts first, in subordinate construction, and holding back the main thought till the last. The mind is thus held intent; the subordinate thought cannot be dismissed till one hears the main thought which puts it in its right relation.

[1] Cp. Demetrius, c. 11.

When the main thought does come, it gives an impression of completion and a feeling of satisfaction ; the circle is complete, the runner
has rounded his course and is back at the goal.[1]   For this principle we
may conveniently use the term *sensus suspensio*.[2]

48. We have an example of *sensus suspensio* in the following
period (25. 18) :

> εἰ δὲ οἴεσθε χρῆναι
> οὓς ἐκεῖνοι παρέλιπον ἀδικοῦντες
> ὑμεῖς ἀπολέσαι .
> οὐδεὶς τῶν πολιτῶν ὑπολειφθήσεται.
>
> *But if you think it right*
> *that those whom they forebore to wrong*
> *be destroyed at your hands*
> *no citizen will be left.*

The first three cola prepare the way for the fourth, and have value only
as they contribute to its force.

49. This form of sentence structure is, of course, common in all
writers.   Wherever the protasis stands first, or subordinate acts are
expressed by participles before the main verb, or by preliminary subordinate constructions of any form, we have *sensus suspensio*.

50. But often such expressions are periodic in form only.   The
real test of periodic structure in this type lies in the degree to which
the preliminary cola contribute to the effect of the final one, and so

---

[1] Herbert Spencer, in his essay on the *Philosophy of Style*, gives a discriminating discussion of the relation of such structure to lucidity.   But
lucidity is only one of several aims in periodic structure.

[2] Aristotle holds that there are periods composed of a single colon
(*Rhetoric*, 3. 9. 5).   Such a period he calls ἀφελής.   He probably had in mind
the case of a single colon of considerable length, based on *sensus suspensio*
of words.   Aristotle does not recognize the type of period that is based on
sensus suspensio of cola, for he divides all periods of more than one colon
into λέξις διῃρημένη and λέξις ἀντικειμένη, that is, periods based on parallelism
and those based on antithesis.   We do not know whether any rhetorician in
the time of Lysias had recognized the fact of *sensus suspensio* as a basis of
periodic structure.   In the matured rhetoric of Demetrius it is fully recognized (Περὶ ἑρμηνείας, c. 10).   In antithetic structure the basis of periodic
effect is really a *sensus suspensio*, but it is convenient to distinguish it from
that which comes from placing subordinate cola before principal ones.

unite with it in one larger thought. A sentence like the following has periodic form, but is not in the full sense a period:

12. 97 ὅσοι δὲ τὸν θάνατον διέφυγον
    πολλαχοῦ κινδυνεύσαντες
    καὶ εἰς πολλὰς πόλεις πλανηθέντες
    καὶ πανταχόθεν ἐκκηρυττόμενοι
    ἐνδεεῖς ὄντες τῶν ἐπιτηδείων
  οἱ μὲν ἐν πολεμίᾳ τῇ πατρίδι τοὺς παῖδας καταλιπόντες
  οἱ δ' ἐν ξένῃ γῇ
    πολλῶν ἐναντιουμένων
ἤλθετε εἰς τὸν Πειραιᾶ.

  And so many of you as escaped death
    after manifold dangers
    and after wanderings to many cities
    and rejection from all
    in want of food
  some leaving your children in your own land turned hostile
  others in a foreign land
    against the opposition of many
came to the Piraeus.

So far as the effect of the final colon is concerned, the long sentence might equally well have been broken up into several short sentences. Moreover, the final colon is not strong or emphatic enough to carry the weight of the long-suspended thought.

51. Yet even this purely formal type of period has value, particularly in narrative. Instead of stringing along one detail after another, it gathers them into groups, giving compactness and rounded form. Admirable periods of this type are found in XVI. 13–16.

52. The length of a period was closely limited by the Greek rhetoricians. Aristotle did not recognize a period as of more than two cola.[1] Demetrius limited the cola to four.[2] The Roman theorists enlarged the number. Quintilian says (9. 4. 125): Habet periodus membra minimum duo. Medius numerus videntur quattuor, sed recipit frequenter et plura. The Greek orators seem not to have troubled themselves with any of these limitations as to number of cola in a period. They wrote as freely as do modern authors, and produced large, strong

---

[1] κῶλον δ' ἐστὶ τὸ ἕτερον μόριον ταύτης (sc. τῆς περιόδου) *Rhet.* 3. 9. 5.

[2] Περὶ ἑρμηνείας, c. 16.

units by the combination of many cola. Neither they nor their critics would have named these 'periods,' but such sentences have the unity of thought and the rounded form that are the essentials of periodic structure. Modern students of their works may wisely ignore the arbitrary limitation of number of cola, and treat these larger combinations as true periods.[1]

53. Modern rhetoricians assume that a 'period' will make a complete sentence. No such idea prevailed with the Greeks; they saw a period wherever there was unity of thought and form in a group of cola; the group might be a pair of cola in the midst of a long sentence; again, a sentence might contain several periods together with non-periodic clauses, or be made up of a group of periods.

54. The following examples show how the true period may lie within the longer sentence:

12. 7 ἔδοξεν οὖν αὐτοῖς δέκα συλλαβεῖν
    τούτων δὲ δύο πένητας
      ἵνα αὐτοῖς ᾖ πρὸς τοὺς ἄλλους ἀπολογία
        ὡς ‖ οὐ χρημάτων ἕνεκα ταῦτα πέπρακται ‖
          ‖ ἀλλὰ συμφέροντα τῇ πολιτείᾳ γεγένηται ‖
          ὥσπερ τι τῶν ἄλλων εὐλόγως πεποιηκότες.

The sentence as a whole is of the running type, but a clear, true period is embedded in it:

12. 33 ‖ οὐ γὰρ μόνον ἡμῖν παρεῖναι οὐκ ἐξῆν ‖
    ‖ ἀλλ᾽ οὐδὲ παρ᾽ αὐτοῖς εἶναι ‖
      ὥστ᾽ ἐπὶ τούτοις ἐστί
    ‖ πάντα τὰ κακὰ εἰργασμένοις τὴν πόλιν ‖
    ‖ πάντα τἀγαθὰ περὶ αὐτῶν λέγειν. ‖

[1] The reason for the refusal of the Greek rhetoricians to use the term 'period' of a large group of cola lay in the feeling that the unity which is the foundation of the period was marred when too much was demanded either of the breath of the speaker or the attention of the hearer. The feeling was a true one. Gildersleeve (A. J. P. 24. 102) quotes the following from James Russell Lowell: "If I have attained to any clearness of style, I think it is partly due to my having had to lecture twenty years as a professor at Harvard. It was always present to my consciousness that whatever I said must be understood at once by my hearers or never. Out of this, I, almost without knowing it, formulated the rule that every sentence must be clear in itself and never too long to be carried, without risk of losing its balance, on a single breath of the speaker."

Here two antithetic periods are linked by a single clause in one grammatical sentence.[1]

C. RHETORICAL FIGURES

55. The Greek rhetoricians from Theophrastus on[2] distinguished two groups of rhetorical " figures," σχήματα λέξεως and σχήματα διανοίας.

56. I. Σχήματα λέξεως, *figures of speech*, modifications of speech for rhetorical effect.

57. (*a*) *Figures connected with balance of cola.*

1. **ἀντίθεσις** *antithesis*.[3] The fondness for antithesis, already marked in the earlier literature, reached its height in the rhetorical work of Gorgias and his pupils. As compared with them, Lysias is moderate in its use. Yet we find it everywhere in his works, and often manifestly the result of studied art. He sometimes uses it with great effect, as in 12. 39 (see p. 53). Cp. 12. 32 f. ; 12. 93 ; 24. 16–18 ; 25. 18.

2. **παρίσωσις**, precise or approximate equality of cola as measured by number of syllables.[4]

---

[1] Aristotle's theory of the 'period' was faulty in that it restricted it to the two types of the antithetic and the parallel structure. But the modern rhetoricians have gone to the other extreme in making the *sensus suspensio* the only basis of the period. From that error it has resulted that they speak of a period as being always a full sentence. They have lost sight of the fact that the unity of form and thought that makes a period may be quite independent of the unity of thought that makes a sentence. The error is already embodied in Whately's definition (*Elements of Rhetoric*, 3. 2. 12), although in his examples he gives due attention to periods based on antithesis. We should obtain a better theory of the rhetorical period by returning to the sound doctrine of Demetrius, modifying it only by removing the restriction of four cola. We should then treat the period as something quite independent of the sentence (though often coinciding with it), and should recognize as the three fundamental types those based on antithesis, parallelism, and *sensus suspensio*.

[2] Theophrastus (372–287 B.C.) was Aristotle's successor in the Peripatetic School.

[3] Aristotle, *Rhetoric*, 3. 9. 7–9.

[4] Aristotle, *Rhetoric*, 3. 9. 9 παρίσωσις δ' ἐὰν ἴσα τὰ κῶλα. Cp. Anaximenes, c. 27. Demetrius (Περὶ ἑρμηνείας, c. 25) calls this ἰσόκωλον. Some rhetoricians used ἰσόκωλον of precise equality, and παρίσωσις of approximate equality. See Volkmann, p. 482.

Cp. 12. 4 ὥστε |μήτε εἰς τοὺς ἄλλους ἐξαμαρτάνειν
|μήτε ὑπὸ τῶν ἄλλων ἀδικεῖσθαι.
12. 7 ὡς οὐ χρημάτων ἕνεκα ταῦτα πέπρακται
ἀλλὰ συμφέροντα τῇ πολιτείᾳ γεγένηται.

So 12. 6 (twice); 25. 18, three pairs of approximately equal cola; 25. 3²; 34. 5.

3. **παρομοίωσις**, equality of cola, heightened by the use of the same or similar words at corresponding points, particularly at beginning or end.[1] So μήτε— μήτε— in the first example above; — πέπρακται— γενένηται in the second.

Cp. 12. 1 { τοιαῦτα —
{ τοσαῦτα —

12. 7 { — περὶ οὐδενὸς ἡγοῦντο
{ — περὶ πολλοῦ ἐποιοῦντο

12. 1 { ἢ τὸν κατήγορον ἀπειπεῖν
{ ἢ τὸν χρόνον ἐπιλιπεῖν

12. 19 { — ἀφίκοντο
{ — ἐποιήσαντο

12. 26 { ἀντέλεγες μὲν ἵνα σώσειας
{ συνελάμβανες δὲ ἵνα ἀποκτείνειας

12. 32 { οὐχ ὡς ἀνιωμένου
{ ἀλλ' ὡς ἡδομένου

12. 47 { — ἐνόμιζον
{ — παρέβαινον

12. 33 { πάντα τὰ κακά —
{ πάντα τἀγαθά—

12. 54 { — μισεῖσθαι
{ — φιλεῖσθαι

12. 57 { — δικαίως ἔφευγον | ὑμεῖς ἀδίκως
{ — ὑμεῖς δικαίως | οἱ τριάκοντα ἀδίκως

12. 67 { διὰ τὴν πρὸς ἐκείνους —
{ διὰ δὲ τὴν πρὸς ὑμᾶς —

12. 70 { — ἀναγκαζόμενος
{ — ἐπαγγελλόμενος

12. 78 { τῶν μὲν παρόντων καταφρονῶν
{ τῶν δὲ ἀπόντων ἐπιθυμῶν

12. 79 μηδὲ { μαχομένους μὲν κρείττους εἶναι τῶν πολεμίων
{ ψηφιζομένους δὲ ἥττους τῶν ἐχθρῶν

12. 89 { ὑπὲρ ὧν ὑμεῖς —
{ ὑπὲρ ὧν οὗτοι —

25. 16 { — ὀργίζεσθε
{ — νομίζεσθαι

25. 20 { ἀλλὰ τὴν αὐτὴν κατελθόντες περὶ ἡμῶν γνώμην ἔχετε
{ ἥνπερ   φεύγοντες περὶ ὑμῶν αὐτῶν εἴχετε

25. 23 { — σωτηρίαν
{ — τιμωρίαν

25. 26 { — ἀφιέναι
{ — ἀπολλύναι

25. 30 { — πεποιήκασιν
{ — κατηγγέλκασι

So 19. 54; 25. 13; 25. 22; 32. 28; 34. 2; 34. 4; 34. 5; 34. 6.

---

[1] Aristotle, 3. 9. 9; Anaximenes, c. 28; Demetrius, c. 25.

4. **ὁμοιοτέλευτον**, rhymed cola.[1] This becomes especially marked in παρομοίωσις, as in most of the examples cited above.[2]

Cp. 32. 25 $\begin{cases} -\ ἀποδείξει \\ -\ ἕξει \\ -\ ἐγγράψει \\ -\ πλουτήσει \end{cases}$ 12. 77 $\begin{cases} -\ δεδωκώς \\ -\ εἰληφώς \end{cases}$ 24. 3-4 $\begin{cases} -\ ἔξω \\ -\ διάξω \\ -\ διοίσω \\ -\ εἰρήσθω \end{cases}$

5. **ἐπαναφορά**, the repetition of the same word at the beginning of successive cola.[3] A fine example is that in 12. 21, πολλοὺς μέν —, πολλοὺς δέ —, πολλοὺς δέ —, πολλῶν δέ — (see p. 348, § 46). Beside the examples under παρομοίωσις, cp. the following: 12. 77 ὀνειδίζων —, ὀνειδίζων —. 12. 78 δικαίως μέν —, δικαίως δέ —. 12. 94 ἐνθυμηθέντες μέν —, ἐνθυμηθέντες δέ —. 16. 8 πολλοὺς μέν —, πολλοὺς δέ —. 19. 9 ἐστερημένοι μέν —, ἐστερημένοι δέ —. 32. 16, the striking and effective repetition of οὐ μετά — at the climax of the mother's complaint. Cp. 12. 68; 34. 4; 34. 8.

Isocrates avoids this figure; Demosthenes is very fond of it; Lysias stands between the two.

6. **ἀντιστροφή**, the repetition of the same word at the close of successive cola.[4] So 12. 57 — ἀδίκως, — ἀδίκως. 25. 20 — ἔχετε, — εἴχετε. But neither is an effective case of ἀντιστροφή, or to be compared with the famous example from Aeschines : —

3. 198 $\begin{cases} ὅστις\ δ'\ ἐν\ τῷ\ πρώτῳ\ λόγῳ\ τὴν\ ψῆφον\ αἰτεῖ \\ ὅρκον\ αἰτεῖ \\ νόμον\ αἰτεῖ \\ δημοκρατίαν\ αἰτεῖ. \end{cases}$

7. **ἐπαναστροφή**, the final word of one colon becomes the initial word of the next.[5]

So 25. 31 ἐκεῖνοι μὲν ὀλιγαρχίας οὔσης
ἐπεθύμουν ὧνπερ οὗτοι
οὗτοι δὲ καὶ δημοκρατίας
τῶν αὐτῶν ὧνπερ ἐκεῖνοι.

[1] Aristotle, 3. 9. 9; Demetrius, c. 26.

[2] As rhyme was not an ordinary feature of Greek poetry, its use in prose did not seem to the Greek hearer as incongruous as it does to us.

[3] Demetrius, c. 268, where ἀναφορά and ἐπαναφορά are used as synonyms. Cp. c. 141.

[4] Hermogenes, Περὶ ἰδεῶν (Spengel, II. 335).

[5] Hermogenes, Περὶ ἰδεῶν (Spengel, II. 336).

34. 11 ἐμαχόμεθα Λακεδαιμονίοις ἵνα κατέλθωμεν
κατελθόντες δὲ φευξόμεθα ἵνα μὴ μαχώμεθα.

8. **κύκλος**, a sentence or period begins and ends with the same word.[1]
The first period cited under ἐπαναστροφή (7) shows perfect κύκλος also.

9. **συμπλοκή**, the first and last words of one colon become the first
and last words of the next.[2]

> Aeschin. 3. 202 ἐπὶ σαυτὸν καλεῖς
> ἐπὶ τοὺς νόμους καλεῖς
> ἐπὶ τὴν δημοκρατίαν καλεῖς.

58. (b) *Figures not connected with balance of cola.*

A second group of figures of speech is independent of balance of
cola, and so is less frequently found in Lysias.

1. **ἀναδίπλωσις**, the repetition of one or more words for rhetorical
effect.[3] This is too passionate a figure for Lysias's restrained style.
Cp. Aeschin. 3. 133 Θῆβαι δέ, Θῆβαι, πόλις ἀστυγείτων, μεθ᾽ ἡμέραν μίαν
ἐκ μέσης τῆς Ἑλλάδος ἀνήρπασται.

2. **συνωνυμία**, amplification by the use of synonyms. A favorite
figure with Demosthenes; used sparingly by Lysias.[4]

> Cp. 22. 21 ἐὰν ἀντιβολῶσιν ὑμᾶς καὶ ἱκετεύωσι.
> 32. 11 ἠντεβόλει με καὶ ἱκέτευε.
> 21. 21 ἐγὼ δ᾽ ὑμῶν δέομαι καὶ ἱκετεύω καὶ ἀντιβολῶ.
> 12. 19 εἰς τοσαύτην ἀπληστίαν καὶ αἰσχροκέρδειαν ἀφίκοντο.
> 12. 24 ὅσιον καὶ εὐσεβές.

12. 3	{ ἀναξίως ἀδυνάτως	12. 68	{ μέγα πολλοῦ ἄξιον
12. 22	{ κακόν αἰσχρόν	22. 16	{ πανουργίας κακονοίας
12. 31	{ ἔλεγχον βάσανον	24. 10	{ τοῦτο ζητεῖν τοῦτο φιλοσοφεῖν
12. 55	{ στάσιν πόλεμον	24. 23	{ καλλίστων μεγίστων

[1] Hermogenes, Περὶ εὑρέσεως (Spengel, II. 252).

[2] Alexander, Περὶ σχημάτων (Spengel, III. 30): τοῦτο τὸ σχῆμα μικτόν
ἐστιν ἐκ τῆς ἀναφορᾶς καὶ τῆς ἀντιστροφῆς, διὸ καὶ οὕτω κέκληται.

[3] Demetrius, c. 140.

[4] Alexander, Περὶ σχημάτων (Spengel, III. 30). Demetrius (c. 280) calls
it ἐπιμονή *ondwelling*, a happy term to bring out the real force of the figure.

3. **ἀσύνδετον**, the omission of the conjunction in a series of coördinate words or phrases.[1] A remarkable example is in the closing sentence of XII : ἀκηκόατε, ἑωράκατε, πεπόνθατε, — ἔχετε · δικάζετε. Cp. the impassioned words of the mother in 32. 16.

4. **πολυσύνδετον**, the repetition of the conjunction in a series of coördinate words or phrases.[2] Cp. 12. 78 καὶ τοσούτων καὶ ἑτέρων κακῶν καὶ αἰσχρῶν καὶ πάλαι καὶ νεωστὶ καὶ μικρῶν καὶ μεγάλων αἰτίου γεγενημένου. Cp. 12. 19; 12. 99; 22. 14.

5. **παρονομασία**, play on the sound and meaning of words.[3] The Gorgian school delighted in this artificial word play. Lysias did not entirely escape their influence. Cp. 12. 32 ἀνιωμένου, ἡδομένου. 12. 33 παρεῖναι, παρ᾽ αὐτοῖς εἶναι. 12. 59 εὐνούστατον, κακονούστατον. 24. 3 δυστυχήματα, ἐπιτηδεύμασιν. 24. 7 δικαίως, ἀδίκως. ἀδικῆσαι, ἀθυμῆσαι. 25. 23 σωτηρίαν, τιμωρίαν. 25. 24 πονηρίαν, σωτηρίαν. 32. 22 γράμματα, χρημάτων.

59. II. Σχήματα διανοίας, *figures of thought*.

Lysias does not make frequent use of the so-called figures of thought. Some of these figures appear, of course, in the unstudied speech of any man. In Lysias the following only demand especial attention.

1. **τὸ πυσματικὸν σχῆμα**,[4] the rhetorical question. A question is asked, not for information or advice, but only for rhetorical effect. Sometimes the speaker answers his own question. The rhetorical question sometimes stirs the emotions of the hearers, sometimes confounds the opponent, sometimes gives an air of candor to the claims of the speaker, and always quickens the attention of the hearers. The ordinarily quiet style of Lysias has little place for such questions, but they are occasionally used with great effect. They are oftenest used in appealing to the good sense of the jury as the speaker draws his con-

---

[1] Aristotle, 3. 12. 2 and 4; Demetrius, c. 268; Hermogenes, Περὶ μεθόδου δεινοῦ (Spengel, II. 435).

[2] Demetrius (c. 63) calls this συνάφεια.

[3] Alexander (Spengel, III. 36) limits the term to the particular case where the play is upon slight changes in the *form* of the word. For play on several meanings of the same word he has the terms ἀντιμετάθεσις, or σύγκρισις, or πλοκή (*Ibid.* p. 37).

[4] Tiberius, Περὶ σχημάτων (Spengel, III. 64).

clusions on the particular point under discussion. Cp. 12. 26–29; 12. 34, 36, 49, 52, 89; 16. 21; 19. 17, 23, 33, 34, 38; 22. 10, 16, 17, 18, 21 · 24. 2, 3, 9, 12, 13, 21, 23; 32. 15, 27; 34. 2, 3, 11.

2. ὑποφορά,[1] the speaker raises objections, often in the form of questions, which the hearers or the opponents may be supposed to make. He answers the objections, sometimes putting the answer also in the form of a question. Lysias sometimes has an effective series of such questions and answers. Cp. 12. 39; 12. 82–4; 19. 29; 24. 23–5; 34. 6.

IV. MONEY AND PRICES AT ATHENS

60. The pre-Solonian system of weights, measures, and coinage of Athens was essentially that of Aegina and the Peloponnesus.[2] Solon introduced the Euboean system, based on a foot 297 mm. long; the square of this foot gave the surface unit; its cube, the unit of capacity; and the weight of this cubic foot of water (or wine), the unit of weight. After the time of Pisistratus these units seem to have been slightly reduced, and made to correspond to a linear foot of 296 mm.   While Solon's other units of measure came into universal use in Athens, his linear foot failed to displace, for common purposes, the old Aeginetan foot of 330 mm.; but this old foot was reduced, probably to correspond to the reduction in the Solonian foot, giving the common working foot of about 328 mm.[3]

61. Attic coinage was based on the talent, the weight of a cubic foot of water (or wine).[4]   The unit of coinage was the drachma, a coin of pure silver, weighing one six-thousandth of a talent, and equal to

[1] Tiberius, Περὶ σχημάτων (Spengel, III. 77).

[2] Busolt, *Griechische Geschichte*, II.[2] 262 f.

[3] Nissen, Müller's *Handbuch*, I.[2] 876 ff. Nissen bases his computation of the reduced Solonian foot upon the diminished weight of our specimens of Attic drachmas after the early period; then, assuming that the common (Aeginetan) foot was reduced in the same ratio, he computes its length as 328.89 mm. Dörpfeld concludes by comparison of the description of dimensions of parts of the Erechtheum (*C.I.A.* I. 322) with the measurements of such of these parts as survive, that the common Attic foot was one of 328 mm. (*Ath. Mittheil.* XV. 167 ff.).

[4] This cubic foot being based on the reduced Solonian linear foot of 296 mm.

4.32 grams,[1] or 66.667 + grains Troy. The modern bullion value of the drachma would be, for the period 1899–1903,[2] $0.08+, and its value in U.S. coined silver[3] would be $0.1795+. The following table gives the Attic system with approximate equivalents in U.S. silver dollars:

$$
\begin{array}{rll}
\text{1 obol} & = & \$0.03 \\
6 \text{ obols} = \text{1 drachma} & = & \$0.18 \\
100 \text{ drachmas} = \text{1 mina} & = & \$18.00 \\
60 \text{ minæ} = \text{1 talent} & = & \$1080.00
\end{array}
$$

62. The Persian daric and the Cyzicene stater were the chief gold coins of the ancient world until the Macedonian supremacy. The daric, a coin of pure gold, passed in Athens as equal to 20 drachmas. The Cyzicene stater was a coin of electrum (gold and silver); its current value in the time of Lysias was above that of the daric,[4] but the exact value in drachmas is not known. We learn that about 328/7 it passed at Bosporus in the Crimea as equal to 28 Attic drachmas.[5]

63. The real value of the drachma must be measured by its purchasing power.[6] In the time of Lysias a drachma would pay a day's wages of a carpenter, or stone cutter, or superintendent of building operations.[7] It was the daily pay of a senator.[8] A half-drachma a

---

[1] Here, as in all computations in this chapter, the modern equivalents are based on Nissen's tables, Müller's *Handbuch*, I.[2] 835 ff.

[2] The average bullion value of silver in London for the period 1899–1903 was $0.5776+ per ounce, *U.S. Treasury Report*, 1904, p. 405.

[3] The standard silver dollar contains 371.25 grains of fine silver. Our silver "quarter" (our coin nearest to the drachma) contains only 347.22 grains of fine silver per dollar, but as our concern is chiefly with considerable sums of drachmas, the value is better taken on the dollar standard.

[4] Xen. *Anab.* 1. 3. 21 compared with 5. 6. 23, 7. 3. 10.   [5] [Demos.] 34. 23.

[6] There was a continuous rise in nominal prices from the time of Solon to that of Demosthenes, caused in part by the increasing supply of silver. The period of Lysias includes a few years of abnormal conditions in the closing years of the Peloponnesian War. Cp. Speck, *Handelsgeschichte des Altertums*, II. 388 f.

[7] Workmen on the Erechtheum, 408/7 B.C., *C.I.A.* I. 324, cp. *C.I.A.* IV. i. 321. That the Erechtheum wages were normal, although the work was perhaps a relief measure, appears from the fact that they bear about the same proportion to the cost of living at the close of the fifth century as do the higher wages of the Eleusinian inscription (*C.I.A.* II. ii. 834, b, c) to food prices in the later period to which it belongs (329/8 B.C. and the years following).

[8] Hesychius, *s.vv. βουλῆς λαχεῖν.*

day was the pay of an unskilled laborer,[1] of a rower in the fleet,[2] a juror's pay for a sitting,[3] and the voter's pay for attendance on a session of the Ecclesia.[4] Four obols ($\frac{2}{3}$ dr.) was the minimum pay of a hoplite in the field.[5] The Attic drachma therefore bought labor that would with us cost from $2.50 to $3.75 ; that is, a given amount of silver coined in Attic drachmas would purchase from fourteen to twenty times as much Athenian skilled labor as the same silver coined in our money would purchase in our labor market.[6]

64. We have some data for determining the real value of the drachma as measured by its purchasing power in the food market. A drachma would buy $\frac{1}{4}$ to $\frac{1}{2}$ medimnus of barley meal ($= 1\frac{1}{2}$ to 3 pecks),[7] the common food of the people.[8] We have the following quo-

[1] Aristoph. *Eccles.* 310. Jevons argues for a drachma as the pay of an unskilled laborer at the close of the fourth century, *Jour. Hellenic Studies*, XV. 239 ff.; but cp. Beloch, *Griechische Geschichte*, I. 415.

[2] Thucyd. 8. 45. 2, Xen. *Hell.* I. 5. 7. Thucydides (6.31. 3) notes the pay of a drachma a day to rowers in the fleet on the Sicilian expedition as extraordinary.

[3] Schol. Aristoph. *Vesp.* 88, 300.

[4] Arist. *Resp. Ath.* 41. 3.

[5] Busolt, *Griechische Altertümer*,[2] p. 305.

[6] The average day's wages in the United States in 1900 for men corresponding to the Athenian one-drachma workmen were: for carpenters, $2.63; stone cutters, $3.45 ; brick layers, $3.84 ; stone setters, $3.82. *U.S. Bureau of Labor, Bulletin No. 53*, July, 1904.

[7] The medimnus = 51.84 li. = 5.88 pk.

[8] A sacrificial calendar from the Attic Tetrapolis, of the early part of the fourth century (the period of most of Lysias's speeches), published in the *Papers of the American School of Classical Studies at Athens*, Vol. VI. 374 ff., gives numerous quotations of prices. So far as we can test these by other evidence, they seem to be higher than the average. This table gives a ἑκτεύς of barley meal at 4 obols ($= 4$ dr. per medimnus). But from Aristoph. *Eccles.* 547 (392 B.C.) we infer that wheat was 3 dr. per medimnus at this period. We find later in the century the price of wheat to that of barley as 2:1 (*C.I.A.* IV. ii. 834 b) or 9:5 (*C.I.A.* IV. ii. 196, Beloch, II. 356 Anm. 4); assuming this ratio for the time when wheat was 3 dr., we have $1\frac{1}{2}$ to $1\frac{2}{3}$ dr. for unground barley. This agrees with the 2 dr. for barley meal mentioned in an anecdote of Socrates preserved by later writers (see Beloch, I. 411 Anm. 1).

tation of prices for live animals for sacrifice (naturally choice animals at a maximum price) in the Tetrapolis inscription: a cow (or ox?), 90 dr. = \$16.16; a sheep, 11 to 17 dr. = \$1.97 to \$3.05; a goat, 12 dr. = \$2.15; a sow, 20 dr. = \$3.59; a pig, 3 dr. = 54 cts.[1] The cattle for a hecatomb in Athens in 410 B.C. cost on the average about 51 dr. (= \$9.15) a head;[2] for the Delian festival of 374 B.C. about 77 dr. (= \$13.82).[3] Oil and wine were cheap. An early fourth-century inscription[4] has oil at ½ obol a κοτύλη = about 20 cts. a gallon. At a later period, when all prices were higher, wine was 8 dr. a μετρη-τής = about 14 cts. a gallon.[5] It is in accord with these prices that we find in a decree of thanks to a Delian who has rendered service to Athens, and is temporarily residing there, an appropriation of one drachma a day for his support (τροφή).[6]

65. These prices show that in reckoning the real value of any sum of Attic drachmas for the time of Lysias we must make large allowance for the high purchasing power of silver. Its value was greatest in the labor market, where slave labor kept wages at a minimum, while in the food market it was in all departments greater than with us, — in some, much greater.

66. But it must be remembered that a small fortune made a man rich in the Athens of the fourth century B.C., not only because the necessaries of life were cheap, but still more because the simplicity of life was such that even the rich demanded few luxuries.[7]

[1] We find the same price for a pig in Aristoph. *Peace*, 374.

[2] *C.I.A.* I. 188. This is upon the assumption that a full hundred cattle were bought for the 5114 dr. recorded. Possibly this was not done. It is difficult to understand how cattle could have been so cheap at this period of the war.

[3] *C.I.A.* II. 814.

[4] *C.I.A.* II. 631.

[5] *C.I.A.* II. ii. 834 b (329/8 B.C.).

[6] *C.I.A.* II. i. 115 b (p. 408), to be dated not long after the middle of the fourth century.

[7] We have most interesting details as to the increased prices of labor and of many commodities later in the fourth century, in the accounts preserved from building operations at Eleusis, 329 B.C. and after, *C.I.A.* II. ii. 834 b, IV. ii. 834 b, II. ii. 834 c. Cp. Speck, *ibid.* II. 532 ff.

V. THE MANUSCRIPTS

67. Thirty-one speeches ascribed to Lysias have come down to us in the *Codex Palatinus* X (Heidelbergensis 88). All our other Mss. of Lysias were copied from this. Two of these speeches, however, numbered I and II, have also been preserved in another group of Mss. as a part of a collection of speeches by several authors.[1] We have also parts of three more speeches (in modern editions numbered XXXII, XXXIII, and XXXIV) in the Mss. of the treatise of Dionysius on *Lysias*, where they were transcribed as specimens of Lysias's style.[2] The Ms. X was written in the twelfth century. From an entry in a four-teenth-century hand on a blank leaf it appears that the Ms. was originally at Nicaea.[3] It was taken to Italy, thence to Heidelberg; in 1622 it was taken to Rome, thence to Paris by command of Napoleon in 1797; in 1815 it was taken back to Heidelberg.[4] The Ms. con-sists of one hundred and forty-two leaves of parchment. Before it reached Italy it had lost one whole quaternion,[5] two leaves in another place, and a single leaf in still another.[6] The fact that all the other Mss. have *lacunae* at the places where X is mutilated is the conclu-sive proof that they were copied from it. The archetype of X had a considerable number of variant readings, which are preserved in X. The readings of the other Mss., where they differ from those of X, are conjectures of critics or copyists. Readings of C (*Laurenti-anus plut.* 57, 4) are occasionally cited in the following notes, not as ancient testimony, but as giving the origin of current corrections of X.

---

[1] Erdmann has shown that Speeches I and II in the Ms. X came to it from a different archetype from that which furnished the others. This other arche-type was the common source of I and II of Ms. X and I and II of the other group. Erdmann, *De Pseudolysiae epitaphii codicibus*, Lipsiae, 1881 ; *Lysi-aca*, Strassburg, 1891.

[2] On the Mss. of Dionysius see Appendix, XXXII, introductory note.

[3] Schöll, *Hermes*, XI. 203.

[4] For the history of the Ms. see Sauppe, *Epistola Critica ad Godofredum Hermannum scripta*, Lipsiae, 1841.

[5] This contained the close of Speech XXV, the whole speech entered in the index of the Ms. as Κατὰ Νικίδου ἀργίας, and the beginning of XXVI.

[6] These two leaves contained the close of Speech V and the beginning of VI. The single leaf was between §§ 49 and 50 of VI.

There are many impossible readings in X, which must be corrected by pure conjecture. Of the speeches printed in this volume, the nineteenth has the greatest number of corruptions of text.

VI. BIBLIOGRAPHY

1513. Aldus, Venice. In the *Rhetores Graeci*, I. 86–197.
1575. Stephanus, Geneva. In the *Oratorum Veterum Orationes*.
1739. Taylor, London. *Lysiae Orationes et Fragmenta*.
1772. Reiske, Leipzig. Vols. V and VI of Reiske's *Oratores Graeci*. Containing with his own notes those of Taylor and Markland. With scholia, variant readings, and indices.
1823. Bekker, Berlin and Oxford. Vol. I of Bekker's *Oratores Attici*; Antiphon, Andocides, Lysias.
1828. Dobson, London. Vol. II of Dobson's *Oratores Attici*. Containing notes of Stephanus, Taylor, Markland, Reiske, and others, and Dobree's *Adversaria ad Lysiam*.
1838. Baiter and Sauppe, Zurich. *Oratores Attici*, Fasc. I, Antiphon, Andocides, Lysias. Also the Lysias alone in a small text edition of the same date.
1852. Scheibe, Leipzig. *Lysiae Orationes*. 1855, *Editio altera*. Text edition (Teubner text) with critical apparatus.
1854. Westermann, Leipzig. *Lysiae Orationes*.
1863. Cobet, Amsterdam. *Lysiae Orationes*. Revised by Hartman, Leyden, 1890.
1863. Van Herwerden, Groningen. *Lysiae Orationes Selectae*. Speeches I, XII, XIII, XVI, XXV, XXXII.
1888. Weidner, Leipzig. *Lysiae Orationes Selectae*. Speeches I, VII, X, XII, XIII, XVI, XIX, XXII–XXV, XXX–XXXII.
1899. Van Herwerden, Groningen. *Lysiae Orationes in quibus etiam Amatoria a Platone servata, cum Fragmentis*.
1901. Thalheim, Leipzig. *Lysiae Orationes*. *Editio Maior*. Containing full critical apparatus.

STANDARD EDITIONS OF SELECTED SPEECHES WITH COMMENTARY

1848. Rauchenstein, Berlin. *Ausgewählte Reden des Lysias*. Revised by the author in 1853–59–64–69–72–75. Divided into two parts and revised by Fuhr, 1880. Part I is now in the eleventh edition (1899), and Part II in the tenth edition (1897), revised repeatedly by Fuhr. Part I, Speeches XII, XIII, XVI, XXV, XXXI. Part II, Speeches VII, XIX, XXII, XXIII, XXIV, XXX, XXXII.

1865-1870. Frohberger, Leipzig. *Ausgewählte Reden des Lysias.* Vol. I, Speeches XII, XIII, XXV, 1865. Vol. II, Speeches I, X, XIV, XV, XXXII, 1868. Vol. III, Speeches XVI, XIX, XXIV, XXX, XXXI, 1870. Each volume has commentary and a critical appendix, and Vol. III has full indices for the three volumes.

Vol. I is in a second edition, revised by Gebauer, 1880. Gebauer has enlarged the critical appendix from 46 pages to 310, making it a great storehouse of information on both grammatical and rhetorical usage.

1873. Frohberger, Leipzig. *Ausgewählte Reden des Lysias, Kleinere Ausgabe.* Speeches VII, X, XII-XVI, XIX, XXII, XXIV, XXV, XXX, XXXI, XXXII.

Speeches XII, XIII, XVI, XXV, XXXI, revised by Gebauer. 1882. Revised by Thalheim, 1895.

Speeches VII, X, XIV, XV, XIX, XXII, XXIV, XXX, XXXII, revised by Thalheim, 1892.

1882. Shuckburgh, London. *Lysiae Orationes* XVI, with analysis, notes, appendices, and indices. Speeches V, VII, IX, X, XII, XIII, XIV, XVI, XVII, XIX, XXII, XXIII, XXIV, XXVIII, XXX, XXXII. Now in the fifth edition, 1892.

1885-1887. Kocks, Gotha. *Ausgewählte Reden des Lysias.* Vol. I, Speeches VII, XII, XIII, XVI, XIX, 1885. Revised by Schnee, 1898. Vol. II, Speeches XXI-XXV, XXVIII, XXX-XXXIII, 1887.

1895. Morgan, Boston. *Eight Orations of Lysias*, with introduction, notes, and appendices. Speeches VII, XII, XVI, XXII, XXIII, XXIV, XXXI, XXXII.

VII. CRITICAL NOTES

In the following critical notes the statements of Ms. readings are taken from the notes of Thalheim's critical edition of 1901. Minor orthographical errors of X in which Ms. authority is not significant are corrected in the printed text without comment; otherwise all variations of the printed text from the readings of X are recorded, as are all variations (except in punctuation) from the text of Thalheim's critical edition (1901).

The following abbreviations are used in the critical notes:

Bekk., Bekker.	Rn., Rauchenstein.
Cob., Cobet.	Rs., Reiske.
Cont., Conter.	Sch., Scheibe.
Dobr., Dobree.	Steph., Stephanus.
F., Fuhr.	Tayl., Taylor.
Frb., Frohberger.	Th., Thalheim.
Geb., Gebauer.	Turr., Baiter and Sauppe.
Herw., Van Herwerden.	Us.R., Usener-Radermacher.
Markl., Markland.	Wdn., Weidner.
Mor., Morgan.	West., Westermann.

XII

1. **εἴργασται ·** Th. Clauses introduced by τοιοῦτος, οὕτως, and the like, following the main statement without other connective, fall into two classes: (a) exclamatory clauses, often expressing indignation or surprise (so Lys. 12. 84, 13. 31, 12. 17, 12. 44, 13. 60, 28. 6), sometimes giving the general fact or principle of which the preceding statement is an illustration (so Lys. 1. 2, 1. 32, 32. 21), sometimes expressing the writer's final reflection called out by a series of statements (so Thuc. 2. 65. 13); (b) clauses which, like the one under discussion, give the ground for the preceding statement (so Herod. 3. 85; Dem. 20. 141, 22. 68; Eurip. *Medea* 718, 789). In class b the preceding statement is *in effect* a ὥστε clause, so that the connection is much closer than in class a; οὐκ ἄρξασθαι δοκεῖ, τοιαῦτα εἴργασται = τοιαῦτα εἴργασται ὥστε οὐκ ἄρξασθαι δοκεῖ. When two such clauses are followed by a ὥστε clause, the last clause tends to draw the middle (τοιοῦτος) clause toward itself, giving the effect of a harsh asyndeton after the first clause. Thalheim's punctuation helps to resist this.

2. **πολλῆς ἀφθονίας οὔσης ὑπὲρ τῶν δημοσίων ὀργίζεσθαι** Herw.; Rn.-F.; πολλῆς ἀφθονίας οὔσης ὑπὲρ τῶν ἰδίων ἢ ὑπὲρ τῶν δημοσίων ὀργίζεσθαι X, Th. Even if we accept the single ἤ where we should expect ἤ . . . ἤ, the statement as it stands in X is not true. It is not a fact that all citizens have *either* public *or* private grounds of anger; all have public grounds, and many have private grounds in addition. Th. interprets ἤ as *than* through the comparative force of ἀφθονία, citing δεξαίμην ἂν ἤ 10. 21.

3. **ποιήσωμαι** Vulg., Sch.; ποιήσομαι X, Th. The probability of the contamination of ποιήσωμαι by the following πειράσομαι seems

greater than that Lysias used so rare a construction, found nowhere else in the orators.   Weber, *Entwickelungsgesch. der Absichtssätze*, II. 94; GMT. 367.

5. **πονηροὶ** Rs., Th.; πονηροὶ μὲν X. — **προτρέψαι** Wdn.; τραπέσθαι X, Th., a reading which requires an awkward change of subject. — **τοιαῦτα** Markl.; καὶ τοιαῦτα X.

6. **πένεσθαι** Markl.; γενέσθαι X. — **τὴν δ' ἀρχὴν** Scaliger; τὴν ἀρχὴν X; τὴν ἀρχὴν δὲ Rs., Th.

7. **ἕνεκα** C; οὕνεκα (for οὕνεκα) X (Lampros, *Hermes*, X. 264).

11. **ἐπειδὴ δὲ** F.; ἐπεὶ δὲ X, Th.   I have accepted Fuhr's conclusion that Lysias did not use ἐπεί temporal (Rn.-F. on 32. 2, *Anh.*), and that ἐπειδή must be substituted wherever ἐπεί temporal has been handed down.   In all of these cases ἐπεί is followed by δέ.   Of Fuhr's cases only three are attested by the Mss. of Lysias (12. 11, 13. 43, 23. 14). In Fr. 88 ἐπεί is clearly causal; in 32. 2 it is more causal than temporal. — **ὡμολόγησεν**: ὡμολ°ͺ X (Schöll, *Hermes*, 11. 215).   Pison had agreed to accept a talent; he now broke his agreement.   I have written ὡμολόγησεν (repeated from § 9) as preferable to ὡμολόγησα C, ὡμολόγουν Sch. (conj.), ὡμολόγητο Fritzsche, Th. - - **δαρεικοὺς**: Maussac; καρικοὺς X.

12. **ὅποι** Codex Vindob.; ὅπη X. — **εἰς τἀδελφοῦ** Cob.; εἰς τὰ τοῦ ἀδελφοῦ X, Th.

15. **ᾔδη**: ᾔδειν X, Th.   I have followed Morgan in restoring the older form here and elsewhere.   Kühn. § 213. 5.

17. **τοὐπ' ἐκείνων** Fritzsche; τὸ ὑπ' ἐ. X; τὸ ἐπ' ἐ. Aldus.

18. **ἐξ οὐδεμιᾶς** Cob.; οὐδὲ μιᾶς X. — **κλεισίον** Sauppe (Meisterhans³ 51); κλίσιον X.

19. **κτήσεσθαι** Dobr.; κτήσασθαι X.   See GMT. 127, Kühn. 389, Anm. 7. — **ὅτε πρῶτον** Hertlein (*Hermes*, 13. 10), Rn.-F.; ὅτε τὸ πρῶτον X, Frb.-Geb., Th.   ὅτε τὸ πρῶτον can mean only *when . . . the first time*, or *when once*. — **ἦλθεν** X; ἦλθον Th., with the comma after οἰκίαν instead of after Μηλόβιος.

20. **ἀξίους γε ὄντας**: ἀξίους ἔχοντας X. — **πάσας μὲν** Rs.; πάσας X. — **εἰσενεγκόντας** Markl.; ἐνεγκόντας X.

21. **ἀτίμους** Markl.; ἀτίμους τῆς πόλεως X.

22. **τοσοῦτον**: τοιοῦτον X.

24. **ὅσιον**: ὅσον X. — **ὅ τι** Brunck; εἴ τι X.

25. **Ἦ**: ἦν X, Th.   I have followed Morgan in restoring the older Attic form (Kühn. § 298. 4). — **'Ἀντέλεγον, ἵνα μὴ ἀποθάνητε** Usener

(*Rhein. Mus.* 25. 590) ; ἀντέλεγον. ἵνα ἀποθάνωμεν ; ἵνα μὴ ἀποθάνητε X. The reading of X can stand only as a sarcastic question, ill fitted to the direct, rapid series of questions, and weakening the force of the outburst Εἶτ', ὦ σχετλιώτατε κτλ. 'Αντέλεγον. Ἵνα ἀποθάνωμεν ἢ μὴ ἀποθάνωμεν ; Ἵνα μὴ ἀποθάνητε. Rs., Th.

26. ἀποκτείνειας Kayser ; ἀποκτείνῃς X, Th. ; ἀποκτείνοις Author Περὶ ἐρωτήσεως Spengel, I. 166. The change of mood within the sentence would not in general be surprising, but where the two verbs are in antithesis the change is less likely, and for this speech very unlikely, when it carries with it the destruction of the rhymed ending. — οἴει δεῖν ἐμοὶ F. ; οἴει ἐμοὶ X ; δεῖν before δοῦναι Th. after Madvig.

27. προσετάχθη Rs. ; ἐτάχθη X. — ἧττον Canter ; πίστιν X.

29. αὐτῆς X ; om. Dobr., Th. For examples of the intensive standing alone in oblique case, see Kühn. 468, Anm. 1. — παρὰ τοῦ Canter ; παρ' αὐτοῦ X.

30. μὲν δὴ C ; μηδὲν δὴ X. — σῴζειν τε . . . παρόν Sauppe ; σῴζοντα . . . ὃν X. — πᾶσιν Rs. ; πάντες X.

31. τοῖς Rs. ; τούτοις X.

34. ποτ' ἐποίησας Dobr. ; πότε ποιήσαις X. Gildersleeve defends ποιήσαις, "as the question may safely be taken as a generic question" (GS. 439). But the parallelism with ἀπέκτεινας makes the distinctively past form more probable. — ἐτυγχάνετε . . . ἀπεψηφίσασθε : ἐτύχετε . . . ἀπεψηφίσασθε X ; ἐτυγχάνετε . . . ἀπεψηφίζεσθε Kayser ; ἐτύχετε . . . ἀποψηφίσαισθε Th. (opt. after Markl.). The aor. indic. with ἄν, to express an unreal conclusion belonging to time immediately future, is rare, but this passage is perhaps supported by ἂν χαρίσασθαι 19. 26 ; see GMT. 414 (to the examples there add Eur. *Medea*, 426) and cp. Haley on Eur. *Alcestis*, 125. The unusual aor. of the apodosis probably led to the corruption of the protasis in the Mss. — ὑεῖς F. ; υἱεῖς X.

35. ὑμέτεροι Rs. ; ἡμέτεροι X. — πότερον Hamaker ; ὅτι ἢ X, Th. ; ἢ ὅτι Fritzsche. The reading of X gives the absurd statement that 'the citizens will learn to-day that wrong-doers will either be punished or go free.' Fritzsche's remedy is simple, but we feel the lack of ὅτι with the second ἢ (cp. ἢ ὡς . . . ἢ ὡς, § 34). — σφᾶς γ' F. ; σφᾶς X ; σφόδρα σφᾶς Wdn. Lysias says either ἢ που . . . γε or ἢ που σφόδρα ; see 7. 8, 13. 69, 25. 17, 27. 15, 30. 17 ; cp. Dem. 55. 18 ; Thuc. 5. 100, 6. 37. 2 ; Andoc. 1. 24, 90. — ὑμῶν : ἡμῶν X. — τηρουμένους X, Th. ; τειρομένους Canter ; κηδομένους Rn. ; τιμωρουμένους Markl. ; διατεινομένους Frb. The middle τηρουμένους is appropriate here ; the allies

are 'on their guard' against the exiles in the interest of the Athenians; cp. Thuc. 4. 108. 1; Ar. *Wasps*, 372, 1386.

36. **τεθνεώτων**: τεθνειότων X. — **ἀκρίτους**: ἀκρίτως X. — ὑφ' C; ἀφ' X.

37. **οὐδ' ἂν . . . δίκην δοῦναι ἀξίαν δύναιντο**: οὐδ' . . . δίκην δοῦναι δύναιντ' ἄν X. In favor of the position of ἂν after οὐδ' (Herw.) is the fact that the four passages in Lysias similar to this have ἄν with the introductory word. These passages also have ἀξίαν either immediately after δίκην or separated by a single word. The position of ἀξίαν after δοῦναι (Markl.) breaks up the unpleasant succession of similar initial sounds in δίκην δοῦναι δύναιντ' ἄν. To write ἀξίαν after δύναιντ' ἄν (Fr., Th.) is to add to this unpleasant sound the awkward confusion of sound between ἂν ἀξίαν and ἀναξίαν.

38. **κατηγορημένα** C; κατηγορουμένα (*sic*) X. — **ἢ ὡς πόλεις** Meutzner; πόλεις X; ἢ πόλεις Markl., Th.

39. **ὑμετέραν** Rs.; ἡμετέραν X.

40. **τοσαῦτα ἐσκύλευσαν** Rs.; ἐσκύλευσαν τοσαῦτα Sch., Th.; om. τοσαῦτα X. — **ἀφείλοντο**, . . . **κατέσκαψαν** · Wdn., Th.; ἀφείλοντο; . . . κατέσκαψαν; Vulg. — **ὅτι ἑαυτοῖς** Sluiter after Tayl. and Rs.; οἷς αὐτοῖς X.

41. **αὐτοῦ** Dobree; αὐτῶν X.

42. **ἔπραξεν** Ald.; ἔπραξαν X.

43. **ὑμετέρῳ** Steph.; ἡμετέρῳ X.

44. **φυλὰς** Tayl.; φυλακὰς X. — **χρείη** Bekk.; χρὴ X. — **ψηφιεῖσθε** Cob.; ψηφίσησθε X.

45. **καλῶς** Frb.; καὶ X. — **ὑμᾶς** Markl.; ἡμᾶς X.

47. **καίτοι κἀκεῖνοι** Hertlein (*Hermes*, 13. 10); καίτοι X, Th.

48. **ἐχρῆν αὐτὸν** Bekk.; ἐχρῆν ἂν X. αὐτὸν (intensive) adds greatly to the force and displaces a troublesome ἄν. Goodwin's defense of this ἄν (GMT. p. 410) rests upon the translation "have to" for ἐχρῆν: "*if he had been an honest man, he would have had, first, to abstain from lawlessness in office*," "not being an honest man, he did not have to abstain from lawlessness in office." But "have to" is just ambiguous enough to be misleading; it covers both external and moral necessity. If in Goodwin's phrase we substitute the strict translation of χρῆν, *obligation*, we have, "not being an honest man, he was not under obligation to abstain from lawlessness in office," the fatal absurdity which La Roche pointed out. The apodosis of εἴπερ ἦν ἀνὴρ ἀγαθός is in μὴ παρανόμως ἄρχειν and μηνυτὴν γίγνεσθαι; both are contrary to fact, ἐχρῆν is not. — **ἀλλὰ τὰ** C; ἀλλὰ τἀληθῆ X.

50. αὐτῷ Cont.; αὐτὰ ᾧ X.

51. τὰ πράγματα Geb. (cp. 13. 60); μοι ταῦτα X.

52. εἰ γὰρ Schott; καὶ γὰρ X. — ἦν C; ἂν ἦν X. — **κατειληφότος**: κατειληφότες X. — **εὔνοιαν** Markl., cp. § 49; συνουσίαν X.

53. (1) **πρὸς ἀλλήλους διαλλαγήσεσθαι** (Hamaker)
ὡς ἀμφότεροι ἔδειξαν (Canter);

(2) πρὸς ἀλλήλους ἔσεσθαι, ὡς ἀμφότεροι ἔδοξαν X;

(3) πρὸς ἀλλήλους ἔσεσθαι, ὡς ἀμφότεροι ἔδειξαν (Canter) Th.;

(4) πρὸς ἀλλήλους ἔσεσθαι, ὡς ἀμφότεροι ἐδείξαμεν, Geel, Rn.-F.;

(5) τὰ πρὸς ἀλλ. ἔσεσθαι, ὡς ἀμφοτέροις ἔδοξεν Frb.

With (3) Th. supplies τὰς διαλλαγάς from τῶν διαλλαγῶν above as subject of ἔσεσθαι, but the hearer almost inevitably takes ἔσεσθαι with the subject of εἴχομεν; Fuhr so interprets it, and translates (4) *Wir würden beiderseits gegeneinander sein, wie wir beiderseits zeigten*, a translation that leaves the thought vague and incomplete. The same objection holds against (5). For (1) is the fact that the desire for reconciliation and its defeat by Eratosthenes's friends is the central thought of the passage, and ought to be definitely expressed. — **αὐτοὺς** X. We might expect a more definite word, yet the very vagueness of αὐτούς fits the delicacy with which Lysias is speaking to a part of the jury of their own defeat, and the restrained expression κρείττους ὄντες.

55. γενόμενος Frb.; ὁ τῶν τριάκοντα γενόμενος X. — **καὶ** (after Κριτίᾳ) om. X. — **αὐτοὶ** Markl.; αὐτ°ῖς X. — **τοῖς** Rs.; ἢ τοῖς X.

56. ᾧ καὶ Rn.; οἱ καὶ X.

57. εἰ δ᾽ ὑμεῖς δικαίως, οἱ τριάκοντα ἀδίκως Rs.; εἰ δ᾽ ὑμεῖς ἀδίκως, οἱ τριάκοντα δικαίως X. — **δὴ** Steph.; δι᾽ X.

58. αὐτῶν: αὐτῶν X. — **στρατεύεσθαι** X; στρατεύσασθαι C, defended by F. as perhaps correct, on the ground that πείθειν usually takes the aor. F.'s many Lysian examples owe the use of the aor. to the nature of the verb itself, rather than to the connection with πείθειν. For pres. of an action similar to στρατεύεσθαι cf. Aes. 2. 63 πείθων ὑμᾶς μὴ προσέχειν . . . μηδὲ . . . βοηθεῖν; Dem. 5. 5 ἡνίκ᾽ ἐπειθόν τινες ὑμᾶς . . . βοηθεῖν Πλουτάρχῳ. Other instances of πείθειν with pres. infin. are Xen. *Anab.* 5. 1. 14; Demos. 32. 7; Aeschin. 1. 48, 2. 154; Thuc. 2. 33. 1, 2. 67. 1.

59. ἐδανείσατο: ἐδανείσαντο X.

60. πόλεις ὅλας Cob.; πόλεις X, Th. — **οἷς** Tayl.; οὓς X.

61. οὐκ οἶδ᾽ ὅ τι F., who cites 7. 42, 10. 31, 12. 37, 16. 9, 22. 22, 24. 21; οἶδ᾽ ὅτι X; οὐκ οἶδ᾽ ὅτι Th. — **πλείστων** Cont.; πλεῖστον X.

62. ἄν om. X. — παραστῇ, ὡς X. The thought is clear as it stands ; the supposed objection that may arise in the mind of some juror is precisely the objection that Demosthenes raises in 18. 15 εἶτα κατηγορεῖ μὲν ἐμοῦ, κρίνει δὲ τουτονί, and it is presented in the same terse antithesis. For παραστῆναι ὡς cp. Plat. *Phaedrus* 233 c ; Thuc. 4. 61. 2, 4. 95. 2 : Andoc. 1. 54 ; Demos. *Epis.* 3. 36 (otherwise παραστῆναι is followed by infin., Thuc. 6. 34. 9, 6. 68. 3, 6. 78. 1). — ἀπολογήσεσθαι Markl. ; ἀπολογήσασθαι X. — ἐκείνῳ Tayl. ; ἐκείνοις X.

64. γὰρ ἦν Rs.; γὰρ X. — τοὺς Θηραμένους Franz ; τοῦ Θ. X. — αἰτίου . . . γεγενημένου Bekk.; αἰτίους . . . γεγενημένους X.

65. ταῦτ᾽ Classen ; ταῦτ᾽ X. — αὐτῶν Sauppe, followed by later editors generally ; αὐτοῦ X, Wdn.

66. τῇ πολιτείᾳ Dobr.; τῇ πόλει X ; om. Th. — Κάλλαισχρον : κάλαισχρον X. — προτέρους Canter ; πραοτέρους X.

67. Ἀρχεπτόλεμον : ἀρχιπτόλεμον X.

69. σωτήρια Markl. ; σωτηρίαν X. — ἕνεκα West. ; οὕνεκεν X. Çp. on 32. **10.** — ταῦθ᾽ ἃ πρὸς Vulg. ; ταῦτα πρὸς X. — ἐπετρέψατε Cont. ; ἐπέμψατε X. — γυναῖκας : γυναῖκα X.

70. αὐτὸς Canter ; αὐτοῖς X. — περιελεῖν : περι^{ελεῖν}_{αιρεῖν} X. — ἀποστερήσεσθε Cob. ; ἀποστερηθήσεσθε X, Th.   See Kühn. I. ii. p. 541.

71. ὡμολογημένος West.; λεγόμενος X. — ἐκείνων Markl. ; ἐκείνου X.

72. παρόντος : παρόντ^{ος}_{ων} X. — μηδὲ Emperius ; μήτε X. — διαπειλοῖτο Cob. ; ἀπειλοῖτο X. — ψηφίσαισθε : ψηφίσοισθε X.

73. ὑμᾶς Cont. ; ἡμᾶς X. — ἠκκλησιάζετε Frb. ; ἐκκλησιάζετε X.   The other form of augment, which X gives in Lys. 13. 73 and 76, ἐξεκκλησίαζε, was also certainly current (Kühn. I. ii. p. 415).

74. μέλοι : μέλλοι X. — ποιήσεθ . . . κελεύει Cob.; ποιήσαιθ᾽ . . . κελεύοι X. With the reading of X we have after εἶπε the change from opt. of ind. disc. to indic., then back to opt.   The reason for shifting to the vivid ἔσται is clear, but it is surprising if the speaker shifts back to the opt. as he comes to the culminating and emphatic clause of the period.   Moreover ποιήσαιθ᾽ of X must stand for aor. subj. with ἄν ; but the clause is emphatically minatory, so that we should expect fut. indic. or fut. opt.   These considerations make probable (not necessary) the emendation ποιήσεθ᾽ . . . κελεύει.

76. παρήγγελτο Cob. ; παρηγγέλλετο X, Th. — δέκα δ᾽ Ald. ; δέκα X.

77. δεῖ C ; δοκεῖ X. — οὐδὲν φροντιζόντων Λακ. Dobr. (See on Βοιωτοὺς 16. 13) ; οὐδὲν φροντίζων δὲ τῶν Λακ. X. — αὐτὸς αἴτιος X : αὐτοῖς αἴτιος Kayser, Th. — αὐτοῖς ἔργῳ C ; αὐτῶ ἔργω X.

78. **αἰτίου γεγενημένου** Rs.; *αἴτιοι γεγενημένοι* X. — *ἤδη* X; *δὶς* Sauppe. — **γὰρ** X; *γὰρ πρότερον* Frb.; *γάρ ποτε* Geb. Additions like *πρότερον, ποτέ*, are not needed with *ἤδη* and the aor., however tempting to readers whose language requires a plup. to represent one past act as clearly preliminary to another.

79. **τούτου** Rn.; *τουτουὶ* X. — **μαχομένους μὲν** Cont.; *μαχομένους* X.

80. **μέλλειν**: *μέλειν* X. — **ὑμεῖς ὑμῖν αὐτοῖς** F.; *ὑμῖν αὐτοῖς* X, Th.; *ὑμῖν ὑμεῖς αὐτοὶ* Funkhänel. The clauses *μηδὲ . . . πόλει* and *κάκιον . . . βοηθήσητε* form the culmination of a series of antitheses; it is, therefore, almost necessary to have a word (*ὑμεῖς* or *αὐτοί*) expressed in antithesis to *τύχης*. Thalheim's citation (Fr.-Th. p. 187) of 21. 14 for the omission of *ὑμεῖς* is not to the point, for there the antithesis is not between *ἐμέ* and the subject of *ἀδικήσετε*, but between *ἐμέ* and *ὑμᾶς αὐτούς*. His objection to the disturbing effect of the insertion of *ὑμεῖς* after the long series of verbs where it has not been expressed is met by the closely parallel construction of 18. 15.

81. **κατηγόρηται** Bake; *κατηγορεῖτε* X. — **μὲν** F.; *δὲ* X. Th. *κατηγόρηται* marks the transition from the attack on the career of Eratosthenes and the other moderates. The substitution of *μέν* for the meaningless *δέ* is therefore justified by 27. 1. — **ὁ αὐτὸς** Markl.; *αὐτὸς* X. — **κρινομένων** Rs.; *γινομένων* X.

82. **καὶ οὗτοι** Dobr.; *καίτοι οὗτοι* X. — **ἀκρίτους**: *ἀκρίτως* X.

83. **ἀποκτείναιτε** Bekk.; *ἀποκτείνοιτε* X. — **ἀκρίτους** C; *ἀκρίτως* X. — **δημεύσαιτε** Rs.; *δημεύσετε* X. — **τὰς οἰκίας** Sch.; *οἰκίας* X. — **ἐξεπόρθησαν**; Th. follows Frb.-Geb. in writing *ἐξεπόρθησαν*. Without the interrogation *ἢ . . . ἤ* is less fitting than *καὶ . . . καί*.

84. **αὐτῶν τὴν ἀξίαν** Auger; *αὐτῶν* X; *αὐτῶν ἱκανὴν* Sintenis. — **δύναισθε** Bekk.; *δύνησθε* X. — **δοκεῖ**: *δοκῇ* X. — **τοσοῦτον ἢ** Rs.; *τοσοῦτον δ'* X.

85. **ἐδύναντο** Markl.; *δύναιντο* X. — **ἐλθεῖν** C; *ἐλεῖν* X. — **ἔσεσθαι καὶ** Cob.; *ἔσεσθαι τῶν πεπραγμένων καὶ* X; *ἐσ. τῶν τε πεπ. καὶ* Rs., Th. Cp. 22. 19, 30. 34.

86. **συνερούντων** Rs.; *ξυνεργούντων* X. — **κἀγαθοὶ** Canter; *ἢ ἀγαθοὶ* X. — **τῆς τούτων** Markl.; *τῆς* X. — **ἀπολλύναι** Markl.; *ἀποδοῦναι* X; *προδοῦναι* Cont. — **οὐδὲ** Rs.; *οὔτε* X.

88. **τῶν ἐχθρῶν** Geb.; *παρὰ τῶν ἐχθρῶν* X. — **δεινὸν εἰ**: *δεινὸν οἱ* X. — **ἐπ'** added by Rs.; *ἀπολέσασιν ἧπου* X, with mark in the margin signifying corruption. — **βοηθεῖν** Vulg.; *βοηθεῖεν* X.

89. πολὺ Vulg.; πολλοὶ X; πολλῷ Rs., Th. Lysias has πολλῷ with πλείων in 17. 6, 24. 16, 29. 8; otherwise with the comparative he always uses πολύ. — ῥᾷον Steph.; ῥᾴδιον X.

90. δείξετε Markl.; δείξατε X.

91. ψηφίζεσθαι Bekk.; ἀποψηφίζεσθαι X. — κρύβδην εἶναι Sch.; κρύβδην X.

92. διὰ τούτων C; διὰ τοῦτον X.

93. μὲν Baiter; μὲν ἂν X.

94. πονηροτάτων Rs.; πονηροτέρων X. — σφετέρας Markl.; ὑμετέρας X.

95. ἐξητοῦντο Cont.; ἐζητοῦντο X.

96. ἀπέκτειναν Rs.; ἀπέκτενον X. — ἀφέλκοντες Rs.; ἀφελόντες X.

99. προθυμίας οὐδὲν Canter; προθυμίας X. — ὑπέρ τε τῶν ἱερῶν Sauppe; ὑπὲρ τῶν ἱερῶν X.

100. ἡμῶν: Auger; ὑμῶν X. — εἴσεσθαι X; ὄψεσθαι or εἰσόψεσθαι Hamaker. See Commentary. — κατεψηφισμένους ἔσεσθαι Kayser; καταψηφιεῖσθαι X. — τὰς τιμωρίας Franz; τιμωρίας X.

XVI

1. συνῄδη: συνῄδειν X, Th. I have followed Morgan in restoring the older form here and elsewhere; cp. 12. 15; Kühn. § 213. 5.

2. ἀηδῶς Rs.; ἀηδῶς ἢ κακῶς X.

3. καὶ περὶ Rs., Fr.-Geb.-Th.; περὶ X; καὶ (without περὶ) Herw., Th. — ἵππευον Rn.; ἵππευον οὔτ᾽ ἐπεδήμουν X.

4. ἐπεδημοῦμεν added after πολιτείας by Markl., after καθαιρουμένων by Kayser. — μεθισταμένης τῆς πολιτείας Ald.; μεθισταμένη τῇ πολιτείᾳ X.

5. μηδὲν Francken; τοῖς μηδὲν X, Th. There is no separation of two classes, but close connection of two characteristics of one class, the second, indeed, growing out of the first.

6. ἐγγεγραμμένοι Markl.; ἐπιγεγραμμένοι X. — ἀναπράξητε Harp. s.v. κατάστασις; ἀναπράττηται X; ἀναπράττητε Vulg. before Sch.; ἀναπράξαιτε Sauppe. Mor. defends ἀναπράττητε as referring to "the repeated number of cases"; but Lysias is quite as likely to have thought of the summary result ("upshot aorist") as of the detailed process, so that it becomes purely a question of the weight to be given to the quotation as independent textual evidence.

7. ὡς κατάστασιν παραλαβόντα F.; οὔτε κατάστασιν παραλαβόντα X; οὔτε κατάστασιν καταβαλόντα Bake, Th. The reading of X breaks the connection of thought; the whole argument turns on the absence of the name from the phylarchs' list. — ὅτι Kayser; διότι X. — ἀποδείξειαν Rs.; ἀποδείξαιεν X.

8. ἤ: ἦν X, Th. ˉ I have followed Morgan in restoring the older Attic form. Kühn. § 298. 4. . Cp. on § 1 and on 12. 25. — ὥστε μηδὲν δι' ἄλλο με Tayl.; ὥστ εἰ μηδὲν διαβάλλομαι X.

9. αὐτῆς Frb.; ταύτης X; cp. 19. 55. — μόνων: μόν_{ον}^{ων} X. .

11. διώκηκα Sauppe; διώκησα X; ἤ τὰς F.; ἢ περὶ τὰς X.

13. Βοιωτοὺς Pertz; τοὺς Βοιωτοὺς X. *In nominibus gentium usurpandis Lysias constantem usum sequitur: nomina ubivis sine articulo ponit*, Pertz, *Quaest. Lys.* I. 6. — ἀσφάλειαν εἶναι δεῖν νομίζοντας X. δεῖν has caused much question, but Geb. has successfully defended it by comparison with Thuc. 4. 10. 4 ἀπὸ νεῶν, αἷς πολλὰ τὰ καίρια δεῖ ἐν τῇ θαλάττῃ ξυμβῆναι. Here δεῖ has clearly the force of "may be expected." Geb.'s comparison of Aeschin. 3. 170 is less convincing, for there δεῖν refers to what *ought* to be found to meet a definition, as well as to what one expects to find. — ἡγουμένους: the synonym to νομίζοντας in a parallel clause is quite in Lysias's style, but it is strange that a new infinitive does not come with it. Perhaps Weidner's conjecture is right, κίνδυνον ἐφεστάναι ἡγουμένους. Kayser would erase ἡγουμένους. — εἶπον Dobr., cp. 1. 23; ἔτι X; ἔφην C, Th. (but only one prose instance of φημί = κελεύω is cited, Xen. *Cyrop.* 4. 6. 11). — παρασκευάσαντα marg. Ald.; παρασκευάσαντι X.

15. ἐναποθανόντων Markl.; ἐνθανόντων X. — ὕστερος Cont.; ὕστερον X. — Στειριῶς Cob.; Στειριέως X. See Meisterhans,[3] § 57. 10. — τοῦ πᾶσιν Bekk.; τοῖς πᾶσιν X.

16. προσιέναι X; παριέναι Herbst, on the ground that the post was seized to prevent the victorious Spartans from 'passing on' to the north; but the point here is rather that Mantitheus would voluntarily leave a post which was so strong that the enemy could not approach (προσιέναι) for a place of great danger. — ἀποχωρίσαι X; ἀποκληρῶσαι M. The emphasis is upon the fact that a division was to be *removed* from their position of safety. — σεσωμένους Wdn.; σεσωσμένους X, Th. Kühn. I. ii. p. 544.

18. κομᾷ Hamaker; τολμᾷ X.

19. ἀμπεχόμενοι Dobr.; ἀπερχόμενοι X.

20. τὰ τῆς R.; τῶν τῆς X.

21. τοὺς τοιούτους Francken; τούτους X. — πολλοῦ ἀξίους Cob.; cp. 10. 3, 33. 3; ἀξίους X.; ἀξίους τινὸς P. R. Müller, Th. Lysias is speaking of leadership in public affairs; he would hardly say that the people considered political leaders as the only people worth *anything*; this would reflect on too many of his auditors.

XIX

Title, ΥΠΕΡ: ΥΠΟ X.

2. τὴν προθυμίαν F., after *Frag.* 70; om. τήν X. — ὥσπέρ καὶ West.; om. καί X.

3. τοῦ μεγίστου Francken after Andoc. 1. 1; om. τοῦ X.

4. ὑπὸ πάντων τῶν παραγενομένων Dobr.; ὑπὲρ πάντων τῶν πεπραγμένων X; ὑπὸ πάντων ὑπὲρ τῶν πεπραγμένων Sauppe, Th.

6. ἰδεῖν Cont.; δεινότατον X. — ἐθέλοντες Pertz (Meisterhans,³ p. 178); θέλοντες X.

7. οὐδὲ γὰρ Dobr.; οὐ γὰρ X. — ἀπέδοσαν: ἀπέδωκαν X. See Meisterhans,³ p. 188. Cp. Fuhr, *Rhein. Mus.* 57. 425 ff. — ἡ συμφορὰ Rs.; συμφορά X.

8. ἀπὸ τῶν τοῦ Halbertsma, after ἐκ τῶν τοῦ of Francken; ὑπὸ τοῦ X. — οὕτως ἐν δεινῷ Rn. Cp. Dem. 18. 33 οὕτω δ' ἦν ὁ Φίλιππος ἐν φόβῳ. ἐν οὕτω δεινῷ X, Th. (F. cites τῶν οὕτω δεινῶν Lucian Ἀποκηρυττόμενος 14).

9. ἀνήλωσεν Tayl.; ἀνάλωσεν X.

10. ὑμῖν: the dative with δαπανῶντος is not impossible, though not used elsewhere by Lysias, but the change from εἰς αὐτόν to the dat. gives reason for the suspicion that a word is lost in the second clause (δόντος, Sluiter; χορηγοῦντος Markl.; ἀναλώσαντος Francken; λῃτουργοῦντος P. Müller; ἐπιδιδόντος, Wdn.). — ἄλλοθεν ἔχωσιν F. (ἄλλοθεν after West., ἔχωσιν after Sch.); μὴ δῶσιν X. The correction of the impossible reading of X is pure conjecture; κερδάνωσιν Th. after Cont.; λάβωσιν C; λαβεῖν δυνηθῶσι Rs.; κτήσωνται Dobr.

11. τοῦ ἀγῶνος Halbertsma; καὶ τοῦ ἀγ. X, Th. — ἀκροασαμένους ἡμῶν: ἀκροασομένων ὑμῶν X. — νομίζητε Rs.; νομίζεται X.

12. ἐμὴν ἀδελφὴν Tayl.; ἀδελφὴν X.

13. τῇ τε πόλει Rs.; τῇ πόλει X. — ἔν γε Rs.; ἔν τε X. — βίου παντὸς καὶ: βίου πᾶν καὶ X.

15. ἐθελόντων: θελόντων X; see on § 6. — οὐκ ἔδωκεν Bekk.; οὐ δέδωκεν X. — ὄντι Φαίδρῳ Tayl.; φαίδρω (*sic*) ὄντι X. — τῷ after Φαί-

δρῳ *add*. Rs. — κᾆτ' Sauppe; καὶ X. There were only two daughters (§ 17).

16. ἡ ἐν Ἑλλησπόντῳ: ἡ *add*. P. Müller.

17. τοῖν: ταῖν X. — ὑεῖ Th.; υἱῶ X.

18. ἂν X; δὴ Sauppe. — ἀρκοῦν ἦν P. Müller; ἦν X.

19. Διονυσίου Sauppe; καὶ Λυσίου X. Against the Ms. reading three objections have been raised: (1) It makes Lysias a ξένος of the Athenian Aristophanes. Now while Lysias was not an Athenian citizen, he had lived at Athens as boy and youth, and he had now been back in the city some twenty-five years; it is hard to believe that he would think of his relation to Aristophanes as ξενία. (2) If Lysias was looked upon as a suitable man to help win Dionysius's friendship in 393, it is surprising to find him in 388, in the Olympic speech, urging the Greeks to unite against him. (3) It would certainly not be in good taste for Lysias to dismiss the general Eunomus without a word of appreciation, while calling attention to his own services to the democracy. Sauppe's conjecture restores to ξενίου its normal force, and gives to the participial clauses following τοῦ Εὐνόμου a real meaning, for they bring out the fitness of Eunomus for the embassy by showing his cordial relations to Dionysius on the one side and the democracy on the other. With the Ms. reading there would be a departure from the real point, in order to throw around the memory of Aristophanes something of the popularity that Lysias enjoys.

20. τὰς τριήρεις Frb.; τριήρεις X. — παρεσκεύαστο Bekk.; παρεσκεύασατο X, Th. The context demands either plupf. or impf.

21. δέκα *add*. West. In § 43 the article (τὰς δέκα ναῦς) implies that the number was given here. — τοὺς *add*. Frb.

22. οὖν Frb.; δ'οὖν X. — ἀπορῶν Kayser; εἰπὼν X. — ἥ Steph.; ᾗ X, Rn.-F.

23. μηδενὸς Markl.; μηδὲν X. — ἐκ Κύπρου Th. follows Rn. in omitting these words, and their origin as a gloss is so easily explained that they cannot be defended with any certainty. Yet the expression is a possible one with ἀπορήσειν, as we see when we use the positive form, πάντων εὐπορήσειν ἐκ Κύπρου (see Rn.-F. *ad loc*.). — ὑπολιπέσθαι Lipsius; ὑπολείπεσθαι X. — οὐκ εἰ ἦν: οὐκ ειην (*sic*) X; οὐχ ἃ ἦν Bekk., Th. The Ms. reading presents no difficulty if we understand πάντα to mean all the money required for the expedition, not all of Aristophanes's property (τῶν ὄντων). — ἐφ' ᾧ τε: Rn.; τε X, Th. To the strangeness of the coördination of χαρίσασθαι and κομίσασθαι in the Ms. reading is added the difficulty of explaining μή for οὐ (μὴ ἐλάττω). — Κάλει . . . ΜΑΡΤΥΡΕΣ supplied by West. to fill the *lacuna* involved in τῶν μὲν μαρτύρων immediately following ΜΑΡ-ΤΥΡΙΑ in X.

24. ἔχρησαν τὸ ἀργύριον Rs. ; ἐχρήσαντο X.

25. μὲν . . . φιάλην χρυσῆν: φιάλης μὲν χρυσῆς X ; Sauppe transposed μὲν to its place after ἔλαβε. — ὑποθήσει δὲ 'Αριστοφάνει λαβὼν F. after Rn. (who wrote δὲ εὐθέως 'Αριστ.) ; ὡς ἀριστοφάνην λαβεῖν X ; Th. omits ὡς 'Αριστ. (after Dobr.), and writes βούλεται δὲ λαβεῖν (after Frb.). While ὡς 'Αριστοφάνην is easily explained as a gloss on αὐτῷ, yet the meaning is not quite clear if the name does not appear before § 26. — ἵν' Sauppe; ἂν X; ἆς Ald. — τὴν τριηραρχίαν: X combines τὰς τριηραρχίας and τὴν τριηραρχίαν (see Lampros, *Hermes*, X. 269). — λύσεσθαι Steph.; λύσασθαι X.

26. τὸ *add.* Sauppe. — ἂν *add.* Markl.

27. σύμμεικτα: Meisterhans,[3] p. 188 ; σήμμικτα X. — ΑΠΟΓΡΑΦΗ ΧΑΛΚΩΜΑΤΩΝ wanting in X.

28. πρὶν Sluiter; πρὶν νικοφήμῳ ἦ καὶ ἀριστοφάνει πρὶν X. — Κόνωνα *add.* Bekk. — 'Αριστοφάνει *add.* West. — γῆ μὲν Ald. ; γε μὴν X. — ἀλλ' ἦ: ἀλλ' εἰ X. — ἡ *add.* Rs. — Εὐβουλίδου Meursius; εὐβούλου X.

29. οὐσίας Cont. ; αἰτίας X. — δὶς χορηγῆσαι Rs. ; διαχορηγῆσαι X. — οἴεσθε Rs. ; οἴεσθαι X.

30. ἄξια λόγου ἔχοιεν C ; ἀξιολόγου ἔχοι X. — ἃ *add.* Tayl.

31. τὰ *add.* Sauppe. — ἐν *add.* Emperius. — ἐρήμη P. Müller ; ἐμῇ X. — ἀπεφαίνετο Pertz ; ἀπεφαίνοντο X. — πλεῖν ἦ: πλείω ἦ X. See on 32. 20.

32. μηδὲν West. ; μὴ X. — ἐνοφείλεσθαι Bekk. ; ὀφείλεσθαι X. — τὰς *add.* West.

34. ἄνδρες *add.* F. — ἠξιοῦτε ἂν C ; ἠξίουν X. — τοὺς κηδεστὰς τοὺς ἐκείνου Sluiter, Rn.-F. ; τοὺς . . . ἐκείνου (*lacuna* of four letters) X ; ἐκείνου Th.

35. τοῦτό γε Cob. ; τοῦτον X. — ἂν *add.* Emperius. — πλεῖν: πλείονα X. See on § 31.

36. ὁμοίως Rs. ; ὅμως X. — σᾶ Cob. ; ἴσα X.

37. διένειμεν X ; διένεμεν Steph., Fr., F., Th. The supposition is particular, *i.e.* that of a single action of an indefinite subject (τις), with the potential aorist in the apodosis.

38. δημεύσαιτε Rs. ; δημεύσετε X. — ἀγαθὸν X ; κακὸν Sauppe, who

holds that the suggestion that the confiscation of the property of Timotheus might be justified by the prospect of a great gain to the city, is strange and especially ill-fitted to the character of the speaker. But the "good" (ἀγαθόν) to the city in the supposed case would be, not the gain of so many talents of property, but the "good" sought in every righteous confiscation, the protection of the city by the punishment of crime. — δὲ C ; ἐὰν X ; δ' εἰ Rn., Th. — λάβοιτ' ἢ ἃ X, corrected by the first hand from λάβοι τὴν ; λάβοιτ' ἢ Steph., Th. — τούτου : τοῦτο X. — ἂν ἠξιοῦτε Cob. ; ἠξιοῦτε X.

40. γίγνεται Rs. ; τί γίγνεται X.

41. διέθετο Tayl. ; ᾔσθετο X. — ΜΑΡΤΥΡΕΣ om. X.

42. ᾤήθη ἂν Steph. ; ᾠήθησαν X. — οἰκίαν Markl. ; οὐσίαν X. — πλεῖν : πλέον X. Cp. on § 31. — κατεχορήγησε Rs. ; καὶ ἐχορήγησε X.

43. ἐπὶ Σικελίας Hertlein ; ἐν Σικελίᾳ X. — ναῦς Tayl. ; μνᾶς X.

44. αἰτιάσαισθε Dobr. ; αἰτιᾶσθε X. — ἐπεὶ Rs. ; ἐπὶ X. — πλεῖν : πλέον X. Cp. on § 31.

45. μὲν οὖν Markl. ; μὲν X. — οἱ Tayl. ; καὶ X.

46. πλεῖν : πλεῖον X. Cp. on § 31. — ἐνειμάσθην δὲ τὼ υἱεῖ : ἐνειμάσθη δὲ τῷ υἱεῖ X. On υἱεῖ see Meisterhans,[3] § 17. 4 and § 55. 4. — ἑκάτερος Rs. ; ἑκατέρω X. — πλεῖν : πλέον X. Cp. πλεῖον (X) above. — τάλαντα Rs. ; ταλάντων X.

47. ἔνδον Sch. ; ἔνδον ἦν X. — καταλείπειν Kayser ; καταλιπεῖν X.

52. I have followed Th. in inserting this paragraph after § 47. The instance of the mistaken assumption as to the property of Alcibiades is fitting as one of the series introduced by οἳ ζῶντες μὲν πλουτεῖν ἐδόκουν (§ 45), and closed with the comment φαινόμεθα οὖν κτλ. (§ 49) ; the point in all of these cases is that after the death of the man, his property was found to be far below popular expectation, or wasted away rapidly in the hands of his heirs. With the close of § 49 a new and more surprising instance of misconception is introduced, — that concerning the property of a living man, who himself proved its falsity. From this the speaker draws the telling inference that it is dangerous to act under such rumors. This is followed in the most logical manner by § 53. The insertion here of the instance of Alcibiades would betray not merely looseness of structure, but inability to remember the point of the argument. Cp. Westermann, *Quaestionum Lysiacarum*, II. 17 ff. The position of the paragraph in the Mss. would give a strong presumption against its genuineness were not the text of the whole speech in so poor condition. — πλεῖν : πλέον X.

48. πλεῖστα Baiter and Sauppe; ὃς πλεῖστα X. — φασι Cont.; φησι X. — τὰ αὐτοῦ Sch.; αὐτοῦ X. τὸ δὲ τούτου νῦν West.; τό, τε τούτου τοίνυν X. — κατέλιπεν ἄν Rn.; κατέλιπεν X.

49. οὖν add. Rs. — ἐψευσμένοι: ἐψηφισμένοι X. — τεθνεώτων Markl.; τεθνεῶτος X. — ἐξελεγχθεῖεν: ἐξενεχθεῖεν X.

50. ταλάντοις Francken; τάλαντα X, Th. — ἤ add. C; ὅσων Rs. — ἀπογράφοντος Rs.; ἀπογραφέντος X.

51. ἁπάντων Rs.; ἀπόντων X. — ἔπαθε C; εἰ ἔπαθε X. — πρὶν Steph.; πλὴν X. — εἰδότας Steph.; εἰδότες X. — καὶ ἤδη Dobr.; καὶ ἰδίᾳ X. — γέ τινας Markl.; τέ τινας X. — ἀπολέσθαι οἱ ῥᾳδίως Kayser; ῥᾳδίως ἀπ. οἱ X.

54. μᾶλλον ἤ: ἢ μᾶλλον X. — ἀπολέσαι Rs.; ἀπολέσθαι X.

55. καὶ ᾧ τρόπῳ . . . προσεδανείσατο: Th. follows West. (Quaest. Lys. II. 20) in treating this recapitulation as interpolated. But West.'s argument from its incompleteness is not conclusive. The speaker recapitulates the two great facts upon which he bases his argument; all that has followed the testimony to the impoverishment of Aristophanes by his Cyprian expedition has been to show the reasonableness of that testimony and the danger of rejecting it because of a different preconception. — οὔτε τῷ Rs.; οὐδὲ τῷ X. — οὔτε πρὸς . . . οὔτε πρὸς C, Rs.; οὐδὲ πρὸς . . . οὐδὲ πρὸς X.

57. μόνου τούτου ἔνεκα ἵνα Hertlein; οὐ μόνον τούτου ἔνεκεν, ἀλλ' ἵνα X. Th. suggests οὐδενὸς ἄλλου ἔνεκα ἀλλ' ἵνα. — ἀναγνώσεται: ἀναγνώσετε X¹. — ΛΗΙΤΟΥΡΓΙΑΙ C; om. X.

58. καὶ τοῖς Sluiter; αὐτοῖς X. — δοκοῦντά Markl.; δοκοῦντάς X.

59. παρέσχεν F.; παρεῖχεν X, Th. — εἴσεσθαι: ἔσεσθαι X.

60. μὲν χρόνον Ald.; μὲν οὖν χρονον X. — λάθοι: λάθη X.

61. ὃν ὑμεῖς Rs.; ὃ νῦν εἰς X. — δημεύσαιθ' C; δημεύσηθ' X.

62. ὥσπερ καὶ Sch.; ὥσπερ εἰ X. — τῷ τ' ἔργῳ τῇ πόλει ταῦτ' ἔσται I have written for τῷ τ' ἔργῳ πάλαι ταῦτ' ἐστί X; ὥστε τῷ γ' ἔργῳ πάλαι τῆς πόλεως ταῦτ' ἐστί Th. — οὔτ' ἐγὼ X; οὐκ ἐγὼ Th. — ὑμῖν τε Steph.; ὑμῖν δὲ X, Th.

63. ἀθληταῖς Tayl.; ἀθλητὰς X.

XXII

1. ποιουμένους τοὺς λόγους Hirschig; ποιουμένους λόγους X; λόγους ποιουμένους Frb., Th.

2. ὡς ἀκρίτους: ὡς ἀκρίτως X. — γνώσεσθαι: γνώσεσθε X.

3. **σωτηρίας ἕνεκα** : σωτηρίας οὔνεκα X ; cp. on 32. 10.

4. **δεδιὼς τὰς αἰτίας· αἰσχρὸν δ' ἡγοῦμαι** Dobr. ; δεδιὼς δὲ τὰς αἰτίας αἰσχρὸν ἡγοῦμαι X.

5. **ἀνάβητε.** εἰπὲ Frb. ; ἀνάβηθι εἰπὲ X. — ἢ **ἀξιοῖς** Rs. ; ἀξιοῖς ἢ X.

6. **πλείω** : add. Markl.

7. **χρῆν** Rs. ; χρὴ X. — **διὰ μακροτέρων** P. Müller ; καὶ μακρότερον X.

8. **τέτταρες** Bergk ; δύο X ; νῦν Th. δύο of X is probably from a mis-understanding of δ' = τέτταρες. — **φιλονικοῦσιν** : φιλονεικοῦσιν X.

9. **παρέξομαι.** ΜΑΡΤΥΡΙΑ. **καὶ ὡς οὗτος . . . φαίνονται.** ΜΑΡ-ΤΥΡΙΑ. X has a *lacuna* after παρέξομαι with space for about eight letters, and it has μρα in the margin. Elsewhere Lysias always intro-duces his testimony immediately after παρέξομαι (F. *ad loc.*). With the reading that I propose the speaker calls Anytus to testify to what his advice really was ; he then produces *other testimony*, probably copies of official records, to show that Anytus's term of office fell the year before. With καὶ ὡς οὗτος . . . εἶπε the governing verb is readily understood from the context. Th. transposes ΜΑΡΤΥΡΙΑ from the position after φαίνονται (ΜΑΡΤΥΣ vulg.) to the *lacuna* after παρέξο-μαι, and reads καὶ οὗτος . . . (after Pluygers). — **δὲ τῆτες** Emperius ; δ' ἐπίτηδες X.

10. **ἀπολογήσεσθαι** : ἀπολογήσασθαι X.

11. **ἀλλὰ γὰρ** Rs. ; ἀλλὰ μὲν γὰρ X. — **τοῦτον τὸν λόγον . . . οὐ τρέψεσθαι** Cob. ; . . . ἐλεύσεσθαι X ; τούτῳ τῷ λόγῳ . . . ἐλεήσεσθαι Wdn., Th. — ὑμῖν C ; ἡμῖν X, and Suid. *s.v.* ἄξιον, Th. ; cp. ὑμῶν ἕνεκα § 12.

12. **ὑμῶν** X ; ἡμῶν Th. — **ἕνεκα** : οὔνεκα X. — **νῦν** Hofmeister ; νυνὶ X.

14. **αὐτοὶ** Markl. ; οὗτοι X. — **κεκλῆσθαι** : κεκλεῖσθαι X.

15. **τοῖς αὐτοῖς καιροῖς . . . ἐν οἷσπερ** Cob. ; τούτοις τοῖς καιροῖς . . . ἐν οἷσπερ X ; τοῖς καιροῖς . . . ὥσπερ Th. — ἡμῖν X ; ὑμῖν Bekk., Th., because of τυγχάνητε following. But τυγχάνητε is itself joined with διαφερώμεθα and ἀγαπῶμεν.

18. **ἀμφισβητούντων** Th. after ἀλλ' ἀμφισ. of Frb. ; λαμβάνειν X ; καὶ ἀρνουμένων Dobr. ; Wilamowitz, *Arist. u. Athen.* II. 379, suggests that the language follows the wording of the law as to the Eleven : ἂν μὲν [ὁμ]ολογῶσι, θανάτῳ ζημιώσοντας, ἂν δ' ἀμφισβητῶσιν, εἰσάξον-τας εἰς τὸ δικαστήριον Arist. *Resp. Ath.* 52. 1.

19. **τούτων** Kayser ; αὐτῶν X.

20. **αἱροῦνται** Tayl. ; αἰτοῦνται X. — **παύσασθαι** Vulg. before Sch.

παύσεσθαι X; παύεσθαι Sch., Th.; cp. § 8. Lysias repeatedly uses παύσασθαι, never παύεσθαι.

21. ἐφ' οὖς Tayl.; ἐφ' οἷς X. — παρὰ τούτων Tayl.; παρ' αὐτῶν X. — τίν' αὐτοὺς C; τὴν αὐτὴν X. — εἰσπλέουσιν Rs.; ἐκπλέουσιν X.

22. ὅτου Sauppe; ὅτε X.

XXIV

The superscription in X is ΠΡΟΣ ΤΗΝ ΕΙΣΑΓΓΕΛΙΑΝ ΠΕΡΙ ΤΟΥ ΜΗ ΔΙΔΟΣΘΑΙ ΤΩΙ ΑΔΥΝΑΤΩΙ ΑΡΓΥΡΙΟΝ. But it is clear from § 26, compared with Arist. *Resp. Ath.* 49. 4, that this is not a case of εἰσαγγελία. See Introd. p. 232.

1. οὐ πολλοῦ Markl., cp. Xen. *Anab.* 5. 4. 32; ὀλλοῦ X. — γὰρ *add.* Rs. — ἐφ' ἧς X; ἐφ' ᾗ Dobr. See commentary. — ἄξιον X; ἀξίως or ἄξια Rs.; ἄξιον ὄντ' F. The force of βεβιωκότα so nearly approaches that of γεγονότα that the pred. adj. seems possible; yet no other instance is cited, and βεβιωκώς with adv. is very common. Lysias uses it even in 14. 41, where the parallelism of cola would tempt to the use of the adjective: ἄλλως δὲ κόσμιοί εἰσι καὶ σωφρόνως βεβιώκασιν.

3. ἰᾶσθαι · καλῶς: ἰᾶσθαι καλῶς X; ἰᾶσθαι, εἰκότως P. Müller, Th. κ_ιλῶς is precisely fitted to the sportive tone.

4. οἷός τ' ὦ P. Müller; οἷον X; οἷόν τε Ald., Th.; οἷόν τ' ᾗ Schulze. Lysias elsewhere uses the formula ὡς ἂν δύνωμαι διά . . . (12. 3, 12. 62, 16. 9).

5. τὴν μὲν οὖν: τῆς μὲν οὖν X. — εὐπορίαν καὶ τὸν ἄλλον: εὐπορίας καὶ τῶν ἄλλων X.

6. ἧν ἂν Cont.; ᾗς ἂν X.

7. τοὺς καὶ Rs.; καὶ τοὺς X.

8. ἑπόμενα C; ἐχόμενα X.

9. προκαλεσαίμην Rs.; προσκαλεσαίμην X. — καίτοι πῶς Cob., Rn.-F.; καὶ πῶς X, Th. Cp. καίτοι πῶς οὐκ ἄτοπον κτλ., § 12. — τύχοι τι Emperius; τύχοι τις X. — ὁμολογεῖν ἄν με: ὁμολογεῖν ἂν inserted by Kayser, με by Th. after F. (ἐμὲ).

10. ἐγὼ γάρ, . . . τοῦτ' οἶμαι Wdn.; ἐγὼ γάρ, . . . τοιοῦτο X; εἰκὸς γάρ, . . . τοῦτο Kayser, Th.

11. ἀναβαίνω: after ἀναβαίνω X adds ῥᾳδιόν ἐστι μαθεῖν, omitted by most editors after Sch.

12. τοῦτον ἂν αὐτόν Kayser; τοῦτον αὐτὸν X; τοῦτον ἂν (omitting αὐτὸν) Wdn., Th. — εἰμι Kayser; εἴην X.

13. **θεσμοθέται** add Frb.

14. **οὐθ᾽ οὗτος ὑμῖν · εὖ ποιῶν** Cont., Rs., Th. (without interpunctuation). Mss. omit ὑμῖν. οὐθ᾽ οὐδεὶς εὖ φρονῶν Reuss; οὐθ᾽ οὗτος ἑαυτῷ Kayser.

15. **λέγει** C; λέγω X. — **ὀνομάσειε** Rn.; ὀνομάσαι X. — **πραόνως, ταῦτα** Kayser; πρᾷον ὡς μηδὲ ψεύδηται ταῦτα X; πραόνως ψεύδηται, πιστὰ ποιήσων Wdn.

16. **τοὺς πενομένους** Rs.; πενομένους X.

17. **πρεσβυτέροις** Frb.; ἑτέροις X.

18. **οὓς ἂν**: οὓς ἐὰν X. — **ὑπάρξαντας** Steph.; συνάρξαντας X.

20. **ὁ δὲ** (after μυροπώλιον): οἱ δὲ X. — **ὅποι ἂν τύχῃ**: ὅπη ἂν τύχοι X. — **τοὺς ἐγγυτάτω** Steph.; ἐγγυτάτω X. — **τοὺς πλεῖστον** Steph.; οὐ πλ. X. — **ἀμουγέπου** Mor. (Kühn. I. 1. 614); ἄλλου γέ που X.

21. **περὶ τῶν φαύλων ὁμοίως τούτῳ** Dobr., Rn.-F., Th.; π. τ. ὁμοίως τούτῳ φαύλων X, Fr., Blass (*Att. Bered.* I. 639). The Ms. reading gives a fine, keen thrust, quite in keeping with the tone of the speech, but it breaks the connection of the γάρ clause with the preceding, πρὸς ἓν ἕκαστον . . . τῶν εἰρημένων.

22. **καὶ μὴ**: μηδ᾽ X; μὴ οὖν F.; μὴ τοίνυν Wdn.; μὴ δὴ Herw.; μὴ Th. F. suggests that μηδ᾽ is right and that the necessary preceding negative clause has dropped out. I propose καί as giving the close connection needed with the preceding; this is not an inference (οὖν, τοίνυν) from that, but a continuation of it. — **μόνον** Markl.; μόνον X. — **ἀρχῶν** X, Rn.-F.; *del.* Frb., Th. ἀρχῶν fits the reference in § 13 and καλλίστων of § 23; its erasure destroys a fine bit of humor.

23. **δειλαιότατος** Markl.; δικαιότατος X. — **θῆσθε** Bekk.; θέσθε X. — **τὴν ψῆφον** Cont.; τῇ ψήφῳ X.

24. **βίου**: Francken; βίου πρὸς τὰ τοιαῦτα X.

25. **ἀλλ᾽ οὐδ᾽** C; οὐδ᾽ X. — **Χαλκίδα** Frb.; X adds τὴν ἐπ᾽ Εὐρίπῳ. — **ἀποδημῶν** Reuss; ἁπάντων X, F.; ἀπελθών Bäker, Th.; ἁπάντων of X, an exaggeration at best, is strangely put in so emphatic a position.

26. **ὁμοίων** Cont.; ὁμοίως X.

XXV

On the title see Introd. p. 253.

1. **καὶ σαφῶς** Dobr.; οἳ σαφῶς X; εἰ σαφῶς Rs., Th. — **μηδὲν** Rs.; μὲν X. — **κερδαίνειν ἢ** X, Rn.-F.; omit Dobr., Th., Fr.-Geb. He is speaking of sycophants, who meddle with things that do not concern

them, hoping to be bought off (κερδαίνειν) by the men whom they threaten, or else (ἤ) to carry the case against them through the courts (πείθειν). Francken proposes κερδαίνειν ὑμᾶς πείθοντες, and Reuss κέρδους ἕνεκα; but the gain of the sycophant comes not by his persuading the court, but by being bought off from the attempt.

2. ὅσα Herw.; ἃ Χ; ἅπανθ' ἃ Bartelt, Rn.-F.; Th. (after Rs.) retains ἃ and inserts πάντ' before ἐμοῦ. — γεγένηται Dobr.; γεγένηνται Χ.—ἀποδείξω Steph.; ἀποδείξαι Χ. — ἅπαντα Steph.; ἅπαντας Χ. — ὁ βέλτιστος Rs.; βέλτιστος Χ.

3. καθιστάναι: καθιστάνειν Χ. — χρηματίζοιντο Coraes.; χρηματίζειν τὸ Χ.

4. ἀποφήνω Van den Es; ἀποφανῶ Χ.

5. μοι add. Frb.

7. οὓς add. Cont.

8. καθεστάναι F.; καθιστάναι Χ.

9. τῶν πολιτειῶν Rs.; πολιτειῶν Χ. — αὖθις Brulart; αὐτοῖς Χ. — ἐπολιόρκουν τοὺς μεθ' Sch.; ἐπολιορκοῦντο μεθ' Χ.

10. εἴ τις: Χ has ἥτις with εἰ written above. — τὴν κρίσιν Rn.; κρίσιν Χ.

11. ἦσαν Francken; ἦσαν εὐθύνας δεδωκότες Χ, Fr.-Geb. εὐθύνας δεδωκότες gives an unnecessary limitation to the class of ἄτιμοι, and breaks the symmetry of the three parallel cola, thrusting δεδωκότες into apparent coördination with ἀπεστερημένοι and κεχρημένοι. The origin of the words as a gloss is easy to conjecture. — ὑμῶν Steph.; ὑμῖν Χ. — τὰς περὶ τούτων Auger; τὰς τούτων Χ. — ἀποδέχεσθαι Tayl.; ὑποδέχεσθαι Χ.

12. τετριηράρχηκα Sch.; ἐτριηράρχησα Χ. — μὲν γὰρ Χ; τε γὰρ Geb., Th. — τετράκις δὲ: I have written δὲ for καὶ of Χ (Th.). This makes the trierarchies, four of which included naval battles, the first of the forms of liturgy, the εἰσφοραί, the second form. It avoids treating νεναυμάχηκα as a form of liturgy, as is done with the reading τε. Weidner's substitution of εἰσφορὰς δ' for καὶ εἰσφορὰς accomplishes the same thing, but less clearly.

13. προστραττομένων ἐδαπανώμην Steph.; πραττομένων ἐδαπανῶμεν Χ. — ἀλλὰ Emperius; ἀλλὰ καὶ Χ.

14. οὔτε τῶν Markl.; οὔτε ἐπὶ τῶν Χ. — οἱ τριάκοντα Markl.; οἴδε Χ.

15. χρήσασθαι Frb.; χρῆσθαι Χ.

16. οὐδὲ δίαιταν: οὔτε δίαιταν Χ. — ὀργίζεσθε Ald.; ὀργίζοισθε Χ.

18. ἐχθροὺς C; ἐκ τοῦ X. — ἐκβαλόντας: ἐκβάλλοντας X. — ὑπολειφθήσεται Dobr.; ἀπολειφθήσεται X.

19. ὅτε (before ὑπέρ) Geb.; ὅτι X.

20. ἡγεῖσθαι C; ἡγεῖσθε X. — ἡμῶν Francken; αὐτῶν X.

21. κακὸν C; ἀγαθὸν X.

22. πυνθάνοισθε X; ἐπυνθάνεσθε Francken, Th. With the opt. the following μὴ ἔχοντας is regular; with the indic. it would be very exceptional. — ἐκ τοῦ ἄστεως X has after στασιάζοντας; F. placed before ἐκκεκηρυγμένους. — πλείους δὲ Cont.; πλείους X. — ταὐτὰ Th.; ταῦτα X.

23. τούτων χαλεπώτερον Geb.; χαλ. τούτων X; see commentary.

24. δέξαιντ᾿: δέξαι τ᾿ X.

25. μνησθῆναι καὶ: καὶ add. Baiter. — Ἐπιγένην καὶ Δημοφάνην καὶ Κλεισθένην X. Beloch (Att. Politik, p. 78, Anm. 1) restores Ἐπιγένην in Arist. Eccl. 167 for Ἐπίγονον of the Mss. Schwartz (Rhein. Museum 44, 121 Anm. 1), followed by Busolt (Griech. Gesch. III. ii. 1542 Anm. 1), writes Δημόφαντον and Κλειγένην, probably correctly. Both men were active at the time mentioned. In 410 Demophantus moved the decree of Andoc. 1. 96 ff. Cligenes was clerk of the Senate in the first prytany of 410/9 (C.I.A. I, 188, Andoc. 1. 96); he is reviled by Aristophanes (Frogs, 707 ff.) as ὁ πίθηκος and ὁ μικρός (cp. v. 1085).

27. ὥστε τοὺς: ὥστε add. C.

28. διεκελεύσαντο Tayl.; διελύσαντο X. — ταύτην . . . φυλακήν: Rs. would add μόνην, μεγίστην, or βεβαιοτάτην; so ἱκανωτάτην Herw.; ἀσφαλεστάτην F. — ἂν add. Geb.

31. ὅμως Rs.; ὁμοίως X.

32. δέξαιντ᾿: δέξαι τ᾿ X.

33. τοὺς ἐκ Πειραιῶς κινδύνους X; τοὺς τῶν ἐκ Πει. κινδύνους Sauppe. Sch. would drop κινδύνους or read κινδυνεύσαντας; ἀκινδύνως P. Müller. 34. 2 has τῶν ἐξ ἄστεως (πραγμάτων), an expression parallel with τοὺς ἐκ Πειραιῶς κινδύνους. The expressions ἐκ Πειραιῶς and ἐξ ἄστεως were becoming fixed formulas. Against the insertion of τῶν or its equivalent (making the prosecutors enjoy freedom to act as they will because of the dangers of other men) is the mention of the safety that may afterward come through others; this implies that the former safety came through them (τούτους). — δι᾿ ἑτέρους Tayl.; δι᾿ ἑτέρου X. — σωτήρια Frb.; σωτηρία X. — πεπαύσεσθαι Geb.; ἐπιλύσασθαι X. — οἱ τοιοῦτοι πάντες: I have written this for τὸ αὐτὸ πάντες of X. Th. retains τὸ αὐτὸ πάντες, translating alle wie ein Mann. τῷ αὐτῷ πάντες

Baiter; διὰ τοῦτο πάντως Frb.; τοῦτ᾽ αὐτὸ δείσαντες Sch., Fr.-Geb.; τοιοῦτοί γ᾽ ὄντες West.; αὐτὸ τοῦτο πάντες F.

34. **κατανοῆσαι** C; κατηγορῆσαι X. — **ὑμεῖς τε** Rs.; ὑμεῖς δὲ X.

35. **περὶ ὑμᾶς** C; περὶ ἡμᾶς X. — ὑπο⟨ψίαν καταστήσετε⟩ Francken's conjecture.

XXXII

For the text of speeches XXXII, XXXIII (the Olympic speech), and XXXIV we depend upon the Mss. of Dionysius Περὶ τῶν ἀρχαίων ῥητόρων. For a summary description of the Mss. and for bibliography see the preface of the text edition of Usener-Radermacher, *Dionysii Halicarnasei Opuscula*, Vol. I, Leipzig, 1899.

The Mss. are of the following families:

I. Mss. of a collection of selected works of Dionysius, Philostratus, Callistratus, Aristides.

II. Mss. of a collection of rhetorical works of Dionysius with a Compendium of Rhetoric by Josephus Rhacendytes.

III. Mss. of a collection of speeches and declamations by various orators and sophists, in which is included the treatise of Dionysius on Lysias. This text has been emended by an editor who has often made corrections according to his own judgment, not on authority of other Mss.; but the source of the text of the treatise on Lysias seems to have been a good Ms. of Family I.

In addition we have for §§ 1–3 as far as χείρους εἶναι, and § 4 as far as θυγατέρα, independent testimony in a citation by Syrianus, which has been transmitted also in the anonymous treatise Walz. VII. 1084, and in Maximus Planudes, Walz. V. 546.

In the following notes only the more important variant readings are recorded. Note is made wherever the text adopted differs from that of Thalheim or that of Usener-Radermacher. Mss. are cited as follows (see Usener-Radermacher, p. 2, Thalheim, p. vii.):

> I. F *Florentinus, bybl. Laurent.* LIX. 15.
>
> II. M *Ambrosianus*, D. 119, *sup.*
>
> P *Vaticanus Palatinus gr.* 58.
>
> B *Parisinus, bybl. nat. gr.* 1742.
>
> III. C *Parisinus, bybl. nat. gr.* 1800.
>
> G *Guelferbytanus n.* 806.
>
> T *Parisinus bybl. nat.* 2944.

1. ὦ ἄνδρες δικασταί after διαφέροντα, Mss.; ὦ δικασταί after ἦν,
Syr. — εἰδώς τε ὅτι Syr.; εἰδὼς ὅτι Mss., Us.R. (cp. 13. 11). See
commentary. — πεπονθότες F, G, T, Syr.; παθόντες M, P, B.

2. ἔπεισα τοῖς φίλοις G, Th.; ἔπεισα τοὺς φίλους F, M, P, B, T;
ἔπεισα αὐτοὺς τοῖς φίλοις Syr., Us.R. — δίαιταν Syr.; διαιτᾶν Mss.
Cp. Isae. 2. 29 ἐπιτρέψαι . . . τοῖς φίλοις διαιτῆσαι. But for δίαιταν
cp. [Dem.] 59. 45 συνῆγον αὐτοὺς οἱ ἐπιτήδειοι καὶ ἔπεισαν δίαιταν
ἐπιτρέψαι αὐτοῖς; cp. [Dem.] 34. 44, 40. 43, 59. 68, Isoc. 18. 14. —
τὰ τούτων F, P, G, T, Syr.; τὰ τούτου M, B. — ἐπειδὴ δὲ Syr.; ἐπεὶ δὲ
Mss. See 12. 11 Crit. N. — ἐξηλέγχετο Syr.; ἐξήλεγκτο Mss. — αὐτοῦ
Syr.; αὐτοῦ Mss. — ὑπομεῖναι Mss. (F¹ has ει and αι *in rasura*); καθυ-
πομένειν Syr. — πρὸς τούτους Mss. except F; πρὸς τούτοις V of Syr., F.

3. μηδὲν Syr.; οὐδὲν Mss, Us.R.

4. ὦ ἄνδρες δικασταί Mss.; ὦ δικασταί Syr. — ὑεῖ δύο Morgan (cp.
on 12. 34); υἱοὶ δύο F, M, Us.R.; δύο υἱοὶ G, T.

5. τῶν ὁπλιτῶν: τοῦ ἐπὶ τῶν ὁπλιτῶν G, T. — ἀδελφόν Herw.;
ἀδελφὸν ὁμοπάτριον Mss., probably from § 4. — ἀναγκαιότητας: ἀνάγκας
T. — δικαίῳ περὶ τοὺς αὐτοῦ παῖδας Sauppe; καὶ ὥσπερ τοῦ αὐτοῦ παῖδας
F, M, P, B; ἑτέρῳ εἰς τοὺς αὐτοῦ παῖδας ἐπιτρόπῳ G.

6. ναυτικὰ Markl.; αὐτίκα Mss. — μνᾶς . . .: Sauppe pointed out
the loss of an item in the reckoning. — δὲ (after κατέλιπε) *add*. Rs.

7. ἀνδρός . . .: Fuhr pointed out the *lacuna*, which is seen in the
absence of a correlative to τὴν μὲν θυγατέρα. Wilamowitz (*Hermes*,
36. 536) would, instead of assuming the *lacuna*, read τέως μὲν τὴν
θυγατέρα. Without *lacuna* Us.R.

8. ἐπειδὴ Fuhr; ἐπεὶ Mss.; cp. §§ 2 and 25. See 12. 11 Crit. N.
— χρόνῳ F, M; cp. 1. 8, 13. 83; τῷ χρόνῳ G, T; cp. 1. 20. — ἐπιλειπόντων Rs.; ὑπολειπόντων (-λιπ- G) Mss.

9. καταλίποι Steph.; καταλείποι Mss., Us.R. — διέφερεν: διέφερε
Ald.; διέφερον Mss.

10. κλάοντες Cob. (cp. Kühn. I. i. p. 134); κλαίοντες Mss., Us.R.
— ἕνεκα Dobson (cp. Kühn. I. ii. p. 251); οὕνεκα Mss.

11. ἠντεβόλει Cob. (cp. Kühn. I. ii. p. 35); ἠντιβόλει Mss., Us. R. —
ἱκέτευε G, T; ἱκέτευσε F, M. — εἰ καὶ μὴ πρότερον F; εἰ μὴ καὶ πρότερον
M, P, B; εἰ καὶ πρότερον μὴ G, T.

12. πραγμάτων Mss., Us.R. (cp. τὰ τούτων πράγματα, § 2);
χρημάτων Th. and most editors, after Halbertsma.

13. ἐθέλω Rn. (cp. Kühn. I. ii. p. 408); θέλω Mss. Us.R. — οὗτος
λέγῃ F, M; αὐτὸς λέγῃς G, T. — καταβαλεῖν: καταλιπεῖν Mss.; ἐκλι-

πεῖν Sch.; λιπεῖν Dobr.; ἀπολιπεῖν West.; καταβιοῦν Fuhr; καταναλίσκειν Us.R.; καταλύειν Th. The Ms. reading and the conjectures cited all rest upon the assumption that τὸν βίον is the mother's life; but her life is not involved in perjury over her children's heads more than in any perjury. The point of the argument is that the mother is willing to stake her children upon the truth of her oath; τὸν βίον is then the life of the children, which will be the penalty if her oath is false. I have therefore written καταβαλεῖν, the precise word for the payment of a price or penalty.

14. **αὐτὴ** F², M; αὐτῇ F¹; αὐτὸν G, Th. — **ναυτικὰ** Markl.; αὐτίκα Mss. — **ἐξοικίσει** Cob.; διοικήσει Mss.; διοικίσει Matthaei, Th, Us.R. So **ἐξῳκίζετο** Cob.; διῳκίζετο Mss., Th., Us.R. The analogy of forms like διαπερᾶν, διαπλεῖν, etc., cited by Th. to justify διῳκίζετο in the sense of 'removed' is not valid in view of the familiar and otherwise universal use of διοικίζειν = to scatter a people in different settlements. See Cobet, Var. Lect. p. 68. — **βιβλίῳ** F, M, B, Us.R. (βυβλίῳ F, B); τῷ βιβλίῳ G, Th.; τῳ βιβλίῳ T. — **αὐτήν** Rs.; ταύτην Mss.

15. **ἐγγείῳ** Naber; ἐγγείους F, M, P, B; ἐγγύους G, T.

16. **ἐκβάλλειν** F, P, B, M¹; ἐκβαλεῖν T. The present infinitive is exactly fitted to the picturesque description of how he proposes to 'send them packing.' — **ἠξίωκας** Mss.; ἠξίωσας Pluygers, Th. — **ὁ πατὴρ** T; πατὴρ F, M, P, B.

17. **ἀτίμους** F, M; ἀτίμως G, T. — **προθυμῇ . . . φοβῇ . . . αἰσχύνῃ . . . ποιῇ** Herw. Cp. Kühn. I. ii. p. 60. προθυμῇ . . . φοβῇ Mss.; αἰσχύνῃ Mss. except F, which had αἰσχύνην, corrected by F¹; ποιεῖς F, M, P, B; ποιῇ G, T. Th. and Us.R. have -ει in all but αἰσχύνῃ.

18. **μὴ ἧττον** F, M, P, B; μηδὲν ἧττον G, T, Wdn. The emphatic form is more common; the simple negative with ἧττον appears in Lysias only here and in § 21.

19. **πρὸς ἀλλήλους**: M, P, B, Th., Us.R.; εἰς ἀλλήλους F; om. G, T. The only other instance in Lysias of ὑποψία with prep. is 25. 30, where πρός may be due to the connection with ὁμονοίας. In other prose writers εἰς is used with ὑποψία oftener than πρός. εἰς Thuc. 4. 27. 2, 6. 61. 4, 6. 103. 4; only once with πρός, 2. 37. The two instances in Andocides (1. 51, 1. 68) have εἰς. Antiphon always uses εἰς, but with a word of motion: II. β 3, 6, II. γ 2, 10. The only instance of either in Demosthenes is 23. 103 ἡ γὰρ ἐκείνων πρὸς ἀλλήλους ταραχὴ καὶ ὑποψία, where πρός may be due to ταραχή. [Dem.] 48. 18 has τῆς ὑποψίας τῆς πρὸς τὸν οἰκέτην. Demosthenes has κατά in 29. 24.

Isocrates has ὑποψίαν περὶ αὑτοῦ λαβεῖν 15. 123. In favor of πρός in our passage is Lysias's usage with words of hostile attitude. A full statement of his use of prepositions with words denoting hostility is the following:

A. Of hostile attitude, πρός with acc.,

ἀηδῶς διακεῖσθαι 16. 2.	ὀργή 25. 5.
ἀλλοτρίως διακεῖσθαι 33. 1.	ὑποψία 25. 30, (32. 19?).
διαφέρεσθαι 32. 1, 18. 17.	φθόνος 12. 66.
διαφορά 12. 51, 25. 10.	φιλονικεῖν 3. 40.
ἔχθρα 12. 2, 13. 1, 18. 5.	φιλονικία 33. 4.

B. Of military movements (real or metaphorical),

1. **πρός** with acc.,	2. **ἐπί** with acc.,
μάχεσθαι 22. 8.	ἔρχεσθαι 33. 8.
μάχη 3. 45.	στάσις καὶ πόλεμος 12. 55.
πόλεμος 12. 93, 33. 9.	στρατεύεσθαι 14. 30, 14. 32, 14. 33, 18. 9.

C. Of other action 'against,'

1. **πρός** with acc.,

ἀντειπεῖν 26. 4, 26. 5.	τιμωρία 1. 2.
εἰπεῖν 26. 16.	πράγματα 29. 10.
λέγειν 12. 47.	πράττειν 27. 4.
ἀμιλλᾶσθαι 33. 6.	
ἔγκλημα 25. 23.	
στασιάζειν 26. 22.	

2. **κατά** with gen.,

ἐξευρίσκειν 3. 34.	ὀργὰς παρασκευάζειν 1. 28.
ἐπιορκεῖν 32. 13.	ὁμόψηφοι 13. 94.
κατηγορία 31. 2.	τρόπαια στῆσαι 18. 3.
μηνυτής 13. 2, 13. 18.	ψεύδεσθαι 22. 7.

3. **περί** with acc.,

ἀδικεῖν 31. 24.	κακία 31. 4.
ἁμαρτάνειν 14. 28, 31. 23.	
ἐξαμαρτάνειν Fr. 53. 1 (cp. under εἰς).	
ἀσεβεῖν 14. 42.	

4. **ἐπί** with acc.,

εἰσιέναι 3. 7, 3. 23.	ἔρχεσθαι 33. 8, Fr. 47.
ἐκπηδᾶν 3. 12.	συνίστασθαι 22. 17, 22. 21.

5. ἐπί with dat.,
δωροδοκεῖν 25. 19, 29. 11.
6. εἰς with acc.,
ἐξαμαρτάνειν 12. 2, 12. 89, 25. 9   παρανομεῖν 3. 17.
and often (cp. under περί).   προνοεῖσθαι 4. 18.
ὑβρίζειν 1. 16.
μήτε . . . μήτε Bekk.; μηδὲ . . . μηδὲ Mss.
20. τῶν μὲν F¹, Us.R.; τὰ μὲν F², M, P, B, G, Th. — ἔχειν Rs.;
ἐλεῖν Mss. — τετρακισχιλίας Herw. (cp. § 28); ἑπτακισχιλίας Mss.,
Us.R. Fuhr makes up the 7000 by adding the 7 t.–40 m. loaned on
bottomry, the evidence of which could not be denied, to what Diogiton
first told the boys their father had left them, 20 m. and 30 staters.
See p. 285 n. 2. — ὅποι τρέψειε Cont.; ὅπου στρέψειεν F; ὅπου στρέψειε
P, B, G; ὅπου στράψειε M. — γναφεῖον Rs.; γναφεῖον ἱμάτια Mss.; καὶ
εἰς γναφείαν καὶ εἰς ἱμ. Scaliger, Us.R. The position of ἱμάτια is suspicious; it would be strange to say, " For shoes and for laundry and for
clothing and for the barber's." — κουρέως F, M, P, B; κουρέον T; κου-
ρεῖον Ald. — πλεῖν : πλεῖον Mss. See Kühn. § 50, Anm. 11.
21. αὐτῷ τίθησι, τὸ δὲ τούτοις λελόγισται Rs.; αὐτῶν τίθησι τούτοις
λελογίσθαι Mss. (λελόγισθαι M). — ἐφ᾽ ᾧ Sylburg; ἐφ᾽ ὧν Mss. —
ἄνδρες Mss. Herw. and Fuhr add δικασταὶ from a sign in M that seems
to indicate the loss.
22. τῷ δ᾽ ἐπιτρόπῳ Frb.; τῷ δ᾽ ἐπὶ F, M, P, B; τὸν δ᾽ ἐπὶ T; τῷ δ᾽
ἐπεὶ Ald.; τὸν δ᾽ ἐπεὶ G. G, T add εἰσὶν after πατρῴων.
23. ἀπηλλαγμένον . . . πριάμενον Dobr.; ἀπηλλαγμένοις . . . πριάμενον F, M, P, B; ἀπηλλαγμένος . . . πριάμενος T. — ὁπότερα F, M,
P, B, cp. Isae. 1. 22; ὁπότερον G, T. — καταστήσων T; καταστήσονται
F. M, P, B.
24. ἄνδρες add. Herw. — δεούσας Ald.; δέουσαν F, M, P, B; δεούσαιν G. — συμβαλέσθαι Ald.; συμβάλλεσθαι Mss., Us.R. — τούτοις
Dobr.; τούτων M, P, B; τούτων τοῖς F, G, T. — τῶν θυγατριδῶν F, M,
P, B; τῶν αὐτοῦ θυγ. G, T.
25. ἐπειδὴ δὲ Fuhr; ἐπεὶ δὲ Mss., Us.R. See on § 8. — ἔφασκεν
G, T; φάσκων F, M, P, B; φάσκει Us.R. From the rarity of the
indic. of φάσκω in Lys., Fuhr suggests the loss of a phrase here, as
αὐτὸς τὴν ὠφέλειαν ἔλαβε. But ἔφασκε is used of a false statement precisely as here in 1. 14 and 10. 1.
26. ἄνδρες add. Herw. (cp. § 24). — ἔργον εἴη M, P, B; εἴη ἔργον
F, G, T. — ὁ τῆς Herw.; τῆς Mss., Us.R.

27. ἐπέδειξε Mss., cp. on 16. 3. ἀπέδειξε Pluygers, Th. — δεούσας : δέουσαν Τ ; δεούσαιν G. Cp. § 24. — ἀνηλωκέναι : Fuhr suggests ἀνηλωμένας (the more common construction) and λελόγισται. — ὥστε Μ, G ; ὥσγε F, P, B, T. — αὐτῷ οὐδεὶς F ; οὐδεὶς αὐτῷ Μ, P, B, Th. ; οὐδεὶς Τ. — περὶ τούτων : παρὰ τούτων Sylburg. — ΜΑΡΤΥΡΕΣ om. Mss., except T margin.

28. ἄνδρες add. Herw. — ἔχειν αὐτὸς F, M, P, B ; αὐτὸς ἔχειν G, T. — αὐτῷ F, M, P, B ; αὐτῶν G, T.

29. αὗται ἔτεσι Τ ; αὗται ἔτεσι F ; ἔτεσιν αὗται Μ, P, B, Ald. — καὶ ἀποδείκνυνται found in G, T, but probably an editor's conjecture to supply a *lacuna* in older Mss. For other possible expressions cp. Dem. 27. 37, Isae. 6. 14. Us.R. omit, with indication of *lacuna*. — περιόντα : after περιόντα all Mss. have τῶν ἑπτὰ ταλάντων ; either this must be erased (Markl.) or after μναῖ we must add τῶν τετταράκοντα μνῶν (Us.R.).

XXXIV

For the sources of the text, see introduction to the critical notes on XXXII.

The title is from Dionysius's introduction, *Lysias*, § 32, ὑπόθεσιν δὲ περιείληφε τὴν περὶ τοῦ μὴ καταλῦσαι τὴν πάτριαν πολιτείαν Ἀθήνῃσι.

1. ὦ ἄνδρες Ἀθηναῖοι Us.R. ; ὦ Ἀθηναῖοι Mss., Th. So in §§ 3, 9, 11. Us.R. follow the abbreviation in F, and the Lysian usage. Jahrb. 1873, p. 158. — δὶς ἤδη. καὶ Dobr. ; διὸ δὴ καὶ Mss.

2. ἐστὲ Tayl. ; εἰσὶν Mss. — οἵ G ; ὅτι F, M, P, B. — Πειραιοῖ Us. ; Πειραιεῖ F, M, Us.R. ; Πειραιῶς G, T.

3. ὦ ἄνδρες Ἀθηναῖοι : see on § 1. — οὔτε οὐσίᾳ τῆς πολιτείας add. Us. ; οὔτε οὐσίᾳ add. Sauppe, Th. Cp. 18. 6. — χρήματα Us., Th. ; τὰ χρήματα Mss., Us.R. — ἐκεκτήμεθα Emperius ; ἐκτησάμεθα Mss., Th., Us.R. The context demands "possessed," not "acquired." — ὅπως Steph. ; οὕτως Mss. — τινὰ Ἀθηναῖον Us.R. : ἵνα ἀθηναῖον F[1] ; ἵνα ἀθηναίων G ; ἵνα ἀθηναῖόν τινα F[2], M, P, B margin ; ἵνα ἀθηναίων τινὰ B ; Ἀθηναῖόν τινα Th. — ἀπώσομεν Baiter ; ποιήσωμεν F. M, P, G ; ποιήσομεν B. — νῦν δὲ G ; om. F, M ; Us.R. om. and indicate a *lacuna* between ἐποιούμεθα · and καὶ τοὺς. — ἀπελῶμεν Bekk. ; ἀπολοῦμεν Mss. ; ἀπελοῦμεν Rs.

4. πείθησθε Sluiter ; πιθώμεθα F ; πειθώμεθα M, P, B, G. — τὰ ἐν ταῖς ἐφ' ἡμῶν ὀλιγαρχίαις γεγενημένα Weil, Th. ; ταῖς ἐφ' ἡμῶν ὀλιγαρχίαις γεγενημέναις F[1], M, T (γεγενημένας F pr.) ; πλείστας τῇ πόλει

συμφορὰς ἐν (or πολλὰς συμφορὰς) ταῖς ἐφ᾽ ἡμῶν ὀλιγαρχίαις γεγενημένας Us.; ταῖς ἐφ᾽ ἡμῶν ὀλιγαρχίαις ἐκείνους μάλιστα ἐχθροὺς γεγενημένους Rad. — ἀλλὰ: ἀλλὰ καὶ F pr., G.

5. ἅπερ κτήσονται Steph.; ἀποκτήσονται F, M, P, B; ὅπερ κτήσονται G, T. — λάβωσιν G, T; λάβητε F, M, P, B.

6. τοιούτων Baiter; τοῖς τῶν F, M, T; τούτων Sluiter. — ἡμῖν F;
ὑμῖν M, T. — ἐρωτῶσι Markl.; ἐρῶσι Mss.; ἐροῦσι Desrousseaux,
Us R. — ποιήσομεν: ποιήσωμεν M, P, B. — ἃ Λακεδαιμόνιοι Steph.;
λακεδαιμονίοις Mss. — τούτους M; τούτοις F, G, T. — τίς F, M; τὸ T;
τί G. — περιγενήσεται: περιγενέσθαι F, M, P, B. — ποιήσομεν: ποιήσωμεν F¹; ποιήσαιμεν G, T. — μαχομένοις Us.; μαχόμενοι F, M, P, B;
μαχομένους G, T. — ἢ G, T; εἰ F, M, P, B. — καταψηφίσασθαι Ald.;
καταψηφίσεσθε F, M; καταψηφίσεσθαι T.

7. ἐὰν μὲν πείσω Us.; ἐὰν μὲν πείθω Mss. — ἀμφοτέροις κοινὸν εἶναι
τὸν κίνδυνον: τὸν before κίνδυνον add. Sch.; κοινὸν after εἶναι F corr.,
Us.R.   The obscurity of the passage led Usener to the conclusion that
there is a considerable lacuna after κίνδυνον (so Us.R.), in which stood
the correlative to this ἐὰν μέν. — τὴν αὐτὴν ἔχοντας γνώμην om. F¹, G,
T. — τὴν αὐτῶν οἰκοῦντας om. M, P, B. — τοὺς δὲ . . . οἰκοῦντας om. T.
— ἡμῶν (T); ὑμῶν F, M, P, B.

8. ἴσασι γὰρ Mss.; ἴσασι γὰρ ἐκεῖνοι Dobr., Th.; ἴσασι γὰρ Λακεδαιμόνιοι Us.R.   The definite τούτων in the second clause seems to
me sufficient to make clear, by contrast, the subject of ἴσασι and ἐμβάλλωσι. — ἐμβάλλωσι T; ἐμβάλωσι F, M, Us.R.; ἐκβάλλωσι P. —
καλὸς Ald.; καλῶς F, M, T. — τούτους μὴ Th.; τούτους Mss.; τούτους
οὐ Rs.; τούτους οὐδὲ Us.R. — καταδουλώσασθαι Sylburg; καταδουλώ-
σεσθαι Mss. — ἧττον: add. Rs.; M has a space after τοσούτῳ; τοσούτῳ
οὐκ P, B.

9. ὦ ἄνδρες Ἀθηναῖοι: ὦ Ἀθηναῖοι F, M, P, B, Th.; ὦ ἄνδρες G,
T. — ἡμῖν M, P, B; ἡμῶν F, G, T.

10. ἡμῶν T; ὑμῶν F, M, P, B. — ἐλπίζοντας δ᾽ ἔτι I have written
after West. (κατελπίζοντας δ᾽ ἔτι); καὶ ἐλπίζοντας ἐπὶ Mss.; καὶ ἐλπίζοντας Tayl., Jebb; καὶ ἐλπίζοντας . . . ἐπεὶ (with ἔσται for ἔσεσθαι)
Us.R., the correlative of μέν being assumed to belong in the lacuna.
Th. prints as in X, with the comment "corrupta."   No solution that
has been proposed offers a normal construction and a reasonable explanation of the origin of the corruption.

11. ὦ ἄνδρες Ἀθηναῖοι: see on § 1. — ἐλευθερίας: ἐλευθ. ἑλλήνων
G, T.

Greek Index

[The references are to the commentary (by speeches and paragraphs), unless otherwise designated.]

υἱός 12. 34, 19. 12, 19. 46 Crit. N.

ὑμέτερος = objec. gen. 22. 13.

ὑπάρχειν 12. 23.

ὑπέρ: of ground of action or feeling 25. 5; with words of punishment 25. 28; with ὀργίζεσθαι 12. 80; = περί 24. 4.

ὑπό: with verbs active in form 12. 43; with non-personal object 12. 3, 24. 6.

ὑποφορά p. 357.

ὑποψία: prepositions with 32. 19 Crit. N.

φαίνεσθαι: with partic. or infin. 22. 7.

φανερὰ οὐσία 32. 4, 32. 23.

φάσκω 32. 25 Crit. N.; φάσκων 12. 5.

φέρε 12. 62.

φεύγειν δίκας 32. 2.

φεύγω: as perf. 12. 14.

φεύγων, ὁ 12. 2.

φημί = κελεύω 16. 13 Crit. N.

φθέγξασθαι 32. 18.

φίλος 12. 38.

φοιτᾶν 32. 15.

φορμῶν 22. 5.

φυγή 25. 21.

φύλαρχοι 12. 44, 16. 6.

χαρακτῆρες p. 344.

χείρους 16. 3.

χρή, χρῆν, ἐχρῆν 12. 48.

ψῆφοι p. 339.

ὦ ἄνδρες Ἀθηναῖοι 34. 1 Crit. N.

ὡς: subjective 16. 8, 22. 5; with partic. in ind. disc. 12. 73; ὡς ἐπὶ τὸ πολύ 19. 6.

ὡς: preposition 16. 4.

ὥσπερ ἄν 12. 20.

ὥστε: with infin. 25. 26; with infin. in purpose clause 19. 16; with ἄν and infin. 12. 1.

ᾤχοντο ἀπιόντες 12. 75.

English Index

[The references are to the commentary (by speeches and paragraphs), unless otherwise designated.]

OKLAHOMA SERIES IN CLASSICAL CULTURE

The University of Oklahoma Press is pleased to announce a new series entitled the Oklahoma Series in Classical Culture. This venture formalizes the Press's long tradition of publishing books in the classical fields. The series editor is A. J. Heisserer (University of Oklahoma) and the members of the advisory board for the series are Ernst Badian (Harvard University), David F. Bright (University of Illinois at Urbana-Champaign), Nancy Demand (Indiana University), Elaine Fantham (Princeton University), R. M. Frazer (Tulane University), Ronald J. Leprohon (University of Toronto), Robert A. Moysey (University of Mississippi), Helen F. North (Swarthmore College), Robert J. Smutny (University of the Pacific), Eva Stehle (University of Maryland at College Park), A. Geoffrey Woodhead (Corpus Christi College, Cambridge/Ohio State University), and John Wright (Northwestern University).

The series will publish books of the highest quality in the following areas:
(1) General studies in ancient culture, including literature, history, and archaeology.
(2) General textbooks in English intended primarily for use in undergraduate courses.
(3) Classroom textbooks intended primarily for use in Greek and Latin courses, such books invariably containing the text in the original language together with helpful notes for students.
(4) Specialized monographs in ancient culture, dealing with such areas as ancient medicine, Ciceronian studies, Latin literature in the Late Empire, and the social and political history of Classical Greece.